AIRCRAFT OF THE ROYAL NAVY
SINCE 1908

ROYAL NAVY
044
NO STEP
ROYAL NAVY
RESCUE
LT. HOBBS

AIRCRAFT OF THE ROYAL NAVY
SINCE 1908

DAVID HOBBS

Seaforth
PUBLISHING

Frontispiece:
The author starting up his Gannet AEW 3, 043/R of 849B Flight embarked in *Ark Royal*, prior to the Flight's disembarkation to the US Naval Air Station Norfolk, Virginia, in April 1976.

First published in Great Britain in 2024 by Seaforth Publishing
An imprint of Pen & Sword Books Ltd
George House, Beevor Street,
Barnsley S71 1HN

www.seaforthpublishing.com
Email info@seaforthpublishing.com

British Library Cataloguing in Publication Data
A CIP data record for this book is available from the British Library

ISBN 978-1-3990-8952-4 (Hardback)
ISBN 978-1-3990-8953-1 (ePub)
ISBN 978-1-3990-8955-5 (PDF)

Pen & Sword Books Limited incorporates the imprints of Atlas, Archaeology, Aviation, Discovery, Family History, Fiction, History, Maritime, Military, Military Classics, Politics, Select, Transport, True Crime, Air World, Frontline Publishing, Leo Cooper, Remember When, Seaforth Publishing, The Praetorian Press, Wharncliffe Local History, Wharncliffe Transport, Wharncliffe True Crime and White Owl.

Typeset and designed by Mousemat Design Limited
Printed and bound by Printworks Global Ltd, London/Hong Kong

FSC
www.fsc.org
FSC® C007031

Contents

Acknowledgements

THIS PROVED TO BE THE LARGEST BOOK PROJECT that I have ever undertaken and, as always, I was helped enormously by the encouragement from my wife Jandy, my son Andrew and his wife Lucyelle. Much of the detail about the aircraft themselves came from a variety of primary sources including the archive of unclassified comments and descriptions of aircraft, aero-engines and manufacturers once held by the Naval Aircraft Department in which I served between 1979 and 1982. When I later became Curator of the Fleet Air Arm Museum at Yeovilton I was saddened to learn that this material must have been destroyed or lost when the Department was broken up. Further significant material was gathered from the Naval Historical Branch and the MOD Archive at Hayes when I was carrying out research for my historical books on the Fleet Air Arm and RN aircraft carriers. I owe a debt of gratitude to David Brown, Christopher Page and Stephen Prince, consecutive Heads of the Naval Historical Branch during the period I carried forward my research, and also to Jenny Wraight, the Admiralty Librarian.

This book contains Public Sector information licensed under the Open Government Licence v 1.0 in the UK. I would particularly like to thank Harland Quarrington, the MOD Chief Photographic Adviser and Deputy Defence Imagery Editor, for his kind and effective help in tracking down and making available the Crown Copyright images used to illustrate some of the current aircraft types in service with the Royal Navy.

Chris Sandham-Bailey went to considerable trouble to create three-view drawings for many of the more important aircraft types and get them to me in a timely manner. I am also grateful to him for the images of what the Saunder-Roe SR-177 and Hawker P.1154 might have looked like had they entered service.

I was able to illustrate many of the aircraft with photographs from my own archive and those captions with no credit after them in parenthesis are from this source. Inevitably there were gaps, however, and I am extremely grateful to Philip Jarrett who was able to fill many of them with images from his own extensive collection. Commander David Goble RAN was kind enough to let me use RNAS images from the Goble Family Collection. The Lucy Family had made images available from the collection of Lieutenant W P Lucy DSO RN for my previous books and some of these were used again as were images provided by the Sea Power Centre – Australia. Others who generously helped by providing photographs included Guy Warner, Nigel Edwards, Merv Green, Lee Howard, Paul Waterhouse, Bob Turner, Ces Mowthorpe and Dave Skelton.

My own impression of the various aircraft types that I flew have been augmented in some of the aircraft descriptions by friends and fellow naval aviators with whom I discussed them over the years. I served under Captain Eric 'Winkle' Brown CBE DSC AFC RN for a short while as a junior officer at Lossiemouth but came to know him well when I was Curator of the Fleet Air Arm Museum; we sometimes lectured together and discussed the many types he had flown. Captain Alan 'Spiv' Leahy CBE DSC RN became a friend when we both served on the committee of the Fleet Air Arm Officers' Association and we often discussed the types he had flown in the bar after meetings. Commander Keith Harris OBE RN, a fellow veteran of 849 NAS as well as a long-term friend, proved to be a valuable source of information about many aircraft types. Commander Peter Flutter AFC RN flew with me in Gannet AEW 3s of 849B Flight from *Ark Royal*; despite the constraints placed on space and word count I was delighted to include much of his description of the aircraft and its operation from the observer's perspective. My BRNC Dartmouth contemporary Commander Ken Mackenzie RN provided details about the Buccaneer's strike system. Commander Serena Brotherton RN, who has put so much energy into the creation of the 'Anyface' Association of AEW/ASaC veterans, provided me with insight into the operation of the Sea King in this role from the observer's perspective and her husband, Lieutenant Commander John Brotherton RN, gave a pilot's opinion of the aircraft. I am grateful to them all for their help and enthusiasm. I have drawn other aircrew opinions from the wealth of biographies, autobiographies, articles and papers in my archive but, of course, all errors or omissions in the text are entirely my own.

As always, I am grateful to Rob Gardner of Seaforth Publishing for his continued support and between us I believe that we have, with this book, created the best multi-volume history of the Royal Navy's aircraft, aircraft carriers and flying operations ever published.

David Hobbs

Preface

THIS IS, AS FAR AS I AM AWARE, the first book describing the complete range of aircraft operated by the Royal Navy to be written by a former naval pilot. During my 33 years' service I flew a wide range of fixed and rotary-wing types operationally and embarkations in aircraft carriers allowed me to understand and appreciate other types that I did not fly. Three years spent on the staff of the Naval Aircraft Department were fascinating and gave access to a wealth of archive material as well as the chance to work alongside test pilots and project engineers getting new aircraft and their systems to sea. After retirement from active naval service I was able to gain further knowledge about RN aircraft of every type and era during eight years as Curator of the Fleet Air Arm Museum.

It was always my intention to join the Navy as a pilot and, whilst I was still at school, I saved my pocket money to buy the second, 1962, edition of Owen Thetford's *Aircraft of the Royal Navy since 1912* published by Putnam. For many years this was the standard reference work on the subject but when I decided that a more up-to-date volume was long overdue, I must admit to under-estimating the scale of the task at first. That edition of Thetford's book contained entries for 244 aircraft types; the research that led to this book identified 422 designed or manufactured by 96 different firms.

I decided that the most logical layout was to place designers and manufacturers in alphabetical order with the aircraft they produced listed under them in chronological order. This has the merit that each firm's design progress can easily be followed. Where the firm's identity changed I have kept them under the name of the original rather than risk making multiple entries which might cause confusion. Examples include the Buccaneer, designed and first built by Blackburn, later identified as part of the Hawker-Siddeley Group and then British Aerospace. This is the reason why the Wasp appears under Saunders-Roe who designed it and not Westland who subsequently bought the firm. The Wasp's identity was further complicated by the fact that the airframes were actually manufactured by Fairey, which had also been purchased into the Westland Group, and all had Fairey construction numbers. Both the Merlin and Wildcat are listed under Westland which was responsible for the original design work and not under GKN Westland, AgustaWestland or Leonardo, the Yeovil firm's later identities.

Some aircraft were only flown in prototype form, evaluated and rejected over a short time frame. Others were technically-complex aircraft that earned a place in the affections of those who flew them and a place in history. I have not, therefore, given every type an equal description although nearly every entry has details of size, maximum take-off weight, MTOW, and speed to allow basic comparisons to be made. More noteworthy aircraft have photographs and longer descriptions including the amount of fuel carried to give an idea of relative endurance. Those of the greatest significance are illustrated with multiple photographs together with three-view drawings; many have aircrew comments on their operational capabilities, strengths and weaknesses. Wherever possible I have listed the number delivered to the RN and the squadrons and ships in which they served. Fixed-wing, rotary-wing, lighter-than-air and unmanned aircraft are described within this overall framework. Some aircraft projects were given high priority by the Admiralty but subsequently cancelled after considerable work had been put into both their design and the modifications needed to allow aircraft carriers to operate them. Examples include the de Havilland DH 116, Saunders-Roe SR-177 and Hawker P.1154RN, the latter originally allocated the name Sea Harrier. Since they were important projects in their own right I have included them among the aircraft that did enter service to give a wider picture of RN aircraft procurement and ambitions.

This is not an operational history although there are brief descriptions of how aircraft types were used. It is, of course, intended to stand on its own but it also complements my six-volume series of RNAS/Fleet Air Arm histories and the companion *British Aircraft Carriers*, all published by Seaforth. Aircraft used by the RAN and RCN Fleet Air Arms have not been included since doing so would have increased the size of the book considerably beyond the practical size agreed with Seaforth.

More than a century and a quarter has passed since the RN ordered its first aircraft and this book is intended to keep the memory of both the aircraft and the brave and resourceful men and women who flew and maintained them alive; to commemorate their service and to broaden understanding of naval aviation's remarkable contribution to the nation's defence. The story of the Fleet Air Arm and its aircraft is far from over and new aircraft types will emerge beyond those described in these pages. The operation of unmanned aircraft or 'drones' from *Prince of Wales* in the latter months of 2023 indicate the likely way ahead with large numbers of small, affordable unmanned aircraft operating from both carriers and other types of warship and auxiliary in a range of roles that will be at the forefront of naval operations over the next few decades. I shall enjoy watching their progress.

David Hobbs MBE
Commander Royal Navy (Retired)
Alnwick
February 2024

Abbreviations

AAC	Army Air Corps [UK]
AAM	Air-to-Air Missile
AAR	Air-to-Air Refuelling
A&AEE	Aeroplane & Armament Experimental Establishment
ac	alternating current
ADDL	Airfield Dummy Deck Landing
ADR	Aircraft Direction Room
ADTU	Aircraft Direction Officers' Training Unit
AESA	Active Electronically Scanned Array [radar]
AEW	Airborne Early Warning
AFCS	Automatic Flight Control System
AGM	Air-to-Ground Missile
AH	Army Helicopter
AI	Air Intercept [radar]
AIM	Air Intercept Missile
ALIS	Autonomic Logistics Information System
AMC	Armed Merchant Cruiser
AMRAAM	Advanced Medium Range Air-to-Air Missile
ASaC	Airborne Surveillance and Control
ASH	Air-to-Surface Homing [radar]
ASM	Air-to-Surface Missile
ASR	Air Search and Rescue
ASRAAM	Advanced Short Range Air-to-Air Missile
ASV	Air to Surface Vessel [radar]
ASW	Anti-Submarine Warfare
Avcat	Aviation Carrier Turbine Fuel [JP-5 NATO F-44]
Avgas	Aviation Gasoline
AVPIN	Aviation Isopropyl Nitrate
AS	Anti-Submarine [aircraft]
Avtur	Aviation Turbine Fuel [JP-4 refined for jet engines]
AWI	Air Warfare Instructor
BAC	British Aircraft Corporation
BCF	Battle Cruiser Fleet
BLC	Boundary Layer Control
BHP	Beardmore, Halford and Pullinger [engine]
BPC	British Purchasing Commission [in the USA]
BPF	British Pacific Fleet
BRNC	Britannia Royal Naval College [Dartmouth]
BVR	Beyond Visual Range [in fighter combat]
C	Transport [aircraft]
CAM-Ship	Catapult-Armed Merchant Ship
CAP	Combat Air Patrol
CAS	Chief of the [UK] Air Staff
CBAS	[3] Commando Brigade Air Squadron
CCA	Carrier Controlled [radar] Approach
CDS	Chief of the [UK] Defence Staff
CFS	Central Flying School
CHF	Commando Helicopter Force
CID	Committee of Imperial Defence
CNS/1SL	Chief of the [UK] Naval Staff/First Sea Lord
COD	Carrier On-board Delivery [aircraft]
COMR	Civilian Owned Military Registered
CPE	Central Point of Entry
CSG	Carrier Strike Group
CV	Aircraft carrier
CVA	Strike aircraft carrier
CVE	Escort aircraft carrier
CVS	Support [anti-submarine] aircraft carrier
DAM	Director of Air Material [within the Admiralty]
DARPA	[US] Defence Advanced Research Projects Agency
DBR	Dive Bomber Reconnaissance [aircraft]
dc	direct current
DNAW	Directorate of Naval Air Warfare [within the Admiralty]
DNO	Director of Naval Ordnance
ECM	Electronic Countermeasures
ECU	Engine Change Unit
ehp	estimated horse power
EIF	East Indies Fleet
EOTS	Electro-Optical Targeting System
ETPS	Empire Test Pilot School
EW	Electronic Warfare
F	Fighter
F/A	Fighter/Attack [aircraft]
FAW	All-Weather Fighter
FB	Fighter Bomber
FBC	Future Building Committee
FCBA	Future [RN] Carrier-Borne Aircraft
FG	Fighter – Ground Attack
FGA	Fighter Ground Attack
FFAR	Folding Fin Air-to-air Rockets
FLASH	Folding Lightweight Active Sonar for Helicopters
FOAC	Flag Officer Aircraft Carriers
FOC	Full Operational Capability
FONA	Flag Officer Naval Aviation
FONAC	Flag Officer Naval Air Command
FONFT	Flag Officer Naval Flying Training

FOST	Flag Officer Sea Training
FR	Fighter – Reconnaissance
FRADU	Fleet Requirements and Aircraft Direction Unit
FRS	Fighter Reconnaissance Strike [aircraft]
FRU	Fleet Requirements Unit
FTS	Flying Training School
GA	Ground Attack [aircraft]
GP	General Purpose
GPS	Global Positioning System
HAR	Helicopter – Air Rescue
HAS	Helicopter – Anti-Submarine
HC	Helicopter – Transport
HIFR	Helicopter In-Flight Refuelling
HM	Helicopter – Maritime Warfare
HMA	His Majesty's Airship
HMA	Helicopter – Maritime Warfare/Attack
HMAS	His/Her Majesty's Australian Ship
HMS	His/Her Majesty's Ship
HOTAS	Hands On Throttle And Stick
hp	horse power
HR	Helicopter Rescue
HT	Helicopter – Training
HTP	Hydrogen Peroxide
HU	Helicopter – Utility
HUD	Head-Up Display
HUDWAC	Head-Up Display Weapon Aiming Computer
IFF	Identification, Friend or Foe
IFTU	Intensive Flying Trials Unit
IOC	Initial Operational Capability
IP	Initial Point
IR	Infrared
ISR	Intelligence, Surveillance and Reconnaissance
JASS	Joint Anti-Submarine School
JCO	Joint [UK] Combat Aircraft
JFH	Joint Force Harrier
JHF	Joint Helicopter Force
JHS	Joint Helicopter School
JPO	Joint Project Office [JSF/F-35]
JSF	Joint Strike Fighter
JTIDS	Joint Tactical Information Distribution System
LABS	Low-Altitude Bombing System
LAST	Low-Altitude Surveillance System
lb	pound
LRIP	Low-Rate Initial Production
LST	Landing Ship Tank
MAC-Ship	Merchant Aircraft Carrier
MAD	Magnetic Anomaly Detector
MADL	Multi-function Advanced Data Link
MAEE	Marine Aircraft Experimental Establishment
MAP	Ministry of Aircraft Production
MATCH	Medium Anti-submarine Torpedo-Carrying Helicopter
MDAP	Mutual Defence Assistance Programme
MLU	Mid Life Upgrade
MOD	Ministry of Defence [UK]
MoS	Ministry of Supply
MOU	Memorandum of Understanding
MTOW	Maximum Take-Off Weight
MTP	Maintenance Test Pilot
mw	megawatt
MWDP	Mutual Weapons Development Programme
NAD	Naval Aircraft Department [at RAE Bedford]
NAFDU	Naval Air Fighting Development Unit
NAS	Naval Air Squadron
NATO	North Atlantic Treaty Organisation
NBMR	NATO Basic Military Requirement
NDB	Nuclear Depth Bomb
NF	Night Fighter
NH	NATO Helicopter [Industry]
nm	nautical mile
NSR	Naval Staff Requirement
NSW	Naval Strike Wing
ODIN	Operational Data Integrated Network
OFT	Operational Flying Training
OTS	Over The Shoulder [attack method]
PCB	Plenum Chamber Burning
pdr	pounder [weight of shell fired by a gun]
PMA	Portable Maintenance Aid
PPI	Plan Position Indicator [radar]
PR	Photographic Reconnaissance
QFI	Qualified Flying Instructor
QOI	Qualified Observer Instructor
RAAC	Rear Admiral Aircraft Carriers
RAE	Royal Aircraft Establishment [Farnborough]
RATOG	Rocket-Assisted Take-Off Gear
RFA	Royal Fleet Auxiliary
RFC	Royal Flying Corps
RIO	Radar Intercept Officer [USN]
RNAS	Royal Naval Air Service
RNAS	Royal Naval Air Station
RNAY	Royal Naval Air Yard
RP	rocket projectile
rpg	rounds per gun
rpm	revolutions per minute
RWR	Radar Warning Receiver
S	Strike [aircraft]

SAM	Surface-to-Air Missile
SAR	Search And Rescue
SBAC	Society of British Aircraft/Aerospace Companies
sfc	specific fuel consumption
shp	shaft horse power
SIGINT	Signals Intelligence
SNO	Senior Naval Officer
SS	Sea Scout [airship]
STOVL	Short Take-Off and Vertical Landing
STUFT	Ships Taken Up From Trade
T	Training [aircraft]
TACAN	Tactical Carrier Air Navigation [system]
TANS	Tactical Aircraft Navigation System
TBR	Torpedo Bomber Reconnaissance [aircraft]
TDU	Torpedo Development Unit
TF	Torpedo Fighter
TIALD	Thermal Imaging And Laser Designation [pod]
TMB	Target Marker Bomb
TR	Torpedo Reconnaissance [aircraft]
TSR	Torpedo Spotter Reconnaissance [aircraft]
TT	Target Towing
TTB	Target-Triggered Burst
U	Unmanned [target aircraft]
UAV	Unmanned Air Vehicle
UCAV	Unmanned Combat Air vehicle
USAAC	United States Army Air Corps
USAAF	United States Army Air Force
USAF	United States Air Force
USCG	United States Coast Guard
USMC	United States Marine Corps
USN	United States Navy
V/STOL	Vertical/Short Take-Off and Landing
VTOL	Vertical Take-Off and Landing
WAC	Western Approaches Command
WOD	Wind Over the [flight] Deck
WRE	Weapons Research Establishment [Woomera, Australia]

ALBATROSS

Albatross B II

A single German Albatross B II with a wingspan of 42ft, powered by a Mercedes D II engine developing 120hp giving a maximum level speed of 65 knots, was procured for evaluation by the Royal Aircraft Factory before being requisitioned by the Admiralty in August 1914. It flew at the Isle of Grain experimental establishment until 1918.

ADMIRALTY AIR DEPARTMENT

Type 1000 Seaplane

Designed in 1914 as a torpedo strike aircraft with the type number taken from the airframe number of the only example completed. Built by White, it had a wingspan of 115ft, three 310hp Sunbeam engines, two mounted as tractor units at the forward ends of the two separate fuselages and the third mounted as a pusher behind a central glazed structure which accommodated five aircrew. Delivered to Felixstowe in 1916 but not completed until January 1917, the heavy structure was beyond the strength of the floats to withstand the stress of take-off and landing, even in calm water. It was written off after a crash near Calshot in December 1917.

Admiralty Type 1000.

Sparrow

Intended to intercept Zeppelins, this biplane was designed around a recoilless Davis gun mounted under the pilot's seat on the floor of a nacelle attached under the upper wing. It had a conventional, wire-braced, fabric-covered wooden airframe with a wingspan of 32ft and a single 80hp Gnome rotary pusher engine. The layout led to an extremely tall, narrow-track undercarriage which caused problems taking off, landing and taxiing. Four prototypes were contracted, two from Hewlett & Blondeau and two from Blackburn. The former two were delivered to Chingford in 1915 for evaluation but were considered unsuccessful. The Blackburn examples were also delivered to Chingford but might never have flown. All four were soon deleted.

Admiralty Flying Boat.

Flying Boat

Designed in late 1915, its boat hull had a step design originated by Lieutenant Linton Hope RN. Pemberton Billing was contracted to construct two prototypes but subcontracted one to May, Harden & May. The wings folded forward for hangar stowage and the engine was mounted between them. The fuselage was a wooden monocoque which performed well after initial problems were overcome. Both were evaluated at Isle of Grain in 1917 and limited production followed. Provision was made for wheels to be fitted to the fuselage to allow flight off a carrier deck or removal from the water via a ramp ashore. One embarked in *Furious* during 1917 but was struck off charge at Rosyth in 1918. A further forty were ordered from Pemberton Billing but most were delivered directly into storage after the Armistice.

Flying Boat data

Length:	30ft 7in
Span:	50ft 4in
Height:	13ft 1in
Maximum weight:	3,567lb
Engine:	One Hispano-Suiza 8B pusher rated at 200hp
Fuel:	Avgas. 61 gallons
Performance:	Maximum speed 88 knots at 2,000ft
	Service ceiling 11,000ft (time to height from sea level 33 minutes)
Endurance:	4 hours 30 minutes
Armament:	One 0.303in Lewis gun in bow cockpit with ammunition in 47-round drums
	Small anti-submarine bombs

Navyplane

A two-seat pusher-engined, biplane seaplane intended for the reconnaissance and bombing roles designed in 1916. Pemberton Billing was contracted to build two prototypes but only one was completed. The nacelle was mounted mid-way between the wings with W/T and

Admiralty Navyplane.

a 0.303in Lewis machine gun for the observer. Wingspan was 36ft. At first it was powered by an unreliable American Smith Static radial engine but it was replaced by an AR 1 engine of similar power. Test flights revealed very poor performance; it took 30 minutes to reach 1,300ft and could climb no further.

AEROSPATIALE

AS 365N Dauphin

Two Dauphins chartered from Bond Helicopters, later VERITAIR Ltd, as commercially owned military registered, COMR, helicopters in 1995 are still used in 2024. They have a rotor-diameter of 39ft 2in, MTOW of 9,480shp and are powered by two Turbomeca Arriel 2C turboshafts, each developing 838shp. Maximum level speed is 155 knots. Flown by a crew of two and carrying up to eleven passengers, they operate from Devonport Naval Base supporting Flag Officer Sea Training by moving staff between the shore, ships and on a variety of fleet requirements tasks.

AS 365N Dauphin. (Lee Howard)

AEROVIRONMENT

Puma

A small, battery-powered UAV weighing only 13lb that can be launched by hand and operated in the ISR role. Wingspan is 9ft 2in and it has a Mantis i45 gimballed EO/IR low-light camera mounted under the fuselage. It first flew in 2007 and was adopted by the US Marine Corps in 2008, designated as the RQ-20A. The RN evaluated it from 2019 within 700X NAS and it achieved IOC in August 2020. Three operational flights were designated as Phantom A, B and C Flights, each embarking with a single air vehicle and three personnel, a detachment commander, who integrates Puma with the ship command, a naval air mechanic and an aircraft handler, each qualified to control the UAV remotely, control the camera and download images. Missions can either be keypad and roller ball commanded or pre-planned and autonomous. Early versions had an endurance of 2.5 hours to search an area up to 270 square miles. Maximum level speed is 45 knots and recovery uses a deep-stall technique requiring minimal deck space. The camera has a 50X electronic zoom capability and images can be data-linked to the parent ship from ranges up to 11nm. Developed versions of the Puma have improved batteries and a long-range tracking antenna which give an endurance of 3.5 hours and a data-linking radius of action up to 33nm.

A Puma being launched from a frigate's deck. (Crown Copyright)

AGUSTAWESTLAND

See under Westland for Sea King, Lynx, Merlin and Wildcat.

AIRCO – THE AIRCRAFT MANUFACTURING COMPANY

DH 2

A single DH 2 was transferred from the RFC to the RNAS for evaluation in 1916. It had a wingspan of 28ft 3in, MTOW of 1,441lb and was powered by a single 100hp Gnome monosoupape rotary engine to give a maximum level speed of 80 knots. Evaluated at Hendon in 1916 but never adopted for naval use.

DH 4

Geoffrey de Havilland's DH 4 was one of the outstanding aircraft of its generation, operated by the RNAS as bombers, reconnaissance, anti-submarine and anti-Zeppelin aircraft, replacing the Sopwith 1½ Strutter from 1917. The first prototype was evaluated at St Pol in March 1917. Originally to have had a BHP engine which proved difficult to manufacture, production aircraft had Rolls-Royce Eagle engines which gave the DH 4 a better performance than most enemy

A DH 4 of 5 (Naval) Squadron RNAS. (Goble Family)

A DH 4 of 5 (Naval) Squadron with 65lb bombs on underwing racks.

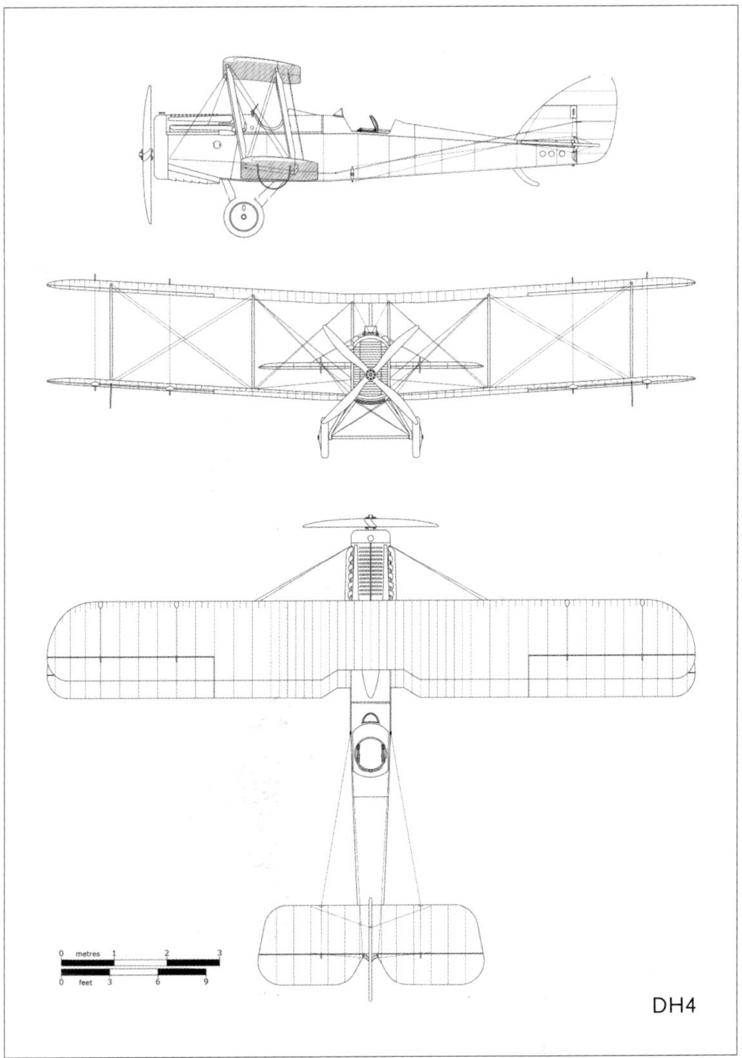

fighters in 1917. It was manufactured with fabric-covered, wire-braced wood and ash wings and the fuselage was built in two sections joined aft of the gunlayer's cockpit. The forward part, containing the two cockpits and the main fuel tanks, was covered with plywood to increase its strength. The wings had two spars and the wooden tailplane structure had variable incidence. Engine power was increased in later batches with larger four-bladed propellers and the undercarriage had to be heightened to maintain ground clearance.

Squadron Commander Bartlett described the DH 4 as an ideal day bomber with a reliable engine. Bombing was carried out in level flight from the greatest height that could be reached to limit the effect of anti-aircraft fire and a typical bomb load was either two 230lb or four 112lb bombs aimed by the gunlayer who lay prone in the rear cockpit looking through a gyroscopic bomb sight fitted in an opening in the bottom of the fuselage. Steering instructions for the pilot on his target run were made by the gunlayer tugging on wires connected to a left/right indicator in the cockpit. Crude by later standards, this simple system was sufficiently reliable to hit the targets RNAS squadrons attacked. Naval DH 4s generally flew to their target in an unescorted formation, separated on a hand signal from the leader to carry out individual runs over the target and rejoined afterwards for the return to base. Later production aircraft had the gunlayer's cockpit rim raised to heighten the Scarff ring and give better fields of fire aft and below.

DH 4 (with Rolls-Royce Eagle VIII engine) data

Length:	30ft 8in
Wingspan:	42ft 4½in
Height:	11ft 0in
MTOW:	3,472lb
Engine:	1 x Rolls-Royce Eagle VIII
Fuel:	Avgas. 65¾ gallons
Performance:	Maximum speed 125 knots with bombs Ceiling 22,000ft 20 minutes to 16,500ft
Endurance:	3 hours 45 minutes
Armament:	Two synchronised 0.303in belt-fed Vickers front guns on forward fuselage decking with 200 rpg; twin 0.303in Lewis guns on Scarff ring in gunlayer's cockpit. Up to 460lb of bombs

A total of 351 DH 4s were delivered to the RN.

RNAS DH 4s saw service with 2, 5, 6, 11 and 17 (Naval) Squadrons; War Flights at Port Victoria, Redcar and Great Yarmouth; 'C' Squadron at Imbros and 'D' Squadron at Stavros and flights at Mudros, Thasos, Mitylene and Andrano.

The DH 4's one weakness was the distance between the cockpits intended to give the pilot a good view and the gunlayer optimal fields of fire; it succeeded in those aims but prevented the verbal communication between pilot and gunlayer that was essential in combat with enemy fighters. The 'Gosport' speaking tube which connected the cockpits was of little practical value in this situation as it required hands to be removed from controls or guns to use it. At first the DH 4's high speed and ceiling allowed it to outpace enemy fighters but as their performance improved combat became more likely they relied on the combined fire of aircraft in formation to drive off enemy fighters. If isolated, pilots relied on their gunlayers to see and engage enemy aircraft coming up behind and below the aircraft and naval squadrons took pains to bring them to a high standard of efficiency. Bartlett wrote in his diary that he and other experienced pilots took up new gunlayers to give them experience over the front lines.

Squadron Commander C P O Bartlett DSC RNAS of 5 (Naval) Squadron in a DH 4. Note the distance between the two cockpits.

In addition to the DH 4s used as bombers from bases in France, RNAS units operated the type on coastal patrols around the UK and for intercepting Zeppelins over the North Sea. Several aircraft were modified with extra fuel to undertake a photographic reconnaissance of the Kiel Canal but when that project was cancelled the aircraft were used on anti-Zeppelin missions from Great Yarmouth. Several DH 4s were used at Isle of Grain for developmental work with flotation bags and others were evaluated with experimental hydrovanes intended to improve the aircraft's ditching characteristics. In the Aegean theatre naval DH 4s attacked the Sofia to Constantinople railway line and in January 1918 attacks were carried out on the Turkish battlecruiser *Goeben* which was aground in the Dardanelles. Most DH 4s were deleted in 1918.

DH 6

Designed to meet an urgent RFC requirement for a two-seat primary trainer. Construction was conventional with doped fabric covering wire-braced wooden frames with the pilots sat in tandem. The instructor occupied the rear seat and had a lever with which he could disengage the pupil's controls if he so wished. Wingspan was 35ft 11in and MTOW 2,027lb. A single 90hp Royal Aircraft Factory 1A engine gave a maximum level speed of 62 knots. Performance was unremarkable but described by the CFS as 'lady-like' and 'utterly viceless'. It was designed to be unstable, a desirable quality in an elementary trainer.

After the Avro 504K became the standard RFC trainer in 1917, over 600 DH 6s were transferred to the RNAS to fill an urgent requirement for aircraft capable of flying coastal anti-submarine patrols. Many were used as a source of spare parts or retained in storage rather than being flown, however. They were usually flown solo with a single 100lb bomb but the type's lack of stability made the DH 6 a difficult aircraft to fly on long operational patrols and they never proved popular. DH 6s operated initially in the Tyne-Tees area but eventually covered the south and south-west coast of England as well. Some unarmed DH 6s were used for convoy control work close to harbours, flown with an observer with an Aldis lamp to communicate with shipping. The type was deleted in 1918.

Airco DH 6. (Philip Jarrett)

Airco DH 9.

DH 9

Intended as an improved DH 4 powered by a 300hp Siddeley-Deasy Puma engine but production problems led to the engine being de-rated to 230hp. This gave the DH 9 a performance inferior to the DH 4 but by 1917 large production orders had been placed and it had to be taken into service. It retained its predecessor's wings and tailplane but the pilot's cockpit was moved aft of the fuel tanks, closer to the gunlayer's cockpit, so that the two crew could hear each other shout over the noise of the engine. Wingspan was 42ft 4in and MTOW 3,325lb but the Puma's unreliability added to the DH 9's unpopularity and a full bomb load limited its ceiling to 13,000ft. The maximum level speed of 92 knots left it at the mercy of enemy fighters and its greater range was negated by the limited range of the fighters needed as escorts. Notwithstanding its limitations, over 600 DH 9s were transferred from RFC production to naval air squadrons or squadrons employed on naval duties after the creation of the RAF. These included 2, 6 and 11 (Naval) Squadrons and units employed on coastal patrols duties at Great Yarmouth, Mullion, Padstow, Durgh Castle and the Mediterranean.

DH 9A

Improved DH 9s were developed with more powerful engines including the 375hp Rolls-Royce Eagle VIII, 400hp Liberty or 450hp Napier Lion. Wingspan was increased to 45ft 11in and the structure strengthened to take the increased MTOW of 4,814lb. 'Nineacks', as they were nicknamed, remained in service with the RAF after 1918 and two Lion-engined DH 9As formed part of the *Eagle* Flight that carried out deck-landing trials in the incomplete *Eagle* between May and October 1920. Two were embarked in *Argus* together with 2F.1 Camels and Fairey IIID floatplanes for the Atlantic Fleet spring cruise in 1920. Others took part in palisade trials in *Eagle* in 1929 and *Glorious* in 1930 which were evidently unsuccessful because one 9A went over the side in *Eagle*. Other 9As operated at the flying schools at Leuchars and Gosport where naval pilots were trained after 1924. A total of fifty-two were used on naval tasks, some of them only briefly.

SS-2 inflated in its construction shed.

AIRSHIPS Ltd

SS-2

In February 1915 the Admiralty issued an urgent requirement for a non-rigid Sea Scout airship capable of 45 knots carrying two crew members and a 160lb bomb load. Airships Ltd produced a prototype in 4 weeks based on Willows' design number 5 with an envelope of $70,000ft^3$ and a 100hp Curtiss engine driving two swivelling propellers. Later designated SS-2, it was recognised as innovative but needed further development. It was evaluated at Kingsnorth in 1915, and later taken to Capel where it was dismantled and scrapped.

AIRSPEED

Envoy

The Envoy was a seven-seat passenger aircraft powered by two 350hp Armstrong Siddeley Cheetah IX engines giving a maximum level speed of 185 knots. A single example was transferred to the RN from the RAF and operated by 781 NAS on light communications duties for 4 months during 1941.

Oxford

Large contracts were awarded by the Air Ministry for the AS 10 Oxford training aircraft from 1937. It was derived from the Envoy and followed the British practice of naming trainers after educational establishments. It was a neat little aircraft with a particularly well-designed cockpit layout. The basic Oxford was a two-pilot, twin-engined monoplane with space in the rear compartment for up to seven seats, light stores or equipment and 264 were allocated to the RN from RAF maintenance units although not all were transferred. RN Oxfords were used as a conversion trainer for pilots destined to fly twin-engined aircraft, for instrument flying instruction and as trainers for observers, aerial photographers and telegraphist air gunners. They were also used to develop carrier blind landing aids, later known as instrument landing systems, radio equipment and for ship's radar calibration. A number carried passengers, light stores and spare parts between naval air stations.

Between June 1944 and October 1957 Oxfords operated at various times in the station flights at Anthorn, Ballyhalbert, Belfast, Bramcote, Burscough, Crail, Dale, Donibristle, Eastleigh, Evanton, Gosport, Halesworth, Lossiemouth, Ronaldsway, St Merryn, Stretton and Yeovilton.

No naval air squadron was completely equipped with Oxfords but between May 1942 and April 1957 Oxfords were operated by 700, 701, 702, 703, 704, 720, 727, 728, 729, 730, 739, 740, 744, 750, 751, 758, 759, 762, 765, 766, 771, 776, 778, 780, 781, 782, 787, 789, 790, 792, 798 and 799 NAS.

Oxford Mark 1 data

Length:	34ft 6in
Wingspan:	53ft 4in
Height:	11ft 1in
MTOW:	7,600lb
Engines:	Two 375hp Armstrong Siddeley Cheetah X
Fuel:	Avgas. 156 gallons
Performance:	Maximum level speed 160 knots
	Ceiling 19,200ft. 13 minutes to 10,000ft
Endurance:	5 hours at economical speed
Armament:	None

Airspeed's Fleet Shadower. (Philip Jarrett)

Fleet Shadower

The AS 39 Fleet Shadower was designed to meet Admiralty Requirement OR 52 in 1937 for a carrier-borne aircraft capable of flying at 38 knots for not less than 6 hours to shadow enemy surface forces. Two prototypes were contracted but only one was completed, powered by four 130hp Pobjoy Niagara V engines which gave a maximum level speed of 110 knots. Wingspan was 53ft 4in, 18ft folded, and MTOW 6,935lb. The pilot's cockpit was high with an excellent view; the nose was extensively glazed for the observer to take bearings and the TAG occupied an enclosed cabin in the centre section. The AS 39's stalling speed with power on was only 32 knots and its endurance was assessed as 'approximately' 6 hours, just meeting the specification. It was never put into production.

An Oxford of 781 NAS at Lee-on-Solent.

ALCOCK

A.1

Whilst serving with 2 Wing RNAS at in the summer of 1917, John Alcock, of later transatlantic flight fame, designed and built a single-seat fighter using components from other aircraft. It was powered by a 110hp Clerget rotary engine and had the forward fuselage and lower wing of a Sopwith Triplane. The upper wing came from a Pup, modified to accept ailerons that extended inboard as far as the inner struts and the tailplane and elevators had once belonged to a Camel. The pilot's eyes were level with the upper wing where it least obscured his field of view and the rear fuselage, rudder and part of the fin were fabricated to his own design in the Wing's workshops. The armament was a single, fixed 0.303in Vickers machine gun on the top decking forward of the cockpit with an interrupter mechanism. Completed in October 1917, it was found to be fast, manoeuvrable and a delight to fly but by then Brown had been taken prisoner by the Turks. Only one example was ever built, referred to by Brown as the Sopwith Mouse. It was eventually written off following a crash.

Alcock's A.1. (Philip Jarrett)

ARMSTRONG-WHITWORTH

SS-27

In May 1915 Armstrong Whitworth was contracted by the Admiralty to investigate SS design improvements. The original Willows envelope was replaced with a 70,000ft^3 Clement Bayard type imported from France. The greater disposable lift allowed an FK 3 fuselage to replace the earlier type and an additional fuel tank was fitted aft of the pilot to give an endurance of up to 12 hours. The Renault engine was retained and the new airship, designated SS-27, was completed in July 1915 and deployed to Marquise where, unfortunately, it was wrecked after colliding with a church steeple in August. The modifications were considered sufficiently successful for the Admiralty to order ten similar airships to be built at Wormwood Scrubs naval air station and they are described in that section.

R-25

One of four airships of the 23 Class described in the Vickers section. Vickers built two and Beardmore a fourth. There were variations between individual ships, R 25's most significant being the method of gas-bag insertion before the keel was attached. This caused gas bag surging which moved the centre of lift unpredictably. Work began in October 1915 but trim trials were not carried out until October 1917 when disposable lift was found to be disappointingly low. A major weight reduction programme was carried out but after arrival at Howden R-25 was considered unfit for operational use and spent most of its short life on training, flying for only 221 hours 5 minutes before being deleted in 1919.

HM Airship R-25. (Philip Jarrett)

R-29

One of four projected air ships of the 23X Class. Another, R 27, was built by Beardmore but two, R 28 by Beardmore and R 30 by Armstrong Whitworth, were cancelled by the Admiralty after examination of the crashed but largely intact German Zeppelin L 33 in September 1916 led to the design of the 33 Class. The 23X class incorporated Admiralty improvements including removal of the external keel. R-29 first flew on 29 May 1918.

HM Airship R-29 as completed. (Philip Jarrett)

A B C D E F G H I J K L M N O P Q R S T U V W X Y Z

R-29 data

Length:	539ft
Diameter:	53ft
Height:	75ft
Gasbag capacity:	990,000ft^3 of hydrogen in 18 gasbags
Gross lift:	30.1 tons
Disposable lift:	8.5 tons
Engines:	Four 300hp Rolls-Royce modified Eagle water cooled
Performance:	Maximum speed 48 knots
Endurance:	Over 30 hours
Armament:	Five 0.303in Lewis guns. Up to eight 112lb or 230lb bombs

Loads were concentrated at bulkheads and suspended from the radial wiring which maintained the hull in its correct polygonal shape. An internal corridor allowed the crew to move between cars and gave access to the petrol and ballast bags. Bombs were suspended beneath the walkway and released by Bowden cables from the control car. Lewis guns were mounted to give defensive fire against enemy aircraft with one each in the control and after cars, two on top of the hull reached by ladders running through tubes between the gasbags, one forward and one aft with a fifth gun mounted in the aftermost part of the hull reached through a 'crawl way' just big enough for a man to get through. As originally built, R-29's fore and aft cars had two swivelling propellers driven through gearing by a single engine. The centre car had two engines, each driving a single propeller. Later, the centre car was replaced by two wing cars mounted abreast, each with one engine driving its own propeller. R-29 was further modified with one propeller on the rear car replacing the two swivelling propellers.

R-29 operated from East Fortune in an operational career of only 5 months which included anti-submarine patrols and escort missions in support of convoys to and from Scandinavia. It was used for wireless trials in early 1919 before being deleted in October after flying for only 335 hours.

R-33

Zeppelin L 33 crashed virtually intact at Little Wigborough in September 1916 and, after examining it, the Admiralty ordered R-33

HM Airship R-33 in post-1918 mooring trials.

from Armstrong Whitworth and R-34 from Beardmore. The allocation of the number 33 was purely fortuitous; it was the next in sequence and nothing to do with the German airship on which the design was based. Larger than its predecessors with a streamlined shape, it broke away from the tubular shape of earlier British rigids.

R-33 data

Length:	644ft
Diameter:	79ft
Height:	95ft
Gasbag capacity:	1,950,000ft^3 of hydrogen in 19 gasbags
Gross lift:	118,000lb
Disposable lift:	58,240lb
Engines:	Five 275hp Sunbeam Maori
Performance:	Maximum speed 53 knots
Endurance:	Over 30 hours
Armament:	Designed to have 0.303in Lewis guns and 230lb bombs

R-33 was launched on 6 March 1919 but never fitted with armament. What appeared to be a single forward car was actually two units separated by a small gap. The front housed the control compartment and the rear one engine driving a two-bladed propeller. Two more engines were fitted in wing cars slung alongside each other slightly forward of amidships, each with reversing gearboxes so that their propellers could check forward momentum when landing or coming up to a mast. The after car contained two engines that drove a single propeller. Whilst still under Admiralty control in 1919 R-33 carried out an extended flight to advertise Government Victory Bonds during which a brass band played on the forward gun platform on top of her hull while it flew over London. In 1920 the few remaining airships were transferred from Admiralty control to the Air Ministry and R 33 was given the civilian registration G-FAAG. It was deleted and scrapped in 1928. It had flown for 735 hours; more than any other British rigid airship. Armstrong Whitworth received two further orders for airships, R 35 in 1918 and R 39 in early 1919 but both were cancelled in August 1919.

FK 8

A single example was ordered in December 1916 and fitted with a 200hp Sunbeam engine. It flew in March 1917 but was damaged in a forced landing in April and never accepted into service.

FK 10

The second in a series of unsuccessful quadruplane designs none of which proved successful. Three were procured for evaluation in 1917 fitted with 110hp Le Rhone rotary engines but found to have very poor performance. The second and third evaluated at Manston were grounded as unsafe. There were no production orders for the type.

FK 12

Triplanes fitted with 250hp Rolls-Royce Eagle engines; two were nominally diverted from a War Office contract to the RNAS but all were cancelled after the General Manager of Armstrong Whitworth wrote that he considered the design to be so unsafe that they should not be flown. Cancellation came as no surprise.

An FK-10 at Manston.

Whitley GR VII

Operated in large numbers by the RAF early in the Second World War and built in the largest number of any Armstrong Whitworth-designed aircraft. Sixteen were transferred to the RN from the RAF in 1944; of these nine were re-wired as flying classrooms and used by 734 NAS from its formation in February 1944 at Worthy Down. RN Whitleys were powered by two 1,145hp Rolls-Royce Merlin X engines giving a maximum level speed of 200 knots, MTOW was 33,950lb and wingspan 84ft. They were used to teach new Barracuda pilots engine handling techniques in a rear compartment fitted with consoles containing fuel flow meters and other instruments demonstrating the effects of boost and throttle settings. The last examples were withdrawn to Stretton in 1946 when 734 NAS was disbanded and subsequently scrapped.

Other firms' designs

During its existence, Armstrong Whitworth built or converted large numbers of aircraft under licence, among them twenty-five Meteor NF 11s into TT 20s for target-towing duties with the RN which are described with other Meteor variants in the Gloster section. The firm built 400 Sea Hawks for the RN which are described in the Hawker section.

AUSTER

Auster Marks I, III and V

The RN received seven Austers transferred from the RAF from 1943 for light utility tasks. Four were Mark Vs with 130hp Lycoming 0-290-3 engines; earlier marks had different engines. Wingspan was 36ft 5in and the aircraft could carry two passengers in addition to the single pilot and they were fitted with full instrument flying panels. Several had short but interesting lives including two fitted with arrester hooks for use in 777 NAS, the carrier trials unit, on *Pretoria Castle* in 1945–6. Another served with 778 NAS, the service trials unit and several were used by target towing units such as 790 and 791 NAS to allow pilots to have some light-hearted general flying practice. At least one was in Singapore during 1946 and others were used by RNVR air squadrons until 1954.

Auster of 1832 NAS.

ASTRA-TORRES AIRSHIP COMPANY

HM Airship Number 3

In 1912 the CID recommended that the Admiralty order a single Astra-Torres airship to follow HMA 1 in 1911. Designated HMA 3, its envelope had a capacity of slightly over 280,000ft^3 and it was powered by two Chenu engines, each driving a two-bladed propeller mounted on brackets high above the enclosed, box-shaped car. Length was 248ft and maximum level speed 45 knots. Armament comprised a single free-mounted 0.303in Hotchkiss machine gun. It was accepted by the RNAS in September 1913 and used for W/T trials. In August 1914 it was at Kingsnorth and made early wartime patrols escorting troopships ferrying the BEF to France before deploying to Ostend with Commander Samson's Eastchurch Squadron. Subsequently withdrawn to Dunkirk, it reported German advances but its vulnerability forced its return to Kingsnorth from where it flew over London at night to give the RNAS Anti-Aircraft Corps' searchlight crews experience in locating and tracking airships. Its last operational missions were patrols over the eastern English Channel in 1915 before deletion in 1916.

HM Airships Numbers 8, 10 and 16

After HMA 3 the Admiralty ordered three further Astra-Torres airships, Numbers 8, 10 and 16. Number 8, delivered in December 1914, was identical to Number 3 and replaced it at Kingsnorth to carry out patrols over British shipping in the eastern Channel. It was deflated in 1915 and deleted in 1916. Number 10 was smaller with an envelope capacity

HM Airship number 8.

of only 150,000ft^3. It may not have been delivered from Astra-Torres but its envelope was used for a prototype Coastal airship design rejected by the RNAS. There is no evidence that Number 16 was ever delivered as Astra-Torres' designs were overtaken by in-house non-rigid airship development at Kingsnorth.

AVRO

Type D biplane

Whilst never officially on Admiralty charge, a single Type D has an important place in naval aviation history. Constructed in 1911 with a 35hp Green engine that was probably second-hand, it was used initially by Avro to give demonstration flights. Commander Oliver Schwann RN, commanding officer of the airship tender *Hermione* at Barrow-in-Furness, flew in it at Brooklands as a passenger and was sufficiently impressed to raise £700 from colleagues and their wives to buy it and have it sent by rail to Barrow. Once there, Schwann had naval air mechanics led by Petty Officer Bobbitt remove the wheeled undercarriage and replace it with floats designed by his team who styled themselves the 'Seaplane Club'. The club paid £1 to insure Bobbitt for carrying out tasks outside his normal naval duties. Schwann had not qualified as a pilot but carried out a series of runs across Cavendish Dock in Barrow which often ended with the seaplane capsizing. After a series of recoveries and repairs by Bobbitt's sailors, Green increased engine power to 45hp by fitting open exhaust ports and this improvement together with the club's seventh float design resulted in partial success. On 18 November 1911 the aircraft lifted off the water unexpectedly and climbed to about 20ft over the dock, the first ever take-off by a British seaplane. Unfortunately Schwann's lack of skill led to a stall after which the aircraft fell back onto the water and capsized. It was salvaged, reconstructed and flown on several more occasions by Schwann, after he qualified as a pilot, and others during 1912. The Type D's operation led directly to major investment in the concept by the Admiralty. Fitting the floats doubled the Type D's MTOW from 500lb to 1,000lb. Wingspan was 31ft and performance with the 45hp engine was just sufficient to get airborne with endurance limited to about 20 minutes, the time it took for the engine's cooling water to boil away.

Commander Oliver Schwann RN in the Type D beginning to taxi across Cavendish Dock at Barrow-in-Furness.

Type 500

A single Avro 500 was ordered by the Admiralty in February 1913 for evaluation at Eastchurch. It took part in the 1914 Royal Fleet Review in July 1914 but was badly damaged in a forced landing a week later and deleted in 1915. A second example was ordered a year later and a third requisitioned in 1914 for use as a training aircraft at Hendon and Chingford. Wingspan was 36ft and MTOW 1,300lb. They were powered by a single 50hp Gnome rotary engine which gave a maximum level speed of 44 knots and could remain airborne for 6 hours.

Type 501

One example was ordered by the Admiralty in 1913 and used at Isle of Grain to evaluate different float designs before being fitted with a wheeled undercarriage. After 1914 it operated from Dover and Dunkirk, taking part in early strikes against Zeebrugge and Ostend. From 1915 it was used as a training aircraft at Eastchurch before being deleted in 1916. The single 100hp Gnome rotary engine gave a maximum level speed of 57 knots. Wingspan was 47ft 6in and MTOW 2,700lb.

Type 503

The Admiralty ordered three Type 503 seaplanes in 1913 for evaluation at Isle of Grain but all had their floats replaced by wheels before the outbreak of war for use as training aircraft. The single 100hp Gnome rotary engine gave a maximum level speed of 55 knots. Wingspan was 50ft and MTOW 2,200lb. All three were deleted in late 1915.

Type 504

The first Type 504 prototype flew at Brooklands in 1913 using wing-warping rather than conventional ailerons but these were replaced by hinged ailerons in production aircraft.

Avro 504C data

Length:	29ft 5in
Wingspan:	36ft
Height:	10ft 5in
MTOW:	1,574lb
Engine:	One 80hp Gnome seven-cylinder rotary engine
Fuel:	Avgas. 21 gallons in main tank; 4½ gallons in gravity tank
Performance:	Maximum level speed 72 knots Service ceiling 13,000ft. 16 minutes to 10,000ft
Endurance:	8 hours
Armament:	As a strike aircraft 4 x 20lb bombs plus 4 small incendiaries; as a fighter one 0.303in Lewis gun with several 47-round ammunition drums. Some variants had a 0.303in belt-fed Vickers front gun

The RNAS received a total of 310 Avro 504s of which 190 were 504Bs, 80 were 504Cs, 30 were 504Gs and 10 504Es.

Units that operated the Avro 504 included 1 Squadron, 2 Wing, 3 Squadron, 4 Squadron RNAS and the type was used for training at Chingford, Cranwell, Fairlop, Frieston, Manston, Port Victoria and Redcar.

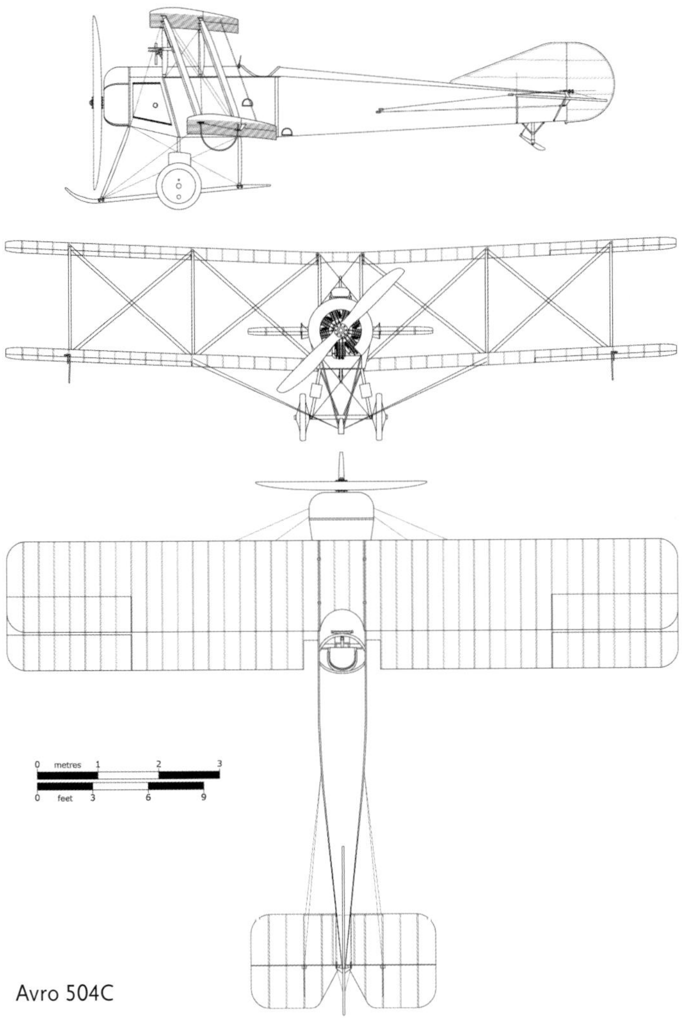

Avro 504C

Flight Commander A W Bigsworth RNAS by the Avro 504 in which he damaged Zeppelin LZ 39 on 17 May 1915.

Orders for the 504 were placed by both the RNAS and RFC during 1914 but, while the War Office accepted Avro's structural design, the Admiralty specified spars of greater cross section, reflecting its intention to use the type in the strike role carrying bombs. The first RN Avro 504 was a single-seater, airframe number 179 and so the type was designated Type 179 under the Admiralty system. As larger numbers came into service it became known, more commonly, as the Avro 504 and never had a name. One was allocated to the Eastchurch Squadron in November 1914 and used to attack enemy submarine docks at Bruges. Bad weather prevented the pilot from finding the docks and so he bombed the Ostend to Bruges railway line instead. Four others were deployed for an even more ambitious attack from the French airfield at Belfort, a few miles from the Franco-Swiss border, on the Zeppelin factory at Friedrichshafen by Lake Constance 120nm away. It was carried out on 4 November 1914 by three aircraft, the other having broken a tail skid attempting to take off. They were all armed with four 20lb bombs and flew low over Lake Constance to escape detection. After locating the target they climbed to 1,200ft and then dived with their engines switched off to release their weapons at about 700ft over the target. Nine bombs were seen to fall in the target area; one impact was not observed and two hung up on their racks. Observed results included a gas works explosion and extensive damage to a hangar together with the airship inside it. One aircraft was shot down but the attack was a remarkable achievement.

Avro 504s were also used by the RNAS as anti-Zeppelin fighters armed initially with small bombs dropped on the airships from above. Most fighter variants were two-seaters but the 504C had an auxiliary fuel tank in place of the front cockpit which increased its endurance to 8 hours. A Lewis gun could be fitted forward of the pilot to fire incendiary ammunition upwards at an angle of 45 degrees, missing the propeller disc. Variants of the type used by the RNAS included the 504B, 504C, 504E and 504G. The 504B was an unarmed two-seat version and the 504G was a modified version of the 'B' used for gunnery training with a Vickers front gun on the decking forward of the cockpit and a Lewis gun on a Scarff ring aft. The 504E had a 100hp Gnome monosoupape radial engine but was used mainly for training.

An Avro 504 in snow at Dover.

Avro 504C. (Philip Jarrett)

Some 504s were used in development of arrester gear and in catapult-launching techniques. A modified 504C, re-designated as a 504H, was one of the first aircraft to be launched by catapult in 1917. Two post-war developments, the 504K and 504N were used by the RAF to train naval pilots at Leuchars until well into the 1930s and a small number were used for deck-landing trials on *Eagle* in 1924 and for deck-landing training on *Argus*. The last RN example was only deleted at Lee-on-Solent in 1939.

Type 510

The 510 was a two-seat biplane seaplane intended for the 1914 Circuit of Britain race. One was purchased by the Admiralty in August 1914 for evaluation at Calshot. Performance was unremarkable and it was only capable of 60 knots in level flight. Despite this, the Admiralty ordered five production examples with a wingspan of 63ft powered by single 150hp Sunbeam Nubian engines. However, their performance was so bad that they could only be flown solo and they were found to be of negligible value. Accounts of their few short flights contain little of interest except for one in which Flight Lieutenant C Draper RNAS flew under the Tay Bridge on 17 May 1915. They were eventually scrapped in 1917 having not flown since 1915.

Type 519

Two single-seat biplane bombers with folding wings powered by a single 150hp Sunbeam Nubian engine were ordered by the Admiralty for evaluation in 1916. They had a maximum level speed of 66 knots, MTOW of 3,000lb and took 30 minutes to climb to 6,000ft. Evaluation at Eastchurch showed little to commend them and no production orders followed.

Type 523 Pike

The first twin-engined Avro design, the Type 523 was a biplane with cockpits for a single pilot and two gunlayers, the latter armed with 0.303in Lewis guns on Scarff ring mountings. Powered by two opposite-handed 160hp Sunbeam engines driving pusher propellers, with MTOW of 4,000lb, the Pike was intended for use as a long-range photographic reconnaissance aircraft or short-range bomber. Two prototypes were evaluated at Isle of Grain in 1917 and, after modifications requested by the Admiralty, their performance was found to be to be reasonable but production contracts with other firms for similar aircraft had already been placed and the Pike was not taken forward.

Type 529/529A

The Admiralty ordered two enlarged versions of the Pike which Avro designated Type 529. The first was a tractor biplane with two 190hp Rolls-Royce Falcon engines and MTOW of 6,309lb. The second, designated Type 529A, was re-engined with two 230hp BHP engines before delivery with MTOW increased to 7,135lb. It achieved a maximum level speed of 102 knots carrying twenty 50lb bombs suspended nose-upwards. The forward gunlayer acted as bomb-aimer, laying prone on the fuselage floor to look through an aperture and guiding the pilot with the aid of a Gosport speaking tube. Evaluation at Hendon showed no improvement over aircraft already in service and no production orders were placed.

Type 555 Bison

Designed to meet a 1921 Admiralty specification for a three or four-seat fleet spotter/reconnaissance aircraft to operate from the growing number of aircraft carriers, the Bison was intended to locate and track an enemy fleet as battle developed and signal corrections for battleship gunfire. Contemporary RN policy was to open fire at extreme range, beyond the visual range of battleship directors and corrections by airborne observers were, therefore, of critical importance.

The open pilot's cockpit was at the top of a high, slab-sided, fuselage forward of the top wing with an unrestricted view for deck landing and surface search. The engine cowling sloped away at an angle of 45 degrees and it was found necessary to fit a horizontal rod forward

Bison Mark II of 421 Flight embarked in *Furious* during 1926. Note the fixed pilot's cockpit access ladder.

of the windscreen to give a failure-proof indication of level flight. The fuselage was fabricated with steel tubes and the central portion formed a plywood observers' cabin which had sufficient space for the aircrew to stand, move about and make use of large rectangular observation windows at either side to plot enemy warships on a chart fitted to a central plotting table. The TAG's W/T installation was within this space. A Lewis gun on its Scarff ring could be reached easily from the cabin if the aircraft had to defend itself against enemy fighters and the pilot could use his front gun to deter enemy attacks from the forward hemisphere, tracer ammunition being used to help him 'hose' his bullets onto the target in the absence of a gunsight. Flotation bags were fitted in the rear fuselage in case the aircraft came down in the sea and an innovative design feature allowed fuel to be jettisoned so that the empty tank would counter the dead-weight of the engine and provide buoyancy for long enough after ditching to allow the crew to abandon the aircraft. Three hooks were fitted to the axle between the main wheels to engage the fore and aft retaining wires fitted in early carriers but these were deleted after 1925 when the wires were removed. Bisons had no wheel brakes and had to be chocked or held in position before take-off and after landing.

Bison II data

Length:	36ft
Wingspan:	46ft; 18ft folded
Height:	14ft 2in
MTOW:	6,132lb
Engine:	One water-cooled 480hp Napier Lion II
Fuel:	Avgas. 93 gallons
Performance:	Maximum level speed 95 knots
	Service ceiling 12,000ft. 24 minutes to 10,000ft
Endurance:	4½ hours
Armament:	One 0.303in Lewis machine gun on Scarff ring aft of cabin with ammunition in 47-round drums. One 0.303in belt-fed Vickers fixed front gun with 500 rounds

The RN received fifty-six Bisons comprising three prototypes, twelve Mark I and forty-one Mark II.

Units that operated the Bison included 421 and 423 Flights which operated from the aircraft carriers *Argus*, *Furious*, *Hermes* and *Eagle*.

The first prototype flew in 1921 with the mainplane mounted directly on top of the fuselage but production aircraft introduced a 15in gap so that a sliding hatch could be fitted in the cabin roof behind the cockpit as an alternative means of communication to the Gosport tube between observers and the pilot, although they had to shout above the noise of the engine. One Bison I was modified with a single mahogany boat-like central float and small stabilising floats under the lower wings for evaluation at Felixstowe but this revealed both longitudinal and directional instability, unsatisfactory behaviour on the water and inadequate elevator control below 70 knots. The evaluation was abandoned.

The first Bisons went to sea with 423 Flight during May 1924 in *Argus* and the various flights equipped with it served in the Atlantic, Home and Mediterranean Fleets. They were withdrawn from service in 1929.

Type 621 Tutor/Type 646 Sea Tutor

Widely used by the RAF as a two-seat pilot training aircraft from the early 1930s, sixteen were used to train RN pilots at Leuchars and Gosport. Wingspan was 34ft and they were powered by a single 155hp Armstrong Siddeley Mongoose IIIC engine. MTOW was 2,182lb. A derivative, the Sea Tutor was equipped with twin floats to train RN floatplane pilots destined to fly catapult aircraft from battleships and cruisers. MTOW rose to 2,894lb and they had a maximum level speed of 80 knots. Of the fourteen delivered, the majority were used at Calshot from 1934. Both types were declared obsolete in 1939.

Type 652

A four-seater charter aircraft that was to evolve into the Type 652A Anson. Some civilian Type 652s were requisitioned by the RAF in 1939 and two of these were transferred for use by 811 NAS during 1941/42 while it was shore-based at Lee-on-Solent, Arbroath and Machrihanish.

Type 652A Anson

Designed to meet an RAF requirement for a land-based general reconnaissance aircraft capable of limited radius patrols over the sea, the first prototype flew in 1935 and was immediately put into large-scale production.

Anson I data

Length:	42ft 3in
Wingspan:	56ft 6in
Height:	13ft 1in
MTOW:	8,000lb
Engines:	Two 335hp Armstrong Siddeley Cheetah IX radial
Fuel:	Avgas. Four 35-gallon tanks in wings
Performance:	Maximum level speed 165 knots
	Service ceiling 19,000ft. 12 minutes to 10,000ft
Endurance:	4 hours
Armament:	One 0.303in Lewis gun in aircraft used for TAG training

Anson of 783 NAS based at Lee-on-Solent in 1948.

None built directly for the RN but 215 transferred from the RAF, RCAF and RAAF.

Naval air squadrons wholly or partially equipped with Ansons at some stage of their existence, included 700, 701, 703, 707, 710, 711, 719, 720, 723, 724, 725, 728, 732, 735, 737, 739, 740, 742, 743, 744, 747, 749, 750, 751, 758, 762, 763, 766, 771, 772, 773, 778, 781, 782, 783, 784, 785, 786, 787, 789, 790, 792, 798 and 799 NAS.

The first was 783 NAS in January 1942 and the last was 700 NAS in 1956. During 1945 there were thirty-five squadrons operating the type and twenty-seven squadrons used Ansons at some stage between 1945 and 1956. At various times between October 1944 and October 1956 Ansons were used by station flights Anthorn, Arbroath, Belfast, Bramcote, Brawdy, Burscough, Crail, Culham, Eglinton, Ford, Gosport, Lossiemouth, Machrihanish, Ronaldsway, St Merryn, Stretton, Ta Kali, Worthy Down and Yeovilton.

Many were converted into flying classrooms but they could alternatively be fitted with up to eight seats to ferry passengers and urgent stores between air stations. Fitted with ASV radar they were used to train observers in the surface search and anti-submarine roles and when fitted with AI radar they were used to train night fighter pilots and observers. Some were fitted to train aircrew in the electronic warfare role, others were used in aerial photography training and to train aircrew in submarine location and tracking techniques using sonobuoys. Others were used in trials which included carrier-controlled landing development. Ansons were also used to give basic airborne instruction to observers and for advanced instrument flying training, twin-engine and refresher flying practice for pilots with associated standardisation checks. They provided airborne targets for the RN fighter direction school and were used for numerous fleet requirement tasks. A basically unremarkable aircraft, Ansons provided useful service for many years.

Type 671 Autogyro

Avro built the Cierva C.30A autogyro under licence as its Type 671 and a single example was lent to the RN by the RAF in 1935 for deck-landing evaluations. These were successfully carried out on *Courageous* in July and *Furious* in September after which the aircraft was returned. It had a rotor diameter of 37ft, MTOW of 1,900lb and was powered by a single 140hp Armstrong Siddeley Civet engine which gave a maximum level speed of 96 knots. Take-off run in still air was 36ft. Although the Type 671 was not assessed as having any operational value, its evaluation demonstrated early Admiralty interest in rotary-wing aircraft. Two similar Cierva-built autogyros were lent to the RN from the RAF in late 1939 for evaluation as radar calibration aircraft. They were returned after 6 months.

Type 683 Lancaster

Three Lancaster Mark VII bombers, each powered by four 1,620hp Rolls-Royce Merlin 24 engines, were transferred to the RN from the RAF in March 1946 and operated by 780 NAS at Hinstock. Since it was a grass airfield, they were flown from runways at nearby Peplow to give multi-engine flying experience for pilots undergoing courses at the Naval Advanced Flying School until 1947. Maximum level speed was 240 knots, MTOW was 68,000lb.

Type 768

In 1959 Avro proposed a variant of its Type 748 turboprop airliner, designated Type 768, as a replacement for the Gannet AEW 3. It had a shortened fuselage and wingspan reduced to 75ft, 40ft when folded. The AN/APS-96 radar antenna was fitted inside a 24ft rotodome over the fuselage which would have blanked the original tail surfaces and so a new twin-finned empennage was proposed. The Admiralty considered the 768 too large for carrier operation and it was not taken forward.

The Type 671 autogyro lent to the RN in 1935 which carried out deck-landing trials on *Furious*. (Philip Jarrett)

BAE SYSTEMS

The Sea Harrier and Hawk both originated as Hawker projects and their details are included under that heading.

BEARDMORE

WB I

A single WB 1 was procured for evaluation at Cranwell in 1917. It was a two-seat biplane bomber with a wingspan of 61ft 6in, MTOW of 5,600lb and powered by a single 230hp Beardmore Adriatic engine which gave a maximum speed in level flight of 80 knots. It took 44 minutes to climb to 10,000ft but it could carry up to six 110lb bombs and stay airborne for up to 7 hours. The observer/gunlayer's cockpit had a Scarff ring fitting for a 0.303in Lewis machine gun. It was intended to attack its targets in a stealthy, gliding approach for which the nose was carefully streamlined, radiators were mounted sideways to reduce drag and the wings were optimised for gliding flight. During tests it only descended 400ft per nautical mile in gliding flight. The observer/gunlayer aimed the bombs laying prone on the fuselage floor and looking through an aperture with cross-hairs and communicating left/right signals to the pilot with a system like a ship's engine-room telegraph. It was described as successful but, with Handley Page 0/100 bombers entering service, there were no production orders.

WB II

Beardmore manufactured BE 2Cs under licence and the WB II started as a private venture improvement later covered by an Admiralty contract. It mated the wings and tailplane of the BE 2 with a new fuselage of circular cross section. Comments from RNAS aircrew led to the pilot's cockpit being placed in front of the gunlayer, reversing the unpopular arrangement in the BE 2c. For the fighter role it had two synchronised, belt-fed, 0.303in Vickers front guns on the decking forward of the pilot and the gunlayer had a single 0.303in Lewis gun on a Beardmore-Richards mounting in the rear cockpit. The latter comprised a 'witch's broomstick' that pivoted on a ball joint in the cockpit floor with its upper end running round a circular ring that surmounted the cockpit. The gunlayer's seat was mounted half way up the 'stick' which could be rotated instinctively and easily or locked in one position. The gun attachment allowed a range of movement from vertically upwards to downwards only 15 degrees off the centreline of the aircraft to cover much of the danger area behind and below the aircraft. The single Admiralty prototype first flew in 1917 with a 160hp Beardmore engine, later replaced by a 200hp Hispano-Suiza which gave a maximum level speed of 105 knots. It was evaluated at Port Victoria and gained favourable reports but was not considered superior to other types already in production and no more were ordered.

WB III

Beardmore was the first manufacturer to receive an Admiralty contract to construct Sopwith Pups under licence. Pups had to be partially dismantled to fit into the small hangars of seaplane carriers and Sopwith was fully committed to the design and production of its later fighter designs and so the Admiralty tasked Beardmore to modify the Pup to improve its carrier compatibility. The resulting WB III was one of the first wheeled aircraft intended specifically for carrier operation.

A WB III in 1918 with jettisonable undercarriage which was embarked on *Nairana* for several periods. (Philip Jarrett)

WB III data

Length:	20ft 2½in
Wingspan:	25ft (10ft 3in folded)
Height:	8ft 1¼in
MTOW:	1,289lb
Engine:	One 80hp Le Rhone 9C or 80hp Clerget
Fuel:	Avgas. 18 gallons
Performance:	Maximum level speed 90 knots
	Service ceiling 12,400ft. 12 minutes to 10,000ft
Endurance:	2 hours 45 minutes
Armament:	One 0.303in Lewis gun

The Admiralty ordered 100 WB IIIs in 1917 in batches of 30 and 70. The prototype was modified from the last Pup of a batch built for the RNAS.

No dedicated units were fully equipped with WB IIIs but the Grand Fleet aircraft parks at Turnhouse and Donibristle maintained a number that were embarked as single-aircraft flights. They saw most use in the seaplane carriers *Nairana* and *Pegasus* which could strike them down into their small forward hangars but the prototype carriers *Furious* and *Vindictive* also embarked some for short periods. WB IIIs were also embarked for short periods in *Manxman* and *Campania* as well as the battlecruisers *Renown* and *Princess Royal* and the cruisers *Cassandra*, *Dublin*, *Phaeton* and *Royalist*.

Since they were essentially 'one-shot' interceptors with no flight deck capable of recovering them if they were too far from land, those that were flown off in the Grand Fleet's normal operating areas in the eastern North Sea had to ditch on completion of their sortie. Those that did so were written off charge although they might only be a few weeks old. Of the last batch, forty-six aircraft were delivered straight into reserve and never used operationally.

In order to fold, the wing structure was redesigned, stagger was eliminated, the dihedral angle reduced and full-gap interplane struts connected the centre section to the lower stub wings. Other modifications included a lengthened fuselage and wingtip skids but the after fuselage and tailplane were identical to the Pup. The prototype and the first thirteen production aircraft had an undercarriage that could be folded into the bottom of the fuselage to reduce the aircraft's stowed volume. This was not a success, however, and subsequent aircraft were fitted with a jettisonable undercarriage consisting of two steel tube V-struts with their upper ends secured by steel tubing intended to reduce the risk of the aircraft nosing over as it ditched. Although it was a distinct type, most RNAS personnel referred to the WB III as the Beardmore Folding Pup. The prototype was delivered to Eastchurch in February 1917, followed by the first production example in June but further deliveries were delayed when a shipment of Le Rhone engines was sunk. At first the Lewis gun was mounted on a tripod in front of the cockpit to fire upwards at an angle of 45 degrees through a cut-out in the upper wing centre section. Later it was moved to a mounting above the upper wing centre section to starboard of the centreline, firing forwards over the propeller disc. The 47-round ammunition drums were loaded with ball, tracer, and Brock and Pomeroy ammunition for use against Zeppelins. The WB III was one of the first naval aircraft fitted with flotation gear as standard. The type never proved popular with pilots because the modified wings impaired the Pup's delightful handling qualities. Most surviving examples were deleted by early 1919.

WB IV

A single-seat fighter intended for operation from aircraft carriers, the WB IV's wings could be folded aft like the WB III but the single 200hp Hispano-Suiza engine was installed at the aircraft's centre of gravity, behind the pilot and directly under the centre section of the upper wing. An extension shaft passed between the pilot's legs to drive a two-bladed wooden propeller and the cockpit was situated well forward to give an exceptionally good view over the steeply-sloping nose for deck landing. Flotation gear was to be capable of keeping the aircraft afloat for at least 6 hours, the whole fuselage was covered with plywood, the cockpit was watertight and a large buoyancy chamber was built into the forward section. To make ditching safer, the undercarriage was jettisonable and the area under the cockpit was hydrodynamically-shaped to reduce splash on impact and keep the cockpit above the water. Only one of three prototypes ordered was completed and it was evaluated at Isle of Grain in 1918. It had a maximum level speed of 97 knots and the 37-gallon fuel tank gave an endurance of 2 hours 30 minutes. Wingspan was 35ft and MTOW 2,595lb. Armament comprised a 0.303in Vickers front gun on the port side of the fuselage where it could be re-cocked if necessary by the pilot and a 0.303in Lewis gun on a tripod mounting in front of the fuselage to fire upwards at an angle of 45 degrees. The WB IV was considered inferior to the Sopwith 2F.1 Ship Camel, especially with regard to climbing performance which RNAS pilots regarded as essential to intercept Zeppelins from deck alert. It was also considered that engine maintenance would have been difficult.

WB V

Designed to meet an Admiralty specification for a single-seat, ship-board interceptor fighter armed with a single 37mm Puteaux cannon and powered by a single 200hp Hispano-Suiza engine mounted conventionally in front of the pilot, the WB V had its cockpit under the upper wing centre section together with flotation gear, folding wings and a jettisonable undercarriage. The gun was mounted between the engine cylinder blocks, firing through a hollow propeller shaft. Pilots had to sit close to the cannon breech to load and fire it and even the designer considered this to be horrible. The first of three prototypes was delivered for evaluation at Isle of Grain in December 1917 modified with a machine gun armament which gave a performance similar to the WB IV. It was written off after an accident in January 1918. The second prototype was completed but abandoned and the third never completed.

HM Airship Number 24

Details of the 23 Class are included in the Vickers section but after it began work on Number 23, the Admiralty contracted Beardmore to build Number 24 and Armstrong Whitworth Number 25. Number 24 flew for the first time in October 1917 but was found to be heavier than its sister-ships, probably because Beardmore used extra-strong rivets and fastenings. Little could be done to remedy this but the engine and propeller were removed from the rear car to give sufficient disposable

HM Airship Number 24.

lift for a delivery flight to East Fortune. Machinery was then re-installed and acceptance trials began in December before moving to Pulham in 1918 as a training airship. After mooring-mast experiments it was deleted in December 1919 having only flown for 164 hours 38 minutes.

R 27

One of the 23X class airships, R 27 was built by Beardmore and a second, R 29, by Armstrong Whitworth. Improvements included modifications to the bow and stern to increase the envelope's gas volume but the most significant change was the removal of the keel. Fuel, ballast and bombs were all re-located into the frame and distributed along the bottom two girders and inverted U-shaped ribs fitted to them created an internal walkway from which every part of the ship could be reached. These two airships also had a modified fuel system with a large diameter aluminium pipe running beneath the tanks which could be used to fill them under pressure or jettison fuel to reduce weight.

R 27 data

Length:	539ft
Diameter:	53ft
Height:	75ft
Envelope capacity:	990,000ft^3
Engines:	Four 300hp Rolls-Royce Eagle
Gross lift:	30.1 tons
Disposable lift;	8.5 tons
Performance:	Maximum level speed 48 knots
Endurance:	Over 23 hours
Armament:	Light bombs and 0.303in Lewis machine guns

R 27 flew for the first time in June 1918; trials at Howden demonstrated its improvement over the basic 23 class and in August 1918 it carried out a flight of 23 hours 15 minutes. A hangar fire destroyed it 6 days later when a USN radio mechanic accidentally caused a spark which ignited fuel spilled on the hangar floor near the un-numbered USN airship he was working on. It was destroyed together with R 27, SSZ 38 and SSZ 54. It had only flown for 89 hours and 40 minutes.

HM Airship R 27.

HM Airship R 34 under construction.

R 34

Beardmore's R 34 was identical to R 33 built by Armstrong Whitworth and its data is listed in that section. It first flew in March 1919 and was accepted by the RN in May after repairs when a jammed elevator cable led to a heavy landing after the second flight. Based at East Fortune, it carried out a 56-hour fully-armed flight around the Baltic coast of Germany as one of a series of measures intended to coerce the German Government into signing the peace treaty at Versailles. In July 1919 it carried out the first double crossing of the Atlantic, landing at Mineola, Long Island after a flight of 108 hours 12 minutes into a westerly wind. The return flight, assisted by the wind, took only 75 hours and 3 minutes. After moving to Howden it was used training until August 1921 when it was caught by worsening weather over the North Yorkshire Moors and struck a hill-top, smashing both fore and aft propellers and damaging the control car. It struggled back to Howden using the two wing engines and landed with the help of a 400-man handling party but strong crosswinds prevented it from being moved into its hangar. After being moored out on the airfield it continually impacted the ground and was damaged beyond repair, a sad end for an effective airship that had flown for over 400 hours.

R 36

The last rigid airship built under Admiralty contract, R 36 was designed using information gathered from examining the wreckage of Zeppelin L 49 which had been brought down relatively intact in France during October 1917. Work on it was suspended in November 1918 but resumed in 1920 to a revised civilian design. For comparison with the earlier airships, it had a gas capacity of 2,101,000ft^3 and a disposable lift of 16 tons. In 1921 it was given the civilian registration G-FAAF.

BEECH AIRCRAFT COMPANY

Traveller

The USN transferred seventy-five Travellers to the RN under Lend-Lease arrangements and shipped them to the UK from February 1944. It was a single-engine biplane powered by a 450hp Pratt & Whitney Wasp Junior R-985-50 engine giving a maximum level speed of 166 knots. Wingspan was 32ft and MTOW 4,250lb. They were capable of carrying three passengers and up to 125lb of luggage in addition to a pilot and aircrewman.

Travellers were operated by 701, 712, 725, 730, 740, 776, 778, 781, 782, 787 and 799 NAS in the light utility role between April 1944 and November 1945 although some of these squadrons only operated a single aircraft for short periods. They were also used by station flights at Anthorn, Dale, Drem, Eglinton, Machrihanish and Stretton and Belfast between November 1944 and November 1945. The USN considered them sufficiently valuable to require their return after the war and fifty-one were shipped back to the USN. The remainder were either written off or otherwise disposed of by the RN.

Traveller.

Navigator

The USN transferred five Navigators, designated SNB-2C, to the RN in 1943 in lieu of a similar number of Grumman Goose amphibians contracted under Lend-Lease arrangements. They were powered by two 450hp Pratt & Whitney Wasp R-985-25 engines which gave a maximum level speed of 198 knots. Wingspan was 47ft 8in and MTOW 7,850lb. The RN retained the name Navigator but not the USN designation and all five were transferred in the USA; one was re-allocated to BOAC and a second was retained by the RN detachment at Anacostia for use by staff officers visiting factories manufacturing aircraft for the RN. It could carry six passengers in addition to two crew members. The remaining three were shipped to Ceylon and used by 742 NAS to provide daily clipper flights between RN airfields in Ceylon and India from 1943 to 1945. At least one flew back to the UK in 1945 and was used by Ronaldsway station flight in 1946.

Expediter

The USN transferred seventy-two Expediters, designated JRB-2, to the RN under Lend-Lease arrangements from 1944. An improved version of the Navigator, they were used widely in the light utility role. The USN name was retained in RN use.

Expediter data

Length:	34ft 3in
Wingspan:	47ft 8in
Height:	9ft 4in
MTOW:	8,000lb
Engines:	Two 450hp Pratt & Whitney Wasp R-985-AN-1
Fuel:	Avgas. 229 gallons
Performance:	Maximum level speed 210 knots
	Service ceiling 26,000ft. 3 minutes to 5,000ft
Endurance:	Up to 7½ hours
Armament:	None

Expediters partially equipped 701, 723, 724, 728, 730, 733, 742, 755, 781, 782, 791 and 799 NAS from 1944 onwards; the last examples were only retired from 728 NAS at Hal Far during 1959. They were also operated by station flights between 1945 and 1955, albeit some of them only for short periods, including Arbroath, China Bay, Coimbatore, Hal Far, Lossiemouth, Ronaldsway and Yeovilton. They carried up to six passengers or an equivalent weight of light stores and proved both reliable and ideal for running clipper flights from RN airfields in in the UK, Malta, Ceylon and Australia. Only five were returned to the USN after 1945; the remainder were purchased for another decade of service. Some were used as Admiral's barges and given special paint schemes.

Expediter of 728 NAS based at Hal Far in 1955.

Beech Avenger T 1 of 750 NAS.

Avenger T1

In 2012 four Beech King Air 350ER aircraft were procured for the UK Military Flying Training System run by Ascent Flight Training as COMR, aircraft, known in RN service as the Avenger T 1. They equip 750 NAS at Culdrose delivering Phase 3 training for RN observers before they move on to operational helicopter types and are flown by a mix of RN and civilian pilots. The QOIs are all RN. Wingspan was 57ft 11in, MTOW 15,000lb and they were powered by two 1,050shp Pratt & Whitney PT6A-60A turboprops, giving a maximum level speed of 313 knots. They have dual controls but are normally flown by a single pilot with up to four student observers and their instructors.

BELL

P-39D Airacobra

One of a batch of fighters ordered by the French but taken over by the UK in 1940, a single Airacobra was used for carrier trials. In 1944 it was used to investigate arrested landings by aircraft with a tricycle undercarriage and effectively became 'Winkle' Brown's personal aircraft after he carried out the first deck landing by an aircraft with a tricycle undercarriage on *Pretoria Castle* on 4 April 1945. He used it as a hack to fly between airfields for his test work. It was powered by a single 1,150hp Allison V-1710-35 V12 engine which gave a maximum level speed of 324 knots. Wingspan was 34ft and MTOW was 8,300lb. The engine was positioned at the centre of gravity, aft of the cockpit, driving the propeller through a shaft under the pilot's seat. It was deleted in 1945.

P-39D Airacobra landing on *Pretoria Castle*.

A Royal Marines Bell 47 Sioux being recovered by a Wessex HU 5 of 847 NAS.

Bell 47 Sioux

Built under licence by Westland in the 1960s for use as unit light helicopters by the British Army; fourteen of these were allocated to the Royal Marines to form 3 Commando Brigade Air Squadron at Sembawang in August 1968. The unit also operated six Westland Scouts. In 1971 the unit moved to a new base at Coypool in Plymouth from where helicopters were deployed in support of amphibious operations from North Norway to the Mediterranean. Westland Gazelles replaced the Sioux in 1975. Rotor diameter was 37ft 1½in and MTOW 2,850lb.

BLACKBURN

Type L

A two-seat hydro-biplane or seaplane with twin floats, the Type L was designed for the Daily Mail Circuit of Britain seaplane race in August 1914. Wingspan was 49ft 6in and it was powered by a single 130hp Canton-Unne engine. The race was abandoned when war was declared against Germany and the Type L was requisitioned by the Admiralty. Flown initially by company pilots from a section of beach north of Scarborough on coastal patrols, some unconfirmed reports say that it was fitted with a machine gun. It hit cliffs while flying from Scarborough to Killingholme and was deleted in 1915.

TB Seaplane

A biplane with two separate fuselages, each with its own cockpit and engine, supported on the water by floats, originally to have been powered by two 150hp Smith engines. These proved unsuccessful and 100hp Gnome rotaries were substituted. The Admiralty ordered nine and the first was completed in August 1915. The last example delivered in 1916 was re-engined with two 110hp Clerget 9b engines but was still under-powered. Two were evaluated at Isle of Grain but not found satisfactory. The remainder may never have flown before being deleted in 1917. The type's shortcomings were explained in the Grain report which explained that the pilot occupied the left-hand cockpit with all the engine and flying controls while the observer occupied the right-hand cockpit several feet away with no controls other than the starting handle for the engine on his side. Starting the engines whilst the aircraft was afloat was said to need discipline, courage and agility because a pool of excess petrol formed on the float under each engine as it was primed which usually ignited when the engine coughed into life. The observer had to lie on the lower wing centre-section, put out the fire on the pilot's side with an extinguisher, scramble into his own cockpit, start the second engine and then jump out again to extinguish the fire on his own float. Because of the engine noise, the only way the pilot and observer could communicate was by hand signals. It was intended to be a Zeppelin destroyer armed with a 70lb container of Ranken darts. Unsurprisingly, there were no further orders for the type.

Triplane

Designed an anti-Zeppelin fighter powered by a single 110hp Clerget pusher engine, later replaced by a 100hp Gnome monosoupape. Wingspan was 33ft 5in and it was to be armed with a Davis gun but it was never fitted. Only one was built and evaluated in late February 1917 but found to be unsatisfactory. It was deleted in March.

GP

A conventional three-seat, twin-engine biplane, the GP was intended as a long-range anti-submarine patrol bomber, identified by Blackburn as the GP, seaplane. It had a long, slim fuselage of small cross section and engines fitted in nacelles between the wings. Wingspan was 74ft 10in and MTOW 8,600lb. The two floats were similar to those on the TB and, like them, were fitted under the engines. The wings could be folded outboard of the engines for hangar stowage although the type was never intended to operate from seaplane carriers. The three aircrew

The prototype Kangaroo in 1918.

sat in open cockpits with the gunlayer in the nose armed with a 0.303in Lewis gun fitted on a Scarff ring and a bombsight mounted outside the cockpit to starboard. The pilot sat in the centre, just ahead of the wing centre-section and an observer or second gunlayer aft of the wings, also with a Scarff-ring mounted Lewis gun. Up to four 100lb or 230lb bombs could be carried on racks under the wings and a torpedo could be carried on the centre section between the floats. Only two prototypes were built, the first fitted with two 150hp Sunbeam Nubian engines and the second with two Rolls-Royce Falcons driving four-bladed propellers. Service trials at Isle of Grain during 1916 found the GP to have a maximum speed of 85 knots and an endurance of 8 hours. Although they were considered successful, no production orders for the GP followed.

Kangaroo

A derivative of the GP with a wheeled undercarriage, the Kangaroo reflected an Admiralty policy change that patrols over the sea were better performed by wheeled aircraft because seaplane take-offs and landings were often limited by sea state. MTOW was 8,017lb and its two 250hp Rolls-Royce Falcon engines gave a maximum level speed of 90 knots. The Admiralty ordered twenty in 1917 and the first was delivered in 1918. Based at Seaton Carew, they equipped RNAS flights that became 252 and 246 Squadrons after the creation of the RAF, still based at Seaton Carew. They were used on coastal anti-submarine patrols off the east coast of the UK.

The fuselage was essentially the same as that of the GP except that there was provision for a single 520lb bomb suspended from its nose in an internal compartment between the main spars of the lower wing. Otherwise the armament was the same. The gunlayer's bombsight was an RNAS Mark IIA. Some Kangaroos were transferred to the anti-submarine observers' school at Aldeburgh in 1919 but all were withdrawn from service by the end of 1919. Wingspan was 74ft 10in and the wings folded outboard of the engines for hangar stowage. Internal avgas tanks contained 215½ gallons which gave an endurance of 8 hours.

N 1B

Known in the factory as the 'Nib', this was a concept design for a single-seat, flying-boat fighter intended to escort flying boat patrols over the North Sea. It was to have been powered by a single 200hp pusher engine giving an estimated maximum level speed of 100 knots but Admiralty policy changed while it was under construction and it was never completed.

Blackburd

The Blackburd was designed as a carrier-borne aircraft capable of carrying a heavier torpedo than the Sopwith T.1 Cuckoo. It had a square-section fuselage and its unusual undercarriage had a transverse axle with the wheels connected to it for take-off which had to be jettisoned before the torpedo could be dropped. Skids were used for the subsequent deck landing. It was fitted with flotation bags and, if it ditched, it was thought that the lack of wheels would prevent it from nosing over. Wingspan was 52ft 6in and MTOW 5,700lb. It was powered by a single 350hp Rolls-Royce Eagle VIII diving a two-bladed wooden tractor propeller to give a maximum level speed of 80 knots whilst carrying a torpedo. The outer wings could be folded. Trials showed the Blackburd's performance to be inferior to the Cuckoo and it lacked a comparable ability to manoeuvre at low level during an attack. Three prototypes were delivered to East Fortune in August 1918 but there were no subsequent production orders.

Swift

Most orders for new aircraft were cancelled after the Armistice in 1918 but Admiralty enthusiasm for torpedo attack aircraft led to their continued development and Blackburn worked on a private venture torpedo aircraft powered by a single 450hp Napier Lion IB engine. A new company designation system identified it as the T.1 Swift, a single-seat biplane that was the first to resolve the problem of folding staggered wings effectively. It was designed to carry the 1,423lb Mark VIII 18in torpedo, a genuine 'ship-killing' weapon instead of the lighter Mark IX carried by the Cuckoo. Three 520lb bombs could be carried as an alternative. There was still insufficient weight to carry an observer, however, and contemporary Admiralty thinking was that strikes would only be carried out over relatively short ranges and the pilot would not need navigational assistance. A single prototype was built for evaluation at the A & AEE Martlesham Heath in 1921 and satisfactory deck-landing trials were carried out on *Argus* during 1921 but no further Swifts were ordered. Wingspan was 48ft 6in, MTOW 6,300lb and a maximum level speed was 93 knots.

Dart

The Swift's successful A&AEE trial report led to the procurement of 3 modified aircraft for further evaluation. They had reduced wingspan and a later mark of engine, differences considered sufficient to justify a new designation, T.2, later named Dart. Handling trials at Martlesham Heath in 1921/22 proved satisfactory.

Darts of 810 NAS from *Courageous* in 1933.

Dart data

Length:	35ft 4½in (40ft 2½in with floats)
Wingspan:	45ft 5¾in (17ft 6in folded)
Height:	12ft 11in (17ft with floats)
MTOW:	6,383lb
Engine:	One 465hp Napier Lion V
Fuel:	Avgas. 78½ gallons
Performance:	Maximum level speed 94 knots
	Service ceiling 10,200ft. 44 minutes to 10,000ft
Endurance:	3 hours
Armament:	One Mark VIII or Mark IX torpedo on centreline.
	Equivalent weight of bombs on under wing hardpoints.
	No gun armament

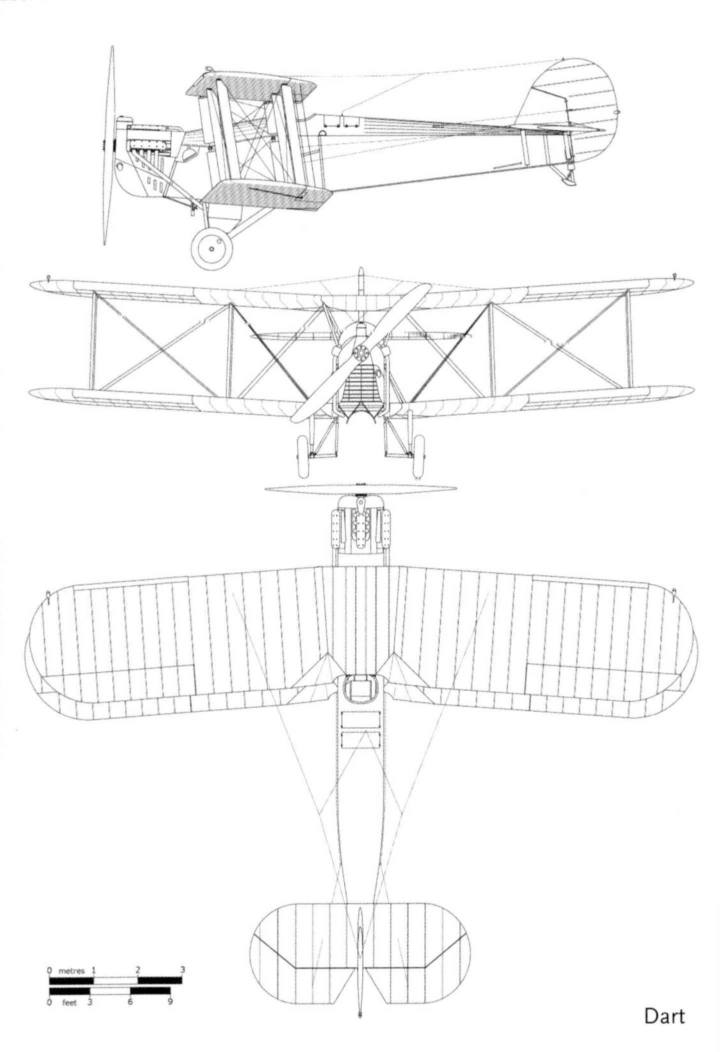

The Fleet Air Arm received 117 Darts, including the three prototypes, produced in small batches over a period of 5 years.

Darts served with 460, 461, 462, 463 and 464 Flights between 1923 and 1933 in the carriers *Eagle*, *Furious* and *Courageous*. The type was also used briefly by 810 NAS after it was formed by amalgamating 463 and 464 Flights in April 1933.

A Dart of 810 NAS on *Courageous*' forward lift.

A Blackburn of 422 Flight embarked in *Eagle* during 1926.

The Dart was large for a single-seater but was rugged and reliable and, with a stalling speed of only 38 knots, it was easy to land on a carrier deck. After replacing the Cuckoo it remained in service for 10 years and played an important part in the early development of RN torpedo attack tactics. Later production batches had alternative wheel or float undercarriages so that aircraft could operate while their carriers were at anchor. The Dart's solid deck-landing reputation led to its selection to demonstrate the feasibility of night operations from an aircraft carrier and on 1 July 1926 a Dart of 462 Flight carried out the world's first night deck landing on *Furious* followed by further, successful night operations in the English Channel and the waters off Scotland culminating in a declaration of IOC. Night operations became routine and in 1928 the Darts of 463 Flight in *Courageous* specialised in night attacks and had their aircraft painted black.

In September 1930, fifteen Darts from 461 and 462 Flights carried out an attack with practice torpedoes on the new battleships *Nelson* and *Rodney* off the Isle of Wight. Eight hits were achieved and no aircraft were assessed as having been shot down because they were difficult targets for the fleet's fighters to intercept and umpires ruled that anti-aircraft gunfire would have achieved little against them. Pilots were trained to drop their torpedoes from only 15ft to minimise their air trajectory and reduce any tendency to dive below set running depth after water entry. This was especially important in shallow, littoral water where they might otherwise hit the seabed. The Dart force began to run down in 1929 and was finally declared obsolete in April 1935.

Blackburn

Imaginatively named after a town in Lancashire in line with contemporary British policy and not the company that built it, the Blackburn was intended to carry out the same reconnaissance and gunnery spotting roles as the Avro Bison, both types having been designed to meet Specification 3/21. Wingspan was 45ft 6½in, reduced to 17ft 6in folded, and it was powered by a single 450hp Napier Lion IIB engine giving a maximum level speed of 107 knots. Avgas capacity of 90 gallons gave an endurance of 4½ hours and MTOW was 5,962lb. Service ceiling was 12,950ft but performance could never be described as lively as it took 49 minutes to climb to 12,000ft. Fortunately reconnaissance missions were usually flown at low level.

To simplify production and reduce the number of spare parts needed in an aircraft carrier, the Blackburn had folding wings and tailplane identical and interchangeable with the Dart but the obvious difference between them was the large cabin for the observer and TAG. The fuselage was made up with lengths of tubular steel fitted into joint clusters machined from solid. The TAG's W/T equipment was against the forward cabin bulkhead and there was a folding table for the observer. Aft of the cabin there was an open space, shielded from the slipstream by a rearward extension of the cabin roof, from which the observer could take bearings or use a camera. It also had a Scarff ring for a 0.303in Lewis gun with three spare 47-round drums of ammunition. Surprisingly, given the aircraft's role, there was provision for a front gun on the port side of the pilot's open cockpit; a Vickers 0.303in belt-fed machine gun with 500 rounds.

The pilot sat in a high, open cockpit just forward of a cut-out in the leading edge of the upper wing and protected from the airflow by a Triplex windscreen. The engine cowling sloped away sharply to give a good view for deck landing. The Fleet Air Arm received sixty-three Blackburns, including the three prototypes, in small batches between May 1923 and December 1926. The last thirty were to an improved Mark II standard powered by the 465hp Napier Lion V. Mark I aircraft equipped 422 Flight in *Eagle* and *Argus* between 1923 and 1928 and 420 Flight in *Furious* between 1926 and 1928. Mark II aircraft equipped 449 Flight in *Furious* and *Courageous* between 1929 and 1931 and 450 Flight in *Argus* and *Courageous* between 1929 and 1931. Some aircraft were modified for trials with float undercarriages which had strengthened keels that, in theory, allowed them to land on the deck of an aircraft carrier. Trials showed this to be possible but damage was caused to both floats and flight deck with the former losing their watertight integrity. Handling trials at MAEE Felixstowe found the seaplane variant to be viceless in the air but unsuitable for operational use and development ceased. A small number of Mark Is were modified for use as deck-landing trainers, known unofficially as Blackburn Bulls. The front fuselage was widened to accommodate student pilot and instructor side-by-side in an open cockpit. The widened fuselage increased drag to the extent that the trainer needed a considerable take-off run and took 10 minutes to climb to 1,000ft. After its withdrawal from operational service in 1931 the Blackburn was declared obsolete in 1933.

Airedale

A three-seat, deck-landing monoplane powered by a 385hp Armstrong Siddeley Jaguar engine designed to meet Specification 37/22 for a Blackburn and Bison replacement. Its wings folded aft along the fuselage sides to reduce wingspan from 46ft to 17ft 6in for hangar stowage. The pilot's open cockpit was forward of the wing to give a good view for deck landing and there was a cabin for the observer and TAG with an open area aft of it fitted with a Scarff ring for a 0.303in Lewis gun. The pilot had a 0.5in Vickers front gun with an interrupter mechanism to fire through the propeller arc. Light bombs could be carried on a carrier under the fuselage, aimed by the observer lying prone under the pilot's cockpit to look through a bombsight mounted in the bottom of the fuselage.

The Airedale incorporated several unusual features including a lever which allowed the pilot to rotate his seat aft so that he could step down into the cabin to talk to the observer. There was also a folding seat at the rear of the cabin with duplicated controls so that the observer could attempt to fly the aircraft back to the carrier in an emergency or, presumably, the pilot could fly the aircraft from the cabin if he chose to do so. Two 60-gallon fuel tanks gave an endurance of 4 hours. MTOW was 4,942lb and maximum level speed was 105 knots. Two prototypes were built for evaluation, one of which was unfortunately crashed by a service pilot when he collected it from Brough to fly to A&AEE Martlesham Heath. The second was tested in 1926 but said to offer insufficient advance over types already in service.

Ripon

The T.5 Ripon was designed to meet Specification 21/23 for a torpedo/reconnaissance aircraft. In the reconnaissance role it was intended to operate out to considerable distances from its carrier and so an observer was considered essential to cope with navigation and communications.

Ripon Mark IIA data

Length:	36ft 9in (41ft 3in with floats)
Wingspan:	44ft 10in (17ft 10in folded)
Height:	12ft 10in (15ft with floats)
MTOW:	7,405lb (7,866lb with floats)
Engine:	One 570hp Napier Lion X, XI or XIA
Fuel:	Avgas. 162 gallons plus an optional 120-gallon auxiliary tank in lieu of a torpedo
Performance:	Maximum level speed 98 knots Service ceiling 13,000ft. 25 minutes to 10,000ft
Endurance :	5 hours. Up to 14 hours with the auxiliary fuel tank
Armament:	One 18in torpedo on centreline or up to three 520lb bombs or six 230lb bombs underwing. One belt-fed Vickers 0.303in front gun with 500 rounds and a 0.303in Lewis gun on a flexible mount in the rear cockpit with three spare 47-round ammunition drums

The Fleet Air Arm received ninety-six Ripons including two prototypes, built in small batches between 1925 and 1932.

Ripons equipped 460 and 461 Flights in *Glorious* together with 462, 465 and 466 Flights in *Furious* from 1929 onwards. After the re-grouping of flights into squadrons in April 1933 Ripons served with 810 NAS in *Courageous*, 811 NAS in *Furious* and 812 NAS in *Glorious*.

The two prototypes were effectively the only Mark Is. The first flew in April 1926 with a wheeled undercarriage and the second in August with floats; contemporary Admiralty policy dictating that naval aircraft should be capable of operating with either. After competitive

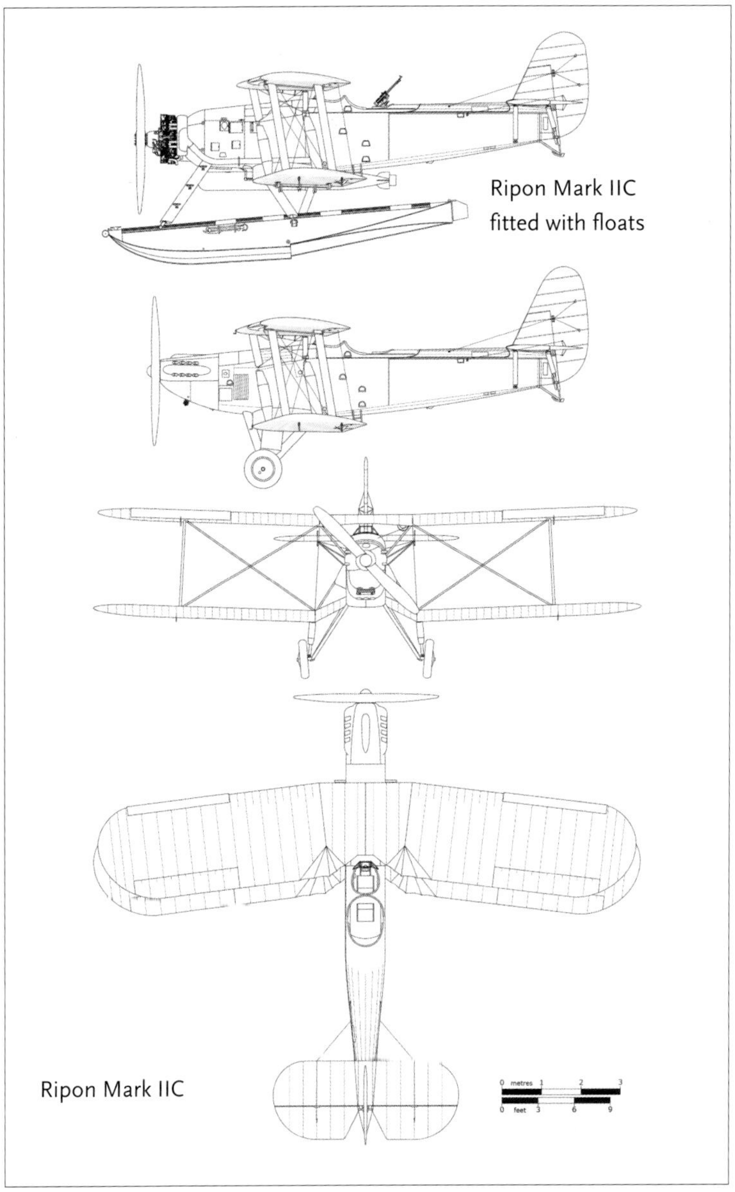

Ripon Mark IIC fitted with floats

Ripon Mark IIC

The all-metal Ripon Mark III prototype in 1930.

Ripon about to launch.

Ripon Mark II fitted with floats for trials at the MAEE in 1929.

tests against other designs a Mark II version of the Ripon was ordered into production with a more powerful Lion engine. It had familiar Blackburn construction techniques with a steel engine mounting, steel tubular centre section and tie rod braced wooden rear section. The wings were hinged to the rear spars of the top and bottom centre sections for folding to the rear. Minor improvements led to the Mark IIA and in 1930 Blackburn produced two Ripons a week. From 1932 modification kits were produced to bring earlier aircraft up to Mark IIC standard, the final sub-variant. There is no reference a Mark IIB in surviving records. A single prototype Mark III featuring all-metal construction and modified fuselage lines was built as a private venture but not ordered into production.

Sprat

The T.R.1 Sprat was designed to meet Specification 5/24 for a deck landing and seaplane training aircraft with interchangeable wheel or float undercarriages. A single prototype was built and flown in 1926 for evaluation at both A&AEE and MAEE. These proved successful but the requirement was cancelled as an economy measure and there were no production orders. Wingspan was 34ft 9in and MTOW 2,648lb with floats or 2,318lb with wheels. The wings folded for carrier stowage. It was powered by a single 275hp Rolls-Royce Falcon III which gave a maximum level speed of 100 knots.

Nautilus

Intended to meet Specification O.22/26 for a carrier-borne, two-seat fleet spotter aircraft with limited capability as an interceptor fighter, a single prototype was built in 1929 for evaluation. Wingspan was 37ft and MTOW 4,750lb. It was powered by a single 525hp Rolls-Royce F.XIIMS engine to give a maximum level speed of 135 knots. Endurance was 2 hours 30 minutes and the armament comprised a single belt-fed Vickers 0.303in front gun in a trough on the port side of the engine cowling with 500 rounds and a single 0.303in Lewis gun on a rotatable gun ring in the rear cockpit with three spare 47-round drum magazines. The front gun could be replaced by a G 3 camera gun for training and there was a W/T set in the rear cockpit powered by a wind-driven generator on the starboard side. The Hawker Osprey was selected to meet the requirement but the Nautilus was considered to be a useful aircraft and it was allocated to 405 Flight in late 1929 and embarked in *Furious* during 1930. The gun ring was removed from the after cockpit and a passenger seat fitted to create an early form of COD aircraft. It was subsequently used as a hack at A & AEE until at least 1933.

B.3

In 1931 a single prototype B.3 was ordered for evaluation against other types to meet Specification M.1/30 for a two-seat, carrier-borne torpedo bomber with folding wings. The pilot and observer had tandem cockpits with a prone bomb-aiming position for the latter under the pilot's cockpit floor for use in level bombing. It was completed in 1932 but lost in an accident at A&AEE in 1933. Blackburn built a modified prototype in 1933 as a private venture designated as the M.1/30A which incorporated features repeated in later Blackburn naval designs. It was powered by an 825hp Rolls-Royce Buzzard IIIMS engine which gave a maximum level speed of 125 knots. Wingspan was 49ft 6in and MTOW 5,853lb. The decking behind the observer's position could be removed to accommodate a TAG for reconnaissance and spotting missions and the fuselage was divided into watertight compartments to give greater buoyancy than flotation bags after a ditching. Internal avgas fuel tankage of 257 gallons gave an endurance of up to 5 hours. Another significant development was the installation of pneumatically-operated brakes; the B.3 being one of the first naval aircraft to have them. Armament comprised the contemporary standard 0.303in Vickers front gun and a Lewis gun for the TAG. Primary armament was a 1,900lb Mark VIII, Mark X or K type torpedo in crutches in the centreline between the undercarriage legs. Alternatively, racks were provided on hardpoints under the lower wings capable of carrying four 550lb, 520lb or 500lb bombs, eight 250lb bombs or eight 20lb anti-personnel bombs. Although not ordered into production the Blackburn M.1/30A was purchased for evaluation by A&AEE in 1934 where it was assessed as having outstanding technical merit although it fell short of M.1/30. After its assessment it was used for ditching trials in 1935 and subsequently deleted.

Baffin

The B.5 Baffin was a re-engined development of the Ripon and replaced it in service but its performance was only a marginal improvement over the Ripon IIC. Two private-venture prototypes were

built, one with a 650hp Armstrong Siddeley Tiger I engine and the other with a 545hp Bristol Pegasus I.MS, and given the manufacturer's Class B markings B 4 and B 5 which then became their Blackburn type numbers under a new system. Both were evaluated at A&AEE during 1933 and the Pegasus-engined B 5 was selected for production. Deck-landing trials were carried out on *Courageous* and catapult trials were carried out at Farnborough in early 1934. Specification 4/33 was written around the B 5 and it was given the name Baffin. Later Baffins were fitted with the Bristol Pegasus II.M3 engine which gave a slightly better rate of climb but an inferior overall performance, higher fuel consumption and increased weight. A 20 per cent reduction in endurance after fitting the Pegasus II.M3 gave urgency to the requirement for a replacement and, although the Baffin could carry the same weapon load as the Ripon it was only considered an interim type.

Baffin data

Length:	38ft 4in
Wingspan:	45ft 6½in (17ft 10in folded)
Height:	12ft 10in
MTOW:	7,610lb
Engine:	One 580hp Bristol Pegasus II.M3
Fuel:	Avgas. 120 gallons
Performance:	Maximum level speed 120 knots
	Service ceiling 13,000ft. 30 minutes to 10,000ft
Endurance:	Over 3 hours
Armament:	Identical to the Ripon

A flight of Baffins from Gosport in 1936.

Of the ninety-one Baffins delivered to the Fleet Air Arm, twenty-seven were built new and sixty-four were converted from Ripons.

Early aircraft were allocated to 812 NAS in *Glorious* in January 1934 and the type became the standard torpedo bomber in March. By late 1934 Baffins equipped 810 NAS in *Courageous* and 811 NAS in *Furious*. It was also operated briefly by 820 NAS between August 1935 and February 1936. Most Baffin squadrons were re-equipped with Fairey Swordfish from 1936 but the last to relinquish them was 810 NAS in March 1937 which replaced them with Blackburn Sharks. Baffins of 810 NAS led the Fleet Air Arm fly-past over King George V's Jubilee Naval Review at Spithead on 15 July 1935.

Shark

The B.6 Shark was a three-seat biplane intended to meet Specification S.15/33 for a TSR aircraft. Other firms submitted aircraft to meet S.15/33 including Fairey with the TSR I which evolved into the Swordfish. The Shark had a buoyant Alclad-skinned fuselage but could only carry Mark VIII or Mark X torpedoes, not the heavier 'K' type. A system of slanting struts replaced the streamlined flying and landing wires used in previous Blackburn designs to form a 'Warren Girder' structure which was strong enough to support a full bomb load while the aircraft was struck down in a carrier's hangar with its wings folded. While this allowed Sharks to be armed before they were ranged onto the flight deck, it made the wings heavy and difficult to fold manually.

A B C D E F G H I J K L M N O P Q R S T U V W X Y Z

Taxi-ing out of the range onto the centreline for take-off was greatly eased by having pneumatic wheel brakes and a lockable tail wheel. The first prototype flew in August 1933.

A course-setting bombsight was fitted on a hinged mounting over a hatch in the observer's cockpit deck which could be closed by a watertight door when not in use. Camber-changing flaps were considered essential for taking-off from a carrier at maximum weight and were also used to land-on at the minimum practical speed. The prototype carried out handling trials at the A&AEE in late 1933 followed by deck-landing trials in *Courageous* in 1934. Further trials at the MAEE evaluated a Shark fitted with floats as the Admiralty intended to operate Sharks as catapult aircraft from battleships and cruisers as well as from aircraft carriers. Water tests proved very successful and the type's performance in rough water received favourable comment. Large-scale production was authorised as the Fleet Air Arm expanded. The Shark's rugged strength and buoyancy attracted favourable comment and it was recorded that an aircraft ditched 20 miles from Gosport with a practice torpedo still attached. Subsequently located floating upside down, it was towed back to Gosport, refurbished and flew again after the engine and waterlogged radio were replaced. Sharks amounted to more than half the torpedo aircraft built by Blackburn but its rugged structure did have a drawback since the contemporary Fairey Swordfish was both quicker and cheaper to manufacture. They were also regarded by many pilots as having the better handling qualities.

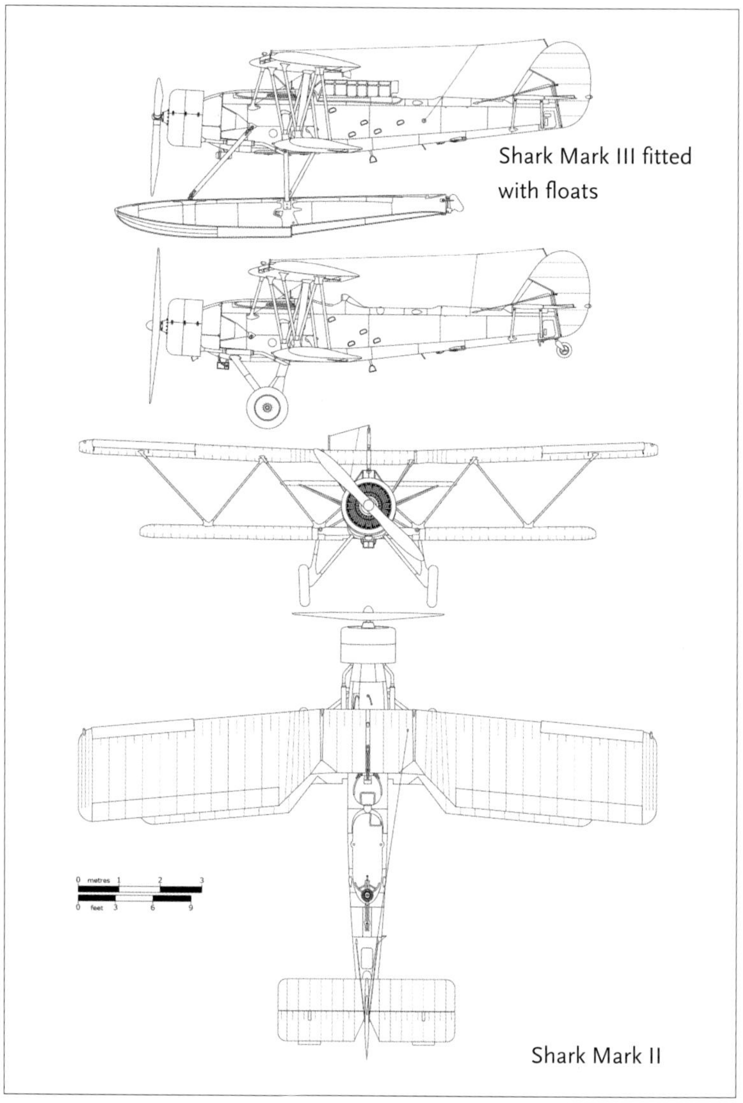

Shark Mark II data

Length:	35ft 3in (38ft 5in with floats)
Wingspan:	46ft (15ft folded)
Height:	12ft 1in (14ft 3in with floats)
MTOW:	8,050lb (8,610lb with floats)
Engine:	One 760hp Armstrong Siddeley Tiger VIc
Fuel:	Avgas. 172½ gallons. An optional 150-gallon overload tank could be carried on the torpedo crutches.
Performance:	Maximum level speed 132 knots Service ceiling 16,000ft. 20 minutes to 10,000ft
Endurance:	4½ hours with internal fuel. Up to 9 hours with overload tank.
Armament:	One Mark VIII or X torpedo or up to 1,500lb of bombs on underwing carriers. One Vickers 0.303in front gun with a 500 round belt. One Vickers K gun on a ring mounting aft for the TAG with ten 60-round pans stowed in the after cockpit

Shark Mark I.

In addition to the single prototype production comprised 16 Mark Is; 126 Mark IIs and 95 Mark IIIs. A total of 238 Sharks were delivered to the Fleet Air Arm.

The first front-line squadron to re-equip with the type was 820 NAS in 1934, followed by 821 and 822 NAS in 1936 and 810 NAS in April 1937. Two Sharks equipped 444 Flight in 1936 for catapult operations from the battleships *Repulse* and *Malaya*. The flight was re-designated as 705 Flight in July 1936. All five units were re-equipped with Swordfish by September 1937.

With a large number of airframes available, Sharks equipped shore-based squadrons with roles as diverse as seaplane pilot training, torpedo attack training, observer training, TAG training, fleet requirements duties and target-towing for both air-to-air and ship-to-air firings. Between July 1936 and October 1943 Sharks were operated for varying periods by 701, 705, 750, 753, 755, 756, 757, 758, 767, 774, 780 and 785 NAS. By far the largest operator of Sharks was 750 NAS, the Observer School at Piarco in Trinidad which had over forty on charge at one time.

Mark Is were followed by Mark IIs with more powerful Tiger VI engines in 1935 and it was these that equipped the front-line squadrons. The Mark III introduced an enclosed canopy offering better crew comfort, built to meet Specification S.19/36 and these were used mainly by shore-based squadrons. At least twenty Sharks were retrofitted with Type D target-towing winches between 1937 and 1939 together with an internal drum with several hundred feet of cable for towing a sleeve target; the re-winding gear was wind-driven by a turbine fitted on the port side of the rear cockpit. Some aircraft were also fitted with attachment points for towing glider targets with a wingspan of 16ft. Shark Mark IIIs intended specifically for training squadrons were delivered without arrester hooks.

Skua

Admiralty Specification O.27/34 called for a considerable advance over earlier designs and the Blackburn B.24 which was selected to meet it became first RN carrier-borne monoplane and the first to be fabricated entirely from metal. It was also the first to have a retractable undercarriage, the first to have a variable-pitch propeller and the first British aircraft designed specifically for dive-bombing. Its weaknesses were the lack of sufficient power from its chosen powerplant and the delay getting it into service. The Admiralty had wanted it to be operational by 1937 but the Air Ministry, which had overall responsibility for aircraft production at that time, forced the B.24 to proceed slowly by placing greater emphasis on the RAF's B.26 Botha. Two prototypes were ordered in April 1935 but the first, powered by an 840hp Bristol Mercury IX radial engine, did not fly until February 1937. Company trials were slowed by the death of Blackburn's chief test pilot and the aircraft was found to be longitudinally unstable at low speed, a problem manifested as a sudden wing drop without warning at deck-landing speed. Wind-tunnel tests also revealed that the aircraft was incapable of recovering from spins using the standard recovery method.

In an attempt to hasten its entry into service, the Admiralty accepted Air Ministry advice to order the whole production run 'off the drawing board' in July 1936, before it had even flown, to meet the revised Specification 25/36; the name Skua followed in 1937. Skua development was further delayed by an Air Ministry decision to replace the Mercury engine with the Bristol Perseus XII because the Mercury was allocated exclusively to expanded RAF Blenheim bomber production. The first three production aircraft were eventually delivered in October 1938 but all written off in accidents, one while carrying out deck-landing trials on *Courageous* in the Firth of Forth during December 1938. Modifications incorporated in the Mark II solved the instability problem but intentional spinning was 'universally and totally forbidden' in pilots' notes. The second aircraft had a lengthened nose which was replicated in production aircraft.

The Skua had a flush-riveted, semi-monocoque, Alclad constructed and covered fuselage that incorporated two watertight compartments to retain buoyancy after ditching; one under the pilot's cockpit deck that could be used as an overload fuel tank and the other in the rear fuselage. The fuselage was watertight up to the cockpit rim and the whole airframe stressed for catapult launching and arrested recovery. The tail hook had a hydraulic damping device to prevent 'hook bounce' over the arrester wires. The wings were also fabricated and covered with Alclad and built as three units with the two-spar, heavy-duty centre section bolted under the fuselage to form the bottom

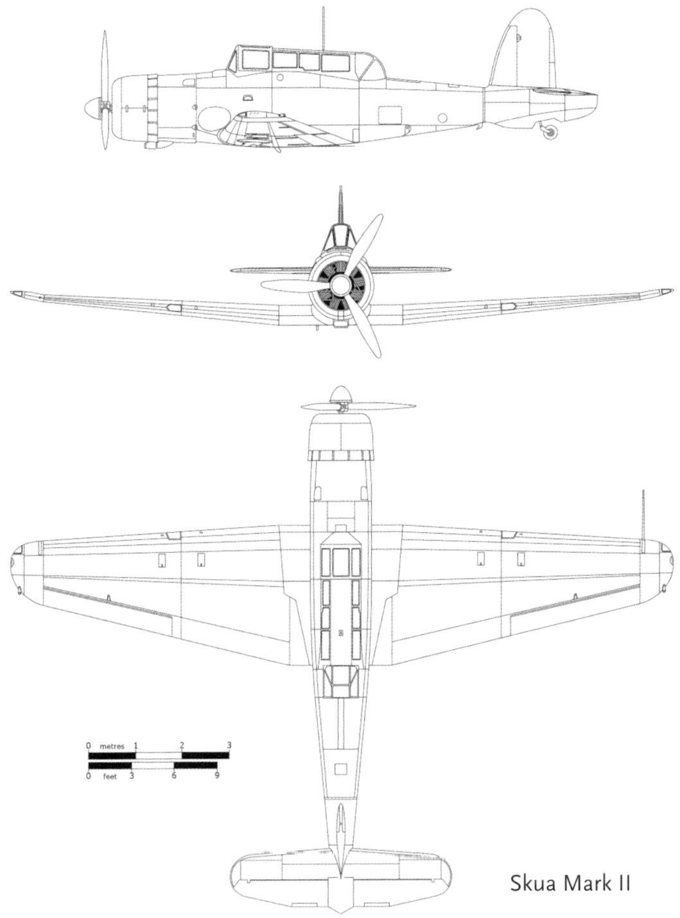

Skua Mark II

Skuas of *Ark Royal*'s 803 NAS in 1939.

of the front watertight compartment. The outer wings tapered in plan and thickness to terminate in detachable, upswept tips. They contained further watertight compartments and Zap-type flaps, the upper edges of which slid aft as they were lowered for take-off and landing and for use as dive brakes. Wing folding was manual, the wings being walked aft by handlers to rotate about an inclined hinge to lay parallel to the fuselage with the leading edge uppermost. Both aircrew sat under an enclosed canopy with strengthened frames to protect them if the aircraft inverted after a crash landing. The pilot's cockpit had a sliding hood and the observer/TAG's cockpit had a curved, rotating cover that acted as a wind shield when the rear gun was used. The gun was mounted on a pillar and lay in a stowage in the rear fuselage decking when not in use. The W/T equipment was fitted within a compartment aft of the pilot's cockpit and fuel was carried in tanks between the cockpits.

Skua Mark II data

Length:	35ft 7in
Wingspan:	46ft 2in (15ft 6in folded)
Height:	12ft 6in
MTOW:	8,228lb
Engine:	One 890hp Bristol Perseus XII
Fuel:	Avgas. 166 gallons
Performance:	Maximum level speed 200 knots Service ceiling 20,200ft. 6 minutes to 10,000ft clean
Endurance:	4½ hours
Armament:	One 500lb SAP bomb semi-recessed under the fuselage centreline with ejector arms to swing it clear of the propeller arc on release. Four 0.303in Browning Mark II front guns, two in each wing firing clear of the propeller arc, with 600 rpg. One 0.303in Lewis Mark IIIE or Vickers K gun in the rear cockpit. Light stores carriers under the wings could each carry four 20lb bombs or flares

After the two prototypes, the RN received 190 Skuas between October 1938 and March 1940.

Skuas equipped 800, 801, 803 and 806 NAS which embarked at various times in *Ark Royal* III, *Glorious*, *Furious* and, for a brief period, the new *Illustrious* between the end of 1938 and May 1941. They also operated from Hatston and were temporarily detached to airfields in southern England during the Dunkirk evacuation.

Between September 1939 and July 1944 Skuas equipped all or part of 755, 757, 758, 759, 760, 768, 769, 770, 771, 772, 774, 776, 778, 779, 780, 787, 788, 791, 792, 794 and 797 NAS for use in the training, target-towing and fleet requirements roles.

When I was curator of the Fleet Air Arm Museum 'Winkle' Brown told me that he flew the Skua as a student in 759 NAS at Yeovilton during 1940. He described the take-off run as 'lumbering', the rate of climb as 'disappointing' and the maximum level speed as a 'stately' 195 knots. On the other hand, he found it to be a good dive-bomber. The standard Fleet Air Arm technique was to cross a target at about 8,000ft, keeping it in sight until it disappeared under the leading edge of the wing and then winging over into a 70-degree dive. Flaps were fully extended and the sight picture maintained by keeping the target at the

A running range of Skuas on *Ark Royal* in 1940.

top of the engine cowling. The ideal release height was 3,000ft and the flaps were retracted as pull-out commenced. The first RN pilot to achieve the five aerial victories that would have given him 'ace' status in the USN in the Second World War was Lieutenant W P Lucy DSO RN, the commanding officer of 803 NAS. Other pilots used Skuas to good effect during the brief Norwegian Campaign in 1940 and, despite the type's poor performance, they earned a place in history with some remarkable achievements. Admiralty records show that in 1939–40 Skuas were engaged in seventy-four air combats with German, Italian and Vichy French aircraft during which they were credited with shooting down twenty. On 26 September 1939 a Skua of 803 NAS from *Ark Royal* flown by Lieutenant B S McEwen RN and his observer Petty Officer B M Seymour was the first British fighter to shoot down an enemy aircraft during the Second World War. On 10 April 1940, the day after the German invasion of Norway, sixteen Skuas of 803 and 800 NAS led by Lucy flew from Hatston to carry out a dawn dive-bombing attack on the enemy cruiser *Königsberg* in Bergen at the limit of the Skua's radius of action. Every bomb was either a hit or damaging near miss and the ship sank; the first major warship ever to be sunk by air attack. An attack on *Scharnhorst* in June was less successful with eight out fifteen Skuas from 800 and 803 NAS shot down. There were also attacks on Vichy French warships at Mers-el-Kebir and Dakar after the French armistice with Germany in 1940.

Roc

In the mid-1930s the RAF was fascinated by the concept of a 'bomber destroyer' fitted with a power-operated gun turret to engage its targets from any angle and the Boulton Paul Defiant was selected for the role. Suitably encouraged to follow this lead, the Admiralty issued Specification O.30/35 for a carrier-borne equivalent. The Blackburn B-25, later named Roc, was selected and a production contract was placed in April 1937. It was developed from, and structurally similar to, the Skua with the same Perseus engine, thus minimising the logistic

Rocs of 759 NAS from Eastleigh in 1940.

support required to maintain the two types. The pilot sat under a sliding canopy in a cockpit similar to the Skua but the central fuselage was widened to take the gun turret and the wings had two degrees of dihedral outboard of the centre section to avoid the need for upturned wing tips like the Skua. Aft of the pilot there was a cramped W/T compartment for the TAG from which there was access into the turret when it was in the stowed position with the guns facing aft. It was hydraulically-powered and he controlled its movement with a single control stick, training it through 360 degrees and elevating the guns up to 85 degrees relative to the aircraft datum. They were fired electrically by depressing a button on the control stick. There was automatic interruption of the firing circuit if the tail unit or propeller disc came into the line of fire and an aerodynamic fairing aft of the turret which was lowered into the fuselage by a device under the turret when the guns were trained aft. The extra weight of the turret made the Roc 25 knots slower than the Skua which was itself chronically slow.

Blackburn subcontracted Roc construction to Boulton Paul; there were no prototypes and the first production aircraft flew in December 1938. The first three aircraft went to the A&AEE in March 1939 where problems were found with trim, control and stability which led to delays while they were resolved. The Roc's performance was immediately assessed as poor but armament trials revealed that the Roc could be dived steeply and safely with the air brakes deployed at up to 260 knots without affecting turret operation although climbing high enough to commence the dive took a long time. Two early production Rocs were sent to the MAEE for evaluation with floats against Specification 20/37 for a seaplane turret fighter. Alclad covers were fitted over the wheel wells and the floats were similar to those designed for the Shark. They added significant weight and performance, already marginal, was now described as dangerous. Early tests showed marked directional instability and one aircraft crashed during take-off in December 1939. The Roc seaplane was obviously useless and work on it was abandoned.

Roc data

Length:	35ft 7in
Wingspan:	46ft (15ft 6in folded)
Height:	12ft 1in
MTOW:	7,950lb
Engine:	One 890hp Bristol Proteus XII
Fuel:	Avgas. 163 gallons internal plus 70 gallons in optional external tank
Performance:	Maximum level speed 170 knots Service ceiling 14,600ft. 6½ minutes to 5,000ft
Endurance:	4 hours on internal fuel; 6 with external tank
Armament:	Four 0.303in Browning machine guns with 600 rpg in a Boulton Paul Type A Mark II power-operated gun turret. Provision for a single 250lb bomb on the centreline plus light bombs or flares on underwing racks

The RN received 136 Rocs before production ceased in 1940.

No front-line squadrons were fully equipped with Rocs but small numbers were operated alongside Skuas in 1940 by 800, 801, 803, 805 and 806 NAS.

Shore-based squadrons that were wholly or partially equipped with Rocs between August 1939 and August 1944 included 725, 754, 755, 757, 758, 759, 760, 761, 764, 765, 768, 770, 771, 772, 773, 774, 775, 776, 777, 778, 787, 789, 791, 792, 793 and 794 NAS. They were used as target-tugs and fleet requirements aircraft.

Early Rocs were received at Worthy Down with little enthusiasm. During 1940 there were never more than ten Rocs in operational units but several were embarked in *Ark Royal* during the Norwegian Campaign. A section of three from 801 NAS was flown in April 1940 to intercept a German He 115 floatplane believed to be homing enemy bombers onto the fleet. They drove it off but lacked the speed to catch it. The same aircraft were flown later against an He 111 shadower. They again drove it off but pilots could not get the gunlayers into a firing position. After failure during their brief embarked career, Rocs were disembarked from *Ark Royal* in May 1940 and re-allocated to second line squadrons.

The majority of Rocs were actually delivered direct to air yards for modification to carry out target towing and other fleet requirements tasks. Some found use on the ground as anti-aircraft defences around naval airfields in the autumn of 1940. Between August 1939 and mid 1944 Rocs with their turrets removed were fitted with Type B Mark IIA wind-driven winches which could let out 6,000ft of cable while the aircraft flew at 10,000ft. Metal containers were fitted under the fuselage to contain sleeve targets; multiple targets meant that, providing the wire was not shot through, they could be replaced if hit. In this guise the Roc carried out important but unspectacular tasks before having to be withdrawn from service in 1944 when spares ran out.

Firebrand

Work on the B.37 Firebrand originated with Admiralty Specification N.8/39 for a two-seat fighter. Unlike the RAF which specified batteries of rifle-calibre machine guns in its fighters, the Admiralty specified four 20mm cannon capable of destroying targets in a single burst. Early war experience led to a modified specification, N.11/40 for a high-

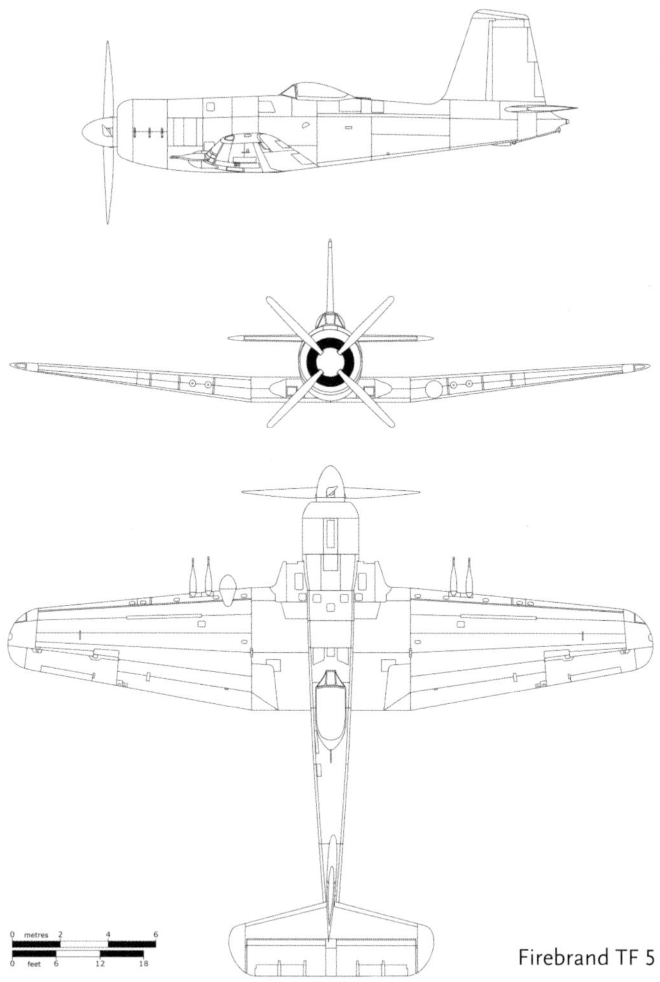

Firebrand TF 5

performance, single-seat interceptor and Blackburn was awarded a contract for three prototypes to be powered by a 2,305hp Napier Sabre III liquid-cooled, 24-cylinder 'H'-type engine expected to give a maximum level speed of 310 knots. It first flew in February 1942 but from then on development was slowed by a succession of design changes and then by a change of role. Firebrands did not equip an operational squadron until the war was over.

Structurally, the Firebrand had a massive two-spar centre section built around a heavy-duty centreline frame; the main undercarriage oleos retracted inwards to give a wide track and the tail wheel was retractable. The folding wings were attached to the centre section by forged steel fork-end fittings and folded manually to lie parallel with the fuselage, leading edge uppermost. The guns could not be re-loaded while the wings were folded. The name Firebrand was allocated in 1941 and the Sabre-engined prototypes and Mark I and II variants were tested at the A&AEE from June 1942. Deck-landing trials were carried out on *Illustrious* in February 1943. In 1943 the MAP decided that the Hawker Typhoon should have priority for Sabre engine production and, with the Seafire entering service, the Admiralty considered cancelling the Firebrand but decided instead to instruct Blackburn, through the MAP, to re-work the design as a fast, carrier-borne torpedo strike aircraft.

The second prototype earned a legendary place in Fleet Air Arm history on 20 February 1943 when a pipe burst while it was returning to Brough and covered the windscreen with oil, the engine seized and the pilot attempted to carry out a wheels-up landing. The oil prevented him from seeing the heavy-duty cable of Earl's Cement Works overhead bucket system and he hit it full on, severing the cable and demolishing the system. The aircraft survived, however, and was rebuilt as the prototype TF II. It had a widened centre section and yet more strengthening to carry an 18in torpedo between the wheel wells. It flew again March 1943, only a month after hitting the bucket system!

Specification S.8/43 was drawn up to cover the change of engine from the Sabre to the Bristol Centaurus. Aircraft built to this standard were given the new Blackburn type number B.45 and designated TF III and used for development flying which revealed a lack of directional stability, subsequently rectified in the B.46 Firebrand TF 4 by fitting a rudder of much increased area to give better control during slow carrier landings and an unusually large fin offset 3 degrees to port to compensate for the swing on take-off. The first TF 4 flew in May 1945. Dive brakes were fitted above and below the mainplane leading edges and there was an automatic torpedo angle setting to give the optimum position on the ground, in flight and on torpedo release. The TF 5 introduced long span aileron tabs and the TF 5A introduced hydraulically boosted aileron control. The last Firebrand was delivered to the RN in 1947.

Firebrand TF 5 data

Length:	38ft 9in
Wingspan:	51ft 3½in (16ft 10in folded)
Height:	13ft 3in
MTOW:	17,500lb
Engine:	One 2,520hp Bristol Centaurus IX
Fuel:	Avgas. 239 gallons internal plus 100-gallon or 45-gallon drop tanks
Performance:	Maximum level speed 295 knots (278 knots with a torpedo) Service ceiling 28,500ft. 2 minutes to 5,000ft
Endurance:	3 hours on internal fuel
Armament:	Four 20mm Hispano front guns, each with 200 rpg; hardpoints on centreline could carry one Mark 15 or 17 torpedo, one 2,000lb or 1,000lb bomb or one Mark 6, 7 or 9 mine or one 100-gallon fuel tank; underwing hardpoints under each wing could carry one 500lb or 250lb bomb or one 250lb Mark 11 depth charge or one 45-gallon drop tank or eight 60lb RP or twelve 25lb RP

After the three prototypes, nine Firebrands were completed to F I standard, 12 to TF II standard and 27 to TF III. Production of the TF 4 variant totalled 102, of which 40 were upgraded to TF 5 standard and 70 aircraft were built to TF 5 and 5A standard.

Between 1945 and 1953 Firebrands equipped 813 and 827 NAS.

A number of different marks partially equipped shore-based squadrons for varying periods between October 1944 and February 1953 for use in the tactical development and training roles. These included 700, 703, 708, 717, 736, 738, 759, 764B, 778, 787 and 799 NAS.

Firebrand TF 5 of 813 NAS embarked in *Indomitable* during 1951.

Firebrand TF 5s of 813 NAS from *Indomitable* in 1952.

Firebrand TF 5s of 827 NAS in *Eagle*.

813 NAS formed with TF 4s at Ford in 1945 and three aircraft took part in the Victory fly-past over London in 1946. It later embarked in *Implacable*. 827 NAS formed in 1950.

Alan Leahy and I discussed the Firebrand when we were both on the committee of the Fleet Air Arm Officers' Association and he recalled a warning in pilot's notes that below 90 knots the ailerons were ineffective; a statement at odds with the normal approach speed for a carrier landing of 80 knots. Performance deteriorated significantly with a torpedo loaded and Maurice Tibby wrote that the 'Firebrick', as it was known, lumbered into the air at its own pace and was quite unable to turn smartly in any direction. It was eventually replaced by the Wyvern, itself the victim of a prolonged period of development.

Firebrand of 827 NAS after a barrier engagement in *Eagle*.

B.48

Designed as an improved Firebrand, it was powered by a 2,475hp Bristol Centaurus 59 engine which gave a maximum level speed of 330 knots. The inverted, gull-shaped wing folded hydraulically in two places and the anhedral centre section allowed a cleaner wing attachment to the fuselage and a shorter undercarriage than the Firebrand. Three prototypes were ordered, one of which was never completed; the others were retained by Blackburn for tests from 1947 but no more were ordered by the Admiralty. Wingspan was 44ft 11½in, 18ft folded, and MTOW 15,280lb.

YB.1

Blackburn offered rival designs to meet Specification GR.17/45, for which the Admiralty selected the Fairey Gannet. They had company identifications B.54 and B.88, later changed to the SBAC designations YA.7, YA.8 and YB.1. The YA.7 was to be have been powered by the Napier Double Naiad turboprop but it was discontinued and the three prototypes were completed with 2,000hp Rolls-Royce Griffin 56 piston engines. Deck-landing trials were carried out on *Illustrious* in February 1950. When the specification was changed to require a third crew member the cockpit was enlarged and the aircraft re-designated as the YA.8. Further deck-landing trials were carried out on *Illustrious* in June 1950 and both prototypes were used as aerodynamic test beds for the

YB.1 carrying out deck-landing trials in *Illustrious* during 1950.

B.88/YB.1. The single prototype YB.1 was powered by an Armstrong Siddeley Double Mamba like the Fairey Gannet, first flew in July 1950 and carried out deck landings on *Illustrious* during October. After the Gannet was selected the three prototypes were used as trial hacks before deletion in 1957. YB.1 wingspan was 44ft 2in, 19ft 6in folded, MTOW was 13,091lb and maximum level speed was 280 knots.

Buccaneer

The B.103 Buccaneer was the last type to be built under the Blackburn name and the Admiralty requirement for it was a response to the contemporary expansion of the Soviet Navy's cruiser fleet. It was conceived as a specialised strike aircraft capable of operation from fleet carriers; able to carry both nuclear and conventional weapons and capable of attacking at high speed and very low level to avoid detection by enemy radar. A DNAW statistical study had revealed that the probability of an attacking aircraft being shot down by defences was under 10 per cent below 200ft. In 1952 both the RAF and USAF were mesmerised by the procurement of supersonic strike aircraft but Admiralty staff calculated that fuel consumption in a high subsonic attack would be up to eight times less than the volume required for a supersonic attack. This gave a significantly greater radius of action for the same amount of fuel. The RN's Korean War experience emphasised the correctness of this thinking and the Admiralty drafted operational requirement, NA.39, around it in June 1952.

NA.39 was to be a two-seat strike aircraft capable of flying at Mach 0.85 at or below 200ft with radar to enable attacks of unprecedented accuracy on ships or discrete land targets. It was to have a hi-lo-hi radius of action exceeding 400nm and the aircraft had to have weight and dimension parameters compatible with the fleet carriers the RN planned to have in service in the late 1950s. The requirement was distributed to industry as MoS Specification M.148T and Blackburn's B.103 submission was accepted by the Admiralty in July 1955. The Admiralty had the wisdom to 'freeze' the design and commit to the production of twenty prototypes, allowing concurrent trials of the aircraft's sophisticated systems to get the aircraft into service quickly. Blackburn's decision to employ BLC significantly reduced the size of wing needed for landing on a carrier. It involved blowing a sheet of air at sonic speed across the upper surfaces of the flaps to prevent airflow separation and increase lift coefficient. The same basic concept had been used by Supermarine in the Scimitar but Blackburn went further, blowing right across the wing from tip to tip immediately ahead of acutely depressed flaps and drooped ailerons to give roughly double the lift of an un-blown wing. A second slit facing rearwards in the upper surface close to the leading edge improved lift still further. An added advantage of the smaller wing area made possible by BLC was reduced gust response in low-level turbulence but it increased the nose-down pitching moment when flaps were selected. Blackburn countered this with a leading-edge blowing slit on the tailplane's underside which allowed its surface area to be halved. A hinged trailing portion was unlocked to act as an 'upside-down flap' when the wing flaps were lowered. A relatively small tailplane thus imparted the necessary down loads at low speed but was not over-powerful at high speed in dense, low-level air. The NA 39 was one of the first British aircraft to feature area-ruling in which the plot of total cross-sectional area was made to form a smooth curve from nose to tail with no sudden change due to the wing. Crudely applied by later standards, it made extra volume

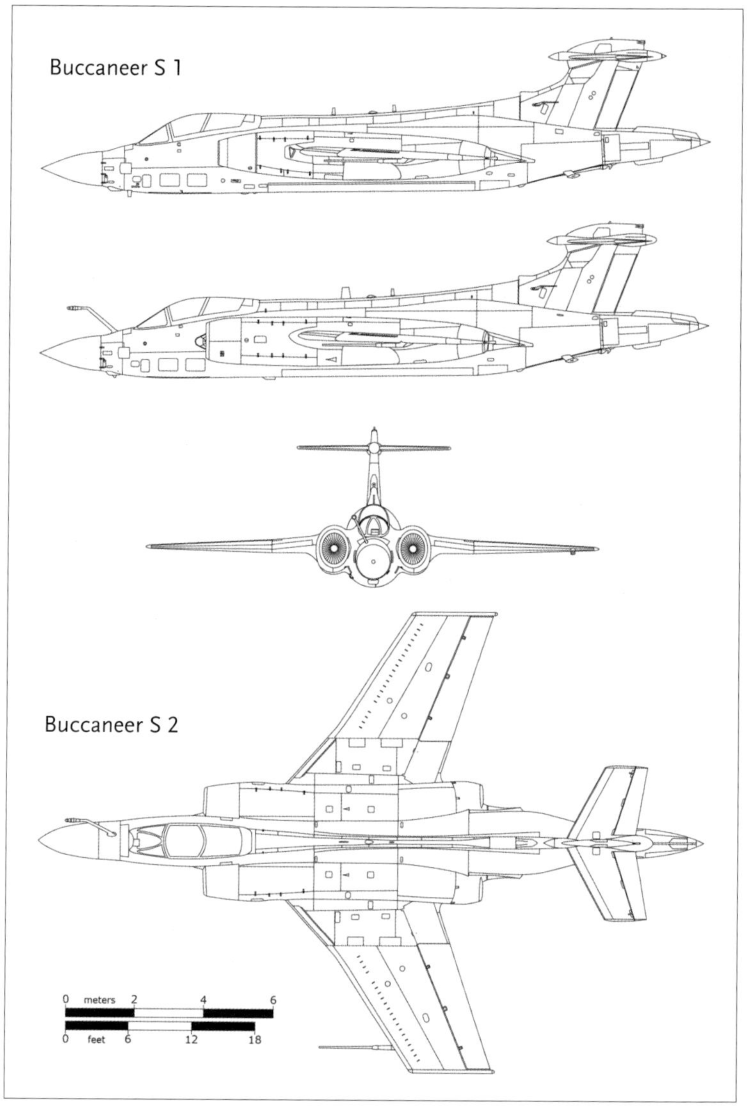

A Buccaneer development batch aircraft carrying out carrier trials on *Victorious* during 1960.

Buccaneer in the original anti-radiation white finish carrying out trials in *Ark Royal* during 1963.

available in the bulged rear fuselage for avionics besides reducing the thrust needed to maintain high-speed cruising flight.

Since operational short take-off and landing capability would be provided by the carrier, Blackburn opted for two de Havilland Gyron Junior turbojets, each with a thrust of 7,100lb, to power the B.103. These were just sufficient to achieve Mach 0.85 but had a lower sfc than more powerful alternatives. This was the most questionable aspect of the design since it left the aircraft dangerously vulnerable during take-off with BLC selected. The B.103 was designed with a robust airframe to give a fatigue life unlimited by low-level flight. The semi-monocoque fuselage was built in three sections, the nose complete with cockpit, the centre section with integral engine mountings machined from solid ingots and the rear fuselage. The prototype contract stipulated that the first aircraft, XK 486, was to fly no later than April 1958 and, after the resolution of last-minute problems, it flew for the first time on 30 April 1958. It was basically an empty shell without folding wings or role equipment but subsequent prototypes were closer to the operational standard. In August 1960 the Admiralty announced that the type had been given the name Buccaneer and the first version designated Buccaneer S 1. Successful carrier trials were carried out on *Victorious* in January 1960. In order to fit onto carrier lifts the air brake at the aircraft's tail had to be in the open position and the nose cone had to be folded as well as the wings.

The S 1's marginal single-engine performance led to early efforts to identify a more powerful engine with low fuel consumption and in May 1959 Rolls-Royce offered the Spey RB.168-1A Mark 101 turbofan engine, originally designed for the Trident airliner, It had 37 per cent more thrust than the Gyron Junior but even better sfc. The re-engined Buccaneer was designated S 2 and had enlarged oval-section intake ducts and larger jet pipes and the change required a re-designed engine structure and new machined forgings onto which the wings were fitted. The first S 2 flew in May 1963 and incorporated other improvement including a constant-speed 30 KVA engine-driven alternator to power a new ac electrical system. Unlike the S 1, the S 2's inner wing was fully blown and wingspan was increased to 44ft by adding glass fibre tips.

Buccaneer S 2 data

Length:	63ft 5in (51ft 10in folded)
Wingspan:	44ft (19ft 11in folded)
Height:	16ft 3in (16ft 8in folded)
MTOW:	62,000lb
Engines:	Two 11,100lb thrust Rolls-Royce Spey RB.168 Mark 101 turbofans
Fuel:	Avcat. 1558 gallons internal plus, optionally, up to 860 gallons in slipper tanks and 440 gallons in a bomb-bay tank plus 100-gallon in-flight refuelling pod
Performance:	Maximum level speed 580 knots, Mach 0.95 Ceiling 40,000ft
Endurance:	Up to 9 hours with two in-flight refuellings
Armament:	Internal bomb bay with rotating door capable of carrying a single Red Beard or WE 177 nuclear weapon, four 1,000lb or 500lb bombs, a photographic reconnaissance pack or fuel tank. Four wing hardpoints, each stressed to carry up to a 3,000lb load, could carry Bullpup, Martel or Sidewinder missiles, 1000lb or 500lb bombs, 2in rocket pods or Lepus flares. The inboard hardpoints 'plumbed' to take 430-gallon or 250-gallon drop tanks or a Flight Refuelling Ltd Mark 2B/C 'Buddy' hose and drogue refuelling pod which allowed the aircraft to act as an air-to-air tanker

RN production included 20 prototypes, 40 built to S 1 standard and 84 to S 2 standard, a total of 144.

Between 1961 and 1978 Buccaneers served with 700Z, 700B, 736, 800, 801, 803 and 809 NAS.

Avionic systems included Blue Parrot radar designed by Ferranti and the Blue Jacket doppler navigation system, the pilot's Rank-Cintel head-up display on which the strike sight was projected, UHF and HF communications and radar-detection devices at the wingtips known as wide-band homers. Both pilot and observer had excellent visibility through the single canopy with the pilot's Martin-Baker Mark 4MS

Buccaneer S 2 and its potential weapon loads including Red Beard, Bullpups, conventional bombs and a bomb-bay fuel tank.

Buccaneers at Lossiemouth.

Buccaneer S 2 of 800 NAS from *Eagle*.

Buccaneer S 2 of 800 NAS from *Eagle* releasing eight 1,000lb bombs.

ejection seat situated slightly to port and the observer's slightly to starboard and higher to give him a view ahead. In high-speed flight at low level there would be very little time to eject in an emergency and the two seats had a command ejection facility, the observer's seat being fired automatically if the pilot initiated ejection. Since there was no time for the canopy to be jettisoned, a system was perfected to allow ejection through it. The pilot's instrument panel was an OR.946 layout in which airspeed and Mach number were displayed on a horizontal tape above a 'roller-blind' artificial horizon.

The Buccaneer weapons system was originally designed to toss nuclear weapons at Soviet *Sverdlov* class cruisers but worked equally well with conventional bombs against other surface targets. Attacks with conventional weapons were usually carried out by groups of aircraft using others with AAR to extend their range if necessary. Toss-bombing attacks used the excellent Blue Parrot radar to detect targets at 250nm or more but it had a distinctive signature which gave away the presence of the aircraft and so it was usually only the leader that transmitted. Target position updates could be provided by AEW aircraft using coded voice transmissions. Primary sensor during the high-level outbound leg was the wide-band homer, later the RWR or programmable detector head of anti-radar Martel ASM were used. Using 'radar advantage' the Buccaneer crew could detect enemy transmissions at a greater range than the return signal could be detected by their receiver. Once detected, the transmission gave a course to steer and an 'under-the-lobe' descent was initiated by losing height until the signal was lost in steps until the aircraft got down to 100ft. The observer also used a radar horizon ruler which when set on his 1:250,000 chart gave height against range in order to stay under the radar coverage. Ken McKenzie explained to me that the observer confirmed that the pilot's radio altimeter was set to 100ft and master armament switch selected on before selecting the weapons stations in the bomb bay and under the wings and feeding weapon delivery data into the control and release computer. This was an analogue 'black box' in the rear cockpit containing an eight-way bomb distributer which was fed with wind velocity, target course and speed for it to calculate the clockwork pre-release timer. At about 30nm from the target the lead aircraft popped up to transmit a few Blue Parrot sweeps to ensure that the Blue Jacket doppler navigator was providing correct information to the radar target marker. The observer then marked the target which automatically ran down. At 20nm to run the leader called 'Bananas' or, in radio silence, accelerated to 580 knots and all aircraft switched on their radars on the 20nm scale and locked onto the target. At 15nm the leader called 'Split' or rocked his wings in radio silence and the attacking aircraft fanned out for 45 seconds before turning back onto the target; by then all aircraft would be travelling at 9nm a minute. Once back on the attack heading the observer locked-on the radar to provide the pilot with a target marker in his strike sight which he had to keep inside the range ring. The pilot could aim visually at the target but computation still relied on radar range data. At 3 seconds to pull-up an event marker appeared on the strike sight and the pilot had to press an 'accept' button on the stick to continue the attack. When the computer calculated the pull-up point at about 4nm from the target the target marker moved up the strike sight and the pilot pulled up at about 3 to 4 G to keep it in the ring. Bombs were released at about 30 degrees nose-up. At about

Buccaneer S 2 of 700B NAS fitted with a bomb-bay reconnaissance pack.

Buccaneer S 2 of 809 NAS taking number 3 wire on *Ark Royal*.

Buccaneer S 2 of 801 NAS about to be catapulted from *Victorious*.

Buccaneer S 2 of 803 NAS at Gan in the Indian Ocean in August 1968. It had just flown non-stop from Lossiemouth with air-to-air refuelling and a day later flew on to embark in *Hermes* off Penang to demonstrate the RN's ability to reinforce a carrier in the Far East Fleet. Admiral Sir Caspar John, the first pilot to become First Sea Lord, flew in the observer's seat.

Wheels down, flaps down, ailerons drooped and hook down. A Buccaneer S 2 of 801 NAS seconds before landing on *Hermes*.

60 degrees nose-up the pilot began the escape manoeuvre, applying 135 degrees of bank in a 4G turn to get down onto a reciprocal heading at low level. This was a disorientating manoeuvre, especially at night or in bad visibility, and the observer could provide some reassurance by looking over the pilot's shoulder at his standby artificial horizon. Toss bombing was an accurate delivery method for its era and was frequently practised on splash targets towed astern of the carrier or its plane-guard destroyer. Improved defensive systems from the 1970s gave urgency to the development of stand-off ASMs.

Ted Anson, who flew it both as a test pilot and a squadron commanding officer, said that the S 1 had not been difficult to fly but when the S 2 entered service the major range and reliability drawbacks were quickly resolved almost overnight, turning an essentially good aircraft into a magnificent one. Talking specifically about the S 1 during his time as the commanding officer of 700Z NAS, Alan Leahy said that once the pilot got used to the idea that our Buccaneer was not going to leap into the air like the Scimitar or Sea Vixen it was a great plane to fly until the time came to get it down on the ground again. The blown wings, flaps and tailplane worked perfectly if correctly selected but tended to concentrate the mind for a few seconds. Keith Harris, the QFI responsible for Buccaneer pilot standardisation for many years, remembers it as being smooth and stable at low level with a roomy cockpit. He considered day and night operation, including toss-

Buccaneer S 2 of 809 NAS refuelling a Phantom FG 1 of 892 NAS.

bombing and air-to-air refuelling, to be straightforward techniques.

The first operational squadron was 801 NAS which commissioned at Lossiemouth in July 1962. It operated from *Ark Royal* and *Victorious* and served with the Far East Fleet throughout much of the period of confrontation with Indonesia, deterring the Indonesian Navy from taking a more effective role against Malaysia and its Commonwealth allies. After disbanding in 1965 it re-formed as the first operational Buccaneer S 2 unit in October 1965 from a nucleus of 700B NAS and re-embarked in *Victorious*, later transferring to *Hermes* before disbanding in 1970.

In January 1963 the nucleus of the IFTU, 700Z NAS, reformed as 809 NAS to act as the headquarters squadron for the Buccaneer S 1 at Lossiemouth before being renumbered as 736 NAS to act as the training unit. It formed part of the RN Strike School at Lossiemouth until February 1972 when it was disbanded. 809 NAS recommissioned with Buccaneer S 2s in 1966 embarked in *Hermes* in the Far East Fleet. It returned in early 1968 and remained shore-based until 1970 when it embarked in *Ark Royal* for service in the Atlantic and Mediterranean. It remained with her until 1978 and disbanded with the carrier.

800 NAS was commissioned in 1964 with Buccaneer S 1s for embarkation in *Eagle*. It, too, served with the Far East Fleet and Buccaneer S 2s replaced the S 1s in 1966. It disbanded when *Eagle* was prematurely retired in February 1972.

803 NAS was the tactical development unit formed at Lossiemouth in July 1967. Whilst nominally shore-based, its aircraft flew from the UK to *Hermes* in the Indian Ocean in a matter of days during 1968 using air-to-air refuelling. It disbanded in December 1969.

BLERIOT AERONAUTIQUE

Type XI

A Bleriot Type XI monoplane, similar to the machine flown across the Channel in 1909, was purchased by the Admiralty for evaluation in 1913. It flew patrols from Eastchurch in August 1914 and deployed to France with 3 Squadron in September where it was wrecked trying to

Bleriot Type XI.

take off in a strong wind. A further twenty-six were procured in 1915 and largely used for training. Wingspan was 34ft 3in, MTOW 1,388lb and Gnome rotary engines of increasing horsepower culminated with the 80hp which gave a maximum level speed of 58 knots. Three examples of the improved Bleriot BG Parasol monoplane were either requisitioned or presented to the RNAS in August 1914 and more were procured in 1915. They had aerodynamic improvements but the same 80hp Gnome engine and served between 1914 and 1916 at Eastchurch and Dover and with both 2 and 4 Wings. The RNAS received forty-five BGs but they saw little active service.

BOREL

Hydro-Monoplane

Eight examples were purchased by the Admiralty in 1913. One was embarked in *Hermes* for the 1913 fleet manoeuvres but damaged by high seas. Others flew from sheltered waters at temporary coastal bases during the same manoeuvres, one of which carried Winston Churchill and another Admiral Jellicoe as passengers to judge for themselves the value of air reconnaissance. Subsequently used for training, those that had not been written off after crashes were struck off charge in December 1914. They were powered by a single 80hp Gnome rotary engine giving a maximum level speed of 56 knots, wingspan was 38ft 4in and MTOW 2,028lb.

Borel operating from *Hermes* during the 1913 Fleet manoeuvres.

BOULTON PAUL

Defiant

Designed to meet an RAF specification for a two-seat monoplane fighter with a power-operated gun turret, the Defiant was expected to take a position near a stream of bombers while the gunner moved the turret to engage them. By 1940 the concept was exposed as a failure and, although some were used as night fighters, uses had to be found for large numbers of mass-produced Defiants. Many, designated Defiant TT 1, had the turret replaced by a target operator's cockpit with a windmill-driven Mark IIB winch and these matched a naval requirement for a target-towing aircraft to serve in fleet requirement units. A number were, therefore, transferred to the RN from the RAF. Subsequent modifications led to TT II and III variants, some of which were also transferred.

A Defiant of 794 NAS at St Merryn in 1944. (Philip Jarrett)

Defiant TT 1 data

Length:	35ft 4in
Wingspan:	39ft 4in
Height:	11ft 4in
MTOW:	8,250lb
Engine:	One 1,280hp Rolls-Royce Merlin XX
Fuel:	Avgas. 104 gallons
Performance:	Maximum level speed 245 knots
	Service ceiling 28,000ft. 9 minutes to 15,000ft
Endurance:	1½ hours
Armament:	None

Most RN Defiants were transferred from the RAF but some were delivered new from late production batches to make an overall total of 150.

Between 1942 and 1945 Defiants equipped or partially equipped 726, 727, 728, 733, 770, 771, 772, 774, 775, 776, 777, 779, 788, 789, 791, 792, 794 and 797 NAS.

The Defiant saw world-wide RN use on fleet requirements and target facilities tasks in Trinidad, Cyprus, Malta, Gibraltar, East and West Africa and Ceylon during the latter half of the war. They were rapidly withdrawn from service in 1945.

Sea Balliol

Designed to meet Specification T.7/45 for a single trainer intended to replace the variety of pilot training aircraft in RAF service in 1945 and as a deck-landing training aircraft for the RN, the P.108 incorporated

Sea Balliols of 781 NAS, Junior Officers' Air Course Flight, at Lee-on-Solent in 1957.

A B C D E F G H I J K L M N O P Q R S T U V W X Y Z

the contemporary CFS view that pupil and instructor should sit side-by-side with the unusual addition that a second pupil was to be seated behind them sideways facing to starboard. It was originally to have had a turboprop engine but their slow development led to the selection of a Merlin piston engine instead. The basic Balliol first flew in 1947 but before it entered service the RAF dropped the idea of a second pupil and the vacated space was used for radio equipment. In 1951 Balliols were ordered in large numbers but again the RAF changed its mind and opted for jet-powered training aircraft. Balliol orders were cut drastically but from the outset a Sea Balliol variant had been intended for carrier operation with an undercarriage capable of deck landing, a fuselage strengthened for a deck hook and folding wings. The first Sea Balliol flew in October 1952 after pre-production aircraft had carried out deck-landing trials on *Illustrious* during November 1950. Full carrier compatibility trials were carried out successfully in 1953, also in *Illustrious.* The RN eventually received thirty aircraft designated Sea Balliol T 21 with the last delivered in 1954. Wingspan was 39ft 4in, 21ft 8in folded and MTOW 8,470lb. It was powered by a single 1,245hp Rolls-Royce Merlin 35 which gave a maximum level speed of 270 knots.

Sea Balliols served with 702, 703, 727, 750, 765, 781 and 796 NAS until 1959 when most were placed in storage at Lossiemouth and ultimately scrapped. Their most interesting role was with *Triumph*'s ship's flight when she was a cadet training ship. They gave young officers experience of carrier flying. The last unit to operate the type was the MTP School at Abbotsinch. Keith Harris flew the Sea Balliol as part of his conversion onto the Skyraider having initially trained on Vampires. He remembers it as a heavy airframe for its Merlin engine and whilst the take-off was reasonable it tended to run out of speed in a loop. It had a rugged undercarriage, however, and was a pleasant aircraft to fly.

BREGUET AVIATION

Chenu-engined biplane

A single example purchased by the Admiralty for evaluation in 1912 was powered by an 80hp Chenu engine. Wingspan was 45ft 9in and, after assembly, it operated from Eastchurch but came down on marshy ground after engine failure in April 1913, suffering extensive damage. It may have been repaired but there is no record of it flying again.

'Tin Whistle' seaplane

Three examples with 200hp Canton-Unne engines were ordered in 1913 and allocated Admiralty serial numbers. Two were never delivered but the third may have been evaluated at Calshot but never accepted.

de Bombe biplane

Two examples powered by 225hp Sunbeam engines were ordered in October 1915 for evaluation. One was never delivered but the other was delivered to 5 Wing at Coudekerque in April 1916 for evaluation. It was found to be unserviceable in May and written off as not worth repairing.

Breguet de Chasse. (Goble Family)

de Chasse

A two-seater biplane with rear-mounted 'pusher' engine; fifteen were ordered from early 1915 in batches of five. The first batch had differing engines, the second had 200hp Salmson engines and the third 225hp Sunbeam engines. Wingspan was 53ft 10 engines, MTOW 3,384lb and up to 660lb of bombs could be carried. Two of the first batch served with 3 Squadron at Tenedos; the others at St Pol and Dover. The second and third batches all served with 5 Wing at RNAS Coudekerque. Most were deleted by the end of 1916.

Type V

Three demonstration examples were followed from August 1916 by twenty-six production Breguet Vs which equipped 3 Wing at Luxeuil-les-Bains for attacks on German industrial targets. A batch of thirty to be built under licence by Grahame White with Rolls-Royce engines was ordered but only one was delivered before it was cancelled. The Type V was a two-seat biplane powered by a single 225hp Renault engine giving a maximum level speed of 72 knots. Wingspan was 57ft 8in, MTOW 4,158lb and they could carry a 660lb bomb load. Attacks on the Mauser factory at Oberndorf by early aircraft revealed the type's disappointing performance and the remainder were delivered to Luxeuil but not used operationally before being deleted in early 1917.

BREWSTER

Buffalo

Designated as the F2A by the USN, a batch was purchased by the UK in 1939 and named Buffalo for RAF and RAAF use in Singapore and the Far East. After Belgium collapsed in 1940, batches of fifteen and eleven were transferred from a Belgian order to the RN and a single aircraft was transferred from an unrecorded source to bring the overall total to twenty-seven. They were powered by a single 1,100p Wright Cyclone R-1820-G105A radial engine giving a maximum level speed of 275 knots. Wingspan was 35ft and it fitted on USN carrier lifts without wing-folding but this made it awkward to embark in British

Buffalo of 759 NAS at Yeovilton. (Philip Jarrett)

carriers. It was only used by squadrons based ashore. MTOW was 6,840lb and armament comprised four wing-mounted 0.5in machine guns firing clear of the propeller arc.

The Buffalo was obviously no match for contemporary German single-seat fighters but the Admiralty shipped at least ten to Dekheila in early 1941 for embarkation in *Eagle*. They were allocated to 805 NAS but after evaluating them, its commanding officer Lieutenant Commander A F Black RN insisted that his unit be equipped instead with Sea Gladiator biplanes. The unit still had some Buffalos at Maleme in May 1941 when the Germans invaded Crete, all of which were destroyed. Others served briefly with 804 NAS at Hatston defending Scapa Flow and some partially equipped 759 and 760 NAS at Yeovilton.

Corsair

Corsairs built under licence from Chance Vought by Brewster were designated as F3As by the USN and those transferred to the RN under Lend-Lease arrangements were identified as Corsair Mark IIIs. The Corsair is described in the Chance Vought section.

Bristol Boxkite. (Philip Jarrett)

BRISTOL

TB 8

A two-seat biplane, powered by a single 80hp Gnome rotary engine which gave a maximum level speed of 66 knots, the first TB 8 was evaluated with floats but most had wheeled undercarriages. A batch of twelve was transferred from the RFC and saw operational service with the RN Dover Command both in the UK and France. Others were used for coastal patrols off the east coast of the UK and for training. Wingspan was 37ft 8in and MTOW 1,665lb. All were deleted by mid-1916.

Boxkite

The Admiralty ordered a single Boxkite with a 50hp Gnome rotary engine in 1912 for pilot training at Eastchurch. Subsequent batches amounted to thirty-one used for training at Eastchurch, Chingford, Redcar and Killingholme. Several were later fitted with 60hp or 80hp Le Rhone rotary engines but the last batch were nearly all used as a source of spare parts rather than flown. Based on a design by Henri Farman with the same dimensions, the Boxkite was regarded by the Admiralty as being better built. Wingspan was 46ft 6in, MTOW 900lb and maximum speed in level flight was 35 knots. It was soon considered obsolescent after 1914 and most were deleted by early 1916.

Scout

A single-seat biplane evolved from a 1913 sporting design which created a sensation at the 1914 Aero Show at Olympia, two were requisitioned by the Army and sent to France with the RFC, named Scouts and retrospectively designated 'B' variants. The Admiralty ordered production batches identified as Scout Cs which differed in detail from the RFC version. They were used as anti-Zeppelin fighters from Chingford, Dover, Eastchurch, Great Yarmouth, Port Victoria and Redcar. They were also embarked in the seaplane carrier *Vindex* which had a flying-off deck 64ft long by 25ft wide over the bow. Her two Sopwith Baby seaplane fighters had proved too cumbersome to fly off the deck on wheeled trollies and her officers gained Admiralty permission to evaluate a fighter with a wheeled undercarriage. Bristol Scout C number 1255 was allocated and embarked, its only modification being a quick-release slip wire to hold it back until the engine reached maximum power with the ship steady into wind. On 3 November 1915 *Vindex* steamed at 12 knots into a 15-knot wind giving a relative wind over the deck of 27 knots. Flight Lieutenant B F Fowler RNAS flew the aircraft off the deck after a run of 46ft. This was a major step forward and the RN put considerable effort into refining the technique with the result that take-off by wheeled fighters was considered routine by 1916.

On 2 August 1916 a Scout, piloted by Flight Lieutenant C T Freeman RNAS, was flown off *Vindex* to intercept a Zeppelin. Lack of an effective weapon was the Scout's weakness and at this time most were armed with pistols, rifles or grenades but on this occasion the Scout was armed with Ranken darts, small free-falling explosive missiles released above a Zeppelin with the aim of ripping gas bags open, detonating and igniting the hydrogen gas they contained. They were not usually successful, although Freeman saw darts hit on his third pass 500ft over the airship. There was no explosion but the Zeppelin was seen to lose height and turn east. Freeman ran out of fuel and had to ditch near the North Hinder Light Vessel where he was rescued after some hours by a Dutch steamer. Later Scouts were fitted with machine guns and the RN evaluated Scouts as part of several anti-Zeppelin weapon systems. One was fitted onto the modified upper wing of a Porte Baby flying boat. It was successfully air-launched on 17 May 1916, proving the concept to be feasible, but it was considered too complicated to be operationally viable and it was not taken forward.

A Scout in the original national markings used by the RNAS.

Scouts at Dover.

Scout C data

Length:	20ft 8in
Wingspan:	24ft 7in
Height:	8ft 6in
MTOW:	1,195lb
Engine:	Single 80hp Le Rhone 9C nine-cylinder rotary engine or 110hp Clerget seven-cylinder rotary engine
Fuel:	Avgas. 16 gallons
Performance:	Maximum level speed 82 knots with Le Rhone engine Service ceiling 15,500ft. 18 minutes to 10,000ft
Endurance:	2½ hours
Armament:	Two 24-round canisters of Ranken darts or a single 0.303in Lewis machine gun. Various hand-held weapons

The RNAS received 154 Bristol Scouts, of which seventy-four were C variants and eighty D variants.

Bristol Scouts operated at RN air stations Redcar, Great Yarmouth, Cranwell, Port Victoria, Chingford, Dover, Eastchurch, East Fortune in the UK and Vendome in France. Others served with 2 Wing at Mudros but the only ship to embark them on a regular basis was *Vindex*.

The Scout D differed from the C in having shorter ailerons and increased dihedral. Machine gun experiments led to some being fitted on the centreline forward of the cockpit, firing through the propeller arc but with no effective interrupter mechanism a prolonged burst would shatter the propeller. The weight of gun and ammunition put the aircraft close to its weight limit. As better aircraft came into service most Scouts were allocated to training units where they were considered such a delight to fly that many were 'appropriated' by officers who used them as their personal aircraft, a testament to their popularity.

Blenheim

A light day-bomber selected by the RAF in the late 1930s which flew for the first time in June 1936 and entered service in 1937 as the fastest aircraft in the RAF. However, such was the pace of development that it was obsolescent by September 1939. Its bomb load was only 1,000lb, half that of the Fairey Swordfish although it did have a significantly greater radius of action. As it replaced them the RAF agreed to transfer surplus Blenheims to the RN for use by fleet requirements squadrons

A Blenheim of 771 NAS from Twatt in the Orkney Islands.

and sixteen Mark Is were transferred from 1941 onwards followed by seventy-two Blenheim Mark IVs from 1944. Guns and bombing equipment were removed and they were fitted with naval radios. The Mark IV wingspan was 56ft 4in, MTOW 14,400lb and it was powered by two 905hp Bristol Mercury XV radial engines which gave a maximum level speed of 235 knots.

Blenheims served in significant numbers with 748, 759, 770, 771, 772, 775, 776, 780, 787 and 798 NAS between April 1941 and 1945. Most were withdrawn from service when their squadrons were disbanded at the end of the war in Europe in May 1945. Some aircraft of 775 NAS at Dekheila continued in use until August 1945, used to work up ships passing through the Mediterranean to join the BPF.

Beaufort

Designed as an RAF torpedo-bomber, the Beaufort first flew in October 1938. After being replaced by de Havilland Mosquitoes, 104 were transferred from the RAF to the RN from 1943 for fleet requirements duties. These included sixty-five Mark Is powered by two 1,145hp Bristol Taurus VI radial engines and thirty-nine Mark IIs powered by two 1,200hp Pratt & Whitney R-1830-S3C4G Twin Wasp radial engines. Both had a wingspan of 57ft 10in, the Mark I had a MTOW of 21,228lb and a maximum level speed of 235 knots. The Mark II had a MTOW of 22,50lb but the same maximum speed.

Beauforts partially-equipped 728, 733, 762, 788 and 798 NAS at Lee-on-Solent, Dale and Ford in the UK, Ta Kali and Luqa in Malta and China Bay in Ceylon.

Beaufighter

Developed as a private venture by Bristol using the wings, tail and rear fuselage of the Beaufort with a new fuselage and more powerful engines, the Beaufighter was an effective strike and night fighter used

RN Beaufighters and other aircraft on the deck of a ferry carrier in 1945.

extensively by the RAF in the UK and Mediterranean theatres. The Mark II had a wingspan of 57ft 10in and MTOW of 21,100lb. The majority had Bristol Hercules engines but the IIF had two 1,280hp Rolls-Royce Merlin XX engines which gave a maximum level speed of 285 knots. Merlin-powered Mark IIs were transferred to the RN for fleet requirements duties and Mark X versions were made available later with the same dimensions but powered by two Bristol Hercules XVII radial engines. They had a slightly lower maximum speed of 280 knots but better endurance. All RN Beaufighters had their armament removed to simplify maintenance and were fitted with RN communications equipment. The RN eventually received ninety-nine Mark IIs and twenty-one Mark Xs from the RAF between 1943 and November 1945 when the last unit to operate them disbanded. A few ex-RAF TT 10 target-towing conversions were operated from Malta in 1949.

Beaufighters partially-equipped 726, 728, 733, 762, 772, 775, 779, 781, 788, 789, 797 and 798 NAS at Ta Kali and Hal Far in Malta; China Bay, Katukurunda and Colombo Racecourse in Ceylon; Port Reiz in Kenya; Wingfield in South Africa; North Front in Gibraltar and Lee-on-Solent, Dale and Machrihanish in the UK.

Type 173

After successful evaluation of the Sikorsky S-55 ASW helicopter in 1953, the Admiralty issued Requirement NA 43 for a helicopter capable of both search and strike in a single sortie. Bristol proposed a development of its Type 173 experimental ten-seat helicopter with tandem rotors powered by two Alvis Leonides piston engines. For NA 43 it would have folding rotor blades and tailplane to fit diagonally into a hangar space 44ft long by 40ft wide. MTOW was estimated at 10,600lb with a crew of three, pilot, observer and sonar operator. A Type 173 prototype was embarked in *Eagle* in November 1953 to examine its suitability and it was found to be too big and cumbersome for routine carrier operations. Rotor spreading and engagement would have made it very difficult to incorporate it into a carrier's deck operating cycle and this led FOAC, Rear Admiral A R Pedder, to strongly state his view that that helicopters could not operate from fleet carriers without degrading their ability to operate fixed-wing aircraft. This view was not accepted by the Admiralty which ordered further development work to meet NA 43.

Bristol Type 173 carrying out deck trials on *Eagle*.

Type 191

The helicopter evolved to meet NA 43 was designated Type 191 by Bristol. It was to be powered by two 1,650shp Napier E.156 Gazelle free-power turbines down-rated for normal flight so that, in the event of a single engine failure, the other could provide high power for a limited time to allow safe single-engined recovery. There were to be two four-bladed rotors, each with a diameter of 48ft 11in and a long fuselage with a bulged weapon bay enclosing a single Pentane or two Dealer-B torpedoes or depth charges, flares and sonobuoys. MTOW was to be 17,800lb. The aircrew comprised two pilots, an observer and aircrewman and it was to have AN/AQS-4 sonar.

Treasury approval for sixty-five Type 191s was given in April 1956, followed by an order for three development aircraft fitted with Leonides engines to speed progress, bringing the overall total to sixty-eight. Ground running by the first development aircraft began in November 1956 but had to be discontinued after engine over-heating and transmission failures. These were resolved but used by the Admiralty, which had never entirely overcome doubts aroused by the Type 173's evaluation in *Eagle*, to justify cancellation of all sixty-five Type 191s in 1957. Unfinished Type 191 prototypes were completed to act as Napier Gazelle ground-running test rigs and the Admiralty turned to the Westland-built licensed version of the Sikorsky S-58, fitted with a Gazelle free-power turbine, to meet NA 43.

BRITISH AEROSPACE

The Sea Harrier and Hawk were latterly marketed under the British Aerospace brand name but they began as Hawker designs and are described in the Hawker section. The Jetstream evolved from a Handley Page design and it is listed under that heading.

BRITISH AIRCRAFT CORPORATION

The Canberra was latterly re-branded under the BAC name but was originally an English Electric design and is described in that section.

BURGESS

Type 0 Gunbus

A two-seat biplane fighter powered by a single 140hp Sturtivant liquid-cooled engine with a pusher propeller giving a maximum level speed of 72 knots. Wingspan was 45ft and MTOW 920lb. The Admiralty purchased thirty-six from the USA in 1915 which had the gunlayer sat in front of the pilot in an elongated nacelle. After evaluation, however, they were already considered obsolete and deleted.

CAPRONI

Ca 4

A three-engined triplane bomber, six were lent to 6 Wing RNAS at Otranto by the Italian Navy in January 1918, then returned in March. They were powered by three 400hp Liberty engines which gave a maximum level speed of 76 knots; wingspan was 98ft and MTOW 16,535lb. Defensive armament comprised four 6.6mm Fiat-Revelli machine guns and they could carry up to 3,200lb of bombs.

CAUDRON

Amphibian Seaplane

Three single-engined, two-seat, tractor biplane seaplanes with the company designation Type H were purchased by the Admiralty for use in the 1913 fleet manoeuvres. Two were powered by 80hp Gnome rotary engines which gave a maximum level speed of 43 knots; the third had a 100hp Gnome monosoupape. Wingspan was 45ft 11in and MTOW 1,455lb. They were used as reconnaissance aircraft fitted with W/T transmitters; weight limitation prevented them from carrying a receiver. One was embarked in *Hermes* on 25 July 1913, replacing the wrecked Borel and it was flown off a trackway over the ship's bow on 28 July while she steamed into wind at 10 knots. It was subsequently disembarked to Isle of Grain but written off in June 1914 after side-slipping into the River Medway. A second was also embarked in *Hermes* but 'fell into the sea' a mile off-shore and the third crashed during its acceptance flight at Grain in August 1913. After repair it struck a buoy whilst attempting to take off and sank in the River Medway. It was recovered, found to be beyond repair and deleted.

G II

A single example with a 60hp Anzani engine, built by the British Caudron Company, was requisitioned by the Admiralty in November 1914. It was a two-seater with a wingspan of 23ft 9in, a maximum level speed of 57 knots and MTOW of 882lb. It crashed in January 1915, was repaired and then crashed again in June 1915 after which it was deleted.

G III

The Admiralty purchased 154 G III two-seat tractor biplanes for use as trainers in the UK and at the RNAS training centre at Vendome in France. The majority had 100hp Anzani air-cooled radial engines which gave a maximum level speed of 60 knots. Wingspan was 43ft 5in and MTOW 1,619lb. It was considered a pleasant aircraft to fly.

Caudron G IIIs used for training at Vendome.

Caudron G IV.

G IV

A twin-engined derivative of the G III which was widely used by Allied air arms as a bomber.

Caudron G IV data

Length:	23ft 6in
Wingspan:	55ft 5in
Height:	8ft 5in
MTOW:	2,970lb
Engines:	Some delivered with two 80hp Le Rhone 9C rotary engines; all subsequently delivered or re-engined with two 100hp Anzani air-cooled radial engines
Fuel:	Avgas. 110 gallons
Performance:	Maximum level speed 72 knots Service ceiling 14,000ft. 33 minutes to 10,000ft
Endurance:	4 hours
Armament:	One 0.303in Lewis gun in front cockpit. Up to 250lb of bombs

A total of sixty-one G IVs were procured for the RNAS, at least six of which were transferred to the French shortly after delivery. A further batch was cancelled. Of those that saw operational service with the RNAS, forty-three were built by the parent company and twelve by the British Caudron Company. They served with 4 and 5 Wings of the RNAS and 7 (Naval) Squadron.

The RNAS formed 5 Wing in early 1916 for operations from Coudekerque with Breguets and Caudron G IVs. In April 1916 it was joined by 4 Wing operating from Petite Synthe. They specialised in night attacks on German seaplane, U-boat and Zeppelin bases in Belgium. On 2 August 1916 a combined force of ten G IVs and a single Farman bombed the enemy airfield at St Denis Westrem, near Ghent, in daylight. They were escorted by five Sopwith 1½ Strutters and attacked in line astern with the timing of their weapon release controlled by a strike co-ordinator in one of the Sopwiths using flares from a Very pistol. G IVs were gradually replaced from early 1917 by the Handley Page O/100. One of their last major operations was a strike on Bruges docks in February 1917 by 7 (Naval) Squadron.

CHANCE VOUGHT

Corsair

Designed to meet a 1938 USN specification for a carrier-borne fighter with the highest possible performance, the company's V-166B, designated F-4U by the USN, combined the smallest possible airframe with the 2,000hp Pratt & Whitney R-2800 Double Wasp air-cooled radial. Its inverted gull wing allowed relatively short undercarriage legs but gave sufficient clearance for the 13ft 4in diameter Hamilton-Standard three-bladed metal propeller. It also allowed upward-folding wings within the height restrictions of US carriers. The metal-clad fuselage used innovative spot-welding techniques to reduce surface friction and here too the gull wing helped since it joined the fuselage at a right angle with no need for fillets to smooth the airflow. The first development aircraft was the most powerful naval fighter ever built and first flew in May 1940 but production aircraft incorporated a number of modifications including an enlarged, self-sealing fuel tank close to the centre of gravity to minimise trim changes as fuel was used. This displaced the cockpit aft by 3ft giving the Corsair its distinctive long-nosed appearance but led to criticism that the pilot's view for deck landing was bad. Production modifications increased MTOW by approximately 25 per cent compared with development aircraft.

Corsair Mark II with undercarriage down

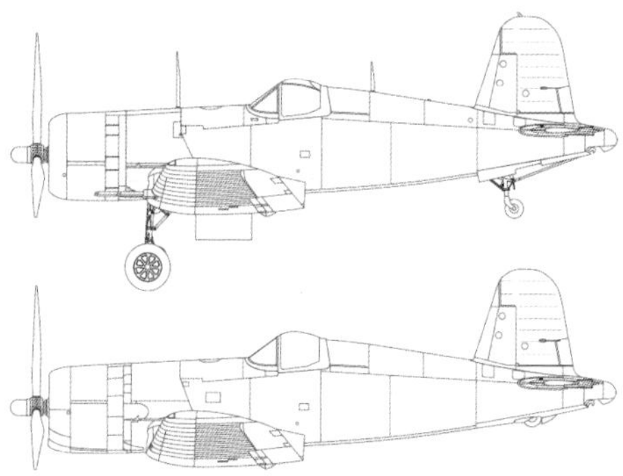

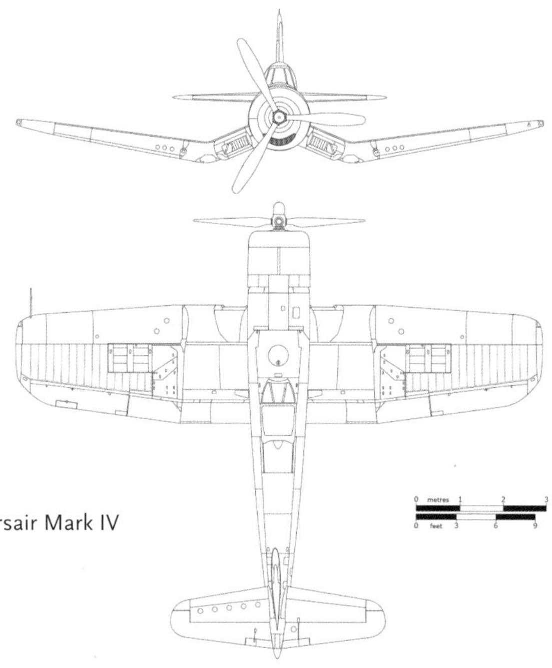

Corsair Mark IV

Corsair of 1833 NAS.

USN testing revealed undesirable deck-landing features. Stiff oleo movement caused an incipient bounce on hitting the deck but worse, there was a tendency to torque stall when applying power quickly in the landing configuration. The long nose meant that a continuous tight, curving approach had to be made to keep the batsman in the pilot's sight on final approach and there was a tendency to drop a wing as the throttle was closed at the 'cut'. The USN desperately wanted the F-4U but had grave doubts about its operability from a carrier, even before carrier qualification trials began on *Sangamon*, CVE-26, in September 1942. After these the Corsair was declared unsuitable for normal carrier operation but by then production aircraft were coming off the production line in large numbers. Priority was, therefore, given to re-equipping shore-based USMC squadrons in the Pacific. Sub contracts for Corsair production had been given to Brewster and Goodyear; the former designated F3A-1s and the latter at FG-1s. The USN's Corsair problems were to the RN's advantage, however, since large numbers were offered for transfer under Lend-Lease arrangements.

Corsair Mark IV data

Length:	33ft 4in
Wingspan:	39ft 8in (17ft folded)
Height:	15ft 1in
MTOW:	13,846lb
Engine:	Single 2,000hp Pratt & Whitney R-2800-8 Double Wasp air-cooled radial engine
Fuel:	Avgas. 197 gallons in fuselage tank. 102 gallons in wing tanks in most aircraft. One 145-gallon centreline drop tank. Total 344 gallons
Performance:	Maximum level speed 345 knots Service ceiling 37,000ft. 6 minutes to 10,000ft
Endurance:	Up to 6 hours with drop tanks
Armament:	Six 0.5in Colt-Browning machine guns, three in each wing. Inboard four 400 rpg, outboard two 375 rpg. Provision for up to two 1,000lb bombs on hardpoints under inner wings

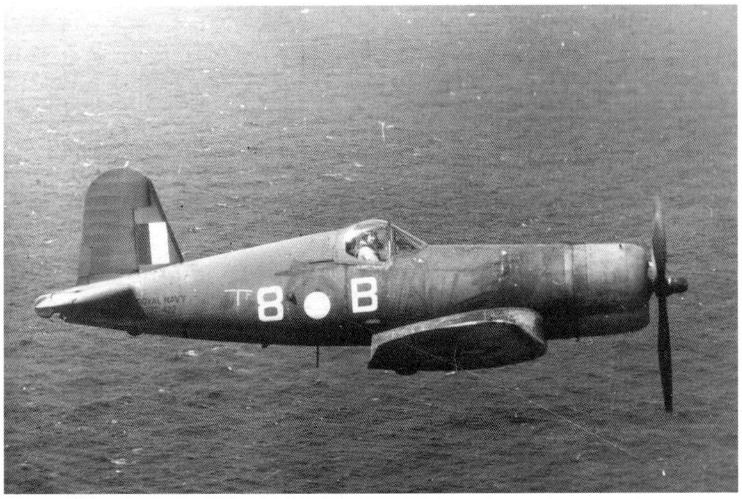

Corsair of 1836 NAS in 1944 with Eastern Fleet roundels and hastily-applied squadron markings; the 'T' is applied in chalk.

A running range of Corsairs in BPF markings on *Victorious* in 1945,

A Corsair turning finals on *Illustrious* being given the 'cut' signal.

Cocooned replacement Corsairs in *Unicorn* during 1945.

The RN had 1,892 Corsairs transferred to it from the USN under Lend-Lease arrangements. Of these 95 were to Mark I standard, 510 to Mark II, 430 built by Brewster designated as Mark IIIs and 857 built by Goodyear designated Mark IVs. Further batches were cancelled after VJ-Day.

Naval air squadrons in the 700-series based ashore operated Corsairs throughout the world on tasks ranging from pilot conversion and training to fleet requirements and tactical fighter development. They equipped, or partially equipped, 700, 703, 706, 715, 718, 719, 721, 723, 730, 731, 732, 733, 736, 738, 748, 757, 759, 760, 768, 771, 772, 777, 778, 787, 791, 794 and 797 NAS between 1943 and 1946.

Front-line squadrons were formed and trained in the USA at Quonset, Lewiston and Brunswick from June 1943 at the rate of roughly one a month until VJ-Day. They included 885, 1830, 1831, 1833, 1834, 1835, 1836, 1837, 1838, 1841, 1842, 1843, 1845, 1846, 1848, 1849, 1850, 1851, 1852 and 1853 NAS. Some of the later squadrons only had a short existence as they were split up to provide manpower for other units when they arrived in the UK or Australia for the BPF.

Corsair squadrons served in the aircraft carriers *Illustrious*, *Victorious*, *Formidable*, *Glory*, *Vengeance*, *Venerable* and *Colossus*. No Corsair squadrons operated from escort carriers on a regular basis but a number were delivered to the UK, deployed between fleets or ferried in *Ruler*, *Trumpeter*, *Pursuer*, *Khedive*, *Atheling*, *Smiter*, *Rajah*, *Trouncer*, *Puncher*, *Ranee*, *Reaper*, *Thane* and *Patroller*. Replenishment carriers with the BPF fleet train carried replacement Corsairs for issue to the fleet carriers as well as Avengers, Hellcats, Seafires and Fireflies.

RN Mark I Corsairs equated to the USN F4U-1 standard but were soon followed by the Mark II which featured unique RN modifications as well as those introduced by the USN. The latter included a higher, single-piece Plexiglas canopy replacing the heavily-framed 'bird-cage' hood and a seating position for the pilot raised by 7in to give an improved view for deck landing. RN modifications included the installation of British radios and the wingtips were squared off with 8in removed from each wingtip rather than the original curve in order to give adequate clearance above the wings in the folded position when stowed in British carrier hangars. This modification was found to improve the Corsair's rate of roll. Another simple modification was the attachment of a small spoiler to the inner leading edge of the port wing to disturb the airflow when the throttle was closed at the 'cut' so that both wings lost lift together and there was no wing-drop. Both navies benefitted from the provision of longer-stroke undercarriages which largely cured the problem of bouncing on landing. All RN Corsairs were modified to carry a single 145-gallon drop tank on the centreline and from the 361st aircraft a 114-gallon drop tank could be carried under the starboard wing hardpoint. From the 441st aircraft 114-gallon drop tanks or 1,000lb bombs could be carried under either wing.

The first RN Corsair squadrons in action were *Victorious*' 1834 and 1836 NAS in April 1944 when they flew top cover for the attack by Barracudas on *Tirpitz* in Kaa Fjord, Operation 'Tungsten'. Later strikes were covered by 1841 and 1842 NAS embarked in *Formidable*. Corsairs gave outstanding service with the BPF during 1945, operating from the fleet carriers *Illustrious*, *Victorious* and *Formidable*, taking part in strikes against the Sumatran oil refineries, the Okinawa campaign and attacks on the Japanese mainland. Notable Corsair pilots included Major R C Hay RM, leader of Number 47 Naval Fighter Wing and strike co-ordinator for the strike on the Palembang refineries in January 1945. Lieutenant L D Durno DSC RNVR of 1834 NAS achieved five 'kills' but the type's top-scoring pilot was Lieutenant D J Sheppard DSC RCNVR of 1836 NAS who achieved six 'kills'. Lieutenant R H Gray DSC RCNVR, Senior Pilot of 1841 NAS, was awarded the Fleet Air Arm's second VC of World War Two. On 9 August 1945 he led a sweep by eight Corsairs from *Formidable* against Japanese ships in Onagawa Bay. They were armed with two 500lb bombs in addition to their front guns and Gray was flying Corsair KD 658 coded 115/X. 'Hammy' Gray took off at 0810 and led his aircraft to Onagawa where a concentration of enemy shipping had been reported by an earlier sweep. They were identified as two destroyers and a minesweeper moored close inshore and he led his aircraft down to low level to attack using the 'skip-bombing' technique, bouncing the bombs across the sea surface into the side of the target. Anti-aircraft fire from the ships and shore was intense and Gray was hit in the lower part of his engine which caught fire. Japanese eye-witnesses saw one of his bombs fall off but he held his aim unflinchingly and hit the target with his remaining bomb. Seconds later his Corsair rolled inverted and crashed into the sea, giving him no chance to bail out. The target was subsequently identified as the escort destroyer *Amakusa* which sank in under five minutes with the loss of 157 lives. The remaining Corsairs sank the minesweeper and damaged the second destroyer. Gray had previously been awarded the DSC for his part in the attacks on *Tirpitz* and his VC was announced by the Admiralty on 12 November 1945.

The fleet carriers landed their Corsairs immediately after VJ-Day to airfields in Australia from where they were taken to sea and dumped since the Lend-Lease agreement required them to be purchased in dollars, returned or destroyed. Ditching was the cheapest alternative; sadly, many Corsairs dumped off Eastern Australia were brand-new aircraft, only just delivered to the BPF. Some Corsairs were retained, however, since 1831, 1846, 1850 and 1851 NAS embarked in *Glory*, *Colossus*, *Venerable* and *Vengeance* had only joined the BPF in July 1945 and it took some months to replace them with Seafires. The last Corsair squadron, 1851 NAS, was disbanded in August 1946 when *Vengeance* returned to the UK.

Rows of Corsairs from *Victorious* and *Formidable* at Maryborough in 1945 awaiting disposal.

Pilots' impressions of the Corsair differed. When Norman Hanson, who later commanded 1833 NAS, arrived at Quonset Point and saw them for the first time he thought they were the most wicked looking aircraft he had ever seen. He was already an experienced pilot but promptly sat down and typed his will. Once they got used to it, however, most pilots found the Corsair's rugged power exhilarating. The principal Japanese naval fighter, the A6M Zero, had poor aileron control at high speed and rolled sluggishly. This allowed Corsair pilots to carry out slashing attacks at high speed from a dive and break port or starboard to shake off any attempt at pursuit.

CURTISS

Small America

Two Curtiss flying boats with the company designation H.1 were purchased by the Admiralty in August 1914 for evaluation at Felixstowe. Found to be under-powered, their two 90hp Curtiss OX-5 engines were replaced by two 100hp Anzanis and they were used for development before being deleted in 1916. They were followed by sixty-two Curtiss H.4 flying boats retrospectively named Small America by the RN after the introduction of larger Curtiss boats. Eight were built by Airco under licence but the others were shipped to the UK between July 1915 and August 1917. Early aircraft had two 50hp Curtiss OX-5 engines but these were replaced by two 100hp French Anzani or 130hp British Clerget engines. Despite these improvements, Small Americas always lacked power and most were used for experiments with modified hull forms and planing bottoms that led to the Felixstowe flying boats designed by Wing Commander John Porte RNAS. The Small America was a boat-hulled reconnaissance aircraft constructed of wood with fabric covering and operated by a crew of four; two pilots, an engineer and a telegraphist. Wingspan was 72ft and MTOW 4,983lb. Maximum level speed was 60 knots and armament included a flexibly-mounted 0.303in Lewis gun in the bow position. Individual aircraft had Lewis guns mounted in other positions and bombs could be carried on underwing hardpoints, typically twelve 20lb or two 100lb bombs. Small Americas operated from Felixstowe, Calshot, Calafrana in Malta, Westgate, Great Yarmouth and Killingholme.

Very few H.4s survived into 1918 because their wooden hulls were easily damaged and deteriorated quickly in use. Their operational value was limited but the development work carried by John Porte to improve what was basically a sound design was an important step in flying boat design for the RNAS.

H 4 Small America beached at Newlyn for maintenance.

Large America

Purchased from early 1916 and named Large America by the RN, these flying boats comprised slightly different sub-types with the Curtiss designations H.8, H.12B and H.16. The final batch had only just entered service when the war ended in 1918. It was an enlarged development of its predecessor delivered with two 160hp Curtiss engines but these were found inadequate and replaced by two 275hp Rolls-Royce Eagle I engines. By 1918 the survivors had been further re-engined with more powerful Eagle VIIIs.

Large America data

Length:	46ft 6in
Wingspan:	92ft 8½in
Height:	16ft 6in
MTOW:	10,650lb
Engines:	Two Rolls-Royce 375hp Eagle VIII
Fuel:	Avgas. 248 gallons
Performance:	Maximum level speed 75 knots Service ceiling 10,800ft. 3 minutes to 2,000ft
Endurance:	6 hours
Armament:	Up to four 0.303in Lewis guns on flexible mountings in nose, cockpit and side hatches. Up to four 100lb or two 230lb bombs on underwing hardpoints

H 12 Large America 8666 on its handling trolley at Felixstowe in 1917.

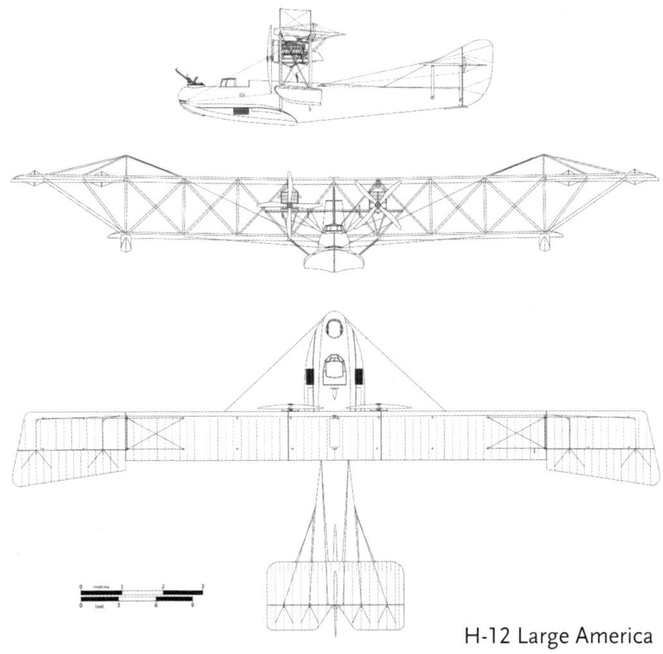

H-12 Large America

Curtiss H 8 Large America. (Philip Jarrett)

Total deliveries to the RN amounted to eighty-six Large Americas.

Large Americas initiated the 'Spider-Web' patrols based on the North Hinder Light Vessel searching for U-boats in transit on the surface and were used as both long-range anti-submarine patrol aircraft and as anti-Zeppelin fighters over the North Sea with considerable success. On 14 May 1917 the German airship L 22 was shot down by 8666 from Great Yarmouth north-north-west of Texel Island; the first Zeppelin to be destroyed by a flying boat. On 14 June 1917 a second Zeppelin, L 43, was destroyed by 8677 from Felixstowe. Others were credited at the time with sinking U-boats although post-war research revealed that they might only have been damaged.

Large Americas operated with the War Flights at Felixstowe, Great Yarmouth and Killingholme. They were worked hard and only eighteen were still in service by November 1918.

JN-3

A two-seat trainer biplane powered by a single 90hp Curtiss OX-5 engine, JN-3s were ordered from 1915 onwards, built in both the USA and Canada. Some of the latter were found to exhibit poor workmanship when re-assembled in the UK and, surprisingly, they were delivered without dual controls. The Fairey Aviation Company was contracted to make modifications, the resulting aircraft identified as JN-3 (Improved). The work included installation of dual controls, strengthening the airframe and fitting enlarged tail surfaces. Propellers were replaced by British-built units less prone to failure. Wingspan was 43ft 10in and MTOW of 1,918lb. Improved JN-3s were used for training at Chingford, Cranwell, Eastbourne, Hendon, Howden, Westgate, Killingholme, Eastchurch, Isle of Grain, Luxeuil-les-Bains, Scarborough, Redcar, Hornsea, Manston, Folkestone and Vendome.

JN-4

Known colloquially in the RNAS as the 'Jenny', the JN-4 was the same size as the JN-3 but structural improvements raised MTOW to 2,130lb. It had the same 90hp Curtiss OX-5 engine giving a maximum level speed of 62 knots. The Admiralty purchased 121 JN 4s in 1916; most went to the RNAS training establishment at Vendome in France but others went to Hendon, Redcar, Eastbourne, Chingford, Cranwell, Eastchurch, Isle of Grain, Manston, East Fortune and Luxeuil-les-Bains in small numbers. Those that had not been written off in crashes had been deleted by March 1918.

Curtiss JN-3. (Philip Jarrett)

Curtiss JN-4 at Vendome. (Philip Jarrett)

Type N (modified)
Six examples were ordered by the Admiralty in 1914, built in Canada and delivered in February 1915. They were two-seat, tractor, biplanes powered by a single 90hp Curtiss OX-5 engine which gave a maximum level speed of 70 knots. Wingspan was 41ft 6in and MTOW was 1,800lb. Some aircraft were issued to Eastchurch, Chingford, Dover and St Pol but found to be of little value. None were used operationally and all six were deleted in August 1915.

R.2
One hundred R.2 two-seat tractor biplanes were ordered by the Admiralty in 1915 and built in Canada. Most were powered by 160hp Curtiss V-X engines which proved unreliable but a few were built with 150hp Sunbeam engines. Delivered from 1916 onwards, some were fitted with hardpoints for bomb carriage and issued to 3 Wing at Luxeuil-les-Bains. Others were used for bombing, gunnery and observer training at Cranwell and Eastchurch. Fourteen aircraft were not delivered and at least twenty-five were never flown. Most were deleted by the end of 1917 but a few survived as trainers into 1918. Wingspan was 45ft 11½in and MTOW 3,092lb. With the Curtiss engine maximum level speed was 75 knots but it took 10 minutes to climb to 4,000ft. Endurance was an impressive 6½ hours. The R.2 was soon replaced in 3 Wing by 1½ Strutters and by better aircraft in training units as soon as they became available.

Type T
This tractor, triplane, flying boat was designed to meet an Admiralty specification for a large patrol aircraft and twenty were ordered by the Admiralty in May 1916. Wingspan was 134ft and MTOW 22,000lb. It was to have been powered by four 250hp Curtiss V-4 engines to give a maximum level speed of 90 knots but they were not developed in time and the first aircraft was shipped to the UK in component form without engines. Four 240hp Renault engines were installed when it was assembled at Felixstowe in October and it first flew in November 1916. On its second flight the tailplane collapsed on landing; it was not repaired and the remaining nineteen were cancelled.

Model C Twin Canada
A single example was ordered in 1915, the first design from the Canadian Curtiss plant in Toronto. Adapted from the H.4 flying boat and powered by two 160hp Curtiss V-X engines, wingspan was 75ft 10in and MTOW 6,300lb. After assembly at Hendon in June 1916 it was used for trials with Sperry-Curtiss automatic stabilising gear which were not considered successful and it was deleted in early 1917.

Seamew
A mid-wing monoplane designed for the USN to operate as either a floatplane or with a wheeled undercarriage. Designated SO-3C and named Seagull by the USN, it first flew in October 1939 but it was plagued by aerodynamic problems. Distinctive turned-up wingtips were a visible attempt to cure them but it was never used widely and withdrawn from service by March 1944 as the requirement for observation flights was no longer considered important. The RN was allocated 250 under Lend-Lease arrangements, not all of which were delivered. It was renamed as the Seamew Mark I in RN service and, as in the USN, the 520hp Ranger SGV-770-6 engine was found to be extremely unreliable. Wingspan was 38ft and MTOW 5,588lb with a wheeled undercarriage. Maximum speed in level flight was 110 knots and it had an endurance close to 8 hours. The RN never used the float plane variant and the wheeled variant proved unpopular because the main oleos were sited well aft, making taxiing difficult. Most were used for TAG training starting with 744 NAS at Yarmouth, Nova Scotia, from March 1943 but they were found to have such poor performance on the rare occasions when they were serviceable that they were withdrawn after a few months and replaced by Swordfish. In October 1942 Seamews replaced Sharks in 745 NAS at Worthy Down and it was the intention to replace the squadron's Lysanders and Proctors in the TAG training role but again bad serviceability was its downfall and when the squadron disbanded in 1944 the remaining Seamews were scrapped.

Helldiver
Designed to meet a USN dive-bomber requirement and designated SB-2C, it first flew in December 1940 but was plagued by aerodynamic issues that led to a number of crashes. It did eventually enter USN service but pilots referred to it as either 'the Beast' or the 'Son of a Bitch Second Class', playing on its SB2C designation. RN Helldivers were manufactured under licence by the Canadian Car and Foundry company, USN designation SBW-1B. It was a two-seat monoplane dive-bomber capable of carrying a 1,000lb bomb under the fuselage and a 500lb bomb under each wing. Wingspan was 49ft 8½in and MTOW 12,256lb. RN Helldivers were designated Mark I and powered by a single 1,650hp Wright R-2600-20 Double-Row Cyclone engine which gave a maximum level speed of 250 knots. Only 26 Helldivers were transferred from the USN to the RN under Lend-Lease arrangements out of an intended total of 450 and they only equipped one squadron, 1820 NAS, which commissioned at Brunswick in April 1944 before being ferried to the UK in *Arbiter*. It spent much of its short existence at Burscough with detachments to *Speaker* for deck-landing qualification but was found completely unsatisfactory for its intended purpose. When 1820 NAS was disbanded in December 1944 it had lost several aircraft and crews in accidents including three aircraft that failed to pull out of vertical dives and had never been cleared to embark operationally by the RN. Some had been issued to 700 and 778 NAS for brief periods of evaluation but no other squadrons received any. Remaining airframes were deleted.

Curtiss Helldiver. (Philip Jarrett)

A B C D E F G H I J K L M N O P Q R S T U V W X Y Z

A
B
C
D
E
F
G
H
I
J
K
L
M
N
O
P
Q
R
S
T
U
V
W
X
Y
Z

de HAVILLAND

DH 60M Moth

A two-seat biplane with a metal-frame fuselage derived from the earlier Gipsy Moth which had a wooden structure. It first flew in 1928 and twelve were acquired for RN use as dual-control deck-landing training aircraft from 1929 onwards. Alternative wheel or float undercarriages could be fitted. Wingspan was 30ft, and MTOW 1,750lb. They were powered by a single 120hp de Havilland Gipsy II engine which gave a maximum level speed of 92 knots as a landplane or 86 knots as a seaplane. Moths were allocated to the flying training schools at Leuchars and Gosport where RN pilots were trained and were sometimes attached to disembarked squadrons for continuation flying and standardisation checks. Examples include 801, 811 and 822 NAS at Donibristle in 1939. Training squadrons including 767 and 769 NAS also used Moths at Donibristle for deck-landing training in *Furious* during 1939. Three further examples were requisitioned in 1939; two of these were used by 767 and 770 NAS at Hyeres and on *Argus* for deck-landing training in 1940 and the third was used by the station flight at Eastleigh until 1941.

Puss Moth

A single DH 80A Puss Moth monoplane was requisitioned by the Admiralty in January 1940 and used by the station flights at Evanton and Fearn until 1943 when it was deleted. It was considered a stable, viceless aircraft and a delight by all who flew it. It was powered a single 120hp de Havilland Gipsy III engine giving a maximum speed of 110 knots. Wingspan was 36ft 9in and MTOW 1,900lb.

DH 86

A graceful four-engined, ten-seat biplane which first flew in 1934 and was intended to carry mail and passengers on the Singapore to Sydney leg of the London to Sydney air route flown by Imperial Airways and QANTAS. It was powered by four 205hp de Havilland Gypsy Six series II engines which gave a maximum level speed of 145 knots. Wingspan was 64ft 6in and MTOW 11,000lb. A number were requisitioned for the RAF after the outbreak of war and from 1940 onwards six were transferred to the RN for use by 782 NAS at Donibristle on inter-airfield clipper flights. One was destroyed during an enemy air attack on Lee-on-Solent in July 1940 and the others were withdrawn from service in 1944.

DH 83 Fox Moth

A single-engined biplane designed as a short-range passenger-carrier which first flew in 1932. It was powered by a single 145hp de Havilland Gipsy Major IC engine which gave a maximum level speed of 95 knots and could carry four passengers in the fuselage forward of the pilot's elevated cockpit. Costs were minimised by using Tiger Moth components wherever possible. Wingspan was 30ft 10in and MTOW 2,100lb. Many were requisitioned for the RAF after 1939 and in 1941 one was transferred to the RN for operation by 781 NAS at Lee-on-Solent, moving to Stretton in 1942 and then Eastleigh in 1943. Among other tasks at the latter it gave air experience to Sea Cadets.

DH 85 Leopard Moth

A monoplane with an enclosed cockpit powered by a single 130hp de Havilland Gipsy Major which gave a maximum level speed of 95 knots. Wingspan was 37ft 6in and MTOW 2,225lb. Many were requisitioned for the RAF after 1939 and two were subsequently transferred to the RN. One was issued to 759 NAS at Eastleigh in April 1940, moved to St Merryn in August but returned to the RAF in 1941. The second was transferred in 1942 and used by the communications flight at Worthy Down. In 1945 it was used by 700 NAS and then Number 6 Ferry Pool, also at Worthy Down, which used it to collect pilots who ferried aircraft around naval air stations. It was discarded in 1946.

DH 87 Hornet Moth

A biplane with an enclosed cockpit powered by a single 130hp de Havilland Gipsy Major IC engine which gave a maximum level speed of 110 knots, the first Hornet Moth flew in 1934. Wingspan was 31ft 11in and MTOW 2,000lb. Four seaplane variants were purchased by the Admiralty in 1939 and used by the communications flight at Lee-on-Solent. In 1940 they were fitted with wheeled undercarriages; two were transferred to 781 NAS, also at Lee. The other two went to Hatston. A fifth aircraft was requisitioned in 1940 and used by 759 NAS at Eastleigh before joining 781 NAS until 1945. The Hornet Moth had dual controls for two pilots seated side by side with bench seating behind them for two passengers, an ideal light communications arrangement. One crashed in 1940 but the others continued in use until 1945.

DH 95 Flamingo

A monoplane short-haul airliner capable of carrying up to seventeen passengers with a crew of two pilots and a radio operator. The DH 95 was de Havilland's first all-metal, stressed skin design and was powered by two 890hp Bristol Perseus XIIC engines which gave a maximum level speed of 215 knots. Wingspan was 70ft and MTOW 17,600lb. It first flew in December 1938 but production was cut short in 1939 and only fifteen were completed. Some aircraft were requisitioned for the RAF but one Flamingo was allocated directly to the RN and issued to 782 NAS at Donibristle. It was used on daily communications flights to naval air stations in the Orkney and Shetland Islands and Northern Ireland until it was deleted in 1946. A second Flamingo was transferred from the RAF in March 1945 and used as a source of spares.

DH 82A Tiger Moth

A two-seat biplane with the Gipsy engine modified to run inverted giving a smother aerodynamic profile. The instructor sat in the front

Flamingo of 782 NAS at Donibristle.

Tiger Moth of the BRNC Flight at Roborough.

cockpit with the student in the rear and it was flown solo from the rear cockpit. It first flew in October 1931 and became the standard British elementary training aircraft from 1932, training RN as well as RAF ab initio pilots. Production expanded greatly in the late 1930s and Tiger Moths were produced by de Havilland factories in Canada, Australia and New Zealand as well as the UK.

Tiger Moth data

Length:	23ft 11in
Wingspan:	29ft 4in
Height:	8ft 9½in
MTOW:	1,825lb
Engine:	One 130hp de Havilland Gipsy Major I
Fuel:	Avgas. 19-gallon tank in upper wing centre section
Performance:	Maximum speed 90 knots
	Service ceiling 14,000ft
Endurance:	3 hours
Armament:	None

No Tiger Moths were built for the RN but 100 were transferred from the RAF to the RN and a further thirteen were transferred from the RAAF during the Second World War. Three were purchased from civilian owners in 1956.

No squadrons were completely equipped with Tiger Moths but examples were issued to 700, 701, 702, 721, 723, 727, 728, 729, 733, 755, 756, 758, 759, 768, 769, 770, 775, 780, 781, 782, 796, 798 and 799 NAS from 1941. They were also taken on charge by station flights at Anthorn, Arbroath, Ayr, Bankstown, Belfast, Brawdy, Crail, Culdrose, Dale, Donibristle, Dunino, East Haven, Eastleigh, Eglinton, Fearn, Gosport, Hal Far, Hatston, Henstridge, Inskip, Lee-on-Solent, Lossiemouth, Maryborough, Maydown, Piarco, Ronaldsway, St Merryn, Stretton, Ta Kali, Worthy Down and Yeovilton for periods between 1942 and 1973.

RN Tiger Moths were used for standardisation checks on operational pilots and to provide continuation flying practice for pilots appointed to 'desk jobs'. After 1945 the RN used Tiger Moths for pre-flying training grading and a flight was retained to give air experience to cadets at the BRNC Dartmouth until 1966. My own first flights were in the Dartmouth Tiger Moths based at Roborough Airfield just outside Plymouth and I have very happy memories of flying an open cockpit biplane and can still visualise having to lean my head to one side in order to get a better view past the instructor for landing on the grass airfield.

DH 82B Queen Bee

A radio-controlled, unmanned target aircraft designed to meet Specification 18/33. It had the same de Havilland type number as the Tiger Moth and identical engine, wings and undercarriage but the fabric-covered metal-tube fuselage of the Tiger Moth was replaced by the spruce and plywood wooden fuselage used previously in the DH 60 Moth which was both cheaper and more buoyant. They also had a 25- rather than 19-gallon fuel tank to increase endurance. The front cockpit had instruments and controls to allow a human pilot to fly a Queen Bee if necessary but a fairing covered it during unmanned flights. The rear cockpit became an enclosed compartment near the centre of gravity for the radio control equipment for which electrical power was provided by a wind-driven generator.

The prototype Queen Bee flew with a human pilot in January 1935 and unmanned in June using a push-button panel to control take-off, manoeuvres and landing. Wheeled undercarriages were fitted for test flights or ferrying but operational Queen Bees were fitted with Short-designed metal floats for water landings. No Queen Bees were contracted directly for the RN but they were used by RAF target facilities flights Gosport, Hal Far and Seletar in Singapore to provide targets for RN warships. Some were embarked in cruisers of the Home, Mediterranean and Far East Fleets. Float-fitted Queen Bees were catapulted to fly up and down a pre-determined course while the fleet's anti-aircraft gunners fired at them. If destroyed they crashed into the sea but any that survived, as most did, could be landed on the water and recovered by crane for further use. Whilst they were certainly live targets, Queen Bees flying at 90 knots in a straight line were hardly representative of an actual attack but production continued until 1944. Some stored Queen Bees had their radio-control equipment removed and were refitted as dual-control trainers; at least five of these were used by the RN. One was used by 775 NAS at Dekheila in 1941 but was written off during a test flight when it hit the sea and another was at Fayid. Most survivors were scrapped after 1945.

Pilotless Queen Bee being launched from *Pegasus*.

de Havilland Dominie.

DH 89B Dominie

A light transport aircraft used by the RN from the 1940s until the early 1960s, the Dominie was a variant of the civilian DH 89 Dragon Rapide airliner which was exported worldwide during the 1930s. Many were requisitioned for the RAF from 1939 and contracts were placed for the military derivative named Dominie. When de Havilland stopped making them in 1942 to begin Mosquito production, assembly was transferred to Brush Coachworks Ltd.

Dominie Mark 2 data

Length:	34ft 6in
Wingspan:	48ft
Height:	10ft 3in
MTOW:	5,500lb
Engines:	Two 200hp de Havilland Gipsy Queen 3
Fuel:	Avgas. 76 gallons
Performance:	Maximum speed 138 knots
	Service ceiling 19,500ft. 12 minutes to 10,000ft
Endurance:	3 hours 45 minutes
Armament:	None

No Dominies were built directly for the RN but sixty-five were transferred from the RAF.

No squadrons were completely equipped with Dominies but between 1941 and 1963 they were allocated to 701, 703, 739, 744, 767, 776, 778, 781, 782, 787, 790 and 799 NAS for use in the light transport role between air stations. A single Dominie from 776 NAS was used as the personal barge of Admiral Sir Max Horton, C-in-C Western Approaches Command.

For varying lengths of time over the same period Dominies were used by station flights at Abbotsinch, Anthorn, Arbroath, Bramcote, Brawdy, Culdrose, Culham, Donibristle, Eglinton, Evanton, Ford, Hatston, Lossiemouth, Machrihanish, Stretton, Woodvale and Yeovilton. The RN still had fourteen on charge in 1961, some of which were modified and equipped to act as air ambulances and painted with red crosses on the fuselage as well as the national insignia.

Mosquito

de Havilland's private venture concept of a wooden bomber with no defensive gun armament that could fly both faster and higher than contemporary fighters was initially rejected by the RAF which saw no merit in anything outside its own pre-conceived ideas but in December 1939 a single prototype was sanctioned and a production contract placed in March 1940. The Mosquito first flew in November 1940 and A&AEE trials showed it to have excellent potential as a long-range fighter and reconnaissance aircraft as well as a bomber. The two crew, pilot and observer, sat side-by-side in an all-wood cantilever monoplane with a slim, tapering fuselage of circular section built with moulded sections of cedar wood separated by balsa wood. To simplify the installation of controls, wiring and pipelines port and starboard halves

'Winkle' Brown gets the 'cut' seconds before taking a wire on *Indefatigable* on 25 March 1944. The first carrier landing by a twin-engined aircraft.

of the fuselage were made separately and the single-piece stressed-skin wings were built around the radiators and ten fuel tanks. Low drag nacelles for the two Rolls-Royce Merlin engines housed the retractable main undercarriage and the tail wheel was also retractable to give a clean, exceptionally low-drag airframe. Large-scale contracts were placed to manufacture Mosquitoes for the RAF in the bomber, fighter-bomber, night fighter and photographic reconnaissance roles and they were eventually manufactured by de Havilland factories in the UK, Canada, Australia and under licence by Airspeed Ltd at Christchurch, Percival Aircraft Ltd at Luton and by the Standard Motor Company.

Mosquito FB VI data

Length:	40ft 6in
Wingspan:	54ft 2in
Height:	12ft 6in
MTOW:	22,258lb
Engines:	Two 1,460hp Rolls-Royce Merlin 21
Fuel:	Avgas. 539 gallons plus two optional 50-gallon underwing tanks
Performance:	Maximum level speed 330 knots Service ceiling 33,000ft. 3½ minutes to 10,000ft
Endurance:	7 hours
Armament:	Four 20mm Oerlikon cannon and four 0.303in Browning machine guns in the nose. Two 500lb bombs in the bomb bay plus 500lb bombs on underwing hardpoints. Alternatively up to eight 3in RP on underwing rails

Admiralty interest in the Mosquito was stimulated in 1942 by its high performance and the FBC's recommendation that new carriers should be capable of operating aircraft up to 30,000lb which meant that Mosquito derivatives could embark in them. Several 'war-weary' aircraft were transferred to the RN for use by fleet requirements units as targets more representative of enemy capability than Queen Bees, Skuas or Martlets. As soon as the Admiralty gained approval to procure its own Sea Mosquito derivative of the DH 98, ex-RAF Mosquitoes were used train RN pilots and observers, including the T III, a dual-control

'Winkle' Brown talking to senior officers after landing on *Indefatigable*.

conversion trainer. By 1945 the RN had received thirty-three FB VIs and seven T IIIs transferred from the RAF and used them to train air and ground crews with 704 NAS. It also received four PR XVIs and two NF XIIIs. Mosquitoes were never built directly for the RN but after 1945 further batches were transferred from the RAF including fifty-eight B 25s, forty-nine B XVIs, thirty-eight PR XVIs, twenty-nine FB VIs, a single NF 30, fourteen PR 34s and thirty-two T IIIs, a total of 221. A single F II and two NF XIIIs in non-flying condition were tested to destruction in trials of new flight deck crash barriers suitable for twin-engined aircraft.

The last Mosquito derivative was a conversion of the B XVI into the TT 39, a shore-based target tug designed to meet Admiralty Specification Q.19/45. It featured a lengthened nose to provide glazed accommodation for a camera to record shell bursts, the installation of an electrically-driven winch in the bomb bay and a dorsal observation cupola for the winch operator. It was equipped to tow either 32ft or 16ft span targets or a small drogue. The original engines were replaced by two 1,710hp Rolls-Royce Merlin 72/73 or 76/77 engines but maximum speed with a target deployed was only 260 knots. Twenty-two aircraft were converted to TT 39 standard from 1947 but further planned conversions were cancelled as a savings measure. The TT 39 followed the naval sequence of mark numbers but, only intended for use ashore, it was never re-designated as a Sea Mosquito variant. TT 39s were used by 728 NAS at RNAS Hal Far and 771 NAS at RNAS Ford until 1952. A handful of PR 34s were used in the electronic warfare training role by 751 NAS at Watton until 1954.

The conversion unit, 704 NAS and a single front line squadron, 811 NAS, operated FB VIs from September 1945 to prepare air and ground crews for the introduction of the Sea Mosquito. Other squadrons that were partially equipped with the type from 1945 until 1954 included 703, 728, 733, 751, 762, 770, 771, 772, 773, 777, 778, 787, 790 and 797 NAS which used them for fleet requirements duties and trials.

The batsman running clear of the Mosquito's path.

Before ordering the Sea Mosquito the Admiralty needed to prove that it was possible to operate an aircraft of this weight and speed from a carrier. Twin-engined aircraft had never operated from a carrier

A B C D E F G H I J K L M N O P Q R S T U V W X Y Z

Mosquito T 3 of 762 NAS after suffering a collapsed undercarriage at Culdrose in 1949.

because a single-engine failure on take-off before safe single-engine speed was reached could lead to a fatal asymmetric roll. The loss of an engine in flight would make deck landing dangerous because of the disparity between the aircraft's minimum single-engined landing speed and the maximum speed, relative to the deck, that the arrester wire system could accept. 'Winkle' Brown was the test pilot selected to carry out a trial in LR 359, a specially strengthened FB VI with a Barracuda-type arrester hook fitted under the rear fuselage in 1944. It was also fitted with four-bladed propellers to improve total thrust and acceleration. He was briefed that the recommended approach speed was 110 knots and the stalling speed with gear and flaps down was 96 knots. The carrier was to be the new *Indefatigable*, the largest RN fleet carrier. Her arrester wires could accept an aircraft up to 20,000lb but only up to a maximum entry speed of 60 knots relative to the deck. A high WOD would be needed and the starboard wingtip would be close to the island if the aircraft landed on the centreline. To counter this, both landing and take-off runs were to be offset slightly to port.

A second FB VI was modified with a hook and both were flown to Arbroath to practice ADDLs. 'Winkle' Brown flew with RAE test observer Bill Stewart and they found that the stalling speed could be reduced considerably but power had to be maintained until seconds before the wheels hit the deck. If throttles were cut too early at low speed the Mosquito would snap into a vicious stall, probably inverting with fatal consequences. Having evolved the best landing technique, 'Winkle' Brown landed on *Indefatigable* on 25 March 1944, the world's first deck landing by a twin-engined aircraft. LR 359 weighed 16,000lb as it turned finals and telemetry showed that it entered the wires at 68 knots. The ship was steaming at over 20 knots so the landing was well inside the arrester wire parameters. Trials continued a day later with increased weight and on the third landing, with the weight calculated as 18,000lb, the hook failed but 'Winkle' Brown managed to open the throttles and fly away. A eventual total of twenty-four landings were made by Brown and Commander H J F Lane RN, commanding officer of the Service Trials Unit at Crail, during March, April and May 1944. The Mosquito could be operated from a carrier but the swing on take-off and the risk of a single-engine failure had to be accepted.

Sea Mosquito

Designed to meet Admiralty Specification N.15/44 and named Sea Mosquito but retaining the same DH 98 company designation as other Mosquito variants, two Mosquitoes were modified into interim Sea Mosquitoes including one that had taken part in the *Indefatigable* trials. The Sea Mosquito had a small nose radome for an ASH surface-search and target acquisition radar scanner, folding wings and a strengthened after fuselage and was designated TR 33. The first production example flew in November 1945 but the first thirteen aircraft were not built to the full specification. The fourteenth aircraft was the first fully-representative example with folding wings. An A-frame arrester hook was fitted under the after fuselage with an extra bulkhead near its attachment points to give greater strength. A new long-stroke undercarriage was fitted to reduce bounce and new four-bladed, large-diameter propellers were fitted to gain maximum free take-off performance, even with low WOD. It was also cleared to use RATOG. Both the TR 33 and TR 37 were fitted with a Type F analogue torpedo-sighting computer identical the one used in the Barracuda. The TR 37 had a larger nose radome to accommodate an ASV Mark XIII radar scanner. This required a re-design of the fuselage forward of the cockpit but it was otherwise identical to the TR 33 and able to carry the same weapons. TR 37s served with 703 and 771 NAS between 1948 and 1950.

Sea Mosquito TR 33 data

Length:	42ft 3in
Wingspan:	54ft 2in (27ft 3in folded)
Height:	13ft 6in
MTOW:	23,850lb
Engines:	Two 1,705hp Rolls-Royce Merlin 66
Fuel:	Avgas. 1,200 gallons internal plus optional 30/50-gallon tanks on underwing hardpoints
Performance:	Maximum level speed 330 knots Service ceiling 30,000ft. 5 minutes to 10,000ft
Endurance:	4½ hours
Armament:	Four nose-mounted 20mm British Hispano cannon with 200 rpg. One 18in torpedo under the fuselage plus eight 3in RP or two 500lb bombs on underwing hardpoints. Two further 500lb bombs could be carried in the bomb bay when a torpedo was not carried

Sea Mosquitoes of 811 NAS in 1946.

Two prototypes and fifty-two Sea Mosquito TR 33s were received by the RN followed by six TR 37s. Total sixty.

Sea Mosquitoes served with the shore-based 703, 739, 751, 762, 771, 778, 787 and 790 NAS for a variety of trials and fleet requirements tasks between 1946 and 1950. TR 33s served with 811 NAS between 1946 and 1947 at Ford and Brawdy but did not embark with them.

The Sea Mosquito TR 33 represented a step-change in strike capability, introducing high speed, long range, radar to search for a target, a computerised sighting system and an 18in torpedo capable of sinking major warships. They were intended to operate from the *Malta* class carriers but when these were cancelled in 1945 the viability of operating from the smaller *Illustrious* class was considered marginal. With the Firebrand TF 5 in operational service and the Wyvern under development to keep the torpedo-attack alive, the Admiralty decided against keeping the Sea Mosquito in operational service.

Sea Vampire

The DH 100 Vampire evolved from an experimental design powered by a 2,700lb thrust de Havilland Goblin 1 centrifugal-flow gas turbine engine. Early Goblin tests revealed that long jet pipes reduced thrust and so de Havilland adopted a short nacelle with the tail unit mounted on

Sea Mosquito TR 33.

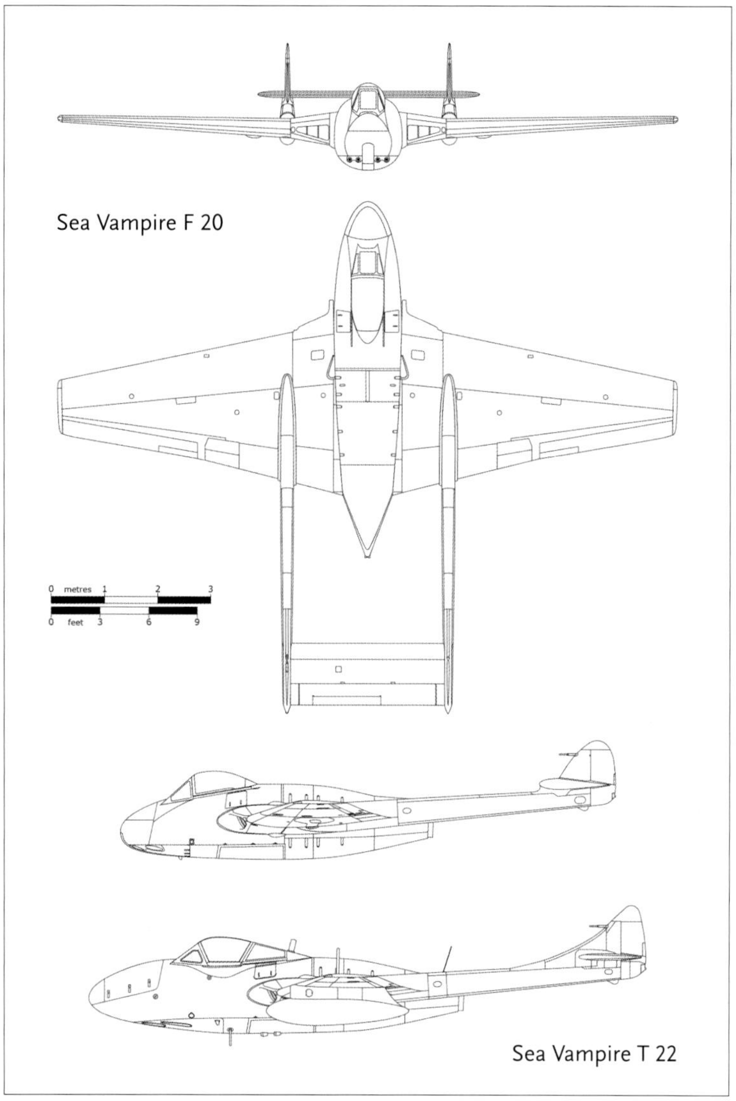

twin booms which were lighter than a conventional rear fuselage. Given the name Vampire, the first prototype flew in September 1943 with wings, tail booms and engine bay of metal construction but the cockpit was made of a plywood and balsa wood sandwich using Mosquito technology. The short-legged nose-wheel undercarriage reflected the lack of need for propeller clearance and the small oleos reduced structure weight. Early Vampires for the RAF were built by English Electric as de Havilland was fully committed to Mosquito production and the first flew in April 1945. It proved to be one of the most successful first-generation jet fighters with thousands built for the RAF, RAAF, RCAF, RNZAF and twenty-two other air arms around the world.

One of two prototypes completed in 1944, LZ 551/G, was modified to an interim Sea Vampire standard with the installation of an arrester hook, a 40 per cent increase in flap area and long-travel oleos. It was designated as a Sea Vampire F 10. The Admiralty had been attracted to the Vampire by its high performance and small size; it was small enough to fit the lifts of the new light fleet carriers without the need for folding wings if placed athwartships. The F 10 gave the RN the chance to land a jet-powered fighter on a carrier before the USN and 'Winkle' Brown flew LZ 551/G to Ford where he carried out ADDLs. Controversially, he used the piston-engined, three-point attitude deck-landing technique, estimating, with the batsman's help, the ideal 'cut' position where the throttle would be closed, allowing the aircraft to sink firmly into the wires. This technique had consequences, however; the Goblin was slow to accelerate from a low throttle setting and without propeller drag the aircraft took time to decelerate after the throttle was closed. The 'cut', therefore, had to be taken early on the final approach at a distance that would be difficult for the batsman to judge. Once he had closed the throttle, the pilot was committed with only a minimal chance of overshooting off a misjudged approach.

On 3 December 1945 Brown left Ford to join *Ocean* which was commanded by Captain Caspar John RN who had previously commanded the trials carrier *Pretoria Castle*. The sea state was marginal but Brown was already airborne when a signal telling him to remain at Ford arrived. Caspar John was announcing over the ship's main broadcast that the trial had been postponed when the Sea Vampire arrived overhead; knowing both the man and his ship he instructed Brown to land-on. Reminiscing in later years, when I was Curator of the Fleet Air Arm Museum, 'Winkle' Brown told me that as he turned finals he was immediately aware of two things. He had a superb view of the deck but now that he was low down, he realised that the ship was moving more violently than he had at first thought in both pitch and roll. The aircraft was steady in its approach, however, and the batsman gave him constant 'steady' signals so it never occurred to him to go round again. He came straight in and made what he felt to be a gentle landing, catching number 1 wire although camera footage showed that the pitching stern had hit the tail booms just before touchdown. The RN had become the first navy in the world to land a jet on an aircraft carrier. The aircraft was immediately refuelled and took off with a remarkably short deck run. Further deck landings followed but on the fourth the bottom of one of the enlarged flaps hit an arrester wire and was slightly damaged. The aircraft was flown back to Ford where the flaps were reduced in size and 4 days later the trials re-commenced without problems.

Sea Vampire F 20 data

Length:	30ft 9in
Wingspan:	38ft
Height:	8ft 10in
MTOW:	12,660lb
Engine:	One 3,000lb de Havilland Goblin 2 centrifugal-flow turbojet
Fuel:	Avtur. 330 gallons internal fuel with two optional 100-gallon drop tanks
Performance:	Maximum level speed 460 knots Service ceiling 43,500ft. 10 minutes to 25,000ft
Endurance:	2 hours at sea level. 2½ hours at 30,000ft
Armament:	Four 20mm Hispano-Suiza cannon in nose with 150 rpg. Two underwing hardpoints could each carry a single 500lb or 1,000lb bomb or eight 3in RP when drop tanks not fitted

Eight Vampires, including LZ 551/G, were modified to development Sea Vampire standard and re-designated as Sea Vampire F 10s and two prototype Sea Vampires were built as such. In 1947 a batch of eighteen

Sea Vampire F 21 carrying out angled-deck trials on the USS *Antietam* in the English Channel during 1953.

Sea Vampire prototype LZ 551/G on *Ocean* in 1945. The first jet aircraft to land on a carrier.

Sea Vampire F 21 catching the single arrester wire during undercarriage-less flexible deck trials on *Warrior* in 1949.

'Winkle' Brown climbing into a Sea Vampire F 21 prior to a catapult launch from *Warrior* in 1949.

incomplete Vampire FB 5s were completed as Sea Vampire F 20s. A further five Vampire F 3s were converted to Sea Vampire F 21 standard to meet Specification N.18/47 with strengthened fuselages for use landing with their undercarriages retracted in the 'rubber deck' trials.

A single Sea Vampire F 20 served with 806 NAS during 1948 when the unit carried out a display tour of Canada and the USA. It was the first British jet aircraft to fly in the USA and took part in thirty demonstrations with the unit's Sea Furies and Sea Hornets over a period of 3 months which included the opening of an International Air exposition in New York and the Canadian National Exposition in Toronto.

Sea Vampire F 20s and F 21s served with 700, 702, 703, 728, 759. 764, 771, 781 and 787 NAS for a variety of trials and for pilot familiarisation with jet operating techniques. Sea Vampire F 10s and semi-navalised 'hooked Vampires' also served with 778 NAS. The Sea Vampire can, justly, be described as the aircraft that led the RN transition from piston-engined fighters into the fast-jet era.

In his report after landing on *Ocean* 'Winkle' Brown stated his opinion that the level of skill required to deck land a Sea Vampire successfully would be beyond that expected from average front-line pilots but the Admiralty ordered further trials in 1946, to be carried out by 'C' Squadron, the RN element of the A&AEE. It was commanded by Commander J A Ievers RN. LZ551/G was used again but this time the carrier was *Ocean*'s sister-ship *Triumph*. Ievers was joined by Lieutenant Commander Randolph Pearson RN and Lieutenant S G Orr DSC AFC RN. All three reported positively on the Sea Vampire's potential as a deck-landing aircraft and their intense programme of ADDLs led them to believe that the throttle 'cut' leading to a sinking approach into the wires was far from ideal. What had seemed to 'Winkle' Brown to be a problem with slow engine response was overcome by flying the aircraft onto the deck without throttling back at all after a flat approach with engine RPM in the higher range where throttle response would be immediate if required for a wave-off. The team made a total of sixteen deck landings on *Triumph*, spread over two days in June 1946 using their new technique. All of which were entirely successful. This technique would not have worked with a piston-engined, tailwheel aircraft since it would cause the aircraft to bounce over the wires after the main wheels impacted the deck but it

Sea Vampire T 22, XA 160, in a green-and-white paint scheme for use as Flag Officer Air (Home)'s barge at Lee-on-Solent in 1962. (Philip Jarrett)

was perfect for the tricycle-undercarriage Sea Vampire and future jet aircraft. Ievers' team advised the Admiralty that the Sea Vampire was actually a very good deck-landing aircraft providing the correct technique was used.

The Sea Vampire F 20 had strengthened oleos and ARI 5272 VHF radio. The V-shaped arrester hook was housed under a fairing that extended over the jet exhaust nozzle and attached to hinges below it. In production aircraft the airbrakes and flaps were 30 per cent larger than those of the Vampire and the airframe was strengthened in the vicinity of the catapult spools fitted near the wing roots. The first F 20s were issued to 703 NAS at Lee-on-Solent which carried out over fifty successful deck landings on *Illustrious* with them. In April 1949 702 NAS was commissioned as part of the Fighter School at Culdrose with six F 20s and two Meteor T 7s to give pilots experience of embarked jet operations and tactics. It embarked successfully in *Implacable* between September and November 1949 and *Theseus* between May and June 1950. Sea Vampires were also embarked in *Vengeance* during early 1949 for a 6-week deployment to the Arctic to assess the effect of extremely cold weather on men, ships and aircraft. This too proved successful and the Sea Vampires acquitted themselves well but the Admiralty decided that they lacked sufficient endurance to be issued to a front-line fighter squadron for embarked operations.

Sea Vampires were heavily involved in evaluating the flexible deck, colloquially known as the 'rubber deck', a concept proposed by Lewis Boddington, Head of the NAD at RAE Bedford. He proposed removing aircraft undercarriages to reduce the weight of aircraft structures by about 7 per cent, transferring the pneumatic absorption of deck-landing impact from the aircraft to the ship in the same way that catapults and arrester gear were used to assist take-off and landing. The obvious drawback was the inability of an undercarriage-less aircraft to taxi after landing or to land on carriers and airfields that did not have flexible decks. A prototype 'rubber deck' was constructed at Farnborough in 1947 to evaluate the concept using three strengthened Vampires flown by 'Winkle' Brown. These proved successful and a flexible deck was fitted to *Warrior* on top of its conventional flight deck in November 1948. Three Sea Vampire F 21s carried out over 200 successful landings on *Warrior* and later the trials carrier *Illustrious*, flown by nine pilots including 'Winkle' Brown. Whilst the landings themselves were successful, practical flight deck operations were impossible since the aircraft had to be lifted by a crane onto a trolley to clear the deck, a process that took about five minutes compared with the 30 seconds or less that it would have taken a wheeled aircraft to taxi clear of the wires. Jet engine technology soon advanced sufficiently to resolve the lack of power which had been the original rationale of the concept.

Experiments with angling the flexible deck mats off the carrier centreline led to the brilliantly simple idea of the angled flight deck and Sea Vampires were among the aircraft used to fly proof-of-concept approaches to an angled deck painted on *Triumph* in 1952. The first carrier to be fitted with a fully-angled deck was the USS *Antietam* and after trials off the USA she carried out further trials off the UK in 1953 which included both landings and take-offs by Sea Vampires. Sea Vampires were considered the ideal aircraft to carry out the first trials of the prototype deck-landing mirror sights fitted in *Illustrious* and *Indomitable* in 1953. At least one of the aircraft was fitted with an early form of head-up display which allowed the pilot to monitor air speed while concentrating on the sight. Appropriately, a single Sea Vampire F 20 flown by Rear Admiral W T Couchman DSC OBE, Flag Officer Flying Training, led the massed fly-past by 327 aircraft from 40 Commonwealth naval air squadrons over Queen Elizabeth II's Coronation Review of the Fleet on 15 June 1953. From 1956 single-seat Sea Vampires were stored at Lossiemouth before being deleted in 1960.

Two-seat trainers

The RAF was responsible for all pilot training up to the award of 'wings', and used a developed Vampire with side-by-side seating for the advanced element of the course in the 1950s. The Admiralty saw the value of procuring a naval variant for use in RN operational training

Sea Vampire T 22s of 736 NAS from Lossiemouth in 1956. (Philip Jarrett)

squadrons, for converting pilots from piston-engined fighters to jets and for annual pilot standardisation checks. Side-by-side seating gave the instructor the same sight picture as the student in weapons delivery training. Vampire/Sea Vampire trainers were all given the generic de Havilland type number DH 115

Two RAF Vampire T 11 trainers were transferred to the RN for evaluation in 1952 by 759 and 781 NAS. This proved successful and Specification T.111 P.2 was issued to cover the production of Sea Vampire T 22 trainers for the RN. They differed from the RAF T 11 in having a TR 1936 VHF radio, a ZBX homing beacon and fittings for the pilots to wear anti-G suits. Two T 22 prototypes were built followed by production batches of fifty-three and twenty. The first production T 22 was delivered to Stretton in September 1953 and the type subsequently equipped, or partially equipped, 702, 718, 727, 736, 738, 750, 759, 764, 766 and 781 NAS,

The Sea Vampire T 22 had a MTOW 13,480lb fitted with two 100-gallon drop tanks but at this weight it was limited to gentle manoeuvres. The full range of aerobatics and combat manoeuvring could only be carried out below 11,710lb. The maximum level speed for a clean aircraft was 455 knots but with full drop tanks it was limited to 390 knots or Mach 0.76 above 15,000ft. The T 22 could be armed with 500lb bombs or 3in RP like the F 20/21 but only had two 20mm cannon. Both pilots had a Gyro Gunsight Mark 5 and a G.45 camera operated during gun and RP firing when the camera master switch was selected on. The T 22 was not intended for deck operation and had no hook but was used for ADDLs. The original Sea Vampire T 22s had framed canopies and lacked ejection seats but from 1956 they were modified with Mark 3B ejection seats, revised clear cockpit canopies and other detail improvements. Later examples were built with them from the outset. T 22s were used in a variety of roles including conversion and continuation trainers for fighter pilots destined for the Sea Venom and Sea Vixen, instrument rating trainers, airborne targets for the ADTU and also as targets for training AEW observers destined to fly in Skyraiders and Gannets. Several T 22s were used as 'Admiral's Barges' by Flag Officers. When HM Queen Elizabeth II presented Colours to the Fleet Air Arm in July 1956 Rear Admiral C L G Evans CBE DSO DSC, FONFT, led the fly-past in a 'box' of four Sea Vampire T 22s flown by himself, his Flag Lieutenant and the six Captains of his naval air stations. The last Sea Vampire T 22 was operated by the Air Direction School at RNAS Yeovilton until July 1970.

Sea Hornet

De Havilland built on the success of the Mosquito with a private venture design for a twin-engine long-range fighter it designated as DH 103, later named Hornet. Its slim, oval section fuselage was made of wood but the one-piece, two-spar cantilever laminar flow wing structure had a composite wood and metal assembly with a stressed birch ply double upper skin and an under-surface of reinforced Alclad. It was the first design in which wood and metal components were cemented together using the newly formulated Redux adhesive. Rolls-Royce developed special variants of the Merlin engine with minimal frontal area to reduce drag and the two engines were 'handed', turning inwards to eliminate torque effect in normal flight with a Merlin 130 in the starboard nacelle and a Merlin 131 in the port. Both drove four-bladed de Havilland Hydromatic variable-pitch propellers and the low-drag radiators were faired neatly into the wing leading edges inboard of the engines. The first prototype flew in July 1944 only 13 months after design work had started and the RAF, which had previously seen no need for long-range fighters, ordered Hornets into production.

From the outset de Havilland saw the DH 103's potential as a naval long-range strike fighter and the handed engines and high drag flaps were always intended for carrier operations. The Admiralty drafted Specification N.5/44 around it in 1944 and the resulting fighter was given the name Sea Hornet but retained the same de Havilland type number as the Hornet. In line with contemporary MAP policy, RAF variants were designed F 1 onwards and RN variants were numbered from F 20. Heston Aircraft Ltd was allocated three production airframes for use as prototypes and contracted to produce the naval variant with a new wing which featured hydraulic power folding similar to that of the Sea Mosquito and a forged steel arrester hook on flush fitting external 'V' frame under the rear fuselage. Catapult hooks to engage the strop needed for a tail-down launch were fitted, together with new Airdraulic undercarriage units capable of withstanding the shock of deck landing. Even with these changes, production Sea Hornets were only 550lb heavier than the basic Hornet. The first prototype Sea Hornet flew in April 1945 and the third was the first built to full naval specification. 'Winkle' Brown carried out the successful carrier qualification deck landings on *Ocean* in August 1945.

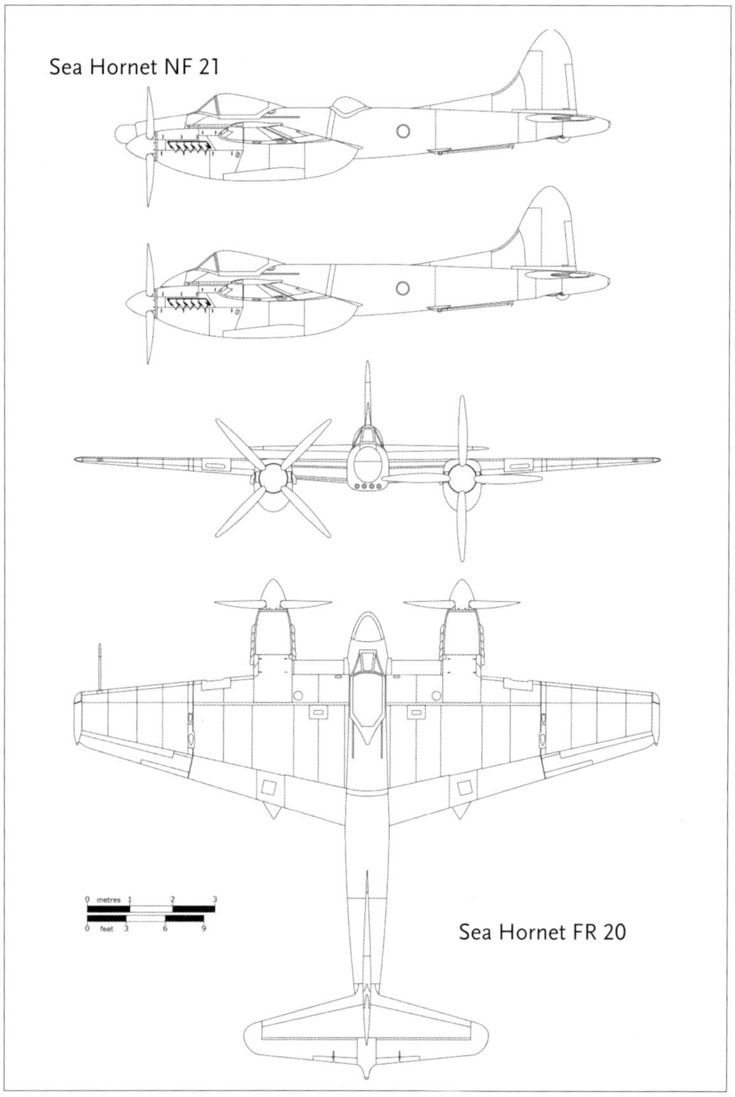

Sea Hornet NF 21 data

Length:	36ft 8in
Wingspan:	45ft (27ft 6in folded)
Height:	14ft folded
MTOW:	19,530lb
Engines:	Two 2,030hp Rolls-Royce Merlin – 134 port/135 starboard
Fuel:	Avgas. 432 gallons plus 2 optional 200-gallon drop tanks
Performance:	Maximum level speed 402 knots Service ceiling 36,500ft. 2½ minutes to 10,000ft
Endurance:	Over 5 hours with drop tanks
Armament:	Four 20mm Hispano front guns with 180 rpg. Underwing hardpoints for up to two 500lb or 1,000lb bombs or up eight 3in RP

Nine aircraft were modified to varying extents for use as Sea Hornet prototypes.

Seventy-seven were built as F 20 or FR 20 variants; seventy-eight were built as NF 21s and twenty-three as PR 22s; a total of 187. Three surplus RAF Hornets were expended in crash barrier trials in *Implacable.*

Between 1947 and 1954 Sea Hornets were operated by 801, 806 and 809 NAS. A single Sea Hornet PR 22 was allocated to 1833 NAS, an RNVR unit at Bramcote, from 1951 to 1952. Sea Hornets were also allocated to 703, 728, 736, 736B, 738, 739, 759, 771, 778, 787, 792 NAS and the un-numbered FRU at Hurn to carry out a wide variety of training, fleet requirements and trials duties until 1957.

The Sea Hornet proved extremely popular with pilots. Alan Leahy described it as a thoroughbred and as a weapons platform its inward-turning propellers gave no torque problems; there was no change of directional trim with variations of power or speed. Front gun attacks were both accurate and deadly but with the four guns firing at 650 rounds per minute, 180 rpg gave only 3.5 seconds of fire. The AN/APS-4 radar in the NF 21 had only limited detection range against the slim wooden fuselage of other Sea Hornets in practice interceptions, about 3½nm. Bomber-sized aircraft could be detected at about 11nm, sufficient to manoeuvre into a firing position.

Sea Hornet F 20 carrying out deck-landing trials on *Implacable* in 1948.

Sea Hornet NF 21 of 809 NAS on *Indomitable* in 1953.

Sea Hornet FR 20s of 728 NAS at Hal Far.

Sea Hornet NF 21 of 809 NAS disembarked from *Eagle* in 1953.

F 20

The first production single-seat F 20 flew in August 1946 and carried out service trials with 703 NAS. The only front-line unit fully equipped with this mark was 801 NAS between July 1947 and April 1951, embarked first in *Implacable* and then *Indomitable*. After the first thirty aircraft, later batches were delivered to FR 20 standard with camera windows built into the rear fuselage for an optional camera fit, largely supplanting the need to embark PR 22s. FR 20 production ceased in June 1951.

NF 21

The two-seat night fighter variant was designed to meet Admiralty Specification N.21/45 and the first production aircraft flew in July 1946. It differed in having a heated observer's cockpit with a small bubble canopy in line with the wing training edge. Other changes included the replacement of the Merlin 130/131 engines with Merlin 133/134 fitted with flame-damping exhaust manifolds that would not interfere with the pilot's night vision. The nose was modified with a thimble radome containing an AN/APS-4 radar scanner and the tailplane had increased span. A pronounced dorsal fillet was also introduced from the leading edge of the tailplane which was later fitted to the other marks as well. The extra weight of the second crew member and radar increased MTOW by 1,000lb compared with the F 20 and reduced maximum speed by 30 knots at medium altitude but it could still carry the same weapons load. It could also be used as a navigation leader for other strike aircraft in adverse weather or at night and could be loaded with 3in RP fitted with Glow-worm flares to illuminate its own target at night as well as RP fitted with 60lb explosive warheads. Sea Hornet NF 21s carried out their first day deck-landing trials on *Illustrious* in October 1948 which went so well that the trials team followed them almost immediately with night deck landings. 809 NAS operated Sea Hornets between February 1949 and March 1954 and during this period they operated from *Vengeance*, *Indomitable* and *Eagle*. On 16 October 1949 a flight of four Sea Hornet NF 21s flew non-stop from *Vengeance* off Gibraltar to Lee-on-Solent, 915nm in 3 hours 10 minutes. A fifth aircraft flew the same distance on 24 November in only 2 hours 45 minutes.

PR 22

The single-seat PR 22 had the guns removed to create a lighter airframe with slightly improved performance. Service ceiling was raised to 37,000ft and endurance was increased. The rear fuselage was modified to accommodate two F.52 cameras for daylight reconnaissance or a single K.19B for night use. Three were allocated to 801 NAS for a short period in 1949/50 but the modification of the F 20 to FR 20 standard limited the need for the specialised PR 22 to be embarked and reduced the number manufactured. Some were allocated to second-line squadrons but most were put into long-term storage and scrapped after the 1957 Defence Review.

Sea Devon

The DH 104 was an all-metal, low-wing monoplane with a semi-monocoque fuselage and a retractable tricycle undercarriage designed to replace the Rapide and named Dove in civilian service. It was

Sea Devon at Yeovilton. (Nigel Edwards)

powered by two 330hp de Havilland Gipsy Queen 174 engines which gave a maximum level speed of 185 knots. MTOW was 8,500lb. It had dual controls for two pilots and seats for seven passengers. It first flew in September 1945.

The RAF procured a military derivative named Devon from 1948 and in 1954 the Admiralty selected the type as a Dominie replacement in the light transport role. A batch of ten was ordered for delivery in 1955 named and designated Sea Devon C 20. All were former civilian aircraft refurbished to meet RN requirements with naval radios. A further three new-build aircraft were delivered in 1956. They first went into service with 781 NAS at Lee-on-Solent in April 1955 and several remained with it until the squadron was disbanded in 1981, flying daily 'clipper' flights between UK air stations. Sea Devons were also allocated to 727, 728, 750, 765 and 771 NAS between 1956 and 1989 and others were allocated to station flights at Arbroath, Culdrose, Hal Far, Lossiemouth, Prestwick and Yeovilton between 1956 and 1983. A single Devon C 2 with uprated 380hp Gipsy Queen 175 engines was transferred to the RN from the RAF in 1978 for use by Culdrose Station Flight until 1978 when it was returned.

Sea Venom

The DH 112 was designed as a fighter-bomber powered by a single de Havilland Ghost engine and first flew in September 1949. It retained the twin-boom configuration of the Vampire but had new wings of greater span with a thinner aerofoil section and swept leading edges. They were stressed to take tip-mounted 75-gallon fuel tanks after wind tunnel tests showed them to be more aerodynamically efficient than pylon-mounted tanks. The RAF procured a single-seat version but initially showed no interest in a two-seat night fighter variant so de Havilland developed one as a private venture and flew a prototype with the temporary civil registration G-5-3 in 1950. It used the same wings mated with an enlarged fuselage which had two crew members side by side with the pilot to the left and the observer/radar operator to the right and slightly further aft. AI radar was contained in an elongated nose. G-5-3 was eventually procured for evaluation and an RAF production order for the Venom NF 2 followed in 1952. Early examples were delivered without ejection seats, making aircrew escape at high Mach numbers marginal.

The Admiralty recognised the two-seat Venom as a potential Sea Hornet replacement and evaluated the prototype, now identified as WP 227, in 1950. It was found suitable for carrier operation, Admiralty Specification N.107 was written around it and three prototypes were ordered. The first flew in April 1951, initially designated Sea Venom NF 20 but this was changed to FAW 20 following an official change from night to all-weather fighter designations. Production Sea Venoms had hydraulically-powered folding wings, an arrester hook which retracted into a 'pen-nib' shaped fairing above the jet pipe, catapult strop pick up points and a strengthened long-stroke, undercarriage which was compressed on retraction to fit into the wheel wells. The early 'bird-cage' canopy design was replaced by a clear-view clamshell canopy which could be mechanically jettisoned under water after ditching and all Sea Venoms had the 75-gallon tip-tanks which could not be jettisoned in flight. If weight had to be reduced quickly fuel in them could be jettisoned. Deck-landing trials on *Illustrious* during July 1951 went well and Sea Venoms were put into production. At first they lacked ejection seats but had AI.10 radar and naval equipment including a ZBX carrier homing beacon receiver, provision for the crew to wear anti-G suits and an interim pressure breathing capability, activated if there was a cockpit pressurisation failure. There was also provision for RATOG. Sea Venoms began to replace Sea Hornet NF 21s from 1954.

Sea Venom FAW 21 data

Length:	36ft 7in
Wingspan:	42ft 11inches (22ft 6in folded)
Height:	7ft 6in (11ft folded)
MTOW:	15,250lb
Engine:	One 4,950lb de Havilland Ghost 104 turbojet
Fuel:	Avcat. 92 gallons in a fuselage tank with a further 220 gallons in eight interconnected wing tanks plus two 75-gallon tip tanks. Total 462 gallons
Performance:	Maximum level speed 500 knots/Mach 0.83 Ceiling 49,200ft. 2 minutes to 10,000ft
Endurance:	2½ hours at altitude
Armament:	Four 20mm British Hispano cannon with 150 rpg. Hardpoints beneath each wing for one 1,000lb or 500lb bomb or four 3in RP

The RN received four prototypes, fifty FAW 20, 167 FAW 21 and thirty-nine FAW 22; a total of 260 Sea Venoms. Thirty-three FAW 21s were modified to FAW 22 standard.

Sea Venoms equipped, or partially equipped, a number of shore-based squadrons including 700, 736, 738, 750, 751, 766 and 787 NAS between May 1955 and March 1970. The last of these was 750 NAS which used the type for fast-jet observer training.

Between 1954 and 1966 Sea Venoms served in 809, 831, 890, 891, 892, 893 and 894 NAS. Those in 831 were modified for the electronic warfare role. Sea Venoms were used by station flights at Anthorn, Merryfield, and Yeovilton between 1956 and 1958 and between 1961 and 1970 they were used by the un-numbered ADTU at Yeovilton flown by civilian pilots and maintained by Airwork Services Ltd.

The FAW 21 introduced improvements including powered ailerons to improve its roll rate. A single FAW 21 prototype carried out development flying including a deck-landing evaluation in *Albion*. The FAW 20's AI-10 radar was replaced by AI-21, an anglicised version of the USN AN/APS-57 that did not include the lock-on or blind-fire capabilities of the full American AN/APQ-35 fire-control system. It was funded by the USN under MDAP at no cost to the Admiralty to give a significant improvement in capability. The FAW 21 also introduced ejection seats; Mark 4A-1 for the pilot and Mark 4A-2 for the observer. Each had a Mark 18A parachute stowed behind the occupant's head, a modified L-type dinghy pack in the seat pan and an emergency oxygen bottle at the front of the seat pan. A lever on the right-hand side allowed the seats to be raised or lowered and, so that the pilot could raise his seat

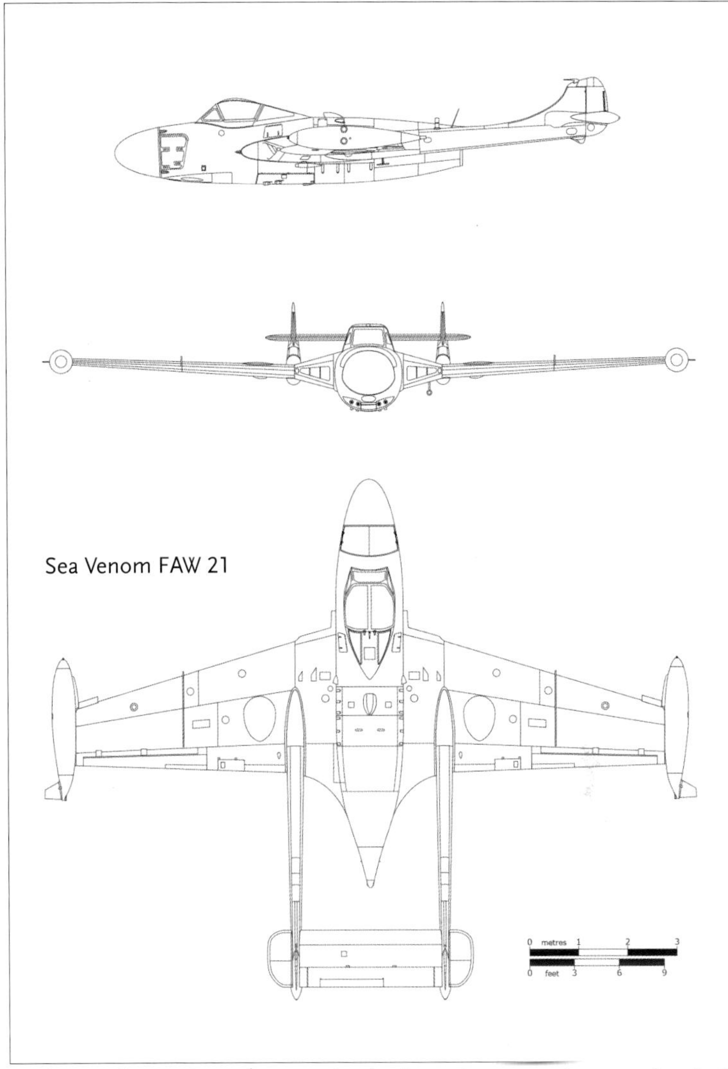

Sea Venom FAW 21

to the maximum in order to gain the best view over the nose for deck landing, the left-hand side of the FAW 21 canopy was domed upwards slightly in later production aircraft. A Green Salad homing indicator replaced the ZBX homing device with its indicator to the left of the retractable Mark 5 gyro gunsight. Other avionics included two ten-channel VHF radios and IFF Mark 10. A single FAW 21 was used in development work on blown flap technology and a deck-landing evaluation on *Ark Royal* in 1956 demonstrated an approach speed 15 knots lower than a standard Sea Venom.

The definitive FAW 22 entered service from 1957 with 894 NAS. It was powered by a 5,300lb thrust Ghost 105; ejection seats were fitted on the production line and the main wheels had Maxaret anti-skid brakes. Aircraft modified for use in the ECM role for 751 and 831 NAS included seven FAW 21s and seven FAW 22s modified to ECM 21/22 standard. They had the guns and ammunition tanks removed and ECM equipment installed in the space made available. Some were modified to dispense chaff. They continued in service alongside ECM Gannets until 1966 when both were replaced by Canberras in the Joint RN/RAF 360 Squadron. Three FAW 21s were modified in early 1958 to carry the de Havilland Blue Jay AAM, later re-named Firestreak. A missile pylon was fitted under each wing inboard of the folding joint and the cannon armament and ammunition were removed to provide space for the missile guidance system. Wiring was installed between the

Sea Venom of 894 NAS landing on *Eagle*.

Sea Venom FAW 21 of 809 NAS on *Albion* during Operation 'Musketeer', the Suez landings in 1956.

Sea Venom FAW 21 of 894 NAS landing on *Albion* in 1960.

Sea Venom of 890 NAS.

Sea Venom of 809 NAS on *Albion*.

missile/pylon interface and the black boxes and a camera was fitted on the port side of the fuselage to film missile behaviour after launch. These aircraft carried out intensive flying trials with 700 NAS at Ford culminating in clearance for the modified aircraft to be allocated to 893 NAS and embarked in *Victorious* for trials in the Mediterranean using Firefly drones operated by 728B NAS from Hal Far as targets during the latter part of 1958. In order to minimise the expenditure of drones, the normal Firestreak explosive warhead was replaced by a magnesium flash head that would show up well on recording cameras but inflict minimal damage on the drone. A direct hit would still destroy the target, however. Film footage analysed after the trials showed that only one missile burst had been outside the lethal distance of a war shot.

At first Sea Venom squadrons had deck hook problems which took time to resolve but the RN carrier task force deployed during Operation 'Musketeer', the Suez Crisis, in November 1956 included 3 FAW 21 squadrons; 809 NAS in *Albion* and both 892 and 893 NAS in *Eagle*. They flew CAP over the fleet and the Anglo/French landings at Port Said but the lack of enemy air opposition soon freed them for use in the ground attack role and Sea Venoms armed with 3in rockets and cannon proved effective against a variety of targets including airfields and military vehicles. None were lost but a single aircraft of 893 NAS was hit by anti-aircraft fire and forced to carry out a wheels-up landing on *Eagle* with a wounded observer.

Keith Harris flew Sea Venoms in 831 NAS and remembers the cockpit as being a very tight fit; pilots with thighs over a certain length were barred from flying it because their knees might have hit the instrument panel on ejection. The observer's cockpit was an even tighter fit. Care had to be taken with the throttle position on start-up as the Ghost engine could produce spectacular sheets of flame if over-fuelled. Sea Venom pilots were converted initially on the Sea Vampire T 22 and Keith remembers that, for some unknown reason, de Havilland had designed the fuel cut-off and air brake levers in reverse order in the two contemporary types which could cause the unwary pilot some embarrassment.

Sea Heron

Work on a civilian aircraft designated DH 114 by the company began in 1949. The first, by then named Heron, flew in May 1950. It proved to be a rugged 14 to 17 seat feeder airliner with a small-field performance that was widely exported throughout the world until 1961. In that year the Admiralty signed a contract for the refurbishment and delivery of five Herons; two formerly operated by Jersey Airlines and 3 by West African Airways. Naval radios were installed and they entered service with 781 NAS at Lee-on-Solent for 'clipper' services, replacing Sea Devons which were passed on to station flights. Renamed as Sea Heron C 2s, they were considered excellent value for money in RN service.

Sea Herons were powered by four 250hp de Havilland Gipsy Queen 30 Mark 2 engines driving two-bladed, variable-pitch propellers which gave a maximum level speed of 145 knots. MTOW was 13,000lb and wingspan 71ft 6in. Sea Herons served with 781 and 728 NAS and the station flights at Culdrose, Hal Far and Yeovilton between 1961 and 1990.

One aircraft, XR 444, ditched in the Irish Sea in June 1972 after suffering a power loss on all four engines. It was recovered for investigation but struck off charge in July. When 781 NAS was disbanded as an economy measure in 1981 the four remaining Sea Herons were used by Yeovilton Station Flight, known appropriately as Heron Flight after the air station ship's name until they were withdrawn from service and sold in 1990. Two Herons were lent to the RN from the RAF. One was a Heron C 4 used briefly by 781 NAS in 1969 before being returned in 1970. The second had formerly been used by the Queen's Flight designated Heron CC 4. After transfer as a replacement for XR 444 it was allocated to Heron Flight and used as the FONAC's 'Admiral's Barge' from 1972. It was eventually sold in 1993.

Sea Heron at Yeovilton.

DH 116 – the projected 'Super Sea Venom'

The Admiralty had appreciated that the Sea Venom had little development potential and would soon be outdated by advances in technology and a new Admiralty Specification, N.114T, was issued to cover competitive evaluation of both day and all-weather naval fighter designs. The all-weather fighters were to be two-seaters fitted with new AI radar, the possibility of carrying AAM was mentioned but the specified performance was little better than the Sea Venom. In 1951 R E Bishop of de Havilland's design department had informal discussions with Admiralty representatives during which he expressed his personal view that the DH 110, described below, came close to meeting N.114T but questioned the need for such a large aircraft since it would only be capable of operation from the larger carriers and then only after their extensive modernisation. He proposed a radical Sea Venom redesign, essentially changing everything except the cockpit. There was to be a new thin wing with greater sweep and the Ghost engine was to be replaced by a single, re-heated Rolls-Royce RA.14 Avon and the twin booms would be replaced by a conventional fuselage containing the engine and jet pipe with an all-moving T-tail. The proposal was given the company designation DH 116 and the Admiralty wrote NSR NA 38 around it in March 1952, followed by Specification N.131T. The MoS referred to it as the Super Sea Venom but this name was never adopted officially. Bishop's design team calculated that the DH 116 would be supersonic in level flight and its development was authorised in September 1952. Two prototypes were ordered although neither appears to have been allocated an airframe number.

The DH 116 was to have been smaller than the DH 110 with better performance but less endurance. Wingspan was to be 42ft, 12ft folded, and MTOW was calculated at 21,400lb. Maximum speed in level flight was to be 600 knots, Mach 1.01 at altitude. All controls were to be power-operated and the wings were to be power-folded about a hinge point just outboard of the main undercarriage legs. The proposed radar was either AI-17 or AI-21 as in the Sea Venom and the initial armament was to comprise two 30mm Aden cannon with 150 rpg under the cockpit floor. To save design effort the cockpit area was to replicate the Sea Venom. Fuel was to have been carried in a 562-gallon tank in the centre section with 120-gallon tanks in each wing and there was to be provision for two 100-gallon drop tanks giving a total of 1,002 gallons of Avcat, calculated to give an endurance of over 2 hours with 5 minutes at high power in combat and a return to the carrier with a 10 per cent fuel reserve. Extensive use of re-heat at low level would have reduced this to a little over an hour. The DH 116 brochure produced for the Admiralty offered an initial un-reheated rate of climb from sea level of 9,900ft per minute and the operational ceiling was to be 51,500ft. Bishop believed that the DH 116 had the capacity for continual upgrades to keep it competitive and that, unlike the larger fighters considered for N.114T, it was capable of operating from light fleet carriers as well as the big fleet carriers; a telling point that deserved greater recognition by the naval staff. The DH 116 had the potential to give the RN a supersonic fighter by the late 1950s but it was not to be.

In the 1950s British aircraft manufacturers lacked drawing office staff to translate their designers' bright ideas into manufacturing drawings within a viable time-frame and de Havilland was no exception. Sadly, the company decided at board level that it could not cope with the extra work that DH 116 would involve and in September 1952 Bishop was instructed to inform the Admiralty that the firm could not proceed with the project. In November 1952 it offered a navalised derivative of the DH 110 in its place since two prototypes had already flown. The MoS advised that the Admiralty must either accept the DH 110 or incur further considerable delay by initiating another competitive design tender and so, aware that the life of the Sea Venom was finite, the Admiralty had little choice but to accept. One of the ironies of the DH 116 cancellation was that the DH 110 was actually nowhere near being a finalised design capable of meeting the NSR and the considerable design effort it required led to significant delays.

de Havilland DH 110.

Sea Vixen

The de Havilland designation for the aircraft that eventually entered RN service as the Sea Vixen was the DH 110. It appears out of sequence because its origins lay in a sketch design proposed as far back as 1946 to meet Admiralty Specification N.40/46 for an advanced all-weather fighter. A two-seat, twin-engine aircraft, it retained the twin boom layout of earlier de Havilland designs. Contemporary radar displays were difficult to view in daylight and the design choice of side-by-side seating for the pilot and observer meant that the observer's position could not easily be darkened with a blind. Viewing the screen through a light-excluding cone was considered impractical and so de Havilland adopted a unique solution. The observer's cockpit was lowered, access being gained by a hatch which lay flush with the top of the fuselage to the right of the pilot's more conventional cockpit which was offset to port. The observer's only view out was through a small window to his right which could be blanked off by a blind when the radar was in use.

DH 110 development moved slowly at first because of de Havilland's commitment to other projects but in 1947 the Rolls-Royce AJ 65, later named Avon, was selected to power it and there was RAF interest in the design. In 1948 the Admiralty refined its specification to include power-folding wings and booms moved outboard to allow inward retraction of the undercarriage. The design team chose a wing with a high wing thickness/chord ratio to give an acceptably low speed for carrier landing and good manoeuvrability. In 1948 the Admiralty still specified that aircraft must be capable of launching from a carrier without catapult assistance and the thick wing made this possible but there was a fatal flaw in its design. There was no front spar but sufficient strength was believed to have been provided by a thick-gauge, D-shaped

Sea Vixen FAW 1s of 890 NAS at Yeovilton.

leading edge skin forward of the main spar. This was lighter than more conventional structures but no representative wing had ever been tested to destruction to define its limits.

Three prototypes were ordered in June 1948 to meet an RAF requirement and agreement was reached that more should be ordered for joint RN/RAF weapons and radar development. By January 1949 further orders for four further prototypes with two modified to meet N.40/46 were anticipated. The Admiralty wrote Specification N.8/49 for a naval strike derivative of the DH 110 and the RAF was considering other roles including photographic reconnaissance. The DH 110's future appeared bright but no work on the naval prototypes had been carried out by March 1949 when the Admiralty issued a revised requirement, NR/A.14 which accepted parameters similar to latest RAF specification to simplify development. It was issued to de Havilland as N.14/49 and in July an order for three naval prototypes was confirmed; two for the night fighter role and one for the strike role. They were never built, however, because of Government pressure to reduce the Naval Estimates since it saw no prospect of war in the immediate future. The naval DH 110 prototypes were cancelled and the Admiralty withdraw from the project in November 1949.

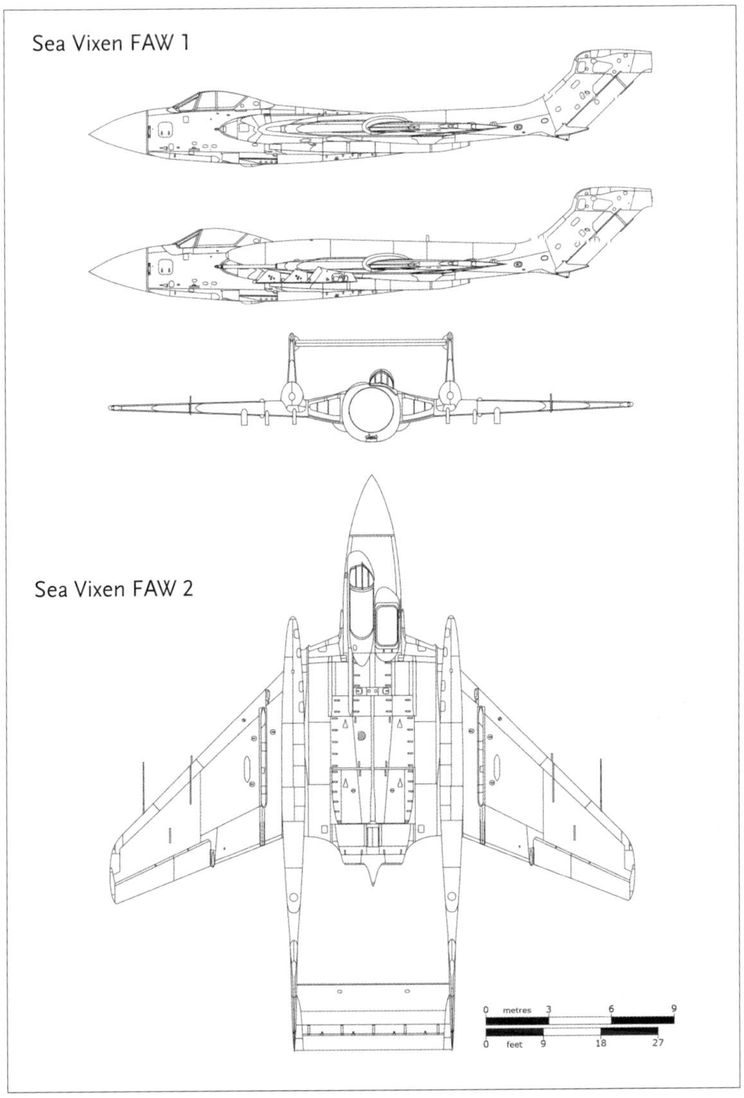

Two of the RAF prototypes were completed and the first, WG 236, flew during September 1951. The second, WG 240, flew in July 1952 but by then the RAF had selected the Gloster Javelin as its all-weather fighter without having a competitive fly-off between it and the DH 110. However, the MoS opted to retain the prototypes as research aircraft. Test pilots found WG 236 to be a pleasant aircraft to fly and it exceeded Mach 1 for the first time in a shallow dive during February 1952; an indicated Mach 1.03, flown by John Derry with Tony Richards as flight test observer. It was the first British twin-engined aircraft to do so. However, the tragic accident that destroyed this aircraft at the 1952 SBAC Farnborough Air Show cast a long shadow over the

Sea Vixen FAW 1 of 890 NAS landing on *Ark Royal*.

Sea Vixen FAW 1s of 890 NAS in *Ark Royal*'s Fly 1 after a recovery in 1962.

DH 110. John Derry and Tony Richards had flown the second prototype throughout the week but on Saturday, 6 September 1952, an unserviceability led to its replacement by WG 236. The display routine began with a supersonic dive from 40,000ft with a pull-out in the vicinity of the airfield for a fast pass along the runway. Derry then turned to port and made a tight, high-speed, left-hand circuit at low level but as he straightened 1½ miles north-west of the public enclosure and began his usual upward roll WG 236 broke up and one of the engines landed in the crowd, killing twenty-nine spectators and injuring a further sixty-three; both Derry and Richards were also killed. An accident investigation was carried out by the RAE structures department led by Dr Percy Walker during which over 1,000 people responded to a request for photographs, one of whom produced a film which showed exactly what had happened. As WG 236 banked towards the crowd the starboard outer wing had detached followed immediately by the port outer wing. With only the centre wing structure left the aircraft suffered a massive nose-up pitch moment causing the cockpit, engines and tail booms to break up in under a second under the excessive 'G' loading. The wreckage was removed to Farnborough and its examination found a compression buckle in the starboard wing which was recreated in structural tests on an identical spare wing. The buckling was put down to an incorrect estimate of the allowable stress at that point and further tests found that WG 236's wing only possessed about 64 per cent of the required ultimate strength. The buckle was believed to be the first part of the aircraft to fail, the result of a single loading and not progressive weakening such as that caused by flutter. The report published on 8 April 1953 cleared Derry of any blame but stated that WG 236 had broken up as the result of torsion, shear and bending loads produced by a manoeuvre that combined both turn and climb inputs at high speed. This had created instability in the structure, the initial form of which was revealed by the buckle. The wing structure of the DH 110 was found to be weaker than it had been thought to be, although the report did admit that it had not been possible to predict from previous experience or calculation the point at which complete failure of the wing would occur. The wing structure of WG 240 was completely re-designed with a new front spar, thicker ribs and reinforced inter-spar stringers and it started flying again in June 1953.

De Havilland's admission in late 1952 that it lacked the resources to proceed with the DH 116 left the RN with no planned replacement for the Sea Venom and the MoS held a conference in March 1953 to discuss the DH 110's suitability to meet Admiralty Requirement NA.38, for an all-weather fighter. Since the earlier cancellation of the DH 110 in 1949 the Requirement had been expanded to include the new 'X' Band AI-18 radar and the ability to carry up to four AAM. The Admiralty representative was concerned about the airframe's strength which was considered minimal for a fighter but the de Havilland representative explained that the design could be modified as required and in July 1953 the Admiralty formally accepted a fully navalised DH 110 to meet NA 38, hoping to avoid the considerable delay of a new competitive tender process. Development still moved at a glacial pace, however, and WG 240 was not taken in hand for naval modifications until 1954. It became the first British aircraft with an all-moving tailplane and other changes included increased fuel capacity, a new 'barn door' airbrake under the fuselage, improved powered

Sea Vixen development aircraft with a dummy Red Beard bomb.

Sea Vixen FAW 2 of 899 NAS on *Eagle*'s waist catapult. (Paul Waterhouse)

control systems and long-travel oleos suitable for deck landing. It never had an arrester hook or folding wings but did make a number of touch and go landings on *Albion* in September 1954 which confirmed that the DH 110 could be operated by the larger light fleet carriers.

In March 1954 a single semi-navalised prototype, XF 828, was authorised but development remained painfully slow. XF 828 was designated DH 110 Mark 20X, the 'X' intended to show the Mark's experimental nature but this was unusual for a prototype. Perhaps it was meant to give the impression that the DH 110 was a developed airframe that merely needed modifications but this was very far from the case. Transforming the DH 110 design into a viable naval aircraft required an 80 per cent re-design. The possibility of replacing the 'coal hole' with a completely clear-view clamshell canopy like that of the Sea Venom was apparently considered but rejected because it would have required even more re-design work. It was also calculated that it would have caused a marginal reduction in speed but I do not know of a single Sea Vixen observer who would not have shouted for joy at the change, whatever it took to achieve it. Other design changes included the selection of more advanced Rolls-Royce Avon 208 engines which required larger intakes and a completely redesigned fuselage and the adoption of a longer nose with a pointed cone to take AI-18; new tailplanes with cropped upper training edges, an arrester hook between the jet pipes and catapult spools. XF 828 lacked folding wings, armament and radar and most development work was carried out by early production aircraft which also had folding wings, a long stroke navalised undercarriage and nose wheel steering. XF 828 first flew in June 1955 and Lieutenant Commander S G Orr RN carried out the first arrested deck landing on *Ark Royal* on 5 April 1956. It was also proved that the Mark 20X could (just) get airborne without catapult assistance. In 1957 it carried out steam-catapult trials at RAE Bedford.

Production began in January 1955 to MoS Specification N.139P, the 'P' standing for production. The name Sea Vixen was announced officially in February 1957 when the first pre-production example was rolled out. Further changes on production aircraft included strengthening which increased weight so the undercarriage had to be strengthened. Hydraulically-folding outer wing panels had the break just outboard of the booms; the pilot's canopy was given a distinctive V-shaped windscreen to better disperse rain and spray and the inner part of each folding wing panel was strengthened and fitted with plumbing to take a 150-gallon fuel tank or Mark 20 in-flight refuelling pod.

In its final iteration of NA.38 the Admiralty deleted the gun armament in favour of an all-missile weapons system; the Sea Vixen was the first British fighter to do so. The primary fighter armament was four Firestreak infrared-homing AAMs. As back-up, fourteen FFAR were to be carried in each of two retractable trays located one either side of the nose-wheel bay. NA.38 also required the Sea Vixen to carry a single 2,000lb Red Beard nuclear weapon, 1,000lb or 500lb conventional bombs, napalm tanks or pods of 2in or 3in rockets on the two inboard pylons on each wing as an alternative to Firestreaks. The Red Beard would have been carried on an outboard pylon balanced by a fuel tank on the other wing. With no RAF interest in the aircraft. mark numbers in the 20 series were an anomaly and in 1959 the first production aircraft were re-designated Sea Vixen FAW 1.

Bearing only a superficial resemblance to the DH 110 sketched in 1946, the Sea Vixen FAW 1 entered operational service in 1959 as the fighter element of a computerised, radar-guided, missile-armed fleet air defence system. It was cleared to use the LABS system for toss-bombing attacks with a nuclear weapon and some aircraft in every squadron were fitted with the modifications needed for this role. The Sea Vixen was also cleared to use the American-supplied AGM-12 Bullpup. An air-

Sea Vixen FAW 2 of 899 NAS landing on *Eagle*. (Paul Waterhouse)

to-air refuelling probe was fitted to the port wing, just outboard of the boom and Sea Vixens were cleared to carry a Flight Refuelling Ltd Mark 20 hose and drogue refuelling pod on the starboard outer pylon so that any aircraft could be used as a an airborne tanker; a technique known as the 'buddy' system.

Two aircraft were used in development work for the FAW 2 variant, implementing some of de Havilland's many ideas for improving the design. Most of these came to nothing but internal fuel capacity was increased by putting fuel tanks in forward extensions of the two booms. The AI-18 radar was continually upgraded and an improved AAM known initially as Blue Jay/Firestreak Mark 4 and later by its colour-code designation Red Top was adopted. It had greater range than Firestreak and a more sensitive IR seeker head that enabled it to engage supersonic targets from ahead using a 'collision-course' intercept method. Red Top was the FAW 2's primary weapon but it could also carry Firestreaks as ample war stocks of the earlier weapon remained. A new observer's hatch was introduced with a frangible panel through which he could eject. The earlier metal hatch had the strength of a manhole cover and prevented ejection if it could not be jettisoned. The new hatch was also bulged slightly to improve the observer's headroom. Nothing would ever have made the 'coal-hole' a popular work space but at least the new hatch was an improvement. Both aircrew had Martin-Baker Mark 4DS ejection seats.

Sea Vixen FAW 2 data

Length:	55ft 7in
Wingspan:	50ft (22ft 3in folded)
Height:	10ft 9in
MTOW:	46,750lb
Engines:	Two 11,250lb Rolls-Royce Avon 208 turbojets
Fuel:	Avcat. 1,688 gallons
Performance:	Maximum level speed 610 knots, Mach 0.95 Service ceiling 48,000ft. 6 minutes to 40,000ft
Endurance:	Over 2 hours
Armament:	Four Red Top or Firestreak AAM; two AGM-12 Bullpup AGM; one 2,000lb Red Beard nuclear bomb; up to two 1,000lb or four 500lb conventional bombs, napalm tanks; up to four 2in rocket pods with 36 rounds in each; 3in rockets including versions with Glow-worm illuminant heads; Lepus flares

The RN received 148 Sea Vixens after the initial DH 110 prototypes. Twenty-nine of these were built as FAW 2s from the outset and sixty-seven FAW 1s were converted to FAW 2s.

They served with 700Y, 766, 766B, 890, 892, 893 and 899 NAS between 1958 and 1972 and with the un-numbered, civilian-manned, FRADU at RNAS Yeovilton between 1972 and 1974. Sea Vixen squadrons operated from the aircraft carriers *Ark Royal*, *Eagle*, *Victorious*, *Hermes* and *Centaur*.

The Sea Vixen FAW 1 first entered service with 700Y NAS, the IFTU at Yeovilton, on 4 November 1958. On completion of this task it disbanded on 30 June 1959 and commissioned a day later as the nucleus of 892 NAS. Sea Vixen training began with 766B NAS at Yeovilton in October 1959 while the main part of the squadron continued to train Sea Venom aircrew until 1960 when 766 NAS re-formed as the Sea Vixen training school. In 1962 the squadron formed a five-aircraft aerobatic team known as 'Fred's Five' led by its commanding officer Lieutenant Commander P B Reynolds RN. A second display team, known as 'Simon's Sircus' after its commanding officer Lieutenant Commander Simon Idiens RN, was formed by 892 NAS in 1968. Both teams proved very popular and their excellent displays demonstrated the manoeuvrability of this large and complex fighter.

Front-line Sea Vixen squadrons made their presence felt in deterrent operations around the world. They formed an important element of the carrier task forces deployed to the Far East Fleet between 1963 and 1966 in support of Malaysia during the Indonesian 'Confrontation'. In 1964 Sea Vixens of 892 NAS embarked in *Centaur* covered landings by 45 RM Commando from the carrier to quell the East African Army mutiny at the request of the Tanganyikan Government. Plan 'Squeeze' was devised to clear one catapult and the landing area of military equipment and RAF Belvedere helicopters to allow the fighters to operate in a ground attack role if necessary. Sea Vixens of 892 and 893 NAS embarked in *Victorious* and *Centaur* took part in Operation 'Vantage', support for Kuwait against a threatened Iraqi invasion on 1961, providing the only British air defence capability in the region. From 1965 to 1966 Sea Vixens of 899 NAS in *Eagle* and 890 NAS in *Ark Royal* flew for long periods during the Beira Patrol,

Sea Vixen FAW 2 of 899 NAS firing 2in rockets.

enforcing UN sanctions to prevent oil reaching the illegal regime in Rhodesia. In 1967 Sea Vixens from *Eagle* covered the British withdrawal from Aden and in 1971 they covered the withdrawal of British forces from the Persian Gulf.

In 1971 Sea Vixens replaced Sea Venoms in the ADTU at Yeovilton but the type proved expensive and over-complicated for this role and they were replaced by Hunters in 1974. Some airframes maintained to taxi-ing standard were used by the School of Aircraft Handling at Culdrose. Consideration was given to converting Sea Vixens into pilotless target aircraft after 1972 and Flight Refuelling Ltd was contracted to carry out the work. It was never adequately funded, however, and only three airframes had been converted when the project was cancelled in 1984.

The Sea Vixen was a far more complicated aircraft than those it replaced; it was operated across a range of strike fighter roles to the very edge of its envelope in all weathers by day and night in every ocean. Inevitably there were casualties. Fifty-one aircrew were killed flying Sea Vixens, to which total John Derry and Tony Richards could be added. Records list forty-three Sea Vixens lost in accidents or crashes with others written off after suffering severe damage.

Chipmunk

Designed by de Havilland's Canadian subsidiary as a Tiger Moth replacement, the DHC-1 was the only Canadian design to be manufactured by the parent company in the UK as well as in Canada. UK versions were designated Chipmunk T 10 and over a thousand were built for the RAF and export to fifteen different air forces. It was a two-seat, low-wing monoplane powered by a 145hp Gipsy Major 8 engine which gave a maximum level speed of 120 knots. The pupil pilot sat in the front cockpit with the instructor behind him, both under a single sliding canopy which was opened and shut manually. Wingspan was 34ft 4in and MTOW 2,100lb. Avgas was carried in two 9-gallon tanks mounted one in each wing with a contents gauge next to the filler cap on the wing surface. Endurance was a little over 2 hours. The first Canadian-built Chipmunk flew in May 1946 and UK-built T 10s were produced from 1950.

No Chipmunks were built specifically for the RN but nineteen were transferred from the RAF from 1965 onwards to replace the Tiger Moths used for grading potential aircrew and giving air experience to cadets at BRNC Dartmouth. Both functions took place at Roborough airfield just north of Plymouth. Some were used by station flights at Yeovilton, Culdrose and Lossiemouth and by 781 NAS for general flying practice. Most RN Chipmunks were retired in 1993 but one was allocated to the RN Historic Flight at Yeovilton to give pilots experience of flying piston-engined aircraft with a tail-wheel undercarriage. It was transferred to the Navy Wings Charity which took over the historic flying task.

Chipmunks of BRNC Flight.

A B C D E F G H I J K L M N O P Q R S T U V W X Y Z

DEPERDUSSIN

Tractor Monoplane

The Admiralty purchased a single two-seat monoplane with a 70hp Gnome radial engine in January 1912. It was evaluated with both wheels and floats, used in the 1912 Army manoeuvres and was one of the first aircraft to be maintained by naval ratings before it was deleted in 1914. A further eight tractor monoplanes with 100hp Gnome or Anzani engines were ordered by the Admiralty from 1915 and one of them was launched from a take-off platform on the cruiser *Aurora* in November 1915. Wingspan was 33ft and MTOW 1,590lb. They were deleted in 1916.

Monoplane seaplane

The Admiralty purchased two monoplane seaplanes with 100hp Anzani tractor engines for evaluation in 1913. Both were found to be unsatisfactory and were discarded by the end of the year.

DEUTSCHE FLUGZEUG-WERKE

Mars

Prior to the outbreak of war in 1914, the Admiralty purchased a single DFW Mars with a 100hp water-cooled tractor engine for evaluation. Wingspan was 56ft and MTOW over 2,000lb. After being fitted with a 120hp Beardmore engine it was used briefly for patrols from Eastchurch after August 1914 but deleted in October following concern that it might be taken for an enemy aircraft.

B.1

A single two-seat DFW B.2 was purchased from the firm by Beardmore for evaluation prior to the outbreak of war and requisitioned by the Admiralty in August 1914. It was used for coastal patrols from Killingholme until the end of the year but deleted in January after a series of accidents. Wingspan was 45ft 11in and MTOW of 2,238lb. It was powered by a single 100hp Mercedes engine.

DONNET L'EVEQUE

Flying Boat

A single example was purchased by the Admiralty in 1912, powered by a single 80hp Gnome rotary pusher engine. Wingspan was 45ft. Evaluation at Isle of Grain found such inadequate control that it was regarded as dangerous to fly. Modifications to improve handling were abandoned after a tent collapsed on it during a gale in 1913 and it was deleted.

DOUGLAS

Boston/Havoc

The DB-7 Boston twin-engined medium bomber was developed from 1937 to meet a USAAC requirement. France was an early export customer but when it collapsed in 1940 many of the DB-7s it had ordered were transferred to the UK. In RAF service they were given the name Boston but by late 1940 a desperate shortage of night fighters led to some being converted for the role. Those modified were renamed as Havocs and some of these were further modified as 'Turbinlite' aircraft with a 2,700 million candlepower Helmore/GEC searchlight and AI-VI radar but no gun armament. Their intended role was to locate and illuminate targets at night for accompanying Hurricanes, a desperate scheme that didn't work. As the RAF received more effective aircraft, thirty-six were transferred to the RN for fleet requirements tasks, not all of which were used. Of these, twenty-one had been Turbinlite aircraft and the balance were of various sub-types transferred on an ad hoc basis when required. Most RN aircraft were powered by two 1,200hp Pratt & Whitney R-1830-S3C4G radial engines which gave a maximum level speed of 260 knots. Wingspan was 61ft 4in and MTOW 19,040lb and they were normally flown by a crew of two, pilot and TAG. The biggest user was 771 NAS at Twatt on the Orkney mainland which operated thirty-one between November 1943 and August 1945 on a variety of fleet requirements tasks. Another served with 772 NAS and one briefly with 778 NAS. All were eventually returned to the RAF.

Boston of 771 NAS at Twatt in the Orkney Islands.

Dauntless

Production orders for the SBD Dauntless two-seat dive-bomber for the USN and USMC were first placed in 1939 and the type earned its place in history on 4 June 1942 in the Battle of Midway when SBDs from the USN carriers *Yorktown*, *Enterprise* and *Hornet* sank the Japanese carriers *Akagi*, *Kaga*, *Soryu* and *Hiryu*. Over 5,000 were built for the USN but it was not considered suitable for Lend-Lease transfer to the RN. However,

Dauntless in RN markings.

six examples were shipped to the UK during 1944–5, all of them former USN aircraft to SBD-5 standard, for use evaluating dive-bombing sight designs and designated Dauntless DB Is in RN service. Wingspan was 41ft 6½in and MTOW 10,855lb. They were powered by a single 1,200hp Wright R-1820-60 Cyclone radial engine which gave a maximum level speed of 200 knots and they could be armed with a single bomb on the centreline up to 1,600lb. There were two Browning 0.5in machine guns in the upper nose cowling with 360 rpg and twin Browning 0.3in machine guns on a flexible mounting in the rear cockpit with 2,000 rpg. Dauntlesses were used by 700 NAS between December 1944 and February 1946 for evaluation and by 787 NAS in the latter half of 1944 for evaluating dive-bombing tactics. None were ever used operationally.

Dakota

The Douglas DC-3 Dakota was one of the outstanding aircraft in the history of aviation, performing in roles ranging from transcontinental transport through parachute and supply dropping, military transport, night flying gun battery to flying classroom. A single Douglas Dakota Mark IV was transferred to the RN from the British Air Force of Occupation Communications Wing for 781X NAS in November 1945. It was used briefly for transporting naval parties carrying out a variety of tasks before being returned to the RAF at Landing Site B.156, Luneburg in May 1946. Wingspan was 95ft and MTOW 26,000lb. It was powered by two 1,200hp Pratt & Whitney R-1830-90C radial engines which gave a maximum level speed of 200 knots. It could carry up to twenty-eight passengers.

Skyraider

After the cancellation of earlier Douglas proposals in 1944 and finding that other forms had been requested to put forward proposals for a re-defined attack aircraft, Ed Heineman was informed by the USN that he could still put forward a proposal if he wished, subject to the same time schedule. He and his team worked overnight on a sketch design, submitted it the next morning and the result became the Douglas Skyraider. A production run was authorised and the first example flew in March 1945. The USN designated it AD-1 and in line with the phonetic alphabet in use at the time it became known as the 'Able-Dog'-1. It was remarkable for its rugged strength and load-carrying ability and gained a solid reputation with the attack community which was enhanced during the Korean War. It remained in production for 12 years with over 3,000 built in twenty-eight sub-variants.

The Skyraider's ability to carry a heavy load combined with a fuselage large enough to install bulky role equipment made it eminently suitable for the AEW role and a prototype was fitted with a ventral search radar. This proved successful and an AEW variant was designed based on the improved AD-4 airframe built in larger numbers than any other Skyraider variant. Designated AD-4W by the USN, 168 AEW versions were built fitted with AN/APS-20A radar which had an aerial 8ft wide inside a large ventral radome between the undercarriage legs. Aerial rotation could be selected to either 3 or 6 rpm to give data rates appropriate for search, fighter control or other functions and it had a peak power of 1 MW. The radar equipment weighed over 2,000lb and was said to cost $1 million dollars in 1951. The AD-4W variant also

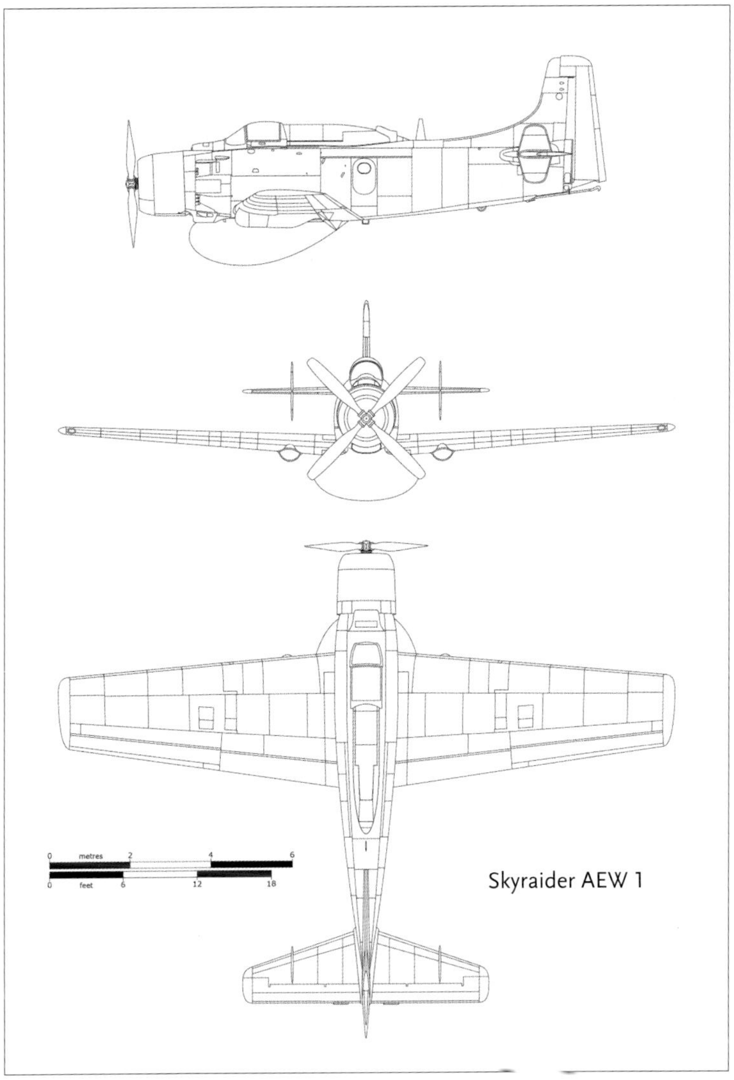

Skyraider AEW 1

differed in having large, fixed leading-edge wing slats to offset the effects of aerodynamic disturbances from the radome at low speeds, especially on the approach to a carrier landing, and small auxiliary fins on the tailplane to improve stability. The cockpit was re-designed with a new instrument panel which incorporated a radar display for the pilot and an autopilot to reduce pilot workload during long sorties. There was a pronounced 'hump' aft of the cockpit canopy which contained avionics. The USN used the AD-4W solely as a flying radar aerial with the picture relayed to the parent carrier for interpretation by means of an AN/ART-28 radar relay transmitter known as 'Bellhop'. The system had an AN/APX-13 IFF system integrated into it. Two seats installed side-by-side in the rear fuselage both had radar displays but they were occupied by technical ratings trained only to ensure that the radar picture was down-linked to the carrier correctly. The small display in the pilot's cockpit was there for him to ensure that his team were obtaining the best radar image although he could use it for searches.

The Admiralty had recognised the need for an AEW capability since the air battles in defence of convoys to Malta and North Russia and had written a staff requirement for it in December 1943. British industry lacked the resources to achieve it quickly, however, and in mid-1944 the Anglo-US Scientific Committee passed work on the AEW requirement to the USA, transferring British cavity magnetron

A Skyraider AEW 1 in 1954.

Skyraider AEW 1 of 849B Flight on *Ark Royal*.

Skyraider of 849D Flight carrying out deck-landing practice with its hook up.

technology created by Birmingham University. The USN awarded a development contract to the Massachusetts Institute of Technology at Mount Cadillac in June 1944 where it became known as the 'Cadillac Project'. It described the cavity magnetron as the most valuable device ever brought to America having failed to produce such a powerful microwave source of its own. The first aircraft fitted with a prototype AN/APS-20 was a modified TBM Avenger which flew 8 months later. By May 1945 there were thirty-five with the US Pacific Fleet but they were just too late to see action against Japan. There were initial problems with the relay equipment but these had been overcome by 1947 when the first AD-4Ws came off the production line.

After 1945 Fairey Aviation proposed derivative of the Spearfish torpedo bomber fitted with AN/APS-20 but the RN lacked the financial resources to fund its development or even to purchase AEW equipment from the USN and the project was not taken forward. After the outbreak of war in Korea in June 1950 the USN was concerned that RN lacked an AEW capability, leaving it vulnerable to low-level air attack. To resolve this shortcoming, it transferred fifty AD-4W Skyraiders to the RN under MDAP arrangements. The first arrived in the UK in November 1951 and were designated Skyraider AEW 1 in RN service. Since it was already in service with the USN, it was considered unnecessary to carry out service trials but one aircraft was used for compatibility tests with RN catapults and arrester gear which proved satisfactory. 778 NAS, commanded by Lieutenant J D Treacher RN, had been formed at Culdrose in October 1951 to introduce the aircraft to operational conditions within the RN. Treacher, another pilot and two observers had been sent to the USA to learn to fly the Skyraider but from the outset the RN thought of the aircraft as a flying operations room and used it in a more proactive way than the USN. Instead of technicians, the rear seats were occupied by observers who interpreted the radar picture to control CAP fighters against incoming enemy aircraft or to direct strike aircraft in addition to providing an AEW barrier. The Bellhop data-link was retained so that the radar picture could be viewed in the carrier's ADR or other ships fitted with a receiver. 778 NAS found that AN/APS-20 could also be used to search effectively for schnorkelling submarines and to direct attack aircraft onto them. On 1 July 1952 the AEW role reached IOC when 778 NAS was absorbed into a front-line unit, 849 NAS, still with Treacher in command.

In January 1952, a 778 NAS Skyraider demonstrated what airborne control could achieve when the merchant ship *Flying Enterprise* was swamped by a storm off Cornwall. The crew were taken off but her captain refused to leave his ship and the episode became the focus of worldwide media coverage. Storms hid the ship's position, sorties by RAF aircraft failed to relocate it and so 778 NAS was tasked to find it. On 5 January Treacher took off into a Force 8 gale with Lieutenant J Winstanley RN in the left-hand observer's seat and BBC air correspondent Charles Gardner in the right. They climbed through cloud to 10,000ft to give radar coverage out to 125nm and Winstanley narrowed down multiple contacts to three probables. He estimated one to be stationary and they descended through cloud to identify it, breaking clear at 500ft and saw the ship on its side with the hull nearly submerged and Captain Carlsen waving to them. Charles Gardner took pictures and recorded the event for a radio broadcast and the position was passed to the RAF which flew a Lancaster to it and dropped safety equipment for Carlsen who finally abandoned his ship when it sank after 13 days adrift.

Skyraider AEW 1 data

Length:	38ft 10in
Wingspan:	50ft (23ft 10½in folded)
Height:	16ft 8in with wings folded
MTOW:	18,300lb for catapult launch (24,000lb from an airfield)
Engine:	One 3,300hp Wright Double Cyclone R-3350-26WA engine driving a four-bladed, metal, variable-pitch propeller
Fuel:	Avgas. 341 gallons internal plus up to two 125-gallon long-range tanks
Performance:	Maximum level speed 305 knots Service ceiling 36,000ft. 2 minutes to 5,000ft
Endurance:	7.8 hours on internal fuel
Armament:	None

The RN received fifty Skyraiders, all from USN production. Of these twenty were new and the rest re-furbished examples, some of which had seen squadron service.

The Skyraider was remembered fondly by all those who flew it. John Treacher remembered that Skyraider aircrew were the first in the RN to wear hard flying helmets or 'bone-domes' issued to them by the USN at Quonset Point. Keith Harris recalled that it had a comfortable, typically American cockpit with superb visibility, well laid-out controls, a pull-out chart board and electric seat raising and lowering. The pilot had his own radar scope and there were even ash trays despite the engine running on avgas! Most controls were miniature replicas of the item; wheel and leg for the undercarriage and aerofoil shape for flaps for instance. The Skyraider was easy to taxi and advancing the throttle on take-off produced a huge and seemingly endless surge of power and acceleration with any tendency to swing easily controlled. There was no limiting speed on lowering the undercarriage which could be used as an air brake. It was stable on carrier approach but there was a strong torque effect on opening the throttle for a wave-off that needed careful attention.

Skyraiders only served with 778 and 849 NAS but the latter was organised with separate flights embarked in carriers, effectively small squadrons with four aircraft each.

At various times between 1952 and 1960 849 NAS consisted of HQ, A, B, C, D and E Flights. HQ Flight remained at Culdrose to provide training, tactical development and support for embarked flights. Flights operated at various times from the aircraft carriers *Eagle*, *Ark Royal*, *Victorious*, *Glory*, *Albion*, *Bulwark* and *Centaur*. The last Skyraiders were not delivered until 1956 but by then there was an acute shortage of spares and some were used as a source of replacement components.

849 NAS operated Skyraiders until Gannet AEW 3s replaced them in October 1960. In June 1953 the squadron, led by Treacher, took part in the Coronation Fleet Review Flypast at Spithead. Pilots were converted to the Skyraider on an individual basis and their training included instruction in radar operation to make use of the display in the cockpit. In 1957 HQ Flight carried out trials of the AN/APS-20C radar which replaced the 'A' version in a Skyraider upgrade programme.

849 A Flight embarked in *Eagle* continuously until 1959. During Operation 'Musketeer', the Suez landings in November 1956, its aircraft flew AEW cover over the Anglo-French task force and delivered urgent supplies ashore. Its last aircraft were replaced by Gannets in 1960.

849 B Flight operated from Hal Far from late June 1953 to develop AEW tactics with targets provided by 728 NAS. In 1954 it joined the air group embarked in *Ark Royal* and remained with her until June 1958 when it transferred to the newly modernised *Victorious*, operating in both the Atlantic and Mediterranean. Its Skyraiders were replaced by Gannets in July 1960.

849 C Flight formed in June 1953 and spent time embarked in *Eagle* before carrying out further development work at Hal Far. It embarked in *Glory* for a short period before returning to Culdrose in 1954. It then formed part of *Albion*'s air group and took part in Operation 'Musketeer' during November 1956. It operated with the Far East Fleet in *Albion* during 1958–9 and replaced its aircraft with Gannets in 1960.

Skyraider of 849C Flight folding its wings after landing on *Albion* during the 1956 Suez operation.

849 D Flight originally formed in August 1953 and spent some months at Hal Far. It embarked in *Albion* for a period in early 1956 and then *Bulwark* for service in the Home and Far East Fleets until October 1958. In January 1959 it embarked in *Centaur* but the air group underwent changes when anti-submarine Gannets had to replace Whirlwind helicopters when they were grounded and D Flight disembarked in June. In February 1960 it embarked in *Albion* for the type's last deployment. After 10 months in the Far East it disbanded at Culdrose in December 1960, ending the Skyraider's service in the RN.

849 E Flight's brief existence from December 1953 included time at Hal Far but it was absorbed into D Flight in October 1954.

DYOTT

Tractor monoplane

A small tractor monoplane powered by a 50hp Gnome radial engine which was procured by the Admiralty in 1915 and evaluated by 5 Wing at Dover for some months without generating much enthusiasm. It was deleted in January 1916 because of what was described as 'fair wear and tear'. Records of performance and dimensions have been lost.

Tractor biplane

The Admiralty ordered 2 examples of this twin-engined tractor biplane for evaluation. The first underwent trials at Hendon and Isle of Grain in 1916, fitted with a Vickers 2pdr gun at the latter. The 2pdr firing trials were unsuccessful and 0.303in Lewis guns were fitted on six spigots fitted onto a rail fitted around the elliptical front cockpit. Presumably they could not all be fitted at once. It was powered by two water-cooled 120hp Beardmore engines and had a tricycle undercarriage with the nose-wheel under the front cockpit. Wingspan was 70ft 6in and MTOW 7,800lb. The second example was evaluated at St Pol in 1917 but found to be useless. A contemporary report condemned it as being 'devoid of the necessary flying qualities required on this station' and it was deleted in March 1917.

ENGLISH ELECTRIC

Aircraft built under licence

As well as the first prototype, the forty-three single-seat Sea Vampire F 20/21s operated by the RN were built by English Electric. Their details can be found in the de Havilland section.

Canberra

A bomber designed for the RAF, the Canberra first flew in 1949 and the name Canberra was confirmed in 1951 when the Australian Government announced its decision to build the type under licence for the RAAF. RAF Canberras were built in bomber, photographic reconnaissance and pilot training variants, all given high priority and ordered in larger numbers than English Electric could cope with so licence-built aircraft were contracted from Short Brothers and Handley-Page. The type entered RAF service in 1951 and the last unit, specialising in PR, was retired in 2006. In that half-century the basic airframe evolved through twenty-one different variants, several of the bombers were capable of carrying tactical nuclear as well as conventional weapons. The B2 variant was the most numerous, many were delivered straight into storage and these later became available for a range of conversions.

The Canberra B 2 fuselage comprised three sections, nose, centre and tail. The nose contained the pressure cabin for the aircrew with the pilot seated under a one-piece bubble canopy slightly offset to the left to allow the navigator access past him to a visual bombsight in the nose. The navigator's position was behind the pilot and in some variants a third crew member was positioned to his right. All had ejection seats. The rear-seat crew only had external vision through a small window in the fuselage side. The pilot's view was reasonable but the canopy was designed before pilots wore protective helmets and I found that if the seat was raised high enough to obtain a reasonable view over the nose my helmet was forced against the canopy. The T 4 pilot training variant was worse because the two pilots were squeezed into the same cockpit dimensions as the B 2 and the ejection seats were canted slightly inwards to achieve this. I found this position extremely uncomfortable and lumbar pain grounded me for a while when I was serving in 360 Squadron with its Canberra T 17s, one of the many B 2 conversions. Access for all crew members was through a hatch in the lower forward fuselage. The centre fuselage comprised a bomb bay under fuel tanks and more fuel was carried in non-jettisonable tip tanks. The tapered rear section supported the tail surfaces. The single-main spar wing was attached to the centre fuselage by a heavy forged bridge members and the engines were built into the wing outboard of the main wheel wells. The basic B 2 wingspan was 63ft 11½in and MTOW was 46,000lb. It was powered by two 6,500lb thrust Rolls-Royce Avon RA.3 Mark 101 turbojets which gave a maximum level speed of 500 knots.

No Canberras were built specifically for the RN but six Canberra pilotless target conversions, designated U 14, were transferred from the RAF in 1961 for use by 728B NAS at Hal Far. The first unmanned flight there was made in August 1961 and U 14s were used as targets for Seaslug and Sea Cat missile firings; one was shot down by a direct hit from a Seaslug fired by the trials ship *Girdle Ness*. The remaining U 14s survived because the trial missiles had telemetry instead of a warhead and only a direct hit could destroy the target. 728B NAS disbanded in December 1961 and the U 14s were returned to the RAF.

A FRADU Canberra T 22 at Yeovilton. (Nigel Edwards)

The U 14 operator's manual explains that it was controlled by a pilot aligned with the runway for take-off and landing and a remote pilot controlled it during its mission. If the Canberra was not shot down it was landed with its brakes on to limit the amount of time it could swerve whilst decelerating on the runway. Burst tyres and damaged wheels were, apparently, easily replaced.

In 1967 the Canberra was selected as a replacement for the Meteor TT 20s used by the civilian-manned FRU at Hurn. A B 2 was modified to TT 18 standard and after successful evaluation at the A&AEE a further ten were modified to this standard to replace the Meteors from 1969. The TT 18 towed sleeve targets on several thousand feet of cable for ships' guns to engage with live ammunition. For systems that required radar tracking or flares onto which optical systems could be locked, Rushton targets were towed from winches fitted to underwing pylons. Endurance on a typical target-towing mission was about 3 hours. TT 18s could also tow sleeve targets suitable for air-to-air gunnery. Three T 4s were transferred to the RN for QFI standardisation checks on the TT 18 pilots. The FRU moved to Yeovilton in 1972 where it combined with the ADTU to form FRADU. The last Canberras to be transferred to the RN were seven PR 7s modified with the Buccaneer's Blue Parrot radar system fitted in the nose, re-designated T 22 and used by FRADU to simulate air-to-surface missile attacks on ships working up under the guidance of FOST. FRADU Canberras were withdrawn from service in the early 1990s and replaced by Dassault Falcons flown by Flight Refuelling Ltd under contract. These were civilian, not RN, aircraft and thus fall outside the scope of this book.

Canberras were also used by 360 Squadron, a joint unit manned by both RN and RAF personnel to provide electronic warfare training for the fleet and UK air defence systems. It used the Canberra T 17 for these tasks, another variant of the basic B 2. Its most distinctive feature was the nose which had a large, hemispherical, radome and four smaller, blister radomes. Twenty-four aircraft were converted. 360 Squadron was formed in 1966 as an amalgamation of the tasks formerly carried out by 831 NAS with Gannets and Sea Venoms and 97 Squadron RAF with Canberras. I served as the Senior Naval Officer within this unit in 1983/84.

ETRICH

Taube

The Taube (Dove) was a two-seat monoplane which first flew in 1910 powered by a tractor 65hp Austro-Daimler engine. Wingspan was 32ft and MTOW 1,875lb. A single example was purchased by the Admiralty in January 1912 for evaluation as a fighting scout by aircrew armed with rifles and pistols. By March 1913 it was considered to be worn out and was deleted.

EUROPEAN HELICOPTER INDUSTRIES

Merlin

Described in the Westland section.

FAIREY

F.2

Design work for the Admiralty on aircraft with the company designations F.1 to F.4 began in November 1915. Constant specification changes caused delays and three of the four aircraft had been cancelled by the time the F.2 flew in 1917. It never had an Admiralty designation and emerged with manually-folded wings and two 190hp Rolls-Royce Falcon engines between the wings driving tractor propellers to give a maximum level speed of 80 knots. The propellers were 'handed' to rotate in opposite directions to eliminate torque reaction, an advanced feature for the time. Wingspan was 77ft and MTOW 4,880lb. It was armed with 0.303in Lewis guns for fore and aft gunlayers and light bombs could be fitted to external racks. The F.2 was evaluated at Isle of Grain during 1917 and found to have a reasonable performance but there were no further orders.

Campania

The first Fairey-designed aircraft to be ordered in quantity, the Campania was a two-seat, biplane seaplane intended for reconnaissance work and specifically intended to operate from the seaplane carrier *Campania* with dimensions that allowed it to be both stowed and winched up through the hangar hatch. Lowering seaplanes over the side to take off from the water took time and often led to damage or even failure to get airborne. Experimentation at Grain led to the use of wheeled trollies placed under the floats which allowed Campanias and other seaplanes to take off from a platform over the fore-deck of a seaplane carrier although they still had to land on the water for recovery by crane. Three development Campanias were powered by different engines and the first of these established a record by flying non-stop from Isle of Grain to Scapa Flow. The definitive version that went into production in 1917 was a biplane made of wood with fabric covering. The folding wings were hinged at the point where they met the fuselage and there were two pontoon-type main floats attached to the undercarriage cross bars; the tail float had a water rudder. Wing tip floats were fitted to the underside of the outer lower wings.

A Campania flying off *Campania* in 1917 using wheeled trollies under the floats.

Campania data

Length:	43ft 0.5in
Wingspan:	61ft 7½in (14ft folded)
Height:	15ft 1in
MTOW:	5,329lb (5,657lb in Eagle VIII-fitted aircraft)
Engine:	One 250hp Sunbeam Maori II. Late production aircraft were fitted with a 345hp Roll-Royce Eagle VIII
Fuel:	Avgas. 88 gallons
Performance:	Maximum speed in level flight 75 knots Service ceiling 6,000ft. 18 minutes to 5,000ft
Endurance:	4½ hours
Armament:	One 0.303in Lewis gun on Scarff ring in rear cockpit. Light bombs could be carried on racks under the fuselage

In addition to the three prototypes, sixty-two Campanias were delivered to the RNAS of which fifty were built by Fairey and twelve by Barclay, Curle & Co.

In addition to *Campania*, Campanias were embarked in *Nairana* and *Pegasus* and were used for coastal patrols from Calshot, Bembridge, Dundee and Portland. Several continued in use after 1918 and five were embarked in *Nairana* during 1919 for operations against Bolshevik forces in Archangel.

The Campania was a popular aircraft that performed well in its intended role but the increased weight with the Eagle VIII engine caused a significant reduction in performance. Maximum speed was reduced by about 5 knots and endurance by a massive 90 minutes. The increase in power was apparently more than used up keeping the heavier aircraft airborne.

Hamble Baby

A single-seat, anti-submarine patrol seaplane with a wooden structure covered by fabric and derived from the Sopwith Baby which Fairey had built under licence. The prototype was a Sopwith-built aircraft which was modified in 1916. It had new wings and hinged flaps were fitted to each mainplane along the full length of the training edge. They acted as ailerons in normal flight but they could be wound down by what was known as camber-changing gear to act as lift-increasing devices for take-off and landing. Lateral control was heavy but effective right down to the stall using a wheel control mounted on a stick which gave fore and aft control. Hamble Babies were produced by Fairey and under licence by Parnall & Sons. Some of the latter were completed with wheeled undercarriages and known as Hamble Baby Converts. Fifty Hamble babies were built by Fairey and further 130 by Parnall, of which seventy-four were Converts.

Hamble Babies entered service in late 1917 embarked in *Empress* and for coastal patrols from Fishguard, Calshot, Cattewater (Plymouth), Seaton Carew, Westgate, Bembridge and Dundee in the UK and Otranto and Santa Maria de Leuca near Taranto in Italy, Suda Bay in Crete, Lemnos and Skyros in the Aegean. *Empress* had four Sopwith Babies and two Hamble Babies embarked while she served with the East Indies and Egypt Seaplane Squadron based at Port Said. Her aircraft made bombing attacks on Turkish installations in Palestine including a railway bridge at Jaljulye.

Hamble Baby data

Length:	23ft 4in
Wingspan:	27ft 9in
Height:	9ft 6in
MTOW	1,946lb
Engine:	One 110hp or 130hp Clerget rotary
Fuel:	Avgas. 24 gallons
Performance:	Maximum level speed 80 knots Service ceiling 7,600ft. 20 minutes to 5,000ft
Endurance:	2 hours
Armament:	One 0.303in Lewis gun mounted on front fuselage synchronised to fire through the propeller arc. Two 65lb bombs on racks under the wings

N 9

The first of two experimental seaplanes from which the long series of Fairey III reconnaissance aircraft evolved, it was designed to meet Admiralty Specification N.2(a) in 1916 for a two-seat aircraft to be operated as reconnaissance aircraft from seaplane carriers. It was a biplane with folding wings, a wingspan of 50ft and MTOW of 3,812lb powered by a single 200hp Rolls-Royce Falcon engine which gave a maximum level speed of 80 knots. Armament was a single defensive 0.303in Lewis gun on a Scarff ring in the rear cockpit. N 9 first flew in July 1917 and was used for catapult launch trials at Isle of Grain and *Slinger* both at anchor and under way. It was bought back by Fairey who sold it on to the Royal Norwegian Navy in 1920.

N 10

Also designed to meet Admiralty Specification N.2(a), N 10 was a two-seat biplane seaplane powered by a single 260hp Sunbeam Maori II engine which gave a maximum level speed of 90 knots. Wingspan was 46ft 2in and MTOW 4,159lb. It was delivered to Isle of Grain unarmed in 1917 and used for trials during which its floats were removed and replaced with a wheeled undercarriage. It was bought back by Fairey.

IIIA

A derivative of N 10 fitted with a wheeled undercarriage for use as a two-seat biplane bomber to replace the obsolescent 1½ Strutter. It was powered by a single 260hp Sunbeam Maori engine that gave a maximum level speed of 96 knots. Wingspan was 46ft 2in and MTOW 3,945lb. Bombs could be carried on a rack under the fuselage and the aft cockpit had a 0.303in Lewis gun on a Scarff ring. A contract for fifty was placed in 1917 and production began in 1918 but hostilities ended before most were delivered. Some might have been used for coastal patrols from Luce Bay and Machrihanish in November. Others were used for trials with flotation gear at Isle of Grain which proved to be able to keep a ditched aircraft afloat long enough for the crew to escape.

IIIB

The Fairey IIIB was a seaplane with a wingspan of 62ft 9in and the same 260hp Sunbeam Maori engine as the IIIA. The type was ordered by the Admiralty to meet its N.2(b) Requirement for a seaplane bomber and its armament comprised a single 0.303in Lewis gun on a Scarff ring for the observer with provision for up to 600lb of bombs below the fuselage carried in tubular containers to protect them from spray on take-off. The first example flew in August 1918 and the first production aircraft were being delivered when the war ended. Maximum level speed was 83 knots and MTOW 4,892lb. The Admiralty ordered sixty but with the end of hostilities only twenty-five were delivered. Some of the remainder were completed later as IIICs; others were cancelled. The first IIIBs reached Westgate and Felixstowe only days before the Armistice and all were deleted by early 1920.

IIIC

Widely regarded as the best seaplane design of the First World War, the IIIC combined design features of the IIIA and IIIB with the float undercarriage and tail of the latter and the equal-span wings with flaps of the former. The Admiralty ordered it as a two-seat general purpose aircraft for use in the bombing and reconnaissance roles. The most significant design change was a different engine.

IIIC data

Length:	36ft
Wingspan:	46ft 1in
Height:	12ft 2in
MTOW:	5,039lb
Engine:	One 375hp Rolls-Royce Eagle VIII
Fuel:	Avgas. 120 gallons
Performance:	Maximum speed in level flight 97 knots Service ceiling 15,000ft. 7½ minutes to 5,000ft
Endurance:	6 hours
Armament:	One synchronised 0.303in Vickers front gun on the forward decking firing through the propeller arc. One 0.303in Lewis gun on a Scarff ring for the observer and provision for up to 250lb of bombs on racks under the fuselage

The end of the war in 1918 brought production to a halt after thirty-six IIICs had been manufactured, most of which were converted from IIIBs on the production line. The first example flew in July 1918 and several were delivered to Isle of Grain before the Armistice. Some arrived at Great Yarmouth in the last days of the war but at least seven – surviving documents do not clarify the actual number – were embarked in *Pegasus* for operations with the North Russian Expeditionary Force based at Archangel in 1919, operating both from the ship and airfields ashore. A bombing attack on Russian warships proved unsuccessful but others attacked railway lines and rolling stock. One aircraft was captured and subsequently used by the Bolsheviks. Surviving aircraft returned to the UK in *Pegasus* and were subsequently used in operations against the Bolsheviks in South Russia, operating from both *Pegasus* and *Ark Royal* until 1921 when the last IIICs were replaced by IIIDs. A single IIIC fitted with a wheeled undercarriage was used for deck-landing trials in the semi-completed *Eagle* in July 1920.

Pintail

A two-seat fighter reconnaissance amphibian designed to operate from land, water or a carrier deck. Only three Pintails were built as prototypes and no production orders followed. There were slight differences between the first, which flew in 1920 and the last in 1921 but they were all powered by a single 475hp Napier Lion V engine giving a maximum level speed of 110 knots and their armament comprised a single synchronised, belt-fed 0.303in Vickers front gun on the decking above the engine firing through the propeller arc and a single 0.303in Lewis gun on a Scarff ring in the rear cockpit. To give the gunner a clear field of fire there was no vertical tailplane, a ventral fin blending into the after float being fitted instead. The outer sections of flap doubled as ailerons and the wings were folded manually. Wheels were fitted within the floats to allow the aircraft to taxi on land but the idea did not prove successful and the Pintail never handled particularly well on water. The third prototype had a wingspan of 40ft, 15ft 8in folded, and MTOW of 4,700lb.

IIID

The IIID followed the IIIC into production and was built in significantly greater numbers as a reconnaissance aircraft for operation from aircraft carriers, other types of warship fitted with take-off platforms or catapults and airfields ashore. It could operate with either wheels or floats and when fitted with the former it was one of the first British aircraft to have an oleo-pneumatic undercarriage. It was also one of the first in which the entire forward fuselage, including the engine and its sub-assemblies fixed into their steel bearing structure, could be removed and replaced by a similar unit to simplify engine changes. Operational IIIDs were three-seaters but seven aircraft in the first batch were modified to act as two-seat training aircraft with dual controls. The fuselage and wings were both made of wood-covered fabric except for one aircraft completed with an experimental steel wing structure and boat-type metal floats. Several IIIDs were modified for use towing targets by FRUs at Lee-on-Solent, Kalafrana and Hal Far.

A float-fitted Fairey IIID of 441 Flight in *Argus* during 1929.

The first IIID was a seaplane and flew in August 1920. The first with a wheeled undercarriage flew in 1921 and Specification 38/22 was drawn up to cover production of the type in batches with different engines identified by different mark numbers. Mark I aircraft were delivered with Eagle engines, Mark II aircraft were powered by Lion II and the final two batches were built as Mark IIIs with Lion VA engines.

IIID Mark II data

Length:	36ft 1in
Wingspan:	46ft 1in (13ft folded)
Height:	12ft (seaplane 13ft)
MTOW:	5,050lb
Engine:	One 450hp Napier Lion IIB
Fuel:	Avgas. 105 gallons
Performance:	Maximum level speed 105 knots (seaplane 100 knots) Service ceiling 20,000ft (seaplane 19,000ft) 4½ minutes to 5,000ft (seaplane 12 minutes)
Armament;	One fixed, belt-fed Vickers 0.303in front gun; one 0.303in Lewis gun on a Scarff ring in the rear cockpit for the TAG. Bombs up to 400lb in total could be carried on underwing racks

A total of 207 IIIDs of all marks were built between 1922 and 1926.

IIIDs served with 422, 440, 441, 442, 443, 444 and 445 Flights of the Fleet Air Arm from the aircraft carriers *Argus*, *Eagle*, *Hermes* and *Furious* serving with the Home and Mediterranean Fleets and the China Station. They were also operated as detached catapult flights in the battleship *Resolution* between 1928 and 1930 and from the cruisers *Dorsetshire*, *Frobisher* and *Norfolk* at about the same time. The hybrid cruiser *Vindictive* had a hangar, catapult and aircraft crane forward, the first RN warship to be fitted with a catapult. She launched a IIID on 3 October 1925, the first British aircraft to be catapulted from a ship under way and embarked 444 Flight in January 1926 for a 2-year commission on the China Station. IIIDs operated ashore at Leuchars where RN pilots were trained from 1924, Kalafrana and Hal Far in Malta in support of the Mediterranean Fleet and Lee-on-Solent where they were used by the fleet spotter reconnaissance training flight. IIIDs from carriers in the Far East were often disembarked for continuation flying at Kai Tak in Hong Kong and at Wei Hei Wei Island. the fleet's summer base. The first units to embark with IIIDs were 441 and 444 Flights in 1924 and the other units were commissioned to tie in with aircraft carrier commissions until 1931 when the last IIIDs were replaced by IIIFs. Four IIID Mark IIIs achieved contemporary fame in 1926 by flying in formation over a number of stages from the UK to Cape Town and back, operating as landplanes or seaplanes as required for the leg in question. When they returned to Lee-on-Solent in June they had travelled 12,232nm without loss or failure.

Ferret

Probably the missing 'E' variant in the Fairey III series, the reason why it merited a name rather than a numeral has never been clarified. It was designed to meet Admiralty Specification 37/22 for a three-seat spotter reconnaissance aircraft and, although it never went into production, it was notable as the first metal-structured Fairey design, albeit covered by doped fabric. Two prototypes were built with the first powered by a 400hp Armstrong Siddeley Jaguar IV radial engine. The second had a 425hp Bristol Jupiter radial engine. The first flew in June 1925 with a

A IIID of 442 Flight disembarked from *Hermes* to Kai Tak in 1927.

wingspan of 39ft 10in and MTOW 4,179lb and a maximum level speed of 115 knots. Armament was a single belt-fed Vickers 0.303in front gun in the starboard fore-decking and a 0.303in Lewis gun on a Scarff ring in the after cockpit for the TAG. The requirement was subsequently cancelled and both prototypes deleted.

Flycatcher

A robust and popular aircraft designed to meet Specification 6/22 for a carrier-borne single-seat fighter, it operated primarily with a wheeled undercarriage but could also be configured with floats. The wings were constructed of fabric-covered wood and had wide chord flaps along their trailing edges, the outer sections serving as ailerons. The aft fuselage was also made of fabric-covered wood but the central and forward sections were fabricated with tubular steel strength members covered by aluminium panels which could be removed for maintenance. It was an equal-span, single-bay, N-strutted biplane with a pronounced 5-degree dihedral and forward stagger on the upper wing which made the lower wing appear to have anhedral. The aft fuselage longeron structure gave the fuselage the appearance of curving upwards towards the squared-off tail assembly. With a wingspan of only 29ft, Flycatchers could be fitted onto the standard carrier lifts of the era and so wing-folding was unnecessary. However, shipment to carriers on foreign stations was facilitated by designing the Flycatcher to be dismantled into sections, none of which was longer than 13ft 6in. The undercarriage assembly was robust and effective and late production Flycatchers were among the first naval aircraft to be fitted with wheel brakes, an innovation that transformed the ability to range and taxi aircraft effectively within the confined area of a flight deck.

Flycatchers over *Furious*.

A Flycatcher over *Eagle*.

This Flycatcher served with 401 Flight between 1924, operating from *Argus*, *Courageous* and *Furious*.

A running range of Flycatchers about to launch.

Armament comprised two Vickers 0.303in machine guns mounted externally on either side of the cockpit where the pilot could reach out to clear jams or re-cock them. Their fittings were complicated because provision had to be made for movement fore and aft and laterally to align them correctly. Both ring and bead and Aldis sights were fitted in operational aircraft, both attached by brackets under the top wing. Whilst the latter was theoretically more accurate, it absorbed the pilot's full attention and the former was preferred as it allowed snap shooting during a dogfight in which the pilot's eyes had to be out of the cockpit for most of time. A G-3 camera gun could be fitted on the lower starboard mainplane to record front-gun effectiveness.

The first prototype flew on 28 November 1922 and the second, completed as a seaplane, in May 1923. The third was completed as an amphibian with wheels fitted inside the floats but protruding partially below them to allow the aircraft to taxi on land but this concept proved unsuccessful. Few aircraft have ever been as popular with both pilots and maintenance personnel as the Flycatcher with a wheeled undercarriage. Several pilots described it as feeling effectively like an extension of the hands and feet that created movement as soon as the pilot thought of it. It was both easy and a joy to fly.

Flycatcher data

Length:	23ft (29ft with floats)
Wingspan:	29ft
Height:	12ft (13ft 4in with floats)
MTOW:	2,979lb
Engine:	One 400hp Armstrong Siddeley Jaguar III or IV radial
Fuel:	Avgas. 53 gallons
Performance:	Maximum level speed 118 knots (110 knots as an amphibian) Service ceiling 19,000ft (14,000ft as an amphibian) 10 minutes to 10,000ft
Endurance:	2 hours
Armament:	Two Vickers belt-fed 0.303in front guns synchronised to fire through the propeller arc. Underwing racks for up to four 20lb bombs

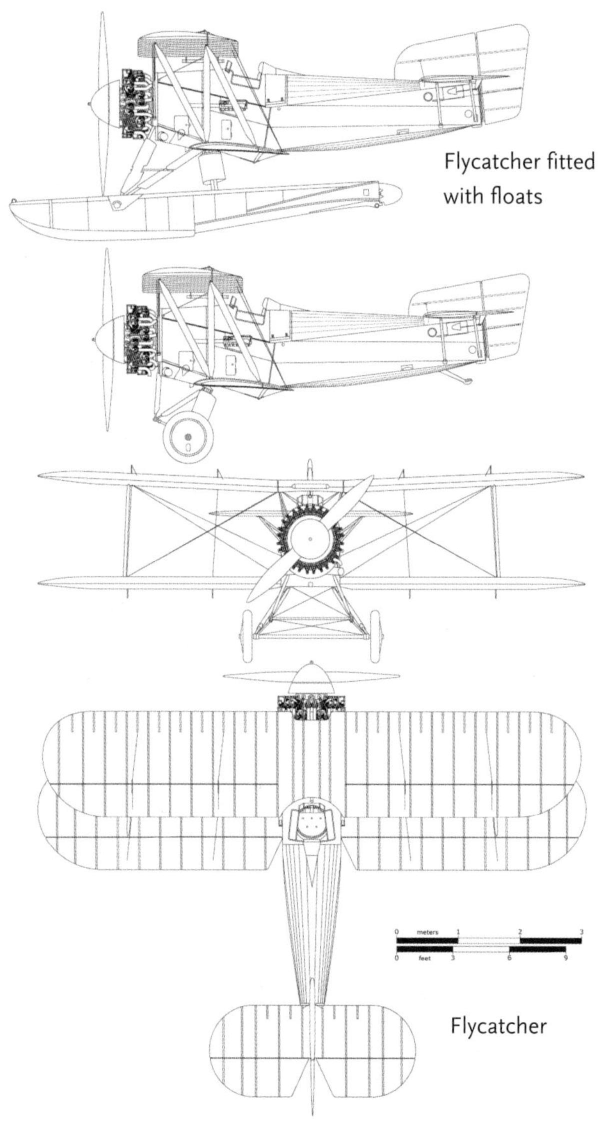

Flycatcher fitted with floats

Flycatcher

A total of 197 Flycatchers, including the three prototypes, was built between 1922 and 1930.

Flycatchers served with 401, 402, 403, 404, 405, 406, 407 and 408 Fleet Fighter Flights and, briefly, with 801 NAS in various commissions between 1923 and 1935.

They served in the aircraft carriers *Argus*, *Hermes*, *Eagle*, *Furious*, *Courageous* and *Glorious*. Battleships and cruisers embarked individual aircraft that flew from turret platforms or catapults. Ships other than aircraft carriers that embarked Flycatchers between 1924 and 1935 included the battleships and battlecruisers *Barham*, *Hood*, *Queen Elizabeth*, *Ramillies*, *Renown*, *Repulse*, *Revenge*, *Royal Oak*, *Royal Sovereign* and *Tiger*. Cruisers that embarked Flycatchers included *Berwick*, *Caledon*, *Cornwall*, *Cumberland*, *Dorsetshire*, *Emerald*, *Enterprise*, *Kent*, *Suffolk* and *Vindictive*.

Flycatchers operated ashore from Leuchars, Gosport and Donibristle in the UK, Kalafrana and Hal Far in Malta, Aboukir in Egypt, Kai Tak in Hong Kong and Wei Hei Wei Island off China. A Flycatcher made the first flight from Hal Far in 1924. Flycatchers were the last fighter to be capable of taking off from the small flying-off deck forward of the upper hangar in *Furious*, *Courageous* and *Glorious*. After fore and aft retaining wires were removed in 1926, landings were made without arrester wires of any kind for several years. The first ever night deck landing by an RN fighter was made by a Flycatcher in *Courageous* during 1929 and early trials with transverse arrester wires were carried out in the same ship by a hooked Flycatcher.

Fairey produced a prototype replacement intended to meet Specification N.21/26 for a deck-landing fighter. Although named Flycatcher II by Fairey, it bore no resemblance to it and was powered by a single 480hp Bristol Mercury IIA radial engine which gave a maximum level speed of 135 knots. It was written off following an accident when the engine cut out on take-off in 1929 and was not ordered into production.

IIIF

The last in Fairey's III series, the IIIF was the most widely-used Fleet Air Arm aircraft between the two world wars. Designed to meet Specification 19/24 for a three-seat spotter/reconnaissance aircraft for naval use and first flew in March 1926. Production aircraft had tubular metal fuselage structures covered by aluminium panels from the pilot's cockpit forward and doped fabric aft. Changes of engine and other details led to IIIFs being produced in three versions, designated Marks I, II and III, of which the Mark III was produced in the greatest numbers. The Mark IIIM had all-metal, fabric-covered wings and the Mark IIIB was stressed for catapult launches. Several were produced with dual controls for pilot conversion training.

The first Mark Is, fitted with a 480hp Napier Lion VA engines, were delivered in February 1927, followed by Mark IIs in August powered by a 570hp Napier Lion XIA. The first Mark IIIM was flown in March 1929. When flown without aircrew in the rear cockpits, a balance weight had to be substituted, a requirement that led to unkind comments about the usefulness of observers. The IIIF could be fitted with either a wheeled undercarriage for carrier operation or twin metal floats for operation as a seaplane either from carriers or from battleships and cruisers with catapults. The float arrangement differed from earlier

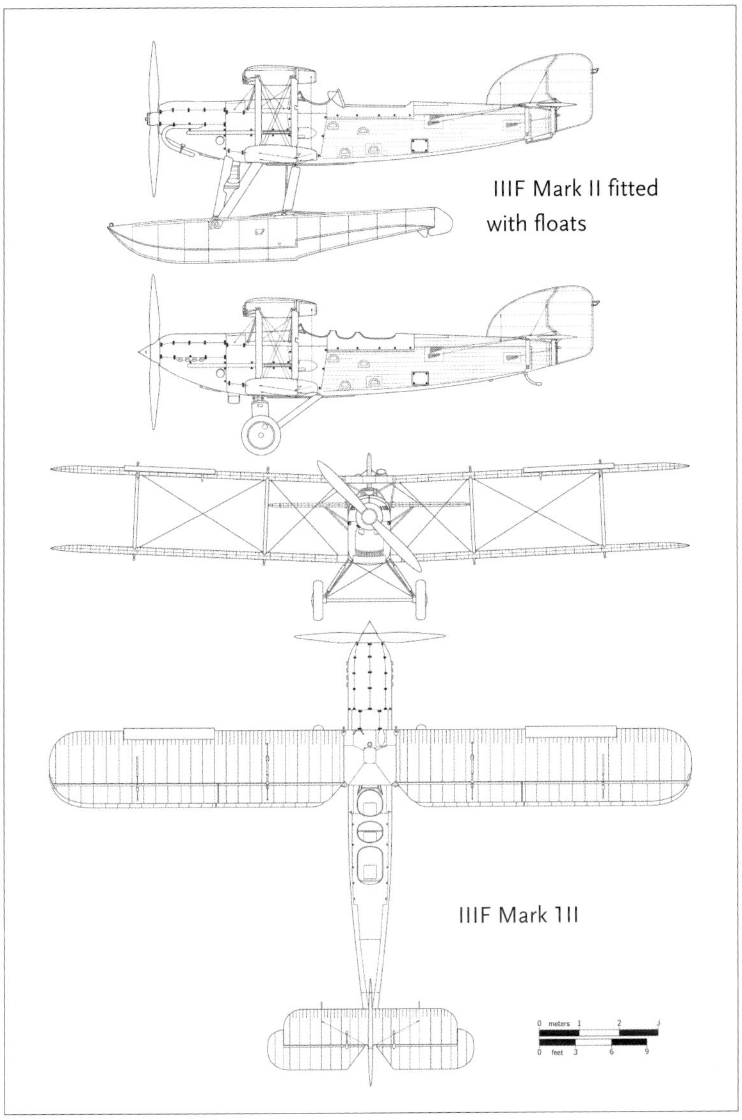

A Fairey IIIF of 443 Flight from *Furious*.

IIIFs of 442 Flight over *Furious* in 1931.

aircraft in the III series by replacing the three-float arrangement with two long floats, each with a water rudder at the rear. The IIIF was more streamlined than its predecessors and was the first British naval aircraft designed with a V-strut undercarriage capable of accepting a vertical descent rate of 12ft per second. It was a biplane with equal-span folding wings and, although designed for the spotter/reconnaissance role, the IIIF could carry a respectable bomb load which could be dropped in level flight with the observer using a bombsight fitted under a hatch in the cockpit floor. Late production aircraft replaced the TAG's Scarff ring with a Fairey 'High-Speed' mounting which allowed the gun to be lowered flush with the upper decking when not in use to reduce drag.

The Fairey Queen was an unmanned variant developed by the RAE that could be catapulted from a warship and flown under radio control as a gunnery target. If it survived, as most target aircraft did, it could be landed on the water and recovered for further use. A prototype was fitted with auto-stabilisation in pitch and yaw but not roll. The wings were, however, given five degrees of increased dihedral to improve lateral stability. A remote control system allowed commands to climb, turn or dive to be sent from the controlling ship and a compensator was fitted to offset the catapult's acceleration effect on the gyro in the control unit. The prototype was embarked in the battleship *Valiant* in 1932 and catapulted but the compensator was clearly inadequate as it crashed into the sea after only 18 seconds. A second Queen was embarked in the same ship but crashed 25 seconds after launch in April due to failure of the rudder control. The third Queen fared better and after a successful launch from *Valiant* in September 1932, the ship deployed to Gibraltar with it in January 1933 for Home Fleet gunnery trials. Two hours after its launch the fleet had used up its entire allocation of anti-aircraft ammunition without even scratching the Fairey Queen and it was landed safely in a rough sea. In May 1933 the Mediterranean Fleet was given its chance and *Valiant* launched the Queen off Malta. After being under fire for 20 minutes it was shot down into the sea by the cruiser *Shropshire*. No production orders for Queens followed but its shortcomings were factored into the design of the de Havilland Queen Bee's control system.

IIIFs withdrawn from operational units were used on fleet requirements duties including target-towing. This was not popular with pilots because dragging a banner on several thousand feet of cable reduced the aircraft's speed to about 80 knots and the fuselage was buffeted by the banner's constant twitching. Despite this, most pilots apparently thought that flying the IIIF was a gentlemanly pursuit and the aircraft had few, if any vices. With an approach speed of only 44

knots when fitted with Handley Page slots on the upper leading edges of later production aircraft, the IIIF was a gentle aircraft to deck land and had little need for the arrester wires introduced in British carriers during the early 1930s. The majority of IIIFs were never fitted with deck-landing hooks.

IIIFs on floats operating from *Hermes* while she was anchored off Wei-Hei-Wei on the China Station.

IIIF Mark IIIM data with wheeled undercarriage

Length:	34ft 4in
Wingspan:	45ft 9in (15ft 4in folded)
Height:	11ft 3in (12ft 7in on floats)
MTOW:	6,301lb
Engine:	One 570hp Napier Lion XIA liquid-cooled engine
Fuel:	Avgas. 110 gallons.
Performance:	Maximum speed in level flight 115 knots
Service ceiling:	Service ceiling 20,000ft. 6½ minutes to 5,000ft
Armament:	One belt-fed Vickers 0.303in front gun in a blast trough on the port side; one 0.303in Lewis gun on a Fairey High Speed mounting at the rear of the TAG's cockpit. A bomb load of up to 500lb could be carried, normally as four 112lb, two 230lb or 250lb with four 20lb bombs for use as sighters

A IIIF of 441 Flight in *Glorious*' netting after a landing accident. Note the sheerlegs rigged to recover it.

Production for the Fleet Air Arm totalled 379 aircraft, of which 55 were Mark Is, 33 were Mark IIs, 114 Mark IIIMs and 177 Mark IIIBs.

Fleet Air Arm IIIFs served with 440, 441, 442, 443, 444, 445, 446, 447, 448, 449, 450 and 460 Flights in the Home and Mediterranean Fleets and on the China Station. Catapult aircraft from some of these flights operated from cruiser squadrons on both the America and West Indies and South Atlantic Stations.

After the 1933 re-organisation IIIFs served with 820, 822, 823, 824 and 825 NAS and with 701, 714 and 718 NAS as catapult aircraft. They served in the aircraft carriers *Argus*, *Hermes*, *Eagle*, *Furious*, *Courageous* and *Glorious* and were familiar sights at airfields around the world from Lee-on-Solent in the UK and Hal Far in Malta to Kai Tak in Hong Kong.

A IIIF of 824 NAS embarked in *Eagle* during 1933.

Between 1931 and 1937 IIIFs were embarked as catapult flights for commissions of varying length in the battleships or battlecruisers *Barham*, *Hood*, *Malaya*, *Nelson*, *Ramillies*, *Renown*, *Resolution*, *Royal Sovereign* and *Valiant*. They were also embarked in the cruisers *Berwick*, *Devonshire*, *Dorsetshire*, *Exeter*, *London*, *Norfolk*, *Shropshire*, *Sussex* and *York* for commissions during the same period.

The IIIF first entered Fleet Air Arm service in 1928 when the type superseded the Fairey IIID and in the following years it replaced the Bison, Blackburn and Ripon. By 1934 the IIIF was itself being replaced in carrier squadrons by the Fairey Seal although the transition was not completed until 1936. The three 700-series catapult units continued to deploy IIIFs to cruisers until 1936 and several IIIFs continued in use as target tugs at naval air stations until the type was declared obsolete in 1940.

Firefly IIIM

A single Firefly IIIM was built to meet Specification N.21/26 for a deck-landing fighter. It was an attractive, streamlined biplane of all-metal construction and was evaluated by the A&AEE from March 1930 and carried out deck-landing trials on *Furious* in June. It was powered by a single 500hp Rolls-Royce Kestrel MS engine which gave a maximum level speed of 165 knots. Wingspan was 33ft 6in and MTOW was 3,479lb. Armament would have comprised two 0.303in front guns with 600 rpg and provision for four 20lb bombs. In 1931 it was fitted with twin floats and was tested at the MAEE but the Hawker Nimrod was chosen to meet the requirement and there was no further interest in the type.

Fleetwing

The Fleetwing was designed to meet Specification O.22/26 for a two-seat spotter/reconnaissance aircraft capable of operating as an interceptor fighter. The rival Hawker Osprey was selected for production but a single, wheeled, prototype Fleetwing had flown in June 1929 and delivered to the A&AEE for comparative evaluation. It could be fitted with either wheels or floats and was to be armed with a single belt-fed Vickers 0.303in front gun and a 0.303in Lewis gun on a Fairey High-Speed mounting in the after cockpit. It carried out deck-landing trials on *Furious* from January 1930 and was tested as a floatplane from *Norfolk* in 1932. It was powered by a single 500hp Rolls-Royce Kestrel engine which gave a maximum level speed of 150 knots. Wingspan was 37ft spread, 15ft 3in folded and MTOW was 4,737lb when fitted with wheels and 5,100lb when fitted with floats.

Seal

Intended as a IIIF replacement to meet Specification 12/29, the Seal was originally identified as the IIIF Mark VI but it had a new engine, a tail wheel replacing the skid, wheel brakes and an arrester hook. A prototype first flew in November 1931 with wheels and then with floats in September 1932. The first production Seal was delivered in 1933 and deliveries continued until 1935. At least one was completed as a dual-control trainer but the majority were delivered as three-seat spotter reconnaissance aircraft.

Seal data

Length:	33ft 8in
Wingspan:	45ft 9in (15ft 4in folded)
Height:	12ft 9in (14ft 4in on floats)
MTOW:	6,000lb (6,400lb as a floatplane)
Engine:	One 525hp Armstrong Siddeley Panther IIA, two-row, air-cooled radial
Fuel:	Avgas. 110 gallons
Performance:	Maximum speed in level flight 120 knots (115 knots as a float plane) Service ceiling 17,000ft (13,900 as a floatplane) 5 minutes to 5,000ft
Endurance:	4½ hours
Armament:	One belt-fed Vickers 0.303in front gun with 600 rpg and one 0.303in Lewis gun on a Fairey High-Speed mounting aft for the TAG. Provision for up to 500lb of bombs on under wing racks

Production for the Fleet Air Arm totalled ninety-one Seals in batches of eleven, twenty-one, eleven, five, twenty-five and eighteen.

A single Seal served briefly with 444 Catapult Flight during 1933. From 1936 to 1938 Seals served with 701 and 702 NAS as catapult aircraft embarked in cruisers. In May 1939 753 NAS was formed with Seals at Lee-on-Solent to become Number Two Observer School and 780 NAS used Seals as pilot conversion trainers briefly in 1939.

Front-line units equipped with Seals were 820, 821, 822, 823 and 824 NAS which operated from the aircraft carriers *Courageous*, *Furious*, *Glorious*, *Hermes* and *Eagle*. Seals were not used in catapult flights as widely as the IIIF but several were embarked in the battleships *Barham*, *Ramillies*, *Resolution*, *Royal Oak* and *Valiant* at times between 1933 and 1938.

The first operational squadrons to embark with Seals were 820 and 821 NAS which joined *Courageous* in late 1933. The last was 822 NAS which took over 821 NAS' Seals when it re-formed with Blackburn Sharks in 1936. 820 NAS only operated Seals until 1935 when it became the first to re-equip with Sharks. The remaining squadrons replaced their Seals with Fairey Swordfish by the end of 1938. A few Seals remained in use as fleet requirements aircraft until 1939 but by then the type was considered obsolete and the remaining examples were deleted.

Fairey Seal. (Philip Jarrett)

Battle

A two-seat, monoplane light bomber designed for the RAF as a Hart replacement, it was powered by a single 970hp Rolls-Royce Merlin G engine and was the reason why the engine was put into mass production. It was the subject of an immense industrial effort in the late 1930s with over 2,000 being produced but by 1940 it was totally outclassed and the aircraft deployed to France were massacred in the brief campaign that ended with the withdrawal of the BEF from Dunkirk and the French collapse. The huge effort to manufacture Battles was intended to make the RAF appear large on paper but it was almost entirely wasted. Its wingspan was 54ft, MTOW 10,792lb and it was supposed to be capable of carrying up to 1,000lb of bombs over a limited radius of action at a level speed of 175 knots.

No Battles were manufactured for the RN but three were transferred from the RAF in 1940. One was used as a ground instructional airframe and two were used briefly on fleet requirements tasks from Gosport. Most were shipped across the Atlantic to Canada where they were used by the RCAF as training aircraft within the Empire Air Training Scheme from 1941 and many Fleet Air Arm pilots flew them.

Seafox

Designed to meet Specification S.11/32 for a light two-seat spotter-reconnaissance seaplane capable of catapult operation from light cruisers. Few of these had hangars so their seaplanes had to remain on their catapults, exposed to the elements while the ship was at sea. Covers were provided for the engine and cockpit but water ingress and corrosion were significant problems that limited availability. The Seafox was an equal-span biplane with slightly staggered, folding wings fitted with the usual flaps and slats. It was one of the first aircraft to have a metal monocoque fuselage consisting of Z-section frames covered with Alclad panels but the wings were fabric-covered. Apart from drain holes, the fuselage was sealed and divided into watertight compartments. The pilot's cockpit was open to give a good view during catapult launch and to provide relatively easy access to the slinging points on the upper wing for recovery by crane. The observer's cockpit, however, was enclosed by a hood to give a secure environment as he worked with his plotting boards, charts, pencils and dividers. It was hinged open from the front to provide access and to make use of the Lewis gun on its Fairey high-speed mounting, providing an windshield for the observer when he used the gun. It was designed to be powered by a single 500hp Bristol Aquila sleeve-valve radial engine but for reasons that are difficult to understand the Air Ministry, which acted as the procurement authority for all military aircraft at the time, selected the 395hp Napier Rapier air-cooled engine instead. Consequently Seafox performance was limited by lack of power throughout its service career.

The first of two prototypes was ordered in June 1934 and flew as a floatplane in May 1936. The second was completed with a wheeled undercarriage in November but was fitted with floats in 1937. Tests at

A Seafox recovering to the AMC *Asturias* in 1942 with the observer on the wing ready to catch the hook. (Philip Jarrett)

the MAEE were generally favourable except for an unusually high landing speed for an aircraft of its size, 50 knots rather than the specified 40 knots but by then the Seafox was already in production. Catapult trials were carried out from *Neptune* off Gibraltar in March 1937. One production aircraft was built as a dual-control trainer and one with a wheeled undercarriage. Test pilots found that the aircraft handled well on the water in wind speeds up to 20 knots with no tendency to swing into wind but at anything approaching maximum take-off weight the lack of power was evident in the length of time it took to get the floats on to the step. In order to un-stick in these conditions, considerable force had to be applied to the control column. When flaps were deployed, the glide angle was steep and there was little chance of holding the aircraft off the surface for a gentle landing unless engine was used.

Seafox data

Length:	33ft 5in
Wingspan:	40ft (16ft folded)
Height:	12ft 2in on floats
MTOW:	5,420lb
Engine:	One 395hp Napier Rapier VI, air-cooled
Fuel:	Avgas. 96 gallons in main and reserve tanks
Performance:	Maximum speed in level flight 110 knots Service ceiling 9,700ft. 15 minutes to 5,000ft
Endurance:	4½ hours
Armament:	One 0.303in Lewis gun on high-speed mounting for the observer. Racks under the lower wings racks could carry two 100lb anti-submarine bombs or eight 20lb bombs

Total Seafox production amounted to two prototypes and production batches of forty-nine and fifteen aircraft.

Seafoxes served with 713, 716, 718 and briefly with 714 Fleet Catapult Flights from 1937 until 1940 when the first three were subsumed into 700 NAS. Others served as catapult flights within 702 and 703 NAS as they were formed from 1940.

From 1939 onwards Seafoxes were also used by 754 NAS, Number Two Observer School at Lee-on-Solent; 764 NAS for floatplane pilot training also at Lee; 765 NAS as a pool unit for floatplane pilots and with 773 NAS for fleet requirements duties. The last unit to operate the type was 702 NAS which gave up its Seafoxes in July 1943 when the type was declared obsolete.

Seafox flights operated from the cruisers *Penelope*, *Ajax*, *Orion*, *Emerald*, *Amphion*, *Arethusa*, *Galatea*, *Neptune* and, briefly, HMAS *Perth*. They also operated in catapult flights embarked in the armed merchant cruisers *Pretoria Castle*, *Asturias*, *Canton*, *Carnarvon Castle*, *Queen of Bermuda* and *Alcantara*.

The Seafox is best remembered for the part played in the Battle of the River Plate on 13 December 1939 by the aircraft flown off *Ajax*. This was the first occasion in the Second World War in which a cruiser-borne spotter reconnaissance aircraft had been used in the role upon which so much emphasis had been placed in the 1920s and 1930s. *Ajax* had the only serviceable Seafox on the station; her sister-ship the New Zealand-manned *Achilles* had no aircraft embarked. *Exeter* had two Walrus but they were not fully worked up. *Ajax* Seafox was flown by Lieutenant E D G Lewin RN with Lieutenant R E N Kearney RN as his observer. They flew throughout the battle and for reconnaissance flights every day while *Graf Spee* was in Montevideo before reporting on 17 December that the enemy ship had blown itself up. *Exeter*'s two Walrus were not launched before the action and both were subsequently jettisoned after being damaged by splinters to prevent fuel leaks adding to fires caused by action damage. By July 1943 most catapult flights had been withdrawn from cruisers as more aircraft carriers joined the fleet and, with more modern American types available for those that remained, the Seafox was declared obsolete.

Swordfish

By every contemporary standard the Swordfish was already obsolescent when the first squadron was equipped with it in 1936 but it went on to serve throughout the Second World War in the strike, reconnaissance and anti-submarine roles. It even outlasted its intended replacement, the Albacore. The Admiralty accepted a slow biplane for the TSR role in 1936 because it wanted an aircraft that could not only operate off aircraft carriers but also from the catapults fitted in battleships and cruisers. To achieve this, the TSR specification included a minimum

Swordfish Mark I with torpedo and long-range tank fitted in the observer's cockpit

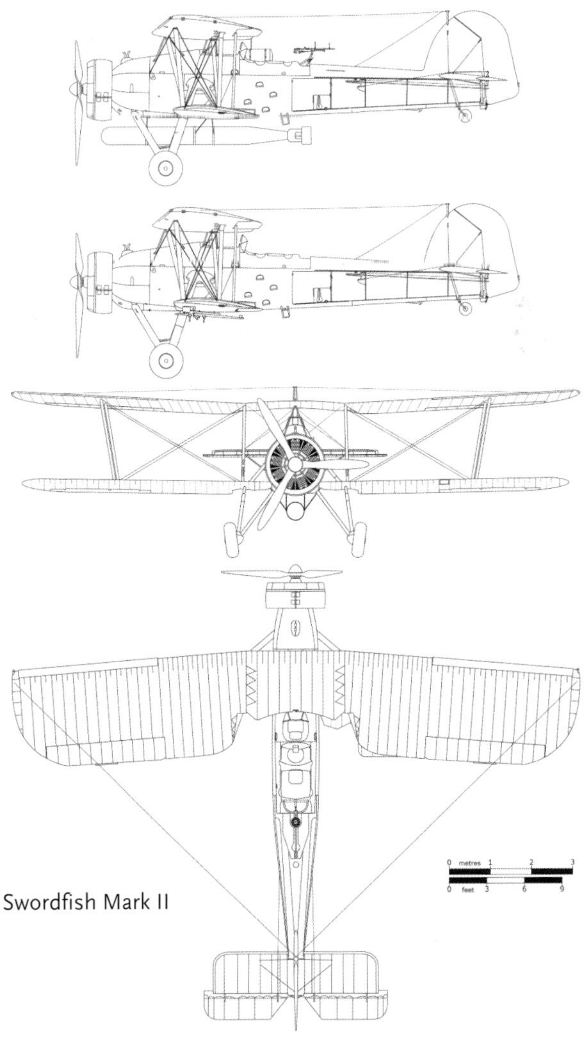

Swordfish Mark II

The TSR-1 prototype in 1933. It was never allocated a British airframe number.

A float-fitted Swordfish of 700 NAS embarked in *Malaya* during 1941.

take-off speed of 60 knots to be compatible with contemporary catapult end speeds. This had been relatively undemanding in the 1920s but made a considerable difference when heavier monoplanes were introduced in the late 1930s. The decision that it should be a multi-purpose aircraft was another factor. The 1932 Mediterranean Fleet exercises had revealed that the number of spotter aircraft embarked in carriers was insufficient to achieve their intended purpose and numbers had to be made up with torpedo aircraft and this experience led to the specification of the aircraft that became the Swordfish as a TSR aircraft.

It was designed by a team under Marcel Lobelle and evolved from an aircraft identified as the TSR I for the Greek Navy. A prototype flew in March 1933 powered by a 625hp Armstrong Siddeley Panther VI radial engine and details were sent to the Air Ministry which had responsibility at that time for procuring aircraft for both RN and RAF use. TSR 1's trials started well but on 11 September 1933 Fairey's chief test pilot, Chris Staniland, failed to recover it from a flat spin. Control inputs had no effect and after twelve turns Staniland attempted to bail out but was blown into the rear cockpit on his first attempt. He succeeded in getting out at the second attempt and the aircraft crashed. A modified second prototype designated TSR II, was manufactured to meet Specification S.15/33, issued under the guidance of Admiral Sir Reginald Henderson, RAAC, for a multi-role aircraft intended to reduce the number of different aircraft types embarked. It was followed by three further prototypes.

825 NAS over *Glorious* in 1936. It was the first to re-equip with Swordfish.

The Swordfish differed from the TSR I in having an extra bay built into the fuselage and strakes ahead of the tailplane leading edges to aid spin recovery and it flew for the first time on 17 April 1934. After Fairey's test programme it moved to the A&AEE for service trials, RAE Farnborough for catapult launch trials and *Courageous* for deck-landing trials. It was then fitted with floats and first flew as a seaplane on 10 November 1934. In January 1935 it underwent evaluation at the MAEE and then to Gosport where it was evaluated as a torpedo-armed strike aircraft. The Swordfish Mark I was powered by a Bristol Pegasus radial engine and the upper wing had a sweepback of 4 degrees to compensate for the lengthened fuselage. The wings had two built-up steel-strip spars and duralumin ribs. The fuselage structure comprised steel-tubing covered by doped fabric. The engine in production aircraft had a wide chord Townend-ring cowling and a three-blade Fairey-Reed, fixed-pitch metal propeller.

A torpedo-armed Swordfish of 816 NAS from *Furious* crossing the Norwegian coast on 11 April 1940.

Swordfish Mark I data

Length:	36ft 4in (40ft 11in with floats)
Wing span:	45ft 6in (17ft 3in folded)
Height:	12ft 10in (14ft 7in on floats)
MTOW:	9,250lb
Engine:	One 690hp Bristol Pegasus IIIM3 air-cooled radial
Fuel:	Avgas. 155 gallons main internal tank. 12½-gallon internal gravity-fed tank. Optional 60-gallon overload tank in rear cockpit. Optional 69-gallon overload tank on centreline crutches
Performance:	Maximum level speed 125 knots Service ceiling 19,250ft. 15 minutes to 10,000ft
Endurance:	Over 4 hours
Armament:	One 1,610lb torpedo or Type A Mark I mine on centreline crutches; up to 1,500lb of bombs or depth charges on centreline and underwing hardpoints. One fixed Vickers 0.303in machine gun to the right of the pilot's cockpit with 500 rpg and one 0.303in Vickers 'K' machine gun on a Fairey high-speed mounting in the rear cockpit

Swordfish at Hatston armed with Type A mines.

The four prototype Swordfish were followed by 692 manufactured by Fairey but after the outbreak of war it was clear that even with its new shadow factories the firm could not cope with the orders that were building up for the newer Albacore, Fulmar, Barracuda and Firefly if it kept the Swordfish production line open. The Admiralty's DAM, Captain M S Slattery RN, arranged for Blackburn to take over Swordfish production and its first example flew on 1 December 1940. Blackburn manufactured fuselages and assembled complete Swordfish but a number of other companies in the Leeds area manufactured the wings, undercarriages, ailerons, fins, rudders, centre-section structure and cockpit floor assemblies. Blackburn had delivered 1,699 Swordfish by the time production ceased in 1944, making a grand total of 2,391 Swordfish.

Swordfish were widely used by 700-series NAS in the training, catapult flight, fleet requirements and utility roles and well as providing pool facilities for pilots waiting to join front-line squadrons and refresher flying for pilots in non-flying appointments. Available in large numbers, reliable and inexpensive to operate, Swordfish were also used for a wide variety of trials tasks and as 'clockwork mice' flying ADDLs ashore and circuits onto deck-landing training carriers to train pilots as batsmen. The Torpedo Trials Unit at RNAS Gosport found the Swordfish to be such a useful and reliable weapon carrier that it retained several in operation until 1951. Shore-based Swordfish units included 700, 701, 702, 705, 707, 710, 722, 726, 727, 728, 730, 731, 733, 735, 737, 739, 741, 742, 743, 744, 745, 747, 753, 754, 756, 759, 763, 764, 765, 766, 767, 768, 769, 770, 771, 772, 773, 774, 775, 776, 777, 778, 779, 780, 781, 783, 785, 786, 787, 788, 789, 791, 796 and 797 NAS, all either fully or partially-equipped between 1936 and 1946.

Between 1936 and 1945 Swordfish served with 810, 811, 812, 813, 814, 815, 816, 818, 819, 820, 821, 822, 823, 824, 825, 826, 828, 829, 830, 831, 833, 834, 835, 836, 837, 838, 840, 841, 842, 848, 860, 886 and 1700 NAS in the strike, anti-surface vessel, anti-submarine, trade protection and reconnaissance roles. 860 NAS was manned by the Royal Netherlands Navy.

The first squadron to re-equip with Swordfish was 825 NAS in 1936 and type was operated with squadrons embarked in carriers and as float-plane detachments in battleships and battlecruisers at first. The need for aircraft to dominate the English Channel after 1939 led to several squadrons operating from shore bases alongside the RAF but by 1942 Swordfish were being replaced by new strike aircraft in the fleet carriers and they were used increasingly in composite squadrons embarked in escort carriers alongside fighters. They proved to be versatile and effective in this role and continued in use until the end of hostilities. 836 NAS provided Swordfish detachments to nineteen MAC-Ships operating in defence of the Atlantic convoys. At one point it had eighty-three Swordfish on strength and was the largest Fleet Air Arm squadron.

Between 1936 and 1945 Swordfish squadrons or flights operated from the aircraft carriers *Activity*, *Archer*, *Argus*, *Ark Royal* (1938), *Atheling*, *Attacker*, *Avenger*, *Battler*, *Biter*, *Campania*, *Chaser*, *Courageous*, *Dasher*, *Eagle* (1924), *Fencer*, *Formidable*, *Furious*, *Glorious*, *Hermes* (1924), *Hunter*, *Illustrious* (1940), *Nairana*, *Stalker*, *Striker*, *Tracker*, *Unicorn*, *Victorious* and *Vindex*. They also operated from the nineteen MAC-Ships.

Floatplane Swordfish were operated at times as catapult flights in the battleships and battlecruisers *Barham*, *Hood*, *Malaya*, *Renown*, *Repulse*, *Resolution*, *Rodney*, *Royal Oak*, *Valiant* and *Warspite*.

The Swordfish was a versatile and reliable aircraft and its ability to carry almost any load from a torpedo to a motorbike on the centreline crutches led to its aircrew calling it the 'Stringbag', a contemporary open-mesh shopping bag that could have purchases of almost any size and shape crammed into it. The admiration its pilots felt for it can be gathered from Terence Horsley's book *Find, Fix and Strike* published in 1943 in which he said that 'perhaps once in the lifetime of every designer will come an inspiration which will result in an exceptionally good aircraft . . . but, whatever the origin, every pilot who lays his hands upon it will instantly know beyond all doubt that it is exceptional. Such an aircraft is the Fairey Swordfish.' Reading through these words again in 2023 I was struck by the author's use of the word 'exceptional' three times in four sentences. He captured the essence of the Swordfish exactly by writing that 'in the beginning, before you start thinking about the 1,500lb of bombs or the 18in torpedo, you know that you have got a friend. And a friend, when you are fighting your way through the darkness towards a lurching flight deck, or are 100 miles out over an empty sea waste, is something worth having . . . it was only when I sat in the cockpit myself, made the . . . run towards the deck at a staggeringly slow speed and felt the firm and instant response to the controls, that I knew at last that I was flying the product of a designer's genius.'

A Swordfish Mark III armed with depth charges about to launch from a tanker MAC-Ship.

The classic RN aerial torpedo attack involved a radical change of height and bearing to confuse an enemy ship's anti-aircraft gunnery control and the technique required extensive training and constant practice. Typically, the approach to a target was made at about 10,000ft in four flights of three aircraft which would attack from different directions, diving vertically onto the target at intervals around it and synchronising dives with the leader. From roughly 2 miles high the descent took about a minute and below 1,000ft pilots eased their aircraft out of the dive and used their sights to aim-off before release to allow for target movement as their weapons ran towards it. The ideal release point was at 1,000 yards from the target. At the moment of release the aircraft had to be at about 200ft, straight and level with no side-slip so that the weapon entered the water cleanly. If the squadron attack was perfectly executed, the target ship would move into the tracks of at least three torpedoes no matter how it tried to evade. The Swordfish torpedo sight was a simple bar forward of the windscreen with notches or lights to help the pilot estimate target speed and aim-off at the ideal 1,000-yard release point.

Swordfish Mark II armed with 3in RP about to take-off from a CVE.

Swordfish Mark III landing on a British-built CVE.

Swordfish and Sea Hurricanes on *Vindex* in Scapa Flow during 1944.

In 1939 the Swordfish was one of only two British aircraft capable of carrying a mine, the other being the RAF Bristol Beaufort. Mark I Swordfish were manufactured without significant changes until 1943 when the Mark II first appeared. It had strengthened lower wings with metal-skinned under surfaces to allow up to eight 3in RP to be carried and launched. Also from 1943 onward, batches of Swordfish were completed as Mark IIIs. In addition to the modified lower wing these had ASV Mark X radar fitted in a scanner between the undercarriage legs which prevented the carriage of a torpedo although RPs, depth charges and bombs could still be carried under the wings. They were also provided with fittings for rocket-assisted take-off gear, RATOG, to facilitate low-wind launches from the decks of CVEs and MAC-Ships. The extra weight of the equipment in the Mark III meant that it had to be flown by a crew of two, the TAG's position being deleted. Both Mark IIs and IIIs were fitted with uprated 750hp Bristol Pegasus 30 engines. No Mark IV Swordfish were built as such but the description was applied to Mark IIs built with enclosed cockpits for use by TAG training units in Canada.

Among the many actions for which the Swordfish is justly famous several stand out including the posthumous award of the VC to Lieutenant Commander (A) Eugene Esmonde VC DSO RN after all six of 825 NAS' Swordfish led by him were shot down attacking *Scharnhorst*, *Gneisenau* and *Prinz Eugen* as they passed through the English Channel in February 1942. The attack on the Italian battle fleet at Taranto in November 1940 changed the course of naval warfare forever. Others include the first airborne torpedo attack in history during the Norwegian Campaign; attacks on German forces as they reached the Channel coast in 1940 and extensive minelaying in the Channel. The operations of Swordfish from Malta, whilst their airfield at Hal Far suffered some of the heaviest bombing attacks of the Second World War, against Italian convoys to North Africa and clandestine operations in Greece and Crete had an effect on operations far beyond that which could be expected from the number of aircraft involved. A Swordfish from *Ark Royal* gained the hit on *Bismarck* that made it possible for the Home Fleet to destroy it and when the Prime Minister Winston Churchill wanted a strategic minefield laid to prevent Swedish iron ore reaching Germany across the Baltic, carrier-borne Swordfish were the only British aircraft capable of carrying it out. Operation 'Paul' was planned but, in the event, not carried out as the German attack in the West began in May 1940. Swordfish proved the ideal aircraft for convoy protection and operated under appalling conditions in the North Atlantic and on the Russian convoy route. The intense cold meant that sometimes aircrew had to be lifted from their cockpits after landing. Swordfish carried out anti-shipping strikes in the Channel and laid mines in support of the D-Day landings, and carried out the first attempt to destroy an enemy dam, the attack on the Tirso Dam in Sardinia in February 1941. They took part in the North African landings in 1942 and acted in support of the British Army in North Africa. All these and many more show what a remarkable aircraft the Swordfish was. It is believed to have sunk a greater tonnage of shipping than any other Allied aircraft in the Second World War and can justly be considered to be one of the greatest and most effective warplanes in history.

Swordfish of 816 NAS in D-Day recognition stripes operating from Perranporth during May 1944.

Albacore

The Admiralty wanted a reliable dive-bomber/reconnaissance, DBR, type to be procured quickly to underpin the Fleet Air Arm's expansion and asked for it to be built by Fairey to dispense with the usual tender procedure and save time. Specification S.41/36 was issued to cover development in June 1936 but there was considerable argument about whether the DBR should be a biplane or monoplane. Admiralty opinion favoured the biplane solution as the quickest and hoped to have the new type replacing Swordfish on the Fairey production line by 1938. A production order 'off the drawing board' for 100 DBR was placed in May 1937, followed only days later by an order for a further 300 but the selected powerplant was the Bristol Taurus which was itself still under development. Production engines had been expected to be available by August 1938 but technical problems caused delays and the first DBR, by then named Albacore, did not fly until 12 December 1938. The Swordfish had to be maintained in production and the biplane conceived as a quick replacement ceased to be so.

The Albacore was an equal-span biplane with folding wings of all-metal structure with an Alclad covered semi-monocoque fuselage and fabric covered wings. The cockpit was fully enclosed and heated and there were hydraulically-operated flaps on both upper and lower wings which could be used as air brakes for dive-bombing and a variable-pitch propeller. There were no prototypes and the first two aircraft off the production line were used for company tests followed by service trials at the A&AEE in which handling was not considered to be as good as the Swordfish. With the leading-edge slots free the stall was described as uncomfortable with pronounced wing-drop and aileron snatch. If the stick was held right back a considerable swing developed into a flat turn, even when full opposite rudder was applied, but it would not enter a spin. With flaps down the wing-drop was less marked and with the slots locked the Albacore could not be fully stalled but remained stable with a very high sink rate. The most positive comments were made about its performance in a steep dive with a torpedo. It remained stable despite the elevators and ailerons becoming extremely heavy and was considered easy and smooth to pullout. Rudder control was always considered heavy. Deck-landing trials were carried out on *Ark Royal* in May 1939 and described as adequate.

The view from the pilot's cockpit was described as excellent but access to it as tortuous and difficult. The enclosed cockpits were not an

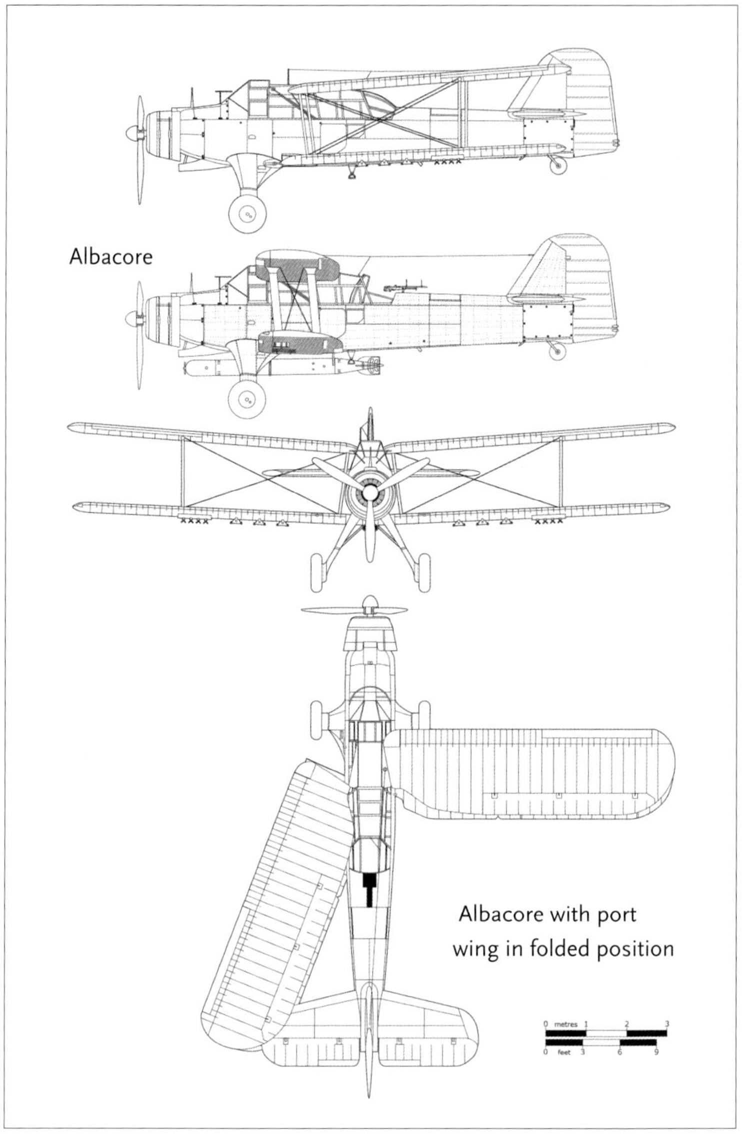

An Albacore lined up for take-off from *Victorious*.

Albacores ranged on *Victorious*.

A strike of torpedo-armed Albacores.

unqualified success. The pilot's position was found to be excessively hot in normal summer conditions, even with the roof slid back and the sliding side windows down but the heater failed to warm it sufficiently in cold conditions. By comparison, the rear cockpit area was always found to be cold and draughty no matter what the heater setting. A large internal fuel tank separated the pilot from the observer and TAG. In summary, the Albacore offered some detail improvements but failed to inspire confidence as a deck-landing aircraft and was even considered by many to have an inferior performance compared to the Swordfish; that was why it was never operated from CVEs in the anti-submarine role. It was only ever intended to be a stopgap and that is precisely what it was. The original concept that Swordfish production would run down and be replaced by Albacores from 1938 never happened and when Albacore production ended in 1943 it was well before that of the aircraft it was intended to replace. 'Winkle' Brown described it to me as 'lumbering', an adjective that described the Albacore perfectly. It was less able to defend itself against fighter attack than the Swordfish because it lacked its predecessor's manoeuvrability.

S.41/36 had included a requirement for the Albacore to be operated as a floatplane for use by catapult flights and the first aircraft was retro-fitted with twin floats for evaluation by the MAEE in March 1940 which were a failure. At speeds above 15 knots water washed over the front of the floats causing the aircraft to 'porpoise', even in calm conditions, and water was thrown up into the propeller disc. Further development was abandoned.

Albacores of 828 NAS climbing out of Hal Far for an attack on enemy shipping.

Albacore data

Length:	39ft 10in
Wingspan:	50ft (17ft 6in folded)
Height:	14ft 2in
MTOW:	10,460lb
Engine:	One 1,130hp Bristol Taurus XII two-row, air-cooled radial
Fuel:	Avgas. 193 gallons
Performance:	Maximum speed in level flight 140 knots Service ceiling 20,700ft. 8 minutes to 6,000ft
Endurance:	5½ hours
Armament:	One 1,610lb torpedo or 1,500lb mine on centreline crutches. Up to four 500lb or six 250lb bombs on underwing racks. One belt-fed Browning 0.303in front gun in starboard lower wing with 500 rpg synchronised to fire through the propeller arc. Two 0.303in Vickers 'K' guns in TAG's cockpit

Total production amounted to 800 Albacores, all built by Fairey.

Albacores equipped or partially-equipped a number of shore-based squadrons between 1940 and 1945 including 700, 733, 747, 750, 753, 754, 756, 763, 766, 767, 768, 769, 771, 774, 775, 778, 783, 785, 786, 787, 788, 789, 791, 793, 796, 797 and 799 NAS in a variety of roles including aircrew training and fleet requirements work in the UK, Malta, Egypt, South Africa and Ceylon.

The Albacore appeared at a time when the RN had very few carriers in operation and as a result several Albacore squadrons operated ashore with distinction both in the UK and the Mediterranean while waiting for their ships to be completed or repaired. Front-line units equipped with the type between 1940 and 1943 included 810, 815, 817, 818, 820, 821, 822, 823, 826, 827, 828, 829, 830, 831, 832 and 841 NAS. They operated from the aircraft carriers *Argus*, *Ark Royal* (1938), *Formidable*, *Furious*, *Indomitable* and *Victorious*.

The first operational unit to be equipped with Albacores was 826 NAS which commissioned with them at Ford in March 1940. After

Albacores being ranged on *Victorious*.

the German attack on the West in May 1940 it laid minefields in the Channel, carried out night bombing attacks on enemy troop movements and escorted Channel convoys. In November 1940 it embarked in *Formidable* with 829 NAS and subsequently deployed to the Mediterranean where both squadrons took part in the Battle of Matapan. Albacores from *Victorious* and *Furious*, escorted by Fulmars, were the only British strike force capable of implementing Churchill's pledge to the Soviet Government that the British would attack German logistic shipping in Petsamo and Kirkenes in July 1941 but they suffered significant losses for meagre results. Albacores proved to be easy prey for German Bf 109 fighters and even Ju 87 dive-bombers in these strikes but the achievement of one crew stands out. Albacore 4K of 827 NAS flown by Lieutenants J N Ball and B J Prendergast RN was attacked more than thirty times as it left the target area at low level. One Ju 87 pilot elected to carry out a slow attack from ahead and slightly above. This gave Ball the chance for a zero-deflection shot with his single front gun and the enemy aircraft was seen to be hit and crash into the sea after a few seconds. After landing on *Victorious* armourers found that Ball had only fired eighty-seven rounds and no enemy rounds had hit 4K. Both Ball and Prendergast were awarded the DSC. Albacores from *Victorious* carried out the only torpedo attack on *Tirpitz* at sea, regrettably without success.

The Albacore carried out some notable operations from shore bases in Malta and North Africa between 1941 to 1943. On 9 July 1942 nine aircraft of 826 NAS flew to a position 250nm behind the German lines in North Africa where they were refuelled by RAF Bristol Bombay tanker aircraft on the ground prior to carrying out an attack on an enemy convoy at Tobruk. Other Albacores spotted for naval bombardments by surface forces and flew anti-submarine patrols. Albacores from Hal Far attacked Axis convoys attempting to carry supplies to North Africa and those based at Dekheila specialised in locating, marking and illuminating targets for RAF bombers. They were painted black to limit detection by searchlight beams and their sleeve-valve engines were so quiet when throttled back in a glide attack that the enemy seldom heard them until after they had marked their targets or dropped bombs and gone. The RN target-marking technique was later copied by RAF Bomber Command's Pathfinder force in the European Theatre. Four Albacore units, 817, 820, 822 and 832 NAS played a significant part in Operation 'Torch', the Allied landings on the North African coast, bombing targets in support of the Army's advance, attacking airfields and carrying out anti-submarine patrols. The last unit to serve in a carrier was 820 NAS which covered the Salerno landings from *Formidable.* 841 NAS was formed in July 1942 to locate and attack enemy shipping in the Channel under RAF radar control. It proved so successful that its aircraft were passed to 415 Squadron of the RCAF when it disbanded and this unit continued the task into 1945.

Fulmar

By 1938 it was clear to the Admiralty that a fighter with better performance than the Skua was urgently required. However, DNAW doubted whether Type 72 aircraft homing beacon development was sufficiently advanced to risk specifying a single-seat fighter for carrier operation. At the time the primary role envisaged for embarked fighters

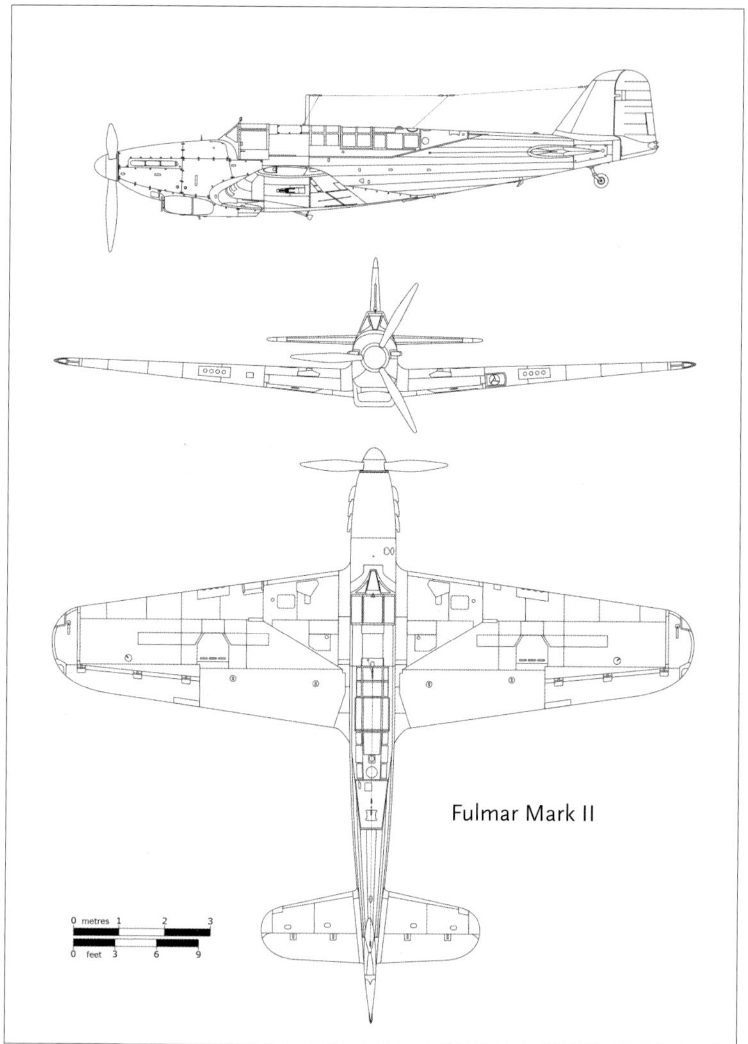

Fulmar Mark II

was the escort of long-range strike and reconnaissance aircraft, both roles that had been carried out by the two-seat Osprey and an observer was thought to be the only sure way of guiding the aircraft back to its carrier. Admiralty Specification O.8/38, therefore, called for a two-seater.

In 1937 Fairey had flown two prototypes designed by Marcel Lobelle to meet an RAF requirement for a two-seat, monoplane, light bomber. They were stressed for dive-bombing with a 500lb bomb and were smaller and lighter than the Battle with significant improvements including an inward-retracting, wide track undercarriage well-suited to carrier operations. The RAF subsequently cancelled the light bomber requirement but the Admiralty accepted the design as the basis of a fighter that could be produced quickly with minimum development effort. The second prototype was modified to meet O.8/38 in March 1938 and evaluated at the A&AEE where it was found to be acceptable in the fighter role. It was difficult to stall and considerable backward force was required on the stick to do so. If held firmly in the stalled condition it would drop its right wing but recovery was immediate when pressure on the column was released. Production Fulmars had manually-folding wings which lay flat along the fuselage sides when folded so that the guns could be reloaded, an arrester hook, catapult spools, new non-continuous canopies for the pilot and observer and stowage for a dinghy. Naval radio and a homing beacon

A Fulmar of 761 NAS from Yeovilton.

receiver were fitted. An instruction to proceed was issued on 5 May 1938 and in this instance the Admiralty's desire to get an aircraft into service quickly met with success. The first aircraft off the production line were used for test and evaluation with the first flying on 4 January 1940. The second was allocated to the A&AEE on 3 May and the third to the RN service trials unit on 10 May. A further eleven had been completed by 17 June and 806 NAS was commissioned at Worthy Down in July for embarkation in the new *Illustrious*. The fact that such a short time elapsed between the first production deliveries and the type's first combat missions in the Mediterranean in the autumn of 1940 emphasised the basic soundness of the Fulmar's design: it was easy and pleasant to fly and pilots liked it. Terence Horsley wrote in *Find, Fix and Strike* that 'it was a fine aeroplane, manoeuvrable, with a good take-off, a moderate climb and plenty of endurance. It satisfied the demands for an observer's seat and several wireless sets considered essential for fleet work. It merely lacked the fighter's first essential quality– speed.' After it entered service, Fairey was instructed to improve the Fulmar's performance and this resulted in the Mark II fitted with a more powerful engine. The prototype flew in January 1941 and production soon followed. Later Fulmars were used for night fighter development; the second seat was considered ideal for the radar operator and the aircraft's excellent handling qualities helped the pilot both to track targets and to recover onto a carrier deck at night or in adverse weather. A flight of radar-equipped Fulmar NF IIs operated from CVEs in defence of some Russian convoys during the winter of 1944/45.

The choice of armament was taken on RAF advice, eight rifle-calibre machine guns, the same as the contemporary Hurricane and Spitfire. The guns weighed 25lb each, a total of only 200lb, and had a muzzle velocity of 2,240ft per second. Rate of fire was 1,200 rounds per minute but the weight of each bullet was only 174 grains and they lacked penetrating power, especially against metal-structured aircraft with armour around vital areas. Effective range was under 400 yards so pilots had get very close to cause serious damage. The contemporary USN fighter weapon of choice was the 0.5in Colt-Browning machine gun which was arguably the best fighter weapon of the war. It weighed 64lb and fired either a solid-shot, explosive or incendiary round at 850 to 950 rounds per minute. It had a muzzle velocity of 2,900ft per second, fired 710 grain bullets and was effective out to 800 yards. To illustrate the effectiveness of a four-gun '50' battery in a Fulmar over eight '303's, the RN Air Weapons School calculated that the energy delivered by the eight '303s' in one minute was 21,047,040ft/lb. The energy delivered by four '50's was 45,316,384ft/lb. Although the gun weight was 56lb greater, the weight of ammunition required for the

A range of Fulmars on *Victorious*.

A 761 NAS Fulmar flying without an observer on an air-to-air gunnery sortie.

'50' option would have been significantly less than for the '303s'. Taking every calculation into consideration, a hit on an enemy aircraft by a single, solid, '50' round would have been seven times as damaging as a single hit by a '303' round. An explosive '50' even more so. Mark II Fulmars modified for the night fighter role in 1944 were fitted with four Colt Brownings.

The positioning of guns in the wings outside the propeller arc after 1936 brought the need to align them accurately with the pilot's gunsight which was on the aircraft's centreline. The RAF favoured an alignment in which the guns were 'toed-in' to converge on a single point 250 yards ahead of the aircraft where they were expected to cause maximum damage. DNAW was unsatisfied with convergent alignment and in 1940 it devised a pattern intended to fill a cylindrical volume of air with as many bullets as possible as opposed to trying to hit a single point with every gun. Put simply the guns were aligned to fire in parallel and the results were found to be remarkably effective. In 1941 two groups of Fulmars fitted with the different alignment systems each shot down thirty-five enemy aircraft but only three Fulmars were shot down by return fire in the group with Admiralty standard alignment. In contrast, the group with the point alignment lost eleven Fulmars to return fire because they had to fire from closer range to achieve their kills and rounds concentrated near the cockpit or engines failed to hit the enemy rear gunners.

Like other fighters of its generation, the Fulmar had a reflector gun sight fitted as standard. The pilot tracked his target through an optically flat glass screen behind his armoured windscreen on which a simple sight picture was projected from below. He had to estimate both range and crossing speed by eye and this was a skill that could only be gained with practice. Once acquired, the sight gave aim-off ahead of the target, allowing hits to be gained. The fuel tank between the cockpits was self-sealing and the pilot's windscreen was made of bullet-proof glass but there was no other protection for the aircrew. The pilot's forward view and the view downwards over the wing leading edge was good. The observer's cockpit had a chart table forward and a T1115/R1116 W/T set aft; the seat being rotatable to access them. The R1147 homing beacon receiver could be controlled from either cockpit. Although it lacked the level speed needed for a fighter, the Fulmar had a very high density which gave it a good diving speed which built up much more quickly than that of light single-seat fighters. This allowed a first, 'slashing' pass against a bomber that compensated to some extent for its lack of level speed.

Fulmar Mark II data

Length:	40ft 3in
Wingspan:	46ft 4½in (17ft 10in folded)
Height:	10ft 8in
MTOW:	10,200lb
Engine:	One 1,300hp Rolls-Royce Merlin 30
Fuel:	Avgas. 155 gallons
Performance:	Maximum speed in level flight 240 knots Service ceiling 27,200ft. 4½ minutes to 5,000ft
Endurance:	4 hours
Armament:	Eight 0.303in Browning front guns with 500 rpg. Underwing racks for two 250lb bombs, 100lb A/S bombs or up to eight 20lb bombs

Fulmar production totalled 600 between 1940 and February 1943, comprising 250 Mark Is and 350 Mark IIs. No NF IIs were built as

A Fulmar NF II with other aircraft in the training carrier *Ravager*'s hangar during 1945.

such; all were converted from Mark IIs.

From 1940 to 1946 Fulmars served with shore-based squadrons in the training, fleet requirements, trials and tactical development roles in 700, 726, 730, 731, 733, 739, 740, 746, 748, 756, 757, 759, 760, 761, 762, 766, 767, 768, 769, 772, 775, 776, 777, 778, 779, 780, 781, 784, 787, 788, 789, 790, 792, 793, 794, 795 and 798 NAS which were wholly or partially equipped with them for varying periods.

Between 1940 and 1943 Fulmars served with 800, 803, 804, 805, 806, 807, 808, 809, 815, 879, 884, 886, 887, 889, 893 and 897 NAS. In 1941 800 NAS was divided into three flights, 'X', 'Y' and 'Z' to provide navigation leaders for single-seat RAF fighters on ferry flights that had taken off from carriers and could not navigate for themselves over the sea. 784 NAS provided operational night fighter detachments that served alongside 813 NAS for embarked periods during 1944–5.

Some squadrons acted as fighter 'pools' for trained pilots awaiting appointments to operational units. Fleet requirements squadrons provided target facilities for fighters, air direction teams and anti-aircraft gunners to maintain their operational efficiency using tactics that would be employed by enemy aircraft. Apart from the UK, fleet requirements units operated Fulmars in Malta, Egypt, Sierra Leone, East Africa, the West Indies, Ceylon and South Africa. Development included, among other things, work on electronic systems to make night and bad weather landings on carriers possible.

Fulmars operated from the aircraft carriers *Argus*, *Ark Royal* (1938), *Campania*, *Eagle* (1924), *Formidable*, *Furious*, *Illustrious*, *Indomitable*, *Nairana* and *Victorious*. They were also embarked for brief periods in the fighter catapult ships *Ariguani*, *Pegasus* and *Springbank*.

With the role equipment removed from the rear cockpit, Fulmars could be fitted with two passenger seats which gave them a useful high-speed communications capability, often providing a 'taxi-service' for senior officers. Between 1942 and 1944 Fulmars were used by the communications flights at Dekheila and Fayid in Egypt.

After embarking in *Illustrious* for service with the Mediterranean Fleet, 806 NAS was immediately effective, destroying twenty-six enemy shadowers, or the bombers that followed them, and damaging as many more. Fulmars formed a component of an effective and evolving air defence system, the first of its kind, which included *Illustrious*' radar, the fighter direction team that interpreted it and the fighters. Fulmars played an important part in the Taranto strike by preventing enemy reconnaissance aircraft from finding or reporting the carrier task force. Other squadrons operated in the UK, 808 NAS gaining the battle honour 'Battle of Britain' for its defence of Scapa Flow. By mid-1941 Fulmars had destroyed fifty-six enemy aircraft and operated from shore bases when their armoured carriers were damaged during operations in the eastern Mediterranean. In the Western Mediterranean Fulmars played an important part in protecting convoys from Gibraltar to Malta. During the 'Pedestal' convoy in August 1942, the Fulmars of 809 and 884 NAS in *Victorious* shot down nine enemy aircraft out of the thirty-one shot down by the fleet's fighters on 11 and 12 August, a considerable achievement for a fighter that was, by then, outmatched by the majority of the aircraft it engaged.

Fulmar squadrons operated from bases in Crete, Egypt, Ceylon and Malta, the latter on night intruder missions against enemy airfields in Sicily for six months during 1941. On 21 May six Fulmars of 800X NAS had been used to lead forty-seven RAF Hurricanes from *Ark Royal* and *Furious* to Malta. After their arrival their night missions destroyed three enemy aircraft over their darkened airfields and many others on the ground by strafing with front guns and shallow bombing with 20lb bombs. They lacked spares and aircraft were kept flying by 'cannibalising' others; the last one flew out to an advanced landing ground in Cyrenaica. On its eventual arrival at Dekheila in Egypt, this battered and much-patched aircraft was condemned as non-airworthy and scrapped. Aircraft from 800Z NAS operated from *Victorious* during the *Bismarck* action during May 1941 and played a gallant part in searching for the enemy battleship in atrocious weather conditions that led to the loss of some aircraft and their aircrew. Fulmars also took part in the Petsamo strike in July 1941 and operated in defence of trade embarked in fighter catapult ships. Between June and September 1941 five combat launches were carried out and a single FW 200 Condor was damaged. During Operation 'Torch', the North African landings in November 1942, Fulmars flew as tactical reconnaissance aircraft in support of Allied forces as they moved inland from the beaches.

The Fulmar's potential as a night fighter was recognised in 1942 and a night fighter training unit, 784 NAS, was formed at Lee-on-Solent in June, moving to Drem in November. In February 1944 this unit formed three operational night fighter flights intended for use in CVEs operating on Russian convoy routes but by then spare parts were in short supply and the Fulmar was difficult to maintain; serviceability was correspondingly poor. On 8 February 1945 a Fulmar NF II attached to *Campania*'s 813 NAS was flown off at dusk in bad weather to intercept a shadower. The observer gained radar contact and the aircraft closed to within 3,000 yards but the AI Mark IV radar failed at that point and the enemy aircraft escaped. On recovery the aircraft's deck hook failed to catch a wire, it crashed into the safety barrier and was subsequently written off. This was the Fulmar's last operational sortie from a carrier.

Barracuda

In May 1937 the Admiralty began to consider options for a torpedo-bomber-reconnaissance, TBR, aircraft to replace the as-yet unbuilt Albacore; these led in October to Admiralty Specification S.24/37 for a single-engined monoplane with a crew of three, pilot, observer and TAG. In January 1938 a joint Admiralty/Air Ministry group selected the Fairey Type 100 design from a number of firms' designs. The rival Supermarine Type 322 was ordered under a supplementary research and development contract to evaluate its variable-incidence wing.

The Type 100, designed by Marcelle Lobelle assisted by R T Youngman, was a shoulder-wing monoplane with a retractable main undercarriage to have been powered by the 1,150hp Rolls-Royce Exe sleeve-valve, high-pressure, air-cooled, in-line 'X' engine. The Exe was designed to be easy to install and have minimal drag unlike contemporary liquid-cooled engines such as the Merlin. An early Exe engine was fitted in a Battle test-bed in 1938 and proved so trouble-free that it was used as Fairey's company 'hack' until 1943. Two prototype Type 100s were ordered in July 1938 and it was appreciated from the outset that this complicated aircraft would require considerable development effort. The fuselage had to accommodate more hydraulic pumps and accumulators than any previous British single-engined aircraft but needed to be narrow to fit into the contemporary British catapult trolley. There was a tough maximum weight restriction and the folded aircraft had to fit within the 45ft by 22ft dimensions of the lifts in the new *Illustrious* class armoured carriers. The Type 100 was considered to be such a promising design that the Air Ministry recommended ordering it 'off the drawing board' before a prototype had flown. The Admiralty agreed in early 1939 and an order for 250 was placed in August with production deliveries expected from 1941. The name Barracuda was chosen for it.

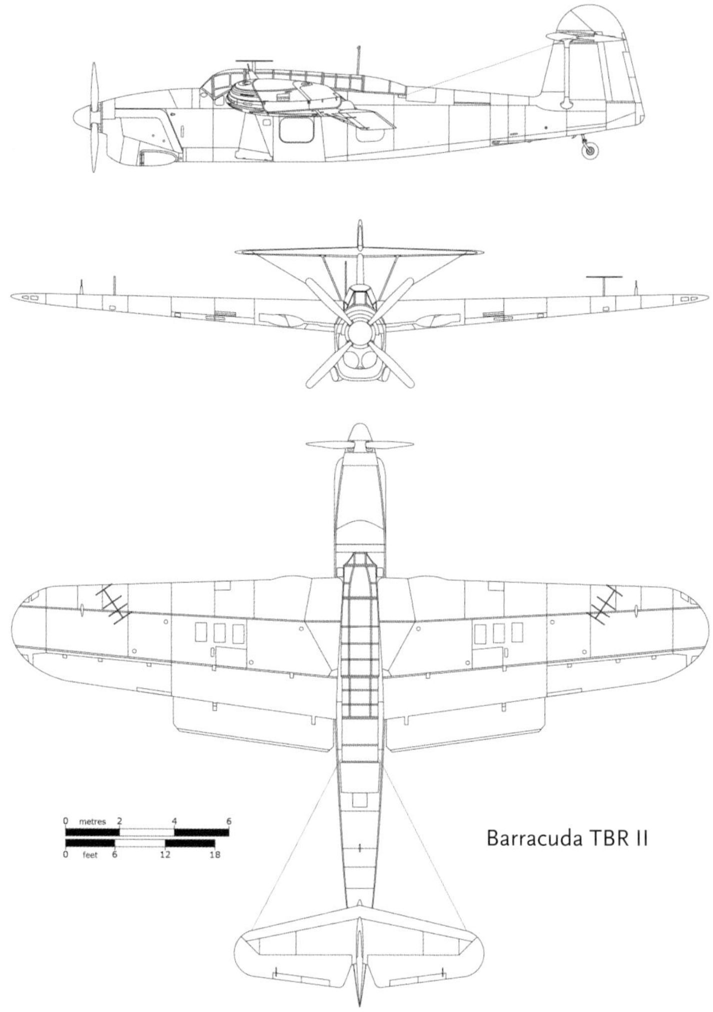

Barracuda TBR II

The first prototype Barracuda in 1940.

A development Barracuda being catapulted from *Victorious* in 1942.

There was a setback in September 1939 when Rolls-Royce ceased work on the Exe in order to concentrate on Merlin production and development and the design team had find an alternative. The Bristol Taurus and the American Wright Cyclone were considered but neither ran on the specified 100-octane avgas. Valve improvements to the Merlin allowed it to run on 100-octane fuel and the Barracuda was re-designed to take the 1,260hp Merlin 30 which had been modified for naval aircraft use but with the liquid coolant and associated radiator and plumbing, it was significantly heavier than the Exe and had a much higher drag factor. A further setback came in the summer of 1940 when the new MAP gave over-riding priority to a small number of RAF fighter and bomber types. It took the Admiralty until September to reinstate work on the TBR.

The first prototype Barracuda flew on 7 December 1940 and in its original form it demonstrated a maximum level speed of 240 knots clean and 220 knots at MTOW. The three crew members were housed under a continuous transparent canopy with separate access to the three positions. The observer's space amidships extended from the canopy to the bottom of the fuselage with his seat on the cabin floor and he had a wide field of view through 'bow windows' below the wing roots. The forward edge of his canopy was hinged to tilt upwards to act as a windshield for the instructor in a proposed dual-control version which was never produced. The undercarriage had an ingenious arrangement comprising an inverted L-shaped assembly pivoted near the bottom of the fuselage and raised or lowered by jack struts attached at the elbow. The base of each inverted L folded into the fuselage side with its fairing and the remainder of the leg, with its wheel and fairing, into wing wells. In this way a broad track was achieved without the necessity for oleos 9ft long retracting fully into the wing.

The specialised flaps were designed by Youngman and subsequently named after him. They were effectively independent aerofoils attached to the inboard trailing edge of each wing by two hinges and a hydraulic jack extension. Four positions could be selected by the pilot; zero incidence for normal cruising flight, a variable positive incidence for take-off and landing, 30 degrees of negative incidence to act as air-brakes in a dive and a folded position. The latter used the flap jack to fold the wing trailing edges inboard of the ailerons upwards and forwards over the mainplane to allow the wings to be folded aft about a hinge on the rear spar. The wings were folded manually, four men being required to unlock each wing, walk it aft and lock a spigot near the tip into a latch on the overlapping tailplane. Retractable hoops under each wing tip allowed men to reach the high-mounted wings and control them as they were moved.

Barracuda Mark II BV 733 was lent to the USN for evaluation in 1944 and is seen here at NAS Patuxent River.

A Barracuda Mark II with the early engine exhaust design.

Prototype evaluation revealed two major shortcomings; a lack of power which was to be remedied by the installation of a more powerful Merlin engine and the effect of the turbulent wake astern of the flaps when they were used as dive-brakes. This led to severe buffeting of the original low-set tailplane and moderate buffeting when they were set in the landing position. This was cured by fitting a taller fin with a high-set tailplane and delivery of the second prototype was delayed until this modification was completed. It was first flown in June 1941. In the meantime the first prototype was lent to 778 NAS to carry out carrier trials on *Victorious*. Afterwards it was returned to Fairey for modifications before being delivered to the A&AEE in October 1941. Unserviceability and the need for modifications delayed the completion of its trials until February 1942 by which time the installation of equipment that had not even existed when S.24/37 was written had increased MTOW from the 10,500lb specified to 14,100lb with a torpedo. Power had been an issue since the cancellation of the Exe but the Barracuda Mark I in operational condition was seriously under-powered. Take-off with the Merlin 30 driving a three-bladed propeller was excessively long and the climb was slow although, given time, 220 knots could still be reached. The first production Mark I flew in May 1942.

The Mark I's shortcomings led to only thirty being built and it was replaced in production by the Mark II with the more powerful Merlin 32 driving a four-bladed propeller. The prototype Mark II flew on 17 August 1942. By the end of 1941 there were already over 1,000 Barracudas on order from Fairey and a consortium of subcontractors including Blackburn, Boulton Paul and Westland. However, Westland's order was cancelled after only eighteen aircraft had been delivered in order to free the firm for Seafire production. Barracuda IIs were equipped with ASV IIN, a metric radar set with fixed yagi antennae mounted on the upper surfaces of the outer wings. It was an effective set for its day but suffered from bearing inaccuracy and poor discrimination between targets. The Barracuda was always intended to have a comprehensive communications fit including MF, HF and VHF sets but development of the latter was slow and the definitive fit was not achieved until 1944 with the British ARI 5206 HF W/T set and either an SCC 522 or AN/ARC-1 VHF R/T set. Both of the latter were made in the USA. Another new equipment in Barracudas was the Type AYD radio altimeter fitted in Mark IIs and IIIs from early 1944. It was intended to give an accurate height for night weapon releases in torpedo and anti-submarine attacks but it was never really trusted by pilots as it developed a reputation for accepting spurious signals. One pilot wrote that 'when the light came on you were as likely to be 100ft under water as 100ft in the air'.

In early 1944 Barracuda III production began with airframes interspersed on production lines with Mark IIs. The Mark III differed mainly in the installation of the British ASV X radar comprising a parabolic antenna in a blister-shaped radome under the after fuselage and its associated 'black boxes'. Later re-designated as ASV XI in December 1944, it was a centimetric set, designed for anti-submarine operations and was capable of detecting a surface vessel at 38nm and a submarine on the surface at 12nm. Both bearing accuracy and target discrimination were good. Mark IIIs could still carry a torpedo but maximum weight was 300lb greater than the Mark II because of the radar installation and the centre-of-gravity was close to the after limit. Barracudas had no front gun but the TAG had a single Vickers 0.303in K gun in early production aircraft, replaced by a twin-gun mounting in the majority. From 1944 the mounting was fitted with a gyro gunsight which allowed accurate deflection shooting. The guns had to be fired from a standing position with the TAG protected from the slipstream by an upward-tilting, hinged canopy but when it was extended, speed was reduced by 10 knots and it caused severe buffeting. This made an aircraft that was already heavy and under-powered even more difficult to handle, especially if the pilot was trying to evade a fighter. Most squadrons forbade the TAG from using the guns and developed 'corkscrew' evasive manoeuvres to confuse the aim of enemy fighters. In 1945 the guns and even the TAG and his seat were removed to reduce weight when Barracudas were deployed to the Far East in light fleet carriers.

The Barracuda's intended primary weapon was the Mark XIIB 18in torpedo which had to be dropped in level flight at 200 knots after a steep, diving approach. During the dive the pilot set his estimate of the target course and speed on the Type F torpedo director and on levelling out he aimed directly at the target for the final low-level run in. The computer adjusted the torpedo's course gyro to give it the correct track to intercept and hit. The weapon's flight in air after release was controlled by a wooden monoplane air tail which prevented roll and corrected pitch to give the ideal angle on water entry at about 180 knots. By the time the Barracuda entered service in 1943 there were very few targets suitable for torpedo attack left at sea in the Atlantic and only sixteen torpedo-armed sorties were flown. These attacked German convoys in the Norwegian littoral and proved very successful. The majority of strike operations used bombs and the six underwing hardpoints could carry weapons weighing up to a total of 1,500lb. To save weight there were only four hardpoints in the Mark III. In the Atlantic theatre three 500lb bombs were carried with two under the port wing and one under the starboard but the aircraft's performance was so degraded in tropical conditions east of Suez that that squadrons refused to accept the risk inherent in asymmetric take-off and substituted one 500lb and one 250lb under each wing. Six 250lb could be carried but the drag induced by this load reduced the type's radius of action so severely that no strikes were carried out in this configuration. In 1943 trials were carried out with the US 1,600lb armour-piercing bomb carried under the fuselage centreline. These proved successful and clearance to carry the weapon was given in December 1943 after aircraft were modified with local strengthening of the airframe around the suspension points. From early 1944 aircraft were modified on the production line.

Plans to give the Barracuda more power led to the Mark IV, a Mark II re-engined with a 1,850hp Roll-Royce Griffon engine. Initially no other changes were envisaged but after its first flight in November 1944 it was evident that extensive airframe modifications would be needed. The Mark IV was, therefore, passed over in favour of the Mark V designed from the outset to be flown by a crew of two, pilot and observer. Wingspan was increased by 4ft and the airframe had greater structural integrity. Fuel capacity was increased, the electrical system modified and a USN-supplied AN/APS-4 radar, known in the RN as an air/surface/homing set, ASH, was fitted in a pod in the leading edge of the port wing. The underwing bomb racks were reduced to two, each capable of carrying a 500lb bomb and there was a single Browning 0.5in front gun. The centreline rack was strengthened to carry a single 2,000lb AP bomb, two 500lb bombs or a torpedo. The first production Mark V flew in November 1945 and the last of only thirty was delivered in 1947; the majority of those on order having been cancelled. The last Barracuda Vs were powered by a single 2,020hp Rolls-Royce Griffon 37 which gave the type the power it had always needed despite a new MTOW 15,900lb with a torpedo. Maximum level speed was 240 knots.

Barracuda Mark II data

Length:	39ft 9in
Wingspan:	49ft 2in (17ft 9in folded)
Height:	14ft 9in
MTOW:	14,250lb
Engine:	One 1,640hp Rolls-Royce Merlin 32 liquid-cooled
Fuel:	Avgas. 228 gallons internal plus optional 116-gallon external tank on centreline crutches for long-range reconnaissance. Total 344 gallons
Performance:	Maximum level speed 210 knots Service ceiling 15,000ft with a torpedo. 6 minutes to 5,000ft with a torpedo
Armament:	Twin Vickers 0.303in K guns in after cockpit (removed in 1945). One torpedo, mine or 1,600lb AP bomb on centreline crutches. Up to three 500lb or six 250lb bombs or depth charges on six underwing hardpoints

Barracudas from *Victorious* on their way to attack *Tirpitz* in Kaa Fjord, 1944.

A Barracuda of 830 NAS taking-off from *Furious* to attack *Tirpitz* in 1944. Like the later 'ski-jump', the wooden ramp gave the effect of lengthening the deck available for the take-off run but in this instance the aircraft is airborne before reaching it.

Between 1940 and 1947 a total of 2,602 Barracudas were manufactured. Of these, 1,192 were built by Fairey, 700 by Blackburn, 692 by Boulton Paul and 18 by Westland. Orders for further aircraft from Blackburn and Boulton Paul were cancelled in 1945.

Barracudas equipped a number of TBR training squadrons and were available in large numbers from 1944 for use in the operational training, observer training, trials, development and fleet requirements roles from bases as far apart as the Orkney Islands, Ceylon, India and South Africa. The last examples were only retired in late 1953 although the majority of squadrons had been disbanded in 1945–6. Units in the 700 series wholly or partially equipped with Barracudas between 1942 and 1953 included 700, 703, 706, 707, 710, 711, 713, 714, 717, 719, 731, 733, 735, 736, 737, 739, 744, 747, 750, 753, 756, 764, 767, 768, 769, 774, 777, 778, 780, 783, 785, 786, 787, 796, 797, 798 and 799 NAS.

Between 1943 and 1953 Barracudas equipped a number of front-line squadrons. These included 810, 812, 814, 815, 816, 817, 818, 820, 821, 822, 823, 824, 826, 827, 828, 829, 830, 831, 837, 841 and 847 NAS.

They operated from the aircraft carriers *Atheling*, *Campania*, *Colossus*, *Formidable*, *Furious*, *Glory*, *Illustrious*, *Implacable*, *Indefatigable*, *Indomitable*, *Nairana*, *Puncher*, *Queen*, *Searcher*, *Smiter*, *Trumpeter*, *Unicorn*, *Venerable*, *Vengeance* and *Victorious*. Barracudas were also used by the Station Flight at Gosport post-war and by the ship's flights of *Vengeance*, *Indomitable* and *Implacable*.

827 NAS became the first operational Barracuda unit in September 1943, using a Fulmar for pilots to gain monoplane experience. Training was carried out on a mixture of Mark Is and IIs for 3 months, a period unfortunately marked by a series of accidents, many of them fatal, which gave the type a bad reputation from which it never entirely recovered. It had its faults but the first Barracuda pilots had gained their previous experience in biplanes with light wing loadings and their monoplane training had been limited and inadequately supervised. Apparently pilots who had been trained on monoplanes and never flown biplanes operationally found less problems with the aircraft than those who had converted from Swordfish and Albacores. In the latter high-speed stalls were unknown and course applications of rudder in a turn did not cause a flick into a spin. Spin recovery in a Barracuda was not difficult but required a considerable amount of height. When used as dive-brakes the Youngman flaps made the aircraft yaw to the right. In theory the rudder trimmer could be used to counter this but in practice the use of rudder with the dive brakes extended was forbidden as excessive sideslip could result in sudden departure from controlled flight. The elevator trimmer was so powerful that it could be used for the recovery from a steep dive but doing so could easily overstress the airframe and great care had to be taken in its use. Retraction of the dive-brakes was followed by a strong nose-down trim change several seconds later. The pilot had, therefore, to re-trim during a torpedo attack while levelling at 200ft, 220 knots and watching the movements of the target and the remainder of his formation while refining the settings on the Type F computer if necessary. Getting this wrong could be fatal and a significant number of trainee pilots were killed whilst carrying out practise attacks. Aware of this danger, the Admiralty sponsored the design and installation of

A Barracuda landing on *Vengeance* during 1945 in the perfect three-point attitude.

the first synthetic training system at Crail. Effectively this was a cockpit simulator within a cyclorama that used lighting effects and an analogue computer control system to allow pilots to practice attacks in the safety of a training facility ashore before practising them for real. It was a considerable success and others were installed at the TBR schools at Fearn and Ronaldsway.

The Barracuda had been designed from the outset for dive-bombing but the increased weight introduced in production Mark IIs meant that the front wing spar, wing-fold locks and the leading edge lacked the strength needed to cope with the higher loadings. Popped rivets were commonplace and there were examples of total wing failure before remedial modification action was taken. There was also weakness in the region of fuselage frame 25 and wrinkling of the monocoque fuselage aft of the cockpit was also frequent, giving early warning of structural failure. Engine bay fires were also among the Barracuda's early shortcomings, caused by the original exhaust system which used collector pipes recessed into the fuselage sides to take hot gasses from the engine exhaust ports to a low point where they were discharged to prevent pilots being blinded by exhaust flames at night. This was achieved but the downpipes were hot and passed close to hydraulic and fuel pipes. Barracudas were grounded on 16 May 1943 until more conventional replacement exhaust stubs were fitted to eliminate the risk.

Pilots found the cockpit comfortable with a good view and in the approach configuration it was a straightforward aircraft to deck land. The observer's cockpit was roomy with ample space for his chart board, notes, maps and Thermos flask. The view was good, as was access to the radar, radio and other controls. By standing on the longerons running under the side windows he could look out of the top canopy to guide the pilot in taking evasive action in combat with fighters. The TAG had a rotating seat facing forward to operate the W/T and aft for a visual surface search.

810 NAS benefitted from 827 NAS' conversion experience and its pilots underwent a supervised monoplane conversion course flying Miles Master trainers. It was the first squadron to take the Barracuda to sea, embarking in *Illustrious* for service with Force H in the Mediterranean in June 1943. With the surrender of the Italian Fleet some weeks later there were no torpedo targets left and most flying consisted of anti-submarine patrols. From the autumn of 1943 the Barracuda force expanded rapidly with as many as three new squadrons forming in some months. They were formed into wings of two squadrons each which trained together for set-piece strike operations.

The type's greatest successes were in the Norwegian littoral between February 1944 and February 1945. Five major attacks on the *Tirpitz* in Kaafjord began with Operation 'Tungsten' in April 1944 which severely damaged the German battleship with fourteen bomb hits. Later strikes found the defences better prepared with the target obscured by smoke. A total of 104 dive-bombing and 16 torpedo-armed attacks were carried out by Home Fleet Barracudas against shipping in Norwegian waters. These achieved outstanding results including fourteen ships sunk, a U-boat driven aground and seventeen ships severely damaged. Barracudas also took part in a number of mine laying strikes and the type's last operation with the Home Fleet was a successful mine lay off Stavanger by 821 NAS from *Puncher* on 22 February 1945. Barracudas operating from shore bases operated against German shipping off the Dutch coast from 1944 onwards. They became adept at hunting midget submarines with Mark IIIs carrying out radar searches and Mark IIs being directed into attacks which claimed one destroyed and at least three probables.

The performance of the Barracuda in tropical conditions deteriorated but the type operated from *Illustrious*, *Indomitable* and *Victorious* in the Eastern Fleet during 1944. They attacked a cement works at Indaroeng, an important rail centre at Sigli and Japanese

Barracudas on the dummy flight deck at East Haven in 1944 training flight-deck officers.

A B C D E F G H I J K L M N O P Q R S T U V W X Y Z

Barracuda Mark IIIs of 815 NAS from Eglinton after 1945. (Merv Green)

defences on the Nicobar Islands before being replaced in the fleet carriers by the more effective Grumman Avenger. In the last weeks of the war four light fleet carriers joined the BPF, each with a Barracuda squadron embarked together with Corsair fighters. Some of these flew patrols as Commonwealth forces re-occupied Rabaul, Northern Formosa and Hong Kong but by 1946 they were all replaced by Fireflies.

After 1945 Barracudas continued in use as observer training aircraft and for the development of anti-submarine tactics with the JASS at Londonderry. 815 NAS retained Barracuda Mark IIIs until May 1953 when the they were replaced by Grumman Avengers, the second time in a decade that Avengers had replaced Barracudas. Specification S.24/37 had been technically advanced when written but the Type 100's slow development and inadequate replacement engine meant that it missed its true generation and was condemned to mediocrity when compared to the Grumman Avenger designed 3 years later.

Firefly

Designed by a team under H S Chaplin to meet Specification N.8/39 for a fast, multi-role, two-seat monoplane fighter with a heavy front-gun armament, good load-carrying capability and reliable deck-landing characteristics, the Fairey submission was accepted by the Admiralty in early 1940 and the revised N.5/40, written around it. A mock-up was approved in June 1940, production drawings issued in November and the name Firefly chosen in December. There were no prototypes as such but the first four Mark 1s were built in the experimental department with production components. British mark numbers changed from Roman to Arabic numerals in 1947 and so, because Fireflies served for a decade after the change, Arabic numerals are used for consistency.

Youngman flaps retracted fully into the lower surface of the wing and extended from the ailerons to the fuselage centreline and A&AEE flying trials revealed that a Firefly with flaps at the take-off setting could out-turn a Spitfire. The wings were folded upwards and then backwards from the centre section around rear spar hinges to lie alongside the fuselage. In the Marks 1 to 4 this operation was manual and required

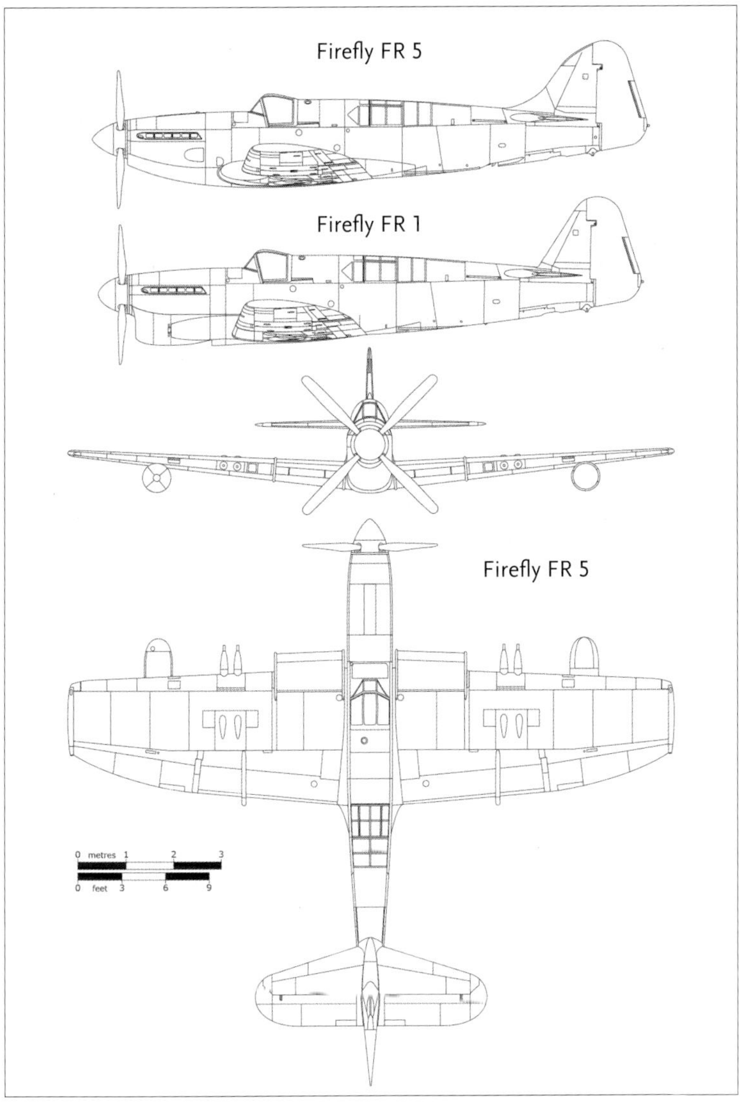

the efforts of a sizeable team of handlers. From the Mark 5 onwards power-folding was introduced and in both cases the locking pins were inserted hydraulically. The pilot's and observer's cockpits were separated by a self-sealing fuel tank and in the Marks 1 to 3 there were tanks in the centre-section leading edges. From the Mark 4 onwards radiators replaced fuel tanks in the centre section leading edges and fuel was carried in a fixed pod on the outer port wing. An equivalent pod on the starboard outer wing carried an ASH radar scanner and its electronics.

The first Firefly flew in December 1941 but the second was lost in June 1942 when the tail assembly collapsed at low altitude due to an elevator overbalance. Alterations were made to the design which included changes to rudder balance and the replacement of fabric-covered ailerons with metal and the third Firefly had them incorporated before carrying out deck-landing trials on *Illustrious* in the autumn. Early production aircraft had a shallow windscreen and a low-topped sliding hood which gave pilots little headroom. This proved unsatisfactory and the majority of Fireflies had deeper windscreens without wipers and revised hoods to give more headroom. The protruding cannon barrels were faired in and the original two-man dinghy in the rear fuselage was replaced by individual 'K'-type dinghies stored in the aircrew seat pans.

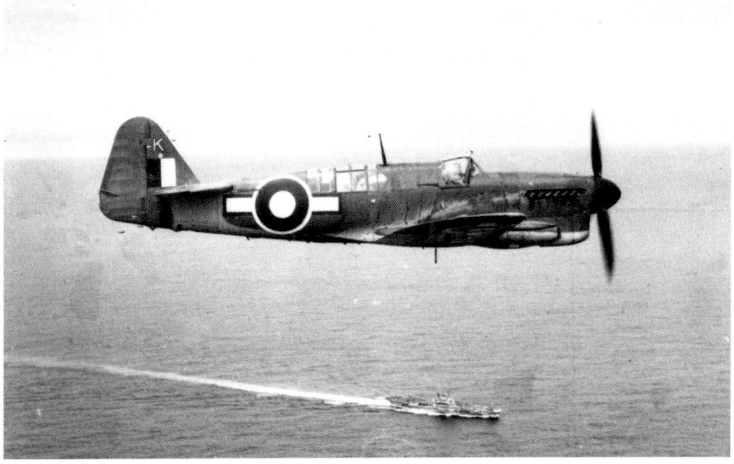

A Firefly Mark I in BPF markings

Different Firefly roles required different equipment fits for the observer, indicated by lettered designations prefixing the mark number. When an individual airframe had its role equipment changed the designator letters were changed. The F 1, a long-range day fighter, came first and when it was fitted with AN/APS-4 (ASH) surface-search radar in a centreline pod under the fuselage it became the FR 1. F 1As were F 1s modified to FR 1 standard. The night-fighter NF 2 was actually produced before the simpler NF 1 and had AI 10, ARI 5526, a British version of the American SCR-720 radar fitted in two pods close inboard on each side of the centre section of the wing. Although derived from the F 1, the NF 2 had significant differences caused by the weight of radar equipment in the rear cockpit which moved the centre of gravity beyond the basic airframe's after limit. To compensate, an 18in bay was inserted into the fuselage aft of the engine firewall and used to house radar equipment. NF 2s were to have been built in significant numbers but production ceased after only thirty-seven because sufficient AN/APS-4 radars were made available from the USN for them to be

A recently-completed Firefly Mark I.

Firefly FR 5s of 820 NAS disembarked to Hal Far from *Theseus*.

optimised in the air-to-air role as ARI 5607. This was carried in a centreline pod identical to the ASH in the FR 1. NF 1s were converted from FR 1s on the production line, accounting for 140 of the 376 built. The NF 2s were converted back into FR 1s from 1945. After 1945 a number of Mark 1s were converted into T 1 dual-control trainers with a raised second cockpit displacing the observer's cockpit. Although this gave them a distinctive appearance the changes were relatively superficial. The instructor in the rear cockpit had a good view ahead over the student in the normal front cockpit making this an ideal type for weapons training. The projected F 3 was a prototype derivative of the F 1 fitted with a more powerful Griffon engine that was never put into production.

Major changes were introduced from the Mark 4 which first appeared in 1945. It had a more powerful Griffon engine driving a four-bladed propeller and to reduce drag the radiators were moved from the 'chin' position under the engine to forward extensions of the wing centre-section. The wings were square-clipped and had fixed nacelles outboard; that on the port side containing fuel and that on the starboard side the radar scanner and its associated electronics. The principal variants were the FR 4 and NF 4, many of which were subsequently modified to TT 4 standard and used by FRUs to tow targets for both air-to-air and anti-aircraft gunnery practice. These had the winch and cable drum from which the target was deployed fitted under the centre section, controlled by an aircrewman in the rear seat. The T 3 was another trainer variant, without the raised rear cockpit, used for training observers in anti-submarine operations. The Mark 5 was a sub-variant of the Mark 4 and was produced in three versions, the FR 5 for daytime fighter reconnaissance missions, the NF 5 night fighter and the AS 5 for anti-submarine warfare search and strike. The first Firefly with power-folding wings was a Mark 5 delivered in January 1949. Aircraft in the AS role were wired to carry sonobuoys with equipment in the rear cockpit that enabled the observer to track the underwater contacts they detected. They could also carry 3in RP or depth charges. With no internal stowage, a mix of sonobuoys or weapons had to be carried on underwing hardpoints and Fireflies often operated in hunter/killer pairs with one loaded with sonobuoys flying in company with a weapon carrier. The T 5 was a derivative of the FR 5 converted by Fairey in Australia as dual-control trainers for the RAN. The AS 6 was a refined anti-submarine variant evolved from the AS 5 but with the 20mm cannons removed to save weight. Whereas the AS 5 had used USN sonobuoys and electronics, the AS 6 was equipped to use the latest British sonobuoys and their tracking equipment.

The AS 7, which first flew in 1951, was an anti-submarine variant with an enlarged rear cockpit covered by a distinctive bulged canopy to take both an observer and aircrewman with radar and sonobuoy displays. Specification M.101P covered the production of this variant which was intended to bridge the gap between the AS 6 as it became obsolescent and the Gannet. The Admiralty also hoped that it would be a useful aircraft for operation from light fleet carriers in the convoy escort role even after the Gannet entered service. This three-seat aircraft was powered by a 1,965hp Rolls-Royce Griffon 59 which required a reversion to the original 'chin' radiator. The AS 7 was thought of at first as a relatively simple development of the AS 6 but the added weight required a larger wing as well as a larger fin and rudder assembly to

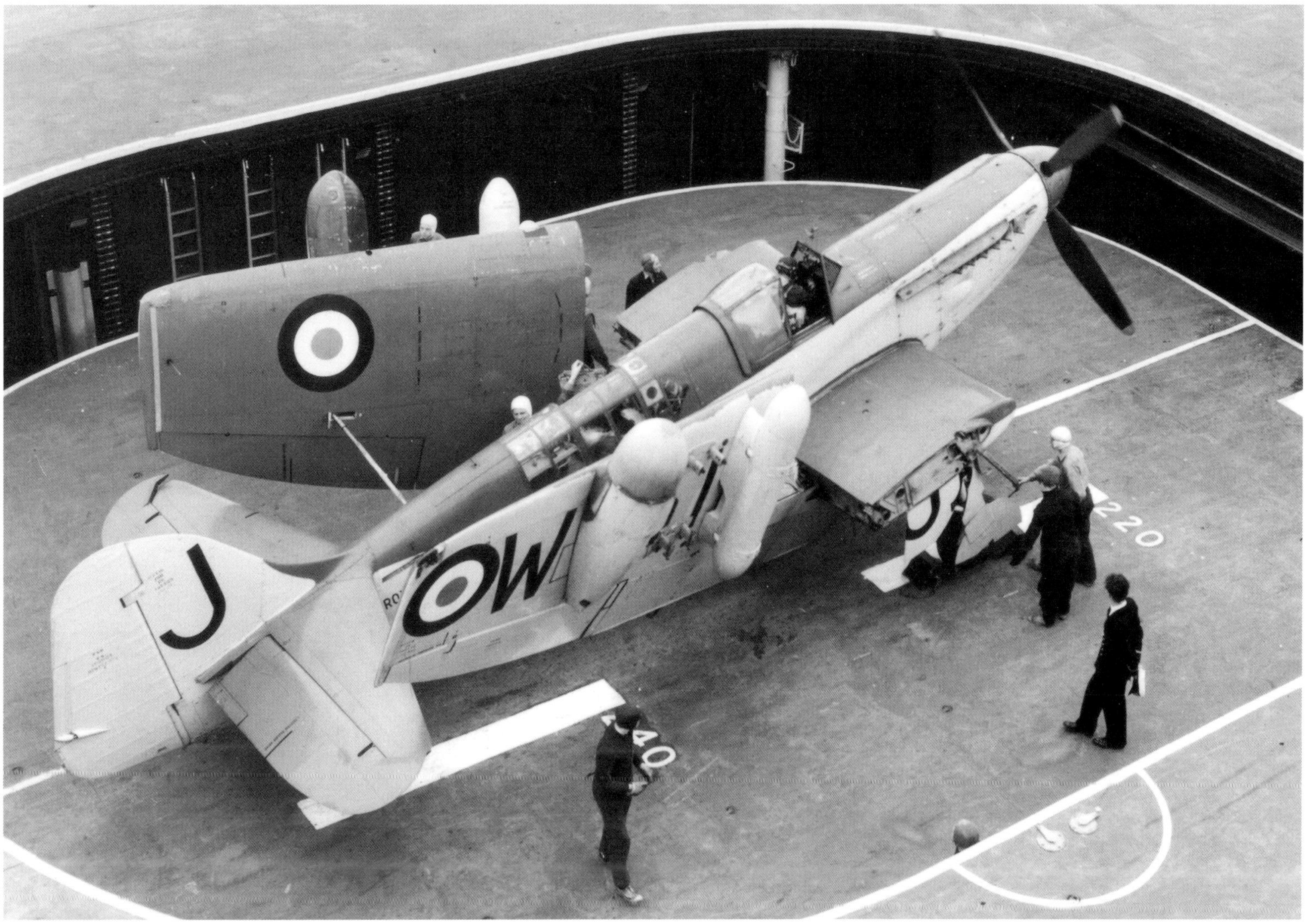

A Firefly AS 6 being raised on *Eagle*'s forward lift.

counteract the destabilising effect of the radiator. The prototype came off the production line in 1951 and flew in May. Production aircraft followed from October 1951 but the type was heavily criticised by the A&AEE for its poor low speed handling that would prevent it from deck landing successfully. Excess weight was another problem and the time gap before the Gannet's arrival was filled by extending the lives of AS 6s and using Avengers made available from the USN under MDAP. AS 7s saw only limited front line service and the majority were delivered as T 7s without deck-landing hooks for use in shore-based squadrons training observers and aircrewmen.

The last Fireflies to be built were thirty-four pilotless target drone derivatives of the Mark 7 designated U 8. A further six were modified from T 7s. They were used at both Llanbedr and Hal Far as targets for guided missile development firings. The first flew in 1953 and the last was delivered in March 1956. They could be radio controlled from a ground station but retained the capability to be flown by a conventional pilot when necessary for deployment or missile system tracking. An increased demand for unmanned missile targets in the 1950s led to forty FR 5s being modified to U 9 standard using the same control equipment as the U 8.

Firefly FR 5 data

Length:	27ft 11in
Wingspan:	41ft 2in (13ft 6in folded)
Height:	14ft 4in
MTOW:	16,096lb
Engine:	One 2,250hp Rolls-Royce Griffon 74 liquid-cooled
Fuel:	Avgas. 146 gallons internal plus 46 gallons in the port underwing pod. Two optional 90-gallon drop tanks on underwing hardpoints
Performance:	Maximum level speed 340 knots Service ceiling 28,400ft. 7 minutes to 10,000ft
Endurance:	Up to 6 hours
Armament:	Four 20mm Hispano cannons in wings with 160 rpg. Two 1,000lb or 500lb bombs on underwing hardpoints. Lighter underwing stations could carry up to eight 3in RP with 60lb warheads

Including prototypes Fairey built 740 Mark 1 variants and General Aircraft built 132. After 1946 Fairey built 591 Mark 4/5/6 variants and 185 Mark 7/8s.

Between 1943 and 1957 Fireflies equipped or partially equipped a large number of shore-based units in roles as diverse as operational,

A replacement Firefly FR 5 being craned onto *Glory* from *Unicorn* at Kure during the Korean War.

Firefly U 8.

A Firefly T 5 trainer in service with the RAN at Nowra.

Firefly AS 6s of 814 NAS in a storm range on *Eagle* in 1953.

conversion and deck-landing training, trials, development, electronic warfare and fleet requirements tasks including target-towing. Unmanned Fireflies were used as targets for guided missile firings in the UK and Malta until 1961. They included 700, 703, 706, 719, 727, 728B, 730, 731, 736, 737, 739, 741, 744, 746, 748, 750, 751, 764, 765, 766, 767, 768, 771, 772, 777, 778, 780, 781, 782, 783, 784, 787, 790, 792, 795, 796, 798 and 799 NAS.

Front-line units equipped with various marks of Firefly between 1943 and 1955 operated in the fighter reconnaissance, strike fighter, night fighter and anti-submarine roles. They included 805, 810, 812, 813, 814, 816, 820, 821, 822, 824, 825, 826, 827, 837, 1770, 1771, 1772, 1790, 1791 and 1792 NAS. A number of RNVR air squadrons numbered in the 1800-series operated Fireflies between 1947 and 1956. These included 1830, 1831, 1833, 1840, 1841 and 1844 NAS.

Between 1943 and 1954 Firefly squadrons embarked in the aircraft carriers *Albion*, *Campania*, *Eagle*, *Glory*, *Illustrious*, *Implacable*, *Indefatigable*, *Indomitable*, *Ocean*, *Premier*, *Ruler*, *Searcher*, *Theseus*, *Triumph*, *Venerable*, *Vengeance* and *Warrior*.

The first operational Firefly unit was 1770 NAS, commissioned in October 1943 and embarked in *Indefatigable* in July 1944 for operations against *Tirpitz* in the Norwegian littoral. 1771 NAS from *Implacable* was the first to locate and photograph *Tirpitz* in October 1944 after her move from Kaa Fjord to Tromso. They subsequently took part in several successful Home Fleet Attacks on enemy shipping off Norway before these two carriers sailed to join the BPF for operations against Japan.. Fireflies took part in the strategically important attacks on the Sumatran oil refineries including Palembang operating as both strike aircraft and escorts. Fireflies from 1771 NAS in *Implacable* struck at Japanese shipping in Truk Lagoon in the Carolina Islands in July 1945 and in August they were joined by 1772 NAS in *Indefatigable* for strikes against the Japanese mainland. The 1790-series NAS were night fighter units formed just too late to see action with the BPF.

After 1945 the first unit to re-equip with FR 4s was 810 NAS and the type equipped squadrons in nearly all the operational carriers in the

Firefly U 9 of 728B NAS being flown from Hal Far without a pilot, photographed from the shepherd aircraft.

Home, Mediterranean and Far East Fleets. With the run-down of the TBR force, Fireflies replaced Barracudas and other wartime types quickly and by the late 1940s the majority of RN air squadrons had them on strength. In June 1953 the Fleet Air Arm fly past over HM Queen Elizabeth II's Coronation Review at Spithead comprised thirty-seven naval squadrons of which seventeen flew Fireflies including one squadron from the RAN and three from the RNVR. Firefly squadrons served alongside Seafires and Sea Furies in the five British and Australian light fleet carriers that operated sequentially in support of UN operations during the Korean War from 1950 to 1953. The Boyd Trophy for 1952 was awarded jointly to 825 NAS with Firefly FR 5s and 802 NAS with Sea Fury FB 11s, both embarked in *Ocean*. Between them they had flown 123 combat sorties and dropped 90 tons of bombs in a single day and in a later period in action they flew 749 combat sorties in nine days. After Gannets entered service, Fireflies were soon withdrawn from the front line but continued in use with RNVR units and training squadrons until 1956.

Spearfish

By 1943 the Admiralty was aware that the Barracuda had missed its intended generation and was incapable of the long-range strike missions experience had shown to be necessary and so Admiralty Specification O.5/43 was issued for a replacement TBR unlimited by the restrictions imposed by the *Illustrious* class. It was intended for operation from the larger fleet carriers recommended by the FBC in 1942 with the MTOW increased to 30,000lb and a team led by H E Chaplin began design work after a development contract was signed in August 1943. He opted for a conventional layout powered by a single 2,600hp Bristol Centaurus radial engine driving a five-bladed Rotol variable-pitch propeller with a diameter of 14ft. Internal fuel was contained in two 183-gallon tanks in the wings with a further 43-gallon tank in the starboard wing. The equivalent position in the port wing was taken up by the engine oil cooler with its leading edge intake. The majority of its offensive weapons were to be carried in an internal bomb bay 18ft long to create less drag than the Barracuda. It was capable of carrying either a single British 18in or American 22.4in torpedo, a single mine, 1,600lb or 2,000lb bomb or four 500lb bombs as well as multi-flare dispensers. A single 180-gallon long-range fuel tank was an alternative bomb-bay load. Bombs were to be carried on ejector racks which would throw the bombs clear of the propeller arc when released in a steep diving attack. Sixteen 3in RPs were to be carried on zero-length launchers under the outer wings and there were two 0.5in Browning front guns, one in each outer wing. The Spearfish was also to have had

Spearfish prototype.

a Frazer-Nash 95 dorsal turret, controlled remotely by the observer, fitted with two 0.5in Brownings. ASV 15 radar was fitted in a retractable radome aft of the bomb bay to reduce drag in cruising flight but lowered for the radar to be operated.

Fairey-Youngman flaps covered 70 per cent of the wingspan, retracting fully into the lower wing when housed. The massive main undercarriage legs were hinged onto the wing centre-section, retracting outwards into the outer wing panels. Wing-folding was hydraulically powered with the outer wings turning to lie flush with the fuselage like those of the Firefly. When in manual control the flying surfaces felt stiff and lateral control was especially difficult and for this reason a servo-assisted control was incorporated which underwent continued development after 1945. Chaplin had hoped to incorporate pitch reversal of the enormous propeller disc as a means of keeping airspeed below 260 knots in a 70-degree dive-bombing attack but this proved difficult to achieve. There was airflow disturbance when the reverse-pitch setting was selected and it also had to be changed with extreme rapidity through the minimum torque angle to avoid over-speeding. These problems were never overcome and the idea was dropped. The pilot had a good view over the nose for deck landing and weapon aiming and the throttle quadrant was designed to give course engine control over the first two-thirds of movement for deck landing and very rapid acceleration to full power in the final third to cope with a wave-off.

Records do not show that Spearfish prototypes carried out carrier qualifications but 'Winkle' Brown and other pilots flew ADDLs which demonstrated that with development of the servo-assisted control system 'feedback' to the pilot's control column the type would have been a satisfactory deck-landing aircraft. However, the cancellation of the big *Malta* class carriers after the war left only the new light fleet carriers and existing *Illustrious* class fleet carriers and the new *Eagle* and *Ark Royal* were some years away from completion so the Admiralty decided to run the TBR force down to the minimum needed to keep skills alive. The Firebrand was closer to operational service, although it was less versatile, and the Spearfish was cancelled.

Spearfish data

Length:	44ft 7in
Wingspan:	60ft 3in (20ft folded)
Height:	13ft 6in
MTOW:	22,083lb
Engine:	One 2,600hp Bristol Centaurus, sleeve-valved radial
Fuel:	Avgas. 409 gallons internal plus optional 180-gallon bomb-bay tank
Performance:	Maximum level speed 260 knots Service ceiling 25,000ft. 8 minutes to 10,000ft
Endurance:	Over 5 hours
Armament:	One Frazer Nash 95 dorsal turret with two 0.5in Browning machine guns. Two Browning 0.5in machine guns in wings. Up to sixteen 3in RP under wings. Bomb bay could contain one British or American torpedo or mine or up to 2,000lb bombs and flares

Eight prototypes were ordered in 1944 of which six were completed and two cancelled. Orders for 150 production aircraft were cancelled in 1945.

The first prototype flew in July 1945 and the second in December. After 1945 Fairey continued to complete prototypes with the last delivered in 1947 for use in several test and development roles, not least to inform its Type Q project that became the Gannet. Several were used by the RN as hacks and the last of these remained in use with the carrier trials unit at Ford until 1952. Designed for carrier operations with an unusually high MTOW it proved valuable for testing new arresting gear. In 1948 one prototype was lent to Napier for artificial ice-accretion trials. The last prototype to be completed was never flown but used as a source of spare parts.

A modified Spearfish design was proposed to meet Specification O.21/44 and can be seen as a precursor of the Gannet in that it was to be powered by two engines in a single-engine configuration. Two Rolls-Royce Merlin engines were to be fitted in tandem driving independent co-axial three-bladed propellers. The forward engine was under the pilot's cockpit and the after one was between the pilot and observer's cockpits. Radiators for the two liquid-cooled engines were situated in the inner wing leading edges. Nothing came of the proposal, however.

Delta One

A design that never led to an operational fighter but which gives insight into Admiralty thinking. Kamikaze attacks on the BPF in 1945 stimulated the Admiralty to request a fighter that could be launched from vertical rails to provide a 'last-ditch' defence against enemy aircraft that had broken through the fleet's outer defences. Fairey's proposal opted for a delta wing because it was efficient at high angles of attack and came to be known as the Fairey Delta One, or FD-One. There were to be no flaps and, in the absence of a tailplane, elevator and aileron control were provided by combined surfaces known as elevons. These and the rudder were to be servo-powered but with a manual back-up. A 3,700lb Rolls-Royce Derwent 8 turbojet was selected as the main powerplant with rocket boosters. Calculations showed that the FD-One would reach a speed of 260 knots at an altitude of 1,320ft after a VTO with an initial acceleration of 3.16 g. Control during take-off and acceleration would have been maintained by swivelling jet-pipe nozzles developed by Rolls-Royce.

In July 1946 the MoS implemented a new government policy that prototypes considered dangerous, including the FD-One, could only be tested using pilotless scale models. This required the design of an unmanned, autonomous, half-scale replica of the FD-One powered by a rocket motor that could be ramp-launched. The complex flight-control system had to be capable of withstanding rapid acceleration during launch. A manned full-size version was to be developed in due course as an experimental aircraft but the Admiralty had opted for the Seaslug SAM rather than a manned fighter to meet the requirement.

The FD-One models had a wingspan of 10ft and were powered by a 1,800lb thrust Beta 1 bi-fuel engine. Launch was boosted by two 600lb-thrust cordite rockets. Control during launch was achieved by swivelling nozzles on the Beta exhaust; one acting laterally and the other vertically to correct errors in yaw and pitch. The behaviour of the model in flight was transmitted to a ground control station by telemetry. Unfortunately, initial acceleration toppled the autopilot gyros, the same problem encountered in pre-war pilotless target aircraft. Early launches from Aberporth resulted in the model rolling over and crashing immediately after launch. German V2 rocket systems were adapted to resolve this issue but telemetry systems proved unreliable and models were lost when it failed. Because of this limitation it was decided to keep flights within sight of the launch pad but this required levelling off and turning hard after a vertical climb when the model had barely gained flying speed. Some rolled over and dived into the sea when given these commands. The Beta engine used 80 per cent HTP as an oxidizer and methanol hydrazine which ignited spontaneously when mixed. The former was extremely corrosive and the model design had to keep the two liquids and their pumps reliably segregated and both tanks and plumbing had to be manufactured with high-grade stainless steel.

The Admiralty retained an interested in the FD-One as a technology demonstrator, however, and offered the LST *Suvla* as a launch platform. The first fully successful model launch was made from her in May 1949. There was still an element of danger from the fuel, however, and it was decided to continue the trials at the WRE Woomera in Australia. About forty FD-One models are believed to have flown successfully and they gave useful data about zero-length launches but this technology was not taken forward into operational capability. A single full-sized FD-One was built and flew in 1951. Peter Twiss, Fairey's chief test pilot, found it very difficult to fly except in calm conditions because of the small wing area and the relatively large rudder and elevon surfaces needed for adequate control at low speed in the original design concept of a ramp launch. It only ever flew conventionally.

Gannet

Fairey's Type Q, subsequently named Gannet, was designed to meet Admiralty Specification GR.17/45 for an anti-submarine aircraft with an enclosed bomb bay and radar housed in retractable radome. Twin-engines were to give reliability but a single-engine layout was desirable to prevent asymmetric control problems deck landing after a single engine failure. The design team led by H E Chaplin asked Armstrong Siddeley to help achieve this by coupling two of its new Mamba turboprops to drive co-axial propellers through a common gearbox and in December 1945 work started on what was to became the Double Mamba ASMD-1. This powerplant had the additional advantage that early turbine engines operated with greater efficiency at full throttle, therefore if half the Double Mamba was shut down in cruising flight, the other half could be run with greater efficiency. Another advantage was that the Double Mamba ran on kerosene,

The first Gannet prototype, VR 546, landing on *Illustrious* in July 1950.

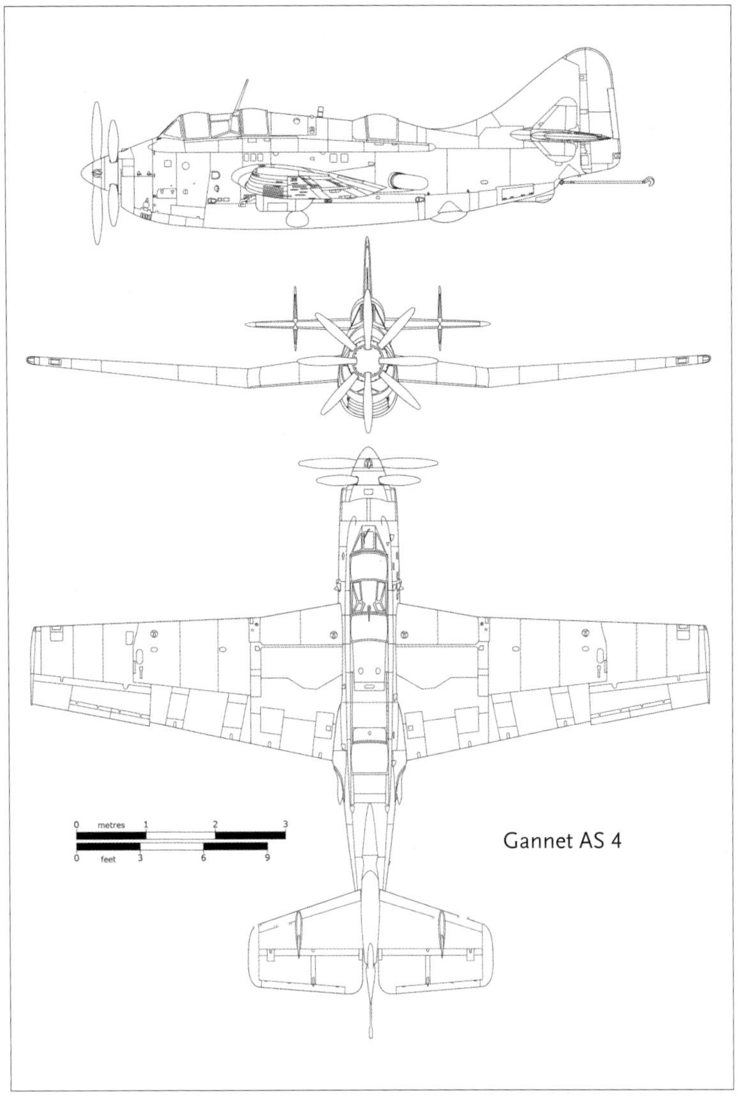

wide-cut turbine fuel or naval diesel fuel which did not require the separate carrier stowage arrangements needed for the more volatile avgas used by piston-engined aircraft.

A contract for two prototypes was awarded on 12 August 1946 and the first, VR 546, flew on 19 September 1949. The second flew in July 1950. Flight control problems led to some early development difficulties and their rectification took until March 1950 when an assessment was carried out by the naval pilots of 'C' Squadron A&AEE. Extensive ADDLs at Ford preceded deck-landing qualification and Lieutenant Commander G R Callingham RN landed VR 546 on *Illustrious* on 19 June 1950; the world's first deck landing by a turboprop-powered aircraft. By that afternoon twenty-five successful deck landings had been completed by Callingham, Lieutenant R Reynolds RN and Fairey's Peter Twiss, a former naval pilot. The Admiralty had amended the requirement in 1949 to introduce an enlarged bomb bay and a third crew position for an aircrewman to monitor sonobuoys and a third prototype was ordered in June 1949 to this standard. It first flew in May 1951. The third cockpit in this aircraft had a larger glazed area than production aircraft because of early uncertainty about whether the aircrewman should face forward or aft. Both positions were provided with the forward-facing one deleted when the aft facing option was selected. The first prototype was modified

Gannet AS 1s of 824 NAS in 1955.

with a dummy retractable radome for the ASV-19 radar moved aft to allow for the longer bomb bay and a metal shape resembling the third canopy for trials. Airflow changes caused by the extra cockpit led to the fitting of distinctive auxiliary fins above and below the tailplane at mid half-span positions. Further carrier qualification took place on *Eagle* during May 1952, with sixty-six successful landings.

In flight, a control unit maintained each engine at a constant 15,000 rpm; changes in propeller thrust were achieved by advancing the throttles to change their pitch. Response to throttle movement was rapid and this helped to make the Gannet a good deck-landing aircraft with maximum thrust available quickly in the event of a wave-off. If one engine failed, an electrically-operated reverse torque switch automatically coarsened its propeller pitch and the appropriate indicator on the pilot's instrument panel showed white. The feathering process was completed by the pilot moving the HP cock lever to the feather and brake setting and pressing the relight button. Either engine could be shut down and feathered in flight and it was usual to rotate them at hourly intervals on a long patrol. All turboprop aircraft run the potential risk of a propeller control unit malfunction fining-off the blades in flight to an angle that would effectively form a flat plate, increasing drag dramatically to the extent that the aircraft would descend rapidly and irrecoverably. To guard against this the Gannet had two fine pitch stops for each propeller. The first was fixed at 6 degrees

Gannet AS 1s of 812 NAS embarked in *Eagle*.

and the second was a removable flight fine pitch stop set at 21 degrees. The latter was automatically withdrawn when the undercarriage was selected down, allowing the propeller to rotate at constant speed with a low power setting on the approach and to take up the fully fine position for ground idling and starting. It re-engaged automatically when the undercarriage was selected up. In anti-submarine and training Gannets the port engine drove the front propeller and the starboard engine the rear. Either engine could be started on deck by a twin-breech cartridge starter with the pushbutton control unit on the pilot's starboard console panel. A spare cartridge was stowed in each main wheel well in case of a landing at a diversion airfield other than a naval air station. After either engine was started it was run up to full power to windmill start the second engine and this was the technique used to re-start engines that had been shut down in flight.

The Gannet's primary sensor was the ASV-19 radar monitored by the observer which could detect snorkels and periscopes at short ranges. Fully submerged targets were tracked by sonobuoys monitored by the aircrewman in the rear cockpit. Two different types of sonobuoy were used, the omni-directional T.1945 and the directional T.1946. Omi-directional buoys were used to gain initial contact with a search 'barrier' and the approximate range of a contact could be estimated from its sound

Gannet AS 4 of 814 NAS with its ASV-19B radome lowered in 1957.

Gannet T 5 of 849HQ Flight at Lossiemouth. It is on an instrument-training sortie with the centre cockpit canopy 'clouded' by metal polish so that its occupant cannot see out and has to fly on instruments throughout the sortie.

level. Directional sonobuoys gave a bearing of their contact and two or more bearings would give a cross-cut to indicate the actual position of a dived submarine with sufficient accuracy to attack it with a homing torpedo. Depth charges or RPs were intended for attacks on submarines on the surface, snorkelling or in the act of diving. At night flares could be dropped so that a submarine on the surface could be seen sufficiently well for a visual depth-charge or RP attack. The advent of nuclear submarines from the mid-1950s made surface contact far less likely.

The Gannet's bomb bay was 17ft long with sufficient capacity for a range of weapons. These could be tailored for a specific mission or make use of standardised load-outs. Load 1(b), for instance, was intended for the location and attack on dived submarines and comprised two Mark 30 acoustic homing torpedoes, five T.1946 directional sonobuoys in the bomb bay and a further twelve T.1945 omni-directional sonobuoys under the wings. Up to six marine markers were carried on the inside of the bomb-bay doors. Load 2 included six 250lb Mark 11* depth charges and sonobuoys for attacks on schnorkelling submarines. Other standardised load-outs included combinations of torpedoes, depth charges and RPs, the latter carried under the wings. The Gannet was a good anti-submarine aircraft when it entered service; it was also capable of attacking enemy surface vessels at night or in adverse weather. In this role the bomb bay could carry up to four mines, depending on type and mark, a single 2,000lb bomb, two 1,000lb or four 500lb bombs. Release parameters for the 500lb bombs in operational load 7 were up to 300 knots in a 50-degree dive. For long-range reconnaissance missions two 81-gallon fuel tanks could be carried in the bomb bay. Underwing hardpoints could carry 1,000lb or 500lb bombs or 100-gallon drop tanks, and either sixteen Mark 8 or twenty-four Mark 5 RPs could be carried on zero length launcher rails under the wings. An alternative store was a G-Dropper containing a dinghy and other equipment that could be dropped to help survivors in the water on an SAR mission.

The need to replace the Firefly AS 6 was regarded as critical after the outbreak of the Korean War and a 'super-priority' order for 100 Gannet AS 1s was placed in March 1951. The first production aircraft flew in June 1953 and the third carried out deck-landing clearance trials, including night deck landings, on both *Illustrious* and *Eagle* in October. Other production aircraft were used for engine, radar and weapons system development. Continuous engine development led to the more powerful Double Mamba 101 which replaced the 100 in the AS 4 and T 5.

A training variant, designated T 2, was manufactured in small numbers by modifying AS 1 airframes on the production line and first flew in August 1954. The front two cockpits had dual controls with a periscope to give the instructor in the second cockpit a view directly ahead. The ASV-19 radar was deleted but the bomb bay could still be used for weapons training and RPs could be fitted under the wings. Two seats, one above the other, were fitted to carry passengers in the rear cockpit but I never heard of anyone brave enough to sit in the bottom one since baling out in case of an emergency would require the occupant of the upper seat to get out first, having folded his seat back before jumping. Weapon sights were provided in both the student and instructor cockpits so that the T 2 could be used for advanced weapon training. For instrument-flying training sorties and standardisation checks the pilot flying on instruments flew in the rear cockpit with a safety pilot in the front cockpit. The rear cockpit canopy and windscreen were made opaque with brass cleaner by the ground crew before the flight so that the pilot flying on instruments could not see out. The practice left one with a distinct association between brass cleaner and instrument check sorties. A few T 5s remained in service for Gannet AEW 3 pilot training and standardisation until 1978.

A small number of AS 4s were upgraded with electronic warfare systems, improved communications and radar to AS 6 standard in 1961 for use in the SIGINT and EW roles with 831 NAS. These were often, but incorrectly, referred to as ECM 6s. Others were modified to COD 4 standard operating as a single aircraft with Gannet AEW 3 flights in carriers to ferry mail, passengers and urgent spare parts to the ships while they were at sea anywhere in the world.

Gannet AS 4 data

Length:	44ft 6in
Wingspan:	54ft 4in (19ft 6in folded)
Height:	13ft 9in (16ft 9in folded)
MTOW:	21,600lb with operational load 1(b)
Engine:	One 3,035hp Armstrong Siddeley Double Mamba 101
Fuel:	Avcat. 463 gallons internal plus optional 162 gallons in bomb bay and two optional 100-gallon underwing drop tanks
Performance:	Maximum speed in level flight 275 knots Service ceiling 25,000ft. 5 minutes to 10,000ft
Endurance:	Up to 4 hours using single engine cruise on internal fuel
Armament:	Mark 30 torpedoes, Mark 11* depth charges, 2,000lb/1,000lb or 500lb bombs, 3in RP, marine markers in various combinations up to 2,000lb in bomb bay and on under wing rails and hardpoints

Gannet COD 4 of 849HQ Flight about to be launched from *Ark Royal*'s bow catapult.

A total of 352 Gannets were manufactured in AS 1, T 2, AS 4 and T5 variants. A number of AS 1s were converted to AS 4 and T 2 standard; six AS 4s were converted to COD 4 standard and nine AS 4s were converted to AS 6 standard.

Between 1954 and 1961 Gannets were operated as all or part of a number of shore-based squadrons including 700, 703, 703X, 719, 728, 737, 744 and 796 NAS. They were used in the training, trials and air-sea warfare development roles as well as fleet requirements tasks. Gannets also operated as part of the station flights at Abbotsinch, Anthorn, Culdrose, Eglinton, Ford and Yeovilton during the same period.

Operational squadrons equipped with Gannets in the 800-series included 810, 812, 814, 815, 820, 824, 825, 826, 831, 847 and 849 NAS embarked in the aircraft carriers *Albion*, *Ark Royal*, *Bulwark*, *Centaur* and *Eagle* for periods between 1955 and 1960. AS 6s of 831 NAS were based ashore until 1966 but embarked detachments in carriers for exercises and 849 NAS used a variety of AS 4, COD 4 and T 5 variants as training, utility and COD aircraft until 1978.

The first RN unit to receive Gannets was the IFTU, 703X NAS, in March 1954 at Ford and the first operational unit was 826 NAS at Lee-on-Solent in January 1955, replacing Firefly AS 6s. Gannet AS 1s and 4s formed the core of the Fleet Air Arm's embarked anti-submarine force in the mid-1950s and served in all the operational carriers from 1955. They took part in a number of exercises in the Home, Mediterranean and Far East Fleets during which they countered the threat from the growing Soviet submarine fleet but were not used in combat. 847 NAS, formed in 1956, operated from Nicosia in Cyprus flying surface-search patrols around the island seeking out vessels attempting to land people or weapons in support of Greek Cypriot terrorists. It returned to the UK to disband in 1959. 831 NAS' electronic warfare detachments often embarked in carriers and the AS 6 updated radar capability allowed jamming targets to be located accurately so that the maximum power could be aimed at them. They had a realistic offensive jamming capability with equipment carried in the bomb bay and on the underwing hardpoints. There were few external differences from the AS 4 other than extra aerial masts but internally they incorporated extensive rewiring, new equipment and an enhanced communications fit that gave them an operational SIGINT capability. Their deployments were always felt to have an air of secrecy about them. The last operational Gannet anti-submarine unit was 810 NAS in *Centaur* which filled a gap while difficulties with the Westland Whirlwind helicopter were rectified. It disbanded in 1960.

Gannet AS 6 of 831 NAS at Hal Far.

The anti-submarine Gannet was withdrawn from service prematurely for several reasons but the main one was the success of trials with Sikorsky/Whirlwind HAS 22 in 1955. Helicopters with active dipping sonar were a better anti-submarine platform for the close-in defence of a carrier task force or convoy against fast conventional submarines and they were agreed to have greater potential for countering nuclear-powered submarines in the future. Gannet production was curtailed; it is difficult to determine the exact number of airframes that were cancelled because some incomplete airframes and components were used to complete aircraft for export to Indonesia but the probable total is nine. For some unfathomable reason, the less capable Short Seamew was left in development and production for another two years. The only task for which fixed-wing aircraft were still superior was surface search over a large or distant area but this could be undertaken as well or better by the AEW aircraft in carrier air groups. The Admiralty therefore accepted a gradual replacement of Gannets in front-line squadrons by Whirlwinds from 1957. The transition was to be complete by the early 1960s when the more capable Wessex was due to enter service. The possibility of operating support carriers, CVS, equipped mainly with anti-submarine aircraft like the older *Essex* class carriers in the USN was considered by the Admiralty but rejected as being too expensive. The decision was taken, therefore, to concentrate anti-submarine aircraft within balanced air groups embarked in the remaining operational carriers, a decision that reflected the fact that the retention of fixed-wing A/S aircraft in addition to helicopters was a capability the RN could not afford, however good the Gannet AS 4 proved to be in service. Gannets were exported to Australia, Germany and Indonesia.

Gannet AEW 3

Early in the Gannet's development, the Admiralty decided to order a modified version as a radar-equipped Skyraider replacement. The designation AEW 3 was reserved for it following in sequence after the AS 1 and T 2 and development work was authorised by Admiralty Directive AEW 154. However, it soon became clear that considerable redesign was needed and the only components that were eventually common between the Gannet AS 1 and the AEW 3 were the outer wing sections. Everything else was to a new design and the Admiralty considered giving the AEW variant a different name but when the decision was taken in 1957 to take the AS variant out of service early, any confusion between the two variants was believed to have been resolved and the name Gannet was retained. The Admiralty required the two observers to sit side by side as they did in the Skyraider and so the original rear cockpits, the ASV-19 radar and bomb bay were deleted and a new, longer and heavier fuselage designed. It was calculated that MTOW would be 5,000lb greater than the AS 1 and so an improved Double Mamba 112 was developed from 1956. Flying trials with the new powerplant were carried out in a modified AS 1. To withstand the impact of deck landing at higher weight new and more robust oleos were designed and these had to be longer than those of the AS 4 to give adequate clearance for the radome located under the fuselage. These in turn required different cut-outs to accommodate them in the inner wing sections when they were retracted and different undercarriage doors. The new fuselage was a foot longer than that of the AS 1 and, together with the weight of the installed avionics, this changed the position of the centre of gravity and so the leading edges of the inner wings were straightened to compensate. The jet exhausts in the AS 1 had run inside the fuselage over the bomb bay to exhaust aft of the wing training edge but this was not acceptable in the AEW 3 because of the observers' seating and the equipment tightly packed into the confined space. In the AEW 3 the engine mounting was larger and shortened jet pipes led from the rear of the engines to exhaust under the inner wing leading edges. They added about 500lb to the thrust from the propellers and improved control at carrier approach speeds. The tailfin was bigger and taller than in the AS 1 to improve stability in yaw and the deck hook was strengthened to cope with the increased weight. The whole structure of the AEW 3 was both bigger and heavier, something pilots who had done their conversion training in the T 2/5 noticed as soon as they climbed up the side into the lofty cockpit. Another difference was that the front propeller was turned by the starboard engine, not the port as in the T 5, so that pilots had to re-learn the rudder reactions to counteract propeller torque that they had practiced so carefully in the trainer. Nobody has ever been able to give me an engineering explanation of why this change was necessary.

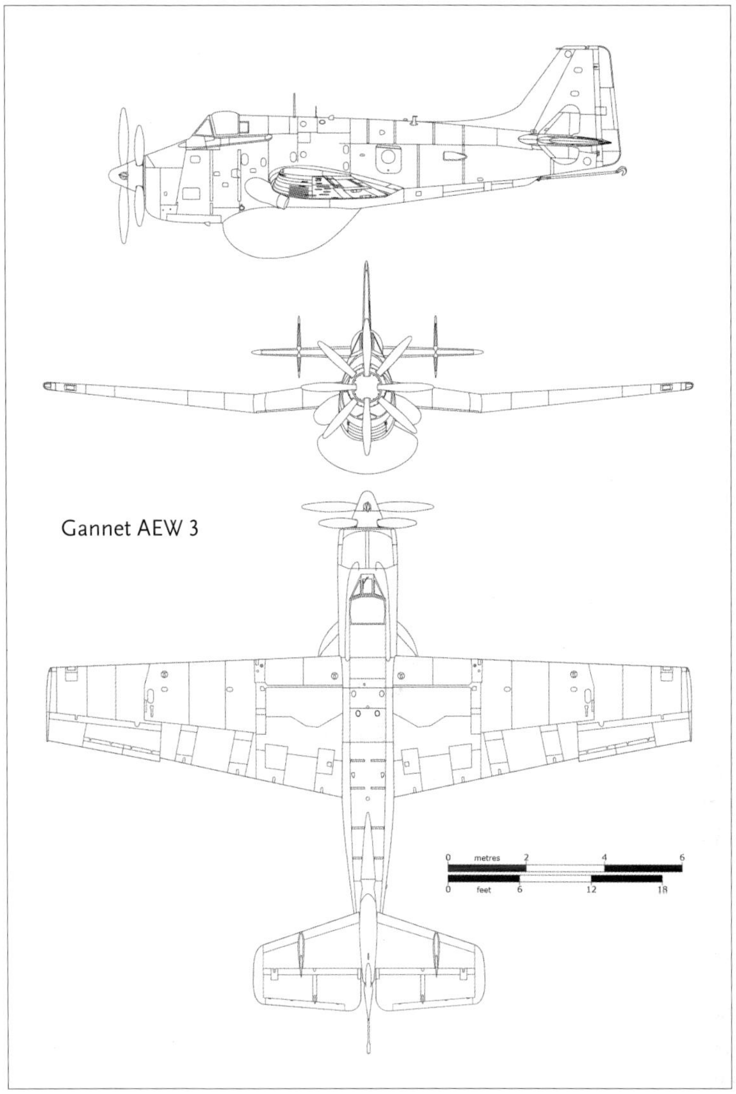

Gannet AEW 3

A Gannet AEW 3 of 849HQ Flight.

The AEW 3 was the last example of Fairey's envelope jigging system in which the fuselage was built inwards. Special templates were manufactured to give the exact shape of the stressed-skin fuselage

A Gannet AEW 3 of 849B Flight about to be launched from *Ark Royal*'s waist catapult.

plating and once the skin was in place the interior was assembled within it and, eventually, the two halves were accurately mated. The system gave better control of external finish and easier access to equipment during construction. The main internal fuel tank was aft of the pilot's cockpit and there were wing tanks in the centre sections. Normal refuelling was by pressure hose with a connection in the right wheel well. Gravity refuelling of the main tank was possible via a filler cap on top of the fuselage but no other tanks could be filled in this way. The AEW 3 carried no weapons but two optional drop tanks could be carried on underwing hardpoints and there was a small fuselage bay aft of the wings controlled by the observers that could carry flares and markers. In addition to the drop tanks the underwing hardpoints could carry Palouste starter pods, G-droppers or baggage pods.

The Gannet AEW 3 was a sophisticated aircraft and the observers fulfilled a range of tasks including air and surface search, fighter and strike aircraft control, communications relay and over-the-horizon targeting, often concurrently. The primary sensor was AN/APS-20F radar procured from the USN, an improved version of the radar fitted in the Skyraider. The radar picture interpreted by the observers could also be transmitted to the carrier's AN/SRR-4 receiver using the AN/ART-28 'Bellhop' data link. An IFF system comprising an AN/APX-6 transponder unit and an AN/APX-7 interrogator unit worked in conjunction with the radar. The ARI 5885 Blue Silk doppler navigation system provided accurate measurements of ground speed and drift angle. These combined with airspeed and heading from the GM4B compass system to allow accurate navigation from the briefed launch position and were fed into the GPI Mark 5 ground position indicator to provide the radar with ground stabilisation.

The observers were separated from the pilot's cockpit by the main fuel tank and they entered through upward-opening hatches on either side of the fuselage level with the wing trailing edges. The mission commander sat on the left with a less-experienced colleague on his right. Both were presented with radar range and azimuth data together with IFF interrogation responses on north-stabilised 7in PPIs with numerous other controls and circuit breakers spread around their working space. Communications comprised two ARC-52 multi-channel UHF transmit/receive units with one control in the pilot's cockpit and one in the rear. Both could be used simultaneously. The single ARI 18032 HF radio had its control unit in the rear cockpit; it was later replaced by a Collins 618T-3 HF single sideband radio as part of an aircraft upgrade. The AEW 3 was also fitted with TACAN which gave the range and bearing of a selected beacon; it worked on UHF and was, therefore, line-of-sight but with the aircraft at altitude the parent carrier's beacon could be tracked for much of an AEW sortie. The AN/APS-20F was a pulse radar with an output of 2.5 megawatts and the aerial was capable of 360 degree search in a clockwise rotation of 2, 4, 6 or 15 rpm. It had provision for sector scanning between 15 and 75 degrees and a tilt gyro-stabilisation unit compensated for the aircraft's pitch and roll up to a maximum of 15 degrees from the horizontal.

Gannet AEW 3 data

Length:	44ft
Wingspan:	54ft 7in (20ft folded)
Height:	16ft 9in
MTOW:	26,000lb
Engines:	One Double Mamba 112 with each unit rated at 1,850shp Total with both units running 3,700shp
Fuel:	Avcat. 613 gallons internal plus one or two optional 100-gallon underwing drop tanks. Total 813 gallons with two drop tanks
Performance:	Maximum level speed 280 knots Service ceiling 20,000ft. 10 minutes to 10,000ft
Endurance:	4 hours on internal fuel flying single-engine barrier patrols
Armament:	None

Including the single prototype, a total of forty-four Gannet AEW 3s were produced for the RN between 1958 and 1963.

Gannet AEW 3s only served with two units, 700G Flight, the IFTU, and 849 NAS. Although listed as a single squadron, 849 NAS could better be described as a wing of five autonomous flights, each effectively a squadron in its own right. These were 849HQ Flight which was responsible for AEW training and tactical development shore-based at Culdrose, then Brawdy and latterly Lossiemouth. The units that embarked in carriers were 849A, B, C and D Flights. 700G Flight received its first aircraft in August 1959 and was re-designated as 849A Flight on 1 February 1960 after its four aircraft had flown 1,855 hours in 5 months.

Initial carrier qualification trials were carried out in *Centaur* during November 1958 and between 1960 and 1978 Gannet AEW 3s operated from the aircraft carriers *Ark Royal*, *Eagle*, *Victorious*, *Hermes* and *Centaur* in the Home, Mediterranean and Far East Fleets.

Gannet AEW 3s operated throughout the latter part of the Cold War and this involved a number of major national, Commonwealth and international exercises but no conflict. Two examples of the type's operational capability give an idea of its capabilities. In 1966 Gannets from C Flight in *Ark Royal* and then D Flight in *Eagle* carried out non-stop surface surveillance operations between March and April as part of the Beira Patrol supporting the UN sanctions against oil shipments to Rhodesia through the port of Mozambique. They located every ship in the area and guided other aircraft to identify them without a single break. In 1972 *Ark Royal* launched two Buccaneers from a position in mid-Atlantic to show a presence over what was then British Honduras when it was threatened by invasion from Guatemala. They were refuelled on the outbound leg by other Buccaneers and a final refuelling, again from Buccaneers, was vital to give the returning aircraft sufficient fuel to reach the carrier at the end of a 2,530nm round trip including 10 minutes making themselves very obvious over the capital, Belize City. They were guided to the rendezvous by the crew of a Gannet that made sure that the precisely-timed interception went without a hitch and sufficient fuel was transferred.

The fundamental importance of embarked AEW aircraft was overshadowed by the debates about the future of the RN that led to the politically inept decision to run down the carrier force from 1966. Gannets were finally withdrawn from service in 1978 when *Ark Royal* paid off despite the fact that big-deck ships including *Hermes* which were capable of operating them were retained in service. *Hermes* had her catapults and arrester wires removed after 1971 and the AN/APS-20 radar systems were removed from Gannets and installed in geriatric RAF Shackletons. These were declared by the government of the time to be capable of the tactical air support of maritime operations but like other RAF aircraft allocated to the role they sat on the ground uselessly while the South Atlantic War to liberate the Falkland Islands was fought by the RN without AEW cover thousands of miles away.

The AEW 3 was an interesting aircraft to fly and had more than its share of eccentricities. I flew with Peter Flutter for many hundreds of hours and he provided me with an excellent description of what it was like from the observers' perspective. The rear cabin could be described as cosy or cramped and claustrophobic depending on the size of the person you shared it with. Two observers were physically separated from the pilot by the main fuel tank amongst other things,

A Gannet AEW 3 of 849B Flight launched from *Ark Royal*'s bow catapult.

Wheels down, flaps down, hook down; a Gannet AEW 3 landing on *Ark Royal*.

preventing physical interaction in the event of an intercom failure. However, if one of the observers unstrapped and reached up he could reach the rudder control rods passing through the cabin to enable synchronised conversation with each of the pilot's feet. He could then respond with a potentially lively yaw-inducing dialogue. Bubble windows offered a fleeting view from the cabin of the world outside, only to be zipped shut once airborne to provide a blackout for a radar view of the same world. Darkened up, the rear cabin was an in-the-womb experience of twins but with fairy lights. Lots of lights, glowing and blinking with both observers encircled by valve-driven analogue black boxes, not just in front but around and behind them. Altitude is the enabler for radar horizon and in this unpressurised aircraft the crew were provided with oxygen supplied through a mask worn throughout the sortie. The pilot's underwater-ejection seat limited the AEW 3's ceiling to 20,000ft and at this altitude the cabin definitely got chilly. The solution was four fan heaters, two in the deckhead and two under the observer's seats. These had advantages and disadvantages; they provided warmth but had a propensity to catch fire. Once unserviceable they had a tendency to be left in this state, so warm 'bunny suits' under the immersion suit were essential when carrying out a high-level surface search.

The essence of the observers' job lay in a 7in glass PPI mounted in front of their faces. Each looked at the world through one of these portals which, at its maximum, compressed over 125,000 square miles into the size of a side plate. The radar was both north and ground stabilised to provide an intuitive map of any coastline accompanied by a myriad of what appeared to be grains of rice but which were in reality returns from shipping. Buried in amongst the rice were aircraft which needed a trained eye to spot in the AEW role. Critical to this was the ubiquitous chinagraph grease pencil which permitted relative movement to be marked and tracks developed allowing intercepts with jets to be achieved. The radar scanner rotated six times a minute to give a 10-second update rate. In reality the return on an aircraft was seldom that reliable, with a 1 in 6 blip/scan ratio not uncommon, allowing an update every minute. An AEW observer therefore had to become good at dead reckoning with a capacity to sound confident when directing a jet sometimes based on near data-free analysis. The other feature of the Gannet's pulse radar was an impenetrable disc of sea return which surrounded its own aircraft origin. The size of this disc increased with sea state and altitude. In practice this gave an annulus of detection outside the sea return before the target disappeared into clutter. Keeping the target outside the clutter required quick control of the Gannet's altitude to reduce the radius of sea return whilst maintaining the target

Gannet AEW 3 of 849B Flight about to take a wire on *Ark Royal*.

Gannet AEW 3s of 849D Flight. Both are flying on one engine with the other propeller feathered. 071 has the port engine (rear prop) shut down; 072 has the starboard engine (front prop) shut down.

in the detection annulus. On windy days this could involve descending to relatively low level with a good pilot anticipating the need to get the aircraft at the right height.

A good pilot was the observers' main obsession when operating from a carrier. A nuance to the uninitiated junior right-hand seat observer was being hit in the throat by the unrestrained chart table as the aircraft accelerated down the catapult. Once that first launch was over, the now-wiser observer learned to keep a hand out to parry the blow. Some cabin activities required unstrapping and kneeling on the seat; access to the Bellhop video relay controls was one of these since they were situated behind the observers' seats. This provided the radar picture to the ship's operations room and, once all indications were good in the aircraft, the observers' war cry of 'fingers green how does my garden grow?' was transmitted to the ship. Many dubious horticultural responses were then possible. An even more acrobatic procedure of almost mythical repute was a potential requirement to tune the magnetron crystals, a maintenance procedure which could, allegedly, be attempted in flight. This required the left-hand seat observer to unstrap and invert himself in the seat to access a hatch in the floor of the aircraft. Only the most obsessive and agile would attempt this manoeuvre.

Having got the aircraft back safely for its planned recovery time, no mean achievement in conditions of radio silence when the ship was inevitably not where it was briefed to be, the observers took a huge leap of faith and put their trust in the pilot and fate. Unlike the passengers in an airliner, the observer was presented with enough information to get worried. For a start he could hear the pilot's breathing and increasingly crisp calls from the LSO indicating that some urgent correction was required. Above all though, eyes were glued to the ASI and ears tuned to the audio ASI. The doom-laden lower tone was a cause for concern with the observers acutely aware that, even with a rudimentary understanding of aerodynamics, aircraft fell out of the sky at the wrong attitude and speed exacerbated by the thought of the very

The Gannet AEW 3 pilot's cockpit.

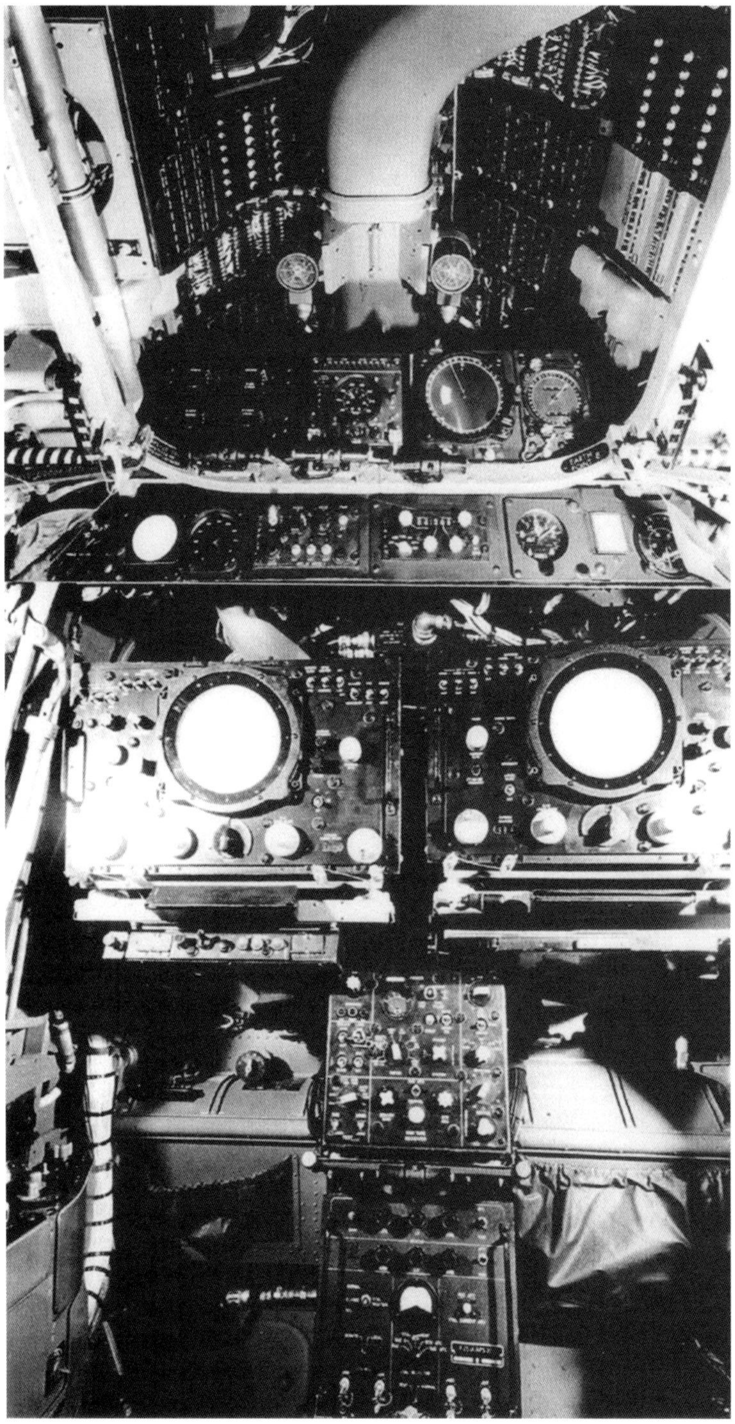

The Gannet AEW 3 observer's compartment looking forward. The sliding chart board is under the right-hand console.

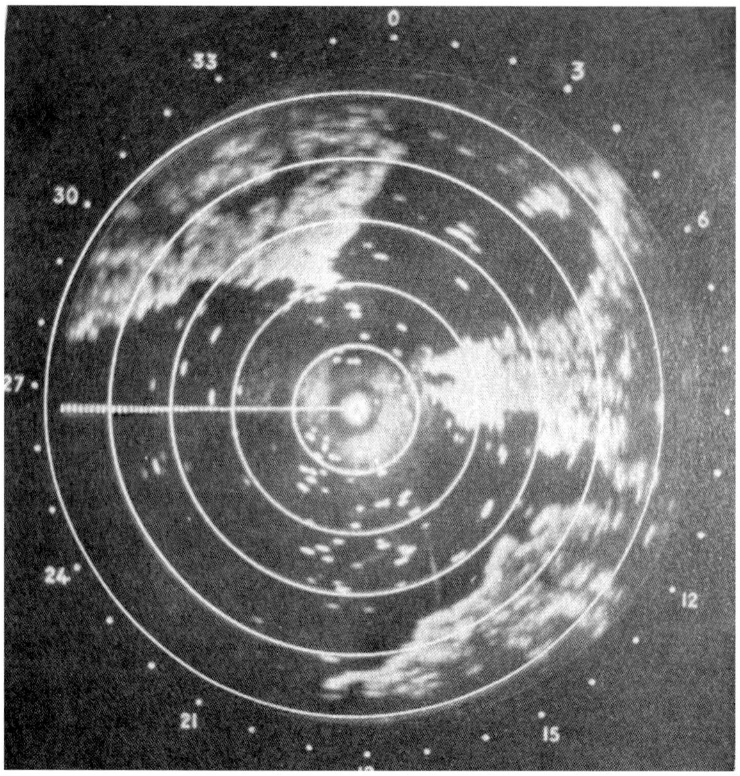

The observer's radar screen. When photographed the aircraft was operating from Brawdy off the south-west tip of Wales. The small contacts like 'grains of rice' are ships.

A Gannet AEW 3 of 849B Flight undergoing maintenance in *Centaur*'s hangar during 1963. The aircraft to the left is a Sea Vixen of 892 NAS.

blunt end of the round down to be negotiated. Generally observers encouraged the pilot to add 5 knots to the calculated approach speed for the wife and kids although overdoing this could lead to the aircraft floating over the wires and a bolter. Then the observers' call of POWER was added to the cacophony of voices shouting at the pilot to the accompaniment of flares as a wobbly overshoot was initiated. When the hook eventually caught a wire, the junior right-hand seat observer was thrust forward by the retardation for another potential encounter with the chart board.

I have many memories of flying the Gannet but perhaps the one that comes to mind most often is changing channels on the pilot's ARC-52 UHF radio control. This was situated well down to the left of the cockpit and changing frequencies and checking that the right one had been selected required the pilot to turn his head nearly upside down. By day this was no problem but when recovering to a carrier on a dark night in bad weather it was the easiest way to get disorientated that I can think of. Usually the observers solved the problem by changing from the homer to the talk-down frequency with their control box in the back but if they were still controlling aircraft up to the last minute or handing over to the next Gannet on task the pilot had to make his own selections. After feeling for the right knob and making what felt like the right selection, the head had to be moved slowly into position to check and then slowly moved back to scan the instruments while commencing the final approach, selecting wheels and flaps down and re-trimming. I will always regard night deck landings on a carrier as something special and being a member of the night flying team the pinnacle of my flying career.

Fairey studied further development of the Gannet and had the carrier replacement programme not been cancelled in 1966, the most likely to have been taken forward was the projected Gannet AEW 7 on which a significant amount of work had been done. It would have been fitted with AN/APS-82 radar with its scanner in a rotodome fitted over the after fuselage. It would have needed more powerful engines but would have provided the new carriers with AEW capability at an affordable development cost. Like so much else of value, it was cancelled in 1966.

Ultra-Light Helicopter

In 1954 the British Army selected a Fairey design for a simple, lightweight helicopter intended for battlefield reconnaissance and casualty evacuation. Economy measures forced its cancellation in 1956 but Fairey proposed a developed version for RN use suitable for operation from small flight decks on frigates. It used rotor-tip drive technology powered by a single Turbomeca Palouste BnPe.2 turbojet built under licence by Blackburn modified with an oversize centrifugal compressor. Air from this was drawn into a casing, through a duct to the rotor head and then, together with metered fuel to the tip-jets. A small rotor diameter gave sufficient lift without needing the tail rotor required by more conventional designs. There were no drag hinges and the two blades formed a 'see-saw' combination to balance lift without needing flapping hinges. The pilot's controls were the same as those of a normal helicopter. There was a collective pitch lever to his left with a twist-grip throttle for increasing engine rpm to increase air pressure to the tip-jets and a cyclic pitch stick between the pilot's legs for control in pitch and roll via a hydraulically-powered system connected to a flexible pylon at the rotor head. Rudder pedals gave directional control by deflecting a metal rudder under the diminutive tail pylon on which the jet exhaust impinged.

Structurally the Ultra-Light comprised a light alloy box containing the fuel tank. The rotor pylon was fixed to the centre of the box and the tiny perspex cockpit was built around it. Two seats, with the pilot to the right, were fitted onto to the box structure and a box-girder boom was fitted to the rear of the box under which the engine was slung together with the rudder and tailplane assembly. The undercarriage consisted of a pair of skids attached to tubes running across the underside of the box. The first of six prototypes flew in 1955.

Rotor diameter was 28ft 3½in and MTOW 1,800lb. Length was only 15ft. Maximum speed was 84 knots and it had an endurance of 2½ hours. When flown by a single pilot it could carry a single Mark 30 torpedo over a sufficient radius of action to be directed onto a release point close to its parent ship's sonar contact. At least two Ultra-Lights were used for RN trials and had 'ROYAL NAVY' painted on their tail booms. One of these operated from a flight deck fitted over the quarterdeck of the frigate *Grenville* in the autumn of 1957 with more than seventy landings and take-offs carried out successfully in winds as high as 62 knots with the deck pitching through 10 to 12ft and rolling up to 14 degrees either side of vertical. During 1958 they carried out further RN evaluations but the Saunders-Roe P-531, which evolved into the Wasp, was eventually selected as the better helicopter to meet the new MATCH requirement and work on the Ultra-Light was terminated.

The Fairey Ultra-Light helicopter in RN markings used in trials on the frigate *Grenville*.

FARMAN AVIATION WORKS

Longhorn

The S.7 Longhorn differed from the Shorthorn by the presence of a forward elevator mounted on outriggers ahead of the nacelle. Sixteen served with the Naval Wing of the RFC before 1914, some of which were fitted with twin floats for reconnaissance missions over the sea. After the outbreak of war they were used mainly for training. Longhorns were built in France and under licence in the UK by a variety of firms including the Phoenix Dynamo Company. The pilot sat in a small nacelle in front of the engine, completely exposed to the elements in early examples but later Longhorns had small canvas screens around the wicker seat to protect him against the wind. A sight glass showed evidence of engine oil pressure and a wool tuft gave evidence of both speed and balanced flight but the pilot relied mainly on his own senses to maintain controlled flight. Wingspan was 51ft and MTOW 1,887lb. They were fitted with engines of varying power, typically the 70hp Renault driving a pusher propeller to give a maximum level speed of 52 knots. The total number operated by the RNAS was 151.

Shorthorn

The Shorthorn featured an elevator situated right aft as part of the tailplane structure. It was a two-seat aircraft intended for both reconnaissance and bombing and the cockpit was a more robust wood and canvas structure than the Longhorn with a windscreen to provide further protection. Some float-fitted examples were used during the 1913 Fleet Manoeuvres, based at Great Yarmouth and Cromarty. Others were used from 1912 as training aircraft. When war broke out in 1914 the RNAS had four Shorthorn landplanes and three seaplanes. The majority of Shorthorns were powered by either 70hp or 100hp Renault engines but one was fitted with a 130hp Canton Unne engine and used by Commander C R Samson RN. In December 1914 he dropped eighteen 16lb bombs from it on German gun batteries near Ostend in the first night bombing mission ever attempted. He then took it the Dardanelles as part of 3 Squadron RNAS in 1915. Wingspan was 30ft 8in and MTOW 2,046lb. Those fitted with a 100hp Renault were capable of a maximum level speed of 58 knots. They had no defensive armament and no standardised bomb load but light bombs were carried on improvised carriers under the wings. The RNAS received a total of sixty-six Shorthorns.

Pusher biplanes

A series of two-seat aircraft powered by Gnome rotary engines driving pusher propellers were procured for the RNAS from 1913, manufactured by Farman in France and, under licence, by Airco and Graham White in the UK. Fuel was contained in a circular drum between the engine and the cockpit. Two of the earliest examples flew over the Grand Fleet battle squadrons as they sailed from Portland to their war station at Scapa Flow in August 1914. They were operated with both wheeled undercarriages and twin floats. Structure was manufactured from fabric-covered steel tubing and some were powered by single 135hp Salmson water-cooled radial engines.

F.20 data

Length:	26ft 6in
Wingspan:	44ft 9in
Height:	12ft
MTOW:	1,440lb
Engine:	One 80hp Gnome radial
Fuel:	Avgas. 20 gallons
Performance:	Maximum level speed 52 knots Service ceiling under 10,000ft. 20 minutes to 3,000ft
Endurance:	3 hours
Armament:	Early trials with machine guns in front cockpit. A variety of bombs could be carried on extemporised underwing racks

A total of 200 Farman F.20 pusher biplanes were procured for the RNAS but a number of these were transferred to the RFC in 1917.

Farman pusher biplanes operated with the original Eastchurch Squadron which later became 3 Squadron RNAS and then 3 Wing when it deployed to the Dardanelles. They also served with 1 and 2 Squadrons RNAS.

Winston Churchill, then First Lord of the Admiralty, being helped into a Farman Shorthorn for a flight in 1913.

Commander C R Samson about to take-off from Imbros in a Farman F.27 armed with the first 500lb bomb ever used in a British bombing mission.

The Eastchurch Squadron, led by Commander C R Samson, flew to Ostend in 1914 with a variety of aircraft, one of which was a Farman. When it became 3 Squadron and deployed to the Dardanelles the unit included 8 F.20s but they lacked the power to lift an offensive load in the high ambient temperatures and proved difficult to maintain. Six replacement F.20s were rejected as being useless for front-line service. Re-engined examples fitted with 140hp Canton Unne engines designated F.27 proved better and were found to survive better in the conditions. F.27s were used as bombers by the RNAS in the Aegean from July 1915 onwards and it was in one of these that Commander Samson dropped a 500lb bomb; the first time a bomb of that weight had ever been dropped operationally by a strike aircraft. His target was a Turkish barracks. RNAS units in Belgium used Farmans for strikes against German submarine pens and Zeppelin sheds in Belgium from 1915 onwards. On the night of 6/7 June 1915 Flight Lieutenant J P Wilson RNAS and Flight Sub Lieutenant J Mills RNAS attacked an enemy airship base at Evere in Belgium and destroyed Zeppelin LZ 38 in its shed. Float-fitted Farmans were also used for coastal patrol work and several pilots attacked U-boats sighted on the surface with 65lb bombs.

FRANCO-BRITISH AVIATION COMPANY (FBA)

Types A, B and H

The Admiralty procured forty-two Type As and 104 of the similar but modified Type Bs for the RNAS. Four Type Hs were presented in 1917 for use at Otranto. The majority of RNAS aircraft were built under licence by Norman Thompson and Gosport Aviation. They were used for training seaplane pilots at RN air stations Calshot and Lee-on-Solent. The Hs were used to fly patrols over the Otranto Barrage and subsequently operated from Calafrana at Malta. The FBA Type Bs built by Norman Thompson had a wingspan of 45ft and MTOW of 2,000lb. They were ordered with Gnome rotary engines but most were delivered with 130hp Clerget rotary engines driving two-bladed pusher propellers. Maximum level speed was 59 knots and they had an endurance of 2 hours 45 minutes.

FBA Type 3.

FELIXSTOWE

F.1

Effectively the prototype of the series, the F.1 was built at Felixstowe after the hulls of four Curtiss H.4s had been rebuilt to improve their handling in rough weather. The F.1 differed in both construction and appearance from them and had a fuselage structure comprising a cross-braced wooden box girder to which a vee-shaped planing bottom and longitudinal fins were added. The hull was 32ft 2in long and used the tailplane and 72ft wings of a Curtiss H 4. It was powered by two 150hp Hispano-Suiza engines and had a wingspan of 72ft.

F.2A

After the F.1 proved successful, Wing Commander J C Porte RNAS turned his attention to improving the larger Curtiss H.12. The original 160hp Curtiss engines could not get the aircraft airborne at MTOW and they were replaced by two 250hp Rolls-Royce Eagles. The F.2's hull was similar to that of the F.1 but larger. The fins were built outside the basic hull structure with intermediate timbers of rock elm running from chine to chine. The top of the hull was fabric-covered except for the area in front of the cockpit which was planked with plywood. The cockpit was semi-enclosed with an open top and the tailplane was set high to keep it clear of spray when taxiing and to give the side gunners a good field of fire astern and below. The wings were similar to those of the H.12. In service the hull proved to be robust and seaworthy and large production orders were placed in 1917. There were some delays at first as responsibility for aircraft production had been moved from the Admiralty to a centralised organisation that had different priorities.

The hull design was basically sound but constant use under wartime conditions led many to deteriorate; the hull bottom planks warped after time, plywood on the fin tops and sides opened up and fabric rotted. These problems were ameliorated by fitting narrower planks to the hull bottom and double-diagonal planking of mahogany and cedar was applied to the fin tops. The hull sides were either given single planking with fabric covering or completely planked with Consuta, a special material developed by S E Saunders consisting of plywood sawn with copper into large sheets. The estimated life of an F.2A moored in the sheltered water of a coastal naval air station was 6 to 8 months but at Great Yarmouth and Felixstowe the boats could be manoeuvred onto wheeled trolleys and hauled up ramps out of the water onto hard-standings or into hangars. Manhandling these large but fragile aircraft was not easy and beaching crews had to be well-practised. The F.2A's main weakness was its fuel system; the main fuel tanks were in the central fuselage and fuel was drawn out of them to a gravity tank in the upper wing centre section by wind-driven pumps. Engine carburettors were fed with fuel from the gravity tank and any blockage in this lengthy plumbing resulted in the failure of one or both engines, forcing the aircraft down onto the sea. A clogged gravity tank

Six F.2A flying boats on a slipway at Felixstowe.

An F.2A modified with open cockpits on patrol over the North Sea.

filter forced the first F.2A to be operated from Great Yarmouth down into the sea on its first operational sortie and a number of reports highlighted similar problems in the months ahead.

F.2A data

Length:	46ft 3in
Wingspan:	95ft 7¾in
Height:	17ft 6in
MTOW:	10,978lb
Engines:	Two 345hp Rolls-Royce Eagle VIII
Fuel:	Avgas. 220 gallons
Performance:	Maximum level speed 84 knots
	Service ceiling 9,600ft. 17 minutes to 6,500ft
Endurance:	6 hours
Armament:	Normally four 0.303in Lewis machine guns; one on a Scarff ring in the bow position and another in the upper rear cockpit and one in each side waist position with ammunition for all in 47-round drums. For offensive missions a double mounting was fitted in the bow and upper rear cockpit positions and a single Lewis gun could be fitted on the cockpit canopy for the second pilot. A single 230lb bomb could be carried on a rack under each lower mainplane

The RNAS received 161 F.2As. The first were delivered in late 1917 and they quickly became the mainstay of the RNAS patrol network operating from Calshot, Dundee, Felixstowe, Great Yarmouth, Killingholme, Scapa Flow and Tresco.

The Felixstowe boats are probably best remembered for their operations from April 1917 within the 'Spider Web' patrol area centred on the North Hinder Light Vessel. Most U-boats had to pass through it on the surface to reach UK waters and flying boat patrols allowed 4,000 square miles of sea to be searched systematically. In the first month of operation alone, twenty-seven patrols were flown, eight U-boats were seen on the surface and forced to dive, three of which were attacked with bombs. Despite their weight and bulk F.2As were manoeuvrable, heavily-armed aircraft and the RNAS used them for offensive patrols against enemy seaplanes and airships in the eastern North Sea. One such mission consisting of four F.2As and a Curtiss H.12, led by Flight Lieutenant R Leckie RNAS, located and attacked a force of fourteen German seaplanes off Borkum and shot down six of them in June 1918. None of the flying boats were lost to enemy fire but one was forced down before the fight ended by a fuel problem and the mechanic of another had to repair a broken fuel pipe during the combat. This action had an interesting consequence since it led to the dazzle-painting of many F.2As so that they could be recognised individually in action or be seen by rescuers if they came down in the sea. At Great Yarmouth the choice of scheme was left to individual pilots and this led to a variety of bizarre combinations of checks, stripes and zig-zags in bright colours.

An interesting scheme to extend the F.2A's radius of action evolved from an idea proposed by Porte in 1916. This involved the construction of specialised lighters on which the flying boats could be towed by destroyers. Orders for four were placed in January 1917 and the first was tested in June. As built, tanks in the lighter could be flooded to lower the stern allowing the F.2A to be fitted onto a trolley and warped into place inside the lighter's bulwarks. Once it was secured in place the tanks were blown dry by compressed air. Towing trials went well and in September a destroyer towed a lighter with a flying boat in place at speeds up to 32 knots. Further lighters were ordered to be built by the Royal Engineers and by the time of the Armistice fifty-one had been delivered. Some, described in the section covering the Sopwith 2F.1 Camel were modified with small wooden decks to carry fighters.

A later evolution of Porte's design, the F.3 had greater range but was less manoeuvrable. This led the RNAS to operate the F.2A in the North Sea where combat with seaplanes and Zeppelins was more likely and to use the F.3 at air stations where long anti-submarine patrols predominated.

F.2C

There is no evidence that an F.2B variant was ever built but there was an F.2C; broadly similar to the F.2A but incorporating a modified hull step to improve planing performance on take-off. Only two were built and they were used by the War Flight at Felixstowe.

Felixstowe F.3.

F.3

With a wingspan of 102ft and MTOW of 13,281lb the F.3 was a larger aircraft than its predecessor and not as well liked by its aircrew but it had a fuel capacity of 400 gallons which gave an endurance of over 9 hours and it could carry four 230lb bombs on racks under the lower wings. The prototype was tested with two 320hp Sunbeam Cossack engines but production F.3s were completed with two 345hp Rolls-Royce Eagle VIII engines giving a maximum level speed of 79 knots. Service ceiling was only 6,000ft. Orders for 263 F.3s were placed from 1917 with a number of contractors including Malta Dockyard but the critical shortage of engines held up deliveries. In Malta there were expert boat-builders in the Dockyard and women were employed as fabric workers under the supervision of Lady Methuen, the Governor's wife. The first Maltese F.3 was delivered in November 1917 followed by seventeen more over the next year. Several were used on development work; one was fitted with one of the world's first servo-operated control systems and another was fitted with a pioneering automatic landing device. After the 1918 Armistice a number of F.3 contracts were cancelled and some completed as F.5s but 117 had been delivered and operated from Cattewater, Felixstowe, Houton Bay, Tresco, Malta and other bases in the Mediterranean. Some remained in service after the war and the last examples were withdrawn in 1921.

Fury

A triplane flying boat with a wingspan of 123ft and MTOW of 25,253lb, the Fury was powered by five 345hp Rolls-Royce Eagle VIII engines installed as two tractor and three pusher units with the outboard units back-to-back. The outboard pushers drove four-bladed propellers since they had to work in the slipstream of the tractor airscrews ahead of them. Even with five engines the Fury was under-powered but still had a maximum level speed of 85 knots. It was found in trials to have superior seaworthiness and take-off characteristics to the earlier Felixstowe boats but only one was built and it was not completed until September 1918. Despite proving effective in trials, the Fury was not put into production when the war ended and, after some use as a trials aircraft, the sole example was deleted in 1919.

F.5

Porte's last flying-boat design was the prototype F.5 built in 1918. The wings were almost identical to those of the F.3 but the fuselage was deeper. When tested it proved to be an excellent flying boat and would probably have been a better proposition for large-scale production than the F.3 but the Ministry of Munitions had taken over aircraft supply arrangements from the Air Board and refused to cover the cost of new jigs and templates. The F.5 that eventually went into production was a hybrid with as many F.3 components as possible to produce a hull that

Felixstowe Fury.

A B C D E F G H I J K L M N O P Q R S T U V W X Y Z

approximated as nearly as possible to the prototype. Most F.5 contracts were cancelled at the end of 1918 but forty were delivered and they were retained in service into the 1920s. Wingspan was 103ft 8in and MTOW 12,682lb. Fuel tankage of 350 gallons gave an endurance of 7 hours and the F.5 powered by two 350hp Rolls-Royce Eagle VIII engines giving a maximum speed of 77 knots.

FLANDERS

B.2

The Flanders B.2 was fitted with several engines before flying with a 70hp Gnome rotary in 1914. Wingspan was 41ft and MTOW 1,500lb. Maximum level speed was 57 knots. A single example was purchased by the Admiralty in August 1914 and allocated to Great Yarmouth but its delivery flight was punctuated by forced landings. After the last of these it was dismantled and delivered in pieces. Subsequently re-assembled, it was never used operationally.

FOLKESTONE NAVAL AIR STATION

SSZ class non-rigid airships

The control car was a boat-shaped, aluminium-covered ash framework with a vee-shaped bottom which allowed it to carry out running landings on land or to alight on relatively calm water. It had three cockpits with the forward occupied by the W/T operator/gunner. He had a single 0.303in Lewis gun that could be mounted on pintles at either side of the cockpit. The pilot occupied the centre cockpit and the rear cockpit was occupied by the engineer. Apart from his instruments and tool bag he had a starting handle to re-start the engine in flight if necessary. It could also be used to turn an auxiliary air pump so that he could maintain air pressure in the aerodynamic ballonets that surrounded the gas bags in the event of engine failure. In practice the Hawk engine proved extremely reliable but situated just aft of the engineer's head, it must have been deafening.

Lift was provided by 70,000ft^3 of hydrogen in two gas bags contained within two ballonets which gave an aerodynamic shape when filled with pressurised air from an air scoop aft of the propeller. Avgas was carried in cylindrical aluminium tanks slung on either side of the car as was the water ballast. The tail surfaces comprised horizontal fins and elevators combined with a single large vertical fin and rudder. Two 110lb or a single 250lb bomb could be carried on racks just forward of the engine mounting. An aerial camera could be fitted but was rarely used on anti-submarine patrol work.

The designation SSZ evolved after the prototype was referred to as the SS-0, spoken as SS-Zero. When its individual identity was first painted on the prototype car it appeared as SS.Z.1 but when it entered service this was amended to SSZ.1 which became the standard format. After a series of very successful trials at Folkestone SSZ.1 was deflated in August 1917 and sent to Frederick Sage & Co, furniture manufacturers, as the pattern from which SSZ cars were mass-produced. It was back at Kingsnorth in August 1917 and used operationally thereafter until it was finally deflated in January 1919.

All RN airship bases had extensive fabric-fitting and repair facilities and were capable of making both gas bags and envelopes for the SSZ class; the cars were sent to them as 'flat-pack' component parts from Sage & Co. Engines were delivered by Rolls-Royce. On average an SSZ took 60 days to assemble.

SSZ class data

Length:	143ft
Diameter:	30ft
Height:	46ft
Envelope:	70,000ft^3
Engine:	One 75hp Rolls-Royce Hawk
Fuel:	Avgas. 102 gallons
Gross Lift:	2.2 tons
Disposable lift:	0.6 tons
Performance:	Maximum level speed 46 knots
	Initial rate of climb 1,200ft per minute
Armament:	One 0.303in Lewis gun
	Two 110lb or one 250lb bomb

SSZ production amounted to seventy-seven built between June 1916 and November 1918. They were assembled at the larger naval air stations where they were to be operated. Those for use from smaller air stations with more limited support facilities were assembled at Wormwood Scrubs and Kingsnorth and then flown to their operating bases. Assembly totals were six at Folkestone, six at Polegate, four at Luce Bay, two at Mullion, two at Pembroke, thirty-two at Wormwood Scrubs, twenty-four at Kingsnorth and one at Anglesey.

Between 1917 and 1919 SSZ class airships operated from Folkestone, Polegate, Luce Bay, Mullion, Laira, Pembroke, Wormwood Scrubs, Howden, Anglesey, Pulham, Cranwell, Kingsnorth, East Fortune and Longside on coastal anti-submarine patrols and as convoy escorts. Several were used for trials including the evaluation of techniques for towing airships by warships and new ways of mooring. SSZ.59 landed on *Furious*' after flight deck in 1918 to demonstrate that it would be possible to refuel, re-arm and change crews on an aircraft carrier to extend the airship's radius of action. SSZ.73 earned place in history by flying under the Menai Bridge shortly after the Armistice, piloted by Squadron Commander T Elmhurst RNAS. Since the gas envelope prevented the pilot from looking up, he judged his height accurately by trailing a sandbag attached to a rope under the car and watching it skip along the surface as he moved under the bridge.

Non-rigid airship SSZ-3.

Graham White Type XV.

GRAHAM-WHITE

Type XV

Given the Admiralty designation Type 1600 after the airframe number of one of the first examples, the Graham-White Type XV Boxkite was a two-seat, dual-control training aircraft which equipped flying training units at Chingford, Eastchurch, Eastbourne and Hendon. Wingspan was 41ft and MTOW 1,150lb. A total of eighty-six was delivered to the RNAS powered by either a 70hp Gnome rotary or 60hp Le Rhone rotary engine giving a maximum level speed of 44 knots. Most naval aircraft featured dual control, a nacelle for the instructor and pupil pilot and upper wing extensions. Earlier examples had been somewhat primitive. The type gave solid but unspectacular service with the majority deleted by 1917.

(ISLE OF) GRAIN NAVAL AIR STATION

Griffin

The Griffin evolved from an Admiralty request to modify a Sopwith B.1 bomber for use as a two-seat, carrier-borne fleet reconnaissance aircraft fitted with wireless and folding wings but the experimental

Grain Griffin.

A B C D E F G H I J K L M N O P Q R S T U V W X Y Z

construction department soon found that it would be better to design and build a new aircraft based on the Sopwith design than to produce a hybrid modification of doubtful value. A single prototype was produced but the changes adversely affected performance. By then the Admiralty had ordered seven more and these were given the name Griffin. Wingspan was 42ft 6in and MTOW 2,858lb. The first had a 200hp Sunbeam Arab engine but later aircraft had a 230hp Bentley BR 2 radial engine which gave a maximum level speed of 100 knots. Internal fuel tankage of 50 gallons gave an endurance of over 5 hours. Only six Griffins were actually completed, the last in October 1918. The first was evaluated from March 1918 and all six were embarked in *Vindictive* by the end of 1918. They were part of her air group in 1919 when she deployed to the Baltic for operations against the Bolsheviks and on 30 July one took part in a strike against Kronstadt. Another bombed a factory in August and one ditched after engine failure. After a brief and little-known career they were all withdrawn from service by 1920.

Sea Gladiator of 801 NAS at Donibristle in 1939.

GLOSTER

Grebe

Six Gloster Grebe fighter trainers were transferred from the RAF to train naval pilots in fighter tactics at Leuchars between 1925 and 1929. Three were Mark I single-seaters and three were Mark II two-seat, dual-control aircraft, the latter used for the longest period. Mark II wingspan was 29ft 4in and MTOW 2,538lb. They were powered by a single 400hp Armstrong Siddeley Jaguar IV radial engine driving a two-bladed Watts fixed-pitch wooden propeller to give a maximum level speed of 142 knots. Service ceiling was 20,500ft which could be reached 24 minutes after take-off. Two gravity tanks under the upper wing had a combined total of 52 gallons of avgas which gave an endurance of 3 hours and armament was two synchronised Vickers 0.303in machine guns on top of the front fuselage decking with 600 rpg.

Sea Gladiator landing on *Eagle*.

TSR 38

A single TSR 38 was submitted to meet the specification for which the Fairey Swordfish was chosen. It carried out deck-landing trials on *Courageous* during 1934 and was evaluated by the A&AEE but no further development was undertaken once the RN selected the Swordfish. Wingspan was 46ft and MTOW 8,038lb. It was powered by a single 690hp Rolls-Royce Goshawk evaporatively-cooled engine driving a two bladed Watts fixed pitch propeller giving a maximum level speed of 135 knots. The Goshawk's notable unreliability contributed to the type's failure.

Sea Gladiator

Originally a private venture, the Gladiator, from which the Sea Gladiator was derived, became the last RAF biplane fighter, already obsolete when it entered service in 1937 but delays with the Skua and Roc forced the Admiralty to seek an interim fighter and the Gladiator was relatively easy to modify. In 1938 the RAF agreed to transfer thirty-eight Gladiators modified to interim Sea Gladiator standard to the RN. They were the first aircraft off the production line built to Mark II standard and modifications included a vee-shaped arrester hook forward of the tail wheel. RN radio was installed and an airspeed indicator that read in knots rather than mph. Designated Sea Gladiator (Interim), they were delivered from December 1938 to Worthy Down, Donibristle, Hatston and Eastleigh and used for fighter pilot training. They were returned to the RAF when production Sea Gladiators were delivered. These were built alongside large batches of RAF aircraft and, in addition to the interim modifications, they had a dinghy stowed in a pod between the undercarriage legs and catapult strong points. A three-bladed, fixed-pitch metal propeller replaced the two-bladed wooden propeller in early RAF aircraft. Sea Gladiators were delivered from February 1939, replacing Nimrods and Ospreys in 801 NAS at Donibristle until Skuas became available. 802 and 804 NAS re-equipped with Sea Gladiators in May and November 1939 respectively and operated in defence of the Home Fleet in Scapa Flow from Hatston.

Sea Gladiator data

Length:	27ft 5in
Wingspan:	32ft 3in
Height:	10ft 4in
MTOW:	5,420lb
Engine:	One 840hp Bristol Mercury IX radial
Fuel:	Avgas. 83 gallons
Performance:	Maximum level speed 225 knots
	Service ceiling 32,300ft. 5 minutes to 10,000ft
Endurance:	Up to 2 hours
Armament:	Four Browning 0.303in front guns; two fitted in fuselage side troughs firing through the propeller disc with an interrupter mechanism and two in pods under the lower wings firing clear of the propeller arc. Fuselage-mounted guns had 600 rpg; wing-mounted guns 400 rpg. With more rounds and a slower rate of fire because of the interrupter mechanism the fuselage guns gave more prolonged fire than the wing guns

The RN received thirty-eight Sea Gladiator (Interim) aircraft and sixty Sea Gladiators. Two former RAF Gladiators were used for trials of the modifications to naval standards and carrier qualification in *Courageous.*

Sea Gladiators served with a number of shore-based squadrons between 1939 and 1944 on tasks including fighter pilot training, deck-

Sea Gladiator of 813 NAS Fighter Flight on *Eagle*.Commander C L Keighley Peach DSO RN, the ship's Commander 'Air', achieved five 'kills' in this aircraft during 1940.

landing training, fleet requirements duties in the UK, Egypt and Ceylon, tactical development and the provision of targets for anti-aircraft gunners to track. Units wholly or partially-equipped with Sea Gladiators included 759, 760, 769, 770, 771, 775, 776, 778, 787, 791, 792 and 797 NAS.

Operational squadrons that used Sea Gladiators between 1939 and 1941 were 801, 802, 804, 805, 806, 813, 880 and 885 NAS. In some instances such as 806 and 880 NAS the Sea Gladiators were a temporary measure awaiting the delivery of Fulmars and Sea Hurricanes. They operated from the aircraft carriers *Courageous*, *Eagle*, *Furious*, *Glorious* and *Illustrious*. A Sea Gladiator from Hatston was the first British aircraft to land on a USN carrier, the USS *Wasp* off Orkney in 1942.

Sea Gladiators were retained by a few station flights until 1943 including Crail, Henstridge and Inskip and used to give dissimilar air combat training for disembarked fighter squadrons. They were also considered a delight to fly.

Sea Gladiators operated from Hatston in defence of the Home Fleet, in the brief Norwegian Campaign of 1940 and in the Mediterranean for a few months before Fulmars and Martlets replaced them. In 1939/40 Sea Gladiators engaged in twenty-four recorded combats against fifty-two enemy aircraft. In the Mediterranean these resulted in seven enemy aircraft destroyed, five of them by Commander C L Keighly-Peach DSO RN, Commander 'Air' of *Eagle* who flew one of 813 NAS Fighter Flight's aircraft. Three enemy aircraft were shot down in the Home Fleet area of operations and, although these numbers might seem small, it should be borne in mind that there were never more than eighteen Sea Gladiators in operational units at any one time throughout 1939 and 1940 and by 1941 there were only six.

Meteor

Designed for the RAF as a single-seat, twin-engined fighter, the Meteor was the first operational British jet. Its twin-engine layout would have made deck landing difficult after a single engine failure but the Admiralty followed Meteor development and the first prototype was allocated to the RN in August 1945 for carrier suitability trials in *Pretoria Castle*. Since it had no hook, it was craned on board in Glasgow and craned off on completion. Two other Meteors were modified by Gloster for deck-landing trials; the guns were removed and a Sea Hornet A-frame arrester hook was fitted under the rear fuselage with local strengthening around its attachment points. Stronger oleos were fitted and the undercarriage doors were removed to prevent them snagging arrester wires and more powerful Derwent engines were installed. 'Winkle' Brown flew ADDLs followed by non-arrested landings on *Illustrious*. After their analysis he made an arrested landing on *Implacable* on 8 June 1948; the first time that a British twin-jet aircraft had landed on a carrier. A total of thirty-two successful landings were made during the trial.

Meteor T 7s used by 702 and 736 NAS at Culdrose during 1952.

Meteor F 3, EE 337. Modified with a hook to carry out the first deck landing by a British twin-jet aircraft during trials in *Implacable* during 1948 being pushed aft by handlers prior to carrying out a free take-off.

A B C D E F G H I J K L M N O P Q R S T U V W X Y Z

In 1947 Gloster produced a trainer variant as a private venture. Based on the F 4, it had a two-seat cockpit in an elongated fuselage with the instructor sat in tandem behind the student and dual controls. It was an immediate success and, designated as the T 7, was ordered in quantity for the RAF. The Admiralty ordered T 7s to convert pilots onto jet operations and provide instrument training and other advanced courses. 702 NAS was the first unit in either the RN or RAF to receive a T 7 in 1949. Other squadrons used them for fighter pilot training, LSO training, refresher flying for pilots returning to the front line and a variety of trials. They were unarmed but did have gunsights for use in tactical training sorties. In 1953 759 NAS had fourteen as well as a number of Sea Vampires and 728 NAS at Hal Far was another long-term user.

When the RAF replaced Meteor F 4s with F-8s, redundant F 4 airframes were modified for use as drones. Gloster designed a remote-controlled, pilotless conversion designated as the Meteor U 15 but the conversion work was subcontracted to Flight Refuelling Ltd. The first U 15 carried out a remotely-controlled take off in 1955, albeit with a safety pilot on board. U 15s were used at the WRE in Australia and the UK range at Llanbedr. The RN received fourteen U 15s for use by 728B NAS at Hal Far as targets for Seaslug SAM development firings from *Girdle Ness*. They were fitted with radio-link equipment and infra-red homing flares to enhance target signature as well as the automatic pilot system. There was also instrumentation and data link equipment to download data to a ground station. Wingtip pods containing cameras were fitted to record the final seconds of a missile's flight path before it hit (or missed) the aircraft. These were jettisonable and recoverable, fitted with a parachute, buoyancy bag and homing beacon with their ejection controlled by ground command. The U 15s were operated successfully by 728B NAS although two crashed off Malta following control malfunctions. Ten were shot down by Seaslug missile hits between 1959 and 1961 and the remaining two were returned to Llanbedr. 728B also operated four Meteor U 16s converted from the later F 8 between 1960 and 1961 but none of these were shot down.

The last variant operated by the Fleet Air Arm was the Meteor TT 20, a target-towing conversion of the RAF's NF 11 night fighter designed to meet an RN requirement for a Sturgeon TT 3 replacement. The conversion work, carried out by Armstrong Whitworth, involved the removal of radar, guns and equipment and their replacement by a winch operator's seat and controls in the rear cockpit. The TT 20 could carry up to four towed targets in the modified rear fuselage; these could be radar-reflective or visual in two sizes; 15ft long by 3ft wide or 20ft long and 4ft wide. These were later replaced by Rushton towed targets. Targets could be streamed and replaced while the aircraft was in flight. An ML Aviation Type G, fully-feathering, windmill-driven winch was mounted in a pod over the starboard wing centre-section between the fuselage and the engine. It was capable of paying out 6,100ft of cable routed from the winch through a cable-cutter to the target exchange and release unit. Near-miss recording gear detected shock waves which indicated near misses. These were relayed to the winch operator's control panel via the towing cable. The cable-cutter could be initiated from either the front or rear cockpit.

Meteor T 7 data

Length:	43ft 6in
Wingspan:	37ft 2in
Height:	13ft
MTOW:	14,230lb
Engines:	Two 3,500lb thrust Rolls-Royce Derwent 8 centrifugal turbojets
Fuel:	Avtur/Avcat. 325 gallons internal plus optional 175-gallon ventral tank and/or two 100-gallon tanks under wing. Total 700 gallons
Performance:	Maximum level speed 520 knots Service ceiling 45,000ft. 6 minutes to 30,000ft
Armament:	None

The RN received a total of eighty-six Meteors comprising one prototype used for carrier compatibility trials; two hooked F 3s used for deck-landing trials; one F 4 used as an instructional airframe; thirty-seven T 7s; two F 8s used for rubber deck and avionic trials; fourteen U 15s; four U 16s; and twenty-five TT 20s.

Between 1948 and 1967 Meteors served on tasks as diverse as trials, jet familiarisation, pilot conversion, LSO training, fleet requirements and target towing. During that period they equipped, or partially equipped 700, 702, 703, 728, 728B, 736, 759, 764, 767, 771, 778, and 781 NAS.

Meteor T 7s served with 806 and 813 NAS during 1953 for standardisation and instrument flying sorties with squadron pilots who normally flew single-seat aircraft. They also served with station flights at Brawdy, Ford, Hal Far, Lossiemouth, Stretton and Yeovilton.

After 728 NAS disbanded in 1967, the last TT 20s were used by the civilian-manned, un-numbered FRU at Hurn which replaced them with modified Canberras in 1971. Both 728 NAS and the FRU had retained a T 7 for instrument and standardisation checks.

GROB AVIATION

Heron

Five G115D Herons were operated by 727 NAS at Roborough airfield outside Plymouth between 2001 and 2004 tasked with new-entry aircrew grading, refresher flying and RN university student air experience work. The aircraft were civil registered and flown by a mix of RN and civilian instructors.

Tutor

In 2004 727 NAS was re-equipped with 5 Grob G115E designated Tutor T 1 transferred from the RAF before moving to Yeovilton in 2006. Maintained by Babcock under contract and flown by a mix of RN and civilian instructors, the Tutor T 1 is a two-seat primary trainer with a fixed tricycle undercarriage powered by a single 180hp Lycoming AE10-360-B1F/B four cylinder piston engine driving a three-bladed propeller to give a maximum level speed of 130 knots. Wingspan is 32ft 10in and MTOW 2,183lb. The type remains in use in 2024.

Grob Tutor T 1 of 727 NAS at Yeovilton.

GRUMMAN

Goose

The G-21 Goose was Grumman's first amphibian flying boat and a number were purchased by the USN for use as seven-seat transports designated JRF. In 1940 several were ordered for the RN by the BPC but these were absorbed later into larger numbers transferred under Lend-Lease arrangements. RN aircraft were to JRF-5 standard with a wingspan of 49ft and MTOW of 8,000lb and powered by two 450hp Pratt & Whitney R-985-AN-6 radial engines which gave a maximum level speed of 175 knots. Of the fifty-five aircraft allocated to the RN, eight were re-allocated and some taken on charge but not used. Of the remainder, forty-two were allocated to 749 NAS at Piarco for use in the Observer School as navigational trainers. Others were used by British staff in the USA as passenger transports and one by the Commander 'Air' of *Indomitable* while she was being repaired at Norfolk in 1943 prior to its delivery to 749 NAS. Twenty-six aircraft were returned to the USN in 1945.

Goose operated by 749 NAS, part of the Observer School at Piarco.

Widgeon used by the Senior RN Officer at the USN Flying Training School at Pensacola in 1944. (Captain W R J MacWhirter RN)

Widgeon

Resembling a scaled-down Goose, the G-44 Widgeon first flew in 1940 as an amphibian flying boat powered by two 200hp Ranger L-440 engines which gave a maximum level speed of 135 knots. Wingspan was 40ft and MTOW 4,525lb. No Widgeons were used by the USN but sixteen were transferred to the RN under Lend-Lease arrangements from 1943 onwards and used in the USA as light utility aircraft capable of carrying two pilots and four passengers. One was used for a while as an admiral's barge and others were allocated to Lewiston, Brunswick and Squantum where Fleet Air Arm squadrons were forming at the rate of one a month on Corsairs and Avengers during 1944. They were used briefly by 738 NAS at Lewiston, 1835 NAS at Brunswick and 857 NAS at Squantum. Another example was the personal aircraft of the Senior RN Officer at Pensacola which trained RN pilots alongside their American counterparts. The surviving aircraft were all returned to the USN in 1945.

Martlet/Wildcat

The G-36, designated the F4F by the USN, was Grumman's first monoplane fighter and followed a series of rugged biplane designs. It evolved from a 1935 competition won by the Brewster F2A but the USN saw merit in the F4F and continued to sponsor it. It out-performed the F2A in trials during 1938 and further development improved its performance significantly by 1939. It was ordered into production with deliveries beginning in February 1940 designated F4F-3 with non-folding wings. A later variant with wings that folded aft neatly to lie alongside the fuselage was designated F4F-4.

With no British single-seat carrier-borne fighter design in immediate prospect, the Admiralty saw merit in the G-36 and ordered a batch of fifty-four to F4F-4 standard to be built alongside USN aircraft. The first was actually delivered on 27 July 1940, ahead of deliveries to the USN. At the time no US name had been allocated to the type and it was named Martlet in RN service. In 1941 the USN gave it the name Wildcat and the different names were used by their respective services until January 1944 when the Admiralty ended confusion by adopting the name Wildcat in the RN. After the collapse of France in 1940 and then Greece in 1941 the RN took over contracts they had placed for F4Fs, adding them to the number purchased. Once America entered the war at the end of 1941 Martlet/Wildcats were transferred under Lend-Lease arrangements and no longer had to be purchased.

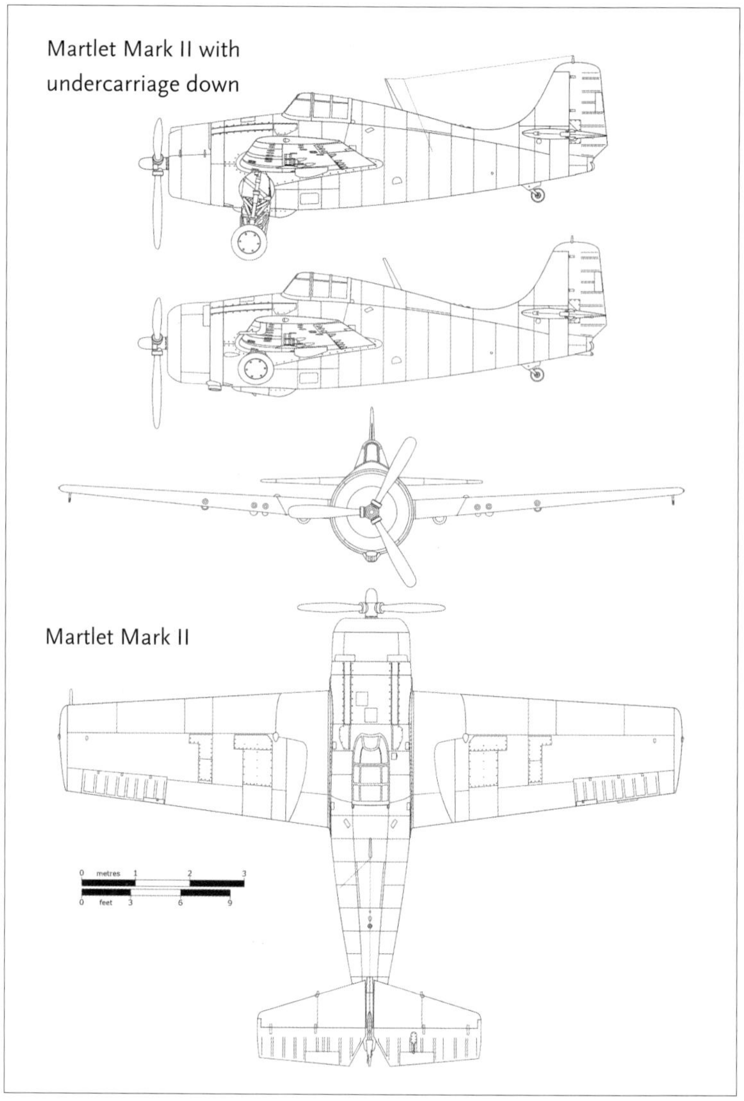

Wildcat Mark IV data

Length:	28ft 11in
Wingspan:	38ft (14ft 4in folded)
Height:	9ft 2in with propeller vertical
MTOW:	7,952lb
Engine:	One 1,200hp Pratt & Whitney Twin Wasp R-1830-86 radial
Fuel:	Avgas. 120 gallons internal plus provision for two 48-gallon drop tanks. Total 216 gallons
Performance:	Maximum level speed 290 knots Service ceiling 34,000ft. 6 minutes to 10,000ft
Endurance:	4 hours
Armament:	Six 0.5in Colt-Browning machine guns, three in each wing firing clear of the propeller arc with 240 rpg

A total of 1,067 Martlet/Wildcats were delivered to the RN. Of these 100 were purchased outright; 131 taken over from French or Greek contracts and 820 transferred under Lend-Lease arrangements. Of the latter 220 were Mark IVs, 312 Mark Vs and 288 Mark VIs.

Between 1940 and 1946 Martlets or Wildcats equipped a number of shore-based squadrons for tasks including operational flying training, air combat training and development, trials, fleet requirements work, deck-landing training, DLCO training, the provision of targets for surface-to-air and air-to-air training, pool units and refresher flying for pilots awaiting front-line appointments. These included 700, 719, 722, 730, 733, 738, 748, 757, 759, 760, 762, 767, 768, 771, 772, 778, 787, 790, 794 and 795 NAS.

For periods between 1940 and 1945 Martlets or Wildcats either fully equipped a number of front-line fighter squadrons or formed fighter flights within composite trade protection squadrons for varying periods. These were 802, 804, 805, 806, 811, 813, 815, 816, 819, 821, 824, 825, 832, 833, 834, 835, 838, 842, 845, 846, 850, 851, 852, 853, 856, 878, 880, 881, 882, 888, 890, 892, 893 and 898 NAS.

From 1940 to 1945 Martlets or Wildcats operated from the aircraft carriers *Ameer*, *Archer*, *Argus*, *Atheling*, *Audacity*, *Battler*, *Biter*, *Campania*, *Chaser*, *Fencer*, *Formidable*, *Furious*, *Illustrious*, *Implacable*, *Indomitable*, *Nabob*, *Nairana*, *Puncher*, *Pursuer*, *Queen*, *Ravager*, *Searcher*, *Striker*, *Tracker*, *Trumpeter*, *Victorious* and *Vindex*.

The former French and Greek aircraft had non-folding wings and were designated as Martlet Marks I and III in service. The Mark I had a single-row Wright Cyclone engine but subsequent marks had Pratt & Whitney Twin Wasps. The Mark IIs purchased for the RN together with the Marks IV, V and VI all had manually-folding wings. Early aircraft were shipped to the UK and completed with British equipment

Wildcat Mark V of 882 NAS about to be catapulted from *Searcher* in 1944. (Philip Jarrett)

Wildcat Mark VI of 853 NAS on *Queen* in 1945.

A Wildcat of 882 NAS in the perfect three-point attitude, but slightly high, about to be given the 'cut' by *Searcher*'s batsman. (Philip Jarrett)

A Wildcat of 881 NAS seconds after landing on *Pursuer* in 1944.

by Blackburn Aircraft but this work was carried out by Blackburn in the USA on later aircraft. From 1944 some aircraft were shipped directly to East Africa and Ceylon for issue to the Eastern Fleet. Sixteen F4F-4s were issued from USN Pacific Fleet reserves to replace aircraft in 882, 896 and 898 NAS embarked in *Victorious* that had been lost while she was on loan to the USN during 1943.

On 25 December 1940 a Martlet of 804 NAS from Hatston was the first American-supplied British fighter to shoot down an enemy aircraft in the Second World War, a Ju 88 attempting to attack the Home Fleet in Scapa Flow. Martlets of 802 NAS operated from the first CVE, *Audacity*, protecting convoys to Gibraltar. They shot down a number of Focke-Wulf Fw 200 Condor four-engined bombers that attempted to attack the ships under their protection. Martlets from *Illustrious* took part in the invasion of Madagascar in early 1942 and in August Martlets from *Indomitable* helped to fight the 'Pedestal' Convoy through to Malta in some of the heaviest air fighting of the war at sea. During Operation 'Torch', the invasion of North Africa in November 1942, Lieutenant B H C Nation RN of 882 NAS in *Victorious* had the unusual experience of seeing men on a French airfield at Blida, over which he was patrolling, wave a white flag. After telling his wingmen to stay overhead he landed to accept its formal surrender.

When Grumman began to concentrate on Hellcat production in 1943, Wildcats were built by Eastern Aircraft, a division of General Motors and designated FM-1 in USN service and Marks V and VI in RN service. They served mainly in composite squadrons with Swordfish or Avengers in CVEs in the convoy protection role and made a valuable contribution to the defeat of the enemy attack on shipping. They operated successfully in the most appalling weather conditions encountered by the Arctic convoys to Russia in 1944–5 and earned a reputation for rugged reliability even though they were out-performed in the air by a later generation of fighters. In the Mediterranean Wildcats took part in the invasion of southern France in 1944 and they also took part in Home Fleet operations against *Tirpitz* in Northern Norway and provided cover over the south-west approaches to the English Channel during the D-Day landings in France.

The Mark VI came into service in 1944; designated as the FM-2 in USN service. It featured a developed version of the Wright Cyclone engine which had first been used in the Mark I and a taller fin and rudder than earlier marks. This variant was used in the Eastern Fleet during 1945 but with higher-performance fighters available in large numbers at the end of the war all marks of Wildcat were withdrawn from service rapidly.

Avenger

The G-40 Avenger evolved from a 1939 USN requirement for a carrier-borne torpedo bomber with an internal bomb bay. It had mid-mounted wings and was designed for a crew of three; pilot, navigator and radio operator/dorsal gunner. The latter had an electrically-powered dorsal turret containing a 0.5in Browning machine gun with 400 rounds at the rear of a long, glazed canopy. The radio equipment was in a small compartment aft of the bomb bay. In USN aircraft there was a ventral 0.3in machine gun but this was not fitted in most RN aircraft. The bomb bay could take a standard USN torpedo or four 500lb bombs but it was too short to take British torpedoes. The G-40, designated

An Avenger of 846 NAS in early 1944. (Philip Jarrett)

TBF-1 by the USN, first flew in August 1941 and the first production aircraft was rolled out in January 1942. USN aircraft acquisition increased dramatically after the Japanese attack on Pearl Harbour and Grumman was instructed to concentrate on the F6F Hellcat and transfer Avenger production to the Eastern Aircraft Division of General Motors, which was already producing Wildcats. Eastern-built Avengers were designated TBM-1 by the USN.

Avenger TBR II data

Length:	40ft 9in
Wingspan:	54ft 2in (19ft folded)
Height:	13ft 9in
MTOW:	17,364lb
Engine:	One 1,700hp Wright Cyclone R-2600-8 two-row, radial driving a 13ft diameter three-bladed Hamilton Standard constant-speed propeller
Fuel:	Avgas. 275 gallons internal plus optional 223-gallon auxiliary tank in bomb bay and two optional underwing 48-gallon drop tanks. Total 605 gallons
Performance:	Maximum level speed 225 knots Service ceiling 21,400ft. 13 minutes to 10,000ft
Endurance:	5 hours on internal fuel
Armament:	Two 0.5in front guns, one in each wing firing clear of the propeller arc with 600 rpg. One 0.5in machine gun in power-operated turret with 400 rounds. One optional ventral 0.3in machine gun with 500 rounds. One Mark XIII torpedo or one 1,000lb or four 500lb bombs in bomb bay. Provision for underwing 3in RP on later aircraft

The first 402 Avengers transferred to the RN under Lend-Lease arrangements were built specifically for the RN by Grumman and designated TBF-1B (for British) by the USN. They were named Tarpon in the RN in 1943 following the line Shark/Swordfish/Albacore etc but it never proved popular and the USN name Avenger was accepted as standard in January 1944. Between 1943 and 1945 the RN received 958 Avengers with the first 402 designated as Mark Is. They were followed by 334 TBM-1s designated as Mark IIs and 222 TBM-3s designated as Mark IIIs. Others intended for the RN were cancelled when the war ended.

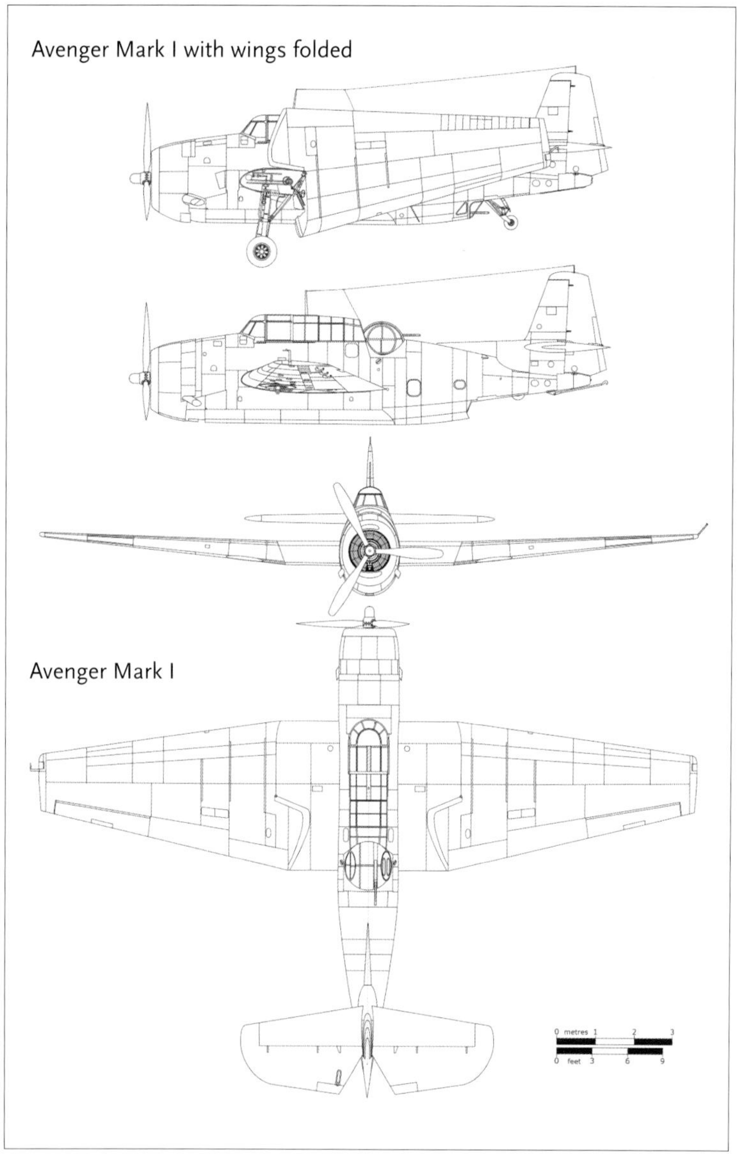

From late 1943 RN Avenger squadrons were formed at Squantum in the USA at the rate of one a month using a few experienced aircrew and others straight from training in the USA and Canada. After a brief work-up squadrons sailed for the UK in one of the newly commissioned CVEs on its delivery voyage to the UK.

Shore-based units equipped or partially-equipped with Avengers between 1943 and 1958 included 700, 703, 706, 707, 711, 733, 736, 738, 744, 745, 751, 756, 763, 764, 767, 768, 777, 778, 785, 787, 797 and 798 NAS. They were employed on a wide range of tasks ranging from aircrew refresher and conversion training in the UK, USA, Australia and Ceylon; trials, fleet requirements, deck-landing training, deck-landing instructor training, air warfare development, TBR training, anti-submarine warfare development and electronic warfare development.

Operational Avengers served with 814, 815, 820, 824, 828, 831, 832, 845, 846, 848, 849, 850, 851, 852, 853, 854, 855, 856, 857, 885, 1700, 1830, 1841 and 1844 NAS at various times between the first commissioning in1943 and the last retiring its remaining aircraft in 1960. Some of these units were composite squadrons which were also equipped with other aircraft types such as the Wildcat.

RN Avengers operated from the aircraft carriers *Albion*, *Arbiter*, *Begum*, *Centaur*, *Eagle*, *Emperor*, *Empress*, *Formidable*, *Illustrious*, *Implacable*, *Indefatigable*, *Indomitable*, *Khedive*, *Nabob*, *Premier*, *Queen*, *Ruler*, *Shah*, *Tracker*, *Trumpeter* and *Victorious*. For short periods they were used by the station flights at Culdrose and Eglinton.

Early production Avengers were modified to RN standards by Blackburn Aircraft in the UK but later examples were modified by Blackburn at Roosevelt Field, New York straight off the production line. Changes included the installation of British gun sights, oxygen systems, radios and radar; the substitution of an F.24 camera for the ventral gun in the majority of aircraft and the modification of the area aft of the pilot to act as an observer's cockpit. Bulged windows replaced the smaller USN-style windows on the W/T compartment and the radio mast on top of the cockpit was made to fold if necessary so that it could fit into the low hangar decks of some fleet carriers. The type's spacious fuselage made it ideal for weapon and equipment trials and at least one RN Avenger was modified with a Frazer Nash FN.95 remotely-controlled turret as part of its development for the Fairey Spearfish.

The first RN Avenger unit was 832 NAS which had TBF-1s supplied by the USN in January 1943 for service in *Victorious* while she was lent to the US Pacific Fleet. It also operated from the USS *Saratoga* when her Wildcats were concentrated in *Victorious* to make better use of the British carrier's superior air direction facilities. 832 NAS covered the American landings on the Solomon Islands, the first time RN aircraft had gone into action from a USN carrier. In the Home Fleet and WAC Avengers augmented Swordfish in the anti-submarine role and carried out a series of strikes against targets in the Norwegian littoral. A number of minelaying sorties off the Norwegian coast were carried out in 1944–5 to prevent enemy convoys from staying close to the shore. During the build up to D-Day several Avenger squadrons helped block the English Channel against German movements. They

Avengers of 846 NAS. (Philip Jarrett)

escorted assault convoys and attacked German minesweepers and both E and R-boats with some success. The last strike by Home Fleet Avengers was carried out against a U-boat base at Kilbotn in northern Norway on 4 May 1945.

Avengers were used in large numbers in the East Indies and BPF, replacing Barracudas. After a series of attacks against Sumatran targets Avengers from four carriers carried out Operation 'Meridian', the largest RN air strike of the war, against the two Japanese-held oil refineries at Palembang in Sumatra in January 1945. They achieved considerable success, cutting off a large percentage of the enemy's aviation fuel supply for the remainder of the war. Between March and May 1945 Avengers and fighters from five fleet carriers supported the American landings on Okinawa and attacked Japanese bases on Formosa. From July onwards they attacked the Japanese mainland with the last Avenger strike, escorted by Seafires, carried out at dawn on VJ-Day only hours before the Japanese surrender. After the end of hostilities Avengers had to be paid for, returned or destroyed and many were literally pushed into the sea to avoid the cost of shipping them back to the USA. The last unit to disband was 828 NAS in 1946.

This was not the end of the Avenger in RN service, however. The USN was concerned about delays with Gannet development and considered RN Barracudas and Fireflies incapable of coping with the growing Soviet submarine threat. It therefore transferred 100 TBM-3E/S Avengers under the MDAP. The 'E's were designated as Avenger

A BPF Avenger being ferried by lighter from the maintenance carrier *Unicorn* to a fleet carrier at Manus in 1945.

849 NAS Avengers preparing to attack Pangkalan Brandan refinery, Sumatra in 1945.

AS 4s and the 'S's as Avenger AS 5s in British service. Mark 4s were pressed into service quickly as received from the USN but AS 5s were modified with British equipment including radar in a fairing under the starboard wing and British communications. Their gun turrets were removed and replaced by a continuation of the glazed canopy aft and some were later upgraded to AS 6 standard with a new radar fitted under the forward section of the bomb bay. When Gannets replaced them, some were further modified for electronic warfare trials and training which continued until they were replaced by Gannets in 1960.

A BPF Avenger being pushed over the bow of *Pioneer* off Eastern Australia in 1945.

An Avenger taking-off from a CVE.

Hellcat

Design work had been initiated on the G-50 by 1940 when the USN instructed Grumman to continue development as a back-up for the F4U Corsair. It had a larger and stronger airframe than the F4F with a low mounted wing allowing a wider-track, inwards retracting undercarriage. Unlike the Corsair, the initial production version of the G-50 was found to be an excellent deck-landing aircraft; two prototypes had been ordered in June 1941 and development proceeded rapidly. Designated F6F by the USN and named Hellcat in line with the feline theme associated with Grumman fighters. A contract for 1,080 was placed in January 1942 and subsequent USN orders brought Hellcat production to 12,275 aircraft by the time the last was delivered in

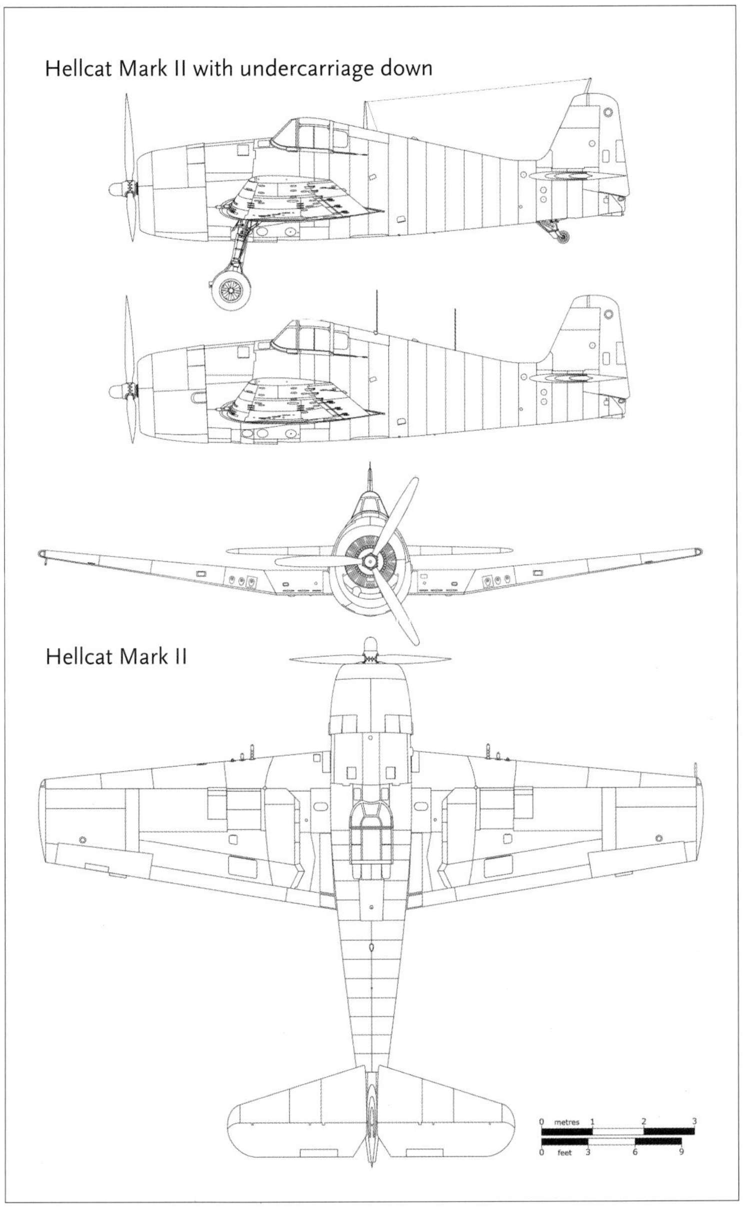

November 1945, all built by Grumman. The first was delivered in October 1942 and by 1943 the USN urgently needed night fighters and Hellcats were modified by Grumman to F6F-3N standard with AN/APS-6 radar in a radome beneath the outer part of the starboard wing. They also featured a radar altimeter, improved IFF and a flat windshield which acted the gunsight reflector. Red cockpit lighting was

A Hellcat Mark I of 757 NAS from Puttalam carrying out deck-landing practice on *Victorious*.

fitted and the instrument panel was redesigned around a centrally mounted radar screen. F6F-3Ns first joined a carrier air group in May 1944. A small number of Hellcats were modified with a long focal length camera in the lower port fuselage aft of the wing. They retained their front guns.

A lightened F6F-4 variant was projected for use from CVEs but not put into production and so production shifted to the F6F-5 standard, the first of which flew in April 1944. They introduced detail changes including additional armour, the flat windshield designed for the F6F-3N and hardpoints for bombs or drop tanks under the fuselage and wings. Within the F6F-5 total a number were completed to F6F-5N standard as night fighters fitted with the AN/APS 6 radar and a small number were modified by the USN after delivery as F6F-5P photographic reconnaissance aircraft.

The Hellcat was second only to the Corsair in the number transferred to the RN under Lend-Lease arrangements. The first 252 were delivered from May 1943 to F6F-3 standard and designated Hellcat F Mark I in British service. A further 849 aircraft were delivered to F6F-5 standard and designated Hellcat F Mark II. Deliveries were completed with seventy-six F6F-5Ns designated Hellcat NF II. Most were put into service initially as received except for the substitution of British R/T and IFF but Blackburn eventually carried out a number of modifications including hardpoints under the wings for 3in RP and cameras in the after fuselages of some aircraft for use in the fighter reconnaissance role designated Hellcat FR IIs. Other conversions were carried out by the RN in Ceylon where sufficient Hellcats were modified to PR II standard to equip 888 NAS for operations with the EIF and BPF. The front guns and ammunition were removed to save weight and F.52 cameras with 36in lenses were fitted in the after fuselage in place of the earlier cameras with their 14in lenses. The bottom of the lens cones projected below the fuselage and special fairings had to be designed and fitted locally to protect them from the airflow and oil seepage from the engine. With full internal fuel and a centreline drop tank a Hellcat PR II had an endurance of over 8 hours.

Hellcat F II data

Length:	33ft 7in
Wingspan:	42ft 10in (16ft 2in folded)
Height:	14ft 5in
MTOW:	14,700lb
Engine:	One 2,000hp Pratt & Whitney R-2800-10W Double Wasp radial
Fuel:	Avgas. Two 73-gallon tanks, one in each wing; one 62-gallon reserve tank under cockpit plus one optional 125-gallon centreline drop tank, total 333 gallons
Performance:	Maximum level speed 325 knots Service ceiling 36,700ft. 1½ minutes to 5,000ft
Endurance:	Up to 8 hours with a drop tank
Armament:	Six 0.5in Browning M2/AN front guns, three in each wing firing clear of the propeller arc with 400 rpg. Provision for two 500lb or one 1,000lb bomb on underwing racks. Provision for up to eight 3in RP with 60lb warheads on underwing rails

A total of 1,177 Hellcats were transferred to the RN between May 1943 and August 1945.

Hellcats were used between 1943 and 1946 in a number of shore-based roles including trials, training, development of both day and night fighter equipment and tactics, fleet requirements and as pool units to refresh and retrain pilots returning to operations. They equipped, or partially equipped, 700, 703, 706, 709, 725, 732, 735, 746, 748, 756, 757, 759, 760, 768, 771, 777, 778, 784 and 787 NAS. They were also used by station flights at China Bay and Lossiemouth.

Between 1943 and 1946 Hellcats served with 800, 804, 808, 881, 885, 888, 889, 891, 892, 896, 898, 1839, 1840, 1844 and 1847 NAS. At various times during the same period they operated from the aircraft carriers *Ameer*, *Arbiter*, *Emperor*, *Empress*, *Formidable*, *Furious*, *Indefatigable*, *Indomitable*, *Khedive*, *Ocean*, *Ravager*, *Ruler*, *Shah*, *Smiter* and *Speaker*.

Hellcats of 800 NAS.

A Hellcat Mark II of 896 NAS about to be catapulted from a CVE in 1945.

Hellcat NF IIs of 892 NAS ranged with Fireflies on *Ocean* during 1945 during a comparative trial of single and two-seat night fighter capabilities.

A B C D E F G H I J K L M N O P Q R S T U V W X Y Z

Hellcat NF II cockpit with the radar controls and screen circled.

The first RN unit to operate Hellcats was 800 NAS which converted from Sea Hurricanes in July 1943. Home Fleet Hellcats took part in strikes against targets in the Norwegian littoral including Operation 'Tungsten' which crippled *Tirpitz* in Kaa Fjord in April 1944. Most of the type's service was with the EIF and BPF, however. In the former they served in CVEs operating in the Burmese littoral in support of the XIVth Army culminating in the capture of Rangoon. 888 NAS was the only specialised PR unit in the RN and between February and March 1945 its aircraft completed twenty-two sorties over the Kra Isthmus, Penang and northern Sumatra to pave the way for Operation 'Zipper', the liberation of Singapore.

In the Pacific Hellcats provided part of the fighter escort for Operation 'Meridian', the strikes against the Palembang oil refineries and took part in operations over the Sakishima Islands in support of the American landings on Okinawa. In August 1945 Hellcats from BPF carriers operated over the Japanese mainland. By then the number of RN Hellcat squadrons was being increased towards the number required for British participation in the projected landings in Japan in the autumn but the unexpectedly early end to the war meant that the majority were disbanded and their aircraft returned to the USN if practical or simply pushed over the side of carriers to avoid the cost of returning them. Some second-line units retained Hellcats until late in 1945 because they were so well regarded that there was a reluctance to replace them. With Seafires and other British-built fighters available in large numbers, however, they could not be afforded.

Only two front-line Hellcat units continued in operation after VJ-Day. 892 NAS, equipped with Hellcat NF IIs, was embarked in the night carrier *Ocean* between December 1945 and April 1946 together with 1792 NAS' Fireflies for a series of evaluations in the Mediterranean to determine whether single or two-seat night fighters were preferable in the post-war fleet. The Firefly was selected as the better option in adverse weather because the observer was able to concentrate on the radar while the pilot flew the aircraft. The Hellcat was probably the better long-term system but would have cost scarce US dollars to maintain in service. The other unit that remained operational was 888 NAS which used its expertise operating under South-East Asia Air Command from Sembawang in Singapore on aerial survey work until June 1946 when its personnel sailed back to the UK to disband and its much-modified aircraft were destroyed.

Tigercat

Designed to meet a USN requirement for a twin-engined, carrier-borne fighter, Grumman's G-51 was named Tigercat and designated F7F by the USN before its first flight in November 1943. Repeated attempts to qualify it for carrier operation failed but it proved to be an excellent night fighter when operated from airfields and it was used as such by the USMC in limited numbers fitted with an AN/APS-6 radar in the nose. The F7F-1 was powered by two 2,100hp Pratt & Whitney R-2800-22W engines which gave a maximum level speed of 390 knots. Wingspan was 51ft 6in (32ft 2in folded) and MTOW 22,560lb. The Admiralty wanted to investigate the single-engined handling characteristics of a large, twin-engined carrier aircraft and the USN agreed to transfer two F7F-1s in 1944 for evaluation. One was tested by 787 NAS and returned to the USN in August 1945. The second was used by both the A&AEE and RAE in 1945/46 to test power-boosted rudder controls. It was returned to the USN in December 1946.

One of the Tigercats evaluated by the RN. It retained US markings but was allocated a British airframe number. (Philip Jarrett)

HANDLEY-PAGE

Type G

A single Type G/100 – the number referring to engine horsepower – two-seat biplane was built in 1913 and used to provide short flights for paying passengers. It had distinctive curved swept-back wings and was powered by a 100hp Anzani engine which gave a maximum level speed of 64 knots. Wingspan was 44ft and MTOW 1,775lb. Purchased by the Admiralty in 1914, its inherent stability was found to make it too easy to fly and instead of training duties it was used for air defence patrols from Hendon, flown by pilots armed with a Webley pistol. After transfer to Chingford in 1915 it was riddled with bullet holes over London by over-zealous gunners who mistook it for a German aircraft, fortunately without shooting it down. It was deleted in 1915.

The first 0/100 allocated to 7 (Naval) Squadron RNAS arriving at Coudekerque in April 1917.

0/100

Handley-Page designed the O/100 at the instigation of Commodore Sueter, Head of the Admiralty Air Department. It was larger than any aircraft built previously in the UK and to ensure the required structural strength, every spar, strut and fitting was tested to destruction and a two-engine layout was selected. Work on the project was given the highest priority during 1915 and the first aircraft was delivered to Hendon in December. Trials at Eastchurch found a number of modifications to be necessary including the substitution of an open rather than enclosed cockpit and the removal of armour to save weight. An open cockpit with a Scarff ring was fitted in front of the pilot for a defensive gunner and provision was made above and below the fuselage aft of the wings for gunners. The long upper wing extensions were supported by bracing wires from king-posts immediately above the outer interplane struts and, since the 0/100's enormous wingspan was expected to cause problems with hangarage, the wings could be folded outboard of the engine nacelles.

Bombs were carried in a bomb bay, suspended vertically from nose rings to take up minimal space around the centre of gravity. Spring-loaded doors were opened by the bombs as they fell through them and the bomb-aimer used a Type HA 1a bomb sight fitted under the gunner's position in the nose of the aircraft. Vertical bomb stowage took up the least space but caused them to tumble after falling through the doors, making accurate delivery almost impossible. Crew sizes varied but by late 1917 usually comprised a single pilot, an observer and two mechanics, all of whom had access to a defensive gun if they were intercepted by an enemy fighter.

Development of a new fuel system led to the O/400 which did not come into service until after the RNAS had been subsumed into the RAF. A few served with the Independent Force in 1918 but fall outside the scope of this book.

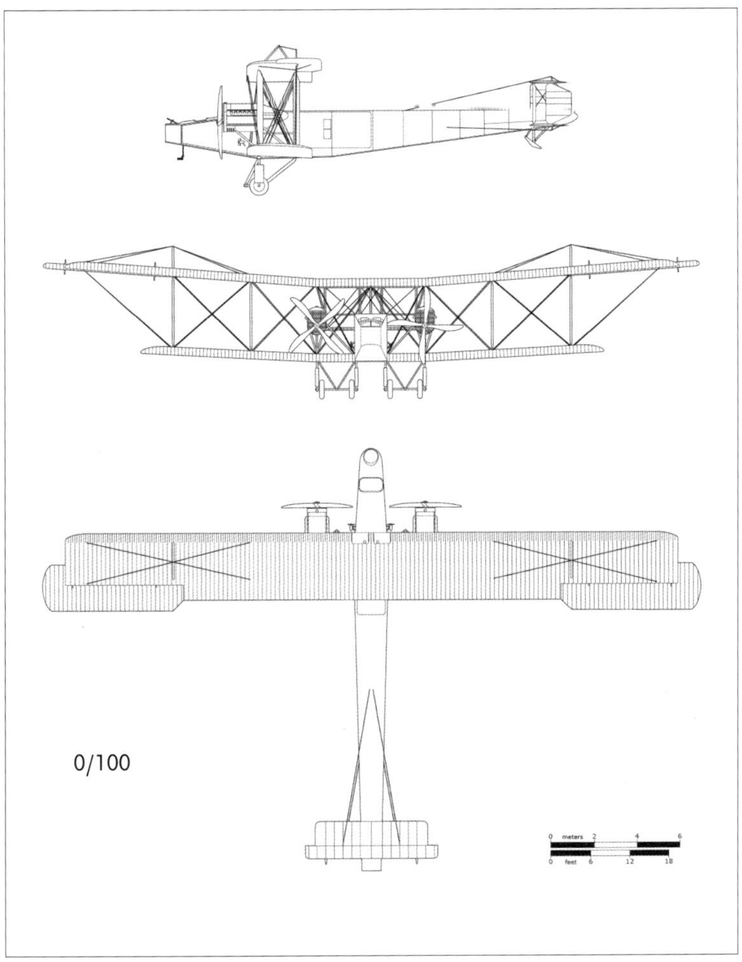

0/100 data

Length:	62ft 10in
Wingspan:	100ft (20ft folded)
Height:	22ft
MTOW:	14,000lb
Engines:	Two 322hp Rolls-Royce Eagle VII water-cooled
Fuel:	Avgas. 370 gallons
Performance:	Maximum level speed 80 knots Service ceiling 7,000ft with full bomb load. 20 minutes to 5,000ft
Endurance:	8 hours
Armament:	Twin 0.303in Lewis guns on Scarff mounting in nose. Two single Lewis guns on brackets either side of cockpit. One Lewis gun aft firing downwards through a trapdoor in the lower rear fuselage. Up to sixteen 112lb bombs

0/100s of 7 (Naval) Squadron. The nearest aircraft has its port wings folded.

An 0/100 photographed next to a Sopwith Triplane and a single-seat Nieuport to give an idea of its size.

The RNAS received forty O/100s which were progressively fitted with more powerful Eagle engines but some early examples were delivered with 320hp Sunbeam Cossacks before being re-engined.

Handley Page O/100s served with 7, 7A, 14, 16 and 'A' (Naval) Squadrons, RNAS; with 3 Wing at Luxeuil-les-Bains, 5 Wing at Dunkirk and at Manston, Redcar, Ochey and Mudros.

The first unit to receive O/100s was 5 Wing at Dunkirk in November 1916. Unfortunately the third aircraft was lost on its delivery flight when its pilot landed at the first airfield he saw after flying over unbroken cloud; unfortunately it turned out to be a German one, 12 miles beyond the front line. At first the 5 Wing aircraft were used for their original purpose flying daylight patrols off the Belgian coast and in April 1917 they attacked a force of German destroyers, leaving one on fire after several direct hits. After an O/100 was shot down on a similar mission they were switched to night bombing missions attacking destroyer and U-boat pens at Bruges, Ostend and Zeebrugge. In the south of France 3 Wing aircraft attacked German industrial centres, paving the way for similar attacks by the Independent Force in the last weeks of the war.

Four O/100s operated from Redcar in September 1917 to counter enemy submarine concentrations off the mouth of the River Tees. They sighted eleven U-boats and attacked seven with bombs; none were sunk but their presence limited U-boat activity. O/100 training was carried out at Manston including 'A' Squadron's preparation for strategic bombing operations. A single 0/100 deployed to Mudros in June 1917. The overall distance flown was 2,000nm, achieved in an airborne time of 31 hours. The crew of five took with them a spare engine, two spare propellers, hammocks, tents and a full set of aircraft spares. It attacked Constantinople on 9 July 1917, achieving hits with 112lb bombs on the battlecruiser *Goeben* in Stenia Bay and on the Turkish War Office.

R/200

Designed in 1917 to meet an Admiralty requirement for a two-seat reconnaissance fighter able to operate either as a seaplane or from a carrier deck, the R/200 had a wingspan of 36ft and was powered by a 200hp Hispano-Suiza engine driving a four-bladed wooden propeller to give a maximum level speed of 82 knots. MTOW was 2,990lb. Six prototypes were ordered but only three were completed; the first two as seaplanes and the last with a wheeled undercarriage. The first two were delivered in December 1917 and evaluated at the Welsh Harp reservoir near Hendon. The third was evaluated at Isle of Grain from February 1918 and later joined by the others but the pressure of bomber construction forced Handley Page to cancel the last three prototypes. The Grain evaluation had already found that the R/200 was inferior to the Parnall Panther which was smaller, lighter and faster with a more reliable Bentley BR 2 engine.

Hendon

In 1924 Handley-Page offered the two-seat HP 25 Hendon for use as a torpedo strike aircraft and six prototypes were ordered for evaluation at the A&AEE. Wingspan was 46ft, MTOW 6,970lb and it was powered by a 471hp Napier Lion II engine driving a two-bladed propeller which gave a maximum level speed of 95 knots. The type was not selected for operational service although one aircraft was attached to 461 Flight in 1924 for evaluation. Deck-landing trials were carried out in *Argus* in September 1925 and *Furious* a month later.

Harrow

The HP 54 Harrow was a monoplane bomber/transport aircraft with a fixed undercarriage designed for the RAF. It could carry up to six 500lb bombs or twenty-four fully-equipped troops and in 1939 one was used as the donor aircraft for successful air-to-air refuelling trials after being fitted with 1,000-gallon fuselage tanks. No Harrows were built specifically for the RN but eight were transferred to the RN from the RAF and modified to ferry aero-engines and passengers between naval airfields. They were all operated by 782 NAS based at Donibristle until 1943 when they were returned to the RAF except for one aircraft that had been lost. Known within the squadron as 'Sparrows', they had a wingspan of 88ft and MTOW of 23,000lb. Two 925hp Bristol Pegasus XX engines drove three-bladed propellers to give a maximum level speed of 175 knots.

Jetstream

Designed for the US market as a civilian twelve to twenty-seat, turboprop feeder-liner with a crew of two, the HP 137 Jetstream first flew in 1967 but Handley-Page was declared bankrupt in 1970. Production and support were taken over by Scottish Aviation which subsequently became part of British Aerospace. Selected by the RAF as a multi-engine pilot training aircraft designated Jetstream T 1, a small production run followed including both re-manufactured civilian aircraft, new-builds and some assembled from partially completed Handley-Page airframes and components. T 1s went into service with the RAF in 1973 but were withdrawn and placed in storage in 1975 as a defence cut. Sixteen T 1s were then transferred to the RN and fourteen of these were modified to T 2 standard as 'flying classrooms' to replace Sea Princes in 750 NAS for observer training. Two further ex-civil aircraft were modified to T 2 standard.

The T 2 had an MEL E190 radar with an 18in scanner within a 'thimble' radome in an elongated nose. They also had TANS, similar to the system fitted in front-line helicopters, which had a doppler input from a Decca Type 71. Fully instrumented consoles were fitted in the rear cabin for both students and instructors with the latter able to move freely about the cabin if necessary. RN Jetstreams were normally operated by a single pilot but there were two seats for pilot training, standardisation and instrument checks. A staff observer usually sat in the right hand pilot seat for take-off and landing. The first T 2 was delivered to 750 NAS at Culdrose in 1978 and the unit was fully equipped by 1979.

Jetstream T 2 data

Length:	47ft 1½in
Wingspan:	52ft
Height:	17ft 5½in
MTOW:	12,550lb
Engines:	Two 940shp Turbomeca Astazou XVI turboprops
Fuel:	Avcat. 384 gallons
Performance:	Maximum speed in level flight 250 knots
	Service ceiling 28,000ft. 2 minutes to 5,000ft
Endurance:	5 hours
Armament:	None

A further four Jetstreams were built to T 3 standard in 1984. These were based on the later civil Jetstream 31 and differed from the T 2 in having Garrett TPE 331 turboprops. They were equipped with Racal ASR360 radars mounted in a ventral radome giving all-round cover rather than the nose-mounted radar in the T 2. They were delivered in 1986 and initially augmented the T 2s in 750 NAS. Later they were used by Yeovilton station flight to maintain a clipper service between air stations. Jetstreams operated with 750 NAS until March 2011 when they were replaced by Beech King Air 350ERs having flown 100,000 hours and trained more than 1.000 student observers.

Jetstream T 2 of 750 NAS at Culdrose.

HAWKER

Hart Trainer

Based on an RAF two-seat biplane day bomber with a performance comparable to contemporary fighters, this variant was a trainer with dual controls. Wingspan was 37ft 4in and MTOW 4,150lb. It was powered by a single 525hp Rolls-Royce Kestrel I B water-cooled engine driving a two-bladed, fixed-pitch propeller to give a maximum level speed of 150 knots. Four Hart Trainers were taken on charge by the Fleet Air Arm for 1 FTS at Leuchars to give advanced flying training to RN pilots between 1932 and 1936 before they moved onto operational types. A single Vickers 0.303in machine gun with 500 rounds was fitted on the port side of the fuselage for weapons training and light bombs could be carried under the wings for glide and dive-bombing instruction. A further seven Hart Trainers were transferred from the RAF stocks to the RN in October 1939 for use by the newly-formed 780 NAS at Eastleigh which converted volunteer civilian pilots to naval standards. It moved to Lee-on-Solent in 1940 and Hart Trainers continued in use until 1942.

Audax

Another Hart variant, the Audax was used by the RAF for tactical support of the Army. It had lengthened exhaust manifolds to prevent pilots' view of the ground being obscured when flying at low altitude and a long message pick-up hook under the fuselage. The Hart's gun armament was retained and there was underwing provision for up to four 20lb bombs or two 112lb supply containers. MTOW was 4,290lb but otherwise the specifications were the same as those of the Hart Trainer. Four Audaxes were transferred to the RN from the RAF for 780 NAS between 1941 and 1942. They were deleted in 1942.

Hoopoe

The single Hoopoe was a private venture tendered to meet Admiralty Specification N.21/26 for a carrier-borne single-seat fighter. It was tested with both a wheeled undercarriage and twin floats although it was found to be significantly underpowered in the latter configuration. Admiralty insistence that it be fitted with a radial engine led to several being tried, the most powerful being a 560hp Armstrong Siddeley Panther III which gave a maximum level speed of 175 knots. Wingspan was 33ft 2in and MTOW 3,910lb. Armament comprised two Vickers 0.303in belt-fed front guns with 530 rpg and provision for four 20lb bombs on underwing racks. Trials at both the A&AEE and MAEE were positive and deck-landing trials were carried out in *Courageous* but by 1930 development of the Nimrod with its liquid-cooled Kestrel engine appeared to show more promise and the Hoopoe was scrapped in 1932.

Nimrod

Admiralty Specification N.16/30 called for a derivative of the Hoopoe powered by a Rolls-Royce Kestrel engine. The result was the Nimrod, a single-seat biplane interceptor fighter which had begun as a private venture with the company designation HN.1, known unofficially as the Norn. By the time the first prototype flew in 1930 it was officially named Nimrod. A second airframe was built for structural testing and ditching/flotation gear trials from the seaplane carrier *Ark Royal*. The Nimrod reflected the view of its designer, Sydney Camm, that aircraft designed for carrier operation need not diverge from those intended for use ashore to anything like the extent that the RAF claimed to be necessary. Structurally it followed Hawker's contemporary methods and had wings with pronounced stagger to give the pilot a reasonable field of view for combat and deck landing. The structure was manufactured with fabric-covered duralumin tubing except for the aluminium panels which covered the engine bay and cockpit area. Deck operations were greatly eased by the type's pneumatic brakes which allowed aircraft to be parked in a 'herring-bone' range and taxied onto the centreline for take-off. The wings were compatible with the 'T'-shaped lifts in the latest carriers and so did not fold. Nimrods had interchangeable wheel or twin-float undercarriages, both fixed to the same attachment points.

Company trials were carried out at Brooklands in 1931, followed by evaluation at the A&AEE and, for the float-fitted version, MAEE. Deck-landing trials combined with sea acceptance trials in *Eagle* during early 1932 and the Nimrod Mark I was accepted into service in June. Development continued and a new specification, N.11/33, was drawn up around a Mark II version with the original Kestrel engine replaced by a more powerful development. It was stressed for catapult launches but lack of a headrest had caused pilot discomfort during catapult acceleration in the Mark I and this was rectified in the Mark II. The new specification also included a requirement to provide better protection against corrosion in the salt-laden sea air and three Mark IIs were constructed with stainless steel tubing. This alteration was not adopted as standard, however, since the greater cost was not offset by significantly improved corrosion resistance. Mark IIs also had slightly swept-back upper and lower wings to compensate for the rearward shift of the centre of gravity that followed the installation of a tail hook and the strengthening around its attachment points when transverse arrester wires were introduced, beginning with *Courageous* in 1931. An A&AEE report in 1931 described the Nimrod's performance as 'impeccable' but later reports, whilst still generally full of praise, commented that the later configuration produced a poor spin to the left.

A Nimrod of 408 Flight embarked in *Glorious* during 1931.

A Nimrod fitted with floats for evaluation at the MAEE Felixstowe during 1932.

Nimrod Mark II data

Length:	26ft 6⅛in
Wingspan:	33ft 6¾in
Height:	9ft 10in
MTOW:	4,059lb with wheeled undercarriage. 4,250lb with twin floats
Engine:	One 640hp Rolls-Royce Kestrel V driving a Watts 2-bladed wooden propeller
Fuel:	Avgas. 61 gallons
Performance:	Maximum speed in level flight 170 knots (125 knots as floatplane) Service ceiling 26,900ft. 6½ minutes to 10,000ft
Endurance:	1 hour 40 minutes
Armament:	Two 0.303in Vickers Mark III front guns with 600 rpg, one either side of cockpit where pilot could reach the breeches to re-cock if necessary. Provision for up to four 20lb bombs on underwing racks

Nimrods of 800 NAS embarked in *Courageous* during 1937.

Hawker built eighty-five Nimrods: of these, two were prototypes, sixty-one were Mark Is and twenty-two were Mark IIs.

Between 1932 and the reorganisation of Fleet Air Arm units in April 1933, Nimrods served with 402, 404, 408 and 409 Fleet Fighter Flights. After the reorganisation they served with 800, 801, 802 and 803 NAS until May 1939 when the last front-line Nimrod unit, 802 NAS, was re-equipped with Sea Gladiators. The 800-series units operated with two flights of Nimrods and one flight of Ospreys. All but 801 NAS, which was the first to relinquish its aircraft in 1936, operated a mix of Nimrods Mark I and II. Nimrods were embarked at various times in the aircraft carriers *Eagle*, *Courageous*, *Furious* and *Glorious*. On the outbreak of war in September 1939, Nimrods remained in use until 1941 with 753, 757, 759 and 780 NAS on training and pilot conversion tasks.

A float-fitted Osprey of 803 NAS over *Hermes* on the China Station in 1935. (Bill Lucy)

Osprey

A two-seat fighter-reconnaissance aircraft intended for operation from both aircraft carriers and catapult-equipped capital ships and cruisers that evolved from the Hart. The prototype Hart was modified at Hawker's expense in 1928 to demonstrate that it could meet Admiralty Specification O.22/26 for the role but production incorporated a number of design changes including greater structural strength to withstand both catapult launches and arrested landings. Wingspan was greater than the Nimrod and so folding wings were incorporated. Mark I Ospreys had aluminium and steel tube structures with aluminium panels over the engine bay. The after fuselage, wings and tailplane were fabric covered. From 1932 the fuselage structure was fabricated with stainless steel to counter the effects corrosion; this and other minor modifications led to the Mark II. Either mark could be fitted with twin floats as alternatives to the fixed wheeled undercarriage using the same attachment points. The wheeled undercarriage included pneumatic brakes. The Mark III introduced in 1933 was equipped with an inflatable dinghy stowed in the starboard upper wing, an engine-driven generator and a Fairey-Reed metal propeller, replacing the wooden propeller of the earlier marks. The final production variant was the Mark IV which replaced the earlier 525hp Rolls-Royce Kestrel II MS with a more powerful variant. All marks had an 'A' frame arrester hook under the rear fuselage forward of the tail skid which could be removed when the twin floats were fitted. Water rudders at the rear of the floats were controlled by the pilot's rudder pedals and water manoeuvring was assessed as good by the MAEE.

A&AEE reports described the Osprey as pleasant to fly, an opinion backed up by many RN pilots who spoke highly of it, but the rear gunner's effectiveness at speeds over 130 knots was questionable. Alarmingly, a test dive in excess of 210 knots in a Mark III caused the hydrostatic valve to operate and inflate the dinghy which broke free and wrapped itself around the tailplane. Despite this, the pilot managed to land safely.

Osprey Mark IV data

Length:	29ft 4in (31ft 10¼in as a floatplane)
Wingspan:	37ft (15ft 7½in folded)
Height:	10ft 5in (12ft 5in as a floatplane)
MTOW:	4,950lb (5,570lb as a floatplane)
Engine:	One 607hp Rolls-Royce Kestrel V
Fuel:	Avgas. 90 gallons
Performance:	Maximum level speed 155 knots (128 knots as a floatplane) Service ceiling 23,500ft (20,700ft as a floatplane) 8 minutes to 10,000ft (11 minutes as a floatplane)
Endurance:	2 hours 15 minutes
Armament:	One belt-fed 0.303in Vickers Mark II front gun with 500 rounds. One 0.303in Lewis machine gun on a Scarff ring in rear cockpit. Provision for up to eight 20lb or two 112lb bombs on underwing racks

Dorsetshire's Osprey taking-off from Hong Kong harbour with other aircraft of the 5th Cruiser Squadron. (Bill Lucy)

A total of 133 Ospreys were delivered including three prototypes, thirty-seven Mark I/IIs, sixty-seven Mark IIIs and twenty-six Mark IVs.

Between 1932 and 1936 Ospreys equipped 403, 404, 405, 406, 407, 409, 443, 444, 445 and 447 Flights. After the re-organisation of floatplane flights in 1936 they operated with 701, 712, 713, 714, 715, 716, 718 Floatplane Flights.

From 1939 Ospreys equipped several shore-based squadrons including 755, 757, 758, 759 and 780 NAS which were used in the TAG training, fighter pilot training and pilot conversion roles. The last unit to give up its Ospreys was 780 NAS which retired them early in 1942; the others had mostly gone by the end of 1940.

After the 1933 reorganisation of Fleet Air Arm units, Ospreys were operated by 800, 801, 802 and 803 NAS. All but the latter operated as mixed units with both Nimrods and Ospreys. They were all replaced by mid-1939.

Between 1933 and 1939 Ospreys operated from the aircraft carriers *Ark Royal*, *Courageous*, *Eagle*, *Furious*, *Glorious* and *Hermes*. As floatplanes they operated as catapult flights from the battleships *Barham*, *Ramillies*, *Royal Sovereign* and *Valiant* and the cruisers *Achilles*,

Ospreys from 800 NAS embarked in *Ark Royal* during 1939.

An Osprey being catapulted from the cruiser *Neptune* in 1934.

Ajax, *Amphion*, *Apollo*, *Arethusa*, *Berwick*, *Cornwall*, *Devonshire*, *Dorsetshire*, *Emerald*, *Enterprise*, *Exeter*, *Galatea*, *Kent*, *Leander*, *London*, *Neptune*, *Orion*, *Penelope*, *Shropshire*, *Sussex* and *York*.

Ospreys were in widespread service by 1933 embarked in aircraft carriers, capital ships and cruisers deployed around the world. They were also used at Gosport as operational training aircraft. 803 NAS embarked in *Eagle* was instrumental in the recapture of the *Tungchow*, a British merchant ship threatened by mutiny on passage from Shanghai to Chefoo with a number of British women and children on board, a mission typical of many carried out by the RN on the China Station during the 1930s. Mark IVs were mostly used as floatplanes embarked in the 3rd Cruiser Squadron in the Mediterranean fleet but some were issued as attrition replacements to the squadrons embarked in carriers.

Henley

A two-seat, light day bomber designed for the RAF, it shared many production jigs with the Hurricane but the RAF lost interest in the concept after prototype trials although a small production run was ordered for use as target tugs. The Henley was powered by a single 1,030hp Rolls-Royce Merlin III driving a three-bladed, two-pitch propeller giving a maximum level speed of 230 knots when towing a sleeve target. Wingspan was 47ft 10½in and MTOW 8,480lb. All armament was removed and a wind-driven winch fitted to operate the cable drum but it needed full throttle to achieve realistic target speeds and this led to excessive engine over-heating and failure. A speed limit of 190 knots was imposed which limited the type's value and even this could not be achieved as larger targets were introduced. No Henleys were built directly for the RN but seven were transferred from the RAF to the RN for target-towing duties in October 1939 and operated by 771 NAS at Hatston and, later, Twatt to provide the Home Fleet with towed airborne targets for live anti-aircraft gunnery practice. Attrition gradually reduced their number and the last was deleted in 1943.

Sea Hurricane

Sydney Camm began design work on the single-seat monoplane fighter that was to become the Hurricane in 1934 despite there being no RAF requirement for such an aircraft at the time. Hawker funded its own work at first although the RAF eventually recognised the design's merit and wrote a specification around it but did not order a prototype until 1935. Hawker suggested improvements to the specification, including the substitution of four 20mm cannon for the rifle-calibre machine guns the RAF wanted. This far-sighted proposal was rejected at the time but when the RAF came belatedly to realise its importance after combat experience the Hurricane was already in large-scale production and modified wings took time to introduce. Unfortunately, a naval version with folding wings was also rejected following RAF advice that it could

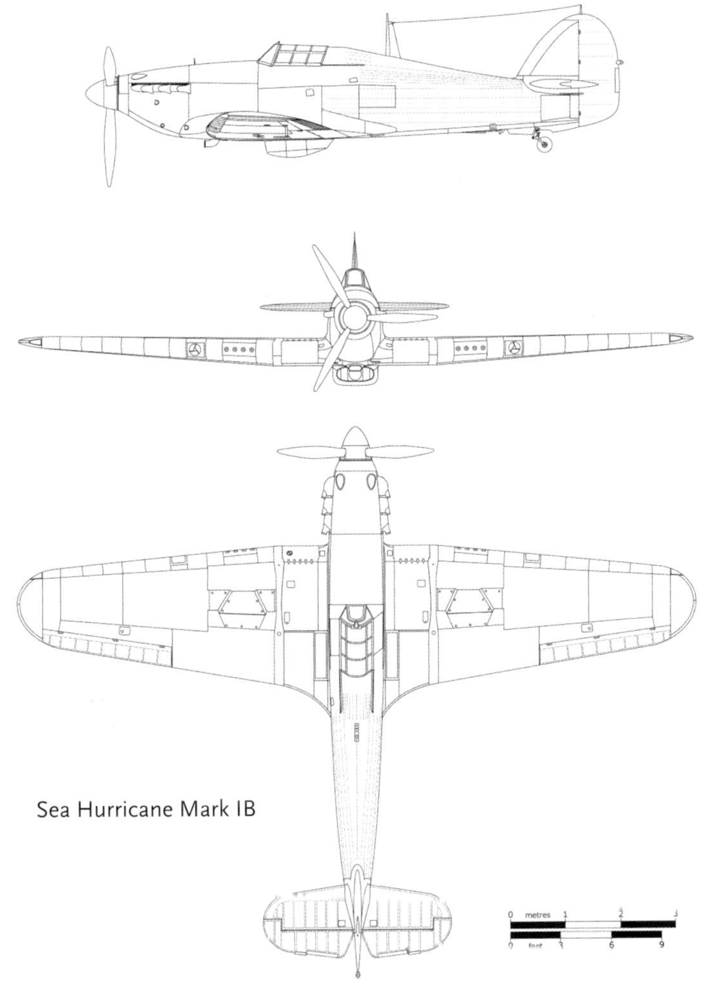

Sea Hurricane Mark IB

Sea Hurricane on a MAC-Ship catapult.

defend the fleet and that the RN would not need such a high-performance fighter. After the prototype was favourably reviewed by the A&AEE Hawker set up production facilities for 1,000 Hurricanes on its own initiative before any official orders were placed and the first production aircraft flew in October 1937.

Structurally, the Hurricane followed Camm's well-proven practice with a tubular metal, cross-braced, fabric-covered after fuselage. The engine bay and cockpit area were covered by aluminium panels. Early production aircraft had fabric-covered wings but these were replaced by metal stressed-skin wings from 1939. As production expanded different

Sea Hurricanes of 880 NAS on *Indomitable* in 1942.

A Sea Hurricane of 880 NAS being re-armed on *Indomitable*'s flight deck.

wings were introduced with different armament features indicated by a letter after the mark number beginning with the 'A' wings which had provision for eight 0.303in machine guns; the 'B' with twelve and the 'C' with four 20mm Hispano cannon. Later examples had wings strengthened to carry bombs or RP. Early aircraft had two-bladed propellers but these were replaced by two-position, three-blade units and eventually by de Havilland or Rotol, three-blade, constant-speed propellers.

The opportunity to manufacture a navalised Hurricane variant having been lost in the early stages of the design, the Admiralty still had to overcome RAF opinion that the operation of high-speed monoplanes from a carrier would be problematical when it resumed full control of naval aircraft procurement in 1939. The catalyst for change came with the brief Norwegian Campaign in 1940 when carrier-borne fighters had provided the only practical means of providing air support for the expeditionary force ashore. The RAF had relied on carriers to carry aircraft to the scene of action and first Gladiators and then Hurricanes were flown off *Glorious* to operate from a frozen lake. The Hurricane pilots had minimal training but managed to land some of their aircraft back on the carrier rather than abandon them when Norway was evacuated. Tragically they were lost a day later when *Glorious* was sunk but the lesson had been learned and desperate steps were taken to convert Hurricanes for naval use. The first were repaired RAF aircraft designated Sea Hurricane Mark IA, some of which had already seen considerable use, fitted with catapult spools for launch from CAM-Ships. Fifty aircraft were converted and thirty-five CAM-Ships were modified with a catapult over their forecastle; they still carried their normal cargo and the final decision whether or not to launch rested with the Master as advised by the embarked RN direction officer. After launch, the aircraft would probably have insufficient fuel to reach an airfield ashore and the pilot was left with the choice of bailing out over the convoy and hoping to be rescued or ditching close to one of the escorts. The large radiator under the fuselage gave the Sea Hurricane very bad ditching characteristics and most pilots elected to bail out. The first CAM-Ship was the SS *Michael E* which sailed in May 1941 but was torpedoed and sunk without launching her aircraft. They were also carried by anti-aircraft escorts designated as fighter-catapult ships manned by the RN and one of these achieved success in August 1941 when it shot down a Focke-Wulf Condor. CAM-Ship aircraft were manned by volunteer RAF pilots, fighter-catapult aircraft were manned by RN pilots.

At the same time modification kits were manufactured to produce Sea Hurricanes that could operate from aircraft carriers. These included an 'A' frame arrester hook fitted under the after fuselage, catapult spools, local strengthening of the airframe and naval radio equipment. The modified aircraft were designated Sea Hurricane Mark IB. They were all either refurbished RAF aircraft or taken from RAF production. The work was mainly carried out by General Aircraft Ltd but some conversions were carried out at naval air yards. Exact numbers have been lost but over 300 Sea Hurricanes were probably produced in this way. From November 1941 Hurricane Mark II airframes were modified

During Operation 'Torch' in 1942 all six of 804 NAS' Sea Hurricanes failed to find *Dasher* after their first operational mission and made forced landings ashore. This is one of them, showing the USN-style markings applied for the operation although the words 'Royal Navy' have not been removed.

to Sea Hurricane standard, the majority converted after completion but some were produced from the outset as Sea Hurricanes on the production lines. Early examples were Mark IIAs with machine-gun wings but the majority were IICs with cannons.

Sea Hurricane Mark IIC data

Length:	32ft 3½in
Wingspan:	40ft
Height:	13ft 3½in
MTOW:	7,800lb
Engine:	One 1,460hp Rolls-Royce Merlin XX liquid-cooled driving a three-blade de Havilland or Rotol constant-speed propeller
Fuel:	Avgas. 97 gallons in three internal tanks plus two optional 44-gallon or 90-gallon drop tanks on underwing hardpoints. Total, with two 90-gallon tanks, 277 gallons
Performance:	Maximum level speed 300 knots Service ceiling 35,600ft. 5 minutes to 10,000ft
Endurance:	2½ hours on internal fuel
Armament:	Four 20mm British Hispano Mark I cannon front guns with 100 rpg, two in each wing firing clear of the propeller arc. Provision on underwing racks for two 250lb or 500lb bombs or eight 3in RP

Since the number of conversion kits manufactured did not exactly match the number of Sea Hurricanes recorded as having been converted it is impossible to say definitively how many Sea Hurricanes were taken on RN charge. Surviving records do reveal, however, that there were at least 630 of which 544 were refurbished RAF aircraft or conversions carried out on aircraft after they had left the production lines. Research is complicated by the fact that many refurbished aircraft were allocated new airframe numbers. A further fifty-eight aircraft were built from the outset as Sea Hurricanes and twenty-eight Hurricane FB IIs were transferred from the RAF to the RN for use by FRUs.

From 1941 Sea Hurricanes served with shore-based squadrons on a variety of tasks including fighter pilot training, type conversion, deck-landing training, DLCO training, fleet requirements duties around the world and naval air warfare development. They included 700, 702, 727, 728, 731, 748, 759, 760, 762, 766, 768, 769, 771, 772, 774, 775, 776, 778, 779, 787, 788, 789, 791, 792 and 794 NAS. The last of these was de-commissioned in 1945.

Operational units equipped with Sea Hurricanes from 1941 included 800, 801, 802, 803, 804, 805, 806, 807, 811, 813, 824, 825, 835, 880, 882, 883, 885, 886, 889, 891, 895 and 897 NAS. Of these 811, 813, 824, 825 and 835 NAS were composite units that operated fighter flights alongside anti-submarine aircraft such as the Swordfish in CVEs.

Sea Hurricanes operated from the aircraft carriers *Argus*, *Avenger*, *Biter*, *Dasher*, *Eagle*, *Furious*, *Indomitable*, *Nairana*, *Striker*, *Unicorn* and *Victorious* and the fighter-catapult ship *Maplin*.

Sea Hurricanes operated from fleet carriers in the Atlantic, Mediterranean and Indian Oceans as well as ashore in North Africa using Hurricanes transferred from the RAF when RN Fulmars, Martlets and Buffaloes ran out of spares support. They also operated from CVEs in the Atlantic, Mediterranean and Arctic in defence of convoys and supporting the Allied landings in North Africa, Operation 'Torch'. They distinguished themselves particularly well in supporting convoys to North Russia through particularly harsh conditions from Convoy PQ 18 onwards in 1942. Some units were still operating the type in 1944 but by then the majority had been replaced by more suitable aircraft such as the Grumman Wildcat. Arguably the Sea Hurricane's greatest achievement was in defence of the 'Pedestal' Convoy for the relief of Malta in 1942. Three carriers, *Victorious*, *Indomitable* and *Eagle*, had 74 fighters embarked between them, of which 50 were Sea Hurricanes, to protect the convoy against 500 enemy aircraft, many of which flew several sorties during 11/12 August, as the convoy passed through the Sicilian narrows. Between them the RN fighters flew 209 sorties during the two-day battle and shot down 39 enemy aircraft. Sea Hurricanes flew 126 sorties with 56 combats in which 26 enemy aircraft were shot down and 13 damaged. Four Sea Hurricanes were lost and others damaged. Lieutenant (A) R J Cork DSC RN shot down six enemy aircraft during the 2 days. Obsolescent by the time the RN received them in any numbers, the Sea Hurricane did at last provide a fighter with sufficient performance to take on opposing fighters with some chance of success and they filled a gap until powerful American fighters became available under Lend-Lease arrangements. It was popular with pilots and 'Winkle' Brown noted that, whilst it lacked the level speed of contemporary German fighters such as the Bf 109F, it could turn inside them easily and the cannon armament of the Mark IIC packed a significant 'punch'. Its wide-track, inwards-retracting undercarriage made it a better deck-landing aircraft than the Seafire and its cross-braced tubular metal construction facilitated relatively straightforward battle damage repair by squadron mechanics.

P.1009

Admiralty Specification N.11/40 for a single-seat carrier-borne strike fighter resulted in the Blackburn Firebrand but Hawker had submitted a rival 'Sea Typhoon' designated P.1009. No prototype was built but drawings show folding wings hinged to lie flush along the fuselage sides like the Skua. Armament was to be four Hispano 20mm cannon with 140 rpg and MTOW would have been about 11,400lb with wingspan similar to the Typhoon at 41ft 7in. Typhoons in RAF service after 1941 were powered by a single 2,180hp Napier Sabre IIA engine which gave a maximum level speed of 355 knots. No work on the P.1009 was continued after the Firebrand was selected.

A single Typhoon was taken on charge by 778 NAS, at Arbroath in 1943 for RN evaluation but was written off after a crash on take-off later in the year.

Sea Fury

In 1943 Sydney Camm designed a fighter to meet Admiralty Specification N.7/43 and suggested that the same basic airframe could also meet an extant RAF requirement. Work on both was taken forward with Hawker preparing drawings for the RAF version and Boulton Paul subcontracted to produce the naval version, beginning with the preparation of drawings. In 1944 the land-based version was named the Fury and the RN version the Sea Fury. The engine selected to power both was the Bristol Centaurus although other engines tested in prototype form included Rolls-Royce Griffons and Napier Sabres. The production standard Sea Fury was described in Admiralty Specification N.22/43 and an initial order for 200 was placed in April 1944, 100 of which were to be built by Boulton Paul. The first Fury prototype flew in September 1944 but by then the RAF had cancelled the entire Fury contract. The first Sea Fury prototype flew in February 1945 and development continued although the Boulton Paul contract was cancelled when the war ended. A second prototype was completed in October 1945 to full RN standard with folding wings, arrester hook, armament and naval radio. A third was completed in January 1946.

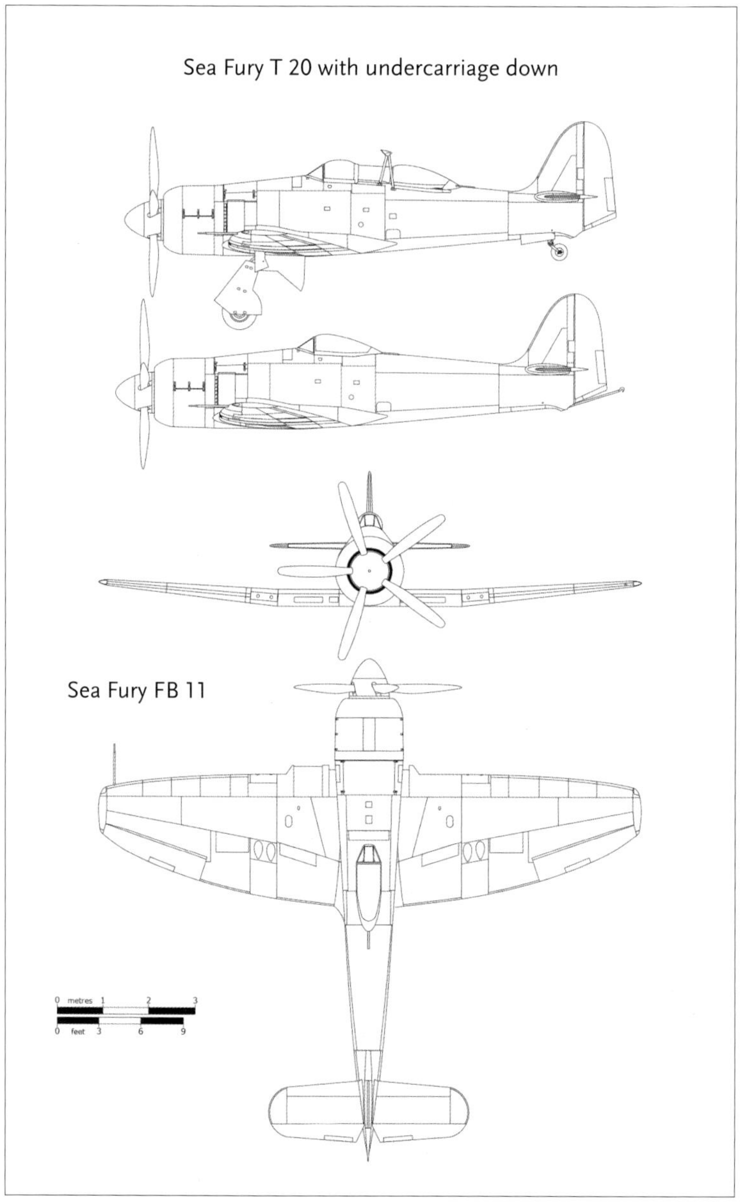

A Sea Fury FB 11 in its factory finish before being delivered to Anthorn in 1951.

A Sea Fury seconds before landing on *Illustrious*.

The Sea Fury was an outstanding single-seat fighter of all-metal, stressed-skin construction that proved popular with pilots and coped well with carrier operations. Trials assumed a more leisurely pace after 1945 but the problems encountered were minor and quickly rectified. An improved hook damper cured an early tendency to bounce and a slightly enlarged tailplane and rudder provided the necessary capability to counter a swing on take-off caused by the massive engine torque when the throttle was opened quickly. Engine vibration at low rpm was cured by a new, resilient, type of mounting. It was superbly aerobatic and deck-landing qualification was achieved after trials in *Victorious* during the winter of 1946/47. A release to service was issued in 1947.

The first version was the Sea Fury F.10, the new Arabic numeral system having replaced Roman numerals in 1947. The mark allocation began at 10 because the numbers 1 to 9 had been allocated to the cancelled Fury. After continued development, Hawker produced strengthened wings to create a more versatile fighter-bomber able to carry bombs, RP, drop tanks and napalm on underwing hardpoints. It also allowed RATOG to be fitted to the inner wings and the improved aircraft, designated Sea Fury FB 11 became one of the outstanding naval aircraft of any generation. As he had said he would, Camm delivered an excellent carrier fighter and what proved to be an outstanding land-based fighter in export versions of the Fury sold abroad from a common basic design. He demonstrated that it is perfectly possible for a good designer to produce a common, successful aircraft that succeeds in both disciplines when allowed the freedom to do so. With the impetus of Korean War operations new batches of Sea Furies were ordered until 1951.

The last variant of the Sea Fury in RN service was the T 20, a two-seat, dual control, training aircraft for standardisation and instrument checks that could also be used for armament training by RN squadrons as well as conversion training for pilots in the RNVR air squadrons. Unusually its development followed an order for a two-seat Fury variant placed by Iraq but the first prototype was produced for the RN. It differed in having two cockpits, each with its own canopy and it first flew in 1948 but during trials at the A&AEE the rear canopy collapsed during a high-speed manoeuvre. The solution was to fit a perspex tunnel that connected the two revised canopies. Hawker designed a periscope mounted on a four-legged structure just forward of the after cockpit to give the instructor a view ahead. Armament was reduced to two 20mm front guns so that equipment displaced from the fuselage by the rear cockpit could be fitted in the wings. They were not fitted with arrester hooks and were never embarked.

Sea Fury FB 11 data

Length:	34ft 7in
Wingspan:	38ft 4½in spread. (18ft 2in folded)
Height:	14ft 9in (with one propeller blade vertical)
MTOW:	14,555lb
Engine:	One 2,280hp Bristol Centaurus XVIII air-cooled radial
Fuel:	Avgas. 200 gallons plus two optional 45-gallon or 90-gallon drop tanks on underwing hardpoints. Total, with two 90-gallon tanks, 380 gallons
Performance:	Maximum level speed 390 knots Service ceiling 35,800ft. 10 minutes to 30,000ft
Endurance:	Over 3 hours with drop tanks
Armament:	Four 20mm British Hispano cannon front guns with 145 rpg, two in each wing firing clear of the propeller arc. Provision on underwing hardpoints for two 1,000lb or 500lb bombs, up to twelve 3in RP, napalm bombs, practice bombs or optional drop tanks

The RN received 729 Sea Furies of which three were prototype single-seaters and one a prototype two-seater. The first fifty single-seaters were delivered to F 10 standard and the balance of 615 to FB 11 standard. There were sixty T 20 two-seat trainers.

From 1947 to 1956 Sea Furies equipped, or partially equipped a number of shore-based squadrons in the advanced, operational, conversion and refresher training roles as well as service trials and development work in fighter tactics, photography and electronic warfare. They were also used by FRUs and for deck landing and DLCO training. They included 700, 703, 736, 738, 739, 744, 751, 759, 766, 767, 771, 773, 778, 781, 782, 787 and 799 NAS.

Sea Furies equipped 801, 802, 806, 807, 810, 811 and 898 NAS and served with 1830, 1831, 1832, 1833 and 1834 NAS in the RNVR Air Branch.

Between 1947 and 1955 Sea Fury squadrons embarked in *Centaur*, *Glory*, *Illustrious*, *Implacable*, *Indomitable*, *Ocean*, *Theseus*, *Unicorn*, *Vengeance*, *Victorious* and *Warrior*.

Sea Fury FB 11 bombing a bridge in North Korea during the Korean War.

All three marks were used at various times by station flights at Arbroath, Brawdy, Culdrose, Eglinton, Ford, Hal Far, Lee-on-Solent, Lossiemouth, St Merryn and Yeovilton.

Keith Harris flew the RN Historic Flight Sea Fury, TF 956, for 2 years and described the exhilarating and impressive performance it demonstrated from his very first flight in it. The teardrop canopy afforded excellent visibility, with throttle, RPM and fuel controls coming easily to the left hand. Performance in the air was superb and the semi-reclining seat enhanced the pilot's ability to pull and sustain high G forces. Long-range, fast cruising could be achieved by hauling back on the RPM control to a seemingly countable blade rotation speed. A very tight deck-landing circuit could be achieved by bleeding off speed in a tight turn, lowering undercarriage and flap and pegging the approach speed with the very controllable max pitch engine control. He ended his description by telling me that he had a greater affinity with the Sea Fury FB 11 than any of the many other types he ever flew.

The first RN unit to take Sea Furies to sea was 807 NAS which embarked in *Implacable* during May 1948. At the same time 806 NAS, a composite unit with two Sea Furies, two Sea Hornets and a single Sea Vampire, deployed to Canada in HMCS *Magnificent* and disembarked to Dartmouth before giving a series of displays in the USA and Canada. In August its display at the opening of Idlewild Airport in New York was described by the press as 'spectacular' and 'having stolen the show'. The squadron returned to the UK to disband later in the year having achieved its aim of increasing awareness of the Fleet Air Arm.

The Sea Fury made an outstanding contribution to the Korean War which broke out in June 1950. The light fleet carriers *Triumph*, *Theseus*, *Glory*, *Ocean* and the Australian *Sydney* maintained flying operations between them over Korea throughout the conflict until an armistice ended it in 1953. *Triumph* had operated Seafire FR 47s and Fireflies but the other carriers operated air groups comprising twenty-one Sea Furies and twelve Fireflies. The maintenance carrier *Unicorn* provided replacement aircraft and operated Sea Furies detached from the light fleet carriers to act as CAP aircraft and free their decks for large ranges of strike aircraft. Two air groups were awarded the Boyd

Sea Fury FB 11 being ranged on *Glory*'s after lift.

Trophy for their actions over Korea; that for 1950 was awarded to 807 NAS Sea Furies and 810 NAS Fireflies embarked in *Theseus* and that for 1952 to 802 and 825 NAS with the same types in *Ocean*. Despite the bitter winter weather in December 1950 that accompanied Chinese intervention in the conflict, *Theseus* flew 338 sorties in seven days in support of UN forces on the ground, attacking bridges, railway rolling stock and enemy troops. In that month her aircraft expended 38,000 rounds of 20mm ammunition and 1,412 3in RP. In 1952 *Ocean*'s aircraft did even better, flying 749 combat sorties in nine days. Priority targets were trucks and road transport but in October they attacked sluice gates in a dam at Yonan. During 1952 Communist forces began to deploy MiG-15 jet fighters against UN operations and on 9 August 1952 one of these was shot down by a flight of 802 NAS Sea Furies led by Lieutenant P 'Hoagy' Carmichael RN. Other MiGs were damaged but none of the Sea Furies were hit. With the end of the Korean War and the increasing number of Sea Hawk squadrons the Sea Fury force was reduced but it still had a strike capability that jets could not match and the last unit to be equipped with the type was 810 NAS which formed the strike element of the first air group embarked in the light fleet carrier *Centaur*, the first to be fitted with a partially-angled flight deck. It filled a gap left by the delayed development of the Wyvern before being de-commissioned in March 1955.

In 1950 Sea Furies began to replace Seafires in the RNVR Air Branch fighter squadrons. The build-up was delayed by the need to provide aircraft for operational squadrons during the Korean War but by January 1955 the Branch had six Sea Fury squadrons. Later in the year their replacement began with Supermarine Attackers and early marks of Sea Hawk. Sea Furies remained in use with the civilian-manned FRU at Hurn until April 1961 when the type was finally declared obsolete.

The Sea Fury had been assessed by the A&AEE from the outset as exceptional and every pilot that flew it enjoyed the experience. Vice Admiral Sir Edward Anson flew Sea Furies with 801 NAS in *Glory* during the Korean War and said that it was everybody's favourite, fondly remembered. Alan Leahy flew 786 hours in Sea Furies, many of them from *Glory* in the Korean War, and amassed 272 deck landings in it. He remembered it as a solid and reliable deck-landing aircraft but one that had one little trick 'up its sleeve'. The final approach to the deck was made just above stalling speed with power on in a perfect three-point attitude ready to 'cut' when the batsman gave the signal. However,

An exhausted crane landed on *Glory* and adopted this Sea Fury as its perch. Kind-hearted sailors fed it on milk and kippers until it regained its strength and flew off.

Sea Fury T 20

if the aircraft was left to its own devices when the throttle was closed, the nose would drop and the main wheels would strike the deck first, the tail hook would then sail over the arrester wires and the aircraft would bounce straight into the barrier. The solution was for the pilot to pull back hard on the stick as the throttle was closed in order to maintain the three-point attitude and let the hook catch a wire. He was an AWI and as well as carrying out the classic attack methods used in Korea, he taught new pilots to use them. These included 45-degree dive-bombing with the attacking aircraft rolling into the dive at 4,000ft, above the effects of light anti-aircraft fire, to release weapons at 1,500ft; any lower and the aircraft might be damaged by fragments from its own bombs. Division attacks were carried out by four aircraft in a 45-degree dive, flown in shallow echelon with 2 seconds between aircraft. RP attacks were also flown in a 45-degree dive but strafing was carried out in a 20-degree dive. Constant practice was needed and every opportunity was taken to make good use of splash targets towed astern of carriers. Every pilot was trained in bombardment spotting techniques. He remembered teaching weapon-aiming techniques in the T 20 but neither he nor his colleagues ever made use of the periscope since he could not imagine anything more foolhardy than diving headlong at a target using a mirror as a reference!

In comparison, my own experience of the Sea Fury was minimal but I did have the opportunity to fly a T 20 of the RN Historic Flight. Its controls were light and it was a joy to fly.

Sea Hawk

Sydney Camm and his team began developing a jet-powered single-seat fighter in 1944. The project, identified by the company as P.1040, in early 1945 centred on the use of bifurcated jet pipes exhausting on either side of the fuselage aft of the wing. This had two advantages over a straight-through jet pipe; they were shorter and space was left in the fuselage for an internal fuel tank aft of the engine. At first the MAP agreed to the development of variants for the RAF named Hawk and the RN named Sea Hawk but the RAF was content with Meteors and Vampires when the war ended and dropped out of the project. The Admiralty, on the other hand, saw merit in the P.1040 and drafted Specification N.7/46 around it in January 1946. Contracts were placed for three prototypes and a static test airframe, the first of which flew at the A&AEE in September 1947.

Structurally the Sea Hawk featured wings attached to stub assemblies mounted at the mid fuselage point which were integral with the centre fuselage assembly and included wing-root engine air intakes. The engine was situated in the centre fuselage exhausting through the bifurcated jet pipes. A single fin and rudder formed part of the tailplane assembly with a conventional tailplane and elevator mounted midway up the fin. The pilot sat on an ejection seat in a cockpit at the extreme nose with the four cannons mounted under it and ammunition stowage behind it. In the prototypes and early production examples all controls were manually operated. Testing revealed the need for minor changes including the fitting of an acorn fairing at the intersection of the fin and tailplane to smooth airflow and the replacement of rectangular exhaust fairings with 'pen-nib' shaped fairings. The first RN prototype flew in September 1948 and featured folding wings, catapult spools and a 'sting' type arrester hook together with full armament and radio

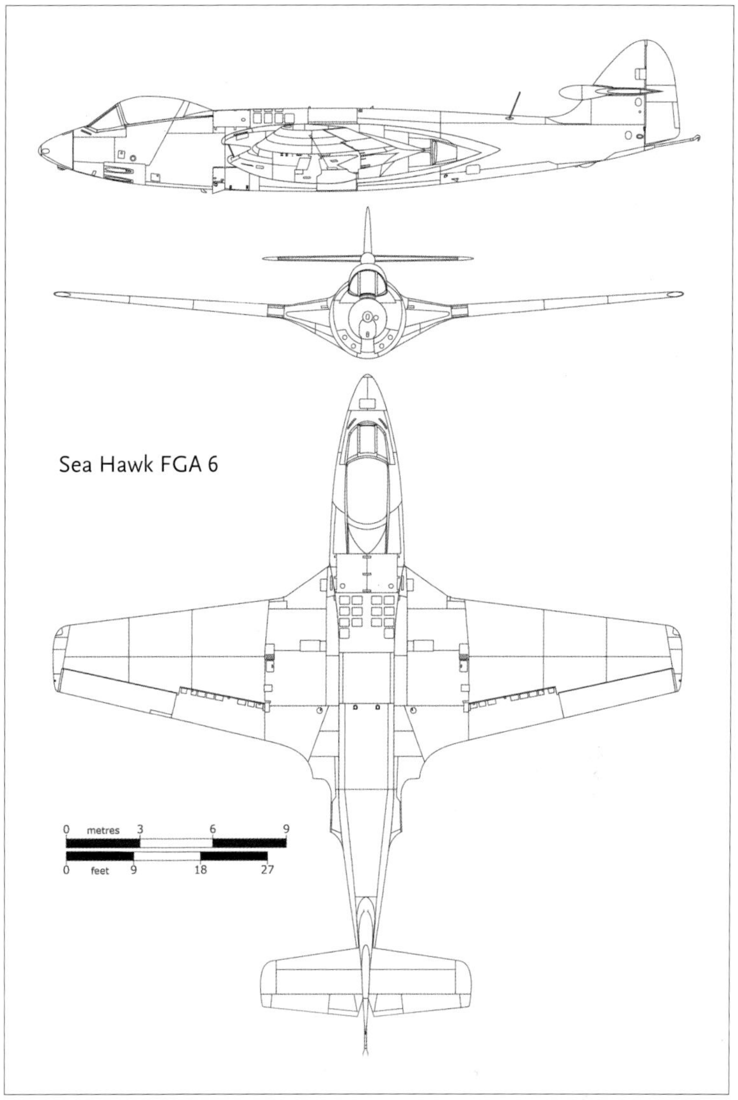

fit. It was plumbed to take two 90-gallon drop tanks on underwing hardpoints. Sea acceptance trials were carried out in *Illustrious* during April 1949 which included both catapulted and free take-offs and a number of arrested landings. Analysis of the type's handling characteristics on final approach led to an increase of 30in in wingspan, the final change made to the airframe structure before series production began. The last prototype flew in 1949, fitted for RATOG and the Admiralty placed a contract for ninety Sea Hawks in 1949.

The first production Sea Hawk F 1 flew in November 1951 and was used by Hawker for stability and control tests which confirmed that lateral control was 'somewhat disappointing'. The solution was power-assisted aileron control and a system was developed and fitted to the fifth production aircraft which effectively became the prototype F 2. Other early production aircraft were used for deck-landing and catapulting trials in *Eagle* during 1952 and cold weather trials in Canada. By then the Korean War was at its height and the government had ordered both the Hunter and Sea Hawk into 'super-priority' production. Hawker was unable to cope and so after thirty-five Sea Hawks had been delivered, its production and development were transferred to Armstrong-Whitworth Aircraft, another member of the Hawker-Siddeley Group. The first AWA-built aircraft was delivered in 1953. After completing sixty F 1s AWA introduced the F 2 with full

One of the initial batch of Sea Hawks built by Hawker being test flown in 1952.

powered aileron control and spring feel. Both F 1 and 2 variants had been able to carry 90-gallon drop tanks but in 1954 production switched to the FB 3 which had extra underwing hardpoints capable of carrying two 500lb bombs or mines in addition to the drop tanks. The next variant was the FGA 4 which also first flew in 1954. This had additional wing strongpoints to allow up to twenty 3in RP to be carried as an alternative to bombs and giving the type a flexible capability for close air support during an amphibious operation. RP also had a potentially devastating impact on small warships but the aircraft had to close within 1,000 yards to fire them accurately. By 1954 the Admiralty was aware that the Sea Hawk's performance with a weapon load needed improvement if it was to remain competitive until the Scimitar came into service and AWA was funded to make improvements. These included the incorporation of powered elevators to improve handling at higher Mach numbers and the replacement of the original Nene with a development that had slightly more thrust. A number of FB 3s were upgraded to this standard, becoming FB 5s. Some FGA 4s were upgraded to FGA 6 standard but the majority were built as such.

Sea Hawk FGA 6 data

Length:	39ft 8in
Wingspan:	39ft spread (13ft 3in folded)
Height:	8ft 8in (16ft 9in folded)
MTOW:	15,225lb
Engine:	One 5,200lb static thrust Rolls-Royce Nene Mark 101 centrifugal turbojet
Fuel:	Avcat. 395 gallons internal plus two optional 90-gallon drop tanks on underwing hardpoints, total 575 gallons
Performance:	Maximum level speed 482 knots/Mach 0.84 Service ceiling 44,000ft. 12 minutes to 35,000ft
Endurance:	Over 2 hours with two 90-gallon drop tanks
Armament:	Four 20mm British Hispano cannon with 120 rpg under the nose. Provision on underwing hardpoints for two 1,000lb or 500lb bombs, up to twenty 3in RP, napalm bombs or practice bombs. Total weapons load up to 2,000lb or up to four 90-gallon drop tanks for ferry flights

The RN received 437 Sea Hawks including 3 prototypes; 95 to F1 standard; 40 to F 2 standard; 116 to FB 3 standard; 97 to FGA 4 standard

Sea Hawk F 1 of 806 NAS landing on *Eagle*'s original straight flight deck.

and 86 to FGA 6 standard. No aircraft were built new to FB 5 standard.

Shore-based units equipped, or partially equipped, with Sea Hawks in the training, trial, development and fleet requirements roles between 1952 and 1967 included 700, 703, 736, 738, 764, 767, 781 and 787 NAS. They were also operated by the civilian-manned FRU at Hurn until 1969. Fitted with four drop tanks the Sea Hawk had a good endurance and was ideal for threat simulation, radar calibration and fighter controller training in the mid-1960s.

Sea Hawks of 898 NAS from *Eagle* in 1958.

Sea Hawks of 804 NAS ranged with Sea Venoms on *Ark Royal*.

Operational fighter squadrons equipped with Sea Hawks between 1953 and 1960 included 800, 801, 802, 803, 804, 806, 807, 810, 811, 895, 897, 898 and 899 NAS. They were embarked at various times in the aircraft carriers *Albion*, *Ark Royal*, *Bulwark*, *Centaur* and *Eagle*.

Sea Hawks were allocated to station flights at Abbotsinch, Anthorn, Brawdy, Ford, Hal Far and Lossiemouth during the late 1950s.

The first unit to re-equip with Sea Hawks was 806 NAS at Brawdy

Sea Hawk of 810 NAS catching a wire on *Albion*

Sea Hawk FGA 6s of 800 NAS rehearsing for their display in the 1958 SBAC Air Show at Farnborough.

in June 1953. By November 1956 seven Sea Hawk squadrons operated from *Eagle*, *Albion* and *Bulwark* during Operation 'Musketeer', the Anglo-French intervention in the Suez Canal Zone. Whilst the affair was a political disaster it demonstrated the latent power of a carrier task force to project power at the point where it is needed and Sea Hawks flew the bulk of the strike missions that destroyed the Egyptian Air Force on the ground in a matter of hours. Strikes began at dawn on 1 November with the carriers 135nm from their targets, just inside the maximum radius of action of a Sea Hawk fully loaded with bombs or rockets and front gun ammunition. Two Sea Hawks were lost to enemy action but both pilots ejected and were rescued. Sea Venoms flew CAP, escort and some strike missions and Wyverns flew strike missions against targets such as bridges. After the Allied landings Sea Hawks proved ideal for close-support missions from 'cab-ranks' over the front line.

Like its predecessor, the Sea Hawk was considered to be a delight to fly and one unit, 738 NAS, gave a superb demonstration of formation aerobatics at the 1957 Farnborough Air Show. For the occasion their Sea Hawks were repainted red with the words 'ROYAL NAVY' painted under their wings in white. Their fuel systems were modified to allow smoke trails which could be selected on and off by the pilot. Alan Leahy, the commanding officer, told me that his aerobatic team was the first in the world to display with selectable smoke although it was grey and not coloured. The squadron's primary task was to convert pilots onto the Sea Hawk and Alan's pilots were all instructors; during 1957 they flew seventeen different displays with five aircraft in the main group and a solo aircraft which displayed while the main group were repositioning. Despite the effort his team put into rehearsing the display routine, Alan took great pride in the fact that every one of his students passed out on time that year, a feat made possible by the work of his maintenance personnel who kept the aircraft serviceable.

Scimitars began to replace Sea Hawks in 1958 but the last unit, 806 NAS, did not disband until December 1960 when *Albion* arrived back in the UK from the Far East. The civilian-manned FRU at Hurn operated black-painted Sea Hawks until 1969. They had bright Harley lights mounted in the nose which could be selected by pilots when requested to make the aircraft easier for trainee gun and Seacat missile crews to track.

P.1052/1081

A swept-wing development of the Sea Hawk was considered as early as October 1945 but the Admiralty was concerned that their high approach speed might make deck landing dangerous. However, two experimental prototypes were ordered under Specification E.38/46 to provide swept-wing data, designated P.1052 by Hawker. At the time there was little UK Government enthusiasm for new fighters and the project proceeded slowly. The P.1052 resembled the Sea Hawk except for the substitution of new wings with a quarter-cord sweep of 35 degrees designed to raise the maximum level speed to Mach 0.86. The non-swept tailplane assembly was retained. Wingspan was 31ft 6in, MTOW 13,488lb and it was powered by the same 5,000lb thrust Roll-Royce Nene as the early Sea Hawks. Work on the prototypes began in 1947 but the first did not fly until November 1948. The second flew in 1949 and established a record by flying from London to Paris in 18 minutes. A&AEE evaluation proceeded at a leisurely pace but one of the prototypes suffered a forced landing and had to be repaired. The second was converted into the P.1081 with a swept tailplane and a straight-through jet-pipe. It was to have been powered by a 7,000lb thrust Roll-Royce Tay reheated, centrifugal turbojet to offer potential as an operational fighter but the RAF had no interest in the 1081 and forced its termination so that Hawker could concentrate on Hunter

Hawker P.1052.

development. The single 1081 therefore flew as an experimental aircraft fitted with a Nene engine configured with a straight-through jet pipe. The remaining prototype, VX 272, remained in P.1052 configuration with an unswept tailplane but its undercarriage was replaced by long-stroke Sea Hawk units and it carried out deck-landing trials on *Eagle* in May 1952. These proved entirely successful but by then the Sea Hawk was in full-scale production, its intended replacement from Supermarine was in development and the Admiralty elected not to introduce a swept-wing Sea Hawk derivative. It transpired that the Scimitar took another 5 years to develop and the Sea Hawk remained in service for another 8 and so, with hindsight, it is clear that a swept-wing Sea Hawk introduced at the FB 3/FGA 4 stage would have been an effective and affordable operational aircraft but the opportunity was lost.

Hunter T 8

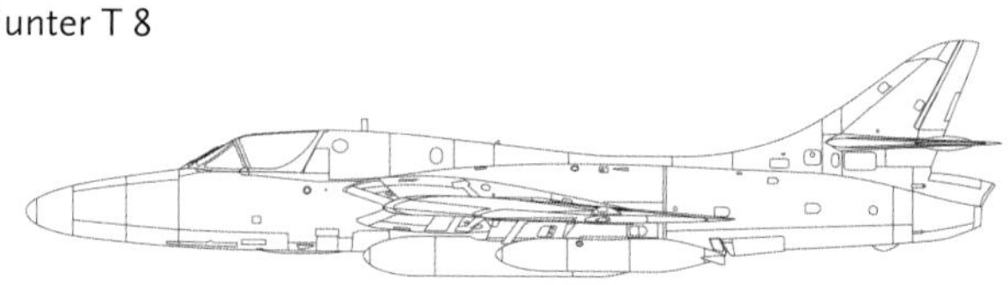

Hunter T 8M

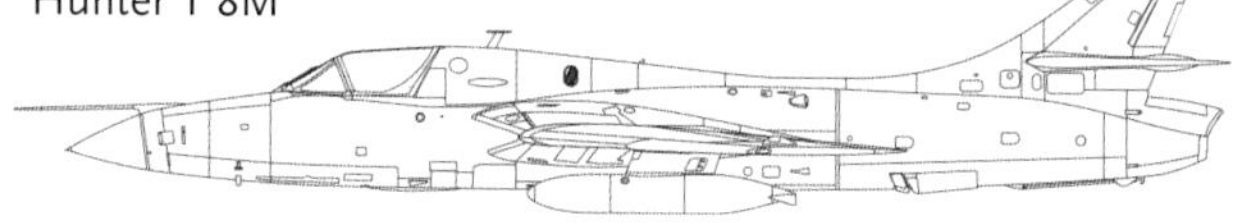

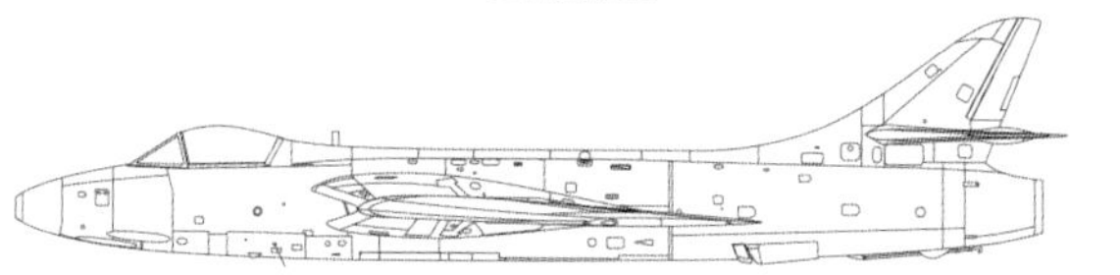

Hunter GA 11

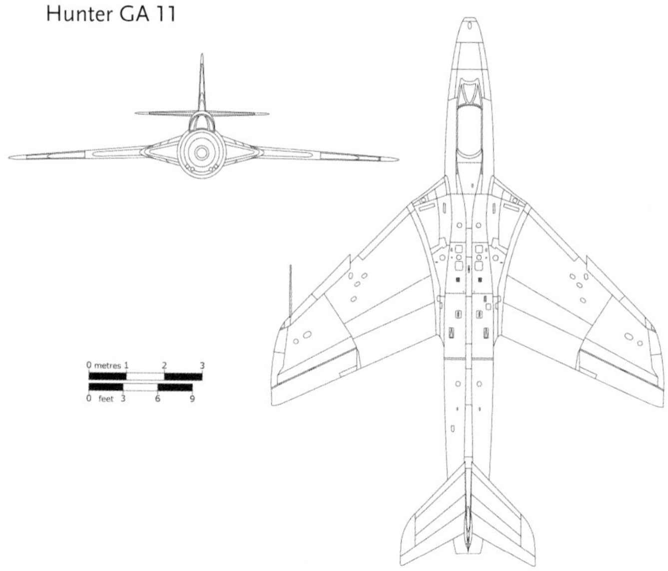

Hunter

After the P.1081, Hawker worked on a new single-seat fighter, designated P.1067, for the RAF powered by the Rolls-Royce AJ-65, later Avon, axial-flow turbojet and subsequently given the name Hunter. Armament comprised four 30mm Aden cannon under the cockpit with gun-ranging radar fitted in the nose. The first prototype flew in 1951, followed by the F 1, F 3 and F 4 variants for the RAF, all powered by Avons and the F 2 and F 5 powered by Armstrong Siddeley Sapphires. Subsequent marks, including those used by the RN, all had Avon engines. The F 4 was the first variant put into in large-scale production.

In 1953 Hawker began work on a two-seat, trainer variant as a private venture but with large numbers of Meteor and Vampire pilots needing conversion onto swept-wing fighters the RAF recognised the requirement and procured it in some numbers. It was basically a two-seat derivative of the F 4 with side-by-side seating. A single prototype was ordered which flew in July 1955, designated P.1101 by Hawker and Hunter T 7 by the RAF.

Hunter T 8 of 759 NAS based at Brawdy in 1964.

With the transonic Scimitar and Sea Vixen due in service in the late 1950s the Admiralty urgently required a transonic training aircraft to act as an advanced and conversion trainer since neither of the new types had a dual control version. The RN Hunter trainer was designated T 8 and, since all training, standardisation and instrument rating checks were carried out ashore, there was no requirement for them to deck land. They offered an effective and affordable way of converting new pilots onto swept-wing techniques and side-by-side seating was regarded as ideal for OFT since both pilots had an excellent view ahead through their gunsights. The Hunter T 8 differed from the T 7 in having naval radios and an arrester hook stressed to take cables on an airfield runway but definitely not those on a carrier. New-build T 8s had a single 30mm front gun but this was later removed to make space for TACAN and

Hunter T 8, XL 580, used as his barge by Rear Admiral Gick, Flag Officer Naval Flying Training, during 1963.

none of the aircraft converted from F 4s had a front gun. The prototype T 8 was a converted F 4 but the ten that followed were new-build. The first aircraft were issued to 764 NAS at Lossiemouth in July 1958, utilisation rates were high from the outset and further batches were ordered from 1963 with all the later aircraft converted from F 4s.

After the type's entry into service, several T 8s underwent modification to suit them for specific tasks. Four designated T 8B had the left-hand pilot's instrument panel replaced by the Buccaneer IFIS display and were fitted with TACAN to act as lead-in trainers for the Buccaneer. A further eleven, designated T 8C, were modified with TACAN but no change to the instrument panel. Three, designated T 8M, were fitted with the Sea Harrier's FRS 1 Blue Fox radar and used initially for trials and later for training pilots in radar intercept techniques with 899 NAS.

In addition to the conversion trainer, the RN also needed a robust, swept-wing, lead-in aircraft to replace Sea Hawks in the tactical and weapons delivery phases of pilot training. Again, the Hunter F 4 was attractive since large numbers of RAF-surplus airframes were available, many of them purchased using US Offshore Procurement funds. The Admiralty purchased them from the US Government and covered the cost of conversion for their new role. Some of these aircraft purchased at minimal cost gave the RN over 30 years of service. This single-seat variant was designated GA 11, the 'F' being omitted because the guns were removed and, initially, it had no other air-to-air weapon. After 1982 some were fitted for Sidewinder AAMs. Naval radios were fitted together with TACAN and an airfield arrester hook. The wings were strengthened to take a variety of air-to-surface weapons or drop tanks on four underwing pylons. Some GA 11s were further modified into PR 11s using the same nose as the RAF FR 10 with its F.95 camera and used for photographic reconnaissance training.

Hunter GA 11 data

Length:	45ft 10in
Wingspan:	33ft 8in
Height:	13ft 2in
MTOW:	21,321 with four 100-gallon drop tanks
Engine:	One 7,575lb Rolls-Royce Avon 122 turbojet
Fuel:	Avtur. 414 gallons plus optional 400 gallons in drop tanks; total 814 gallons
Performance:	Maximum level speed 540 knots/Mach 0.94 Service ceiling 50,000ft. 10 minutes to 36,000ft
Endurance:	2 hours
Armament:	Four underwing hardpoints for drop tanks, practice bombs, 3in RP or 2in rocket pods. Sidewinder AAMs after 1982 in some aircraft

FRADU Hunter GA 11s in the 1970s.

The RN received a total of ninety Hunters between 1958 and 1995. Of these ten were modified on Hawker's production line for completion as T 8s. A further thirty-one were former F 4s converted into T 8s and nine were T 7s transferred from the RAF to the RN in the 1980s as attrition replacements for use by FRADU. They underwent local modifications but were not designated as T 8s. The forty aircraft delivered as GA 11s or PR 11s were all converted from F 4s. (A further batch of ten was cancelled after they had been purchased by the Admiralty and sold back to Hawker.)

Between 1958 and 1972 Hunters equipped, or partially equipped 736, 738, 759, 764 and 766 NAS in the advanced training, operational training, air warfare instructor training, type conversion, standardisation check and instrument checking roles. Three T 8M were used by 899 NAS for pilot conversion training between 1981 and 2005. T 8Bs formed part of 809 NAS when it was the Buccaneer headquarters squadron between 1963 and 1965 and one was attached to 803 NAS briefly in 1960 for instrument and standardisation checks on Scimitar pilots.

From 1958 Hunter T 8 s were issued to station flights at Brawdy, Hal Far and Yeovilton together with the RN unit at Changi in Singapore to provide two-seaters for standards and instrument rating checks for the Home, Mediterranean and Far East Fleets.

Following the UK Government's unfortunate decision to run down the British carrier force in 1966 the RN Hunter squadrons were disbanded between 1969 and 1972 but the aircraft were re-purposed to replace the Sea Hawks of the FRU at Hurn and the Sea Venoms of the ADTU at Yeovilton. The two organisations were combined in 1972 to form FRADU at Yeovilton. FRADU T 8s were also used by the RN Fixed-Wing Naval Flying Standards Flight, also based at Yeovilton, for tasks ranging from standardisation checks for front-line pilots, instrument checks and IRI courses and the provision of dissimilar combat training for disembarked squadrons. Hunters continued to be used by FRADU until 1995 when they were replaced by Hawks. RN Hunters formed two aerobatic teams; the 'Rough Diamonds' of 738

The Hunter T 8 instrument panel.

NAS at Brawdy between 1965 and 1969 and the 'Blue Herons' of FRADU at Yeovilton, both of which used GA 11s, the latter flown by civilian pilots, albeit former service pilots under contract to the RN.

As well as flying the naval T 8 and GA/PR 11 variants, I flew other Hunter marks including the F 6, T 7 and FGA 9 whilst on exchange appointments with the RAF. Like many others, I found the Hunter to be light, responsive and a joy to fly; very much a pilot's aircraft. The cockpit interior was not, perhaps, laid out as well as it might have been but one rapidly got used to it and learned to find switches instinctively. It was easy to fly on instruments and at night and aerobatics in a clear sky were great fun. In simulated 'engine-off' recoveries with the throttle closed the GA 11 covered a nautical mile for every 1,000ft of height lost and this evolution often formed part of the 'Trappers' standardisation checks. Having put out the obligatory practice pan call and checked the TACAN for range and bearing to see if one could reach the long east/west runway at Yeovilton, I always found the next few minutes an enjoyable challenge. Advancing the throttle a little to check that the engine was still responsive could be used stretch the glide a little if necessary but doing it too often would attract criticism. During my flying career I flew an unusual range of aircraft including five marks of Hunter, three marks of Canberra, three marks of Gannet and two marks of Wessex helicopter. If I had to choose one as my favourite it would be the Hunter GA 11 without hesitation. Keith Harris, who flew many more Hunter hours than I did, described it as having that immediate translation of thought into manoeuvre that very few aircraft have achieved.

P.1127

After the 1957 Defence Review a design team under Ralph Hooper began to scheme an aircraft around the Bristol Siddeley BE 53 engine, later named Pegasus, with the aim of developing a strike fighter with VTOL capability. Hawker designated it P.1127 and invested its own funds to develop the concept. Pegasus engine development received significant funding from the US MWDP programme and work began on a prototype in 1959. Before it was complete the MoS purchased it, allocated it the airframe number XP 831, and funded a programme of test and evaluation. Stripped of everything that could be removed to reduce MTOW below 10,000lb it hovered a few inches above the ground in October 1960, restrained by tethering cables. A free hover was carried out in November and more prototypes were ordered. By September 1961 transition from hovering to horizontal flight and the reverse had been achieved and further flights were carried out to widen the envelope.

XP 831 was an experimental aircraft with no role equipment; a semi-monocoque structure of aluminium with local areas of steel in the vicinity of hot exhaust nozzles. It had a conventional structure built to ground attack strength factors with large 'elephant ear' air intakes aft of cockpit. Cold air was exhausted from the large fan forward of the compressor through rotatable fibreglass nozzles and bleed air was fed from the compressor to reaction control nozzles or 'puffers' at the nose, tail and wingtips which replaced conventional controls in non-aerodynamic flight. The rear 'hot' end of the engine consisted of the combustion chamber and turbines exhausting burnt gases through a bifurcated exhaust trunk, using technology developed for the Sea Hawk, to two steel rotatable nozzles. The shoulder-mounted wing was a continuous structure mounted across the top of the fuselage with marked anhedral. The all-moving tailplane was a single-piece unit hinged through the rear fuselage. The most unusual feature was the undercarriage in which the weight was taken mainly on a single

The world's first vertical landing on a carrier by a STOVL fast-jet was carried out by a P.1127. XP 831 landed on *Ark Royal* on 7 February 1963.

A B C D E F G H I J K L M N O P Q R S T U V W X Y Z

A P.1127 development aircraft landing on *Bulwark* during deck-landing trials in June 1966.

midship-mounted main oleo with twin wheels and steering was provided by a conventional nosewheel, originally taken from a Sea Hawk. Balance on the ground was achieved by wing-tip outriggers. Flying controls in normal flight were conventional but converted to the reaction controls when the nozzles rotated through 10 degrees.

P.1127 prototype data

Length:	49ft
Wingspan:	24ft 4in
Height:	10ft 3in
MTOW:	11,800lb at time of first flight, later 14,500lb
Engine:	One 10,500lb Bristol Pegasus I vectored thrust turbofan increased with development to approximately 13,500lb
Fuel:	Avtur. 500 gallons internal
Performance:	Maximum level speed 630 knots/Mach 0.97 Service ceiling 50,000ft. 1 minute to 20,000ft
Endurance:	Over 1 hour
Armament:	None

No P.1127 prototypes were issued to the RN but the Admiralty agreed to allow XP 831 to demonstrate its carrier landing potential. On 7 February 1963 XP 831 landed on *Ark Royal* in Lyme Bay, the first time that a fighter-type aircraft had ever hovered alongside and then carried out a vertical landing on an aircraft carrier. Its civilian test pilot, Bill Bedford, had no previous deck-landing experience and said that the large flight deck had presented few problems with the island giving good cues for both the hover and the landing. In June 1966 another prototype P.1127, XP 984, was embarked in *Bulwark* to evaluate the possibility of operating STOVL fighters alongside helicopters. The results were most encouraging but, only weeks after the cancellation of CVA-01, the MOD saw the trial as a 'back door' tactic by the RN to retain fixed-wing carrier operations and no further action was taken.

P.1154

The P.1127 prototypes generated interest within NATO which issued NBMR-3 for a developed version. German, French and British designs were put forward and the UK Government assumed, naively, that the winning design would generate large orders funded at least in part by NATO. Hawker offered an improved P.1127 designated P.1150 which was larger than its predecessor with a more highly developed engine. In December 1961 the CDS, Admiral of the Fleet Lord Mountbatten proposed the development of a common supersonic fighter/ground attack aircraft based on NBMR-3 for both the RN and RAF. He made no comment on why he preferred NBMR-3 over existing requirements authorised by the Service Chiefs of Staff but the implication is that he saw it as a short-term solution. The Hawker design team under Ralph Hooper evolved their design into the P.1154, basically a clear-weather NBMR-3 strike fighter, but the NATO Committee eventually declared the P.1154 and the French Mirage IIIV to be joint technical winners of the competition to meet the requirement, leaving individual countries to make of that what they would. Neither ever went into production. The relevance of the P.1154 to the RN was that it had become the supersonic close-support aircraft that the RAF decided it could not do without and Mountbatten thought that it was the only project that could deliver a supersonic Sea Vixen replacement for the RN by the end of the decade. Although it never flew, the P.1154 was, therefore, the focus of RN fighter planning between 1961 and 1963.

Naval and Air Staff aspirations for the P.1154 were contained in Naval/Air Staff Requirement 356, Part 1 of which described the RAF requirement for a Hunter replacement close to NBMR-3. Part 2 described what the RN wanted; a fighter capable of intercepting a Mach 2.5 target at 65,000ft in all weathers and at night. Four Red Top IR-guided AAM were to be the minimum armament and a loiter time on CAP 100nm from the carrier of 2½ hours was specified. The Admiralty was prepared to accept a strike radius of action compatible with the fighter-mission fuel load but wanted up to 4,000lb of weapons. Two crew were considered essential to make the best use of a pulse-doppler radar and missile-control system. In summary, the Admiralty wanted a more sophisticated aircraft than NBMR-3 and didn't need V/STOL capability. The RAF seemed only to want a supersonic, V/STOL Hunter. Defence Secretary, Harold Watkinson, was mesmerised by his US contemporary Robert S McNamara who was insisting on a standardised USN/USAF strike fighter, the F-111. Without understanding the issues involved or taking expert advice, he saw the P.1154 as a British equivalent and a lot of money, time and effort was wasted trying to achieve the unachievable. It was immediately obvious to everyone except politicians that the RAF wanted a low-flying, single-seat, clear-weather ground attack aircraft without radar and the RN wanted a high-flying, two-seat, all-weather fighter with the most advanced radar ever fitted in a British fighter and Watkinson had

No P.1154RNs were ever built but Chris Sandham-Bailey drew this impression of what one might have looked like for me. It is shown as an aircraft of 803 NAS embarked in *Eagle*. (Chris Sandham-Bailey)

chosen P.1154 to do both. The MoA, responsible for the supply of aircraft to all three armed services at the time, had pushed hard for the acquisition of a more sophisticated P.1127 as a development tool but now put every obstacle it could think of in the way of modifying the P.1154 to meet the RN requirement. Hawker had designed it with inadequate government funding and was now faced with having to make radical changes to it. 'Winkle' Brown, then Deputy DNAW, discussed P.1154 with Ralph Hooper in April 1962. He agreed that it would be light enough to operate from existing carriers but Hooper noted that meeting the RN requirement would add over 2,000lb to the aircraft's basic weight and double the specified armament. Meeting the CAP requirement required at least a 50 per cent increase in fuel and a larger wing to carry both missiles and drop tanks. A 70 per cent re-design was needed to produce an aircraft that the RAF said it did not want and a low production run would make the variant, now referred to as the P.1154RN, a very expensive aircraft that would still fall short of the Admiralty requirement.

Much could be written about attempts to produce a common aircraft and in nearly all of them it was the RN, not the RAF, that had to make concessions. Roll-Royce complicated things still further by promoting a derivative powered by two re-heated Spey engines. When the evolved design was examined in detail during July 1963 it was found that even the limited performance reluctantly accepted by the Naval Staff could not be met. The Admiralty Secretariat advised the Board the P.1154 was not an airframe capable of delivering a successful outcome. Late in 1963 the Admiralty tried to persuade the Air Staff that the P.1154 suited neither service and should be terminated. The Air Staff took the view that the Hunter must be replaced by 1968; in the end the Admiralty objected alone and the P.1154RN was cancelled in February 1964. It had demonstrated that in the post-1957 era of British defence procurement, the Navy was no longer a big enough player in the fighter market to get aircraft it required in sufficient numbers to make production runs viable. It needed a partner to share the cost; the RAF had shown itself unwilling to make any concessions and could no longer be relied upon. Increasingly the RN had to look towards the USN for collaboration and, after the P.1154RN's cancellation it procured the magnificent McDonnell F4 Phantom II as a Sea Vixen replacement. The P.1154 did leave a legacy, however; the RAF version was to have been named Harrier and the RN version Sea Harrier.

When cancelled, the P.1154RN design had evolved into a two-seat, all-weather fighter with a wingspan of 36ft and a tricycle undercarriage, the outer oleos retracting into mid-wing pods. The nose oleo was to have a nose-tow catapult launch bar like that adopted by the USN. MTOW was estimated at 48,000lb and it would have been powered by a single 39,700lb thrust Bristol Siddeley BS-100 vectored turbofan with four rotating nozzles and PCB, the injection of fuel into the forward nozzles, changing their 'cold' airflow into reheated 'hot' air to give greater thrust. Internal fuel would have been 1,400 gallons. The maximum level speed was expected to be about Mach 1.7 and the initial rate of climb would have been exceptional, figures that make interesting comparison with the Phantom described below.

Sea Harrier

In 1965 the UK Government cancelled the P.1154RAF but authorised development of an improved P.1127 as a Hunter FGA 9 replacement. It was a single-seater capable of carrying 5,000lb of weapons with two podded 30mm cannon but lacked radar and could only be used in clear weather by day. A significant amount of development work had already been achieved by P.1127 prototypes and so progress with the ground attack aircraft by then named Harrier went relatively smoothly. Its lack of realistic fighter capability was reflected in its GR 1 designation when it entered RAF service in 1969. A similar version designated AV-8A, also named Harrier, was built by Hawker for the USMC. The Harrier GR 1 had an obvious niche capability but was expensive both to procure and to operate and the RAF ordered a larger number of Jaguar GR 1 conventional strike aircraft which could carry more than twice the weapon load more than twice as far. If a Harrier squadron had to operate away from a main base it needed hundreds of vehicles to support it which were more vulnerable to interdiction than a hardened, defended airfield. Hawker analysts saw the advantages of operating P.1127s from a carrier with its own logistic and operational support and privately worked on plans for a navalised version. The RN had gained approval for the construction of three *Invincible* class light

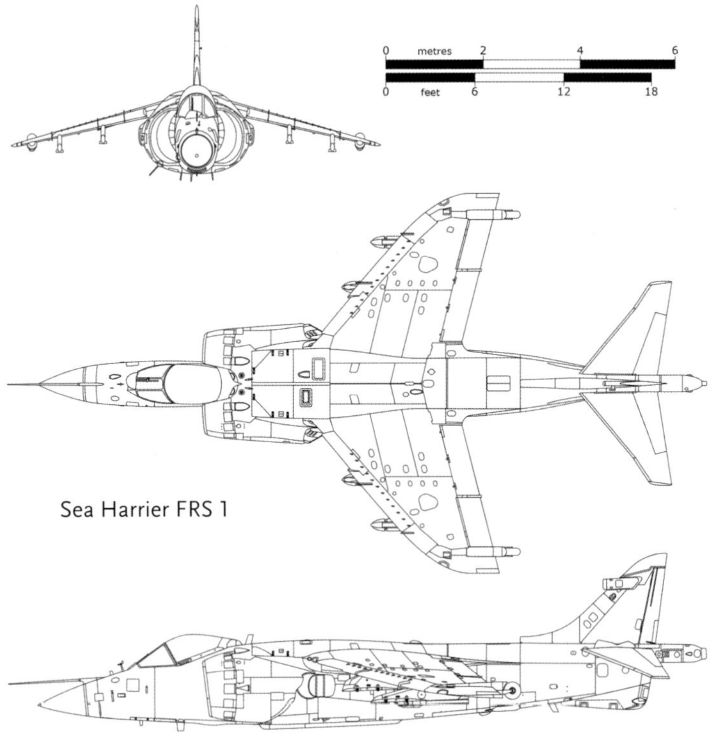

Sea Harrier FRS 1

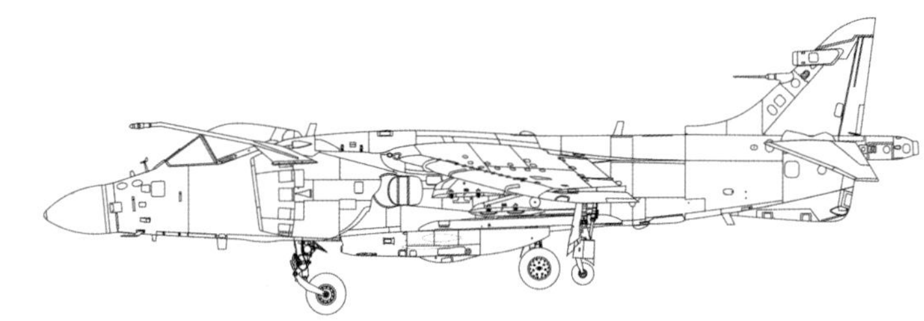

Sea Harrier F/A 2 with undercarriage down

Sea Harrier FRS 1s of 800, 801 and 899 NAS.

carriers and a navalised P.1127 gave them a fighter, reconnaissance and strike capability. The Admiralty had ceased to exist in 1964 and procurement decisions were now taken within a unified MoD, but DNAW and DGA (N) remained at the centre of RN air matters. NSR 6451 issued in January 1972 defined the fighter to be capable of operation from the *Invincible* class to provide a quick-reaction, multi-role capability for tasks which could not be met by any other ship-borne weapons system. These included the area and point reconnaissance of surface contacts, harassment and engagement of enemy air reconnaissance and data-link aircraft, offensive action against surface ships and against airborne missile-launchers. Initially referred to as the Maritime Harrier, the name Sea Harrier was adopted with the designation FRS 1. Full-scale development approval was given in 1972, before *Invincible* was laid down. The RN always intended to operate Sea Harriers from this ship and her sisters.

Structurally the Sea Harrier was a single-seat, vectored thrust fighter with a semi-monocoque structure, principally of aluminium but with steel and titanium components in the vicinity of the engine bay and exhaust nozzles. Wing sweep-back was 34 degrees at quarter chord and the wings, which had integrally-machined skins, were a single structure which had to be lifted off by crane to gain access to the engine for maintenance, one of the less-desirable legacies from the prototype design. A completely new weapons system was installed centred around a Smiths Industries HUD driven by a 20,000-word digital weapon aiming computer, the whole system known as the HUDWAC. Unlike any previous British fighter, the HUD acted as the pilots' primary source of flight information, an analogue 'clockwork' artificial horizon and other instruments being provided as an alternative back-up in case of failure. The primary sensor was the frequency-agile Ferranti Blue Fox radar in the nose developed from the Seaspray radar in the Lynx helicopter. It had both air-to-air and air-to-surface modes but could only lock onto a single target to engage it. Other avionics included TACAN and an I-Band radar transponder to enhance the type's radar signature when carrying out a CCA. Passive electronic surveillance and warning of radar illumination was provided by a radar warning receiver, RWR, with antennae situated on the tailplane assembly to give 360-degree coverage. Five weapon pylons were designed to carry a range of British and US weapons. The inboard pylons could carry up to 2,000lb and were plumbed for drop tanks. Normally these were 100-gallon tanks that made no difference to the type's +7.8 to -4.2 'G' limit. Larger 330-gallon tanks could be fitted for ferry flights but these restricted the aircraft's performance limits. The outer pylons were stressed to 1,000lb and could carry one or two Sidewinder AAMs, 1,000lb bombs, 2in rocket pods or Lepus flares. Sea Eagle ASMs or WE 177 nuclear bombs were carried on the inboard pylon and were usually loaded singly, balanced by a drop tank under the other wing.

The original P.1127 cockpit was re-designed with the pilot raised by 11in, providing space under it for electronics and improving the pilot's view. A Martin-Baker Mark 10, zero-zero, rocket ejector seat was provided with miniature detonating chord, MDC, in the canopy which

An AIM-9 Sidewinder and gun-armed Sea Harrier FRS 1 of 801 NAS on *Invincible* with a display of alternative weapon loads.

exploded the perspex and allowed the seat to be fired through it. The seat's total sequencing time from pulling the handle to clear of the aircraft with parachute deploying was 1.5 seconds. The Pegasus 104 engine, a Rolls-Royce product after it bought Bristol Siddeley, was rated at the same thrust as the 103 in the Harrier but all major casings were changed from magnesium-zirconium to aluminium and all ferrous components were coated with sacrificial aluminium paint to minimise the effects of the salt corrosion. Careful design ensured that despite the extra equipment, Sea Harrier FRS 1 basic weight was only 100lb more than the far less capable Harrier.

Although they were not strictly Sea Harriers, RN two-seat trainers were used as conversion trainers within 899 NAS. The first examples were T 4s, similar to those used by the RAF, lacking both radar and Sea Harrier cockpit layout and their Mark 9 ejection seats required different aircrew equipment assemblies. Later a batch of four T 8s were procured. They were modified from T 4s and still lacked radar but had Sea Harrier-type cockpits and ejection seats.

While the Sea Harrier was in development the RN developed the 'ski-jump' from a concept put forward by Lieutenant Commander D R Taylor MBE RN. It comprised a curved structure at the forward end of the carrier deck which forced an aircraft into an upward trajectory as it left the deck. It was particularly suitable for vectored-thrust aircraft since a small downward deflection of the nozzles on leaving the 'ski-jump' gave both acceleration and lift augmentation until full wing-borne lift was achieved. The first two *Invincible* class ships had 7-degree 'ski-jumps' but *Hermes* had a 12-degree structure and this eventually became the standard. A 12-degree training 'ski-jump' was built at Yeovilton where the Sea Harrier force was based.

The South Atlantic Conflict in 1982 emphasised the need for the Sea Harrier to have a missile capable of BVR target engagement and a more advanced radar to complement it. Funds available to the RN for fixed-wing development were limited and so it was decided in 1983 to incorporate the changes in an MLU of the FRS 1. Before the MLU was completed the Cold War ended and the UK Government decided to withdraw the WE 177 tactical nuclear weapon from service. Sea Harriers were, therefore, upgraded without a tactical nuclear capability and re-designated F/A 2 in line with current USN terminology. The major change was the replacement of Blue Fox radar with the Ferranti (later GEC Marconi) Blue Vixen, a lightweight pulse-doppler, track-while-scan radar operating in I-Band with low, medium or high PRF. It was equally effective over land or water and had a look-down/shoot-down capability. Its operation was controlled by HOTAS cockpit controls which allowed pilots to engage targets instinctively whilst controlling the aircraft. AIM-120 BVR AAM was its primary weapon and it could also carry Sidewinder AAMs for close-in engagements and Sea Eagle ASM for attacks on surface targets. The drop tanks on the inner pylons were replaced by 190-gallon tanks to give over 100nm increase in radius of action. There were two development F/A 2s and a single HS-125 executive jet was used as a test bed for the radar and other avionics. In order to maintain the centre of gravity within limits, the radar black boxes had to be installed in the after fuselage and an 18in extension was inserted just aft of the wing trailing edge, partially to maintain balance and partially to provide extra space. F/A 2s began to arrive with 899 NAS in 1993 and the whole force was re-equipped by 1995.

Sea Harrier FRS 1 data

Length:	47ft 7in
Wingspan:	25ft 3in
Height:	12ft 2in
MTOW:	26,200lb
Engine:	One 21,500lb thrust Bristol Siddeley Pegasus 104 vectored thrust turbofan
Fuel:	Avcat. 650 gallons internal plus two 100-gallon drop tanks. Total 850 gallons. Two 330-gallon ferry tanks could be carried on inboard pylons but limited performance until emptied
Performance:	Maximum level speed 650 knots/Mach 0.97 Service ceiling 51,000ft. Under 1 minute to 20,000ft
Endurance:	Approximately 2 hours with two drop tanks
Armament:	Two 30mm Aden cannon with 150 rpg in detachable pods mounted on either side of the fuselage centreline stores position. One centreline and four underwing stores positions stressed to carry various combinations including a single WE-177 nuclear bomb, Sea Eagle ASM, AIM-9L Sidewinder AAM, 2in rocket pods, conventional 1,000lb bombs and Lepus flares

Sea Harrier F/A 2s of 801 NAS.

The RN received three development aircraft, fifty-four Sea Harrier FRS 1 and eighteen F/A 2, a total of seventy-five aircraft. Of these thirty-three FRS 1s were converted to F/A 2 standard making a total of fifty-one F/A 2s. In addition to the operational aircraft, there were nine Harrier T 4 and four T 8 conversion trainers. The T 8s were all conversions of T 4s.

Sea Harriers served with 700A NAS, the IFTU and with 800, 801, 809 and 899 NAS. Of these, 809 NAS was formed at short notice in 1982 during the South Atlantic Conflict and 899 NAS was the headquarters and training unit which also operated Harrier T 4 and T 8 two-seat trainers and Hunter T 8M radar trainers together with a sophisticated full-motion simulator at Yeovilton which was used by students to 'fly' a significant amount of the conversion syllabus.

Sea Harriers operated from the aircraft carriers *Hermes*, *Invincible*, *Illustrious* and *Ark Royal*. The STUFT ferry carrier *Atlantic Conveyor* was fitted out in days at Devonport Dockyard in 1982 to operate Sea Harriers, if necessary, with vertical launch and recovery from a small deck near the bow. Liquid oxygen, fuel and weapons were provided.

The IFTU, 700A NAS formed in 1979 and evolved into 899 NAS in 1980. The remaining squadrons followed. The FRS 1 was a critical element of Operation 'Corporate', the campaign in the South Atlantic during 1982 to liberate the Falkland Islands. Without the Sea Harriers the operation would not have been possible and both offensive and defensive missions began on 1 May 1982 and continued until 14 June

Sea Harrier F/A 2 leaving *Ark Royal*'s 'ski-jump'. (Crown Copyright)

when Argentine forces surrendered. During this period Sea Harriers flew 2,000 operational sorties and destroyed twenty-four enemy aircraft for no loss to themselves in air combat against an enemy air force that was, on paper, larger and equipped with a wider range of combat aircraft, an outstanding achievement. Unfortunately, two Sea Harriers were shot down by anti-aircraft gun and missile fire and four more were lost in operational accidents.

The FRS 1 played a major role in supporting British troops operating under UN command in the Former Republic of Yugoslavia from the decks of British carriers in the Adriatic. One Sea Harrier was shot down by a Bosnian-Serb anti-aircraft missile during this period. By the time these operations ended in 1996 the F/A 2 had replaced the FRS 1 and demonstrated itself to be the outstanding European fighter of its generation. F/A 2s also took part in policing the UN-declared 'No-Fly' zones over Iraq in 1998 alongside fighters from the USA and other coalition allies. In 1999 F/A 2s took part in Operation 'Palliser', NATO-led operations in Kosovo and demonstrated their 'swing-role' versatility by launching with AAMs and bombs so that they could fly CAP over NATO forces or strike designated targets at short notice.

The Sea Harrier was popular with those who flew it. David Morgan remembered that the Blue Fox radar was a basic system that suffered terribly from clutter over land but worked fairly well at medium to high levels over the sea. At low level, even over the sea it required skilful handling to detect and track targets. Paul Tremelling

Sea Harrier F/A 2 landing on *Illustrious*. (Crown Copyright)

Sea Harrier F/A 2 with practice bomb containers on the outer pylons.

Below: Sea Harrier T 8 of 899 NAS at Yeovilton.

described it as a 'fuselage shrink-wrapped around a Pegasus with aerodynamic surfaces added as an afterthought'.

In 1998 the UK Government carried out a defence review which led to aircraft being operated within a new joint force structure. One of these was JFH which placed RN Sea Harrier squadrons and RAF Harrier squadrons under a single unified command administered by the RAF. The high-minded ideal, like that of the original Royal Flying Corps in 1912, was that the joint force could act together ashore or afloat when needed. In practice, the land-centric administration of the joint force dismissed naval operations as unimportant and, disastrously, the CAS convinced politicians in 2002 that there would be little need for embarked fighters in the short term. At the time the F-35 joint strike fighter was expected to be fully operational by 2012; it is not even fully operational in 2023. JFH also claimed that the F/A 2 needed upgrades for which there was no funding and so the Sea Harrier force was run down from 2004. The last Sea Harrier squadron, 801 NAS, was disbanded in March 2006. Many of the newer aircraft had accumulated very few flying hours. It was a sad end for the Sea Harrier squadrons which deserved far better recognition from politicians for what they had achieved. Some were maintained in taxi-worthy condition for use on the dummy deck at the School of Aircraft Handling at Culdrose. JFH was re-formed with four squadrons, of which two were to nominally to be manned by the RN and two by the RAF based at Cottesmore with a joint training unit at Wittering. They were equipped with the Harrier GR 7/9.

Hawk

Designed as an advanced training aircraft to replace the Gnat T 2 and Hunter T 7 in RAF service, the Hawker P.1182 also did very well in the export market with licence-built versions including the USN's T-45 Goshawk. Tandem seating gave the student good, fighter-type visibility and the instructor in the rear cockpit a good target view over the student's head. Unlike previous trainers it was designed from the outset as an advanced trainer, not modified from an operational type. A 30mm gun pod on the centreline with underwing hardpoints for bombs, rocket pods or Sidewinder missiles gave it a weapon training and limited operational capability. The first example flew in 1974 and 4 FTS at Valley, where both RN and RAF pilots were trained began to operate Hawks in 1976.

It was selected as a suitable Hunter replacement for fleet requirements tasks and aircraft were transferred from the RAF beginning in 1994. They were maintained and flown by civilian contractors for use by FRADU, which moved to Culdrose in 1995, with aircraft used when required by the RN Fixed-Wing Standards Flight at Yeovilton.

Hawk T 1 data

Length:	38ft 10½in
Wingspan:	30ft 9½in
Height:	13ft 1in
MTOW:	12,566lb
Engine:	One 5,200lb thrust Rolls-Royce/Turbomeca 151 turbofan
Fuel:	Avcat. 184 gallons in integral wing tanks, 181 gallons in fuselage tank. Total 365 gallons. Provision for 100 or 190-gallon drop tanks on underwing hardpoints
Performance:	Maximum speed in level flight 540 knots/Mach 0.88 (Mach 1.2 in a shallow dive) Service ceiling 50,000ft. Under 1 minute to 10,000ft
Endurance:	Over 2 hours
Armament:	One 30mm Aden cannon in detachable centreline pod. One hardpoint under each wing for 1,000lb bombs, rocket pods, practice bomb carriers or Sidewinder AIM 9P AAM

No Hawks were built new for the RN but at least thirty-four were transferred to the RN from the RAF. Not all were used at any one time and airframes were cycled through deep maintenance with RAF T 1 s and T 1As.

Hawk T 1 of 736 NAS at Culdrose. (Crown Copyright)

Between 1994 and 2013 Hawks were operated by the civilian-manned FRADU, first at Yeovilton then Culdrose. In 2013 the FRADU task was absorbed into 736 NAS at Culdrose. Maintenance continued to be carried out by civilian contractors but the aircraft were flown by RN pilots and the squadron acted as a pool unit for those waiting to begin F-35B training, holding between appointments or returning to flying duties. It continued to fly fleet requirements missions including FOST's 'Thursday War' in the Channel danger areas and retained the standardisation task.

The Hawk T 1 was withdrawn from service without replacement in both the RN and RAF on 31 March 2022, a defence review having decided that the type could not be retained in service economically beyond that date. The fleet requirements tasking was taken over by virtual training using data-linked command systems. The pool and holding requirement was no longer considered viable because the T 1 was no longer considered representative of a modern fighter with its 'clockwork' instruments. A developed version, the T 2, replaced the T 1 within 4 FTS at RAF Valley for use training RN and RAF fast-jet pilots.

Harrier II

Work was carried out in the UK by Hawker, later absorbed into British Aerospace, and in the USA by McDonnell Douglas to define a second generation development of the Harrier/AV-8A. The UK Government lacked the enthusiasm for a national project and opted for a joint programme based on the McDonnell Douglas design, the AV-8B Harrier II, as a replacement for the Harrier GR 3 in RAF service. The mark numbering sequence of the original Harrier was retained and the first Harrier II for the RAF was designated GR 5. The AV-8B first flew in the USA during 1981 and the first GR 5 in April 1985. The original aluminium alloy fuselage was replaced by composite materials which significantly reduced weight and increased payload or range. The new one-piece wing was also made of composites and there was an elevated bubble canopy similar to the Sea Harrier. The cockpit featured both a head-up display and two head-down displays, the latter known as multi-purpose colour displays. HOTAS allowed weapon selections to be made without moving hands from the flight controls. Unlike its US counterpart, the GR 5 was equipped with the Zeus advanced ECM system. It achieved IOC with the RAF in 1989.

The RAF only intended the GR 5 to be used as a ground attack, interdiction and reconnaissance platform; it had no radar and lacked the letter 'F' in its designation although it could carry Sidewinder AAMs for self-defence. At first it was only a clear air mass, day ground attack aircraft and arguments about the capability of the P.1154 will be recalled when the GR 5 is considered for what it was and what it could have been. The USMC continued to develop the type and produced a variant designated the AV-8B+ fitted with AN/APG-65 multi-mode, pulse-doppler radar and AIM-120 AMRAAM missiles to give a fighter capability similar to the Sea Harrier but the RAF was not interested. A proposal to fit Blue Vixen radar in the GR 5 was dismissed by the MoD as risky, expensive and was not taken forward.

A Harrier GR 7 of 800 NAS landing on *Illustrious*.

A Harrier GR 7 of 800 NAS over Afghanistan.

A developed Harrier II, the GR 7, entered RAF service in 1990 with a nose-mounted FLIR system to give a night attack capability and cockpit compatible with NVG. From 1998 an improved, encrypted communications system was introduced and aircraft were fitted for thermal imaging and laser-designating pods although too few were procured to fit the entire fleet. The final upgrade to GR 9 standard followed the installation of enhanced software, Raytheon's Successor IFF system and improved communications. Link 16 data transfer was to have been installed but the type was politically axed before it could be introduced. New weapons included AGM-65 Maverick ASM and Paveway laser-guided bombs. Reconnaissance capability was greatly improved with the introduction of the Digital Joint Reconnaissance Pod. As well as patrolling No-Fly zones over Iraq from 1993, RAF Harrier IIs operated over Kosovo in 1999 and carried out several short-term embarkations in *Invincible* class carriers. RAF Harriers took part in the 2003 Gulf War flying a total of 870 sorties during a 78-day Allied bombing campaign. From September 2004 a Harrier II detachments of six aircraft from JFH deployed on a long-term basis to Afghanistan with air and ground crews, including those from the naval air squadrons, rotated on a regular basis into theatre from the UK. They proved to be ideal for the purpose and provided 24-hour cover for coalition troops.

Pilot's view through the head-up display of a Harrier GR 7 just before take-off from *Ark Royal*'s 'ski-jump'.

JFH aircraft were deployed to Afghanistan for 5 years continuously before being withdrawn in June 2009. During that period they flew 22,000 hours in 8,500 sorties.

No training Harriers were operated by RN units but 20 Squadron RAF operated two-seat trainer versions of the Harrier II to convert both RN and RAF pilots onto type. Unlike the equivalent USMC TAV-8B, the British aircraft were fully combat capable.

Harrier GR 9 data

Length:	46ft 4in
Wingspan:	30ft 4in
Height:	11ft 8in
MTOW:	31,000lb
Engine:	One 21,750lb thrust Rolls-Royce Pegasus 105 vectored-thrust turbofan
Fuel:	Avcat. 915 gallons internal plus two 250-gallon tanks on inner wing hardpoints
Performance:	Maximum speed in level flight 575 knots/Mach 0.89 Service ceiling 50,000ft. Under 1 minute to 10,000ft
Endurance:	Over 2 hours
Armament:	Two podded 25mm Aden cannon with 100 rpg. Eight underwing hardpoints allow carriage of up to 9,200lb of weapons including AGM-65 Maverick ASM, Paveway III/IV LGBs, rocket pods and Sidewinder AAMs. Different modification states allowed the use of Sniper and TIALD pods and DJRP

No Harrier GR 5/7/9s were built directly for the RN but ninety-four were built for JFH. Together with fourteen Harrier T 10s for pilot conversion; nine of these were upgraded to the same standard as GR 9s, designated T 12s. A few were upgraded with Pegasus 107 engines developing 23,800lb of thrust and re-designated T 12As.

When Sea Harriers were prematurely withdrawn from service in 2006 JFH was re-organised into four squadrons equipped with Harrier GR 7/9s, two to be manned by the RN and two by the RAF. 800 NAS reformed with them in April 2006 and was to have been joined by 801 NAS in October but a lack of manpower prevented it becoming an independent unit and led to the two units being amalgamated into the NSW. 801 NAS was due to re-form out of the NSW in 2010 but JFH became a victim of Government austerity measures and was terminated before this could happen. Training for both RN and RAF front-line Harrier II squadrons was provided by 20 Squadron RAF.

Shortly after being reformed with twelve Harrier GR 7s, 800 NAS spent a short period embarked in *Illustrious* prior to deploying to Afghanistan as part of 904 Expeditionary Air Wing from September 2006. On return to the UK in March 2007 it joined 801 NAS to form the NSW which then deployed to Afghanistan between October 2007 and February 2008. It deployed again between July and December 2008. During this time no aircraft were available for embarkation in the two operational carriers and such fixed-wing practice as they could get had to be provided by USMC, Spanish and Italian Harriers when opportunity allowed. NSW worked up as a carrier squadron for embarkation in *Ark Royal* during 2009 and 2010. The unexpected decision to axe both JFH and *Ark Royal* as a savings measure left the RN with no fixed-wing aircraft capable of embarking in a carrier until *Queen Elizabeth* was completed and the F-35B Lightning II became operational in 2021. On 24 November 2010 a NSW Harrier made its last flight from a carrier, *Ark Royal*, and on 15 December all Harrier flying ceased. In November 2011 the MOD sold the remaining seventy-two Harrier GR 9s along with an extensive store of spare parts to the USMC as a source of components to support the AV-8B fleet. It had been the intention to re-engine the entire GR 9 fleet with the Pegasus 107 engine and retain it in service until at least 2018. Re-engined aircraft were to be designated GR 9A. One of the excuses given by the MOD for the early demise of the Sea Harrier had been the supposed difficulty and expense of fitting the Pegasus 107 but in fact, very few aircraft ever got it. Pilots who flew with it told me that it gave a significant increase in performance.

HAWKER-SIDDELEY

HS-125 CC 1

A derivative of the DH 125 executive jet, two HS-125s of 32 Squadron which acted as both the Royal Flight and a VIP transport unit based at Northolt were transferred to the RN in in 1971 to reflect the unit's joint nature. The scheme was short-lived, however, and they were returned in 1972.

HS-125-600B

A single 600B variant was allocated to the RN in 1988 and modified for use as a development airframe for Sea Harrier F/A 2 avionics. Its distinctive nose carried a Blue Vixen radar and it operated from Dunsfold until 2002, making frequent visits to Yeovilton. Wingspan was 41ft and MTOW 25,000lb. It was powered by two 3,750lb thrust Rolls-Royce Viper 601 turbofans which gave a maximum level speed of 475 knots. On completion of the trials programme in 2002 the sensitive equipment was removed and the aircraft was scrapped in 2003.

A number of aircraft types built originally by companies within the group were re-branded as Hawker-Siddeley types but I have listed them under the firms that originally designed them to maintain a logical sequences. They include:

Buccaneer – see under Blackburn
Sea Vixen – see under de Havilland
Hawk – see under Hawker
748 – see under Avro

The HS-125 used to develop Sea Harrier F/A 2 avionics seen at Yeovilton. (Bob Turner)

Hiller HT 2 of 705 NAS at Culdrose.

HILLER

HT 1

The first naval helicopters were flown by fixed-wing pilots who had undergone conversion courses in Sikorsky Hoverflies but by the early 1950s there was a growing need for ab initio helicopter pilot training. With a similar requirement, the USN had procured the Hiller HTE 1 as a two-seat trainer in 1950. It proved to be under-powered and a larger order for the HTE 2 powered by a single 200hp Franklin 6V4-200 piston engine followed in 1951. Twenty HTE 2s were taken from USN production contracts and transferred to the RN under MDAP arrangements with deliveries starting in 1952. This model had a rotor span of 35ft, MTOW of 2,100lb and a maximum level speed of 74 knots.

The HTE 2 was never allocated a name in Fleet Air Arm service but designated as Hiller HT 1. They had dual controls, a third seat for utility tasks and were operated by 705 NAS in the helicopter training role between May 1953 and January 1963, based at Gosport at first, then Lee-on-Solent from 1955 and finally Culdrose from 1958. One example was used by a flight operating from the survey ship *Vidal* between 1954 and 1957 when it was replaced by a Dragonfly. Another example was used briefly by 706 NAS for a month in late 1953. A single HT 1 led the Coronation Review Fly-Past by the Fleet Air Arm in June 1953.

HT 2

The Hiller HT 1 had proved to be an ideal basic helicopter pilot training aircraft and the Admiralty decided to replace it with a later development. Designated as the nameless Hiller HT 2 these began to replace the HT 1 in September 1962.

Hiller HT 2 data

Length:	28ft
Rotor diameter:	35ft 5in
Height:	10ft 1½in
MTOW:	2,750lb
Engine:	One Lycoming VO-540 B2D piston
Fuel:	Avgas. 36 gallons
Performance:	Maximum level speed 84 knots
	Service ceiling 13,200ft
Endurance:	Over 2 hours
Armament:	None

Hiller HT 2s were procured in two batches, the first for fourteen in May 1962 and another for seven in August 1963.

They were used by 705 NAS in the basic helicopter pilot training role between September 1962 and March 1975 when they were replaced by the Westland Gazelle. Three Hillers were used in the light reconnaissance and utility roles by 845 NAS between March 1964 and August 1965. They were ferried to the Far East in *Albion* and two returned to the UK in *Bulwark*. During the Confrontation with Indonesia they operated from Sibu in Borneo but one was lost in April 1965 when it crashed into a river in Sarawak.

I flew the Hiller HT 2 during my own conversion course and remember it as a delightful little helicopter to fly. The exhilaration of seeing the ground whizz past under my feet through the clear bubble canopy on the first low-flying sortie after being used to conventional enclosed cockpits has remained in my memory. Another memory is the feeling of satisfaction after carrying out a well-judged engine-off autorotation onto the target set out in a sand pit at the centre of the Culdrose runway pattern.

Hiller HT 1 of 705 NAS.

KINGSNORTH NAVAL AIR STATION

The SS Airship class

The First Sea Lord, Admiral of the Fleet Lord Fisher, chaired a meeting at the Admiralty in February 1915 at which he asked for a small airship capable of searching for U-boats in littoral waters with a maximum speed of roughly 40 knots. It was to have a crew of two, pilot and observer, an endurance of up to 8 hours and be fitted with a W/T set with a range of at least 30nm with a weapon load up to 160lb. Above all it was to be cheap, simple and capable of large-scale production without delay. The result was SS-1 which used the envelope of HMA Number 2 taken out of storage with the fuselage of a BE 2c suspended from it. SS stood for Sea Scout.

Work on the prototype had begun immediately at Kingsnorth, it was completed by March 1915 and immediately deemed a success. A rival design by Airships Ltd, designated SS-2, took until May to complete and was considered too complicated and expensive to take forward. There was initial difficulty in sourcing envelopes as all the pre-war suppliers were fully contracted with aeroplane orders but imaginative use of firms that specialised in waterproof clothing or rubber goods solved the problem. Orders were placed and representatives from each of the companies came to Kingsnorth for intensive instruction on the preparation of suitable material. SS-3 was the first production example with an envelope made of rubber-proofed fabric. At the tail of the gasbag a single vertical fin and rudder were fitted ventrally with horizontal fins and elevators fitted to port and starboard. Four coats of dope were applied to the outer surface with a top coat of aluminium varnish to protect against deterioration caused by weather, salt spray and sunlight. The BE 2c fuselage had no wings, rudders or elevators although early examples retained their wheels. These were replaced by skids in later examples. The W/T set had a range of up to 50nm and used a 200ft trailing aerial. SS-1, SS-3 to SS-26 and SS-48/49 had BE 2c cars; SS-27 and SS-39 to 47 had Armstrong-built cars and SS-28 to SS-37 had Farman-built cars.

SS-3 data

Length:	143ft 5 in
Diameter:	27ft 9in
Height:	43ft 5in
Envelope capacity:	60,000ft^3
Engine:	70hp Renault
Fuel:	Avgas. 59½ gallons
Gross lift:	1.85 tons
Disposable lift:	0.64 tons (for crew, fuel, ballast and armament)
Performance:	Maximum level speed 44 knots
	Service ceiling 13,200ft
Endurance:	8 hours
Armament:	One 0.303in Lewis machine gun with 47-round drum magazines. Eight 16lb or two 65lb bombs

SS class production amounted to forty-eight, the majority assembled at Kingsnorth but three were assembled at Barrow-in-Furness and fifteen at Wormwood Scrubs. The number remained with the car and not the envelope, those that had the car replaced had the suffix 'A' added.

SS class airships were based, initially, at Capel and Polegate to cover the eastern Channel. As their numbers grew they were also deployed

SS-14A was built at Kingsnorth in 1915.

to cover the south-western approaches from Mullion and Pembroke Dock. Coverage over the Irish Sea was provided from bases at Luce Bay, Anglesey, Ballyliffin, Bentra, Johnstown Castle and Malahide Castle. Three were deployed to the Eastern Mediterranean and operated from Imbros.

The SS class was regarded as a fairly simple design both to fly and to maintain but rapid construction outstripped the supply of pilots to fly them. The Admiralty considered the task to be within the capabilities of Midshipmen who were competent to operate powered boats and the Grand Fleet was asked to provide volunteers. Midshipman T Elmhirst RN was one of those who volunteered and later recalled that height was maintained by means of turning a wheel with his right hand which was linked to the elevators. Direction was made with foot pedals attached to the rudder and with his left hand he controlled engine rpm, the gas valve, two ballonet air valves and an air pressure control cable. All the SS class airships that survived were deleted in September 1919.

AP-1

By 1915 the Admiralty was frustrated by the lack of any fixed-wing aircraft capable of out-climbing a Zeppelin to get into an attacking position once it was detected. Conventional aircraft also lacked the endurance to carry out standing patrols. Wing Commander N F Usborne RNAS, who commanded Kingsnorth, devised a potential solution; suspending a BE 2c aircraft, complete with its wings and control surfaces, under an SS-airship envelope. His plan was immediately supported by the Admiralty which ordered two prototypes to be prepared and tested. They were designated AP-1 and AP-2, AP standing for Airship-Plane. His idea was that the BE could be released at the same height or even above the Zeppelin instead of having to climb from an airfield after its detection. The AP could also remain on patrol at altitude for up to 8 hours, much longer than a conventional aircraft.

Usborne's plan was that AP-1 could climb rapidly like an airship to the height of the Zeppelin. Once there, the pilot would release the aircraft and fly it into action. Before separation the pilot would open the envelope's gas valve allowing it to fall, gently, back to earth. A first trial was carried out in August 1915 but the aircraft failed to separate. Modifications took until February 1916 when Usborne himself flew AP-1 with Lieutenant Commander de Courcy W P Ireland RN, who had helped with the design, as observer. As they passed 4,000ft the forward suspension points released without being selected. The weight of the engine caused the BE's nose to tip forward and the rear suspension points broke free. The BE tumbled away from the envelope, probably with its controls damaged, and turned over. Ireland was not strapped in and fell to his death in the Medway. Usborne was strapped in but died when the aircraft crashed inverted into a railway goods yard. The Admiralty promptly banned all further experiments of this nature and work on AP-2 was aborted.

AP-1 lifting off for its final, fatal, flight. (Guy Warner)

Coastal class airships

The Kingsnorth design team appreciated that the SS class were an interim type and that an improved design was required for operations further from the coast. Their solution was the Coastal class which, like the earlier design, made use of obsolescent aircraft fuselages to save manufacturing time. They acquired the fuselage of a two-seat Avro 510 with its Sunbeam tractor engine, removed the tapered after section and mated it with another 510 cockpit section, this time with a pusher engine. The result was a four-seat car with an engine at either end which could be produced in quantity. The prototype car was suspended beneath the tri-lobe envelope of Astra-Torres Airship Number 10, which had been kept in storage. It flew for the first time in May 1915 and was used on development work based at Kingsnorth throughout the remainder of the war. Modifications introduced before full production included changes of radiator positioning, a strengthened nose-cone for the envelope and a re-positioned air-scoop to maintain ballonet pressure. Late production Coastals had 220hp Renault engines fitted aft in place of the Sunbeam. Trials with C-1 included securing it to the cruiser *Canterbury* briefly in September 1916 so that crews could be exchanged and fuel tanks re-filled.

The crew comprised a coxswain in the front cockpit with the pilot immediately behind him. Next came the W/T operator's compartment which contained a small petrol-driven generator to provide electrical power even if both main engines failed. By changing the little engine's belt drive it could be used to operate an auxiliary blower to maintain ballonet pressure. The engineer's cockpit was right aft, deafeningly close to the rear engine. All four aircrew wore harnesses in flight and the car was fitted with static-line parachutes so that it could be abandoned in an emergency; one of the first naval aircraft to have such a capability. A space between the pilot and the W/T operator was originally filled by a ballast water tank but this was frequently removed by a local modification to provide an observer's cockpit. Pilots often carried small

Coastal class airship C 4.

C*1 in 1918.

bags of sand slung outboard of the car to give minor alterations of trim.

When fully loaded, Coastals could carry nearly half a ton of bombs or depth charges and once the early snags had been ironed out they proved to be reliable and popular aircraft that formed the backbone of the RNAS airship force throughout the remainder of the Great War. One of the two Lewis guns could be mounted on various positions on the car but the second one could be mounted on top of the envelope to protect against enemy aircraft attacking from above. It was reached by climbing up a 30in diameter tube which ran vertically through the centre of the envelope, ending at a wooden trapdoor near the top. In action the gunner stood on the closed trapdoor and fitted his gun to a Scarff ring attached to a wooden frame laced to the top of the envelope. This mounting was little used at first but after C-17 was shot down by enemy aircraft in April 1917 Coastal crews were ordered to have the upper gun manned at all times when flying more than 3nm from the coast. This applied even if an extra crew member had to be carried to do so.

C-1 data

Length:	196ft
Diameter:	37ft
Height:	52ft 1in
Envelope capacity:	170,000ft^3
Engines:	Two. One 150hp Sunbeam tractor; one 220hp Renault pusher
Fuel:	Avgas. 220 gallons
Gross lift:	4.94 tons
Disposable lift:	1.6 tons (for crew, fuel, ballast and armament)
Performance:	Maximum level speed 45 knots Service ceiling 8,000ft
Endurance:	Up to 22 hours
Armament:	Two 0.303in Lewis machine guns with 47-round drum magazines. Four 112lb, two 230lb bombs or depth charges of equivalent weight

A total of twenty-seven Coastal class airships was built, some of which were rebuilt and given 'A' suffixes when damaged. All of them were built at Kingsnorth.

From early in 1916 Coastal class airships operated from Mullion, Pembroke Dock, East Fortune, Longside, Howden, Polegate, Pulham and Folkestone. They often lacked the speed to attack U-boats sighted at a distance before they dived but several attacks were carried out which might have damaged their targets. Their major value was in keeping the enemy dived wherever they operated, limiting their speed and endurance and, thus, their ability to attack merchant shipping. Once U-boats were sighted, the W/T operator could call up destroyers or other aircraft to prosecute them. The surviving Coastals were deleted in 1918.

Coastal * class airships

Another interim design produced quickly by the design team at Kingsnorth, the Coastal * class was produced in 1917 to cover the late arrival of the North Sea class airships. The design followed that of the earlier Coastals but incorporated improvements that operational experience had shown to be necessary. The car of C-12 was used as a prototype and re-numbered as C*1 but the tri-lobe envelope was new and slightly larger. Open cockpits were retained but the car was covered with plywood rather than canvas and featured taller sides with glass portholes on either side. There was also a glass panel in the floor to give downward visibility. The small petrol engine was retained to power the generator and maintain ballonet pressure in an emergency and fuel was carried in four tanks attached to suspension wires inside the envelope. The Lewis gun position on top of the envelope was omitted and static-line parachutes were provided for the aircrew with pre-fixed lines at positions where they could be reached quickly.

C*4 data

Length:	217ft
Diameter:	49ft
Height:	56ft
Envelope capacity:	210,000ft^3
Engines:	Two. One 110hp Berliet tractor forward; one 220hp Renault or 240hp Fiat pusher aft
Fuel:	Avgas. 400 gallons
Gross lift:	6.46 tons
Disposable lift:	1.8 tons (for crew, fuel, ballast and armament)
Performance:	Maximum level speed 50 knots Service ceiling 9,500ft. 1 minute to 1,000ft
Endurance:	Up to 20 hours
Armament:	Two 0.303in Lewis machine guns with 47-round drum magazines. Two 230lb bombs plus two 100lb bombs or depth charges of equivalent weight

Originally twenty Coastal * airships were ordered but the number was cut back to ten in July 1918, all built at Kingsnorth.

They proved to be a successful design and operated on patrols from East Fortune, Howden, Longside and Mullion. The last of them were withdrawn from service in early 1919.

North Sea class airships

The Kingsnorth design team intended the North Sea class to fill the gap caused by the unexpectedly long delay bringing the big rigid airships into service. The prototype, NS-1, first flew in February 1917 with a trilobe envelope design but it suffered problems with fuel lines and the complicated engine drive shafts. The completely-enclosed control car marked a distinct step forward; it was 35ft long with 6ft headroom and was constructed with steel tubes covered with duralumin sheets and fabric. The control room occupied the forward end with a W/T office and navigation room facing each other aft of it. The after part comprised sleeping and messing facilities for a crew of ten who operated in two watches of five. They had the 'luxury' of a hot plate attached to an engine exhaust that allowed rudimentary cooking in flight. Astern of the control car, and connected to it by a walkway fixed over steel cables, there was a small engine car with the engines mounted outboard of it on either side. It had space for two mechanics, although only one was usually on watch, plus the engine controls. Communication with the control room was by ship-type engine telegraphs. The drive-shaft problem was partially resolved by replacing the Rolls-Royce engines with 240hp direct-drive Fiat engines and the fuel line problem was resolved by re-positioning fuel cells inside the envelope directly above the control car where flexing was minimal. There was an observation/gun platform on top of the envelope with access to it gained through a canvas tube above an open ladder from the roof of the control car. Up to five Lewis guns could be fitted but the normal outfit was three; one on top of the envelope and one on each side of the control car, firing through the control room windows. The design problems were resolved in two ways. A team at East Fortune combined the separate cars into one long structure with the engines still outboard but driving the propellers directly. Kingsnorth's solution was similar but retained the separate cars and by 1918 all the class were modified to one scheme or the other. From late 1918 the Fiat engines began to replace the original Rolls-Royce Eagle but the change-over was incomplete when the war ended.

NS 6 in 1918.

A B C D E F G H I J K L M N O P Q R S T U V W X Y Z

NS-3 data

Length:	260ft
Diameter:	57ft
Height:	69ft
Envelope capacity:	360,000ft^3
Engines:	Two 250hp Rolls-Royce Eagle later replaced by two 240hp Fiat direct-drive engines
Fuel:	Avgas. 220 gallons
Gross lift:	10.85 tons
Disposable lift:	3.8 tons (for crew, fuel, ballast and armament)
Performance:	Maximum level speed 50 knots Service ceiling 9,500ft (1 minute to 1,000ft)
Endurance:	In excess of 24 hours
Armament:	Three 0.303in Lewis machine guns with 47-round drum magazines. Up to six 230lb bombs

Kingsnorth built fourteen North Sea class airships with the last, NS-16, delivered in January 1919. Three others were completed but never delivered or flown after the Armistice. NS-13 made only one flight before being purchased by the US Navy and re-numbered as NS-14 in November 1918.

Once its teething problems were sorted out the North Sea class proved to be particularly effective and adaptable airships of greater operational use than the delayed rigids. They operated from East Fortune, Longside and Pulham.

In May 1918 NS-1 was towed astern of the destroyer *Vectis* at 30 knots and a month later it landed on the sea alongside her for crews to be exchanged by sea-boat. Both NS-7 and NS-8 flew over the German fleet as it sailed into the Firth of Forth to surrender in November 1918. NS-11 established a world endurance record in February 1919 when it covered 4,000nm in 100 hours 15 minutes on a patrol searching for mines. In March 1919 it accompanied NS-12 on the first airship flight to Norway in a flight of over 24 hours' duration. In January 1919, NS-16 took part in an experiment to see if it would be possible to clear mines with a sweep wire towed by an airship.

SSP class airships

The Kingsnorth team produced the SSP, Sea Scout Pusher, to meet an Admiralty requirement for a small non-rigid airship that could carry out patrols previously flown by Coastals and incorporate other operational improvements and the first, SSP-1, flew in January 1917. It had a three-seat, purpose-built car with a rear-mounted pusher engine suspended beneath one of the 70,000ft^3 envelopes produced for the later SS airships. The original powerplant was a 75hp Rolls-Royce Hawk engine designed especially for airships but this suffered problems and it was replaced in production by a 100hp Green engine.

SSP-1 data

Length:	143ft
Diameter:	30ft
Height:	43ft
Envelope capacity:	70,000ft^3
Engine:	100hp Green water-cooled
Fuel:	Avgas. 102 gallons
Gross lift:	2.2 tons
Disposable lift:	0.6 tons (for crew, fuel, ballast and armament)
Performance:	Maximum level speed 45 knots Service ceiling 9,500ft (1 minute to 1,000ft)
Endurance:	Up to 16 hours
Armament:	One 0.303in Lewis machine-gun with 47-round drum magazines. Eight 16lb or one 112lb bomb

Only six SSPs were built; the first at Kingsnorth and the remaining five at Wormwood Scrubs. Production was terminated when the prototype SSZ class airship was evaluated and found to be an even better design. They operated from Folkestone, Anglesey and Caldale.

LEONARDO HELICOPTERS

Merlin – See under Westland

Wildcat – See under Westland

LOCKHEED MARTIN

Hudson

Developed as a maritime patrol aircraft for the RAF, the Hudson evolved from the Lockheed Model 10 Electra, a small pre-war airliner. Four were transferred to the RN from the RAF in 1944 although one was returned unused. RN Hudsons were modified for use as transport aircraft with up to ten seats and used by the Admiralty Flight within 781 NAS to support RN contingents in Europe after the D-Day landings, As the Allied armies advanced they moved into airfields in France and then Germany. In July 1945 they were transferred to 782 NAS at Lee-on-Solent from where they were deleted in 1946. One of them, AM 550, was the personal 'barge' of Admiral Sir Bertram Ramsey, the Allied Naval Commander for the Normandy landings, and he was killed when it crashed on take-off on 2 January 1945.

Wingspan was 65ft 6in, MTOW 17,500lb and they were powered by two 1,200hp Pratt & Whitney Twin Wasp radial engines which gave a maximum level speed of 214 knots.

The Joint Strike Fighter Project

The RN project to replace the Sea Harrier proved to be a long and complicated affair. From the outset it was accepted that, with a relatively small production run, a partner was required to boost numbers and share development costs. The RAF had no interest and talks between the UK MoD and the Pentagon in the late 1980s led to an investigation into the joint development of a supersonic STOVL fighter to replace the RN Sea Harrier and the USMC AV-8B. At the same time the USN and USAF were considering a range of fighter options intended to be affordable, stealthy or just an improvement on existing types. With the end of the Cold War in 1991, US legislators imposed collaboration to achieve what they thought would be economy with a basic fighter design put into large scale production with different versions for the USN, USMC, USAF and export customers. By 1994 this evolved into

An F-35B Lightning launching from *Queen Elizabeth*. (Crown Copyright)

the JSF, to be produced in three versions, each with the same sensors, weapons and an intended 80 per cent commonality in airframe design. The UK joined the project and designated its variant as the UK FCBA. The UK paid a share of the projected development cost and provided some RN and civilian staff for the JPO in the USA; the first time that overseas officials had participated in a US Government procurement programme. This made the UK a Level 1 partner and although other nations bought into the project, none matched the UK level of commitment. With its recent Sea Harrier experience and the future carrier design not yet finalised, it was assumed that STOVL would be the most likely RN variant and this gained the most UK input. The other variants were a conventional version for the USAF to operate from land bases and a bigger-winged version with a tail hook for the USN to operate from carriers. British involvement changed with the 1998 Defence Review when, despite the RAF having said that it did not intend to replace the Harrier, the Government announced that the STOVL JSF variant would now be procured to replace the Harrier in RAF service as well as the Sea Harrier. FCBA was re-designated as the Joint Combat Aircraft, JCA, although it was generally still referred to by its US designation. Three aerospace groups were invited to make proposals and, surprisingly, the first to be eliminated was the McDonnell Douglas/British Aerospace team who had designed and manufactured the AV-8B Harrier II. Their design was dismissed by the US DARPA as being 'not sufficiently advanced in concept' (I am afraid there seems to be no way of avoiding acronyms when describing the JSF and its systems). Boeing's proposal was eliminated in 2001 and Lockheed Martin was awarded a contract to design and develop the JSF. At the time the project was expected to take 10 years to complete.

F-35B Lightning II

The Lightning II is a single-seat, singled-engine all-weather strike fighter that makes unprecedented use of software and innovative systems to deliver air combat, electronic warfare, intelligence, surveillance and network node tasks concurrently. It has an exceptionally dense, mid-wing airframe with a double fin. Fuel tanks fill every available space in the fuselage, wings and even the vertical stabilisers and sequencing from the various tanks is controlled by software. Airframe components are manufactured in a number of countries and shipped to Fort Worth in the USA for assembly. BAE Systems in the UK manufactures the after fuselage and other components. Rolls-Royce makes the swivelling engine nozzle and lift fan for the STOVL variant. Fifteen per cent of the F-35B airframe is built in the UK.

The Lockheed Martin design developed to meet the JSF

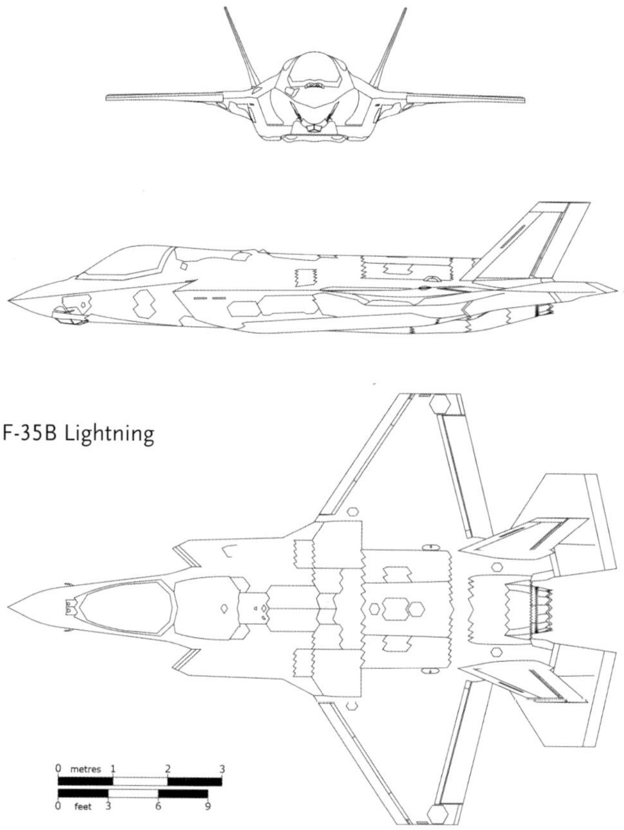

F-35B Lightning

requirement was designated F-35 and named Lightning II and is manufactured in three variants which differ in the way they take-off and land. The USAF F-35A has a relatively small wing and a very high landing speed. The F-35B STOVL variant for the USMC, RN and RAF has the same wing but a lift fan and swivelling engine exhaust for vertical landing. The USN F-35C has larger wings to reduce the landing speed within an acceptable limit for deck landing and a nose-tow catapult launch system. Its MTOW is 10,000lb greater than the other variants and it has more fuel and weapon carriage capability. It is fair to say the 'A' and 'C' variants were heavily penalised to achieve commonality with the very specialised 'B' version which had to be light enough to land on a ship vertically with unused weapons. Designed separately they would have been very different, probably with twin engines in both single and two-seat versions with a significantly greater radius of action. By 2015 many US analysts agreed that it would have been cheaper, quicker and far more efficient to build two separate designs, conventional and STOVL, using common avionics but by then it was too late. It is also obvious that the RN should have selected the F-35C carrier version from the outset, developed it in close co-operation with the USN and built the *Queen Elizabeth* carriers with catapults and arrester wires.

The Lightning II is unique in that it has no British designation; it was taken into UK service with its American designation, F-35B. It is the heaviest aircraft ever operated from a British carrier and also the most complicated aircraft ever taken into British service with flight and engine controls, radar, communications, navigation, electronic warfare, sensor fusion, weapons control and many other systems driven by software. Software programmes are delivered in numbered blocks with Block 3F as the first operational example from 2019. It offers combat capability, the use of wide range of weapons and full transfer of imagery and data but is still far from definitive. Block 4 is in development and there will be others for decades to come.

The F-35B's primary sensor is the Northrop-Grumman AN/APG-81 AESA radar. It has hundreds of transmit/receive modules built into the nose of the aircraft which have no mechanical motion. Beams are shaped by software to give thirty-two radar functions, twelve of which are air-to-air, twelve air-to-surface including ship tracking and sea surface search, four are electronic warfare, two navigation and two weather warning. The AESA is designed to last for the life of the airframe with an anticipated 10,000 hours between failures and even then the failure of a single module would have minimal impact on the overall performance of the radar. Its components are checked by an inbuilt monitoring system that specifies which line-replaceable unit to change if a fault develops. Track information from the radar is fed into an integrated core processor that fuses data with information from other sensors digitally and feeds it to the pilot via a helmet-mounted display and the panoramic cockpit display. There is no head-up display.

The AN/AAQ-37 distributed aperture system, DAS, comprises infrared sensors positioned around the aircraft to provide uninterrupted spherical vision which is fed into the integrated core processor and fused to give missile and aircraft detection, tracking and warnings including ballistic missile launches which can be detected at considerable distance. It also gives the pilot a complete view around the aircraft through the helmet-mounted display, even allowing him or her to see what is under the aircraft. In whatever direction the pilot looks he will see through the sensor that best supports his or her eye line. The sensors are passive and do not reveal the aircraft's presence to an enemy but some of them are positioned close to airframe hot-spots and have to be cooled by a cryogenic system that adds to the aircraft's complexity. Everything that moves in the aircraft is electrically actuated, generating heat inside the airframe and fuel is used as 'heat-sink' to cool it.

F-35B Lightnings of 617 Squadron 'transformed' into vertical landing mode recovering onto *Queen Elizabeth*. (Crown Copyright)

An F-35B Lightning of 809 NAS at the squadron's commissioning ceremony in December 2023. (Crown Copyright)

The Lockheed Martin AN/AAQ-40 EOTS feeds information to both the helmet-mounted display and the panoramic cockpit display via the integrated core processor. It has to fit into a cramped space between the radar and the cockpit and so its optical path is 'folded' by mirrors and prisms to create the most compact optical system devised to date. The primary lens is fitted inside a 'stealth window' assembly under the fuselage comprising seven sapphire facets. It complements the radar and DAS to provide designation for laser-guided weapons, a laser spot tracker for co-operative engagements and forward looking infrared air-to-air and air-to-surface tracking over a wide area with digital zoom capability and the generation of geo-coordinates to allow the use of GPS-guided weapons. Mounting it internally meant that AAQ-40 is another system that requires its own dedicated cooling system using a specialised liquid.

BAE Systems' AN/ASQ-239 Barracuda electronic warfare system inter-operates with the other sensors through the integrated core processor and, through networks, with other aircraft, ships and ground stations. Data is transferred via a MADL which allows transfer in real time. Like EOTS, Barracuda has to be mounted internally to avoid compromising the aircraft's low-observable stealth shape and it uses ten sensors located around the airframe and the radar receiver array itself to provide radar warning and to analyse and identify the emitter. The system provides electronic surveillance including the geo-location of detected radars allowing the F-35 to evade, jam or attack them on its own or within a network-connected force. It can collect signals intelligence and the APG-81 can be used as a stand-off jammer although its use at high power would betray the presence of the aircraft. The US maintains a joint unit that constantly updates the system's emitter library and both a theatre and worldwide threat list. The UK and Australia share a similar capability to support their F-35 fleets.

The Lightning's cockpit is remarkably clean and uncluttered, with very few switches. The panoramic cockpit display comprises four touchscreen panels known as 'portals', each 20in by 8in, within which the pilot can select any preferred arrangement. Most set tactical information on the left and a display of fused sensors on the right. A strip across the top shows digital engine temperature and fuel gauges, caution and warning panels, weapon status, undercarriage position and other administrative data. The aircraft is manoeuvred by a side-stick controller on the right of the cockpit with an arm rest aft of it. The throttle on the left-hand side has linear rather rotary movement and both have HOTAS switches so that the pilot does not have to release his hold on either control to make selections. There is a small battery-powered standby flight display on the centre console which provides sufficient information, in the event of engine failure or combat damage, to allow the pilot to fly the aircraft until the engine is re-lit or ejection becomes the only option.

The F-35B has eleven weapons stations numbered from 1 on the outboard port wingtip to 11 on the outboard starboard wing which are capable of carrying up to 12,000lb of weapons or stores. Numbers 4, 5, 7 and 8 are in two internal bays and can be used when the aircraft is flown in stealth mode but the others can only be used with external pylons fitted which are not stealthy. The internal weapons bays in the F-35B are smaller than those in the F-35A and F-35C. The inner wing pylons, 3 and 9, can each carry weapons up to 5,000lb or 355-gallon drop tanks. The pylons immediately outboard of them, 2 and 10, can carry 1,500lb weapons and the outermost stations at the wingtips, 1 and 11, are designed for air-to-air missiles only. The initial range of

F-35Bs of 617 Squadron embarked in *Queen Elizabeth* during 2023. (Crown Copyright)

weapons included AIM-120 AMRAAM AAMs, GBU-12 laser-guided bombs, GBU-32 joint direct attack munitions, AGM-154 joint stand-off weapons, GBU-39 small diameter bomb and Paveway IV precision-guided bombs. British weapons will be incorporated gradually, including the Meteor AAM which requires Block 4 software.

All three variants of the F-35 are powered by Pratt & Whitney F-135 engines, the most powerful production engine ever fitted in a fighter. The PW-600 variant in the F-35B is unique in that the spool to which the two low power turbines are attached turns a drive-shaft, through a clutch and gear box, to drive a horizontal Rolls-Royce lift fan situated just aft of the cockpit. When it is clutched in for hovering flight this delivers 18,000lb of thrust downwards making the Lightning arguably the world's most powerful turboprop aircraft, albeit with a vertical rather than horizontal thrust line. The PW-600 has other features designed by Rolls-Royce to give vertical thrust. The swivelling tail nozzle deflects hot exhaust from the engine's high pressure core downwards and the roll post puffer jets give roll control and some lift to balance hovering flight using high pressure air bled form the engine. The total vertical thrust from the swivelling tail pipe, lift fan and roll posts is 40,650lb and this sets the weight limit for a carrier landing. With full re-heat in conventional, horizontal flight the F-135 develops 41,000lb of thrust giving a maximum level speed of Mach 1.6.

The aircraft is only part of the system; it cannot be operated without the Lockheed Martin ALIS which manages flight operations, planned maintenance, aircraft diagnostics and repair, supply chain organisation, both pilot and technical training and qualification and all aircraft documentation. A laptop computer known as a PMA communicates with the aircraft systems by Wi-Fi and forms part of the ship or squadron hardware together with standard operating unit servers. The PMA also gives access to paperless aircraft manuals, maintenance details, low-observability management and mission planning software. Data from the server is sent to a central server, known as the CPE in every country that operates Lightnings; the UK CPE is at Marham. Individual aircraft information held within each CPE cannot be accessed by other nations but a core set of data is passed to the global sustainment system run by Lockheed Martin to provide maintenance data for the global Lightning fleet. *Queen Elizabeth* and *Prince of Wales* have ship operating kits that exchange data digitally with the UK CPE. ALIS downloads data from the PMA into individual aircraft mission systems and passes the required weapon load and fuel state information to the maintenance team. It calls up routine aircraft inspections and maintenance routines and is constantly updated via the CPE. If an aircraft develops a fault it sends a code to the PMA together with 'troubleshooting' information, a video clip of the appropriate repair procedure, the identity and location of line replaceable units needed to cure the problem and a list of technicians qualified to do the work. Information about every fault is passed to the global sustainment system to add to the total statistical knowledge of the aircraft systems and their support requirements. ALIS was more than two decades old when F-35 squadrons in the US and UK reached IOC and already obsolescent in software terms. After heavy criticism the US has produced a replacement system named ODIN which was in use with a USMC squadron in 2023. It demonstrated immediate improvement with servers that were a fraction of the size and weight of their predecessor that worked much faster. ODIN is a cloud-native system with applications that can be regularly updated from user feedback. During the change from ALIS to ODIN squadrons must have hardware that supports both but eventually ODIN will replace ALIS one unit at a time. This is another area where work will remain in progress throughout the life of the aircraft.

It took 20 years from design selection to IOC and the F-35 has still not entered full-scale production. DARPA's advanced design proved extraordinarily difficult to deliver and early LRIP batch aircraft have had to be modified at considerable expense to later standards. The F-35B has proved to be extremely expensive both to procure and to operate leading many critics to question whether even the USAF can afford the large numbers it originally wanted. Legacy types have had to be retained in service while development continues. Software has proved to be a difficult area with unpredictable time-scales and soaring costs. Block 4 software, under development in 2024, is expected to cost as much as the original JSF project; it was supposed to be rolled out in 2021, delayed until 2027 and the US Government Accountability Office says that that even this cannot now be achieved.

F-35B Lightning II data

Length:	51ft 2¼in
Wingspan:	35ft
Height:	14ft 3½in
MTOW:	60,000lb
Engine:	One Pratt & Whitney F-135-PW-600 capable of delivering 41,000lb of thrust with re-heat in conventional flight or 40,650lb thrust with lift fan in hovering flight
Fuel:	Avcat. 500 gallons (600 US) internal plus optional 355 gallons (426 US) in drop tanks on inner pylons. Total 855 gallons (1,026 US) in non-stealth operations
Performance:	Maximum level speed Mach 1.6 Service ceiling 50,000ft. 1 minute to 30,000ft
Endurance:	500nm radius of action on internal fuel
Armament:	Two internal weapon bays each capable of holding one AAM and one 1,000lb bomb equivalent. ASRAAM and AMRAAM AAM with software for Meteor AAM in development. Extensive array of laser and GPS guided bombs and stand-off munitions described in text

The UK Government committed to the procurement of 138 F-35s when it became a Level 1 partner and continues to confirm that figure with the qualification that it refers to the number that will be bought throughout the life of the project which may run for another three decades or more. In late 2023 it is understood that thirty-eight F-35Bs had been delivered with 10 more in production.

The UK elected to operate the F-35B within a joint force based at Marham, manned on a 50/50 basis by RN and RAF pilots and technicians. By 2023 the joint force included 17 Squadron which is permanently based in the USA as part of the international development effort and 207 Squadron which is the UK training unit at Marham. The first front-line unit was 617 Squadron which spent much of 2021 embarked in *Queen Elizabeth* for the RN carrier strike group deployment to the Pacific together with a USMC squadron , VMFA-211. There have also been token embarkations in *Prince of Wales*. A second operational unit, 809 NAS, was announced in 2013 but was not commissioned until December 2023 because manpower issues caused delays. Progress since the 2021 carrier deployment has been painfully slow with very few embarked periods; too few to keep the ship and squadrons up to the operational standard they are capable of. There can be little doubt that the failures of earlier politically-derived joint forces are being repeated and that the STOVL F-35B was the wrong choice for the RN; too complicated, too expensive both to buy and fly and operated by a joint force that appears not to have carrier operations as its first priority. The F/A-18E/F Super Hornet operated in close co-operation with the USN would have been a better and more affordable choice. A significant number of RN pilots have flown USN Super Hornets as part of an inter-Navy agreement since 2010 and continue to do so in 2023 to widen RN knowledge of carrier operations.

F-35B landing on *Queen Elizabeth* with 'barn door' open and jet-pipe nozzle rotated. (Crown Copyright)

MANN, EGERTON & Co

Type B

Short 184s were built under licence as Type As before the firm modified the design into its own Type B. It incorporated Type 184 components but had shorter-span lower wings with no ailerons. Wingspan was 63ft 6¼in and they were powered by a single 225hp Sunbeam engine. Only ten were built and delivered in 1916 and they operated on patrol duties from Calshot alongside Short 184s.

Type H

The 1917 Type H was a single-seat fighter intended for shipboard use powered by a 200hp Hispano-Suiza engine driving a two-bladed wooden propeller to give a maximum level speed of 99 knots; it was Mann, Egerton's first original design. Five prototypes were ordered but only two were built. The first had external float attachments along the underside of the fuselage to keep it afloat after ditching and an undercarriage that could be jettisoned to prevent it nosing over on hitting the water. The second differed in having inflatable air bags of balloon fabric. Both were tested at Isle of Grain but proved unimpressive and there were no production orders. Wingspan of the second prototype was 30ft 9in and MTOW 2,326lb. Armament included a single Vickers 0.303in machine gun on top of the fuselage synchronised to fire through the propeller arc and a single 0.303in Lewis machine gun mounted above the upper wing centre-section.

MARTIN

Maryland

Light bombers which first flew in 1939, Marylands were purchased from the USA for the RAF in 1940. Five were transferred to the RN from the RAF in 1940 and two others in 1943. Three of the five were returned to the RAF after a few weeks but two were used by 771 NAS at Hatston until July 1942 and then Twatt for fleet requirements tasks with Home Fleet ships based in Scapa Flow. One of these made history on 22 May 1941 when it flew from Hatston to Bergen to confirm that the German battleship *Bismarck* had sailed out into the Atlantic. The aircraft's gallant crew flew through weather described by the RAF as awful and too bad for flight. RAF Marylands of 431 Flight based in Malta were the aircraft used to photograph the Italian fleet in Taranto before the historic Swordfish strike from *Illustrious* in November 1940.

The Maryland Mark I had a wingspan of 61ft 4in and MTOW of 16,809lb. It was powered by two Pratt & Whitney Twin Wasp radial

Baltimore of 728 NAS at Hal Far. (Philip Jarrett)

Maryland of 771 NAS at Hatston in 1941.

engines which gave a maximum level speed of 264 knots. 771 NAS was the only RN squadron to operate the type which was used mainly for target-towing.

Baltimore

The Martin 187 Baltimore was a twin-engine bomber used extensively by the RAF, RAAF and RCAF during the Second World War. It replaced the Maryland in production and early examples were ordered off the drawing board by the French Government. After the French collapse the orders were transferred to the UK before the type's first flight in 1941. Early examples were purchased but the majority were provided under Lend-Lease arrangements. Wingspan was 61ft 4in, MTOW 27,850lb and two 1,600hp Wright Cyclone R-2600-29 radial engines gave a maximum level speed of 280 knots. From 1944 onwards seven were transferred to the RN from the RAF in the Mediterranean; the last in 1946. Armament was removed and seats fitted for operation by the RN Communications Flight, Malta, and 728 NAS on fleet requirements duties from Hal Far and Takali. By 1947 all were either returned to the RAF, written off after accidents or deleted.

McDONNELL

Phantom II

One of the most successful fighters of all time, the Phantom II evolved after McDonnell had lost out to Chance Vought's F-8U Crusader in a USN competition for a supersonic day fighter but boldly decided to design a private venture 'all can do' fighter even though there was no stated requirement for such an aircraft. Named Phantom II in 1954 (the original Phantom was McDonnell's first USN fighter) it was initially envisaged as a single-seat, twin-engined, radar-equipped strike fighter with four 20mm cannon capable of carrying every type of weapon in the USN inventory and powered by licence-built Armstrong

Phantom FG 1 with undercarriage down and nose oleo in the fully extended position for catapult launch.

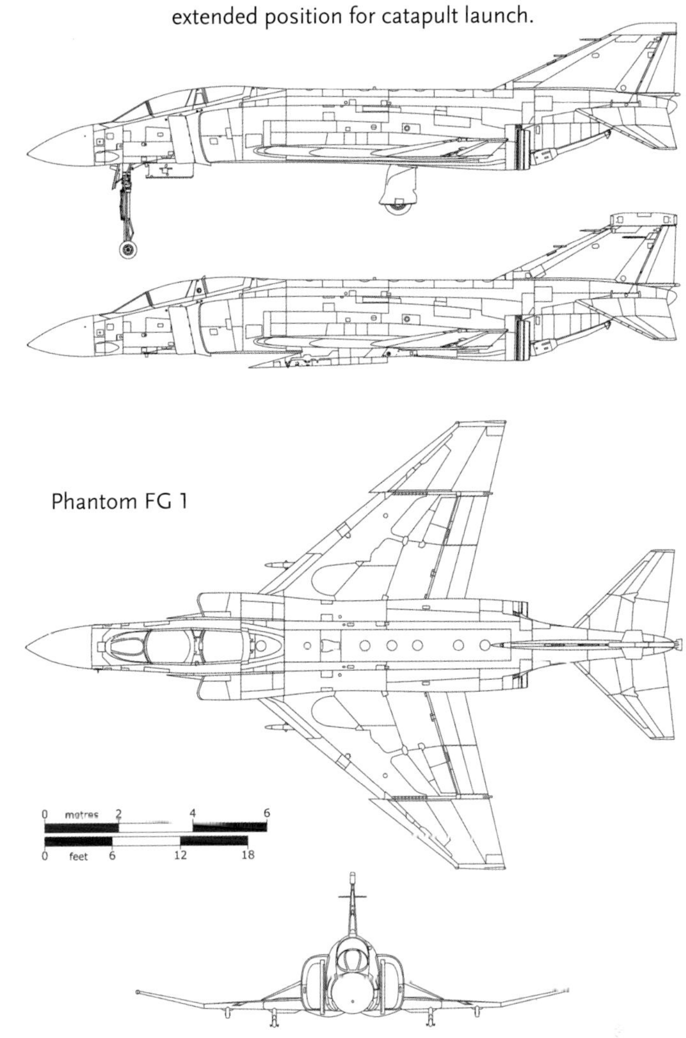

Siddeley Sapphires. The USN was impressed and ordered two technology demonstrators in November 1954 but there was still no official requirement. In 1955 senior naval officers visited the firm to give the project sharper focus in a meeting that reputedly lasted for under an hour. The Phantom II design emerged as two-seat fleet fighter with a low mounted wing of 45 degrees sweep at quarter-chord and distinctive 12-degree dihedral on the outer, folding, wing panels, 'dog-tooth' wing leading edges, a one-piece slab tailplane with 23 degrees anhedral and variable-geometry air intakes. Four Sparrow radar-guided AAM were to be carried semi-recessed under the fuselage so that that they would not prevent pylon-mounted strike weapons, Sidewinders and drop tanks being carried on the centreline and under the wings. It was to be capable of 2 hours on CAP 250nm from a carrier armed with both radar and IR-guided AAM. A second crew member, radar-intercept officer or RIO, controlled the radar and took some of the high operational work load off the pilot. The USN designated it F-4H and it first flew in May 1958. Twenty-three development aircraft were ordered in December 1958 and during test flights the Phantom was found to have such exceptional performance that the USN decided to attempt world records with it. Those achieved included absolute height,

Phantom FG 1 of 892 NAS taxi-ing in at Yeovilton after disembarking from a detachment in the USS *Saratoga* in 1969. (Nigel Edwards)

times to various heights, 310-mile (500km) and 62-mile (100km) closed-circuit speeds, low altitude and absolute air speed records, all gained by production aircraft except for the absolute speed record for which a water-injection system was installed to cool the incoming air ahead of the compressors. The first operational USN Phantoms were delivered to VF-101 NAS, 'Grim Reapers' in 1960 only 2 years after the development batch aircraft were ordered.

By 1961 the USAF had carried out competitive evaluations of the F-4H against aircraft in its own inventory and found it to be a better interceptor and capable of carrying a larger weapon load further than any tactical aircraft in the USAF, with clear potential as a reconnaissance aircraft. It also demonstrated superior flying hours per maintenance hours than any of the aircraft it was evaluated against and the USAF immediately ordered it for its Tactical Air Command. At first it was given the USAF designation F-110A but when standardised Department of Defence designations were introduced in 1962, some say because of confusion among politicians about whether F-110A and F-4H were the same aircraft or not, the designation F-4 was adopted by all three forces that operated the Phantom. The early Navy and Marine Corps versions were redesignated as F-4A and F-4B; the first USAF version F-4C, a minimal change version of the 'B'.

The electrifying performance of the Phantom immediately attracted Admiralty attention as a potential Sea Vixen replacement. It lobbied hard to procure it as the tortuous development of the politically-inspired P.1154 ground on through 1963 and agreement was reached to send pilots and observers to USN squadrons to gain Phantom familiarity. In 1964 the UK Government finally accepted the

Phantom FG 1 of 767 NAS from Yeovilton.

A development Phantom carrying out deck-landing trials on *Eagle*.

Admiralty's case, cancelled the P.1154RN and an agreement was negotiated with McDonnell to procure 140 Phantoms with the first batch of 60 estimated to cost £45 million. By then the USN had funded the development of an improved variant designated F-4J and this would have been the logical choice for the RN, purchased 'off the shelf' with minimal development cost. This simple logic proved too difficult for British politicians, however, and the Government made it part of the agreement that a substantial percentage of the RN Phantom airframe should be manufactured by British firms. Rolls-Royce had proposed a Spey-powered Phantom for the US armed forces in 1962 but McDonnell had dismissed the idea as being too expensive and complicated to implement for the sake of the theoretical benefits that might accrue. Now, however, Rolls-Royce managed to convince the MoA that Speys would deliver increased power to make operation from the smaller decks of British carriers safer. Re-heated Speys of a new design that had never been tested or flown were, therefore, specified for the British Phantom which was designated F-4K by the US authorities. The USN-sponsored Westinghouse AN/AWG-10 pulse-doppler radar designed for the F-4J was built under a licence agreement in the UK by Ferranti as the AN/AWG-11 and most of the cockpit instruments and systems were made in Britain. The outer wings were manufactured by Short Bros and the rear fuselage and tailplane were manufactured by BAC. About half the aircraft content and structure were made in the UK but had to be shipped to St Louis for assembly, adding still further to the higher unit price tag of the 'K' when compared to the 'J'. The Spey was heavier and wider but shorter than the J-79 engine in the F-4J and its installation meant that the after fuselage had to be redesigned. The revised shape increased airframe drag and actually led to the 'K' having a lower performance than the 'J'. Furthermore, the two Speys needed intakes that were 20 per cent bigger than those in J-79 engined aircraft to cope with the greater mass airflow they required and this contributed yet more to the airframe drag. Auxiliary air inlet doors had to be introduced into the re-designed rear fuselage. Although the standard Spey 101 turbofan in the Buccaneer S 2 had proved a great success, Rolls-Royce found a reliable, re-heated derivative difficult to achieve and the solution caused delays and further cost increases. Engaging re-heat rapidly for a late overshoot from a carrier approach proved to be a particularly difficult problem to resolve and a special variant, the Spey 203 with fast light-up augmentation had to be developed before the F-4K could be cleared for carrier operation. Even

Phantom being catapulted from *Ark Royal*.

after the 'K', designated the Phantom FG 1 in RN service, was cleared for operation at sea, engine lives as low as 20 hours were common at first and there were frequent failures. One other significant design change was the need to reduce the Phantom's length sufficiently for it to fit onto the lifts of British carriers which were only 54ft long. This was achieved by folding the nose aft through 180 degrees to starboard.

Apart from its engines, the RN Phantom had other unique features. The Spey nozzles were nearer the fuselage skin and hotter than those of the J-79 so titanium had to be used extensively on the after fuselage to prevent it from melting. The F-4J had a nose oleo that could be extended by 20in to give optimal attitude for catapult launch. To improve launch performance still further off shorter British steam catapults the Phantom FG 1 doubled that extension to 40in which reduced the catapult end-speed required by 10 knots. Like the Buccaneer the British Phantom had 'blown' flaps and drooped ailerons but it also had a tailplane with an inverted slat on the leading edge to optimise airflow over it and hence its performance. All of these modifications increased airframe weight and British Phantoms had to have stronger undercarriages than all other Phantom variants together with stronger tail hooks than the USN versions. The cost of Phantom FG 1 procurement had to include the cost of all these changes and their development. By 1968 the unit cost was more than double that of the F-4J. Despite the recommendation that Spey power would allow Phantoms to operate from small British carriers, subsequent calculation revealed they could never, realistically, have operated from *Hermes*. To 'rub salt' into this self-inflicted wound USN F-4Js could, and aften did, land on *Ark Royal* and *Eagle* during cross-deck operations. Operation from CVA-01 would have presented no problems had she been built and, with some modification to her arrester gear, *Victorious* could have operated them. For all the extra cost and delay, the RN ended up with a Sea Vixen replacement that was double the cost it should have been and which was slower with a worse performance at altitude than the F-4J it had chosen. The one thing the Spey did offer was slighter greater endurance. Despite the need for extensive re-development work, the first of two YF-4K prototypes flew in June 1966.

Phantom FG 1 data

Length:	57ft 7in (53ft folded)
Wingspan:	38ft 5in (26ft folded)
Height:	16ft 1in
MTOW:	56,000lb
Engine:	Two Rolls-Royce Spey 203 turbofans; each 12,250lb thrust dry, 20,515lb with re-heat
Fuel:	Avcat. 1,660 gallons internal plus one optional 500-gallon centreline drop tank and two optional 310-gallon drop tanks on outer wing hardpoints
Performance:	Maximum level speed Mach 2.1 Service ceiling 70,000ft. 1 minute to 30,000ft
Endurance:	Over 2 hours with drop tanks.
Armament:	Four fuselage-mounted AIM-7 Sparrow III radar-guided AAM; four AIM-9 Sidewinder infrared-homing AAM on underwing pylons; four underwing and one centreline hardpoints capable of taking up to 16,000lb of weapons or drop tanks including WE-177 nuclear bombs, conventional 500lb, 750lb or 1,000lb bombs, Bullpup ASM or 2in rocket pods. Lepus flares

892 NAS Phantom over a USN carrier.

The RN was the first Phantom export customer and planned to replace the Sea Vixen on a one for one basis but after the cancellation of CVA-01 in February 1966 and the subsequent decision to run down the carrier force the order was reduced. Some Phantom FG 1s were transferred to the RAF when *Eagle* was taken out of service prematurely and the eventual total received by the RN included two prototypes, two pre-production aircraft used for trials and thirty-four production Phantoms.

After completing service acceptance trials with the A&AEE Phantoms served with 700P NAS the IFTU, 767 NAS the training squadron and 892 NAS which embarked in the reconstructed *Ark Royal* until it was withdrawn from service in 1978. Once the engine shortcomings were overcome it was arguably the most capable fighter operated by the RN in its first century of carrier operations. 700P NAS operated at Yeovilton between April 1968 and March 1969. 767 NAS, also based at Yeovilton, was commissioned in January 1969 and operated until August 1972 when it was de-commissioned. 892 NAS commissioned in March 1969 and a detachment embarked in the USS *Saratoga* in October to gain experience before *Ark Royal* completed her refit. The squadron's shore base was Yeovilton until 1972 and then it had to move to Leuchars to be co-located with RAF Phantoms. Between 1969 and 1978 892, NAS operated extensively from *Ark Royal* in the Atlantic and Mediterranean. They saw no action but played a considerable role in Cold War NATO plans and exercises. Keith Harris, responsible for standardisation checks on Phantom pilots for several years, had previously flown Skyraiders and found the American layout of its cockpit very familiar with well laid-out controls. It was straightforward to control but very easy to go supersonic unintentionally. It was very stable in the approach condition with a comfortable undercarriage 'feel' on landing.

Of interest, the RAF also procured a Phantom variant, the F-4M, British designation Phantom FGR 2. Notwithstanding RAF insistence throughout 1963 that a simple NBMR-3 type aircraft was what it wanted, that no longer seemed such a good idea when it saw that the RN was procuring the Phantom. All interest in the P.1154 RAF evaporated and the RAF ordered the Phantom FGR 2. Given the political climate at the time with a government that had forgotten about sea power, the RAF was allowed to spend even more money to modify its Phantoms so that they could not be operated from a carrier. The first RAF Phantom pilots and RIOs were trained by 767 NAS at Yeovilton.

MILES

Requisitioned aircraft

Three Miles monoplanes were requisitioned in 1940. The M.3B Falcon was a two-seater with a wingspan of 35ft, MTOW of 2,650lb powered by a single 200hp de Havilland Gipsy Six. The M.11B Whitney Straight was another two-seater with a wingspan of 35ft, MTOW of 1,896lb powered by a single 130hp de Havilland Gipsy Major. The M-18 was a proposed improvement of the Miles M.14A Magister two-seat monoplane training aircraft which it resembled with a wingspan of 31ft, MTOW 1,903lb and powered by a single 130hp de Havilland Gipsy Major.

Magister

The M.14 Magister was a tandem two-seat monoplane training aircraft produced for the RAF built largely of wood. It proved to be an ideal lead-in training aircraft for pilots destined to fly fighters and had evolved from the Miles Hawk but featured enlarged cockpits that allowed pilots to have parachutes and the provision of full blind-flying instruments. Both cockpits were open but a hood could be deployed over the front, student's, cockpit when he was practising instrument flying. Wingspan was 23ft, MTOW 1,900lb and the 130hp de Havilland Gipsy Major gave a maximum level speed of 125 knots. Magisters were used widely by the elementary flying schools run by the RAF and many naval pilots, including Hugh Popham who wrote *Sea Flight* after the war, had their first experience of flight in them. Seventeen Magisters were transferred to the RN from the RAF for use as standardisation/check aircraft and for general refresher flying at Eastleigh, Worthy Down, Gosport, Lee-on-Solent, Fearn, Dekheila and Arbroath. Between 1939 and 1942 a small number were used by 780 and 778 NAS on light communications duties.

Master

The M.9A Master Mark 1 was a low-wing monoplane advanced trainer powered by a 715hp Rolls-Royce Kestrel 30 liquid-cooled engine that gave a maximum level speed of 200 knots. It was an ideal lead-in trainer for fighter pilots. The first production contract was the largest yet placed by the RAF for a training aircraft and when it first flew in March 1939 it was the fastest training aircraft in the world. Wingspan was 39ft initially, reduced to 35ft 9in in 1942 when rounded wing-tips were removed. MTOW was 5,573lb. The tandem cockpits were enclosed, access being through sliding hoods. The Master's construction included new techniques; a track was installed in Miles' factory on which the whole production line moved forward as a unit every four hours. Assembly was divided into stages and workers carried out the same assembly task on each block as it was presented to them; a process believed to have been the first of its kind in the UK for aircraft manufacture.

Masters were built in three Marks; Mark I had Kestrel engines, Mark IIs had 870hp Bristol Mercury engines and Master IIIs had 825hp Pratt & Whitney Wasp Junior engines. None were built under Admiralty contract but 77 Mark Is and 68 Mark IIs were transferred to the RN from the RAF after their completion.

Masters equipped or partially equipped 700, 715, 718, 719, 736,

Miles Magister.

Master Mark II of 794 NAS at Dale. (Philip Jarrett)

740, 748, 759, 760, 761, 762, 766, 772, 780, 785, 794 and 798 NAS for a variety of uses ranging from standardisation and instrument flying checks for front line pilots and conversion, pool or refresher flying. They were also used to collect pilots who had ferried aircraft to and from RN air yards and other light communications tasks.

Between 1940 and 1946 they operated from Donibristle, Worthy Down, Yeovilton, St Merryn, Eglinton, Machrihanish, Eastleigh, Henstridge, Lee-on-Solent, Charlton Horethorne, Crail and Stretton.

The second M.20 prototype which was evaluated by the Admiralty against Specification N.1/41 but rejected. (Philip Jarrett)

M.20

MAP fears that fighters might be lost faster than they could be replaced in the summer of 1940 led Miles to propose a simple but effective fighter that could be produced quickly. The resulting M.20 design was endorsed by the MAP, a specification drawn up to cover it, and a prototype flown only 9 weeks after Miles was authorised to proceed. It was a low-wing, single-seat fighter of wooden construction with everything about it intended to reduce production delays. Hydraulics were eliminated; it had a fixed, spatted undercarriage and Master parts wherever possible. Since wheel wells for a retractable undercarriage were not required, there was space for twelve 0.303in Browning machine guns with 410 rpg and with an internal fuel capacity of 154 gallons, the M.20 had greater firepower and twice the endurance of the

Martinet of 771 NAS based at Twatt in the Orkney Islands streaming a towed target.

Hurricane with an endurance of about 5 hours. Wingspan was 34ft 7in, MTOW 7,758lb and the single 1,300hp Rolls-Royce Merlin XX gave a maximum level speed of 308 knots, slightly faster than a Hurricane but slower than a Spitfire Mark II. The bubble cockpit canopy gave the pilot excellent visibility.

An emergency fighter proved to be unnecessary and there were no RAF orders for the M.20 but the Admiralty had issued Specification N.1/41 for a new naval fighter and the M.20 was an obvious contender for it. A second prototype was built for RN evaluation and 'Winkle' Brown flew it in mock combat against a Hurricane. He found that whilst faster, the M.20 was significantly less manoeuvrable and when he attempted to follow the Hurricane in a hard turn it departed controlled flight suddenly without warning. He also considered it less than ideal for deck landing. At low speed the controls were sluggish and on closing the throttle at the 'cut' the nose dropped sharply, requiring firm backward stick movement to prevent the mainwheels hitting the deck first and bouncing. His report informed the Admiralty that although the M.20 was surprisingly fast, it could not match the Martlet, Hurricane or Spitfire for manoeuvrability and it was not, therefore, considered suitable for further development or production.

Martinet

Until 1941 target-towing had been performed by obsolescent aircraft types as they became available but after 1939 there was a big increase in the number required. Miles was asked by the MAP if, as a matter of urgency, it could produce a target-tug based on the Master. The deletion of dual controls and installation of heavy target-towing equipment meant that the engine had to be moved forward to compensate and modifications had to be made to its cooling arrangements because it would be operating at lower speed and higher power when dragging a target. Miles accepted the challenge and designed the M.25 Martinet; Specification TT.12/41 was drawn up around it. Provision was made for the installation of either a wind-driven or motorised winch, six flag and sleeve replacement drogue targets and a cable drum. It first flew in April 1942 and replaced the Master on the production line.

Martinet TT 1 data

Length:	30ft 11in
Wingspan:	39ft
Height:	11ft 7in
MTOW:	6,750lb
Engine:	One 870hp Bristol Mercury XX or 30
Fuel:	Avgas. 130 gallons internal
Performance:	Maximum level speed 210 knots
	Service ceiling 20,000ft. 8 minutes to 10,000ft
Endurance:	5 hours
Armament:	None

No Martinets were built to Admiralty contract but 533 were transferred to the RN from RAF production blocks as they were completed, about one third of the total built.

Between 1943 and 1951 Martinets equipped or partially equipped 722, 723, 725, 726, 728, 728B, 733, 736, 740, 757, 766, 770, 771, 772, 773, 775, 776, 779, 789, 792, 793, 794 and 797 NAS. They were used in the target towing role for fleet requirements work including live anti-aircraft firings from ships and shore training establishments and for air-to-air firings by fighters. The latter including advanced training work, refresher flying and conversion courses at the naval fighter school, night fighter school, and the school of naval air warfare.

Martinets operated from Tambaram, Bankstown, Jervis Bay, Nowra, Schofields, Stamford Hill, Wingfield, Gibraltar, Luqa, Hal Far, China Bay, Puttalam, Katukurunda, Eglinton, Ballyhalbert, St Merryn, Machrihanish, Ayr, Lossiemouth, Rattray, Drem, Dunino, Crail, Twatt, Lee-on-Solent, Burscough, Dekheila, Woodvale, Piarco, Dale and Henstridge. Detachments operated for short periods at numerous other sites. The last units, 771 and 773 NAS continued to operate their Martinets from Lee-on-Solent until 1951.

A derivative of the basic Martinet was developed during 1943 as the M.50 Queen Martinet, a radio-controlled drone to meet Specification Q.10/43. Intended to provide a realistic high-speed target for anti-aircraft fire, it was not removed from the secret list until 1946. The Queen Martinet was only built in limited numbers but three were transferred to the RN in late 1945. Two were operated by 728 NAS at Hal Far in support of Mediterranean Fleet firings and one was operated by 773 NAS at Brawdy.

Monitor

The M.33 Monitor was designed to meet Specification Q.9/42 for a twin-engined aircraft capable of towing a target at more than 260 knots for over 3 hours. It was a shoulder-wing design with a crew of two and was an unusual Miles product in that the fuselage was made from metal although the wings were of wood. Powered by two American 1,700hp Wright Cyclones it reflected contemporary concern over potential shortages of British engines for non-combat aircraft. The first of two prototypes, a T I and a T II, flew in April 1944; by then the RN requirement for a high-speed target tug was recognised as more urgent than that of the RAF and the design had RN-specific features. Wingspan was 56ft 3in, MTOW was 21,075lb and maximum level speed was 290 knots. An initial order for 600 was split between the RAF T I and the RN T II but with the end of the war in Europe, the order was cut to 200 T IIs for RN use. A few months later it was cut to fifty but after twenty had been built it was cancelled altogether. Ten of these were evaluated at the A&AEE but none were issued to the RN. They were all scrapped.

M.39B

A concept evaluation, tandem-wing design powered by two 140hp de Havilland Gipsy Major IC engines on the after wings which allowed the cockpit to be placed right forward giving the pilot an excellent view for deck landing. The front wing had a span of 25ft and the rear 37ft 6in; MTOW was 22,800lb and it had a nose-wheel undercarriage. Maximum level speed was only 140 knots and the single prototype was built without MAP approval in 1944. 'Winkle' Brown flew it but told me that he could never imagine it being developed seriously and there was little Admiralty interest in it.

MORANE-SAULNIER

Type G

Requisitioned from Lord Carbery for the RNAS in 1914, the Type G was a two-seat sports monoplane with which he had won a prize at the San Sebastian seaplane meeting in 1913. Wingspan was 30ft, MTOW

The Type L, 3253, in which Flight Sub Lieutenant R A J Warneford VC RNAS destroyed Zeppelin LZ 37 on 8 June 1915. (Philip Jarrett)

815lb and it was powered by a single 80hp Le Rhone, tractor, rotary engine. It was operated at Eastchurch by 2 Squadron and the naval flying school and suffered several minor crashes before being wrecked and written off in 1915.

Type L

A monoplane with a shoulder-mounted parasol wing raised well over the fuselage, twenty-five were built in France and delivered directly to the RNAS Depot at St Pol from April 1915.

Type L data

Length:	20ft 9in
Wingspan:	34ft
Height:	11ft 5in
MTOW:	1,472lb
Engine:	One 80hp Le Rhone rotary
Fuel:	Avgas. 25 gallons
Performance:	Maximum level speed 67 knots
	Service ceiling nominally 10,000ft. 3 minutes to 1,000ft
Endurance:	3 hours
Armament:	No standard armament. Warneford's aircraft carried six 20lb bombs. The pilot could carry a rifle or pistol

The last of the twenty-five RNAS machines was delivered in June 1915. Most were used by 1 Squadron, later 1 Wing at St Pol but six were shipped to the Aegean for use by 3 Wing and later 2 Wing at Imbros. Three were used briefly by 4 Squadron at Dover and one by 2 Wing at Eastchurch. The majority were deleted by mid-1916.

The most famous Type L pilot was Flight Sub Lieutenant R A J Warneford RNAS of 1 Squadron who was awarded the VC in June 1915 for destroying Zeppelin LZ 37 in the air. He was flying 3253 on a night attack against the German Army airship base at Berchem St Agathe in Belgium but had lost contact with the three other aircraft that had taken off with him. At 0100 on 7 June 1915 he saw the airship emerge from fog into moonlight near Ostend. Turning towards it, he climbed and nearly got into an attacking position at 0150 over Bruges but the airship's defensive fire forced him to evade. It chased him briefly but Warneford managed to gain height advantage at 11,000ft, switched off his engine ignition to avoid over-speeding as he dived along its length, about 150ft above it, and dropped his six 20lb bombs on the envelope. A terrific explosion blew the envelope apart and tossed 3253 upwards and onto its back. Warneford regained control in a steep dive and saw LZ 37 already burning on the ground. The blast had broken a petrol feed pipe so he could not re-start the engine. Visibility was good in the moonlight, however, and he landed in a field behind the German lines where he spent 35 minutes repairing the pipe after which he swung the propeller to start the engine. This took several attempts and, with no brakes, he had to scramble to get into the cockpit as the engine started. After take-off he identified Cap Griz-Nez, landed behind the Allied lines to refuel and then returned to St Pol. A day later he was awarded the VC. Tragically, he was killed in a flying accident 10 days later. 3253 was displayed at Hendon until 1918 but there is no record of its subsequent fate.

Type BB

A single two-seat tractor biplane, company designation MS.7, was purchased for evaluation in October 1915. Wingspan was 28ft 5in, MTOW 1,650lb and it was powered by a single 110hp Le Rhone rotary engine which gave a maximum level speed of 80 knots. It was armed with a single 0.303in Lewis gun for the observer and light bombs and allocated to 3 Squadron, 1 Wing at Eastchurch in 1915 and A Squadron of 5 Wing at Coudekerque in 1916 before deletion in 1916. No more were ordered.

NIEUPORT

IV.G Tractor Monoplane

A single example was purchased by the Admiralty in 1912 but transferred to the CFS at Upavon and never used by the RNAS. Wingspan was 38ft, MTOW 1,322lb and it was powered by a single 50hp Gnome rotary engine which gave a maximum level speed of 56 knots.

Tractor Monoplane Seaplane

Twelve were ordered in 1915 with 80hp Le Rhone engines but delivered with 100hp Gnomes, all built in France and delivered in 1915. Wingspan was 40ft, and MTOW 1,750lb. The first four were used for seaplane training at Calshot but three were soon wrecked. Others went to Windermere for use training seaplane pilots but were not considered a success and the survivors were deleted in 1916.

Tractor Biplane Scout

The first in a series of two-seater, tractor, biplane scouts was delivered to Eastleigh for assembly in 1915. It was powered by a 100hp Gnome rotary engine and after evaluation by 4 Wing it was deleted in November.

Two-Seater Scouts

These were procured for the RNAS in two basic variants, the Type 10 and the Type 12. Both were tractor biplanes of fabric-covered wooden construction delivered directly from the French factory to RN air depots for assembly from February 1915 as fighting, bombing and reconnaissance aircraft. Some bombers were operated as single-seaters and it was in one of these that Squadron Commander R Bell-Davies RNAS of 3 Wing earned the RNAS' second VC during an attack on Ferrijik Railway Junction in Bulgaria, through which German supplies travelled by rail to Turkey. He saw one of the other aircraft, flown by Flight Sub Lieutenant G F Smylie RNAS, brought down on a dry watercourse near the Maritza River by anti-aircraft fire and decided to land nearby and rescue him. After landing he taxied toward Smylie and saw Bulgarian troops approaching. Bell-Davies' aircraft was a Type 10 and he was flying it from what had been the rear cockpit; the space where the front cockpit had been was covered over. Smylie ran up to the aircraft and had to climb over Bell-Davies, slide under the cowl and crouch on all fours between the rudder bar and the engine bearers with his head bumping on the oil tank. Once in, he looked most uncomfortable but they took off and flew to safety. The citation for

Nieuport two-seater. (Philip Jarrett)

Bell-Davies' VC described his action as 'a feat of airmanship that can seldom have been equalled for skill and gallantry'.

Nieuport Type 12 data

Length:	23ft 11¼in
Wingspan:	29ft 7⅛in
Height:	8ft 9in
MTOW:	2,026lb
Engine:	One 110hp or 130hp Clerget rotary
Fuel:	Avgas. 33 gallons
Performance:	Maximum level speed 69 knots Service ceiling 13,000ft. 10 minutes to 5,000ft
Endurance:	3 hours
Armament:	Single 0.303in Lewis machine gun free-mounted in rear cockpit. Single fixed 0.303in Lewis front gun on top wing when flown as a single-seater. Nominally up to six 20lb bombs

The Admiralty procured a total of 181 two-seat Scouts comprising 38 Type 10s and 113 Type 12s, all built in France and 30 manufactured under licence by Beardmore.

Nieuport two-seaters operated with 1, 2, 3 and 4 Wings RNAS at Dunkirk and Imbros and with 7 (Naval) and 10 (Naval) squadrons at Petite Synthe.

They were used extensively in operations on the Western Front from 1915. None were ever embarked in ships. A typical engagement occurred on 14 December 1915 when a Nieuport two-seater from Dunkirk shot down a German seaplane as it attempted to bomb an Allied merchant ship stranded on a sandbank.

Single-Seater Scouts

The Admiralty procured three single-seat Nieuport Scout variants, Types 11, 17bis and 17B. They were sesquiplanes; biplanes in which the upper wing had greater chord than the lower. They entered service in 1915 with 3 Wing in the Dardanelles and 'A' Squadron RNAS received Type 17bis at Furnes in June 1916, the first RNAS unit completely equipped with a single aircraft type. Until replaced in 1917 Nieuports fought with distinction, defending the vast base complex at Dunkirk, escorting both RNAS and RFC bombing missions and destroying enemy seaplanes when they tried to interfere with Allied shipping. They also supported the offensive on the Somme using Le Prieur rockets to destroy enemy spotter balloons over the German 'Tirpitz' heavy gun battery.

Type 17bis data

Length:	19ft 6in
Wingspan:	27ft 3in
Height:	7ft
MTOW:	1,233lb
Engine:	One 110hp Le Rhone rotary
Fuel:	Avgas. 20 gallons
Performance:	Maximum level speed 94 knots Service ceiling 17,400ft. 4 minutes to 5,000ft
Endurance:	2 hours
Armament:	Single fixed 0.303in Lewis front gun on top wing firing clear of the propeller arc at first. Later examples had a synchronised Vickers 0.303in front gun over the engine cowling and provision for four Le Prieur rockets on each of the vee-interplane struts

The RNAS received 112 Nieuport single-seat scouts; of these 21 were Type 11s, 81 were Type 17bis and 10 were Type 17Bs. Fifty of the Type 17bis were built in the UK by Nieuport and General Aircraft which had been set up to build Nieuports under licence. In the event, it only built this batch and subsequently built Sopwith Camels under licence to Admiralty contracts.

Single-seat Nieuport of 2 Wing RNAS.

Nieuport single-seat scouts operated with 1, 2, 3, 6, 8, 9, 10 and 11 (Naval) Squadrons on the Western Front and with 3 Wing in the Dardanelles. They were also used for training at Eastchurch, Hendon and Chingford.

Triplane

Two examples of the Nieuport Triplane were evaluated by the RNAS in 1917; both powered by a single Clerget 9B rotary engine, one of 110hp and the other 130hp. They were evaluated by 11 (Naval) Squadron but were clearly not well thought of as no orders followed.

Nightjar

One of the first fighters intended for aircraft carrier operation, the Nightjar was created by Henry Folland who had produced a series of original designs identified by Nieuport as Mars I, II, III and IV after 1918, some of which were ordered for the RAF and named Nighthawk. By the time the final derivative emerged, the Mars X Nightjar, Nieuport and General had ceased to exist and Folland moved to Gloster taking his designs with him. The Nightjar was a single-seat, deck-landing fighter powered by a Bentley rotary engine and they were assembled by Gloster using Nighthawk components modified to meet the new design. The undercarriage was re-designed with a wider track and long-stroke shock absorption to improve its deck-landing characteristics with hooked jaws on the axle to engage with the fore and aft retaining wires.

Nightjar data

Length:	18ft 4in
Wingspan:	28ft
Height:	9ft
MTOW:	2,165lb
Engine:	One 230hp Bentley BR 2 rotary driving a 2-blade wooden propeller
Fuel:	Avgas. 40 gallons
Performance:	Maximum level speed 105 knots Service ceiling 19,000ft. 23 minutes to 15,000ft
Endurance:	2 hours
Armament:	Two belt-fed Vickers 0.303in front guns synchronised to fire through the propeller arc

Gloster assembled twenty-two Nightjars and delivered components for a further twelve as attrition reserves.

The type had a brief service career, replacing Sopwith 2F.1 Camels in 203 Squadron at Leuchars in July 1922. Six of the unit's Nightjars were deployed to the Middle East in September 1922 embarked in *Argus* during the Chanak Crisis in the Dardanelles. Other Nightjars were used at Leuchars by an un-numbered unit to train pilots in deck-landing techniques but the type developed an evil reputation after at

A Nightjar which served with 401 Flight embarked in *Argus* during 1923.

least five fatal accidents that involved aircraft stalling and spinning during turns on final approach to the airfield. Nightjars remained with 203 Squadron until it was disbanded in April 1923. Six Nightjars and, apparently, a single Nighthawk served with 401 Flight until they were replaced by Flycatchers in 1924. *Argus* was the only carrier to operate the type.

NORMAN THOMPSON

NT. 4 and 4A

Designated by the company as the NT.4, this was a biplane flying boat similar to the Curtiss H.4 Small America and the '4' in the company designation may have reflected that. The RNAS referred to both as Small Americas but the NT.4 differed in that it was larger, had a different hull form and two pusher, rather than tractor, engines. Later examples with more powerful engines were designated NT.4As. The engines were un-cowled to provide easier access for mechanics in flight with large rectangular radiators mounted on the forward interplane struts. The first NT.4 was fitted with a 2pdr Davis recoilless gun over the cockpit roof for trials which proved unsuccessful and it was later removed. The cockpit design was continually modified to provide greater transparency and the final batch had the top completely glazed over.

NT. 4A data

Length:	41ft 6in
Wingspan:	78ft 7in across the upper wing
Height:	14ft 10in
MTOW:	6,469lb
Engine:	Two 200hp Hispano-Suiza liquid-cooled
Fuel:	Avgas. 100 gallons
Performance:	Maximum level speed 84 knots Service ceiling 11,700ft. 15 minutes to 10,000ft
Endurance:	6 hours
Armament:	None standardised. Most carried a single free-mounted 0.303in Lewis machine gun with provision for light bombs under the wings

The RNAS received twenty-six NT.4/4As which operated from Calshot, Cattewater, Dundee, Felixstowe, Killingholme, Invergordon and Scapa Flow on coastal patrols and as a training aircraft. Production ended in mid-1918.

Norman Thompson NT.4A.

Norman Thompson NT.2B trainer.

NT.2B

The NT.2B two-seat flying boat trainer followed the NT.4 into production. The designation seems illogical but was probably chosen to align with Admiralty category N.2B for an aircraft of this type. Its boat-shaped hull had a single step and two thicknesses of planking with a layer of oiled calico between them were built over a framework of wooden formers and stringers. There was a neat enclosed cockpit with dual controls for the instructor pilot and his pupil. Early batches were powered by a single 160hp Beardmore pusher engine mounted between the wings driving a four-bladed wooden propeller. Later batches had a 200hp Sunbeam Arab and the last batch had Hispano-Suiza engines.

NT. 2B data

Length:	27ft 4½in
Wingspan:	48ft 43¾in across the upper wing
Height:	10ft 8in
MTOW:	3,169lb
Engine:	One 200hp Hispano-Suiza liquid-cooled in later batches
Fuel:	Avgas. 60 gallons
Performance:	Maximum level speed 75 knots
	Service ceiling 11,400ft. 35 minutes to 10,000ft
Endurance:	Approximately 4 hours
Armament:	None

Surviving records show that 106 NT.2Bs were built but demand exceeded Norman Thompson's manufacturing capacity and batches were built under licence by both Saunders and Supermarine. After 1918 some records were lost among mass cancellations and more aircraft may have been completed but not delivered.

NT.2Bs operated with training units at Calshot, Lee-on-Solent and Felixstowe but they were quickly withdrawn from service in 1918.

N.1B Tandem Fighter Flying Boat

In 1917 Norman Thompson began work on a two-seat flying boat to meet Admiralty category N.1B for a high-performance fighter. Wingspan was 34ft 3in, MTOW 2,673lb and the single 200hp Hispano-Suiza pusher engine driving a two-bladed wooden propeller gave a maximum level speed of 80 knots. It was evaluated at Isle of Grain in 1918 where its performance was found to be well short of that required for a fighter and no production order followed.

N.2C

Developed from the NT.4A, the N.2C retained the wings of the earlier design but the hull was designed by J C Porte. Two prototypes with a wingspan of 78ft 7in were begun in early 1918 powered by two 200hp Sunbeam Arab engines driving four-bladed wooden pusher propellers. They were completed but with other types available in quantity, there were no production orders.

NORTH AMERICAN

Harvard

A low-wing cantilever monoplane advanced training aircraft with two seats in tandem for the student and instructor designed in 1935 and adopted by both the USN as the SNJ and by the USAAC as the T-6, both named Texan. Development led to an aircraft with machine guns and hardpoints capable of giving student pilots both advanced flying, instrument and weapons-delivery instruction. It had a retractable undercarriage and a metal structure which was initially fabric covered

Harvard Mark III of 1833 NAS at Bramcote in 1949.

but later metal-clad. Variants of the type in British and Canadian service were given the name Harvard and they were used extensively in the British Commonwealth Air Training Scheme in Canada within which thousands of Fleet Air Arm pilots carried out their advanced training. Those trained by the USN flew SNJ-4s and -5s. Harvards were procured for the RAF by the British Purchasing Commission and these differed from US variants in having 24-volt electrical systems as well as other detail changes. Some were transferred later under Lend-Lease arrangements.

Harvard Mark III data

Length:	29ft 6in
Wingspan:	42ft 0¼in
Height:	11ft 8½in
MTOW:	5,617lb
Engine:	One 550hp Pratt & Whitney R-1340-AN-1 air-cooled radial
Fuel:	Avgas. 110 gallons
Performance:	Maximum level speed 180 knots Service ceiling 24,750ft. 3 minutes to 5,000ft
Endurance:	Over 4 hours
Armament:	Two 0.3in front guns, one in each wing and provision for a single 0.3in gun on a flexible mount in the rear cockpit. Light series carriers under wings for both light or practice bombs

No Harvards were procured directly for the RN but 235 were transferred from the RAF. These comprised 77 Mark IIs and 158 Mark IIIs. Some Harvards were fitted with deck-landing hooks for use with deck-landing training squadrons and the carrier trials unit. Between February 1943 and April 1955 the RN operated Harvards in a variety of roles including trials support, pilot refresher flying courses, instrument rating checks, air experience for junior officers, fleet requirements, DLCO training, standardisation checks for fighter squadrons and advanced flying training. RNVR units used them for conversion and refresher flying as well as instrument and standardisation checks.

During that period they partially equipped a number of shore-based squadrons, albeit some of them only briefly in 1945. These included 700, 701, 702, 715, 718, 719, 726, 727, 728, 729, 732, 733, 736, 738, 741, 748, 756, 757, 758, 759, 760, 761, 766, 767, 768, 771, 778, 780, 781, 782, 784, 789, 791, 794, 795, 797, 798 and 799 NAS. RNVR Air Branch squadrons that operated Harvards included 1830, 1831, 1832, 1833, 1834, 1840 and 1841 NAS.

Between 1945 and 1954 they were used by the station flights at Anthorn, Arbroath, Ballyhalbert, China Bay/Trincomalee, Culdrose, Eglinton, Lossiemouth and St Merryn.

A Shelduck pilotless target aircraft based at Hal Far in Malta about to be launched.

Chukar target aircraft on the deck of an RFA before being prepared for use.

NORTHROP

Shelduck

The MQM-36 Shelduck was a pilotless target aircraft designed in 1946 which first flew in 1947. Designated Shelduck D 1 in RN service, it was powered by a single 95hp McCulloch air-cooled engine. Wingspan was 13ft 3in and MTOW 360lb. It was launched from a zero-length launcher assisted by a solid-propellant rocket booster which accelerated it to 80 knots in 0.7 seconds. The launcher could be fitted in any type of vessel with a clear space 20ft by 15ft and flight up to an hour was radio-controlled by an operator in the ship using a AN/ARW-79 radio command guidance system with a programmable automatic height hold. Wingtip pods housed radar reflectors or flares and acted as buoyancy aids to keep the wreckage afloat when the drone was shot down into the sea. Later examples had a sophisticated near-miss recording device which registered TTBs. The RN procured its first examples in 1959. They were operated by a dedicated but un-numbered unit known as the Pilotless Target Aircraft Squadron based at Portland. Later separate flights were established in Singapore and Malta. All three embarked in suitable ships when necessary and in 1962 a specialist flight was formed at Devonport to support the Seacat SAM trials carried out by the destroyer *Decoy*. UK Shelduck procurement continued into the 1980s by when 824 had been delivered, the majority for the RN. The average Shelduck 'life' was 10 sorties and if it was not shot down, it was flown back close to the launching vessel and recovered by cutting the engine and releasing a parachute. After descending into the sea it was kept afloat by buoyancy aids until recovery by sea boat. Once recovered, the air vehicles were given a fresh-water wash and refurbished for further use.

Chukar

The Chukar was a recoverable, remote-controlled, subsonic aerial target capable of speeds up to Mach 0.86 and altitudes up to 40,000ft designed to meet a USN requirements and designated MQM-74A. The RN had a similar requirement and purchased the type as the Chukar D 1. (Chukar is an Asian species of Partridge and the name was only applied by Northrop to export versions.) Development began in 1960, it first flew in 1965 and entered USN service in 1968. It had a cigar-shaped fuselage, straight mid-mounted wings and a single underslung 121lb thrust Williams J400-WR-404 turbojet which gave a maximum level speed of 527 knots. MTOW was 549lb. It was flown off a zero-length launcher either mounted ashore or on a suitable vessel and, like the Shelduck, the RN operated it in a dedicated pilotless target aircraft unit. Like the Shelduck, those that were not shot down were recovered into the sea by parachute, fresh water washed and prepared for future use. Buoyancy chambers to facilitate this were built into the fuselage and wings. In the early 1970s the USN procured a faster version which was put into production as the MQM-74C with a 180lb thrust Williams WR24 7 turbojet. The RN designated its version as the Chukar D 2.

The RN procured at least ninety-eight Chukars, of which fifty-eight were D1s and forty D 2s. They were used from the 1980s into the early twenty-first century. Both variants could be fitted with telemetry to allow analysis of the performance of missile engagements if the drone was not destroyed. SAMs were usually launched against drones with inert warheads to minimise losses and the telemetry showed whether a kinetic warhead would have destroyed or damaged the target.

PARNALL

'Zepp Strafer' Night Flyer Scout

Intended to intercept Zeppelins attacking Britain at night, two prototypes were ordered by the Admiralty but only one was built. It was a single-seat biplane with a wingspan of 44ft intended to climb rapidly and engage the Zeppelin with a single 0.303in Lewis gun angled to fire upwards at an angle of 45 degrees above the aircraft centreline. It was powered by a single 250hp Sunbeam Maori II water-cooled engine driving a two-bladed, wooden propeller to give a maximum level speed of 105 knots. Although delivered in 1917, it never flew because stress calculations showed it to be excessively heavy; it was condemned as unsafe and broken up.

A Panther landing on *Argus*

Panther

A biplane of wooden monocoque construction designed to meet Admiralty specification AD/N.2A for a two-seat spotter/reconnaissance aircraft capable of operation from an aircraft carrier. It had a unique method of folding; the rear fuselage was hinged just aft of the observer's cockpit to be swung to starboard and lie parallel with the wings. To allow the tail unit control runs to remain connected, they ran through a dedicated channel on the starboard side of the fuselage. The two fuselage elements were made of plywood with a fabric covering.

Named Panther when it entered service, the two aircrew sat high in the tall fuselage to give the pilot an exceptionally good view for deck landing. The pilot's cockpit was on top of the main fuel tank just under the upper wing which was mounted low over the fuselage. He gained access through an opening in this wing which allowed a good view overhead when he was strapped in. Production aircraft had flotation gear which comprised three inflatable bags, one in the rear fuselage and one in each of two containers attached to the top of the undercarriage struts. They were initiated by a T-shaped handle situated either to the right of the instrument panel or in the upper wing centre section. Hydrovanes were fitted to the undercarriage to prevent the aircraft nosing over as it hit the water. A production contract was placed with Parnall during 1918 but post-Armistice cancellations caused friction and a smaller order was eventually placed with the nearby British & Colonial Aeroplane Company. Some aircraft had already been built by Parnall and it is likely that a number of components were passed on so the exact split between the two manufacturers is uncertain. They were delivered from 1920.

Panther data

Length:	24ft 11in (14ft 6in folded)
Wingspan:	29ft 6in
Height:	10ft 6in
MTOW:	2,595lb
Engine:	One 230hp Bentley BR.2 rotary
Fuel:	Avgas. 48 gallons in main tank. 10 gallons in two gravity tanks in upper wing. Total 58 gallons
Performance:	Maximum level speed 95 knots Service ceiling 14,500ft. 10 minutes to 10,000ft
Endurance:	4½ hours
Armament:	One 0.303in Lewis gun on a pillar in rear cockpit

Production was terminated after 108 had been delivered. There were also six prototypes giving a total of 114.

Between 1920 and 1926 Panthers served with 205 Squadron, 441 and 442 Flights together with the *Eagle* Flight formed for the ship's early flying trials.

They operated from the aircraft carriers *Argus*, *Hermes* and *Eagle*. During 1921 Panthers were evaluated for their ability to launch from the turret platforms still fitted to capital ships and successful launches were carried out from *Valiant*, *Warspite* and *Hood*. A launch from *Repulse* was unsuccessful as the aircraft fell off the platform and was badly damaged.

The Panther was relatively popular with its pilots and regarded as a pleasant aircraft to fly with few vices despite several being lost in accidents. Whilst not a remarkable aircraft, the Panther played a significant part in the early development of carrier aviation.

Puffin

An experimental two-seat fighter/reconnaissance amphibian capable of operating from an aircraft carrier, the Puffin had a large central float fitted with wheels and small balancing floats under the outer lower wings. Wingspan was 40ft, MTOW 5,000lb and the single 450hp Napier Lion II water-cooled engine gave a maximum level speed of 95 knots. Three prototypes were built and evaluated at Isle of Grain but they were not considered successful and there were no production orders.

Plover

A single-seat biplane fighter designed, like the Fairey Flycatcher, to meet Specification 7/21 for a carrier-borne fleet fighter. It had staggered, equal-span wings with N-shaped interplane struts. The fuselage and wings were made from fabric-covered wood and the wheeled undercarriage was designed to be interchangeable with twin floats. The latter had wheels so that the aircraft could taxi on land in amphibian configuration and had water rudders at the rear. The first Plover flew in 1923; there were two further prototypes and two small production batches. Intended as a replacement for the Nightjar, it was outshone by the Flycatcher which pilots very much preferred. Its unpopularity was exacerbated by structural weakness demonstrated in 1924 when the centre section of a Plover on test collapsed during aerobatics. The pilot had no parachute but managed, by skilful handling, to walk away from a crash landing near Leuchars.

Plover data

Length:	23ft
Wingspan:	29ft
Height:	12ft
MTOW:	2,984lb
Engine:	One 436hp Bristol Jupiter IV air-cooled radial
Fuel:	Avgas. 50 gallons
Performance:	Maximum level speed 125 knots Service ceiling 23,000ft. 25 minutes to 20,000ft
Endurance:	2½ hours
Armament:	Two belt-fed 0.303in Vickers front guns forward of the cockpit synchronised to fire through the propeller arc

Three prototype and fifteen production Plovers were delivered.

Plovers served with 403 Fleet Fighter Flight for a year from June 1923 to July 1924 and 404 Flight from July 1923 to March 1925. One example served briefly with 405 Flight in mid-1924. 403 Flight operated briefly from *Hermes* 1924 but for the remainder of the Plover's time in service it was operated ashore at Leuchars. By 1925 most had been withdrawn except for a few used as trials aircraft.

Parnall Plover fitted with floats. (Philip Jarrett)

Perch

Proposed to meet Specification 5/24 for an aircraft suitable for deck-landing training, the Perch had side-by-side seating for the student and instructor so that both would have a good view of the deck on final approach. Their view was further enhanced by the high cockpit and the pronounced downward slope of the fuselage over the engine decking. It was constructed largely of fabric-covered wood and had alternative wheeled or float undercarriages. Only one was built which first flew in 1926. It was tested extensively at both the A&AEE and MAEE during 1927 but despite favourable reports there were no production orders for the type because of naval budget cuts. Wingspan was 40ft, MTOW 4,500lb and the single 270hp Rolls-Royce Falcon III water-cooled engine giving a maximum level speed of 100 knots.

Peto

Designed to meet Specification 16/24 for a spotter/reconnaissance biplane capable from operation from the submarine *M-2* which was modified with a small hangar, catapult and handling crane in place of the original 12in gun mounting. The hangar was constructed as a watertight structure with a door at the forward end 9ft 3in high and 8ft 9in wide. A crane was fitted on top of it and the catapult was 34ft long with a system of pulley wheels and wires to accentuate the movement of a ram actuated by either compressed air or a cordite charge. It was designed to launch an aircraft of up to 7,000lb at an end speed of 40 knots. Tanks within *M-2*'s hull contained 200 gallons of avgas, considered sufficient for one month's aircraft operations. The embarked pilot and observer had to undergo submarine training and thus qualified for both flying and submarine pay in addition to their basic pay.

Inside the hangar with its wings folded the Peto rested on a trolley on top of a short set of rails. Prior to a launch the hangar door was lowered downwards to form a platform over which a continuation of the rails connected the trolley to the catapult. The aircraft was rolled into position on the catapult, wings spread and engine started. Recovery followed the reverse process with the aircraft taxi-ing alongside to be picked up by the crane and lowered onto the trolley. Once the engine was shut down and wings folded it was pushed back along the rails into the hangar on its trolley and the hangar door was winched shut. The boat was then able to dive. Unfortunately, *M-2* was lost off Portland on 26 January 1932. It was located on the sea-bed on 3 February and

A Peto being hoisted out from *M-2* for water taxi-ing trials in Gibraltar.

divers found that both the hangar door and the upper conning tower hatch were open. It was lying in a bows-up attitude with damage to the propellers showing that it had hit the bottom stern first. The entire ship's company, seven officers and fifty-three ratings, was lost but only two bodies were located, both believed to be part of the aircraft handling party. The precise cause of the loss was uncertain but the open hangar door and the discovery of some of the handling party suggested that she was surfacing to launch the aircraft. It is, therefore, possible that the hangar door was opened too soon but an alternative theory was that the after ballast tank vent valves had been left open as she surfaced, allowing them to refill and drag the stern down; by the time the handling party realised what was happening it would have been too late to close the hangar door.

The Peto was carefully designed to fit exactly into *M-2*'s small hangar. Two prototypes were ordered in 1924 and the first flew in 1926. It was a compact biplane with staggered wings of unequal span and pronounced sweepback; the upper centre section was at the aircrew's eye level to give them the best view above and below the aircraft. The mainplanes were constructed with spruce spars, ribs and the fuselage comprised spruce longerons braced with spruce and stainless steel struts. It was fabric-covered up to the front cockpit and had aluminium panels forward of that. The twin floats were attached by streamlined N-struts and lacked any sort of shock absorption. On trials, the MAEE found the Peto's manoeuvrability on water to be good and it could taxi easily across wind and tide. It was described as ideal for its intended role and was said to be both easy to fly and to maintain. It failed to reach the intended service ceiling of 11,000ft but the Admiralty accepted this shortcoming as there was no alternative aircraft capable of operating from *M-2*. The pilot occupied the rear cockpit and an interesting feature of the design was a hand-turning gear for the engine in the observer's front cockpit. Once he had manned the aircraft, the observer's first task was to use it to rotate the engine as quickly as possible until it fired. It was, apparently, initially stiff to turn and this can have been no easy task.

Peto data

Length:	22ft 6¼in
Wingspan:	28ft 5in (8ft folded)
Height:	8ft 11in
MTOW:	1,950lb
Engine:	One 135hp Bristol Lucifer IV air-cooled radial later replaced by a 135hp Armstrong Siddeley Mongoose IIIC air-cooled radial
Fuel:	Avgas. 14½ gallons
Performance:	Maximum level speed 100 knots when powered by the Mongoose Service ceiling 9,500ft. 11 minutes to 5,000ft
Endurance:	2 hours
Armament:	None

There has been some confusion about the number built as some records list two batches of two. In fact the first prototype was rebuilt after a crash and given a new airframe number, N 255. The second batch was to have comprised this and a another Peto which was cancelled after the loss of *M-2*. N 255 was the aircraft embarked in *M-2* when it was lost. It was actually removed from the hangar by divers and taken to Portland where it was found to be too badly damaged for a second rebuild and was sold for scrap in 1932.

Both Petos operated from *M-2* between 1928 and 1932. N 181/N255 spent two periods embarked; the first ended in 1930 when it was damaged by a heavy landing in the water alongside the boat and it was further damaged by a dockyard crane when it was hoisted onto a jetty in Gibraltar.

After the loss of *M-2* the Admiralty decided that the disadvantages of aircraft operations from a submarine outweighed the advantages and the concept was abandoned. That said, the Peto performed exactly as intended and can be considered a success.

Pike

A single prototype was built to meet Specification 1/24 for a three-seat biplane capable of carrier operation or, alternatively, with twin floats catapult-equipped capital ships and cruisers. A single 450hp Napier Lion V water-cooled engine gave a maximum level speed of 110 knots, wingspan was 46ft and MTOW 6,350lb. It first flew in 1927 but A&AEE trials criticised it for having a cold and draughty cockpit which caused considerable discomfort. The distance between pilot and observer made communication between them almost impossible, even with a Gosport Tube and controls were described as sluggish. There were no production orders.

Pipit

Two prototypes were built to meet Specification 21/26 for a single-seat carrier-borne biplane fighter. A single 495hp Rolls-Royce F.XI water-cooled engine gave a maximum level speed of 152 knots, wingspan was 35ft and MTOW 3,980lb. It could be fitted with either wheeled or twin-float undercarriages. Armament comprised two Vickers 0.303in belt-fed front guns firing through the propeller arc with an interrupter mechanism. The first was evaluated by the A&AEE in 1928 but severe tail flutter in a terminal velocity dive caused the tailplane spar to fracture and the aircraft crashed out of control despite the pilot's recovery efforts. He survived with a broken neck from which he subsequently recovered. The second prototype had a modified fin and rudder fitted for A&AEE tests in 1929 it, too, developed violent tail flutter, the stern post failed and the fin and rudder broke away. This time the pilot bailed out and parachuted to safety but the aircraft crashed and was totally destroyed. These losses ended Parnall's aspiration to build naval aircraft and it turned to the manufacture of light aircraft and components.

PEMBERTON-BILLING

PB.9

Conceived in 1914 as fast single-seat scout capable of rapid construction, the only PB.9 built was designed in only 8 days as a conventional biplane to be powered by a single 80hp Gnome rotary engine. No 80hp Gnomes were available and so it was fitted with a reconditioned 50hp Gnome which gave a maximum level speed of 69 knots. MTOW was 750lb and wingspan 26ft. After its first flight in

Pemberton-Billing PB.9.

Pemberton-Billing PB.23.

Pemberton-Billing PB.25.

August 1914 it was purchased by the Admiralty and used as a training aircraft at Hendon and then Chingford before being deleted in 1915.

PB.23E

A single-seat pusher biplane built in 1915, the PB.23E had a single 80hp Le Rhone rotary engine which gave a maximum level speed of 85 knots. A complex arrangement of struts supported the streamlined cockpit nacelle midway between the wings and it was covered with sheet metal, a revolutionary feature at the time. A single 0.303in Lewis front gun was mounted in the nacelle nose. Wingspan was 33ft, MTOW 1,576lb and the only example built was delivered to Hendon in 1915 where it was known as the 'Pusher Projectile' and used for training until deleted in 1917.

PB.25

The design impressed the Admiralty sufficiently for it to order twenty PB.25s, basically improved PB.23Es with single 100hp Gnome monosoupape, pusher, rotary engines which gave a gave a maximum level speed of 87 knots. The wings were swept back by 11 degrees and the nacelle was covered with fabric to simplify construction. The single 0.303in Lewis front gun was mounted directly in front of the pilot's eyes. Six were delivered to Eastchurch in 1916 and used by the design flight, gunnery school and spotting school before being deleted in 1917. The remainder were delivered to Killingholme in 1917 without engines where they were stored before being broken up for spares.

PB.29E

Designed to fly as slowly as 30 knots to increase the gunner's accuracy in night Zeppelin interceptions with a patrol endurance of 12 hours, the PB.29E was a frail-looking quadruplane powered by two 90hp Austro-Daimler engines driving four-bladed pusher propellers. No weight details have survived but the only example built had two pilots' cockpits in tandem and a searchlight in the nose. The gunlayer with his single pillar-mounted 0.303in Lewis gun occupied a deep nacelle that filled the gap between the upper two wings. It was evaluated at Chingford in 1916 but destroyed in a crash.

PB.31E

This aircraft marked the change of this firm's name from Pemberton-Billing to Supermarine. It was designed by the former, delivered to the RNAS in 1917 as a Supermarine product but retained its PB designation. It was a quadruplane resembling the PB.29E and intended for the same role but had a more robust airframe. The only example built had five crew positions but only ever flew with three. The two pilots had an enclosed, glazed cabin on top of the fuselage but there was only one set of controls. It had a nominal endurance of 9 hours, the control runs and avgas pipes were armoured and wooden structures in the cabin were bound with fabric to minimise the risk of splinters if they were damaged in action. The searchlight in the nacelle nose was powered by a small 5hp engine and could be trained over wide arcs controlled by the gunlayer. It also provided a cockpit heating system. Armament comprised a 1½pdr non-recoil Davis gun with 20 rounds on a gunlayer's mounting above the top wing and two 0.303in Lewis guns on a Scarff ring forward of the cabin. Two 100hp Anzani engines driving four-bladed tractor propellers gave a maximum level speed of 65 knots. Wingspan was 60ft and MTOW 6,146lb. It was delivered to Eastchurch in February 1917 and only flew on a few occasions which showed it to be useless. It was deleted in 1917.

Pemberton-Billing PB.29.

PERCIVAL

Vega Gull

This low-wing fixed-undercarriage monoplane touring aircraft capable of carrying three passengers first flew in 1935. Wingspan was 39ft 6in, MTOW 3,250lb and the single 200hp de Havilland Gipsy Six engine gave a maximum level speed of 150 knots. Four were requisitioned by the Admiralty in 1939/40 and used as light communications aircraft by 780, 781 and 782 NAS. These and a further example transferred from the RAF in 1941 were all to Mark I standard and remained in use until 1943. Two Mark IIs with 205hp Gipsy Six II engines were transferred from the RAF in 1939 and used initially by 754 NAS for observer training. In 1940 they were transferred to 781 NAS as light communications aircraft and used until 1943.

Q.6

A twin-engined commercial aircraft with six passenger seats, several were requisitioned in 1939 and four allocated to the RN. One was destroyed at Lee-on-Solent by enemy bombing before being issued to a squadron but the other three were used by 781, 782, 730 and 787 NAS as light communications aircraft between 1940 and 1944. Wingspan was 46ft 8in, MTOW 5,500lb and the two 205hp de Havilland Gipsy six II engines gave a maximum level speed of 170 knots.

Proctor

Developed from the Vega Gull to meet an RAF requirement for a radio training and light communications aircraft, the Proctor was a single-engined low-wing fabric-covered wooden monoplane with a fixed undercarriage which had larger rear cabin windows and a fuselage lengthened by 6in to allow room for equipment. First flight was in October 1939 and the Mark IA, company designation P.28, was a three-seat, dual-control variant built specifically for the RN as a deck landing and TAG training aircraft. It had dinghy stowage and naval instrumentation. The Mark IIA, company designation P.30, was a three-seat TAG training aircraft, again designed specifically for RN use. The Mark III, company designation P.34, was designed for training RAF radio operators but a small batch was transferred to the RN for fleet requirements tasks. The RN used Proctors for a variety of shore-based duties including observer training at Piarco and Arbroath, TAG training at Worthy Down, dual-control deck-landing instruction, pilot continuation and conversion flying, fleet requirements tasks, light communications and as airborne targets for both day and night fighter pilot training.

Proctor IIA data

Length:	25ft 10in
Wingspan:	39ft 6in
Height:	7ft 3in
MTOW:	3,500lb
Engine:	One 208hp de Havilland Gipsy Queen II liquid-cooled engine driving a two-bladed variable-pitch propeller
Fuel:	Avgas. 40 gallons
Performance:	Maximum level speed 140 knots Service ceiling 17,000ft. 6 minutes to 5,000ft
Endurance:	Over 3 hours
Armament:	None

The RN received 277 Proctors of which 99 were to Mark IA standard,

Percival Proctor Mark II. (Philip Jarrett)

16 to Mark II standard, 150 to Mark IIA standard and 12 to Mark III standard

Between 1939 and 1944 they were allocated to 746, 748, 752, 754, 755, 756, 758, 759, 767, 770, 771, 772, 778, 780, 781, 782, 784, 787, 792 and 794 NAS, some of which only used Proctors for short periods.

Between 1941 and 1943 they were also used by the station flights at Arbroath, Crail, Donibristle, Eglinton, Hatston, St Merryn, Stretton and Yeovilton. Proctor-equipped squadrons operated regularly from Piarco, Worthy Down, Twatt, Machrihanish, Ayr, Charlton Horethorne, Lee-on-Solent and Drem. Virtually all of them had been withdrawn by 1945 and none survived into the post-war era.

Sea Prince

Conceived as a small commercial aircraft in 1947 with the company designation P.50 and the name Prince, it was a twin-engined, high-wing monoplane of all-metal semi-monocoque construction with dual pilot controls and cabin space for eight seats. After its first flight in 1948 the Admiralty selected it to meet two separate requirements; T.17/49, for a radar-equipped 'flying classroom' equipped for observer training and C.18/49 for either the eight-seat configuration or modified with VIP seating to act as an 'Admiral's Barge'. Orders were placed for both types in 1949 named Sea Prince. The trainer variant, company designation P.57, was designated Sea Prince T 1 and the communications variant, company designation P.66, Sea Prince C 1. Both had naval communications and enlarged, double opening doors on the port side aft of the wing so that bulky items of equipment could be loaded and transported, a feature other light communications aircraft lacked.

The trainer variant had the rear cabin fitted with three work stations for student observers and their instructors. Each had a radar display, instruments and navigation equipment. The nose was extended with a 'thimble-shaped' radome for an ASH radar scanner. T 1s were first used for training anti-submarine observers and later by RNVR anti-submarine units for observer refresher flying and training as well as light communications tasks. A specialised derivative of the original T 1, retaining the same designation, was produced in 1952 for basic observer training, replacing Barracudas, Fireflies and Ansons. This had a modified, rounded, nose containing an ASV-19A radar scanner and

Sea Prince T 2 of 750 NAS.

more extensive communications and it was used in this role for 26 years with several equipment upgrades before being replaced by the Jetstream in 1979. A final variant, the C 2, was procured which was basically the T 1 with the radar and instructional consoles removed and replaced by seating.

Sea Prince T 1 data

Length:	46ft 4in
Wingspan:	56ft
Height:	16ft 1in
MTOW:	11,860lb
Engine:	Two 550hp Alvis Leonides 125 air-cooled radials
Fuel:	Avgas. 80 gallons
Performance:	Maximum level speed 195 knots
	Service ceiling 22,000ft. 4 minutes to 5,000ft
Endurance:	Over 2 hours
Armament:	None

The RN procured forty-six Sea Princes from 1949 comprising thirty-nine T 1s, three C 1s and four C 2s.

A single Sea Prince T 1 was operated by 831 NAS in the electronic warfare training role between 1962 and 1966, using its radar when necessary and providing detachments with light transport.

Between 1950 and 1979 Sea Princes formed part of 702, 744 and 781 NAS. The only squadron completely equipped with the type was 750 NAS, the Observer School which flew the type between 1953 and 1979 at Culdrose, Hal Far, Lossiemouth and then Culdrose again.

RNVR squadrons partially equipped with T 1s between 1950 and 1956 included 1830, 1840, 1841 and 1844 NAS at Abbotsinch, Ford, Stretton and Bramcote.

Sea Princes of all three marks were used at various times between 1955 and 1971 by the station flights at Arbroath, Brawdy, Culdrose, Eglinton, Lee-on-Solent, Lossiemouth and Yeovilton. Several of these were T 1s converted to the communications role with seating in the rear cabin but retaining their original designation. One of these was allocated to the SNO at 1 FTS Linton-on-Ouse in the late 1960s. It moved to Church Fenton with 1 FTS in 1969 but was lost after a mid-air collision with a Jet provost in 1971.

The first Sea Prince C 1 was delivered in 1950 and used as a Admiral's Barge. The second supported the RN element of the UK Joint Services Mission to the USA at Washington DC. The Sea Prince was an unspectacular but faithful 'workhorse' that is remembered with affection by many of those who flew it.

PERRY, BEADLE & Co

T1/T2 Tractor Biplane

The T1 flew in 1913 powered by a single 25hp Anzani air-cooled radial engine. Unsurprisingly, it was found to be underpowered and re-engined with a 45hp Anzani with which it was re-designated T2 and flew with it in 1914. It was requisitioned by the Admiralty in December 1914 and evaluated at Hendon where its mediocre performance was criticised. It was a single-seat tractor biplane with a wingspan of 35ft, MTOW was not recorded but its maximum level speed was 55 knots. No more were procured.

PHOENIX DYNAMO MANUFACTURING Co Ltd

P.5 Cork

In 1917 Lieutenant Commander Linton Hope RN designed a new type of flying boat hull and the Admiralty ordered two P.5 flying boats of similar size to a Porte boat with Linton Hope hulls for comparison. Their hulls were built by May, Harden and May with a continuous keel from stem to sternpost and were remarkably strong. Their two 350hp Rolls-Royce Eagle VIII water-cooled engines gave a maximum level speed of 92 knots. Wingspan was 85ft 6in and MTOW 12,511lb. The two pilots sat in tandem cockpits situated aft of the bow gunlayer's position and the engineer sat inside the hull. They were delivered in 1918 for evaluation at Isle of Grain which went well. One was launched during a storm to fly in a 40-knot gale and subsequently moored to a buoy for 3 days and nights with winds gusting up to 45 knots, heavy rain, hail and snow. When brought ashore it was found to have suffered no damage and shipped no water. Despite its success, the P.5 was not put into production because there were more than enough Felixstowe F. 5 flying boats left after the Armistice to equip the post-war squadrons. They were deleted in 1924.

POLEGATE NAVAL AIR STATION

Polegate specialised in the operation of airships between 1916 and 1918 and during that period its air engineering department assembled six SSZ class non-rigid airships from components manufactured elsewhere. These were SSZ-6, SSZ-7, SSZ-8, SSZ-9, SSZ-10 and SSZ-19. Their data can be found in the section on Folkestone naval air station.

PORTE

Baby

The Porte Baby evolved from experiments with Curtiss America hulls at Felixstowe and construction was probably begun before the Felixstowe F.1 had flown. The name Baby was ironic since for much of its time in service with the RNAS it was the largest operational flying boat. The outboard engines were tractors and the midship one a pusher. Components including the plywood-covered wooden hull were manufactured by subcontractors but the boats were all assembled at Felixstowe. The two pilots had an enclosed, extensively-glazed cockpit and Lewis machine guns could be fitted in hatchways aft of the cockpit and in the fuselage aft of the wings. Some Babies were used for torpedo-carrying experiments in 1918 but these were not far advanced when the war ended. Sea trials found that the prototype wallowed badly in a following sea but this was resolved by lengthening the nose by 3ft. The Baby was ordered into production but before many had been completed the Porte II, subsequently re-named Felixstowe F.2, flew and its superior performance led to the remaining Babies being cancelled before assembly.

Porte Baby and Scout combination.

Baby data

Length:	63ft
Wingspan:	124ft
Height:	25ft
MTOW:	18,600lb
Engine:	Three 325hp Rolls-Royce Eagle VII, Vee-12 water-cooled in later examples, two tractor, one pusher
Fuel:	Avgas. 250 gallons
Performance:	Maximum level speed 80 knots Service ceiling 8,000ft. 6 minutes to 2,000ft
Endurance:	4 hours
Armament:	0.303in Lewis guns on flexible mountings. Prototype had a single 6pdr Davis gun; others took part in torpedo trials

Twenty Porte I Babies were ordered in February 1916 but only the first eleven were completed. Incomplete hulls were delivered to Killingholme in 1917 as a source of spares.

Babies operated from Felixstowe and Killingholme but only two remained operational in 1918.

Its size meant that the Baby lacked the manoeuvrability to stand much of a chance against other aircraft in combat and this led to the decision that they would not be used in areas of the North Sea where they might be attacked unless they were escorted by Curtiss H.12 or Felixstowe F.2 boats which were considerably more manoeuvrable. The type did, however, achieve one remarkable feat on 17 May 1916. The RNAS was seeking new ways to use Bristol Scout fighters to intercept Zeppelins over the North Sea. One was to launch them from small take-off decks fitted on seaplane carriers but at Felixstowe the prototype Baby was modified with attachment points for a Scout. These comprised crutches carried on struts forward of the upper wing's leading edge in line with its central engine to take the Scout's wheels and a quick-release mechanism further aft by its tail-skid. Release was activated by the Scout pilot. The Baby was flown by Porte himself and the Scout was flown by Flight Lieutenant M J Day RNAS. The Scout played no part in the take-off but its propeller windmilled with the ignition switches off. When the combination had climbed to 1,000ft over Harwich, Porte turned onto a safe heading; Day switched his ignition on and, once he had achieved full power, released his holding mechanism and climbed away successfully. The experiment had been perfectly successful but was never repeated and never used operationally.

PORT VICTORIA

PV.1

The Port Victoria experimental construction department near Isle of Grain began its work in early 1916 seeking ways to improve the Sopwith Baby seaplane's bomb load. The PV.1 design that resulted comprised a Baby fuselage with new high-lift wings of the same span and enlarged floats; the original lower wing spars were sawn off flush with the fuselage sides and left in situ and the new wings changed the centre of gravity but it was restored with lead weights in the floats. Powered by a 100hp Gnome monosoupape, the PV.1 was about 300lb heavier than a production Baby and the lead weights adding a further 300lb. Test pilots reported that controls had no 'sogginess', the complaint levelled at bomb-laden Babies, but it was about 20 knots slower. Only one conversion was carried out.

PV.2

An original design for a fast, anti-Zeppelin seaplane fighter armed with two 0.303in Lewis machine guns forward of the cockpit firing through the propeller arc with an interrupter mechanism, the PV.2 was a sesquiplane; the lower wing being much smaller than the upper. It was a remarkably clean seaplane with the wing structure attached to the upper fuselage longerons, its low position giving the pilot an unobstructed view of the upper hemisphere. It first flew in June 1916 but test pilots found that the upper wing obscured the pilot's view of the water surface on landing so it was raised level with the pilot's eyes. In this form the only prototype was re-designated as the PV.2bis in 1917 and re-evaluated. It proved popular with pilots but by then the seaplane fighter concept was out-dated and no more were ordered. The single 100hp Gnome rotary engine driving a four-bladed wooden propeller gave a maximum level speed of 80 knots. Wingspan was 29ft and MTOW 1,702lb.

PV.4

Work on a design designated PV.3 for a two-seat fighter with a wheeled undercarriage never reached the prototype stage but a seaplane derivative was designated PV.4. It was a compact sesquiplane with the aircrew and engine occupying a nacelle with the upper wings attached to the longerons aft of the cockpit. The gunlayer occupied the front cockpit with a single 0.303in Lewis gun on a Scarff ring and the pilot sat immediately behind him. Designed at first with a single 150hp Smith radial engine, this failed to materialise and delayed construction until 1917 when a 110hp Clerget rotary engine was substituted in the only prototype built. The change made the aircraft longitudinally unstable; with the tailplane rigged to give correct balance at full power the aircraft became tail-heavy with the engine off and test pilots found that control was lost below 55 knots. It was flown but each landing proved to be an adventure that pilots were not keen to repeat. Work on it was terminated.

PV.5/PV.5a

Designed to meet an Admiralty requirement for a single-seat seaplane fighter and light attack aircraft, the PV.5 was a sesquiplane layout with wings braced by struts to the float supports and a high-lift aerofoil section. Two 65lb bombs were to be carried inside the fuselage and there was to be a fixed 0.303in Vickers machine gun mounted in front of the

Port Victoria PV.2.

Port Victoria PV.4.

cockpit firing through the propeller arc with an interrupter mechanism. One prototype, designated PV.5, was ordered and, to provide comparative data, a second prototype designated PV.5a was ordered which differed in being a biplane but both shared the same fuselage and tailplane design. Both were complete in 1916 but the failure of the Smith radial engine meant that a 150hp Hispano-Suiza had to be substituted and this led to delay. It was decided to abandon the PV.5a but to complete the PV.5 which proved to be a satisfactory aircraft described as pleasant to fly by test pilots. Despite the decision to abandon it, the PV.5a was eventually completed with a 200hp Hispano-Suiza engine. Its performance was better than the PV.5 but it was criticised for its inferior manoeuvrability and pilot's view. PV.5

Port Victoria PV.5.

Port Victoria PV.7 Grain Kitten.

wingspan was 32ft; PV.5a 33ft 1in. PV.5 MTOW was 2,456lb; PV.5a 2,518lb. Maximum speed of the PV.5 in level flight was 82 knots; PV.5a 90 knots.

PV.7 Grain Kitten

By 1916 the concept of using fighters with wheeled undercarriages taking off from warships to intercept Zeppelins had been proved but even the smallest could not operate from destroyers. To fill this perceived gap, the Admiralty instructed Port Victoria to investigate the possibility of building a small fighter and the resulting PV.7 was the first wheeled design to be translated from the drawing board into hardware. It was a tiny, single-bay sesquiplane of otherwise conventional design to have been powered by a single 45hp ABC Gnat engine driving a two-blade wooden propeller. This was not available in time, however, and ABC's 35hp Gnat was fitted instead, giving a maximum level speed of 74 knots. With a Lewis gun, three 47-round drums of ammunition, a 140lb pilot and fuel for 2½ hours MTOW was still only 491lb. Wingspan was 18ft. It proved to be another innovative Port Victoria design that was let down by its engine; the only engine that ever survived more than an hour's flying was a handmade prototype. Production engines gave up regularly on their first flight and consequently it was necessary to remain within gliding distance of the airfield on every test flight. The PV.7 was deleted in 1917.

PV.8 Eastchurch Kitten

The experimental flight at Eastchurch was tasked by the Admiralty to produce an aircraft to the same specification as the PV.7 but its design was transferred half complete to Port Victoria, designated PV.8 and named Eastchurch Kitten. Like the PV.7 it had been designed around the 45hp Gnat engine but it was slightly larger and there was no

Port Victoria PV.8 Eastchurch Kitten.

Port Victoria PV.9.

tailplane, only a balanced elevator surface. The undercarriage was a rigid structure relying on tyres for shock absorption and the flying wires ran through the undercarriage axle from their fixed ends on the outer part of the upper wings. This led one test pilot to write that if the undercarriage was broken on take-off the wings might fold up! The pilot sat with his eyes in line with the trailing edge of the upper wing with the single Lewis gun on the centre section but offset to starboard. There was a small rounded cut-out under the gun to allow its elevation for reloading but this was criticised as being very awkward for the pilot in his cramped cockpit. Like the PV.7, the PV.8 had to be fitted with the 35hp Gnat which proved just as unsatisfactory. It was said to perform better than the PV.7 in most respects but was still not regarded as a viable operational machine and no more were ordered. Wingspan was 18ft 11½in; MTOW 586lb and a maximum level speed 82 knots.

PV.9

Last of the Port Victoria designs, the PV.9 was a single-seat seaplane fighter of sesquiplane configuration with a conventional fuselage structure mounted between the wings to give the pilot a relatively good all-round view. It first flew in December 1917 with the single 150hp Bentley rotary engine giving a maximum level speed of 97 knots but engine problems delayed full evaluation until May 1918. It was described as the best seaplane fighter yet tested but by then the need for such aircraft had disappeared and the sole prototype was deleted. Wingspan was 30ft 11in and MTOW 1,965lb. It was armed with a single 0.303in Vickers front gun mounted on top of the fuselage in front of the pilot firing forwards through the propeller arc with an interrupter mechanism and a single 0.303in Lewis gun above the centre section firing over the propeller arc.

QINETIQ

Banshee Jet 80+

Developed from a pilotless target aircraft designed by Meggitt in the 1980s, QinetiQ took over design authority from 2010. RN interest in Banshee followed Navy Command's Project Vampire and in 2021 a Banshee Jet 80+ was flown off *Prince of Wales* using a launcher fitted to the flight deck but subsequently had to be recovered ashore by parachute. Powered by two small gas turbine engines giving a maximum level speed of 400 knots, Banshees can carry a payload of up to 220lb, enabling developed versions to be fitted with an EO/IR camera and its associated data transmission system or even a small AESA radar. Wingspan is 8ft and it is flown off a 60ft pneumatic launcher. It is operated in flight by a controller using a dedicated ground station. It

Banshee Jet 80+ of 700X NAS at Culdrose. (Crown Copyright)

was selected to meet Phase 1 of Project Vampire in 2022 and the first of a number of air vehicles was delivered in 2023 for operation by 700X NAS which both operates RN unmanned systems and acts as an experimental unit, hence the 'X' in the unit identity. It has a dedicated flight for Banshees which launches them from Culdrose's satellite airfield Predannack. Banshees replaced some of the target simulations formerly carried out 736 NAS' Hawks but they also represent a step in Project Vampire's approach to absorbing new technologies.

REP

Parasol monoplane

A two-seater armed with a single 0.303in Vickers front gun and capable of carrying up to six 65lb bombs. Wingspan was 36ft 11in, MTOW is not known but the aircraft's empty weight without aircrew, fuel and weapons was 695lb. The single 110hp Le Rhone rotary engine gave a maximum level speed of 68 knots. The Admiralty procured twelve in 1915 and they served with 4 Wing at Eastchurch, 1 Wing at Dunkirk and the Eastchurch War Flight, attacking German coastal airfields to prevent enemy air attacks on Allied shipping and carrying out patrols over the English Channel. Those that survived were deleted by May 1916.

ROBEY-PETERS

Davis gun carrier

The only Robey-Peters design to fly was armed with a Davis gun. This was an American 2pdr recoilless gun, a long, unwieldy weapon comprising a tube within which a charge was fired along an aft-facing barrel to compensate for the discharge of an explosive shell along the forward barrel to prevent recoil but it proved to be a failure that was never used operationally. Peters designed his aircraft in 1917 to carry two of them with the pilot occupying an open cockpit just forward of the tailplane with very little view ahead and down for landing. Transparent panels were added to the cockpit sides to give some view of the ground. The gunlayers were expected to stand in two nacelles attached to the upper mainplanes at about a quarter of the distance between the fuselage and the wingtips. The word 'remarkable' hardly does justice to this odd-looking aircraft and test pilots must have thought twice about flying it. Wingspan was 54ft 6in and it was powered by a single 250hp Rolls-Royce Eagle but no record of its estimated performance or MTOW has survived. Two were ordered by the Admiralty but, mercifully, one was cancelled. It was test flown at the manufacturer's aerodrome in 1917 but only just. During the first attempted take-off it tipped onto its nose, injuring the pilot. Fortunately the gunlayer's nacelles were empty. Three days later it succeeded in taking off after repairs but as it tuned downwind on its first circuit the pilot lost control and it crashed into a mental hospital. This time the pilot escaped unhurt but the aircraft was destroyed. No more were ordered.

ROYAL AIRCRAFT ESTABLISHMENT

Larynx and the RAE 1921 Target

One of the most interesting projects evaluated by the Admiralty in the 1920s was an unmanned aircraft designed by the RAE and known as the 1921 Target to mask its true purpose as a cruise missile. It was launched by catapult with the first example fitted to the destroyer *Stronghold* in 1924. It comprised a lattice structure on the bow angled upwards at 40 degrees from which the aircraft was accelerated by a wire hooked onto the aircraft with the other end attached to a large canvas bag full of water which was dropped into the sea. Improbable as it may sound, the system worked and twelve successful launches were carried out in 1924/25. The aircraft was controlled by an autopilot system and designed to hit targets on land with a 200lb warhead from a warship offshore. An improved version named Larynx was produced in 1927 to be launched from an improved cordite-powered catapult fitted to *Stronghold* and her sister-ship *Thanet*. Larynx was designed to carry a 250lb warhead for a distance of 300nm at 175 knots under autopilot control. Again trials went well with five launches achieving varying degrees of success during 1927. The aircraft's course was followed by taking D/F bearings of radio transmissions from it. The pitch of the interrupted continuous wave transmission was used to measure speed and at intervals signals were interrupted to enable distance flown to be deduced accurately. Once the aircraft was calculated to be over its target a signal was sent to cut its engine and dive. Larynx was powered by a single 200hp Armstrong Siddeley Lynx IV radial engine and it could also be used as a gunnery target in addition to potential applications against warships. Despite successful trials afloat and ashore, Larynx was not put into production and development was terminated. It occupies that grey area between drones and cruise missiles in modern terminology, but its guidance was more sophisticated than the German V-1 and Larynx makes a fascinating comparison with twenty-first century concepts.

Larynx on the upward-sloping launcher fitted to the destroyer *Stronghold*.

Commander Samson about to fly a sortie in a BE.2a from Dunkirk in 1914.

ROYAL AIRCRAFT FACTORY

BE.2

A reconnaissance aircraft for the RFC in which stability was considered of prime importance, this was a two-seat biplane with a wire-braced wooden structure covered with doped fabric and the wheeled undercarriage incorporated long skids to prevent nosing over on landing. Wingspan was 35ft ½in, MTOW 1,600lb and the 70hp Renault engine driving a four-bladed wooden propeller gave a maximum level speed of 60 knots. There was no standardised armament but at various times RNAS aircraft carried a 100lb bomb on improvised racks under the fuselage and the aircrew carried pistols or rifles. The RNAS received five, one of which, number 50, was used by Commander C R Samson RNAS as his personal machine; he flew it in the Fleet Review Fly-Past of July 1914, took it to Dunkirk with the Eastchurch Squadron in August and then took it to Tenedos during the Dardanelles Campaign. During its historic career it located German troops moving through Belgium, attacked enemy installations at Ostend, Zeebrugge and Middelkerke, spotted for shore bombardment of Turkish positions by battleships and in its last few days carried out a night bombing attack on Kilia Liman. Except for spotting missions, Samson usually flew it as a single-seater with an extra fuel tank in the front cockpit. The pilot's cockpit was always the rear of the two. Number 50 was finally written off in late 1915 and broken up at Tenedos.

BE.2c

Design improvements led to the B.E.2c which first flew in June 1914. It had the same fuselage, engine and undercarriage as the 2a but new wings with marked stagger replaced the earlier wings and double-acting ailerons replaced wing warp control. The fuselage was a wire-braced wooden box girder made in two parts with a break-joint just aft of the cockpits. The wings had wooden spars, ribs and riblets with external bracing by cables. The fin and rudder were shaped with steel tube with the whole airframe covered by doped fabric. On the outbreak of war, immediate orders for the type were placed with subcontractors but lack of sufficient working drawings caused delays and many of the firms had never built aircraft before.

B.E.2c data

Length:	27ft 3in
Wingspan:	37ft
Height:	11ft 1½in
MTOW:	2,374lb
Engine:	Early aircraft one 70hp Renault; later aircraft one 90hp RAF 1a. A few were built with 90hp Curtiss OX-5. All drove a four-bladed wooden propeller
Fuel:	Avgas. 32¾ gallons
Performance:	Maximum level speed 75 knots Service ceiling 10,000ft. 10 minutes to 3,500ft
Endurance:	3¼ hours
Armament:	Typically one 0.303in Lewis front gun mounted in front of the pilot when flown solo or on a socket in front cockpit when flown as a two-seater. Pistols, rifles and grenades carried by aircrew. Bomb racks for a single 112lb or smaller bombs up to that weight. Pilots of bomb-armed aircraft usually carried a rifle as a defensive weapon

The RNAS received 293 B.E.2c between 1915 and 1917. Some were still in use as training aircraft in 1918 but all the remaining examples were deleted after the Armistice. All B.E.2c operated by the RNAS were manufactured by subcontractors.

RNAS B.E.2c operated with 1 Wing at Dunkirk; 2 Wing at Imbros and Mudros; 3 Wing at Imbros and Tenedos; the Eastchurch Squadron at Dunkirk and 7 (Naval) Squadron in East Africa. They also operated as part of un-numbered units and flights at Great Yarmouth, Bacton, Holt, Burgh Castle, Covehithe, Sedgeford, Redcar, Hornsea, Scarborough, Eastchurch, Eastbourne, Chingford, Cranwell and Port Victoria.

The type was used as a bomber, anti-submarine patrol aircraft from coastal air stations and for both day and night Zeppelin interception missions. An illustration of its use occurred in November 1915 when a B.E.2c of 2 Wing flown by Flight Commander J R W Smyth-Pigott RNAS carried out a daring night strike on the bridge at Kuleli Burgas which spanned the Maritza River, a vulnerable point on the Berlin to Constantinople railway. He dropped his bomb from 300ft and received the DSO for his gallantry but did not destroy the target. In November 1916 a flight of three B.E.2c, led by Flight Lieutenant E Cadbury RNAS, patrolling off Lowestoft sighted and intercepted the Zeppelin L 21 and shot it down.

The second CE.1 flying boat on its handling trolley.

CE.1 Flying boat

A two-seat biplane intended for coastal patrol work and the Royal Aircraft Factory's only flying boat design, the hull was a planked wooden structure with a single step and the wings could be folded aft, hinged on the rear spars. Only two were built; the first in late 1917, flying in January 1918 had a single 230hp RAF 3a engine which gave a maximum level speed of 75 knots. Wingspan was 46ft, 20ft 7in folded, and MTOW was 4,912lb. The second prototype had a single 260hp Sunbeam Maori engine which gave a maximum level speed of 79 knots. Both were evaluated at Isle of Grain and continued in use for a while after the Armistice but were deleted in 1919.

HRE.2

Designed to meet an Admiralty requirement in 1913, the single prototype was designated as a Hydro-Reconnaissance-Experimental aircraft. It was a two-seat tractor biplane first tested with a wheeled, twin-skid, undercarriage in July 1913 with a 70hp Renault engine. Later tests with twin floats emphasised its lack of power; it failed to get airborne and suffered damage on hitting the far bank of a lake. Rebuilt with a 100hp Renault, new wings and ailerons in pace of wing warping, it saw limited service on coastal patrols in 1914 but was never reliable. It was deleted in February 1915.

RE.5

Work started in 1913 on this two-seat tractor biplane with a 120hp Austro-Daimler engine, built under licence by Beardmore, giving a maximum level speed of 68 knots. One was transferred to the RNAS from the RFC in 1914 and deployed to Dunkirk from where it carried out an attack on Courtrai railway station. With no bomb racks, the observer carried improvised bombs in his cockpit which he threw over the side as the aircraft passed over the target. Pilot and observer carried pistols for their own defence. It was not retained by the RNAS for long into 1915.

SAGE

Type 2

A two-seat biplane of wire-braced wooden construction with Vee-shaped interplane struts and ailerons on the upper wings only with a single 100hp Gnome monosoupape rotary engine driving a four-bladed wooden propeller to give a maximum level speed of 99 knots. Wingspan was 22ft 2½in and MTOW 1,546lb. A partially-glazed fairing filled the space between the fuselage and the upper wing inside which the pilot lacked a good all-round view but the gunlayer in the rear cockpit could stand with his head and shoulders through an opening in the upper wing to mount his 0.303in Lewis with a relatively good field of fire. It flew for the first time in August 1916 and evaluation at Cranwell went reasonably well. However, in September it hit a tree when attempting a forced landing and was not considered worth repairing.

Type 3

Designed to meet an Admiralty requirement for an elementary training aircraft, it was a conventional biplane of wire-braced wooden construction with a 75hp Rolls-Royce Hawk engine giving a maximum level speed of 62 knots. Wingspan was 34ft 6in and MTOW 1,980lb. The prototype flew in January 1917 and the Admiralty ordered a production run of at least 28 more but then cancelled the order and instructed Sage to concentrate on the development of seaplanes. Only one was delivered and tests showed its performance to be mediocre.

Type 4

With an airframe similar to the Type 3 and many common components but built from the outset as a seaplane with twin floats this was a two-seat biplane of wire-braced wooden construction covered by doped fabric, powered by a single 150hp Hispano-Suiza engine driving a four-bladed wooden propeller. The observer occupied the rear seat which had a W/T installation, provision for a 0.303in Lewis gun and a sliding floor panel which gave him a view of the sea below the aircraft. The first of only two Type 4s ever built flew in July 1917. When evaluated it was not accepted as a patrol seaplane but, given its Type 3 ancestry, was recommended for adoption as a seaplane training aircraft. The prototype was, therefore modified with dual controls and a forward fuselage modified to take a 200hp Sunbeam Arab engine. As such it was designated Type 4b, the original variant retrospectively designated 4a. Conversion took time, however, and the 4b did not fly until May 1918. The second prototype had folding wings and other modifications including the installation of a 200hp Hispano-Suiza engine driving a two-bladed wooden propeller which made it sufficiently different to be designated Type 4c which first flew in October 1918. It handled well and was even said to be aerobatic but the Armistice was signed before a production contract and no more were built. The Type 4c was the largest of the three sub-variants with a wingspan of 39ft 7¼in, MTOW of 2,215lb. Its 200hp Hispano-Suiza gave a maximum level speed of 85 knots.

SAUNDERS-ROE

SR-177

The SR-177 was regarded by the naval staff at one stage as one of its most important projects. Intelligence agencies in the 1950s had given dire warnings of Soviet bombers expected to be in service by the early 1960s capable of attacking the fleet at supersonic speeds from high altitude with ASM. To defend against such a threat the Admiralty sought a missile-armed supersonic interceptor with excellent high-level performance; a challenging requirement because turbojet engine power decreases with altitude, limiting a fighter's high level speed, acceleration and ability to sustain hard turns in combat. Saunders-Roe proposed a mixed-powerplant interceptor fighter with a turbojet for take-off, landing and cruising together with a rocket to give unprecedented rate of climb and high-altitude performance. The design team calculated that this combination would reduce the fighter's acceleration time from Mach 0.8 to Mach 2 above 45,000ft by as much as 90 per cent and it would have a considerable edge over conventional aircraft, a higher service ceiling and greater agility at altitude. The firm had already demonstrated the concept's practicality with two SR.53 mixed powerplant development aircraft which had flown successfully and now offered a more powerful, radar-equipped single-seat design and it was this which attracted the Admiralty's attention.

A DNAW team under Captain F H E Hopkins DSO DSC RN issued Specification NA 47 for an RN variant of the improved design and, shortly afterwards, the RAF issued its own Specification OR 337

Sage Type 2.

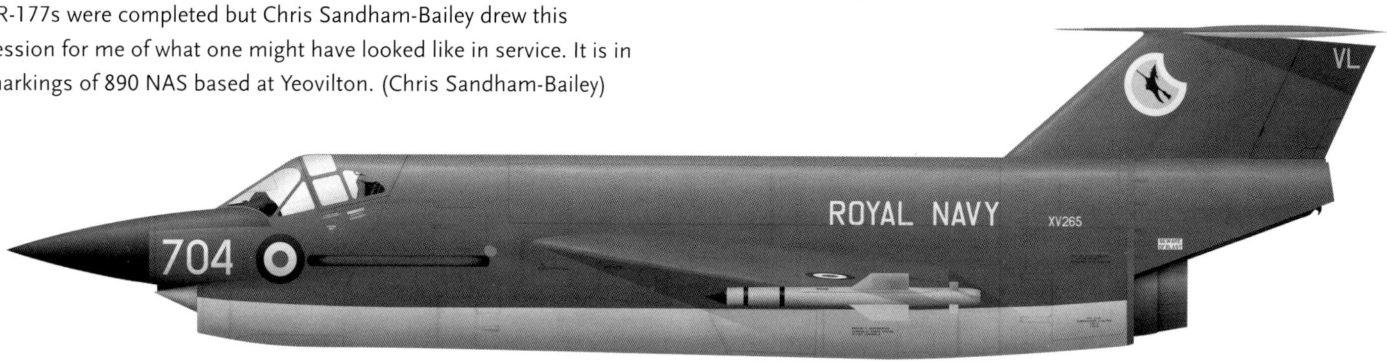

No SR-177s were completed but Chris Sandham-Bailey drew this impression for me of what one might have looked like in service. It is in the markings of 890 NAS based at Yeovilton. (Chris Sandham-Bailey)

for its own variant. Procurement of both was considered so urgent that no time was to be lost with competitive tendering and the MoS ordered both versions of the rocket fighter to be developed with a common airframe designated F.177D. The only significant difference between NA 47 and OR 337 was that former was to have a strengthened undercarriage, tail-hook and naval radios. Unusually, Saunders-Roe adopted the MoS designation and the aircraft became known as the SR-177. In September 1956 the firm was given an order for twenty-seven aircraft of which nine were to be for common development, nine for RN-specific work and nine for RAF development. A project team headed by a Commander RN was established and the ability of the Naval and Air Staffs to achieve a near-common specification for two un-penalised versions of this supersonic multi-role fighter was an outstanding achievement. The RN planned initially to buy 150 SR-177RNs; the RAF at least that number as an initial batch with more to follow. There was considerable foreign interest.

This 1957 model gives a more three-dimensional impression of the SR-177RN; it has Red Top AAM on wingtip rails.

SR-177 was too big for Saunders-Roe to cope with alone and it established partnerships, just as Lockheed Martin would do 40 years later with the F-35. Marshalls were to make the wings with Armstrong Whitworth assembling components made throughout the UK and carrying out flight testing. Both turbojet and rocket engines were designed and built by de Havilland. In its final iteration SR-177 was to have provision for underwing pylons capable of carrying a variety of weapons including both nuclear and conventional bombs, ASM and drop tanks. Red Top IR-guided AAM were to be carried on the wing tips and as an alternative load on pylons. Wingspan was to be 30ft which meant that wing-folding was not required and MTOW was calculated at 28,174lb. Wind tunnel tests demonstrated that its wing offered good low-speed performance for deck landing but was equally capable of speeds beyond Mach 2 at altitude. Maximum level speed was calculated to be Mach 2.35.

The turbojet engine selected was the de Havilland Gyron Junior PS 50 delivering 14,000lb thrust with reheat. The rocket was to be a de Havilland Spectre 5A capable of delivering 10,000lb of thrust for up to 7 minutes at full power. It burnt the same kerosene-based aircraft fuel as the turbojet with HTP as an oxidant using a fine mesh of silver as a catalyst to form a jet of steam and oxygen that delivered thrust. Endurance after using both engines in a fast climb followed by a single combat was estimated at 1½ hours and service ceiling was to be 67,000ft with dynamic excursions possible beyond. Time from catapult launch to 60,000ft was calculated at 2 minutes and at the top of climb acceleration from Mach 1.4 to Mach 2 would have taken 66 seconds. These figures are still impressive decades later. Saunders-Roe also proposed that flushing the HTP tanks with demineralised water would allow them to be filled with Avcat to give long-range sub-sonic strike capability using only the turbojet with weapons rather than drop tanks carried on pylons. A foldaway in-flight refuelling probe was fitted on the left side of the fuselage and the airframe was designed to be immensely strong with a number of components machined from solid blocks.

A P.531 taking-off from the small flight deck fitted to the frigate *Grenville*.

The RN took measures to prepare for SR-177 operations; *Eagle's* modernisation was designed around an air group that was to include twelve SR-177s and HTP was to be stored in exceptionally clean facilities including four aluminium tanks built into the spaces formerly occupied by the forward 4.5in magazines. Special aluminium pipes were installed to carry the fluid to the flight deck where aircraft would be refuelled by men wearing specially-designed protective rubber suits. A significant sum was spent on perfecting methods of replenishing HTP at sea from RFA tankers fitted with aluminium tanks and plumbing similar to that in *Eagle*.

It was not to be, however. Defence Secretary Duncan Sandys arbitrarily cancelled the SR-177RAF in April 1957 because of his privately-held belief, unsupported by any professional advice, that the RAF was unlikely to require manned aircraft beyond those in or just entering service. Work on the SR-177RN continued with urgency until August 1957 when, without warning or any consultation with the Admiralty, Sandys announced while on a visit to the WRE at Woomera in Australia that he had now decided to cancel the RN version as well. Lewis Boddington, head of the Naval Air Department at RAE Bedford and a member of Captain Hopkins' Admiralty team, said after the traumatic cancellation that if Sandys had told the Admiralty that he wanted to axe a naval aircraft programme, they would have elected to lose the Buccaneer because the SR-177 was considered so much more important.

Frustratingly, in 1961 Sandys' successor Harold Watkinson criticised the Admiralty and Air Ministry for failing to agree a common strike fighter design that could be used by both the RN and RAF. They had, it was designated SR-177 and had shown significant export potential right up to the moment 4 years earlier when a politician had arbitrarily cancelled it. No one thought to tell Watkinson.

Skeeter

A small helicopter design that originated with Cierva, Saunders-Roe designated it the P.501. Named Skeeter, small numbers were procured for the AAC. The RN procured three in 1949 for evaluation by 705 NAS at Gosport. Only one was used for any length of time until it was damaged by ground resonance, a common problem with early helicopters, in 1952. All three were sold back to Saunders-Roe in 1954. Rotor diameter was 32ft, MTOW 2,100lb and it was powered by a single 180hp Blackburn Bombardier 702 piston engine giving a maximum level speed of 85 knots.

P.531

Originally intended as a turbine-engined replacement for the AAC's Skeeter, the firm had the imagination to design a slightly larger airframe to give greater capability. The first prototype flew in July 1958 powered by a 400shp Blackburn-Turbomeca Turmo de-rated to 325shp. It had a simple airframe riveted from light gauge aluminium alloy sheet except for a thin stainless steel box under the externally-mounted engine. The cabin had accommodation for a pilot in the right-hand seat and an observer to his left and a bench seat for up to three behind them. The canopy structure was welded from aluminium tube and the windscreen panels were of flat glass to minimise optical distortion. All four cabin doors were non-load-bearing and the P.531 could be flown with any or all of them removed to save weight. For most of the trial period P.531s flew with skid undercarriages. Three P.531s, designated P.531-0/N, were evaluated by 700 NAS at Yeovilton from 1959 to 1961. They carried out deck landings on a platform built over the quarterdeck of the frigate *Undaunted* and evaluation of various undercarriage options included landings on a rolling platform built at RAE Bedford. After 1961 P.531s were operated by 771 NAS at Portland for further trials including deck landings on the frigate *Ashanti* to prove its flight deck/hangar design. The three P.531s differed in detail but shared a rotor diameter of 32ft 3in, MTOW was 5,000lb and maximum level speed was 118 knots. Two of the three ditched but were recovered.

Wasp

The Wasp was an operational derivative of the P.531 produced after Saunders-Roe had become a part of the Westland Group. They were manufactured by Fairey, which had also been absorbed into the same group. For the sake of continuity and simplicity, however, the Wasp is described under the Saunders-Roe heading where its design originated.

Two small helicopters were evaluated by the RN for the MATCH role, the Fairey Ultra-light and the Saunders-Roe P.531-0/N and when the latter was selected in 1961 two pre-production aircraft were ordered for trials. The first flew in October 1962, followed by the first production example, designated Wasp HAS 1 in January 1963. MATCH Wasps formed part of their parent ships' anti-submarine

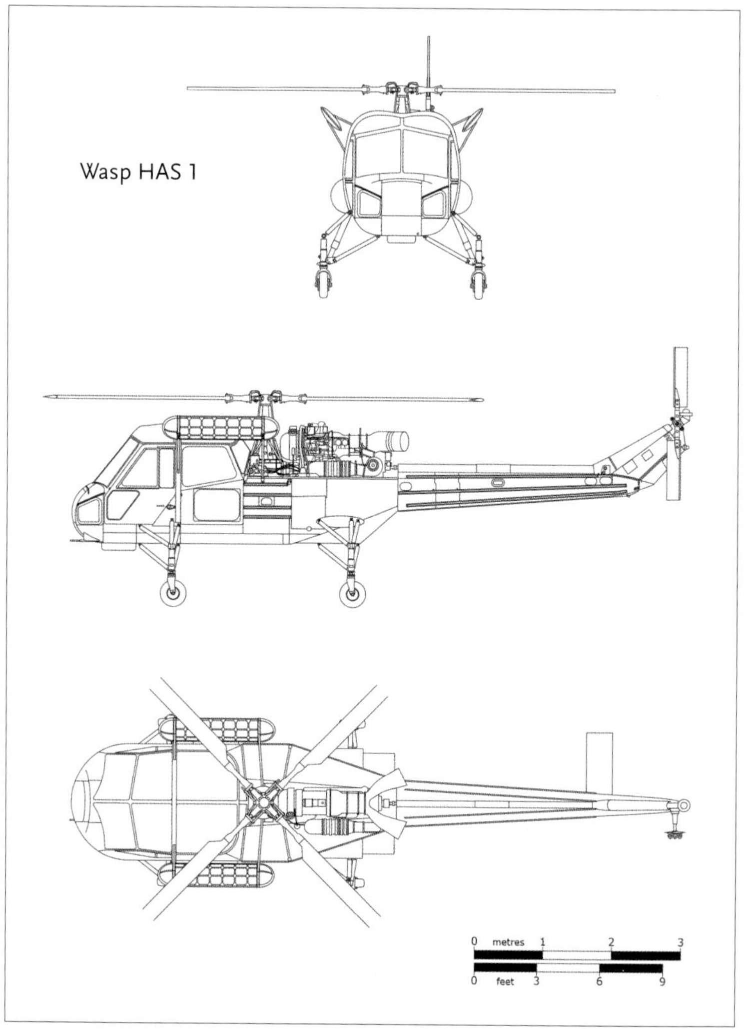

Wasp HAS 1 of *Yarmouth* Flight off Portland.

weapon system, attacking medium-range sonar contacts out to 10nm. They could be armed with a single nuclear depth bomb, up to two homing torpedoes or two depth charges. From 1969 Wasps were equipped to carry the Nord AS-12M wire-guided ASM with the aimer sat in the left-hand seat, giving them the potential to engage small surface targets beyond the range of the parent ships' guns. Wasps also operated effectively from survey ships in support of parties operating ashore and from the ice patrol ship *Endurance*.

Production Wasps differed from the P.531-0/N in having a more powerful engine, four individual undercarriage legs with castoring wheels and a folding tail-boom to fit within the confined hangar space of 'Tribal' class frigates. The distinctive bulged rear cabin doors allowed a stretcher to be carried athwartships on the rear bench seat. When the requirement was written during 1961 it appears that there was no standard specification for a British stretcher; they literally came in a variety of lengths at the whim of the manufacturer and the bulged door was intended to accommodate all but the most extreme examples.

MATCH was a step change from earlier anti-submarine weapons but the Wasp's fuel state, hence endurance, depended on its weapon load. With a nuclear depth bomb or two torpedoes it might only have 20 minutes endurance, enough to fly to the target datum and return with the 200lb minimum landing allowance. Wasp pilots had to react instantly to engine failure since they normally flew at 400ft or less. The skill needed to lower the collective lever, flare, enter auto-rotation and turn into wind before ditching whilst transmitting a MAYDAY call can be imagined, especially if this had to be done on instruments at night in adverse weather. Production Wasps were fitted with rather cumbersome flotation gear comprising panniers above cockpit level held in place by brackets attached to the fuselage. They had the obvious drawback that the cockpit would soon be submerged after a ditching but it kept the airframe afloat for long enough to be salvaged in most cases. The gear added significant weight and in wartime Wasps would have flown without it to carry more fuel.

Two commando helicopter squadrons each operated a single Wasp in the 1960s and 70s, used in the reconnaissance, light observation and communications roles. They were painted green and identified by letters rather than numbers. 845 NAS' Wasp was 'O' and known throughout the squadron as 'Little Oscar'.

Wasp HAS 1 data

Length:	40ft 4in (25ft 9in folded)
Rotor diameter:	32ft 3in (10ft folded)
Height:	8ft 10in
MTOW:	5,300lb
Engine:	One 710shp Bristol (Rolls-Royce) Nimbus 103 shaft turbine
Fuel:	Avcat. Up to 158 gallons
Performance:	Maximum level speed 120 knots Service ceiling 13,400ft
Endurance:	Over 2 hours with maximum fuel
Armament:	One WE-177 nuclear depth bomb; up to two Mark 44 or Mark 46 anti-submarine homing torpedoes; up to two Mark 11 depth charges or up to two Nord AS-12 wire-guided ASM on pylons

The ship's Flight Deck Officer signalling *Falmouth* Flight's Wasp to land.

In addition to the two pre-production aircraft, the RN received ninety-six Wasps. A further batch of thirty was cancelled.

Wasps were operated by 700W NAS, the IFTU, from June 1963 at Culdrose. In March 1964 it became the nucleus of 829 NAS at Portland, the headquarters unit for flights allocated to specific ships. For much of its existence it was the largest naval air squadron with flights deployed all over the world. Wasp pilots were initially trained by 706 NAS at Culdrose but 703 NAS was re-formed at Portland in 1972 to take over the task. It was subsumed into 829 NAS as the Wasp force was run down in the 1980s. They also replaced Dragonflies to give BRNC cadets air experience in the 1970s.

Commando Wasps were operated by 845 and 848 NAS operating from the commando carriers *Albion* and *Bulwark* during the late 1960s and early 1970s, disembarking for periods at RN air stations Sembawang, Culdrose and Yeovilton.

Between 1963 and 1988 Wasp flights operated for varying periods from HM Ships, RFAs and merchant auxiliaries *Achilles*, *Active*, *Ajax*, *Alacrity*, *Amazon*, *Ambuscade*, *Andromeda*, *Antelope*, *Apollo*, *Ardent*, *Arethusa*, *Argonaut*, *Argus*, *Ariadne*, *Arrow*, *Ashanti*, *Aurora*, *Bacchante*, *Berwick*, *Brighton*, *Charybdis*, *Cleopatra*, *Danae*, *Dido*, *Diomede*, *Endurance*, *Engadine*, *Eskimo*, *Euryalus*, *Falmouth*, *Galatea*, *Gurkha*, *Hecate*, *Hecla*, *Herald*, *Hermione*, *Hydra*, *Juno*, *Jupiter*, *Leander*, *Londonderry*, *Lowestoft*, *Minerva*, *Mohawk*, *Naiad*, *Nubian*, *Olna*, *Penelope*, *Phoebe*, *Plymouth*, *Rhyl*, *Rothesay*, *Scylla*, *Sheffield*, *Sirius*, *Tartar*, *Tidepool*, *Vidal*, *Yarmouth*, *Zulu*, *Contender Bezant* and *St Helena*.

Although largely replaced by the Lynx, ten Wasps took part in the South Atlantic War in 1982 and operated in the light communications and casualty evacuation roles as well as their basic MATCH tasking. The two Wasps of *Endurance* Flight together with another from *Plymouth* located the Argentinian submarine *Santa Fe* off South Georgia Island and attacked it with AS-12 missiles, scoring hits on its conning tower which prevented it from diving.

The Wasp HAS 1 was finally withdrawn from RN service on 31 March 1988 after an outstanding career in which had advanced the role of helicopter operations from ships other than carriers for over two decades.

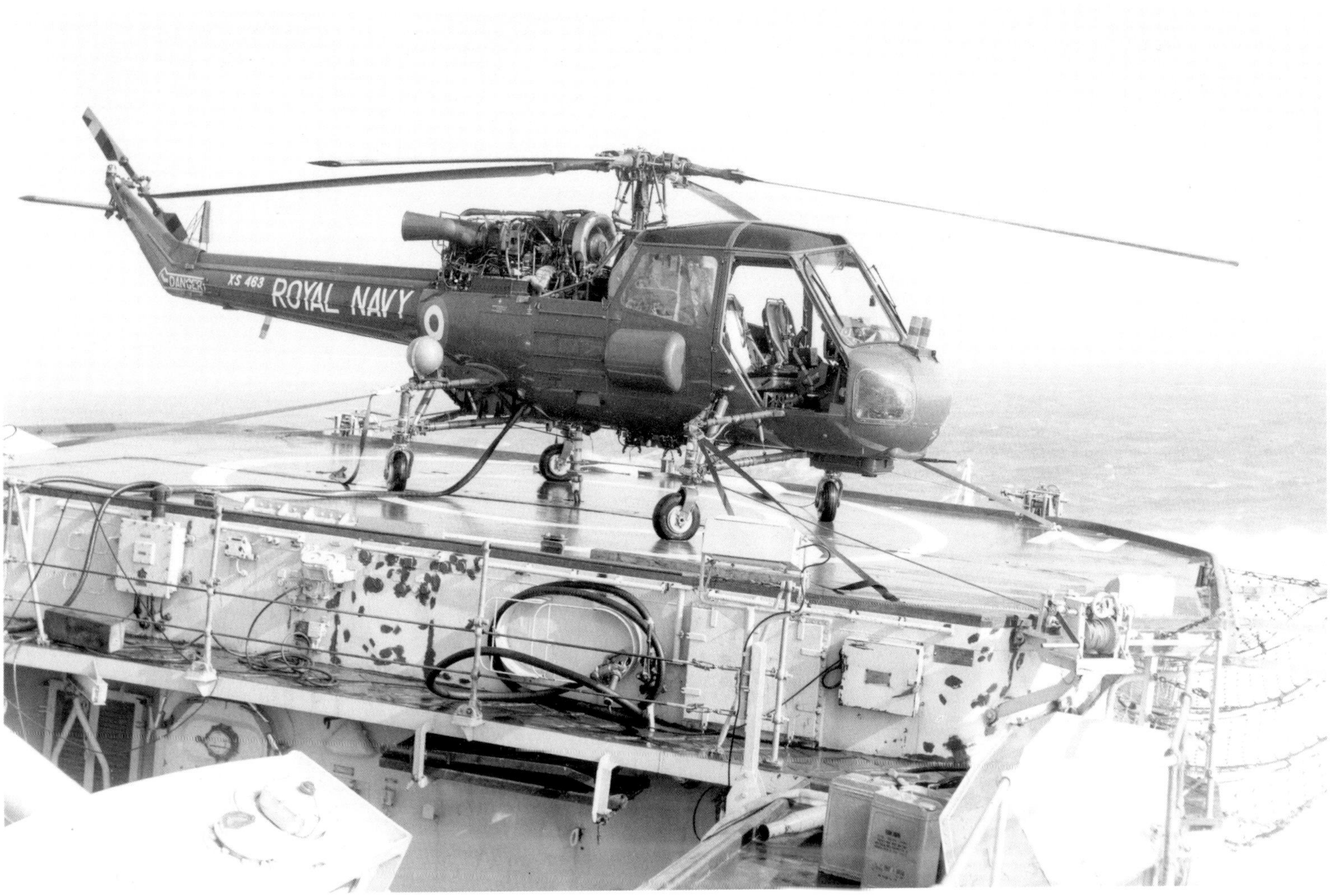

Nubian Flight's Wasp lashed to the frigate's tiny flight deck. Note the absence of flotation gear on the aircraft.

A Scout at RN Air Yard Wroughton in 1974. All Scouts were lent to 3 Commando Brigade Air Squadron by the Army Air Corps and some, like this one, initially retained the word 'Army' rather than 'Royal Marines' on the tail cone. (Nigel Edwards)

Scout

Also developed from the P.531, the Scout closely resembled the Wasp except for its skid undercarriage. Several were transferred from the Army for use by the Royal Marines in 1971 when 3 Commando Brigade Air Squadron moved from Singapore to Coypool on the outskirts of Plymouth. Six were on strength in 1982 and they operated alongside Gazelles with distinction during the South Atlantic War. They were used for reconnaissance, casualty evacuation and light strike roles, the latter armed with Nord SS-11 wire-guided ASM. They were replaced by four Lynx AH 1 helicopters when the unit returned from the South Atlantic. They were returned to the AAC after replacement.

SFECMAS

CT-10

A ground-launched, radio-controlled pilotless target aircraft evolved by this French firm from reverse-engineered German V-1 'flying bombs' captured from the Luftwaffe in 1945. The CT-10 was smaller, 19½ft long rather than 27¼ft and a split tailplane replaced the original. Electronics, IFF and a parachute were installed for remote radio control and recovery and it was powered by a pulse-jet engine based on the original German Argus AS014 which gave 750lb of thrust. It was a simple steel tube with a flap-valve grid at the front which opened to

A B C D E F G H I J K L M N O P Q R S T U V W X Y Z

admit air and closed when ignition took place many times a second to give the distinctive 'doodlebug' sound. The only other components were a fuel inlet valve and a spark plug and it could run on almost any type of fuel. Maximum speed was 280 knots and endurance 40 minutes. It was launched from a ramp with initial acceleration provided by booster rockets which fell away after launch.

CT-10 pilotless target aircraft launch from Marsaxlokk in Malta.

A small RN team was trained to operate CT-10s in France and then based at Hal Far in 1953 with a launching site at Fort Benghaisa at Marsaxlokk to provide targets for the Mediterranean Fleet. Few, if any, were shot down but in fairness the gunnery systems were only permitted to use inert practice rounds rather than live, proximity-fused rounds and only a direct impact would have destroyed the target. Some were lost through control malfunctions, however. They were controlled by RN pilots situated in a control van and offered much more realistic targets than those towed by Sturgeons. On completion of the flight the air vehicle was flown directly over the recovery vessel RFA *Sea Salvor* and the engine stopped by radio signal, a recovery parachute released and it descended slowly into the sea. During the descent the fuel tank was emptied to give extra buoyancy and after recovery the air vehicle was washed, serviced and re-used.

SHORT BROTHERS

The early Naval Short biplanes

Early Short biplanes were frequently rebuilt, some retained their original company designations and some had Admiralty airframe numbers. Frank McClean offered the Admiralty the use of two of his six Gnome-engined pusher Shorts in 1911 with flying instruction for four officers at Eastchurch. The Admiralty subsequently purchased two Shorts, construction numbers S.34 and S.38, and established its own flying school at Eastchurch. S.34 became Naval Aeroplane Number 1 and S.38 Number 2.. In its first weeks in naval service Number 1 became B1, then T1 and then 1 again before being replaced by a new Number 1 in 1913, formerly Short's S.86. Number 2 survived into 1915; its wingspan was 52ft, MTOW 1,540lb and the single 50hp Gnome rotary pusher radial driving a two-bladed, wooden propeller gave a maximum level speed of 35 knots.

Commander C R Samson RN, one of the first four pilots, collaborated with Shorts to develop naval aircraft and had rubber air bags fitted to S.38 to provide buoyancy and Lieutenant A Longmore RN landed successfully with them in place on the Medway off Isle of Grain in December 1911. The aircraft was towed to shore and, after a short period to dry out, took off from the beach and flew back to Eastchurch. In January 1912 Samson flew S.38 to Isle of Grain, landed by the sea wall at Cockleshell Hard from where the aircraft was manhandled over planks across the sea wall onto a lighter from which it was hoisted onto a wooden runway built over the forecastle of the battleship *Africa* moored off Sheerness Dockyard. Half an hour later Samson took off and flew back to Eastchurch successfully. Later S.38 was fitted with a 70hp Gnome which increased its maximum speed to 50 knots. In May 1912 it was loaded onto the runway which had been transferred to *Africa*'s sister-ship *Hibernia* and on 2 May Samson carried out the world's first take-off from a ship under way. She was steaming at 5 knots near Portland. Eleven aircraft similar to S.38 were delivered by 1914 and used as training aircraft but a further thirty-two delivered in 1915/16 were soon deleted.

Naval aeroplane Number 3 delivered in 1911, Short's S.39, was known as the 'Triple Twin' because its two 50hp Gnome rotary engines drove three two-bladed wooden propellers. The nacelle contained two seats side-by-side with dual control; one Gnome was mounted at the rear as a pusher, the other was mounted at the front rotating in the opposite direction to counter gyroscopic effect and drove two wing-mounted tractor propellers through chain gears, that to port being crossed to achieve counter-rotation. Wingspan was 34ft, MTOW 2,100lb and maximum level speed 48 knots. After considerable reconstruction in 1912 it survived until 1916.

Another one-off was nicknamed the 'Tandem-Twin' or, more unkindly, the 'Gnome Sandwich', a reconstructed S.27 delivered in 1912. It had a similar layout to the S.39 but the front Gnome drove a single wooden tractor propeller. Size and performance were also similar but the draught around the pilots was so considerable that it acquired another nickname, the 'Vacuum Cleaner'. It was deleted after the 1913 manoeuvres.

S.41 was a tractor biplane seaplane powered by a single 100hp Gnome pusher radial and fitted with twin floats. The rectangular rear fuselage was covered by doped fabric. It was delivered in 1912 and used in the naval manoeuvres that year. It was modified with a wheeled undercarriage in 1913 and fitted with a 140hp Gnome in 1914. It operated from Eastchurch with continuing modifications until the end of 1915 when it was probably destroyed by fire. Wingspan was 50ft and maximum level speed was 52 knots. Its empty weight was 1,100lb but MTOW details have not survived. The RNAS received five S.41s which operated from Great Yarmouth and Eastchurch.

Short pusher biplane, RN airframe Number 2, being hoisted onto the battleship *Hibernia* in 1912.

Commander Samson flying Number 2 off *Hibernia* on 2 May 1912 in Weymouth Bay.

Naval Aeroplane Number 8, Short's S.42, was a monoplane with a wingspan of 29ft 3in but records of its weight have been lost. It was powered by a single 50hp Gnome rotary and delivered in 1912. A series of repairs followed accidents and it was only used to give instruction in taxi-ing after 1913 before being deleted in 1914.

The single Short S.45 was delivered in 1912 as Naval Aeroplane Number 5. It was used as a single-float seaplane with a 70hp Gnome pusher rotary engine and operated from Port Laing near the northern end of the Forth Bridge during the 1912 manoeuvres but was deleted after capsizing in October.

Short's S.46, evaluated by the RN in 1912, was a monoplane powered by two 70hp Gnome rotary engines in the same tractor/pusher configuration as the 'Tandem Twin' biplane. It was a two-seater with the pilots sat side-by-side and both occupants were exposed to the fierce castor oil (engine lubricant) laden slipstream which earned it the nickname 'Double Dirty'. It operated briefly from Isle of Grain but suffered damage and, despite repairs, it was deleted in 1913. Data about this aircraft has not survived but it was known to have been considered a failure. It was deleted in 1913.

Naval Aeroplane Number 4, Short's S.47, was a two-seat biplane powered by two 50hp Gnome rotary engines, both fitted under a common cowling forward of the cockpit. One drove a two-bladed

'Short 'Triple-Twin'. (Philip Jarrett)

Short 'Tandem-Twin' in 1911.

wooden propeller on the nose and the other drove two two-bladed wooden propellers between the wings by chain-drives. The excessive heat generated by the engines around the cockpit and its effect on the pilots earned it the nickname 'field kitchen'. Wingspan was 34ft, MTOW 2,100lb and maximum level speed was 48 knots. In late 1912 it was used for early W/T experiments with a Rouzet transmitter but it was badly damaged in early 1913 and deleted.

Early Seaplane evolution

Naval Aeroplane Number 19, Short's S.54, was a one-off design delivered to Eastchurch in 1913, the first in a series of fabric-covered two-seat tractor biplanes. The single 140hp Gnome rotary tractor engine gave a maximum level speed of 52 knots. Wingspan was 42ft but records of its MTOW have not been traced. In April 1914 the First Lord of the Admiralty, Winston Churchill, flew in it between Eastchurch and Felixstowe but it was wrecked when it came down in the sea during a war patrol off Felixstowe in December 1914.

Naval Aeroplane Number 42, Short's S.60, had a single 80hp Gnome rotary tractor engine giving a maximum level speed of 57 knots. MTOW was 1,970lb. Converted to a wheeled undercarriage after taking part in the 1914 fleet manoeuvres it was at Eastchurch when war broke out and deployed with Commander Samson's heterogeneous squadron in August. In late September it suffered an engine failure on take-off when being flown by Samson, hit a tree on landing and was found to be beyond repair.

S.79 differed in having a 100hp Gnome rotary giving a maximum level speed of over 60 knots. It was a side-by-side, two-seat biplane with twin floats delivered to Isle of Grain for evaluation in early 1914. Wingspan was 57ft and MTOW 2,100lb. It was used for coastal patrol duties from Calshot but suffered damage landing and was written off in 1915.

Admiralty Type 74 seaplane

Four were delivered to Eastchurch in early 1914 and took part in the Naval Review Flypast in July. A further seventeen were built after the outbreak of war designated by the Admiralty as the Type 74 after the first to be delivered, airframe number 74, Short's S.69. Wingspan was 57ft, MTOW 2,700lb and the 100hp Gnome rotary tractor engines drove two-bladed wooden propellers. Like their predecessors they had twin floats and a small tail float aft. Three Type 74s took part in the strike by aircraft from the seaplane carriers *Riviera* and *Empress* against the German Zeppelin base believed to be at Cuxhaven on Christmas Day 1914, all armed with four 20lb bombs. None knowingly located their target but one successfully returned to *Riviera* and was recovered. The other two failed to locate *Empress* and were abandoned after landing on the sea. Their crews were rescued by the submarine *E-11*.

Type 74 taxi-ing to shore.

Short Folder.

Admiralty 'Folders'

Two aircraft that resembled the Type 74 were the earliest naval aircraft to have folding wings for stowage in warship hangars. Width was reduced from 56ft to 15ft. The first, airframe number 81, was built specifically for the 1913 fleet manoeuvres for which the cruiser *Hermes* was modified to operate seaplanes. It embarked on 18 July 1914 equipped with a W/T transmitter and operated with some success from *Hermes* but was wrecked off Isle of Grain in 1914. The second Folder operated from both *Hermes* and *Riviera* after the outbreak of war but went down in *Hermes* when she was torpedoed and sunk by *U-27* off the Ruylingen Bank in the Straits of Dover on 31 October 1914.

Four repeat Folders, designated Type 81, were delivered from May 1914 with 160hp Gnome rotary tractor engines driving two-bladed wooden propellers to give a maximum level speed of 69 knots. On 28 July 1914 one of them, number 121, was the first British aircraft to get airborne with a torpedo and release it successfully. This was not yet an operational capability because simply getting airborne with the weapon nearly exceeded the aircraft's limits. Three aircraft from this batch were

Type 166 on the fore-deck of *Ark Royal* at Kephalo in 1915

embarked in *Engadine* for the Cuxhaven strike on Christmas Day 1914. One failed to start and took no part in the strike; the other two failed to locate their targets. One was rescued by the destroyer *Lurcher* and towed home after alighting on the sea. Another came down short of fuel and its crew were rescued by *E-11*. One was subsequently used in successful operations against the German cruiser *Königsberg* in East Africa in 1915.

S.81 'Gun Carrier'

Designed to test the 1½pdr Vickers semi-automatic gun, the single S.81 was an aberration in Short's steady seaplane development. Wingspan was 56ft, MTOW 3,100lb and the single 160hp Gnome rotary pusher engine gave a maximum level speed of 69 knots. Only the wings, cockpit nacelle and tailplane were fabric-covered and the gun was mounted at the bow with the gunlayer in the front cockpit and the pilot in the rear. It had twin floats and a tail float. During gun trials in 1915 it was said that the recoil on firing was so great that the aircraft stopped dead and fell by 500ft. Whether this was entirely true or not, the trials were clearly not successful the S.81 was modified with a dynamo and searchlight for night operations. Later in 1915 a 6pdr recoilless gun was evaluated but this, too, proved a failure and the aircraft was deleted.

Admiralty Type 135

Only two were built, the first delivered in 1914 with a 135hp Salmson water-cooled radial engine and the second with a 200hp Salmson. These engines were alternatively identified as Canton-Unne after the surnames of their designers. The large radiator in front of the pilot's cockpit was a distinctive feature of the design that was replicated in many Short seaplanes that followed. Wingspan was 54ft 6in and MTOW 3,700lb. The first example had a maximum level speed of 53 knots; the second 57 knots. Both took part in the Cuxhaven Raid on Christmas Day 1914 operating from *Riviera* and both survived. The second was embarked in *Ark Royal* when she sailed from Sheerness for the Dardanelles in February 1915. It was regarded as her best aircraft and the only one capable of operation in adverse weather. It was written off in April 1915 after suffering action damage.

Admiralty Type 166

Evolved from the Type 135 and intended to carry a 14in torpedo weighing 810lb, wingspan was extended to 57ft 3in in order to bear the extra weight and the 200hp Salmson radial engine had a bulky radiator in front of the pilot. The wings could be folded for carrier stowage reducing the width to 16ft. The main floats were typical wooden pontoon-like structures spaced apart by steel tubes arched in the centre to carry the torpedo. Shorts built six Type 166s but in 1916 a further batch of twenty was built by Westland under licence. These were not fitted for torpedoes but could carry three 112lb bombs instead. The observer's cockpit was fitted for a single 0.303in Lewis gun. Type 166s operated from *Ark Royal* off Salonika in 1916, 'A' Squadron at Thasos and from Calshot.

'Nile' Pusher Seaplane

Short's S.80 pusher biplane was ordered by Frank McClean in 1913 and fitted with floats for an airborne expedition down the Nile in 1914. Wingspan was 67ft, MTOW 3,600lb and it had dual controls. The 140hp Gnome rotary engine gave a maximum level speed of 52 knots. After the expedition it was crated at Khartoum for return to Eastchurch where it was requisitioned by the Admiralty in August and re-engined with a 100hp Gnome but when found to be underpowered it was deleted in November.

Admiralty Types 827 and 830

These types shared a common airframe but were ordered with different engines in June 1914. Half of the first batch of twelve had 135hp

A Type 827 operating in South Africa, hence the warm sea and lack of handlers' clothing.

Salmson engines and the other half 150hp Sunbeam Nubian water-cooled engines, both driving two-bladed, wooden propellers. Those with the Sunbeam engine were identified by the Admiralty as the Type 827; those with the Salmson as the Type 830. Both resembled the Type 166 but were slightly smaller since they were not intended to carry a torpedo. They were among the first types to be put into large-scale production in 1914 and some remained in use until the Armistice. Production amounted to 19 Type 830s but the Sunbeam engine was standardised and at least 107 Type 827s were built by Shorts and subcontractors. Wings could be folded for carrier stowage.

Type 827 data

Length:	35ft 3in
Wingspan:	53ft 11in (16ft folded)
Height:	13ft 6in
MTOW:	3,400lb
Engine:	One 150shp Sunbeam Nubian water-cooled engine
Fuel:	Avgas. 35 gallons
Performance:	Maximum level speed 54 knots Service ceiling not recorded
Endurance:	3½ hours
Armament:	112lb or 20lb bombs could be carried on racks under the fuselage. One 0.303in Lewis gun on flexible mounting for the observer

One Type 830 operated from the seaplane carrier *Ben-my-Chree* and aircraft of both types operated from Great Yarmouth, Calshot, Killingholme and Dundee on coastal patrols and with RNAS units in East Africa including the improvised seaplane carriers *Manica*, *Himalaya* and *Laconia*. Several operated in Mesopotamia and as part of the Otranto patrol as late as 1917.

One of the Great Yarmouth 827s attempted to bomb German warships in April 1916 as they bombarded Lowestoft. Those deployed to East Africa operated successfully in the photographic reconnaissance role and covered the British landings at Lindi, Sudi Bay, Kilwa and Kisiju. On completion they were given to Belgian forces. Those deployed to Mesopotamia operated from Basra but found conditions too hot for them to get airborne. At least two were fitted with 'home-made' wheeled undercarriages and flew successfully with them. Two flew bombing missions against Turkish troops advancing against Kut al Imara in December 1915. A few examples survived until November 1918.

Admiralty Type 184

In 1914 the Admiralty contracted Short Brothers to design a seaplane for embarked operations capable of carrying a torpedo. The result was a two-seat biplane powered by a 225hp Sunbeam Mohawk engine with a massive radiator blocking the pilot's view ahead. It had twin floats and a tail float with a water rudder. The fuselage and wings were made of wood but the undercarriage and interplane struts were made of faired steel tubing. The wing trailing edges were shaped with wire which produced a characteristic scalloped appearance under the tension of doped fabric. The main floats were wooden pontoons 16ft long and 2ft 10in across and the single torpedo was carried on crutches between

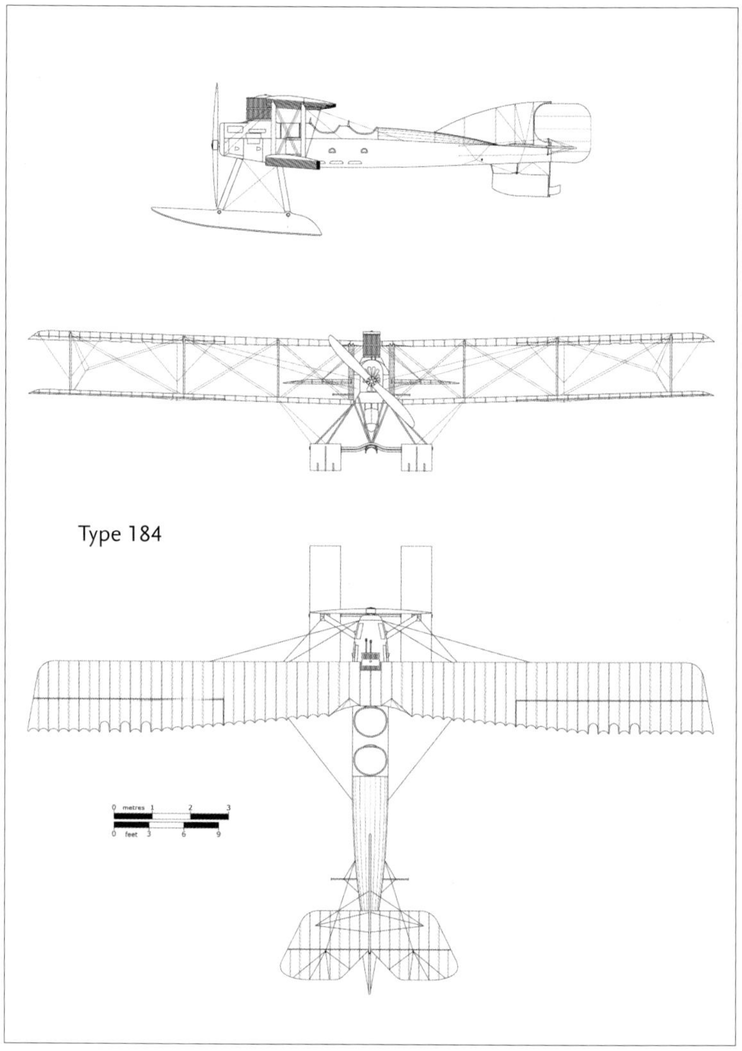

Type 184

them. There were small floats under the wingtips fabricated from steel rings covered in balloon fabric. It had folding wings. The first aircraft, number 184, was delivered in 1915 and this became its Admiralty type number. Shorts lacked the capacity to produce 184s in the numbers the Admiralty wanted and many were built by subcontractors. Early shortages of working drawings meant that subcontractors' draughtsmen had to start by measuring an actual aircraft to produce them quickly.

Despite being fitted with one of the most powerful engines in existence, Type 184 performance with a torpedo was marginal. Fuel had to be limited and even then take-off was only possible with the engine running perfectly from a calm sea surface with a slight breeze. Later Type 184s had 240hp Renault or 260hp Sunbeam engines which improved the maximum level speed by 10 knots and nearly doubled the service ceiling but performance with a heavy weapon load was never good, especially in hot conditions. Other improvements included a bomb rack under the fuselage mounted high above the floats to keep bombs clear of spray on take-off and a Scarff ring mounting for the observer's gun. Some late Type 184s had 275hp Sunbeam Maori engines and one was modified into a prototype single-seat bomber designated the Type D which could carry nine 56lb bombs hung by their noses in a bomb bay. Its evaluation was unsuccessful and no more were built.

A Type 184 being lowered into the River Dart from *Riviera.* (Philip Jarrett)

Admiralty Type 184 data

Length:	40ft 7½in
Wingspan:	63ft 6¼in (16ft folded)
Height:	13ft 6in
MTOW:	5,100lb
Engine:	One 225hp Sunbeam water-cooled engine driving a two-bladed wooden propeller
Fuel:	Avgas. 80 gallons
Performance:	Maximum level speed 66 knots Service ceiling 5,700ft. 8 minutes 2,000ft
Endurance:	up to 4½ hours
Armament:	One 0.303in Lewis gun for the observer in aft cockpit. One 14in torpedo on crutches between the floats; alternatively one 520lb, four 100lb or three 65lb bombs could be carried on the bomb rack under the fuselage

Admiralty figures show 827 Type 184s were delivered to the RNAS between 1915 and 1919. Late orders were cancelled and some aircraft completed after the Armistice were retained by their manufacturers and either scrapped or sold to export customers.

Type 184s operated from the seaplane carriers *Ben-my-Chree*, *Raven II*, *Anne*, *Campania*, *Empress*, *Engadine*, *Furious*, *Nairana*, *Pegasus*, *Riviera*, *Vindex* and *City of Oxford*. They also operated from the cruisers *Arethusa* and *Aurora*.

Ashore, Type 184s operated from Bembridge, Calshot, Cattewater, Dover, Dundee, Felixstowe, Fishguard, Great Yarmouth, Hornsea, Houton Bay, Killingholme, Lee-on-Solent, Newhaven, Newlyn, Portland, Scilly Isles, Scapa Flow, Seaton Carew, South Shields, Strath Beg, Torquay, Westgate, Cherbourg, Dunkirk, Otranto, Taranto, Santa Maria, Mudros, Suda Bay, Syra, Alexandria, Port Said and Basra.

Type 184s made history on two occasions. The first was on 12 August 1915 during the Dardanelles Campaign when an aircraft from *Ben-my-Chree* flown by Flight Commander C H K Edmonds RNAS took off with a torpedo in the Gulf of Xeros. He flew without an observer and limited fuel to save weight and flew across the isthmus at 800ft to Injeh Burnu where he saw a Turkish steamship and glided down to launch his torpedo from 15ft at a range of 300 yards. It detonated abreast the main mast and he believed that he saw it settle in shallow water but in fact the vessel had been shelled by a British submarine on the surface a day earlier and left partially beached. On 17 August Edmonds carried out another attack against Turkish shipping and his torpedo hit a vessel off Ak Bashi Liman. He left it badly damaged and on fire but it was eventually towed to Constantinople for repair. On the same day another 184 sighted and attacked an enemy tug in False Bay successfully. These strikes proved the concept of torpedo-attack for the future but they could not yet be considered fully operational.

The other historic flight took place on 31 May 1916 when number 8359 was launched from *Engadine* at 1508 to track the German fleet during the opening phase of the Battle of Jutland; the first time that an

Type 184s in *Riviera*'s hangar. (Philip Jarrett)

Left: The Short Type 184, airframe number 8359, flown by Flight Lieutenant F J Rutland RNAS from *Engadine* during the Battle of Jutland.

aircraft had taken part in a battle at sea. It was flown by Flight Lieutenant F J Rutland RNAS with Assistant Paymaster G S Trewin RNAS as observer. *Engadine* was attached to the BCF and enemy positions, courses and speeds were transmitted successfully to *Engadine* but after 40 minutes the engine suffered a broken petrol feed pipe. Rutland alighted, repaired the pipe with a piece of rubber tubing cut from his lifejacket and took off again. Although willing to carry on he was ordered to return and was hoisted in at 1600.

Five Short 184s were sent to Mesopotamia in early 1916 for operations from the River Tigris during which they dropped supplies to the beleaguered British garrison at Kut. In home waters Type 184s were used extensively on coastal anti-submarine patrols and on strikes against German submarine bases at Zeebrugge and Ostend. A number were still in service at the end of 1918 and some of the newer aircraft took part in British operations against the Bolsheviks in Northern Russia; deployed to Archangel in *Pegasus*. They were also deployed to the Baltic in *Vindictive* but operated from shore bases when they got there, bombing Bolshevik positions in Kronstadt. Some Type 184s remained in use on mine clearance operations through 1919, others were retained in storage but in 1922 the survivors were scrapped.

Type 320

A long-range, two-seat torpedo-armed biplane with twin floats designed in 1916, wingspan was 75ft, 16ft folded, and MTOW 7,021lb. The single 225lb Sunbeam Cossack water-cooled engine drove a two-bladed wooden propeller to give a maximum level speed of 68 knots. Armament comprised a single 1,000lb Mark IX torpedo or two 230lb bombs and a 0.303in Lewis gun on a Scarff ring for the observer. Admiralty records show that 137 were ordered but ten might have been cancelled. They operated from Calshot, Felixstowe, Killingholme, Great Yarmouth and Isle of Grain in the UK and from Otranto, Brindisi and Calafrana in the Mediterranean. Two examples were used by the Mediterranean torpedo school at Calafrana in Malta in 1918.

310hp Seaplane Type B

Also known as the North Sea Scout, it resembled the Type 184 but had a deeper fuselage and a 310hp Sunbeam Cossack engine. The sole prototype was evaluated at Isle of Grain but details do not seem to have survived. Its armament was a 5pdr recoilless Davis gun in the after cockpit operated by the observer who also had a Lewis gun for defence. The Davis gun proved to be a failure and no production orders followed.

Bomber

Designed in 1915 to meet an Admiralty requirement for a shore-based, single-engine, two-seat bomber capable of carrying six 112lb bombs giving an interim capability until deliveries of the Handley Page 0/100 began, the Bomber's design was based on the Type 184 and the prototype was built alongside the first production 184s. It differed in having a four-wheeled undercarriage and the pilot was moved to the rear cockpit with the observer in front of him, an arrangement criticised at Isle of Grain. Production aircraft reversed them to put the pilot in front. The wings were based on the Type 166 seaplane and could be folded. Early Bombers had fuselages like the Type 184 but later aircraft were longer to improve longitudinal control. Unusually, they were known within the RNAS as Short Bombers and not given an Admiralty type number.

Bomber data

Length:	45ft
Wingspan:	85ft (16ft folded)
Height:	15ft
MTOW:	6,800lb
Engine:	One 225hp Sunbeam water-cooled engine driving a two-bladed wooden propeller
Fuel:	Avgas. 80 gallons
Performance:	Maximum level speed 68 knots Service ceiling 9,500ft. 22 minutes to 6,500ft
Endurance:	up to 6 hours
Armament:	One 0.303in Lewis gun for the observer in aft cockpit. Racks under the inner, lower wings could carry four 230lb or up to eight 112lb bombs

Short Brothers built forty and subcontractors a further fifty-eight.

The first production aircraft were delivered to 7 (Naval) Squadron, part of 5 Wing RNAS at Coudekerque in late 1916 and four aircraft attacked docks at Ostend in November. The Admiralty had wanted 3 Wing RNAS at Luxeuil-les-Bans to be equipped with fifteen Short Bombers and twenty Sopwith 1½ Strutters but an urgent appeal was made by the RFC for aircraft prior to the Somme offensive. Fifteen Bombers were transferred with a number of 1½ Strutters, postponing plans for 3 Wing until the autumn. The Wing eventually formed with 1½ Strutters and no Bombers.

Experimental Scout Seaplanes

Several scout seaplane designs were proposed in 1917 and some were built as prototypes. The first was a two-seat biplane with a 200hp Sunbeam Afridi engine evaluated at Isle of Grain in 1918 but by then the day of the seaplane fighter had passed. Records of its performance have not survived.

The last wartime Short seaplane design was the two-seat N.2B with a single 275hp Sunbeam Maori engine. Two prototypes were built

Short Bomber of 5 (Naval) Squadron.

A B C D E F G H I J K L M N O P Q R S T U V W X Y Z

Sturgeon TT 2 being given the 'cut' landing on *Illustrious.*

for evaluation at Isle of Grain in 1918 where they demonstrated a maximum level speed of 80 knots. Wingspan was 55ft, MTOW 4,922lb and they had a Lewis gun on a Scarff ring for the observer. Two 230lb bombs could be carried on racks under the wings they were outclassed by wheeled fighters and soon discarded.

Shirl

Proposed as a single-seat, carrier-borne, torpedo-attack biplane with a wheeled undercarriage, three prototypes were built one of which was evaluated at Isle of Grain in 1918 and found to be slower and less manoeuvrable than the Sopwith Cuckoo. The others carried out torpedo-drop trials in the Firth of Forth but all development ceased after the Armistice. The third prototype had a wingspan of 52ft, MTOW of 5,951lb and the 360hp Rolls-Royce Eagle water-cooled engine driving a two-bladed wooden propeller gave a maximum level speed of 82 knots. Flotation gear was fitted over the undercarriage.

Sturgeon

Designed initially to meet Admiralty requirement S.6/43 in 1943 for a high-speed TBR aircraft for operation from *Malta* class fleet carriers but the torpedo requirement was deleted and the revised Specification S.11/43 sought an aircraft with a smaller internal bomb bay capable of carrying a single 1,000lb, two 500lb bombs or four 250lb depth charges. Four 0.5in front guns were to be fitted under the nose and up to sixteen 3in RP were to be carried on zero-length launchers under the wings. If bombs were not carried internally, a 180-gallon fuel tank could be carried in the bomb bay and ASV radar was to be fitted in a nose radome. In the reconnaissance role the Sturgeon was to carry two F.52 and one F.24 camera, all mounted vertically in the rear fuselage. Originally designated S.38 by Short Brothers, it was later re-designated SA.1. The Admiralty named it Sturgeon following the 'aggressive fish' theme of earlier strike aircraft and the Sturgeon S 1 emerged as a mid-wing monoplane of Alclad monocoque construction but the ailerons, elevators and rudder were fabric covered. The Admiralty accepted that two engines were required to achieve the high speed it wanted and two Rolls-Royce Merlins were selected. The centre-wing section formed the roof of the bomb bay with four flexible self-sealing fuel tanks above it. The power-folding wings were hinged outboard of the engine nacelles to lie flush along the fuselage sides. The pilot occupied a self-contained cockpit at the wing leading edge and the observer and TAG occupied a separate cabin aft of the wing. No TAG was carried in the reconnaissance role because of the weight of the cameras aft of the C of G. Two prototype S 1s were built and a structural test airframe. First flight was in 1946 and service trials included deck-landing evaluation on *Illustrious* during May 1947. Further trials in 1948 with 703 NAS included deck landings on *Implacable* and catapult launches at various weights. 'Winkle' Brown described the Sturgeon as a sturdy and robust aircraft that revealed no problems in its deck-landing assessment with both engines. It had few vices and the view ahead was excellent but, even with contra-rotating propellers and the engines as close to the fuselage as possible, he reported that a single-engined, asymmetric approach would not be safe. Nevertheless the type was cleared for normal carrier operation by day.

Despite the prototype's success the Admiralty was forced to make economies and the S 1 was not ordered into production. There was, however, a pressing need for a fast target tug capable of carrier operation, the Sturgeon was ideal and Specification Q.1/46 was drawn up around it. Some changes had to be made to the fuselage but the existing jigs could be used and the wings, engines and tailplane were retained for the new variant designated Sturgeon TT 2. There were two prototypes, one modified from an S 1 prototype during build. The first TT 2 flight was in 1948 with the most obvious change being an elongated nose to house the Vinten camera that filmed shell bursts from throw-off shoots in which the ships' directors aimed at the target aircraft but the guns were pointed 20 degrees off it. Analysis of the film revealed how accurate the gunnery systems were but from a pilot's perspective there was always the worry that the throw-off switch might not be in the correct position when fire was opened! Such shoots could not be described as popular. The TT 2 usually flew with a crew of two; pilot and aircrewman, the latter operating the Miles power-driven winch from a new position aft of the wings.

The TT 2 was described as easy and pleasant to fly by A&AEE pilots and it was cleared for carrier operations after deck-landing trials on *Illustrious* during May 1949. To fit on carrier lifts, the long nose was folded downwards and propellers turned to the minimum width position after the wings were folded. During modification to TT 2 standard the airflow over the cooling duct entries in the inner wing was modified and the change improved low-speed handling sufficiently for experienced pilots in current deck-landing practice to be cleared to carry out asymmetric landings. The TT 2 was required to tow both 32ft and 16 ft winged targets; 4ft and 2ft low-drag sleeves and the winch was capable of providing a tow length of 6,000ft.

In 1951 the RN introduced improved radar gunlaying systems and the requirement for throw-off shoots ended. In hindsight it seems strange that the requirement for the Vinten camera in the extended nose lapsed at about the time TT 2s entered service but this could not have been predicted at the time of the re-design. Sturgeons did embark in carriers, especially in the Mediterranean, for short periods but by the mid-1950s the deck-landing requirement was no longer considered to be important. Shorts were instructed to simplify the aircraft and offered the Sturgeon TT 3 in which all carrier equipment was removed and a new, shorter, nose similar to that of the S 1 was fitted. No new TT 3s were built but nineteen TT 2s were converted from 1954 onwards, all of which operated with 728 NAS at Hal Far until the type was withdrawn from service in 1958. All the surviving examples were scrapped.

Sturgeon TT 2 data

Length:	48ft 11in
Wingspan:	59ft 11in (20ft between outer propeller tips when folded)
Height:	13ft 2½in
MTOW:	22,050lb
Engine:	Two 2.080hp Rolls-Royce Merlin 140 driving six-bladed contra-props
Fuel:	Avgas. 410 gallons
Performance:	Maximum level speed 320 knots (220 knots towing a 32 foot winged target) Service ceiling 35,700ft
Endurance:	Up to 3¼ hours including one hour towing a target
Armament:	None

Short built twenty-nine Sturgeons of which two were S 1 prototypes, two were TT 2 prototypes (one of which was converted from the third S 1 prototype in build), twenty-three TT 2s and two were SB.3 anti-submarine prototypes.

Between 1951 and 1958 Sturgeons served with 703, 771 and 728 NAS at Ford and Hal Far. 728 NAS provided targets for a range of trials and live firings in the ranges off Malta and was the largest operator of the type.

The most bizarre development of the type was the Short SB.3, conceived as a stopgap anti-submarine aircraft to meet Admiralty Requirement NA 9 in 1948. Two prototypes were built retaining the basic Sturgeon airframe but the Merlin engines were replaced by two 1,475shp Armstrong Siddeley Mamba turboprops with four-bladed propellers. The forward fuselage was completely remodelled to accommodate two observers in a cabin forward of and below the pilot with a radome containing ASV 15 radar underneath it. It flew for the first time in 1950 but company test pilots found that the Mambas' downward-directed jet pipes had a serious destabilising effect; the Sturgeon's good handling qualities were lost and it proved difficult to trim, especially with one engine idling. Because of this no full assessment of the SB.3 was ever carried out by the A&AEE and the second prototype never even flew. Both examples were broken up to provide spare parts for TT 3 conversions in 1951.

Seamew

In 1948 the threat posed by the expanding Soviet submarine fleet led the Admiralty to issue Specification M.123 for a simple but rugged anti-submarine aircraft that could operate from CVEs as the Fairey Swordfish Mark III had done. Short's SB.6 design, later named Seamew, was accepted and a contract for two prototypes was placed in 1952. It was a basic, two-seat, single-engined aircraft with a fixed undercarriage. The radome for the ASV-19B radar was fitted forward of the weapons bay in the space that would normally have been occupied by the nose oleo and so it had a tail-wheel layout. It did, however, have power-folding wings which were hinged to lie flat along the fuselage sides when folded. Both cockpits had an excellent view for deck landing and visual searches. First flight was in August 1953 and from the outset the Seamew proved to be a very difficult aircraft to fly with controls overbalanced and badly harmonised. There was also a pronounced nose-

Seamew AS 1. (Guy Warner)

down attitude with flaps fully deployed and insufficient elevator control at low speed to correct it. The prototype was damaged during its first attempted landing. None of the attempts to resolve the problems proved satisfactory. The airframe was stressed for dives at up to 325 knots but test pilots found it impossible to exceed 280 knots at full power in a vertical dive.

The second Seamew flew in 1954 fitted with operational equipment and trials included a deck-landing evaluation on *Bulwark* during 1955. The RAF became interested and the first production contract included equal numbers of aircraft for the RN and RAF with deck-landing equipment deleted from the latter designated MR 2. The first Seamew AS 1s were delivered to 700 NAS for trials in 1956 and two carried out carrier trials in *Warrior* making 200 take-offs and landings including catapult launches. By then the intention was to issue the type to the RNVR air squadrons as an Avenger replacement but the 1957 Defence Review disbanded them and the Seamew project was terminated.

Seamew AS 1 data

Length:	41ft
Wingspan:	55ft (22ft folded)
Height:	13ft 5in
MTOW:	15,000lb
Engine:	One 1,590shp Armstrong Siddeley ASM-6 Mamba turboprop
Fuel:	Avcat. 360 gallons
Performance:	Maximum level speed 205 knots Service ceiling 20,000ft. Two minutes to 3,000ft
Endurance:	Up to 4 hours
Armament:	Internal weapons bay could be loaded with one Mark 30 homing torpedo or combinations of up to four 250lb depth charges and 20 sonobuoys. Hardpoints under each wing for three 3in RP

Shorts built two prototype Seamews, one structural test airframe and twenty-four to AS 1 standard, of which only nineteen were delivered to the RN at Lossiemouth where they were mothballed in 1957 and then sold to a local scrap dealer. Of the twenty-four AS 1s, fourteen were begun as MR 2s but converted to AS 1s when the RAF cancelled its order. One other Seamew was completed as far as running its engine at Belfast but was never delivered.

Seamews only served with 700 NAS for a brief period between the end of 1956 and the beginning of 1957. The Seamew certainly adds weight to the theory that if a requirement specifies cheap mediocrity the result will almost certainly not be impressive and it is difficult to understand why development lasted as long as it did.

SIKORSKY

Hoverfly

The first practical military helicopter, the Sikorsky R-4, was developed for the US Army but a number were transferred to the UK under Lend-Lease arrangements from 1944. Basic training was provided for an initial handful of RN pilots in the USA and early deliveries were shared between the RN and the RAF. Initially R-4s were named Gadfly in British service but Hoverfly was substituted in 1945. The largest number operated by the RN were to USAAF R-4B-S1 standard designated Hoverfly Mark I in British service. It was a two-seat, dual control helicopter with a single three-bladed main rotor and a three-bladed tail rotor. It had a single 185hp Warner Scarab air-cooled engine and a fixed, tail-wheel undercarriage. The fuselage comprised fabric covered chrome-molybdenum steel tubing except for the tail pylon which was left uncovered. The cockpit was extensively glazed with engine air intakes aft of it. Unlike in a fixed-wing aircraft, the first pilot sat on the right and each of the two pilots had a cyclic pitch stick that resembled a fixed-wing control column and rudder pedals but there was only a single collective pitch lever, with its twist throttle grip, situated between the seats. Instruments were fitted in a line on a horizontal bracket in front of the pilots and the aircraft could be flown with or without doors in place. The Hoverfly I was distinctly underpowered but the RN was sufficiently impressed by it to purchase the Hoverflies that had been delivered under Lend-Lease for use in a series of trials and evaluations at sea and ashore until 1951. In addition to Mark Is, the RN received a small batch of improved models designated R-6A in the USA and Hoverfly Mark II in Britain. These arrived in 1949 and had an improved, streamlined, metal-covered fuselage; a more powerful 345hp engine and other detail improvements including a combined instrument and switch panel between the two pilots' seats.

Hoverflies formed the initial equipment of 705 NAS at Gosport and played a significant part in developing the techniques used to instruct pilots in the intricacies of helicopter flight including hovering, fast stops, instrument flying and rescue techniques. Hoverflies also took part in trials from a helicopter platform fitted to the frigate *Helmsdale*.

A float-fitted Hoverfly of 771 NAS on a slipway at Portland.

A B C D E F G H I J K L M N O P Q R S T U V W X Y Z

Hoverfly Mark I data

Length:	35ft 5in
Rotor diameter:	38ft (12ft folded)
Height:	12ft 5in
MTOW:	2,535lb
Engine:	One 180hp Warner Super Scarab R-550-1 air-cooled radial engine
Fuel:	Avgas. 20 gallons
Performance:	Maximum level speed 65 knots Service ceiling 8,000ft. 45 minutes to 8,000ft
Endurance:	Up to 2 hours
Armament:	None

The RN received forty-eight Hoverflies, some of them for only short periods for a particular trial or evaluation. This total included a prototype, seven development helicopters and thirty-six Hoverfly Mark Is. The last batch comprised four Hoverfly Mark IIs plus a single development example used as a source of spare parts.

Between 1945 and 1951 Hoverflies operated with 703, 705 and 771 NAS as well as the RN training element at Floyd Bennet Field in the USA.

The first ship to be fitted with a helicopter platform was the US tanker *Bunker Hill* in 1943 and landings were performed to prove their feasibility. Subsequently a 90ft by 40ft platform was fitted to the SS *Daghestan* and landings were made on her off the US East Coast. After these she embarked two R-4s and sailed for the UK as part of an Atlantic convoy. One RN, two RAF and one USCG pilot were embarked but bad weather limited flying. The potential was recognised, however, and in September 1946 Lieutenant Alan Bristow RN landed a Hoverfly on *Helmsdale* for the first time to initiate a series of trials connected with anti-submarine warfare. A Hoverfly landed on the battleship *Vanguard* in February 1947, the first time a helicopter had landed on a major British warship. Hoverflies of 771 NAS were used for a variety of fleet requirements tasks including acting as targets for ships' radar calibration, photography, light communications and trials to expand knowledge of helicopter operations. Evaluations of the SAR role included carrying a casualty on an externally-mounted stretcher with a cover over it to give the victim a measure of protection from the airflow. With the casualty the Hoverfly had to be flown by a single pilot.

S-55 Whirlwind

Westland Aircraft had signed a licence production agreement for the S-55 Whirlwind in 1950 but took several years to establish its own production line, a task made more complicated by the decision to use a British engine. However, the Admiralty regarded evaluation of helicopters' potential in the ASW and amphibious roles as urgent and arrangements were made to transfer Sikorsky-built S-55 Whirlwinds from the USN to the RN under the MDAP. The type's first flight had been in 1949 and it entered USN service at the end of 1950. The aircraft supplied to the RN were taken from new USN production batches and comprised two distinct sub-variants. The first was designated HRS-2 by the USN and HAR 21 by the RN. It was powered by a 600hp Pratt & Whitney Wasp R-1340-40 air-cooled radial piston engine and had bench seating along the cabin sides capable of accommodating eight fully-equipped marines with self-sealing fuel tanks under the cabin floor. The second was designated HO4S-3 by the USN and HAS 22 by the RN. It was powered by a single 700hp Wright Cyclone R-1300-3 air-cooled radial piston engine and was equipped with AN/AQS-4 active dipping sonar which displayed target information for the operator on a paper trace which showed range, range-rate and bearing. The HAS 22's one weakness was its reliance on manual hovering which was impractical at night and they were usually flown with two pilots on A/S sorties which limited the amount of fuel that could be carried, especially in hot conditions.

The S-55 had a single three-bladed main rotor and an anti-torque tail rotor at the end of a tail-boom powered by a drive shaft off the main rotor gearbox. The heavy piston engine was mounted at an angle under the cockpit, forward of the cabin with drive shaft running to the main rotor gearbox which was situated over the cabin at approximately the centre of gravity. There were dual controls but the S-55 could be flown by a single pilot sat in the starboard seat; the cockpit area was extensively glazed with pilot access through large sliding side windows. A winch was fitted over the large, sliding cargo door on the starboard side operated by an aircrewman in the helicopter air rescue role.

Whirlwind HAS 22 data

Length:	42ft 2in
Rotor diameter:	53ft (13ft folded)
Height:	13ft 4in
MTOW:	7,900lb
Engine:	One 700hp Wright Cyclone R-1300-3 air cooled radial
Fuel:	Avgas. 179 gallons
Performance:	Maximum level speed 95 knots. 8 minutes to 5,000ft
Endurance:	3 hours
Armament:	None when fitted with sonar

The RN received ten Whirlwind HAR 21s and fifteen HAS 22s from the USN under MDAP arrangements between 1952 and 1953. One further example, basically a HAR 21, formerly used as a pattern by Westland, was transferred to the RN, raising the overall total to twenty-six Sikorsky-built Whirlwinds.

848 NAS formed with HAR 21s at Gosport in October 1952, the first operational RN helicopter squadron. It embarked in *Perseus* in December 1952 for passage to Singapore and until 1956 it deployed flights to Kuala Lumpur for anti-communist operations during the Malayan Emergency. 848 NAS' efforts in difficult conditions led to it being awarded the Boyd Trophy in 1953. During Operation 'Cato' in 1953 it moved 650 troops and 4,000lb of equipment in 183 sorties comprising 103 flying hours. During the Malayan campaign eight HAR 21s suffered engine failures, three had to be written off in theatre and virtually every one had a close encounter with a tree operating from tiny jungle clearings. The survivors were shipped back to the UK in 1957.

The fifteen HAS 22s were used to form 845 NAS, also at Gosport in March 1954, the first operational RN helicopter anti-submarine squadron. Prior to that they had equipped 706 NAS which had re-formed in September 1953 to evaluate helicopters in the ASW role and devise tactics. Between 1953 and 1970 Whirlwind HAS 22s were also

A Whirlwind HAS 22 of 728 NAS based at Hal Far winching a senior officer off the forecastle of a frigate.

operated by 701, 705, 728, 728C, 737, 771 and 781 NAS. 845 NAS' helicopters with their sonar removed to provide cabin space embarked in *Theseus* for Operation 'Musketeer', the brief Suez Campaign, and carried out the first helicopter assault in history on 6 November 1956, ferrying marines from both *Ocean* and *Theseus* together with the Army/RAF helicopter trials unit. This success led to 728C NAS being formed at RN air station Lee-on-Solent in January 1958 with four HAS 22s to develop the role of helicopters in amphibious operations. After a series of trials in the Mediterranean it was re-designated as 848 NAS.

HAS 22s embarked for varying periods in the aircraft carriers *Ark Royal*, *Eagle*, *Centaur*, *Ocean* and *Theseus*. In June 1958 the aircraft of 728C NAS were ferried from Hal Far to Cyprus in the cruiser *Bermuda* and used on internal security operations with 45 RM Commando. The Whirlwind HAS 22 was a reliable helicopter and it remained in use with Hal Far SAR Flight until 1965 and on fleet requirements and specialist tasks with 771 and 781 NAS. One example was used as an Admiral's 'barge' and another was used to instruct HRH Prince Philip, the Duke of Edinburgh, to qualify as a helicopter pilot.

The Whirlwinds manufactured under licence in the UK by Westland are described under the Westland heading.

SLOANE-DAY

H.1

A single Sloane-Day H.1 tractor biplane was ordered from this New York based company in 1915 and shipped to Hendon for evaluation, arriving in November. Few details of it remain but it was clearly unsuccessful. It crashed into a parked aircraft when attempting to take off in January 1916 and was deleted after attempts to repair it were abandoned.

SOPWITH

School Biplane/D.1

A one-off design delivered to Eastchurch in 1912 with a 70hp Gnome rotary engine but rebuilt as the D.1 in 1913, a three-seater with an 80hp Gnome rotary giving a maximum level speed of 65 knots. It had wing-warping lateral control rather than ailerons and was evaluated with a gun mounting in April 1914 but subsequently deleted in May. Wingspan was 40ft and MTOW 1,750lb.

Three-Seater Biplane

Resembling the D.1, a single three-seater was delivered to Hendon in 1913 but returned for modifications. With these completed it was used at Eastchurch in 1913/14 and deployed to Ostend after the outbreak of war in 1914 with the War Flight that became 3 Squadron RNAS. It was returned to Eastchurch in September 1914 and deleted.

Bat Boat

A single example of this amphibian pusher biplane was delivered to Calshot in June 1913 but sank at its moorings during bad weather after a flight to Brighton and salvage caused further damage. The hull was then used in a replacement aircraft and three further Bat Boats were ordered. One of these, number 118, carried out the first RN night flight using a motor-car headlight to provide illumination and was used for other experimental work including bomb-dropping trials. It took part in the fly-past over the Royal Fleet Review in July 1914 and flew over the anchored fleet at night, illuminating ships with its headlight. The Bat Boats were fitted with different engines starting with a 90hp Austro-Daimler radial and then a 100hp Green. Number 118's wingspan was 41ft, MTOW 1,700lb and maximum level speed was 56 knots. Number 118 deployed to Scapa Flow on 24 August 1914 and maintained daily patrols over the fleet until 24 November. It was eventually deleted in March 1915. A further Bat Boat built to a revised design and then requisitioned had a wingspan of 55ft, side-by-side seating for two pilots and MTOW of 3,180lb. A 200hp Canton-Unne engine, later replaced by a 200hp Sunbeam, gave a maximum level speed of 66 knots.

HT Seaplane

Effectively a Three-Seater with twin floats replacing the wheeled undercarriage with a 100hp Anzani radial engine driving a two-bladed wooden propeller. Wingspan was 40ft and MTOW approximately 2,000lb. The Admiralty acquired three in 1913 for use in that year's fleet manoeuvres. The first was accepted at Calshot and used for W/T and bomb dropping trials; Winston Churchill, First Lord of the Admiralty, flew in it during August 1913. The second flew from Cromarty during the manoeuvres and the third flew from Great Yarmouth. The first two were used for early war patrols before being deleted in January 1915 but the third was written off after an accident.

A Sopwith Bat Boat, the first RN aircraft to fly at night after being fitted with a car headlight.

Sopwith HT Seaplane.

Admiralty Type 137 Seaplane

Two examples of this single-seat biplane torpedo aircraft were delivered to Calshot in August 1914; the number of the first becoming the Admiralty type number. The first had a 120hp Austro-Daimler engine but was later re-engined with a 200hp Canton-Unne before being deleted after an accident in January 1916. The second had a 200hp Canton-Unne from the outset, got airborne with an 810lb torpedo in August 1914 and carried out a controlled drop although it was still a long way short of operational capability. It was also deleted in January 1916 after being used for development work during 1915. Data on it has not survived.

Sociable (also known as the 'Tweenie' or 'Churchill')

This two-seat, dual-control, biplane derived its name from the pilots' side-by-side seating which allowed them to hear each other above the noise of the single 100hp Gnome monosoupape rotary engine. The sole example was delivered to Hendon in February 1914 and Winston Churchill made several flights in it during which he was effectively taught to fly. After the outbreak of war it served with 1 and 3 Squadrons RNAS in Belgium until October when it was abandoned during the British retreat from Antwerp. Wingspan was 36ft but other details have been lost.

Admiralty Type 806 Gun Bus

Three groups of pusher biplanes known as Gun Buses, designated Admiralty Type 806, were built from 1914. The first was a two-seat pusher biplane with twin floats and a 200hp Salmson engine giving a maximum level speed of 70 knots. Wingspan was 50ft but other details including MTOW have been lost. The pilot sat behind the gunlayer. It was used for gunnery trials from Calshot with a 1½pdr Vickers gun and a belt-fed Vickers 0.303in machine gun. The machine gun was found to be the most effective and was adopted. A similar aircraft

Sopwith Gun Bus.

bought by the Greek Navy in 1913 proved so successful that it ordered six more but they were requisitioned by the Admiralty in August 1914. They had a 150hp Sunbeam Crusader pusher engine, wheeled undercarriages and were armed with a single 0.303in Lewis gun in the front cockpit. Delivered from October 1914, they operated from Hendon but were relegated to training. The Admiralty type designation was the number of the last one delivered. At least one was shipped to Dunkirk but might not have flown operationally and they were all deleted in 1915. A third batch of thirty was ordered from subcontractors in 1915 for delivery in 1916 but by then the design was obsolescent; only seventeen were delivered and all were deleted within weeks. The remainder were scrapped.

Admiralty Type 807 Seaplane

The Type 807 was initially a private venture, two-seat tractor biplane seaplane with the aircrew sat in tandem, the pilot occupying the rear cockpit. It attracted Admiralty interest in 1914 and seventeen examples, designated Admiralty Type 807, were ordered. They had a wire-braced wooden fuselage and the wings folded to the rear about hinges on the rear spars; ailerons were fitted to the upper wings only. Records show that dimensions varied slightly between aircraft but a wingspan of 36ft was typical and a 100hp Gnome monosoupape rotary engine driving a two-bladed wooden propeller gave a maximum level speed of 70 knots. They were used widely throughout 1915 flying coastal patrols from Calshot and Great Yarmouth and two operated from Niororo Island during operations against the German cruiser *Königsberg* in the Rufiji river delta. Three were deployed to the Dardanelles in *Ark Royal* but the hot conditions limited their performance and they proved unable to climb high enough to spot effectively. Take-off in any but the calmest conditions was almost impossible but a single Type 807 did spot for the bombardment on 18 March 1915. One was transferred to the cruiser *Minerva* for patrol work in the Gulf of Smyrna in April and another was transferred to the light cruiser *Doris* in April to make reconnaissance flights over Bulair and the Gulf of Xeros but its fabric was stripped off by blast when the ship fired its after 6in guns and the this aircraft played no further part in operations. All Type 807s were deleted by the end of 1915.

Type C Seaplane

A large, experimental, two-seat biplane seaplane designed to carry a 14in torpedo between its twin floats. Three were delivered to Calshot in November 1914; few of their details survived but it is known that they were incapable of taking-off with a torpedo. The 200hp Canton Unne engine drove a two-bladed wooden propeller and wingspan is believed to have been about 80ft. Whilst not itself successful, the Type C did lead to the Type 860 which was.

Admiralty Type 860 seaplane

A contemporary of the Short Type 184 powered by a 225hp Sunbeam engine, it took its Admiralty designation from an aircraft number in the first batch. It was a two-seat biplane with ailerons only fitted to the upper wings. Torpedo crutches were constructed at the centre of two cross-bars that joined the floats and the type flew successfully with a single 810lb 14in torpedo but performance figures have been lost. The pilot flew the aircraft from the rear cockpit and a single 0.303in Lewis

Sopwith Type 807, airframe number 818, which operated from *Engadine* for attacks on Zeebrugge during 1915.

Sopwith Type 860. (Philip Jarrett)

gun could be fitted to the upper wing centre section for use by the observer in the front cockpit. Deliveries began in 1915 with a batch of ten although not all were used operationally. A further batch of twelve was ordered but eight of these were either cancelled or used for spare parts. After evaluation at Calshot, Type 860s were embarked in *Ben-my-Chree*, *Engadine* and *Ark Royal* from 1915, seeing limited use in the North Sea and Aegean. A few anti-submarine patrols were flown from Calshot and Dundee but by 1916 the survivors were relegated to training duties before being deleted.

Tabloid

The fastest aircraft produced in Britain before 1914, a 100hp Gnome monosoupape rotary engine gave a maximum level speed of 81 knots when it was flown by Harry Hawker, Sopwith's Australian chief test pilot. A distinctive metal cowling enclosed the engine and extended aft to the cockpit sides and the fuselage was a wire-braced wooden box girder covered by doped fabric with a 'V'-shaped wheeled undercarriage. It was a biplane with a single pair of interplane struts to keep drag to a minimum and lateral control was by wing-warping rather than ailerons. The prototype was a side-by-side two-seater but the sixteen production aircraft delivered from 1914 were single-seaters. The wingspan of RNAS Tabloids was 25ft 6in, MTOW was 1,120lb and they were used as both fighters and bombers. The first three were transferred from the RFC and armament varied but could include a single 0.303in Lewis machine gun mounted on the decking forward of the pilot or beside the cockpit. Interrupter mechanisms had not been invented and bullets were prevented from hitting the two-bladed wooden propeller by deflector plates, at least in theory. In practice the blades were often hit and damaged.

Three Tabloids served with Commander Samson's Eastchurch Squadron at Antwerp in October 1914, one of which was flown by Flight Lieutenant R L G Marix RNAS on 8 October to attack Zeppelin sheds at Dusseldorf armed with two 20lb bombs on improvised underwing racks. He dived on the sheds and released his bombs at 600ft, hitting one which exploded and destroyed Zeppelin Z.IX inside it. Other Tabloids served with 3 Squadron RNAS at Tenedos and at least two were embarked in *Ark Royal*. Performance in the high temperatures was not good, however. During 1915 several found their way into training units in the UK and at least one was operated from Great Yarmouth. The surviving examples were deleted by mid-1916

Gordon Bennett Racer

Two examples of this single-seat biplane were built for the 1914 Gordon Bennett Air Race with a slimmer fuselage and tailplane than the Tabloid from which they evolved. Wingspan was similar to the Tabloid but the lower MTOW enabled the 80hp Gnome rotary engine to achieve the remarkable level speed of 92 knots. Both were requisitioned by the Admiralty in August 1914 and used by a Fast Flight at Hendon. One was transferred to St Pol and operated with 1 Wing RNAS fitted with a 0.303in Lewis machine gun and deflector plates before being returned to Dover and deleted in 1916. The other operated from Chingford before being deleted in 1915

Two-Seater Scout/'Spinning Jenny'

A derivative of the Type 807 seaplane with the same fuselage and tail unit but this biplane had a wheeled undercarriage instead of the twin floats. The Admiralty ordered twenty-four in 1914 for use as anti-Zeppelin fighters with 100hp Gnome monosoupape rotary engines which gave a disappointing maximum level speed of only 60 knots. A climb to 3,000ft took 20 minutes and since, realistically, the aircraft was unable to climb much higher, the chance of engaging a Zeppelin was minimal. Wingspan was 36ft but other details such MTOW have been lost. It showed an alarming tendency to spin, hence its nickname, and at least five were lost to this cause in crashes. In 1915 there was no standard spin recovery but when Flight Lieutenant J C Brooke RNAS from Killingholme inadvertently span his 'Spinning Jenny' he managed to regain control and land. A day later he took off, climbed to 3,000ft and made two deliberate spins, regaining control after losing about 1,000ft on both occasions before landing safely. He was probably the first British pilot to perform an intentional spin and recover from it and his technique formed the basis of training techniques that continue in use today. Two-Seater Scouts were based at Eastchurch, Cromer, Chingford, Dover, Dundee, East Fortune, Hendon, Killingholme and Great Yarmouth from where they flew anti-Zeppelin patrols armed with a variety of hand-held weapons including rifles fitted with Hales grenades, pistols, a shot-gun firing chain-shot and Very pistols. A number were fitted with racks to drop small bombs on Zeppelins but since the aircraft could never get into a position to drop them they were of little value and merely added weight. For short periods they were used by 2 and 4 Squadrons RNAS. Having failed in their intended role the survivors were deleted during 1915.

Schneider

In 1914 the Admiralty anticipated that single-seat seaplanes would be the fighter to combat Zeppelins. The sea was thought of as a limitless runway and the seaplane carrier as a floating hangar and after its mission the fighter would land on the water close to the parent ship and be hoisted in. A Tabloid seaplane had won the Schneider Trophy in 1914 and so a production derivative named Schneider was ordered in 1914; the first Sopwith design to be ordered in quantity for the RNAS. It retained the same bull-nose cowling as the Tabloid and early examples retained wing-warping but the fin and rudder were made slightly larger and an additional diagonal strut was introduced in each side of the undercarriage to hold the twin floats in place. A slot in the mid upper wing allowed the installation of a 0.303in Lewis machine gun firing upwards at an angle to clear the propeller arc; Schneiders were unlikely to climb above a Zeppelin and attacks would invariably be made from below. They were delivered from early 1915. They proved unsuccessful in the embarked role for which they were intended, however, because the seaplane carrier had to stop to hoist out its aircraft when a Zeppelin was seen and by the time the Schneider got airborne, if it could do so at all, the Zeppelin would have climbed beyond the fighter's ceiling and be safe from interception. A successful launch also required a suitable sea state and this was seldom the case in the North Sea.

One solution was to fit wheels to the floats and take-off from a platform fitted over the seaplane carrier's forecastle. This was tried from *Ben-my-Chree* in May 1915 but the engine backfired so violently after starting that the aircraft fell off the platform. In June 1915 another Schneider was actually launched from a platform on the cruiser *Arethusa* against a Zeppelin but the pilot returned to the ship without pressing home an attack because he thought he had seen a recall signal. Worse followed in July when three recently-delivered Schneiders were hoisted out from *Engadine*; rough conditions led to the floats of all three breaking up and only one could be salvaged. No successful interception was ever made in this way. Trials using the wheeled float combination and a take-off deck continued but the aircraft still had to alight on the water. By August 1915 *Campania* had been fitted with a flying-off deck over the bow 120ft long. Seaplane floats rested on two-wheeled dollies which fell into the sea as the aircraft left the deck and the first take-off was carried out by Flight Lieutenant W L Welsh RNAS with the ship steaming into wind at 17 knots but the technique was still considered marginal since the take-off run was 113ft and *Campania* was modified with a lengthened deck. Schneiders were operated from ships off the east coast of the UK on anti-Zeppelin patrols and continued in use until late in the war, gradually being replaced in the seaplane fighter role by the Baby.

Schneider data

Length:	22ft 10in
Wingspan:	25ft 8in
Height:	10ft
MTOW:	1,715lb
Engine:	One 100hp Gnome monosoupape rotary driving a two-bladed wooden propeller
Fuel:	Avgas. 25 gallons
Performance:	Maximum level speed 81 knots Service ceiling 8,000ft. 30 minutes to 8,000ft
Endurance:	2¼ hours
Armament:	One 0.303in Lewis machine gun mounted to fire upwards at an angle of 45 degrees through an opening in the upper wing centre-section to avoid the propeller arc. Later examples had the gun on the coaming in front of the pilot, synchronised to fire through the propeller arc. A single 65lb bomb could be carried on a rack under the fuselage. Ranken darts were also used for anti-Zeppelin work and several aircraft had Le Prieur rocket-launcher tubes fitted to the interplane struts

Sopwith delivered 136 Schneiders to the RNAS. They operated from the seaplane carriers *Ark Royal*, *Ben-my-Chree*, *Engadine*, *Furious*, *City of Oxford*, *Riviera*, *Campania*, *Vindex*, *Anne*, *Raven II*, *Empress* and *Manxman*. They were also embarked in the cruisers *Arethusa*, *Undaunted* and *Doris* together with the paddle minesweepers *Brocklesby* and *Killingholme*, the gunboat *Halcyon* and even the submarine *E-22* which carried two on deck out to an area they were to patrol.

Shore-based Schneiders operated from Calshot, Dundee, Dunkirk, Great Yarmouth, Felixstowe, Scapa Flow, Westgate, Killingholme and Fishguard in the UK and also in France. In the Mediterranean they operated from Otranto and Santa Maria di Leuca, Thasos, Suda Bay, Syra, Port Said and Alexandria.

A Schneider being hoisted back onto *Brocklesby* after an anti-Zeppelin patrol over the North Sea.

Below: Disassembled Schneiders undergoing maintenance in *Ark Royal*'s hangar during 1915.

A Sopwith Baby seaplane fighter on its beaching trolley in 1918.

Baby

Progressive Schneider development led to a derivative widely referred to as its 'baby' and the name was eventually accepted officially. They had the same wood and canvas construction as the Schneider but a Clerget engine replaced the Gnome. It had a revised, open-fronted, metal cowling, open at the bottom, known as the 'horse-shoe' and wing-warping was replaced by ailerons for lateral control. Babies were delivered from September 1915 and, apart from some early examples, they had the Lewis gun mounted on the coaming in front of the pilot, firing through the propeller disc with an interrupter mechanism. Despite the improvements, the Baby was no more successful than its predecessor. In an attempted attack on the Zeppelin base believed to be at Tondern in May 1916, eleven Babies were lowered onto the water off the island of Sylt from the seaplane carriers *Vindex* and *Engadine*. Four had their propellers shattered by spray, three suffered engine failures during their take-off run and one overturned as it hit the wake of an escorting destroyer. Only three got airborne but one hit a destroyer's W/T aerial and crashed, one had to return with a rough-running engine and the lone aircraft that reached the target found it shrouded in mist. It dropped two 65lb bombs but both missed anything important.

Campania re-joined the Grand Fleet in Scapa Flow with an extended flying-off deck and on 29 May 1916 she launched five Baby seaplanes in quick succession using wheeled dollies under their floats. Once airborne the aircraft landed near the seaplane base at Scapa Bay. This 'no-fuss' demonstration showed the way forward but left the ship anchored near Scapa Bay to retrieve its aircraft, 9nm away from the battlefleet moored off Flotta and at 2254 on 30 May she missed the order to sail for the sortie that developed into the Battle of Jutland. She sailed two hours late but was ordered back.

Baby data

Length:	23ft
Wingspan:	25ft 8in
Height:	10ft
MTOW:	1,715lb
Engine:	One 130hp Clerget rotary driving a two-bladed wooden propeller
Fuel:	Avgas. 25 gallons
Performance:	Maximum level speed 88 knots Service ceiling 10,000ft. 35 minutes to 10,000ft
Endurance:	2¼ hours
Armament:	One 0.303in Lewis machine gun on the coaming in front of the pilot, synchronised to fire through the propeller arc. Two 65lb bombs could be carried on a rack under the fuselage and several aircraft had Le Prieur rocket-launcher tubes fitted to the interplane struts

A rare photograph of a Sopwith Baby firing Le Prieur rockets.

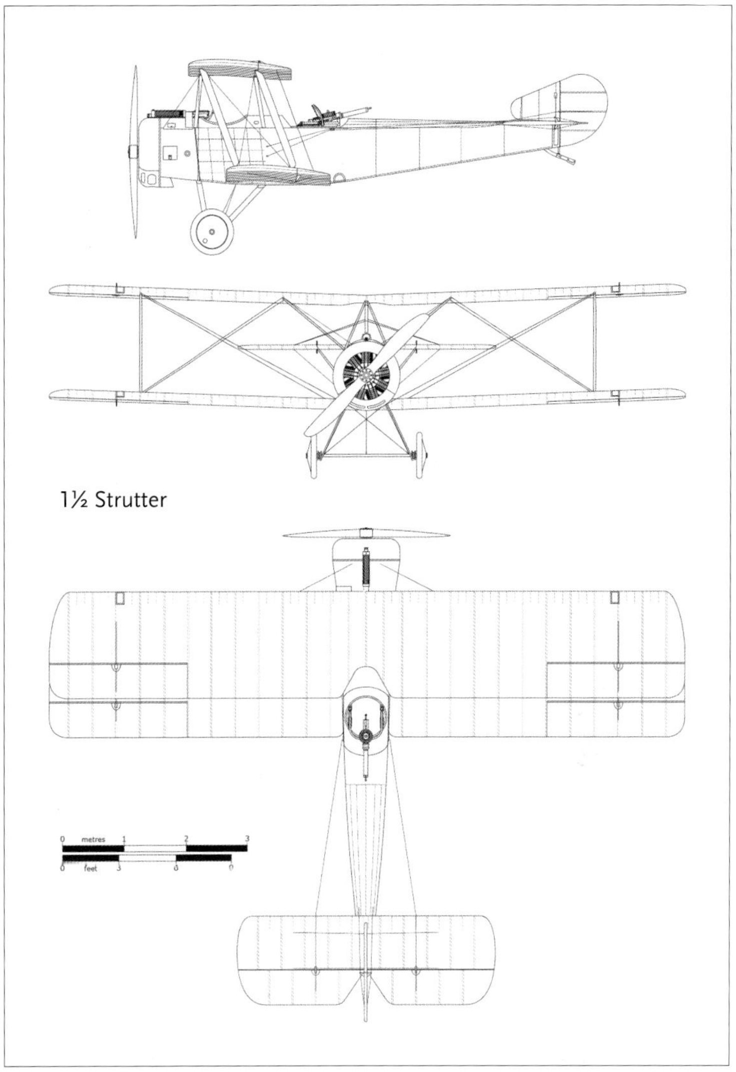

The RNAS received 286 Babies of which 71 were built by Blackburn. They operated from the same seaplane carriers and air stations as the Schneider.

In December 1916, three Babies lowered from *Ben-my-Chree* managed to take off from the water and successfully bomb the Chikaldir railway bridge over the River Jeihan, delaying the transport of enemy guns to Baghdad. In January 1918 two Babies from Imbros attacked the German battlecruiser *Goeben* but failed to hit it. The type was also extensively used for patrol work around the UK coast. For these pilots usually carried a packet of sandwiches, a sea anchor and a pigeon for use if the aircraft ditched. One pilot at Great Yarmouth described it as the machine for the lover of solitude, independence and a wandering kind of life.

1½ Strutter

On 24 September 1918 Commander Richard Bell-Davies VC RN made history in Sopwith 1½ Strutter F 2211 by making the world's first landing on an aircraft carrier, *Argus*. In his autobiographical book *Sailor in the Air* he described making his final approach off a left-hand circuit and was rather daunted at first by the big, square appearance of the after end of the ship since it had no round-down and the dark structure had the appearance of a cliff. He kept well above it and landed safely about half way up the deck. Later landings moved aft as his confidence grew. By then the 1½ Strutter had been in RN service for over 2 years and had a solid reputation in roles that would now be described as fighter, reconnaissance and strike.

Its design evolved from a two-seat biplane built as a private venture by Sopwith in 1915 in which Harry Hawker gained a British altitude record by climbing to 18,393ft. It was a conventional two-seat biplane with a fuselage made of spruce longerons and spacers braced by wire to form a box girder. The bay immediately aft of the engine had panels of aluminium sheet and the wings were made of wood with steel tubing tips and trailing edges with ailerons on both upper and lower wings. Unusually the upper wing had no centre section and the two halves met at a trestle-shaped cabane with additional struts run from upper fuselage longerons to its spars. Thus the wing was supported by parallel systems of 'W'-shaped struts; one about half the length of the other, and it was this feature that gave the 1½ Strutter its name. The lower wings were attached to a centre section with spars that passed through the fuselage. The trailing portions of this lower centre section formed moveable panels pivoted at about one third of their chord on a spanwise axis allowing them to rotate through 90 degrees to act as dive brakes when the pilot turned a handwheel. Another novel feature was an adjustable tailplane that allowed pilots to trim the aircraft accurately as the weight of fuel and stores reduced. The elevator cables were taken upwards from the control shaft in the pilot's cockpit to a pair of fairleads on the outside of the upper longerons beside the after cockpit. They could thus be touched by the observer and by moving them he could gain the pilot's attention more easily than shouting over the noise of the engine. Fuel tanks were mounted between the spars of the lower centre-section, keeping the two cockpits apart; the pilot sat under the upper wing with a good view forward but the observer's cockpit was well aft. Communication between the two, even using a Gosport tube, was extremely difficult. Initially the two-seat fighter version was designated Type 9400 by the Admiralty, a number derived from an aircraft in the first batch but use of the unofficial name 1½ Strutter became so widespread that it was eventually adopted officially. Confusingly, the single-seat bomber variant was initially designated

A 1½ Strutter fighter being prepared by 3 Wing RNAS air mechanics for a bomber-escort sortie.

Type 9700 but they too were eventually accepted as 1½ Strutters. Two-seat 1½ Strutters modified with W/T for use as fleet spotter/reconnaissance aircraft operated from warship platforms and aircraft carriers were known as Ship Strutters.

The first RNAS variant was a two-seat long-range escort fighter armed with a single Vickers belt-fed 0.303in front-gun on the coaming in front of the pilot firing through the propeller arc with a Scarff-Dibovsky interrupter mechanism; the first British fighter thus fitted. The observer's 0.303in Lewis gun was mounted on a Scarff Number 2 ring, another example of the inventive genius of Warrant Officer F W Scarff RNAS. The Admiralty appreciated that the 1½ Strutter would make a capable bomber and ordered a single-seat variant for this role in which the after cockpit was eliminated and covered by rounded top-decking. An internal bomb bay was provided aft of the lower wing with bomb doors on the underside of the fuselage opened by the bombs falling through them and pulled shut afterwards by rubber chords. The two versions were structurally identical and it was possible for either to be converted into the other.

Ship Strutters were modified from both single and two-seaters in 1918 and fitted with W/T for the observer. The front gun was deleted but the Lewis gun was retained for self-defence. By 1918 they were embarked in the new carrier *Argus* and capital ships to search for and shadow enemy ships and to spot the fall of shot of battleships' long-range gunfire when action was joined. Platforms had already been fitted to warship turrets to allow fighters to be launched against Zeppelins and these were extended to allow a Ship Strutter at MTOW to take off when the turret was rotated into the relative wind. On 7 March 1918 Flight Lieutenant D G Donald RNAS took off from 'Q' turret in HMAS *Australia* in the Firth of Forth when it was rotated into a 'felt wind' of 20 knots. The deck covered the turret and gun barrels and was made of 2in planks which could be removed quickly after the launch to allow the guns to elevate and fire. Subsequently Ship Strutters were carried on battleships every time the Grand Fleet put to sea but the aircraft had to ditch close the fleet after its mission if, as was usually the case, it had insufficient fuel to fly to an airfield in the UK. Once *Furious* re-joined the fleet after having a landing deck fitted, she embarked Ship Strutters in place of Short 184s but landing

A 1½ Strutter flown off HMAS *Australia*'s 'Q' turret by Flight Lieutenant D G Donald RNAS in March 1918; the first successful turret-platform launch.

them on in the turbulence aft of the central bridge and funnel would have been hazardous. *Argus* solved the problem.

1½ Strutter data

Length:	25ft 3in
Wingspan:	33ft 6in
Height:	10ft 3in
MTOW:	Two-seater 2,150lb. Single-seater 2,342lb
Engine:	One 130hp Clerget 9 B rotary driving a two-bladed wooden propeller
Fuel:	Avgas. 40 gallons
Performance:	Maximum level speed 93 knots Service ceiling 15,500ft. 21 minutes to 10,000ft
Endurance:	Up to 4¼ hours depending on variant
Armament:	One fixed, belt-fed Vickers 0.303in front gun firing through the propeller with an interrupter mechanism in fighter variant. One 0.303in Lewis gun on a Scarff ring for the observer. Single-seat bomber variant could carry four 65lb bombs or twelve 20lb Le Pecq bombs

Exact figures are complicated by aircraft from RN production batches being transferred to the RFC in 1916 and others being transferred from RFC and French 1917 production batches to the RNAS for conversion to Ship Strutters. Records show that at least 536 were received by the RN.

1½ Strutters served with 1, 2, 3, 5 and 6 Wings of the RNAS and 2, 3, 4, 5, 7 and 9 (Naval) Squadrons on the Western Front. They also served with A, B, C and D Squadrons in the Aegean Theatre and with E and F Squadrons in Macedonia. They were also used on coastal anti-submarine patrols from Great Yarmouth, Mullion, Padstow, Pembroke, Prawle Point and Otranto.

Ship Strutters embarked in *Argus* after her early trials and also in the seaplane carriers *Furious* and *Vindex*. Battleships that embarked Ship Strutters on turret platforms included *Barham*, *Emperor of India*, *Queen Elizabeth*, *Warspite*, *Australia*, *New Zealand*, *Bellerophon*, *Courageous*, *Glorious*, *Indomitable*, *Inflexible*, *Malaya*, *Renown*, *Repulse*, *Royal Sovereign* and *Valiant*.

Commander Bell-Davies VC RN taking-off in a Sopwith 1½ Strutter during deck trials of the world's first aircraft carrier, *Argus*, in October 1918.

Commander Bell-Davies VC RN landing into *Argus*' fore and aft retaining wires in October 1918.

A 1½ Strutter stopped in *Argus*' retaining wires showing how difficult it was for the handling party to extricate themselves and the aircraft.

Sopwith was an Admiralty Contractor and built the majority of naval variants; others were built by subcontractors. The first RN 1½ Strutter flew at Brooklands in February 1916, then went to the War Flight at Eastchurch. The first operational RNAS missions were carried out in August 1916 by 5 Wing at Coudekerque; they consisted of attacks on enemy airship sheds at Evere and Berchem St Agathe together and an ammunition dump at Lichtervelde. The Admiralty intended 3 Wing at Luxeuil les Bains to specialise in strategic bombing but the RFC desperately needed more aircraft in advance of the Somme offensive and it appealed to the Admiralty for assistance. RN plans for the 1½ Strutter were postponed in order to transfer sixty to the RFC.

Anti-submarine patrols were flown by 1½ Strutters armed with two 65lb bombs. Few attacks were made but the patrols forced U-boats to dive when they saw an aircraft, limiting their speed and time deployed. 1½ Strutters could get airborne more quickly than a flying boat or seaplane to respond to a U-boat report. Several 1½ Strutters were used at Isle of Grain for deck-landing experiments with both a tail-hook to catch athwartship wires and clips on the undercarriage axle to engage fore-and-aft retaining wires. They were also used to evaluate flotation gear. Some 1½ Strutters were deployed to the Baltic in *Vindictive* during 1919 for operations against the Bolsheviks but the type was soon withdrawn from the Grand Fleet air pool after the Armistice and none remained by 1920.

Pup

The Pup combined effective design with delightful handling qualities and few of its contemporaries could match its performance when it entered service in 1916. It was developed from a single-seat tractor biplane built as a private venture by Sopwith for Harry Hawker in 1915 and it bore such an obvious family resemblance to the 1½ Strutter that it became known as its offspring or 'pup'. The Admiralty officially designated it as the Type 9901 from the airframe number of the first aircraft built under licence by Beardmore but it was only ever known as the Pup in service and the name was eventually accepted officially. Naval Pups were built by Sopwith and by Beardmore under licence. Structurally the Pup was conventional with a fuselage made of ash longerons and spruce spacers forming a fabric-covered wire-braced box girder over most of its length. The fabric-covered wings had spruce spars and ribs with the small ailerons on both upper and lower wings hinged to the rear spars. Steel tubing was used to form the fin, rudder and elevators and the undercarriage comprised simple 'V' units with a dividing axle. The engine cowling and fuselage side panels aft of it were fabricated from aluminium sheet and the fuselage top decking around the cockpit was covered with plywood. Pups built by Beardmore were invariably distinguished by red, white and blue stripes on the elevators as well as the standard national markings.

RN Pups that operated on the Western Front had a single belt-fed 0.303in Vickers front gun mounted in front of the cockpit firing through the propeller arc by means of a Scarff-Dibovski interrupter mechanism. It was fired by depressing a lever on the rear of the breech rather than by a button on the control column, an awkward arrangement but practice obviously gave pilots the proficiency they needed. Pups operated from ships had other armament variations which included a tripod of steel tubes forward of the cockpit on which a 0.303in Lewis machine gun could fitted to fire at upward angles to engage a Zeppelin from below. The pilot could vary the angle from nearly vertical down to a lower level that would just clear the propeller arc. This made the gun more difficult to aim but did allow a higher rate of fire without the interrupter mechanism.

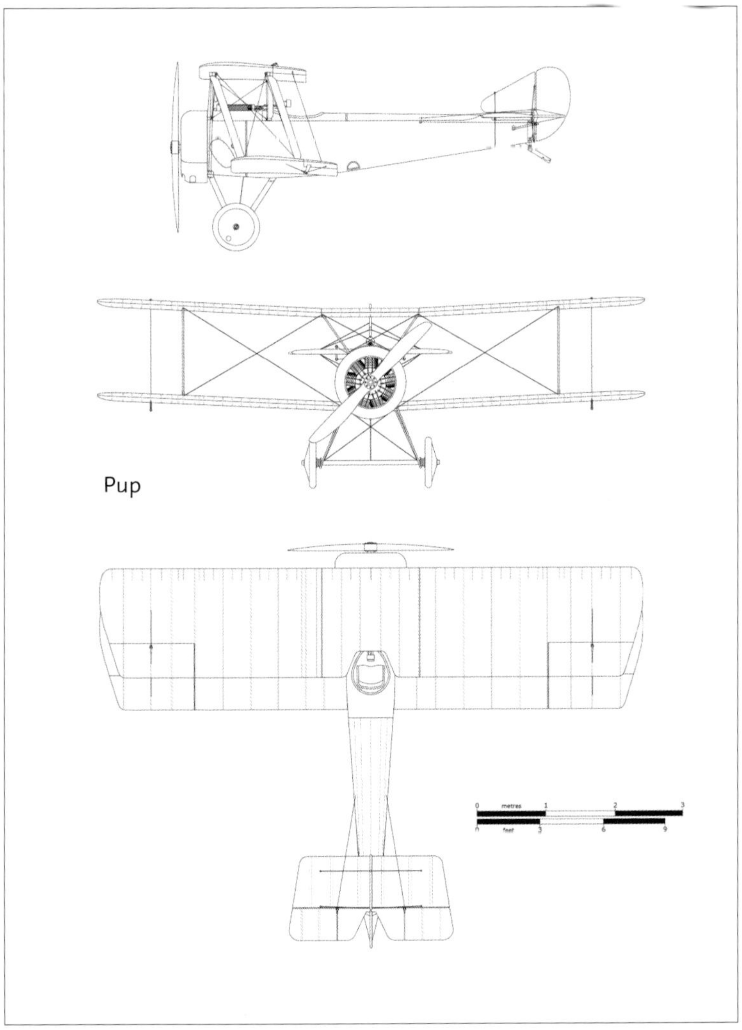

Pup data

Length:	19ft 3¾in
Wingspan:	26ft 6in
Height:	9ft 5in
MTOW:	1,225lb
Engine:	One 80hp Le Rhone rotary driving a two-bladed wooden propeller
Fuel:	Avgas. 19¼ gallons
Performance:	Maximum level speed 98 knots
	Service ceiling 17,500ft. 29 minutes 10 seconds to 15,000ft
Endurance:	3 hours
Armament:	One fixed, belt-fed Vickers 0.303in front gun firing through the propeller with an interrupter mechanism or one 0.303in Lewis machine gun mounted forward of the cockpit to fire at an upward angle. Some Pups were modified to carry four Le Prieur rockets on each of the outer interplane struts for a total of eight

A total of 176 Pups were built for the RN under Admiralty contract by Sopwith and Beardmore. A further 248 manufactured by the Standard Motor Company and Whitehead Aircraft were transferred to the RN from Army contracts.

A Pup on the cruiser *Yarmouth*'s tiny take-off platform.

A skid-fitted Pup used for landing trials on the dummy ship's deck at Isle of Grain. Note the arrester hook.

Pups served with Naval 'A' Squadron, 1 Wing RNAS and with 3,4,8, 9 and 12 (Naval) Squadrons on the Western Front. They also served with Naval 'C' Squadron in the Aegean.

Trials in 1918 involved Pups as well as other types operating from the new aircraft carrier *Argus*. They also operated from flight decks on *Furious* and *Campania* as well as the seaplane carrier *Manxman*.

Pups operated from turret platforms fitted to capital ships in the Grand Fleet including *Repulse*, *Tiger*, *Renown*, *Princess Royal*, *New Zealand*, *Australia* and *Lion* and from small take-off platforms fitted to the cruisers *Yarmouth*, *Caledon*, *Dublin*, *Cordelia*, *Cassandra*, *Chatham* and the RAN *Sydney*.

The first production Pup was allocated to Naval 'A' Squadron at Furnes for evaluation and proved an immediate success. One of the pilots that flew it described its handling qualities as impeccable. The first production Pups went to 1 Wing in September 1916 and Flight Sub Lieutenant S J Goble RNAS shot down the type's first victim. An appeal by the RFC for support from the RNAS on the Western Front led to the formation of 8 (Naval) Squadron, drawn from other units at Dunkirk, which exchanged other types for Pups and shot down twenty enemy aircraft by the end of the year. During the Battle of Arras in early 1917 Pups of 3 (Naval) Squadron shot down a considerable number of enemy aircraft for no loss to themselves; the Pup's ascendancy was so great that German pilots avoided combat with it. By early 1917, however, it was becoming outclassed but by then two Sopwith types, the Triplane and Camel were ready to replace it. Pups continued in use for a while replacing Baby seaplanes in 4 (Naval) Squadron to defend ships off the Belgian coast against enemy air attack and protect of merchant shipping anchored in the Downs off Kent.

Pups replaced Baby seaplanes at sea; first embarked in the seaplane carriers *Manxman* and *Campania* which could launch them from flying-off decks but not recover them. The Gunnery Officer of *Yarmouth*, Lieutenant Commander C H B Gowan RN, devised a short

Squadron Commander E H Dunning DSC RNAS carrying out the world's first deck landing on a moving warship, *Furious*, on 2 August 1917.

Pup N 6453 in which Dunning carried out his historic first deck landing photographed at Smoogroo on the north shore of Scapa Flow.

flying-off platform forward, only 20ft long, from which a Pup could be launched when the ship turned into wind. He later devised an improved, rotatable, deck that could be turned into the felt wind to simplify the launch procedure. In August 1917 Flight Sub Lieutenant B A Smart RNAS was launched in a Pup from *Yarmouth* against Zeppelin L-23 off the Danish coast and succeeded in shooting it down in flames; something a seaplane fighter had never succeeded in doing. Pups were soon embarked in a number of cruisers and on capital ships of the Grand Fleet for operation from turret ramps.

Pups parked on *Furious*' forward deck with protective windbreaks partially raised. They show the amount of space available for Dunning's landing.

Pups were also used in some of the earliest RN deck-landing experiments at Isle of Grain. Some had tail hooks for use with athwartship arrester wires or hooks on the undercarriage axle to engage fore-and-aft retaining wires. When *Furious* first joined the fleet in July 1917 her senior aviation officer, Squadron Commander E H Dunning DSC RNAS, calculated that her flying-off deck, 228ft long and 50ft wide at its widest point, gave ample space to land a Pup even though it was forward of the central bridge and funnel. He made history on 2 August 1917 just south of the Hoxa entrance to Scapa Flow by landing Sopwith Pup N 6453, which had a wheeled undercarriage, accurately on *Furious*' deck. A white eyeline had been painted across the deck to help him judge his position and the ship was steaming at 20 knots into a 26 knot wind which gave 46 knots over the deck. This was just above the Pup's stalling speed and allowed him to move slowly up the port side until he was clear forward of the superstructure and level with the eye line. The Le Rhone rotary engine had no throttle; low speed control was achieved by switching the engine ignition on and off using a button on the control column, a process known as 'blipping'. Flying just above stalling speed Dunning 'blipped' the engine to effectively hover alongside and then carefully used aileron and rudder controls to move across the deck. His 'three-point' attitude was maintained using the elevators. Once in position he 'blipped' the engine ignition off and descended onto the deck where a handling party grabbed the aircraft.

This was the first time an aircraft had ever landed on a moving warship and the age of carrier-borne aircraft in which aircraft could land after a sortie had dawned due in no small measure to the skill and bravery of Dunning and the superb handling qualities of the Pup. The handling party was important because the Pup had no brakes and the wind remained higher than the aircraft's stalling speed after it had landed, especially when the pilot climbed out of the cockpit and made it even lighter. Early aircraft would have fluttered like kites if they were not secured or protected against the wind. Dunning made another successful landing on 7 August but died attempting a third landing hours later when his Pup's engine stalled during an attempt to abort a landing and fly away for another circuit. Pups were used for deck-landing trials on *Furious*' new after landing deck in 1918 but turbulence from the central funnel meant that these were largely unsuccessful. Other Pups took part in deck-landing trials on *Argus* and a significant number were used ashore for training. After the Armistice the type was declared obsolete and the survivors soon disappeared from service.

Flight Lieutenant R P Minifie DSC* RNAS stood next to the Triplane in which he shot down a German Albatross D V in August 1917. (Philip Jarrett)

Triplane

The Triplane replaced the Pup in naval service to become the outstanding fighter on the Western Front in early 1917. Its configuration was chosen to give the pilot the most uninterrupted view possible and to ensure good manoeuvrability. The central wing was level with the pilot's eyes and the narrow chord of all the wings meant that the top and bottom wings masked less of his vision than the larger wings of a biplane. The narrow chord also meant that the shift of the centre of pressure with changes of incidence was comparatively small and this allowed a short fuselage and the distribution of wing area over three wings minimised wingspan and conferred an exceptional rate of roll. Construction was similar to the Pup but stressed to take the 110hp Clerget rotary engine. Late production aircraft were modified to take the 130hp Clerget. Each wing had two main spars and were internally cross-braced with wire. The most unusual feature of the Triplane was its interplane bracing with a single, broad interplane strut on each side which was continuous from the bottom to the top wing, passing through shaped slots in the middle wing. The centre-section struts were also continuous from the top wing centre section to the bottom longerons of the fuselage. The middle wings were secured by long pins to special aerofoil-shaped stubs on the centre-section struts. There were very few bracing wires; a single landing wire and double flying wires were fitted on each side and there were additional drag wires on the middle wing. Ailerons were fitted on all three mainplanes, hinged to the rear spars.

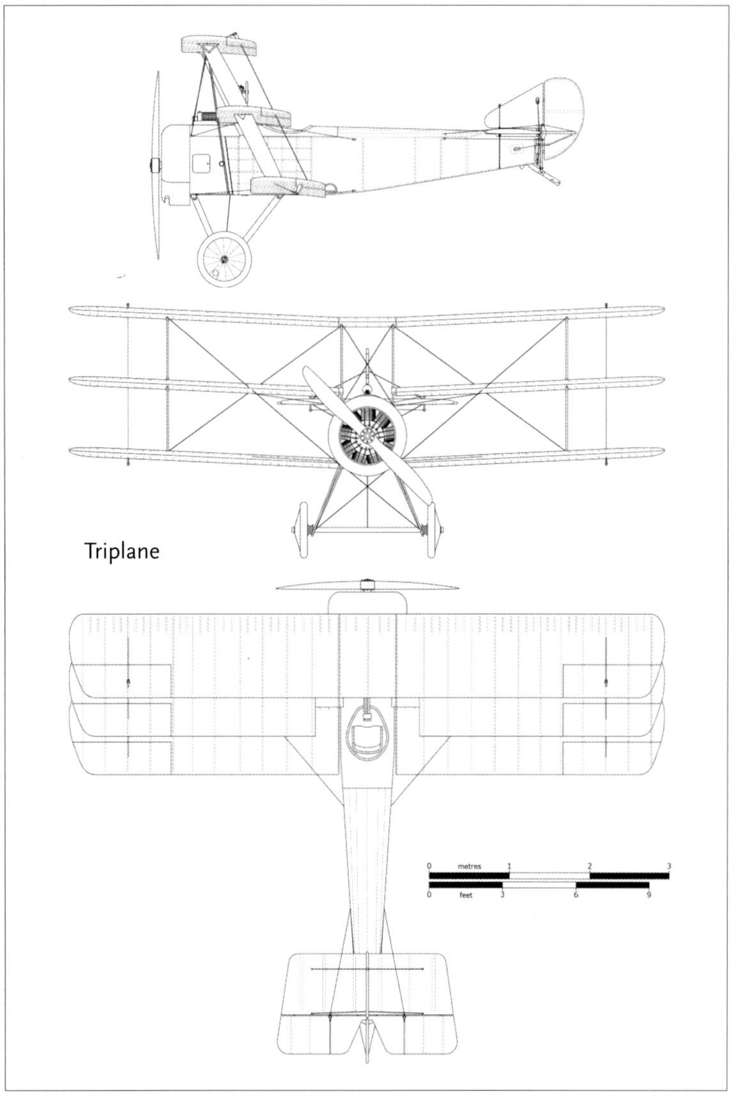

The Triplane was ordered by the Admiralty in quantity for the RNAS from Sopwith and originally the RFC ordered further examples from subcontractors. By late 1916, however, the air situation over the Somme battlefield was desperate and the Army asked the Admiralty to provide all the help it could for the RFC. It agreed to transfer 60 of the Spad S.7 fighters it had on order and increased this offer in February 1917 by transferring all 120 contracted Spads in exchange for the Triplanes on RFC order. In fact most of the subcontracted Triplanes were cancelled and the majority of the aircraft delivered to the RNAS were built by Sopwith.

Triplane (130hp engine) data

Length:	18ft 10in
Wingspan:	26ft 6in
Height:	10ft 6in
MTOW:	1,541lb
Engine:	One 130hp Clerget driving a two-bladed wooden propeller
Fuel:	Avgas. 20 gallons
Performance:	Maximum level speed 103 knots Service ceiling 20,500ft. 10 minutes to 10,000ft
Endurance:	2¾ hours
Armament:	One fixed, belt-fed, synchronised Vickers 0.303in front gun mounted on the top decking forward of the cockpit. Some examples had two synchronised Vickers front guns but suffered a degraded performance

The RN received 150 Triplanes.

Triplanes were operated by 'A' Squadron and 1, 8, 9, 10 and 12 (Naval) Squadrons on the Western Front. A single example was also used by 'E' Squadron of 2 Wing at Mudros in the Aegean. Some were used by the RNAS War School at Manston and at Port Victoria.

Triplane deliveries to operational units began in late 1916 with a successful operational evaluation by 'A' Squadron at Furnes and by February 1917 the first of four naval air squadrons tasked to support the RFC on the Western Front was in action. During the Battle of Arras Triplanes gained an outstanding reputation with some remarkable engagements fought by RNAS pilots such as Squadron Commander C D Booker and Flight Sub Lieutenant R A Little of Naval 8 and Flight Sub Lieutenant R Collishaw of Naval 10. The Triplanes of Collishaw's 'B' Flight, known as the 'Black Flight' and given the names *Black Death*, *Black Maria*, *Black Roger*, *Black Prince* and *Black Sheep* gained complete ascendency in their sector between May and July 1917 and destroyed eighty-seven enemy aircraft. Collishaw shot down sixteen of these in 27 days. From August 1917 they were replaced by Sopwith Camels.

Triplanes of 1 (Naval) Squadron RNAS in 1917. (Philip Jarrett)

Hispano-Suiza Triplane

Two prototypes of this aircraft, sometimes erroneously thought to be a Triplane development, were produced for evaluation by the RNAS. A unique design with wings of different construction and wider chord than the Clerget-powered Triplane, wingspan was 28ft 6in but other figures such as MTOW have been lost. The first had a 150hp Hispano-Suiza engine. The second had a geared 200hp Hispano-Suiza but crashed at 105 knots during a high-speed run at Eastchurch in late 1916 when tail flutter led to a break-up of the after fuselage. The 150hp example was evaluated in 1917 but, while speed and climb must have been good, the pilot's view was poor and manoeuvrability cannot have equalled the Clerget-powered Triplane. There were no production orders.

F.1 Camel

The F.1 Camel reverted to the biplane configuration because the drag imposed by the triplane layout had limited maximum speed. The Admiralty ordered two prototypes, the first of which flew in February 1917. Armament comprised two synchronised, belt-fed Vickers machine guns mounted forward of the cockpit and partially enclosed in a fairing, or 'hump', that quickly earned the aircraft the nickname 'Camel'. It became so popular, so quickly, that it was used officially rather than an Admiralty type number. The Camel airframe had the weight of engine, fuel, guns, ammunition and pilot placed close to the centre of gravity, an arrangement that enhanced manoeuvrability but placed the cockpit between the rear centre-section struts which restricted the pilot's view slightly. The fuselage was a wire-braced box girder with rounded top decking. Aluminium panels covered the bay behind the engine and the sides were then covered by plywood as far aft as the cockpit, the remainder was fabric-covered. The wings were conventional wire-braced, fabric-covered, wooden structures with a straight upper wing and marked dihedral on the lower wings. The centre-section was unusually wide, extending some way outboard of the supporting struts which were splayed outwards. Ailerons were fitted to both upper and lower wings. F.1 Camels built to Admiralty contracts were powered by either 130hp Clerget or 150hp Bentley BR.1 rotary engines driving two-bladed wooden propellers; the latter developed under Admiralty contract and known initially as the Admiralty Rotary Number 1.

The Camel's flying qualities differed from its Sopwith predecessors; it was an unforgiving aircraft for novice pilots but for those who mastered it, it excelled as a dogfighting machine and reports spoke of phenomenal manoeuvrability when it was well-handled. At full throttle it was tail-heavy and with no adjustable tailplane it was tiring to fly for long periods. The short fuselage and concentration of weight forward meant that it could turn in an exceptionally small radius but the torque effect of the propeller meant that in a right-hand turn the Camel tended to drop its nose. In a left-hand turn it tended to rise. These effects had to be countered with rudder, considerably so in the case of a hard turn with the result that the aircraft could easily flick out of controlled flight into a spin when pushed to its limit. Because it was so sensitive some Camels were converted into two-seat trainers for use at the RNAS training depot at Cranwell. Another problem for student pilots who had learnt to fly on the Avro 504 was that the Camel had two engine controls, a throttle and a fine adjustment petrol mixture control but the 504 only had the latter. Clerget engines had a tendency to choke at about 200ft after take-off unless a slightly leaner mixture had been selected. Inexperienced pilots might not act quickly enough to resolve this problem with the result that the tail-heavy Camel at low forward airspeed could easily stall and depart controlled flight into a spin too low for a recovery to be carried out. Improved engines and better training methods eventually resolved the problem.

F.1 Camels of 10 (Naval) Squadron RNAS. (Philip Jarrett)

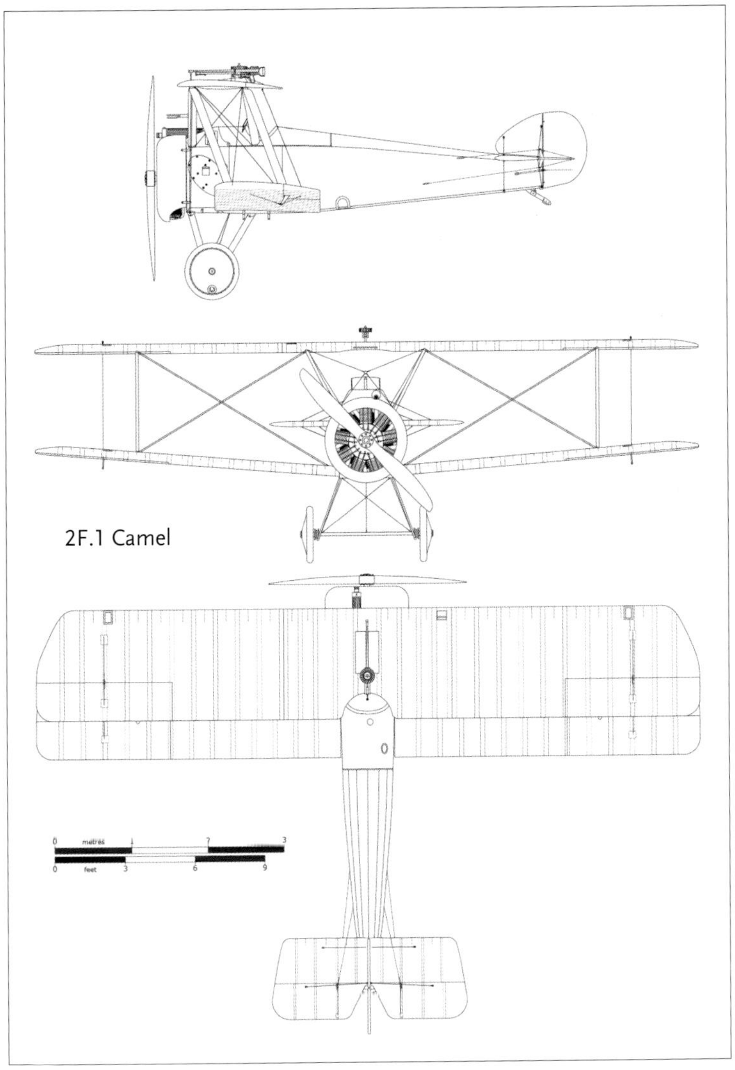

F.1 Camels of 3 (Naval) Squadron RNAS. (Philip Jarrett)

F.1 Camel (Bentley engine) data

Length:	18ft 6in
Wingspan:	28ft
Height:	8ft 9in
MTOW:	1,471lb
Engine:	One 150hp Bentley BR.1 rotary driving a two-bladed wooden propeller
Fuel:	Avgas. 30 gallons in main pressurised tank plus 7 gallons in a gravity tank. Total 37 gallons
Performance:	Maximum level speed 102 knots Service ceiling 22,000ft. 10 minutes to 10,000ft
Endurance:	2½ hours
Armament:	Two fixed, belt-fed, synchronised Vickers 0.303in front guns mounted forward of the cockpit. Some examples were fitted with underwing racks for light bombs

A total of 1,493 F.1 Camels were delivered to the RNAS. Of these two prototypes and fifty production aircraft were ordered under Admiralty contract and the remainder were drawn from bulk production runs after aircraft production was centralised in mid-1917. Many of the last batches went straight into storage, however, and were never used operationally.

Clerget-engined F.1 Camels served with 6, 8 and 9 (Naval) Squadrons on the Western Front and Bentley-engined examples served with 1, 3, 4, 8, 9 and 10 (Naval) Squadrons on the Western Front as well as with the Seaplane Defence Squadron at St Pol which later became 13 (Naval) Squadron. They also flew with defence flights at Burgh Castle, Eastchurch, Great Yarmouth, Felixstowe, Cranwell, Manston and others. In the Mediterranean they operated from Otranto and Taranto and in the Aegean they operated from Thasos, Imbros, Mitylene, Lemnos and by 'D' Squadron at Stavros.

RNAS Camels first went into action in July 1917 when aircraft from Dunkirk attacked German Gotha bombers returning from a raid over England. Apart from fighting for air superiority over the Western Front, naval Camels escorted shipping in the Channel and provided top cover for RNAS bombing attacks on enemy installations. Records show that RNAS Camels shot down 386 enemy aircraft in 1917/18. On 21 April 1918 a Bentley-powered Camel of what had been 9 (Naval) Squadron until a few days earlier shot down the German ace Von Richthofen.

A number of F.1 Camels augmented the 2F.1 in trials including operations from lighters towed by destroyers and a small number were taken to the Baltic in 1919 in *Vindictive* and landed for operations against the Bolsheviks but by 1920 there were none left in service.

A new F.1 Camel in its packing crate ready for delivery.

2F.1 Ship's Camel

The 2F.1 was a derivative design intended specifically for operation from ships. It evolved from a projected FS.1 seaplane design built in prototype form in 1917 but wrecked three days later at Isle of Grain. The 2F.1 differed from the F.1 in having a fuselage built in two halves butt-jointed together aft of the trailing edge of the lower wings and locked in place by brass turnbuckles. The rear portion could be completely detached to reduce the space taken up in a ship's hangar. Elevator control had to be modified by connecting the pilot's control column with control cables running through fairleads and rocking bars to run outside the rear fuselage fabric covering. Removal of the rear fuselage or re-assembly could be carried out in minutes apparently. The upper wing centre-section was shorter in span than that of the F.1, reducing the wingspan and the centre-section struts were made from slender steel tubes rather than spruce to improve the pilot's view. 2F.1s were semi-officially known as Ship's Camels.

The 2F.1's armament also differed from the F.1. A single synchronised belt-fed Vickers front gun was retained under the hump forward of the cockpit, mounted to port of the centreline, and a Lewis gun was mounted above the upper wing centre-section on a mounting that allowed it to be swung back and down for upward firing or reloading. The Lewis gun fired clear of the propeller arc and this made it ideal for explosive bullets. Interrupter mechanisms were not totally reliable and some rounds did hit propellers. This was not a major problem with solid shot but a hit by an explosive round could be disastrous; hence the Lewis gun mount and its position. The Admiralty used Brock and Pomeroy-designed explosive rounds together with tracer and solid shot.

Initially the 2F.1 had the same undercarriage as the F.1 but variations soon appeared. Some were fitted with jettisonable undercarriages to improve the aircraft's ditching properties on one-shot missions. Once *Argus* joined the fleet and 2F.1s operated from her they were fitted with a more robust undercarriage structure with a propeller guard and axle clips to engage the fore and aft retaining gear. Without the guard there was a chance that the propeller would cut into the cables as it nosed forward on stopping with consequent damage to the propeller, retaining wires and deck. The aircraft launched from turret platforms on capital ships and the short runways on cruisers invariably had a tail-guide trestle which raised the tailplane into a flying attitude. This shortened the take-off run to less than 20ft from the aircraft's stowed position when it was launched into a suitable wind.

In addition to take-off platforms on ships, 2F.1s were also flown off high-speed lighters towed astern of destroyers. Originally built to carry flying boats across the North Sea to extend their radius of action, some were fitted with a wooden platform to launch fighters and extend the fleet's air defences. The first attempt, flown by Commander Samson in May 1918 in a 2F.1 with a skid undercarriage, proved spectacularly unsuccessful. The deck had been built level when the lighter was stationary but at high speed the bow rose up significantly to give the deck a pronounced upward slope. The skids were supposed to run in troughs to keep the aircraft straight and it was raised into a flying attitude by a second pilot lying under the tail and pushing up with his legs but with the upward slope caused by the lighter moving at 32 knots the skids jumped out of the troughs and slowed the aircraft to the extent that it stalled and ditched under bow. Samson managed to extricate himself from the wreck as the lighter ran over it and the destroyer's sea boat saw his distinctive white flying helmet bob to the surface 400 yards astern. His first words on climbing the Jacob's ladder up the side of the destroyer were apparently 'I think it well worth trying again'. The deck was rebuilt to be level at high speed and a proper trestle was installed to raise the tail. A second launch by a wheeled 2F.1 flown by Flight Lieutenant S D Culley RNAS in July proved the concept to be viable..

N 5, the prototype 2F.1 Camel was delivered to the RNAS in 1917.

Another experiment involved the launch of a 2F.1 from a rigid airship to defend it against enemy aircraft. R-23 was fitted with a horizontal surface under the keel against which the aircraft's upper wing was held by a quick-release mechanism which passed through the cut-out portion of the centre-section. The first release was carried out over Pulham with the controls locked and a dummy pilot in the cockpit.

A 2F.1 Camel with its rear fuselage detached being delivered to *Furious* in 1918 from the Grand Fleet Air Park at Donibristle.

A 2F.1 Camel taking-off into wind from HMAS *Sydney*'s rotating platform in 1918. (Sea Power Centre – Australia)

An extremely rare but unfortunately poor-quality image of a 2F.1 Camel landing on *Argus* during 1918.

A B C D E F G H I J K L M N O P Q R S T U V W X Y Z

This was successful and a second release was made with Flight Lieutenant R E Keys RNAS in the aircraft. After the release he dived to start the engine and then flew round the airship before landing safely at Pulham. The concept was put in abeyance after the Armistice and not revived.

2F.1 Ship's Camel data

Length:	18ft 8in
Wingspan:	26ft 11in
Height:	9ft 1in
MTOW:	1,530lb
Engine:	One 150hp Bentley BR.1 rotary driving a two-bladed wooden propeller.
Fuel:	Avgas. 30 gallons in main pressurised tank plus 7 gallons in a gravity tank. Total 37 gallons
Performance:	Maximum level speed 107 knots Service ceiling 17,300ft. 11 minutes 30 seconds to 10,000ft
Endurance:	2¾ hours
Armament:	One fixed, belt-fed, synchronised Vickers 0.303in front gun mounted forward of the cockpit. One 0.303in Lewis gun on Admiralty top-plane mounting. Underwing racks for two 50lb bombs

Including the single prototype, 230 2F.1 Camels were delivered to the RN. Of these, 51 were built by Sopwith and 179 by subcontractors.

2F.1 Ship's Camels saw extensive use with the Grand Fleet in the last year of the war and some remained in service until as late as 1922.

2F.1 Camels ranged on *Furious* prior to the Tondern attack in 1918

A 2F.1 Camel lashed to the deck of Lighter H 3 which is being towed at high speed by a destroyer.

They operated from the aircraft carriers *Argus*, *Eagle* and *Furious* and the seaplane carrier *Pegasus*. They were operated from turret platforms in the Grand Fleet battleships and battlecruisers *Ajax*, *Barham*, *Canada*, *Courageous*, *Emperor of India*, *Glorious*, *Indomitable*, *Inflexible*, *Iron Duke*, *Lion*, *Malaya*, *New Zealand*, *Orion*, *Princess Royal*, *Queen Elizabeth*, *Renown*, *Repulse*, *Ramillies*, *Revenge*, *Royal Oak*, *Royal Sovereign*, *Tiger*, *Valiant*, *Warspite* and the RAN *Australia*.

Grand Fleet cruisers that operated 2F.1 Ship's Camels from short take-off platforms included *Aurora*, *Birkenhead*, *Caledon*, *Calliope*, *Carlisle*, *Caroline*, *Cassandra*, *Chatham*, *Comus*, *Cordelia*, *Delhi*, *Dublin*,

Galatea, *Inconstant*, *Penelope*, *Phaeton*, *Royalist*, *Southampton*, *Undaunted*, *Yarmouth* and the RAN *Melbourne* and *Sydney*.

Destroyers of the Harwich Force known to have towed lighters with 2F.1s on them included *Truculent*, *Redoubt* and *Springbok*.

During a sweep by the Harwich Force in June 1918 a 2F.1 was flown off HMAS *Sydney* to intercept German seaplanes in the Heligoland Bight, one of which was forced down into the sea. This is believed to be the first air combat with an enemy fixed-wing aircraft by a fighter launched from a warship. Weeks later 2F.1s from *Furious* took part in further air combats over the fleet. In August Culley was launched from a lighter towed by *Redoubt* to intercept a Zeppelin and succeeded in destroying L-53 after a 30-minute chase.

The most significant embarked 2F.1 achievement was an attack by seven aircraft from *Furious* in July 1918 on the German airship sheds at Tondern, something repeated seaplane strikes had failed to achieve since the first months of the war. Each aircraft was armed with front guns and two 50lb bombs and they flew in two waves, attacking shortly after dawn. One was forced to ditch after engine failure but six reached the objective. The first flight caused a fire in one of the two sheds which destroyed the Zeppelins L-54 and L-60 inside it. The second wave destroyed another hangar but there were no airships inside it. This was the first air strike in history in which the aircraft had taken off from the deck of a carrier. Only two made it back but both had to ditch; *Furious*' landing deck was considered unsafe because of turbulence and funnel smoke. Three other pilots became lost and landed in neutral Denmark and one was missing, presumed to have drowned after ditching.

2F.1s remained in service after the Armistice and in 1919 several formed part of the force deployed to the Baltic for operations against the Bolsheviks in *Vindictive* and one was embarked in the cruiser *Delhi*. Others were used in deck-landing experiments. In May 1920 2F.1s were included in the special Flight that carried out trials in the semi-complete *Eagle* to test the effect of her starboard-side island. They formed part of *Argus*' first post-war air group in January 1920 and sailed with her on the Atlantic Fleet Spring Cruise to the Mediterranean. The last examples were deleted in 1922.

B.1

A single B.1 was delivered to the RNAS for evaluation as a possible 1½ Strutter replacement in 1917. A 200hp Hispano-Suiza 8B engine driving a two-bladed wooden propeller gave a maximum level speed of 104 knots. Wingspan was 38ft 6in, MTOW 3,035lb and it could carry up to 560lb of bombs. After the initial evaluation it was issued to 5 Wing at Dunkirk and took part in several bombing missions with the unit's DH 4s. Whilst there it was fitted with a single synchronised 0.303in Lewis gun forward of the cockpit and was considered to be a good aircraft but it was not ordered into production. It was later used for experimental work at Isle of Grain.

T.1 Cuckoo

Once it was proved that wheeled aircraft could be safely flown off a ship's deck, the Admiralty asked Sopwith to design a torpedo-armed biplane. A subsequent Admiralty memorandum specified an aircraft with a wheeled undercarriage capable of carrying a 1,000lb torpedo from the deck of an aircraft carrier and an endurance of 4 hours. The result was the T.1 and the first example was completed in June 1917 with a Hispano-Suiza engine. It had to be a single-seater to minimise weight and bore a superficial resemblance to the B.1. The wings folded aft with the hinge point at the interplane struts fitted at the outboard extremities of the wide centre-section. The vees of the undercarriage were fitted under the inner struts and the torpedo was carried externally on crutches fitted under the fuselage centreline. Construction of the wings, fuselage and tail unit was conventional with wooden framework cross-braced internally with steel wire and covered in doped fabric except the plywood top decking around the cockpit. The engine cowling was fabricated from aluminium and faired into the flat fuselage sides. Weight considerations also prevented a front gun being fitted

T.1 Cuckoo with wings folded

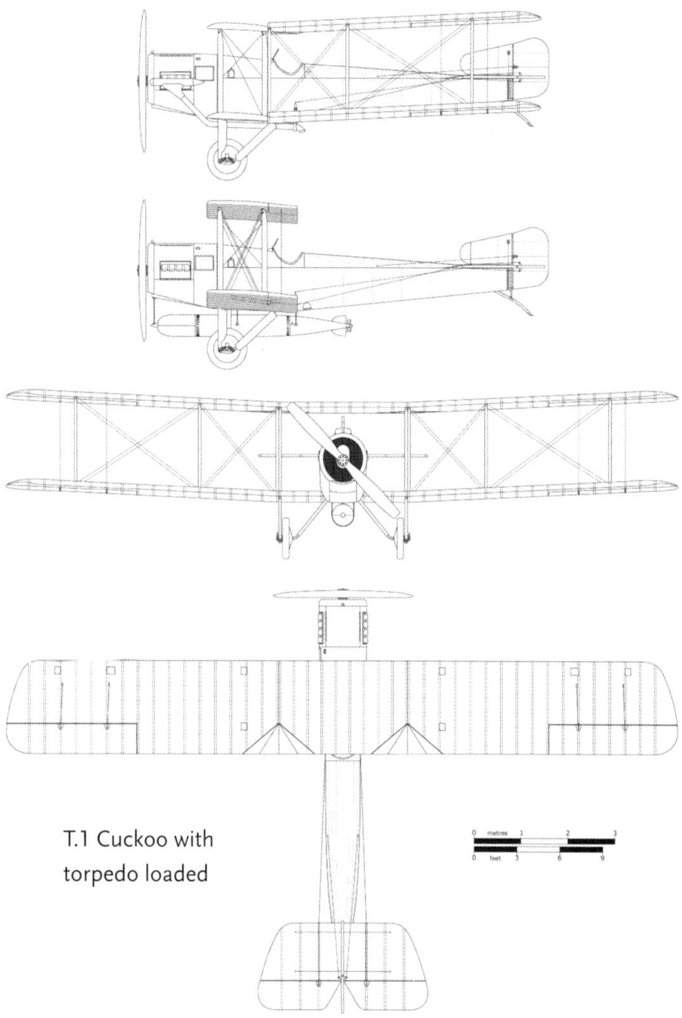

T.1 Cuckoo with torpedo loaded

A T.1 Cuckoo with a loaded torpedo stripped to show its interior structure.

forward of the cockpit as the Admiralty had wanted. The name Cuckoo was selected in 1918.

Service trials at Isle of Grain in 1917 went well and there was considerable enthusiasm within the Grand Fleet for the T.1 to be ordered in sufficient quantity to attack the German fleet in its harbours, flying from the decks of ships converted into carriers. However, the Admiralty was reluctant to convert the number of ships requested and instructed the Grand Fleet to concentrate on *Argus*, *Furious* and *Vindictive* once they were ready. Priority for the Hispano-Suiza engine was given by the new Joint Air Board to SE.5 production and production T.1s were have the 200hp Sunbeam Arab engine instead. This meant significant re-design and revised production drawings which caused delay. Sopwith was fully committed to fighter production and the T.1 was out-sourced to subcontractors with an order for 100 placed with the Fairfield Shipbuilding and Engineering Company and 50 from Pegler & Co. Neither was experienced in aircraft construction, they could not meet the timescale that the Grand Fleet wanted and so fifty T.1s were ordered from Blackburn in February 1918 with the first delivered in May. The first Fairfield aircraft was not delivered until September and the first Pegler aircraft was only delivered in October.

The Sunbeam Arab was a heavier engine and this led to a slight reduction in performance. It also proved to be unreliable and an alternative engine, the 200hp Wolseley W.4A Viper, was selected to replace it. Fairfield-built aircraft were built with Viper engines and designated Cuckoo Mark II; Arab-engined aircraft were retrospectively designated as Mark Is. In 1919 a further development, the Mark III, saw limited production with the 275hp Rolls-Royce Falcon III.

T.1 Cuckoo Mark I data

Length:	28ft 6in
Wingspan:	46ft 9in (18ft folded)
Height:	10ft 8in
MTOW:	3,883lb
Engine:	One 200hp Sunbeam Arab driving a two-bladed wooden propeller
Fuel:	Avgas. 48 gallons
Performance:	Maximum level speed 91 knots Service ceiling 12,100ft. 31 minutes to 10,000ft
Endurance:	4 hours
Armament:	One 1,000lb 18in Mark IX torpedo

The RN received 221 T.1s out of a total of 350 ordered before the Armistice; the remainder were cancelled. Those completed included the single prototype built by Sopwith, 162 built by Blackburn, 50 built by Fairfield and eight built by Pegler. By November 1918 there were 69 in service including 30 serving in units attached to the Grand Fleet.

Cuckoos served with 201 Training Depot at East Fortune, 185 and 186 Squadrons at East Fortune and with the TDU at Gosport. 186 Squadron was subsequently re-numbered as 210 Squadron. The type remained in service after the war and operated from the aircraft carriers *Argus*, *Eagle* and *Furious*. They were finally withdrawn service in April 1923.

The Cuckoo was well thought of by its pilots and a 1919

T.1 instrument panel.

A T.1 Cuckoo releasing a practice torpedo in the Firth of Forth.

T.1 Cuckoos in *Argus*' hangar in 1918. The aircraft to the left is on the after lift ready to be ranged.

publication described it as being a fast, handy machine that provided exactly the right performance needed for close-range attacks on enemy ships at sea or in harbour. *Argus* joined the Grand Fleet in October 1918 and 185 Squadron embarked to prepare for the attack on the German fleet in harbour, an operation that would have pre-dated the Japanese attack on Pearl Harbor by 23 years. They were ready in November but the Armistice was signed before it could happen. The *Argus* attack would have been on a smaller scale than the original Grand Fleet plan which had envisaged 121 aircraft attacking from eight carriers with five aircraft allocated to each target and a strike leader (hence the '1' in '121'). However, 185 Squadron was given the chance to show its potential on Saturday 6 September 1919 when eleven of its Cuckoos carried out a demonstration attack on Atlantic Fleet battleships moored in Portland harbour using running torpedoes with inert warheads. Eight aircraft carried torpedoes and three carried smoke bombs to confuse the defences. Since it was intended primarily as a demonstration, the aircraft attacked at a pre-set time in clear daylight rather than at dawn or dusk but they did fly tactically at low level in two groups, the larger

The 'demonstration' attack on the Atlantic Fleet in Portland Harbour by T.1 Cuckoos in 1919.

of five torpedo aircraft and two smoke bombers using land to the north to mask their approach. The smaller group comprised three torpedo aircraft and one smoke bomber attacking from the sea to the south slightly later than the northern group. The shallow water at Portland presented a technical problem since torpedoes that dived below their set running depth might hit the seabed but this was largely overcome.

The results were impressive; the northern group achieved four hits on three battleships. The southern group gained two hits on the flagship of Admiral Madden, C-in-C Atlantic Fleet. One torpedo from each group struck the bottom and some smoke bombs failed to ignite but the remainder did confuse the defences. The demonstration convinced Admiral Madden that torpedo attack by aircraft was extremely effective and that, despite its limitations, the Cuckoo was an important aircraft. The Fleet Gunnery Officer conceded that even with the exact nature and hour of the attack known beforehand, gunfire could have done little to stop it. The Cuckoo introduced a new era in naval warfare and, as Admiral Madden observed, an enemy fleet was no longer safe in wartime, even in its harbours, since the RN now had carrier-borne aircraft able to move across the oceans of the world to get at them.

7F.1 Snipe

The Sopwith 7F.1 Snipe was evaluated in February 1918 and selected as the replacement for the F.1 Camel. Large orders followed, placed with Sopwith and a number of subcontractors but after the Armistice most were cancelled. After the demise of the RNAS, none were issued directly to a naval unit but several were issued to former naval squadrons re-numbered by the RAF and deployed on the Western Front in the days before the Armistice. These included 201 and 208 Squadrons formerly 1 and 8 (Naval) and 204 Squadron, formerly 4 (Naval) at Eastchurch. After the war 203 and 205 Squadrons, formerly 3 and 5 (Naval), had some Snipes on charge for naval operations. Two examples were issued to the Grand Fleet aircraft parks for potential embarkation but neither was actually used operationally. At least four Snipes were used for deck-landing trials on *Argus* in 1923; one is known to have crashed on deck and one crashed into the sea during these trials. Wingspan was 31ft 1in, MTOW was 2,121lb and the 230hp Bentley BR.2 rotary engine driving a two-bladed wooden propeller gave a maximum level speed of 110 knots. The armament of two Vickers front-guns was the same as the F.1 Camel and there were racks for four 25lb bombs under the wings.

SOCIETE POUR AVIATION et ses DERIVES (SPAD)

S.7

The Admiralty took note of the SPAD S.7's performance with French armed forces in 1916 and ordered Mann, Egerton & Co to produce seventy-five for the RNAS under licence. In the event the Admiralty transferred them to the RFC in exchange for Sopwith Triplanes but a single SPAD-built S.7 was delivered to the RNAS at St Pol as a pattern aircraft. It was used operationally by 6 (Naval) Squadron until December 1916 and then transferred to the Design Flight at Eastchurch before being transferred to the RFC in March 1917. A single-seat biplane fighter with a wingspan of 25ft 8in and MTOW 1,632lb powered by the 140hp Hispano-Suiza water-cooled engine driving a two-bladed wooden propeller to give a maximum level speed of 105 knots. Armament comprised a single synchronised, belt-fed, 0.303in Vickers front gun mounted on the decking forward of the cockpit.

STINSON

Reliant

A high-wing monoplane produced for the US civil market which first flew in 1933 and remained in production until 1941. The AT-19 variant was produced for the USAAF and as its production wound down some were offered to the UK as Lend-Lease transfers. It had dual controls but was usually flown by a single pilot and there was seating for two or three passengers in the rear cabin. The US Government insisted that Reliants were returned rather than destroyed in 1945 because it appreciated that there would be a significant civil market for them and so some priority was given to their return shipment and all but a few were withdrawn by the end of 1945.

Reliant data

Length:	29ft 6in
Wingspan:	41ft 11in
Height:	8ft 6in
MTOW:	4,000lb
Engine:	One 290hp Lycoming R-680 radial
Fuel:	Avgas. 68 gallons
Performance:	Maximum level speed 120 knots
	Service ceiling 21,000ft. 8 minutes to 10,000ft
Endurance:	4 hours
Armament:	None

The RN was allocated 500 Reliants from 1943, although not all were used. In addition to bases in the UK they were shipped to naval air stations in India, Ceylon, Australia and the Admiralty Islands north of New Guinea.

From 1943 Reliants equipped, or partially equipped, 700, 703, 722, 723, 725, 730, 733, 740, 742, 744, 746, 747, 748, 752, 758, 772, 776, 781, 782, 784 and 787 NAS albeit some of them for only a short time. In addition to light communications, Reliants were used for refresher and instrument training, observer training, training support and target simulation. They were ideal for deploying or collecting the pilots who ferried new aircraft to RN air stations or collected 'tired' aircraft for RN air yards to refurbish.

For periods between 1943 and 1945 Reliants were issued to the Station Flights at Abbotsinch, Arbroath, Ayr, Ballyhalbert, Bankstown, Belfast, Burscough, China Bay/Trincomalee, Cochin, Colombo, Crail, Culham, Dale, Drem, Dunino, East Haven, Eastleigh, Eglinton, Evanton, Fearn, Ford, Hatston, Henstridge, Inskip, Jervis Bay, Katukurunda, Machrihanish, Nutts Corner, Ponam, Puttalam, Rattray, Ronaldsway, St Merryn, Schofields, Speke, Stretton, Tambaram, Twatt, Woodvale, Yeovilton and Zeals. They provided an important service that stretched literally around the world in support of front-line operations. In addition to Station Flights, Reliants were allocated to Ferry Units at RN Air Stations Culham, Donibristle and Worthy Down. These were among the last to be stood down and returned to the USA in early 1946.

SUNBEAM

Bomber

In addition to manufacturing aero-engines, the Sunbeam Motor Car Company built Short and Avro-designed aircraft for the Admiralty as a subcontractor during the First World War but only produced one design of its own. The Sunbeam Bomber first flew in 1917 but evaluation of the prototype by the RNAS was unsuccessful and a second prototype was cancelled. The bomb bay and fuel tanks were situated close to the centre of gravity, displacing the single cockpit well aft. A single synchronised Vickers front gun was placed on top of the engine more than 9ft in front of the pilot, far beyond his reach to re-cock or clear a jam. Pilots disliked it and an unreliable engine cannot have helped. Its 200hp Sunbeam Arab water-cooled engine driving a two-bladed wooden propeller gave a maximum level speed of 98 knots. Wingspan was 42ft and MTOW 2,952lb. The internal bomb bay could contain three 100lb bombs. No production contracts were placed.

Stinson Reliant. (Philip Jarrett)

Sunbeam Bomber. (Philip Jarrett)

SUPERMARINE

Seal

Derived from an earlier commercial design, the Seal flew in 1920 and had a boat hull with a wheeled undercarriage that could be partially retracted manually for operation from water or lowered for deck landing or operation ashore. It was a spotter-reconnaissance biplane with a crew of two in open cockpits; the pilot well forward in the bow and the observer aft of the wings. The tractor engine was mounted between the wings and its noise was amplified by a 'box' comprising the upper wing and radiators, making it impossible for the pilot and observer to communicate, a failing that made the type immediately unpopular. It had a wooden structure with a single 450hp Napier Lion IA water-cooled engine driving a four-bladed wooden propeller to give a maximum level speed of 93 knots. Wingspan was 48ft and MTOW 4,800lb but other details have been lost. After delivery in 1921 it carried out deck-landing trials on *Argus* off Spithead in November. From then on it was used for catapult and radiator test flying before being returned to Supermarine for conversion in 1925.

Seagull

The first Seagull was the rebuilt Seal, retrospectively designated Seagull Mark I. A third cockpit was incorporated and it was re-engined with a 450hp Napier Lion II. It was a three-seat amphibian capable of operation from an aircraft carrier or from the water; in the latter case hoisted out and recovered by crane. The rebuilt example was delivered in 1922, soon followed by a second prototype. Both were used for deck-landing trials on *Argus* but proved just as unpopular as the Seal as they suffered from the same operational deficiencies. Production Seagulls were built to Mark II standard constructed from wood covered with doped fabric. The wings were hinged to fold aft along the fuselage sides for carrier stowage. The boat hull was fabricated by shaping sheets of plywood into the appropriate form and attaching them to the wooden framework. The undercarriage was a significant improvement in that landing loads were carried by a vertical telescopic strut to the centre-section of the lower wing's front spar; no loading was transmitted directly to the hull. The upper end of this strut could be moved inwards manually towards the centre of the aircraft to semi-retract the wheels clear of the water when the aircraft was floating, a process that took several minutes. The lower wing was set in the shoulder position and the single tractor engine was mounted in a nacelle slung from the upper wing. The problem of the hull fuel tanks blocking access between the cockpits was partially resolved by moving the main tank to a position under the top wing centre-section, a solution with the added advantage of transferring fuel to the engine by gravity feed rather than a mechanical pump. Movement by crawling through the fuselage between the rear cockpits was possible but not easy. A W/T set between the rear cockpits was fitted as standard.

Seagull Mark II.

Seagull Mark II data

Length:	37ft
Wingspan:	46ft (16ft folded)
Height:	12ft
MTOW:	5,691lb
Engine:	One 492hp Napier Lion IIB
Fuel:	Avgas. 100 gallons
Performance:	Maximum level speed 86 knots Service ceiling 9,150ft. 20 minutes to 6,000ft
Endurance:	4 hours
Armament:	One 0.303in Lewis machine gun on Scarff ring for the gunner

After the two prototypes twenty-three Seagull Mark IIs were delivered to the RN. They carried out deck-landing trials on *Argus* in 1922 but only equipped one front-line unit, 440 Flight which was issued with six Mark IIs in May 1923. The Flight embarked in *Eagle* and operated from her in the Mediterranean using Kalafrana as a shore base while the ship was in Malta. The heat of the Maltese summer was said to make the type's marginal performance even worse. Seagulls never proved popular and they were replaced by Fairey IIIDs which could be operated with either wheels or floats from January 1925. Seagulls were deleted by 1926.

Seamew

Designed as a potential twin-engined, three-seat carrier-borne amphibian, development was slow and the first of two prototypes did not fly until 1928. Both were powered by two 238hp Armstrong Siddeley Lynx IV engines driving four-bladed wooden propellers to give a maximum level speed of 83 knots. Wingspan was 45ft 11½in and MTOW was 5,800lb. The hull was wooden but the wings were of wood and metal composite construction. Early evaluation was hampered by extreme nose-heaviness and damage caused to the propellers by spray as the aircraft attempted a water take-off. The failure of a mainplane fitting in one aircraft during 1930 ended any chance of this underpowered type being ordered into production.

Seagull V

In 1932 Supermarine's chief designer, R J Mitchell, began work on a projected three-seat, single-engined biplane amphibian with the company designation Type 223. The RN showed little interest after its experience with the Seagull but the RAN was enthusiastic and ordered twenty-four in 1934. Although it was an entirely new design, the RAN gave the Type 223 the name Seagull Mark V. Prototype testing with one of the prototypes included operation from *Courageous* off Gibraltar with 444 Flight and from the battleship *Nelson* in 1935 by 702 NAS during a cruise to the West Indies. Of interest, the project pilots were Lieutenant Commanders Caspar John RN, who was to become the first naval pilot appointed as First Sea Lord in 1960, and W T Couchman RN who also became an Admiral. The trials proved very successful and stimulated RN interest in the type. Work on the Type 223 had begun as a private venture and it was first flown by Supermarine's chief test pilot 'Mutt' Summers in June 1933. He was so impressed by the type's strength and manoeuvrability that he looped it over Hendon whilst demonstrating it at the second SBAC Show. The Seagull V initially had a 625hp Bristol Pegasus II.M2 radial engine but was otherwise identical to the Walrus Mark I described below.

Walrus

The RN Walrus differed from the Seagull V in having a more powerful engine and Supermarine designated it Type 236. The Admiralty wrote Specification 2/35 around and placed an initial order for twelve in May 1935. This was followed by an order for a further 204 in 1936 and the original Supermarine prototypes were purchased for the RN. The Walrus Mark I was a three-seat, biplane spotter/reconnaissance aircraft with a pusher engine to keep the propeller well aft of the aircrew member who had to climb onto the top wing centre-section to catch the hook being lowered from a ship's recovery crane. It was of mixed construction with stainless steel front and rear wing spars and both spruce and plywood secondary elements. The leading edge was plywood-covered for strength but otherwise the wings were covered by doped fabric. The tailplane was an integral part of the light alloy fuselage which was built as a single-step boat hull and the Walrus was one of the first British aircraft with a fully retractable undercarriage

Walrus Mark II with undercarriage down and Vicker 'K' machine guns mounted on fore and aft hatches.

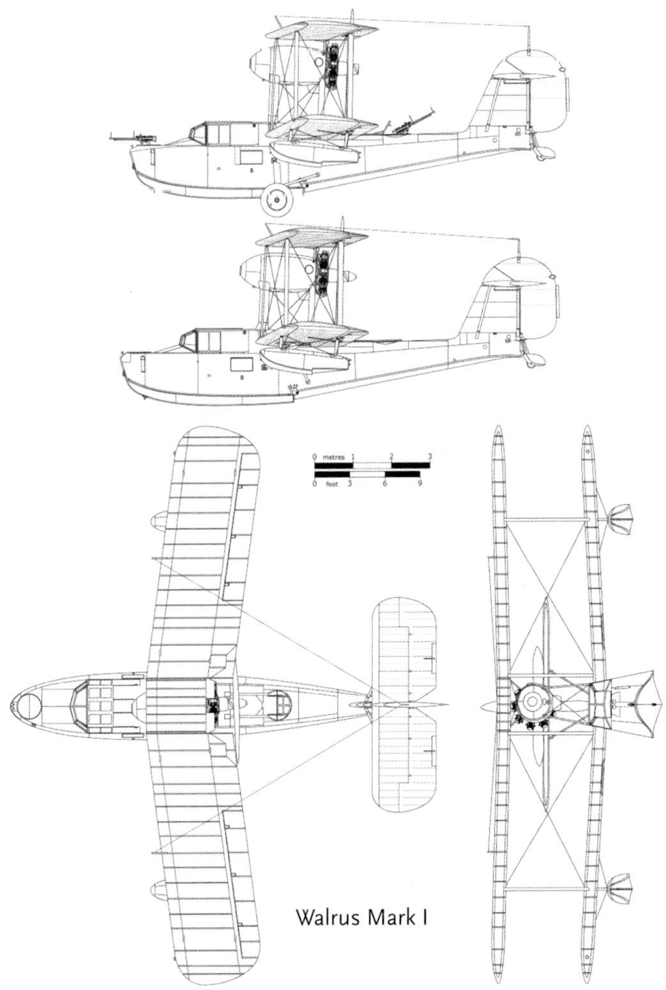

powered by an engine-driven hydraulic system. It also had a fully glazed cockpit to prevent water ingress in rough water conditions. The aircrew member who 'volunteered' to climb onto the upper wing to grab the hook of the Thomas Grab for recovery, usually the TAG, climbed up through a hatch in the cockpit roof. The normal crew comprised a pilot, observer and TAG but a jump seat to the right of the pilot and a control stick extension allowed the Walrus to operate with dual controls for training. Several extra people could be carried in the rear cabin enabling it to operate in both the light communications and ASR roles.

The Admiralty decided in 1936 to concentrate on the Walrus as the primary RN spotter/reconnaissance aircraft for operation from battleships and cruisers but its large orders clashed with RAF orders for Spitfires from Supermarine and so Walrus production was transferred to Saunders Roe. Tools and jigs were transferred and it began manufacturing Mark Is with identical alloy fuselages but in order to make use of skilled wood-workers and free priority alloys for other aircraft, Saunders Roe changed production to a wooden-hulled variant designated Mark II. MTOW was slightly greater than the Mark I but test pilots reported that it was both smoother and quieter, generally preferring it to the Mark I. Another detail change was the substitution of a rubber-tyred tailwheel for the metal wheel of the Mark I. This was also seen as a distinct improvement.

The cruiser *Suffolk*'s Walrus 'Just Jake' being swung inboard by the ship's aircraft crane with the TAG on the upper wing helping with the steadying lines.

Walrus Mark I data

Length:	38ft
Wingspan:	45ft 10in (17ft 11in folded)
Height:	15ft 3in
MTOW:	7,200lb
Engine:	One 750hp Bristol Pegasus II.M2 radial driving a four-bladed wooden pusher propeller
Fuel:	Avgas. One 75-gallon tank in each upper wing. Total 150 gallons
Performance:	Maximum level speed 120 knots Service ceiling 18,500ft. 12½ minutes to 10,000ft
Endurance:	4 hours
Armament:	Two 0.303in Vickers K machine guns, one each on Scarff rings in bow and midships hatches. Underwing racks for two 250lb bombs or depth charges, one under each wing

A total of 686 Walrus were produced including 271 Mark 1s and 190

Walrus 'Just Jake' taxi-ing.

Mark IIs built by Saunders Roe. Between 1936 and 1946 Walrus equipped or partially-equipped 700, 701, 702, 703, 710, 711, 712, 714, 715, 716, 718, 720, 721, 722, 728, 730, 733, 740, 742, 747, 751, 754, 763, 764, 765, 771, 772, 773, 777, 778, 781, 783, 787, 788, 789 and 796 NAS. Between 1936 and 1940 the squadrons numbered between 700 and 720 were operational units providing catapult aircraft for battleships, cruisers and catapult-equipped ships but in 1940 these aircraft were all absorbed into a greatly-expanded 700 NAS.

Apart from their embarked spotter/reconnaissance role with ships of the Home, Mediterranean and East Indies Fleets Walrus embarked in carriers of the BPF as ASR aircraft as well as operating from shore bases around the world in a variety of roles. These included operational anti-submarine patrols off West Africa, ASR from Hong Kong and Malta; fleet requirements duties from Sierra Leone, South Africa, Ceylon, Dartmouth Nova Scotia, Bermuda and the Orkney Islands. They were used for catapult, observer, radar, communications and refresher training and for service equipment trials.

Between 1936 and 1944 Walrus were embarked in the seaplane carrier *Albatross* to provide anti-submarine protection for convoys off Sierra Leone and for catapult training in *Pegasus*. They also operated from *Argus* and *Hermes*. For varying periods Walrus were embarked in *Courageous* and *Glorious* for trials and *Ark Royal* III for passage during the withdrawal from Norway. Individual aircraft were embarked in the aircraft carriers *Ameer*, *Emperor*, *Hunter*, *Khedive*, *Shah*, *Stalker* and *Victorious* for ASR duties. The maintenance carrier *Perseus* embarked a single Walrus for light communications duties in 1945.

Walrus catapult flights were embarked for varying periods in the battleships and battlecruisers *Anson*, *Barham*, *Duke of York*, *Howe*, *King George V*, *Malaya*, *Nelson*, *Prince of Wales*, *Queen Elizabeth*, *Renown*, *Repulse*, *Resolution*, *Rodney*, *Valiant* and *Warspite*.

At various times, catapult flights were embarked in the cruisers *Achilles*, *Ajax*, *Belfast*, *Bermuda*, *Berwick*, *Birmingham*, *Ceylon*, *Cornwall*, *Cumberland*, *Devonshire*, *Dorsetshire*, *Edinburgh*, *Effingham*, *Exeter*, *Fiji*, *Gambia*, *Glasgow*, *Gloucester*, *Jamaica*, *Kent*, *Kenya*, *Leander*, *Liverpool*, *London*, *Manchester*, *Mauritius*, *Newcastle*, *Newfoundland*, *Nigeria*, *Norfolk*, *Sheffield*, *Shropshire*, *Southampton*, *Suffolk*, *Sussex*, *Trinidad*, *Uganda* and *York*.

Known to a generation of naval aircrew as the 'Shagbat' or

A Walrus being catapulted from the cruiser *Bermuda* in Scapa Flow.

'Pusser's Duck' the Walrus established an enviable reputation for reliability and the sheer range of tasks it could carry out, in almost any climate, ranging from admiral's barge to dive-bomber. The latter was first achieved attacking German troop concentrations near Narvik from a temporary base at Harstad during the 1940 campaign in Norway. Some months later a Walrus from *Dorsetshire* dive-bombed an Italian fuel dump on the Red Sea coast successfully. Another Walrus landed in Tobruk harbour under fire at night to deliver urgent supplies while it was under siege. *Albatross* moved its Walrus squadron from Sierra Leone to the Indian Ocean in 1942 for further trade protection duties but by 1944 the number of aircraft carriers in service meant that catapult flights were rapidly stood down. From 1944 the remaining Walrus in RN service were embarked in carriers to give ASR cover during strike operations. The two aircraft embarked in *Victorious* were known as 'Derby and Joan'. During 1942 with the Walrus in service and the Seafire entering service, a Supermarine official told the press proudly that Supermarine were responsible for both the world's fastest and slowest deck-landing aircraft, both designed by R J Mitchell.

Sea Otter

The Type 309 Sea Otter was designed to meet Specification 5/36 as a Walrus replacement and the first of two prototypes flew in September 1938. It differed in having a tractor engine driving a three-bladed, variable-pitch metal propeller. The prototypes had 796hp Bristol Perseus VI radial engines but these overheated and production aircraft had Bristol Mercury radials. The Sea Otter had an alloy hull but mixed fabric-covered wood and alloy wings like the Walrus. Development was slow but included catapult launches and crane recoveries from *Pegasus* in 1939 after which the decision was taken to transfer Sea Otter production to Saunders Roe and design changes were reflected in Specification S.14/39. The first order was not placed until January 1942, however. By then there were doubts about the need for an aircraft to replace the Walrus at all but the requirement for an ASR-capable amphibian was increasing and comparative trials were carried out. These showed that the Sea Otter had a greater radius of action and could take off in an overload condition, both desirable attributes for the ASR mission. Early production aircraft were produced to ABR Mark I standard but later aircraft were modified to ASR Mark II (Naval) standard specifically for this mission. Records do not show that any Sea Otters replaced Walrus before spotter/reconnaissance flights

Sea Otter. (Merv Green)

were withdrawn in 1944. With their low landing speed and sting-type arrester hooks, Sea Otters could operate from a carrier deck under almost all practical conditions. Trials during 1944 cleared the type to use RATOG and the airframe was stressed for both catapult launch and dive-bombing.

Sea Otter ASR Mark II data

Length:	39ft 10¾in
Wingspan:	46ft (18ft folded)
Height:	15ft 1½in to upper propeller tip, undercarriage down
MTOW:	10,000lb
Engine:	One 965hp Bristol Mercury XXX driving a three-bladed Rotol variable pitch metal propeller
Fuel:	Avgas. One 81-gallon tank in each upper wing plus an optional 44-gallon auxiliary overload tank. Total 206 gallons
Performance:	Maximum level speed 142 knots Service ceiling 17,000ft. 6 minutes to 5,000ft
Endurance:	Approximately 5 hours
Armament:	Weapons were seldom carried on the ASR II but the ABR I was designed to have a single 0.303in Vickers gas-operated machine gun on the fore hatch and twin Vickers K guns on the amidships hatch. Racks for four 250lb bombs or depth charges could be fitted under the wings

The RN received two prototypes and 140 Sea Otters.

Between 1944 and 1952 Sea Otters equipped or partially equipped 700, 712, 716, 721, 728, 729, 730, 733, 740, 742, 744, 771, 772, 778, 781, 799, 1700, 1701, 1702 and 1703 NAS. Those in the 1700-series were commissioned specifically for ASR duties in the BPF and Mediterranean Fleet.

Although they never operated in their original spotter/reconnaissance role, Sea Otters operated in a variety of tasks around the world including ASR, light communications, trials, training and fleet requirements work. Examples operated from Hatston, Eastleigh, Kai-Tak, Hal Far, Katukurunda, Ayr, Trincomalee, Machrihanish, Coimbatore, Eglinton, Lee-on-Solent, Arbroath and Henstridge.

Between 1944 and 1952 Sea Otters were embarked in the aircraft carriers *Campania*, *Ocean*, *Theseus*, *Khedive*, *Stalker*, *Hunter*, *Ameer*, *Emperor*, *Shah*, *Attacker* and *Trouncer*. Those in *Campania* provided reconnaissance and communications back-up for Operation 'Hurricane', the British atomic bomb test at Monte Bello Island off north-west Australia in 1952; those in *Trouncer* took part in mine clearance operations in the Eastern Mediterranean in 1945/46.

Between 1945 and 1952 Sea Otters were allocated to station flights to provide an ASR capability at Abbotsinch, Arbroath, Ayr, Belfast, Culdrose, Dale, Eastleigh, Eglinton, Kai-Tak, Lossiemouth, Machrihanish, St Merryn and MONAB-4/Ponam in the Admiralty Islands.

A Sea Otter ASR II from Eglinton carrying out a practice water rescue. (Merv Green)

Type 322 'Dumbo'

Designed to meet the same specification as the Fairey Barracuda but not selected, Supermarine's Type 322 was nicknamed 'Dumbo' because its bulky fuselage and high wings bore a fanciful resemblance to the Disney cartoon character. Two prototypes were ordered which, like the Barracuda, were to have Rolls-Royce Exe engines but when these were cancelled, it too was modified to take the Merlin. Work was slowed by Supermarine's concentration on Spitfires but the Type 322 was, in some ways, more advanced than the Barracuda despite its fixed undercarriage. The wings had slotted leading edges and the trailing edges had extensive flaps but their most distinctive feature was variable incidence. Jacking the wing up to high incidence in low-speed flight kept the fuselage level and gave the pilot a good view of the deck in a three-point landing attitude. When the wings were lowered to the normal flight position they gave good aerodynamic efficiency in the higher speed range but by the time the first example flew in 1943 the Barracuda was already accepted and in full-scale production. Two 'Dumbos' were completed for research into variable-incidence wing designs.

They had a stalling speed of only 50 knots and with the fuselage

Supermarine Type 322 'Dumbo' designed to meet the same Naval Staff Requirement as the Fairey Barracuda. (Philip Jarrett)

level at approach speed it would have been a good deck-landing aircraft. The fixed undercarriage was accepted because the design team believed that the specified performance could be achieved without the weight and complication of an undercarriage retraction system. Never given an official name, the Type 322 had a wingspan of 50ft, MTOW of 12,000lb and the first prototype had a 1,300hp Rolls-Royce Merlin 30. The second had a 1,645hp Merlin 32 which gave a maximum level speed of 240 knots without armament or service equipment. The wings were hinged at the after part of the centre-section to fold aft along the fuselage sides to give a folded width of 18ft. Intended armament was a single torpedo under the fuselage or up to six 500lb bombs on underwing racks. A single 0.303in Vickers K gun could be fitted to a flexible mounting on the rear cockpit hatch. The second 'Dumbo' was still flying in 1947, used as a company chase-plane to observe Attacker low-speed handling trials.

Seagull ASR I

From 1940 Supermarine worked on a monoplane, follow-on amphibian it designated Type 347 which had variable-incidence wings like the Type 322 with full-span, 40 per cent chord slotted flaps, inset ailerons and full-span leading-edge slats to create a high-lift wing mounted above the hull on a pylon. Its designer, Joseph Smith, described it as a combination of Walrus and Spitfire experience to give seaworthiness and performance. The wings folded upwards for carrier stowage and the undercarriage retracted into the fuselage sides when it was afloat. Work was slow but three prototypes were ordered in 1943, only two of which were completed. The first flew in July 1948 and the second in 1949. Successful deck-landing trials were carried out on *Illustrious* in 1949; the high-lift wing performed well and one test pilot demonstrated an approach speed of only 30 knots. By then, however, the replacement of amphibian ASR aircraft by helicopters was envisaged and there were sufficient Sea Otters available for the role until they came into service. The two prototypes were sold for scrap in 1952. Wingspan was 52ft 6in, 23ft 6in folded, and MTOW was 14,500lb. The single 1,815hp Rolls-Royce Griffon 29 gave a maximum level speed of 230 knots.

Spitfire

Spitfires were transferred from the RAF to the RN for trials and training tasks; some of them were issued to new fighter squadrons for use while they awaited Seafires. The majority of 'used' Spitfires transferred were Mark VA and Mark VB but there were some PR XIIIs and even a few Mark Is and IIs. The largest RN users were the School of Air Warfare at St Merryn and the Naval Fighter Schools at Yeovilton and Henstridge. Some were fitted with arrester hooks, described as hooked-Spitfires, and used for deck-landing training. The letters after the Roman mark number indicated the gun armament, the 'A' having eight machine guns and the 'B' two 20mm cannon and four machine guns.

Seagull ASR 1 taking the 'cut' during deck-landing trials on *Illustrious* in October 1949.

Spitfire Mark IA of 759 NAS at Yeovilton in 1943. (Philip Jarrett)

The Mark V was a single-seat fighter with a 1,470hp Rolls-Royce Merlin 45 liquid-cooled engine driving a three-bladed variable-pitch propeller to give a maximum level speed of 330 knots. Wingspan was 36ft 10in and MTOW 6,785lb.

The RN received 279 Spitfires from the RAF between 1942 and 1945. They equipped, or partially equipped 715, 718, 719, 736, 748, 759, 761, 762, 768, 778, 787, 790, 791, 794 and 798 NAS.

Front-line fighter squadrons that used Spitfires to work-up whilst awaiting delivery of their Seafires included 801, 808, 809, 879, 880, 884, 885, 886, 887, 897 and 899 NAS

Seafire

Supermarine had offered a folding-wing design with an arrester hook derived from the Spitfire which it referred to as a 'Sea Spitfire' in January 1940 but this initiative was rejected by the then First Lord of the Admiralty, Winston Churchill. MAP approval for the Admiralty to procure a Spitfire derivative was finally agreed in late 1941 after successful deck-landing trials with a 'hooked Spitfire' had been carried out by Lieutenant Commander H P Bramwell DSO DSC RN on *Illustrious* to prove that carrier operations were viable. Initially a Spitfire VB was modified by Supermarine with an 'A'-frame arrester hook under the after fuselage and it flew from Worthy Down in January 1942 as the prototype Supermarine Type 340 with the new name Seafire Mark I, the name Sea Spitfire having been quietly dropped as it was considered too difficult to say quickly. An initial contract for forty-eight conversions was followed by large production batches built from the outset as Seafires, single-seat fighters with stressed-skin monocoque, Alclad, fuselages. The wings comprised a 'D'-spar leading-edge built onto the front spar to form a torsion box designed to absorb landing shock and front-gun recoil. Aft of this there was an auxiliary rear spar. The wing centre section was built integrally with the front fuselage frames with stiffening members around the wheel wells and gun bays. Wing tips were detachable so that they could easily be replaced if damaged but some units elected to fly without them to increase the aircraft's rate of roll. Ailerons were metal-covered and the split training edge flaps were attached to the secondary spar. Wing folding was introduced in the Seafire Mark III.

Mark IB

Early conversions were designated Seafire IB with minimal modification to get them into service quickly. The 'B' referred to the type's 'B'-type wings designed to take a two cannon/four machine gun front-gun armament. The arrester hook was an 'A'-frame hinged on the bottom longerons on frame 15 with legs 6ft long and faired into the fuselage, except for the bill, to reduce drag. Local strengthening on the bottom longerons was introduced around the hook attachments and also the damping jack hinge points. The hook was held in the up position by a scissors-type snap gear and released by a Bowden cable activated by a lever in the cockpit. Once lowered it could not be raised in flight and had to be clicked back into place by ground crew once the aircraft had landed. The IB did not have folding wings and could only be struck down into hangars by the large lifts in *Argus*, *Furious* and the US-built CVEs. Typically, IBs had either a 1,470hp Rolls-Royce Merlin 45 or 1,415hp Merlin 46 giving a maximum level speed of 320 knots. Only two front-line squadrons were fully equipped with Seafire Mark IBs, 801 in *Furious* and 842 in *Fencer*. Total Mark IB production amounted to 186 aircraft.

F.IIC, FR.IIC and LR.IIC

Seafire Mark IIs, designated Type 357 by Supermarine, were built new

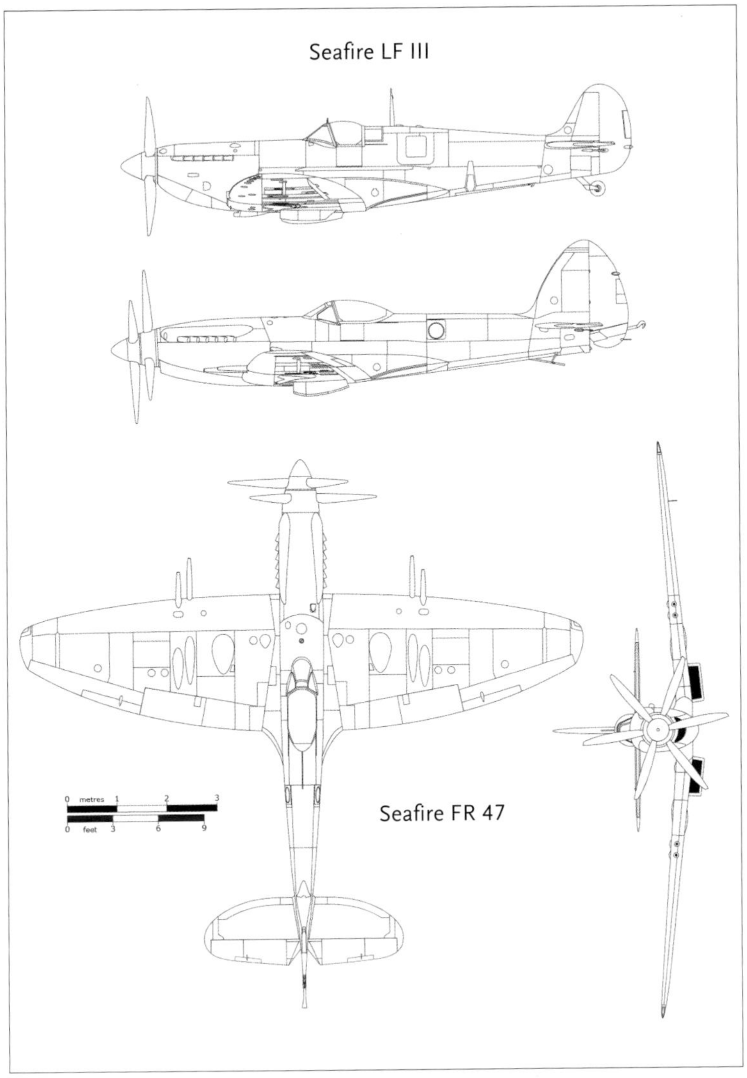

by Supermarine and under subcontract by Westland, introducing detail improvements including the 'C'-type wing which could accommodate differing armament options and catapult spools were fitted as standard but they still lacked folding wings. Early Mark IICs were retrospectively re-designated F.IIC when other specialised sub-variants were introduced. They had a 1,415hp Rolls-Royce Merlin 45 or 46 driving a three-bladed, variable-pitch propeller but their performance at low level, where most interceptions took place, was not considered good enough. Some F.IICs were modified for tactical reconnaissance duties by the addition of two F-24 cameras aft of the cockpit, one vertical, one oblique, and designated as FR.IIC. The extra weight of the cameras aft had to be compensated by the addition of a ballast weight in the engine bay which increased their basic weight. In general F.IICs were about 10 knots slower than Mark IBs in level flight because of their added weight. The most successful of the Mark II variants was the L.IIC, the 'L' indicating optimisation for the best performance at low level. They had a 1,645hp Rolls-Royce Merlin 32 which gave a maximum level speed of 325 knots and to absorb the extra power the L.IIC had a four-bladed, variable-pitch propeller The extra power reduced the take-off run or the WOD required for a free take-off. Mark IIs were modified in service to use RATOG and to carry a single 250lb bomb on a centreline pylon. A total of 372 Seafire Mark IIs were delivered to the RN between 1942 and 1943. Of these 262 were built by Supermarine and 110 by Westland.

F.III, LF.III and FR.III

The Mark III Seafire, identified by Supermarine as Type 358, introduced folding wings with two straight, chord-wise folds; the inner positioned just outboard of the wheel wells from where the wing was

Seafire IICs of 885 NAS on *Formidable* in 1943 showing signs of the harsh environment in which they operated.

A Seafire LIIC of 807 NAS just prior to taking-off.

folded through the vertical into a slight angle towards the fuselage. The wingtips were folded downwards to reduce height for hangar stowage. The hinges were at the top of the front spar and at the rear spar with the locking point at the bottom of the front spar where a tapered bolt was screwed into mating lugs. Both folding and spreading had to be carried out manually and required a well-practised flight deck party. Wing-fold poles could be locked in place to provide strength for aircraft in a deck park with their wings folded. The unique folding wing made it unnecessary to add the suffix 'B' or 'C' and they were not used from the Mark III onwards. They were built in the same sub-variants as the Mark II and the fuselage was basically the same with the basic versions powered by the 1,470hp Rolls-Royce Merlin 55 which had automatic boost control fitted to give good performance at a range of altitudes. LF.IIIs had the Merlin 55M with a cropped supercharger impeller to give 1,585hp at low level. The FR.III designation was applied to LF.IIIs fitted with the two F24 cameras aft of the cockpit but they did not require balance weight in the nose because of the 55M engine was slightly heavier than the 45/46. Four-bladed variable-pitch propellers were fitted as standard and other improvements included underwing hardpoints for two 250lb bombs, one under each wing. Alternatively a single 500lb bomb could be carried under the fuselage centreline. Mark IIIs entered operational service in November 1943 and 1,263 were delivered to the RN of which 913 were built by Westland and 350 by Cunliffe Owen. Within that total, the final 129 aircraft built by Cunliffe Owen were to FR.III standard.

Seafire LF.III data

Length:	30ft 2½in
Wingspan:	36ft 10in (13ft 4in folded)
Height:	11ft 5½in (13ft 6in with wings folded)
MTOW:	7,232lb
Engine:	One 1,585hp Rolls-Royce Merlin 55M driving a four-bladed, variable-pitch metal propeller
Fuel:	Avgas. 85 gallons internal plus optional drop tanks up to 90 gallons. Total 175 gallons
Performance:	Maximum level speed 315 knots Service ceiling 36,000ft. 5 minutes to 15,000ft
Endurance:	Up to 3 hours at low speed
Armament:	Two 20mm Hispano cannon, one in each wing, with 120 rpg. Four Browning 0.303in machine guns, two in each wing, with 350 rpg. Provision for one 500lb bomb on centreline hardpoint. Late production aircraft had provision for four 3in R/P on Mark VIII launchers, two under each wing

F.XV/F 15

In 1943 the MAP decided that there should be no gap between Spitfire and Seafire marks, as both progressed to unusually high numbers. There was no Seafire Mark IV, therefore, and the next version followed the Spitfire Mark XIV to become the Seafire Mark XV. It remained in service after 1947 when British mark numbers changed from Roman to Arabic numerals and so it became the F 15. I refer to it as such to differentiate it from the earlier marks.

It was designed to meet Specification N.4/43 for a single-seat carrier-borne fighter of improved performance and was initially designated Type 377 by Supermarine. Design modifications after testing led to production aircraft being identified as Type 386. The first examples retained the 'A'-frame arrester hook but the majority had the more efficient 'sting'-type hook anchored to the fuselage stern at the base of the rudder. It significantly reduced the nose-down pitching moment caused by the action of the arrester wire on the 'A'-frame arrester hook that had been a Seafire problem since it first went to sea, but the lower part of the rudder had to be sacrificed and so, to compensate, the upper part was enlarged. The hook housing was enclosed in a fairing which joined the lines of the rudder to the fuselage and provided extra fin area until the hook was lowered. The hook was spring-loaded in its housing and when released it extended by 18in. Another of its advantages over the 'A'-frame was that it could pivot by up to 30 degrees either side of centre to compensate for a deck landing that was not exactly fore and aft. As in earlier marks there was an oleo-pneumatic damper to prevent hook bounce when the bill struck the deck. Once deployed, it could not be raised in flight but had to be retracted by a handler on deck after landing.

The F 15 had a 1,950hp Rolls-Royce Griffon VI engine which gave a maximum level speed of 345 knots and the initial rate of climb was over 4,000ft per minute despite the slightly increased MTOW of 8,000lb. Whilst it had the advantage of greatly increased power, the Griffon's huge torque meant that course use of throttle on the final approach to the deck could easily result in a torque-stall with the aircraft flicking from controlled flight into an irrecoverable spin. Another drawback was that it rotated in the opposite direction to the Merlin and this gave a tendency to swing towards the island when the throttle was opened for take-off; a problem that was not resolved until the introduction of contra-rotating propellers on a later mark. Early Griffon VIs had a problem with supercharger clutches which tended to slip at high rpm and boost settings and this meant that F 15s were not cleared for carrier operation until the problem was resolved by a new clutch design fitted in 1947.

Following BPF experience fitting extemporised drop tanks to the Mark III, the F 15 was designed to take a 60-gallon drop tank on the centreline as an alternative to the 500lb bomb. The underwing hardpoints could carry either 250lb bombs or 22½-gallon tanks, known as combat tanks because they caused no degradation to performance. Another alternative underwing load was two pairs of Mark VIII 3in R/Ps. F 15s were just entering service when the war ended but a number of trials were carried out to determine what could be done to make the Griffon-engined Seafire into the best carrier fighter it could be. These led to a number of improvements subsequently incorporated into the Seafire F 17. By August 1945 the Admiralty had placed contracts for 790 F 15s but 407 were cancelled. The 383 that were delivered were all built by Cunliffe Own and Westland.

F 17, FR 17

The F 17 incorporated the improvements found to be necessary in its extensive testing. These included a strengthened undercarriage with long-stroke oleo legs to reduce rebound on hitting the deck. Another, more obvious, change was a cut-down rear fuselage to the level of the upper longerons to allow a 'bubble' canopy, with better all-round visibility, to be fitted. Design work was carried out by Westland and the last F 15s built by the firm had 'bubble' canopies and long-stroke oleos. Identified as Type 384 by Supermarine, the F 17 had a more aerodynamic, curved windshield in front of the bullet-proof screen and a strengthened main spar which allowed a greater weight of stores to be carried on underwing hardpoints. These included 500lb bombs,

Seafire LIIIs of 899 NAS ranged on *Khedive*.

A BPF Seafire III on *Implacable* showing how labour-intensive spreading and folding wings manually was.

22½-gallon combat tanks or up to eight 3in RP. It was the first Spitfire or Seafire mark to have a 24-volt electrical system. The space aft of the cockpit was made adaptable so that it could be fitted with either a 33-gallon fuel tank or two F24 cameras; one vertical and one oblique. Aircraft with the camera fit were designated FR 17s. The first Seafire F 17s were delivered in late 1945 and proved immediately popular. The engine was the same Griffon VI as the F 15 but extra weight reduced the maximum level speed by 4 knots. The F 17 remained in service with RN shore-based training squadrons until 1954. A total of 232 Seafire F 17s was received by the RN. Of these 20 were built by Cunliffe Owen and 212 by Westland. The single prototype was a converted F 15.

F 45

The mark numbers 20 onwards were allocated to a series of advanced Spitfires and so the MAP decided in 1944 to give Seafires mark numbers in a block commencing with 45. The Admiralty issued Specification N.7/44 for a Seafire derivative of the Spitfire F 21 and the result was the Type 388 Seafire F 45. Supermarine retained design authority but subcontracted Cunliffe Owen to make the necessary changes. The F 45 was regarded as an interim type that would not be embarked and had non-folding Spitfire F 21 wings. A 2,035hp Rolls-Royce Griffon 61 engine driving a five-bladed variable-pitch propeller gave a maximum level speed of 390 knots and a rudder of larger chord than earlier marks gave better directional stability but the more powerful Griffon exacerbated the torque problem. F 45s equipped several shore-based units from late 1945 and carrier trials carried out in *Pretoria Castle* included 239 deck landings by five aircraft with only two minor undercarriage malfunctions. Some were fitted with 2,300hp Griffon 85 engines driving two three-bladed, contra-rotating, variable pitch propellers which solved the torque problem and effectively made them prototype F 46s. During diving trials a Seafire F 45 was recorded to have reached Mach 0.88, the highest speed ever recorded by an RN propeller-driven aircraft. The last F 45s were withdrawn from service in 1950. The RN received fifty F 45s and many more were cancelled

Seafires of 887 and 894 NAS ranged on *Implacable* leaving Sydney in 1945.

in 1945. They were built by Supermarine together with the single prototype converted from a Spitfire F 21 bringing the total number to fifty-one.

F 46

Developed from the F 45 but having contra-rotating, variable pitch, propellers the F 46 was cleared for carrier operation but still lacked folding wings. Cunliffe Owen carried out the detail design work and a modified F 45 acted as prototype. The fin and rudder had increased chord to counteract the forward side area of the elongated spinner and additional fuel tankage comprised the 32-gallon tank in the rear fuselage as standard, the two 22½-gallon underwing combat tanks and an optional 50-gallon drop tank on the fuselage centreline. Production F 46s had a 2,300hp Rolls-Royce Griffon 87 engine driving two three-bladed contra-rotating propellers giving a maximum level speed of 390 knots. MTOW was 9,400lb and the armament now comprised four 20mm cannon in the wings with underwing provision for bombs or rockets. They were used mainly by shore-based squadrons but some saw semi-operational service with 1832 NAS of the RNVR. Like the F 45 they were withdrawn from service in 1950. Production amounted to twenty-four, all built by Supermarine plus the prototype.

FR 47

A logical development of the F 46 with folding wings which had a single hinge point outboard of the four cannons. A few early production aircraft had manual folding and spreading but the majority had hydraulically-powered folding selected by a switch in the cockpit. All those that equipped front-line squadrons were to this standard. The FR 47 carried more fuel than any other mark of Spitfire or Seafire and every aircraft could be fitted with two electrically-heated F24 cameras aft of the cockpit, one vertical and one oblique, for reconnaissance sorties hence the FR designation. After its service acceptance trials the FR 47 was cleared for all forms of flight at a MTOW of 11,100lb but, for take-off and gentle manoeuvres, the MTOW was 12,900lb. The first Seafire 47s were delivered in 1946. There were no prototypes and the first production aircraft were used in the test programme. R J Mitchell had designed the original Spitfire but his successor Joe Smith transformed the fragile Seafire IB into the FR 47.

Seafire FR 47 data

Length:	34ft 6in to tip of arrester hook
Wingspan:	36ft 11in (25ft 5in folded)
Height:	12ft 9in (16ft with wings folded)
MTOW:	12,900lb
Engine:	One 2,350hp Rolls-Royce Griffon 88 driving two three-bladed, contra-rotating, variable-pitch metal propellers
Fuel:	Avgas. 84 gallons in forward fuselage tank; 32 gallons in rear fuselage tank; 11 gallons in wing root tanks; and 25 gallons in wing tanks. Total 152 gallons. Additionally a 90-gallon drop tank could be carried under the fuselage centreline and a 45-gallon tank under each wing hardpoint to give a total of 332 gallons
Performance:	Maximum level speed 398 knots Service ceiling 43,100ft. 5 minutes to 20,000ft
Endurance:	Up to 3 hours with 90-gallon drop tank
Armament:	Four 20mm Hispano cannon, two in each wing, with 134 rpg on the inboard guns and 114 rpg on the outboard guns. Provision for two 500lb or 250lb bombs under wings or up to eight 3in R/P on Mark VIII launchers, four under each wing

The RN received ninety Seafire FR 47s, all built by Supermarine.

Including prototypes, total Seafire production amounted to 2,602 aircraft, a number only exceeded by the Fairey Barracuda.

Between 1942 and 1954, Seafires equipped, or partially equipped, 700, 703, 706, 708, 709, 715, 718, 719, 721, 727, 728, 730, 731, 733, 736, 737, 738, 741, 744, 748, 751, 757, 759, 761, 764, 766, 767, 768, 770, 771, 772, 773, 775, 776, 777, 778, 779, 780, 781, 782, 787, 790, 791, 794, 798 and 799 NAS. They flew with these shore-based units in the fighter training, refresher flying, tactical development, conversion training, deck-landing training, trials and fleet requirements roles in the Home, Mediterranean, East Indies and British Pacific Fleets.

Between early 1942 and the end of 1950 Seafires saw operational service with 800. 801, 802, 805, 806, 807, 808, 809, 816, 833, 834, 842, 879, 880, 883, 884, 885, 886, 887, 889, 894, 895, 897 and 899 NAS. Of these, 816, 833, 834 and 842 NAS were composite squadrons that operated both Swordfish and Seafires from CVEs in the trade protection role.

At various times Seafires were embarked in the aircraft carriers *Argus, Atheling, Attacker, Battler, Chaser, Fencer, Formidable, Furious, Glory, Hunter, Illustrious, Implacable, Indefatigable, Indomitable, Khedive, Ocean, Pretoria Castle, Stalker, Theseus, Tracker, Triumph, Unicorn, Venerable, Vengeance* and *Victorious.*

Between 1947 and 1954 Seafires operated with 1830, 1831, 1832 and 1833 NAS as part of the RNVR Air Branch.

In addition to the squadrons based at air stations across the world, Seafires were allocated to Station Flights at Anthorn, East Haven, St Merryn, Schofields, Sembawang, Stretton and Yeovilton between 1943 and 1946.

Despite its shortcomings as a deck-landing aircraft, there were few fighters that could out-perform the Seafire once it was airborne and development kept the various marks competitive. They first entered service with 807 NAS in June 1942 and participated in Operation 'Torch', the Allied landings in North Africa, during which the first Seafire 'kill' was achieved by Sub Lieutenant George Baldwin DSC RN. In September 1943 there were 106 Seafires embarked in Force V, *Unicorn, Stalker, Attacker, Hunter* and *Battler*, to cover the Allied landings at Salerno, Operation 'Avalanche'. They in turn were covered by Force H with the fleet carriers *Illustrious* and *Formidable* which had fifteen Seafires and sixty Grumman Martlets embarked. The Allied Commander's tasking for Force V Seafires was less demanding than expected but carried out effectively. However, they suffered a high proportion of deck-landing accidents and there can be no doubt that Force V's experience off Salerno was responsible for the type's bad reputation as a deck-landing aircraft for the remainder of its career. Admiral Vian who later commanded both the BPF carrier force and the Home Fleet was particularly vocal in his condemnation. No Seafires were lost in combat during Avalanche but forty-two were lost or written off in accidents. In 713 sorties there were 32 catastrophic deck-landing accidents in which Seafires were sufficiently badly damaged to be written off. Four more were lost after engine failures and six from accidents whilst airborne. Added to these, twenty-four Seafires suffered wrinkling of their rear fuselages beyond the capacity of ships' engineering staffs to repair while their attention was focused on keeping the serviceable aircraft flying. Seventeen more suffered undercarriage damage which could not be repaired because insufficient spares were available in the CVEs. Put simply, one out of every nine sorties resulted in the loss of, or serious damage to a Seafire; an appalling casualty rate that was never repeated in any other operation.

It is fair to say that many of the pilots embarked in Force V's Seafire squadrons were inexperienced, lacking the finesse that only hours flown on type could have given them. There were many instances of propeller tips 'pecking' the deck when as aircraft pitched forward on being arrested or when the pilot raised the tail on take-off. This could be cured by filing down the tips and, following *Hunter*'s initiative, roughly 2in were filed off the tips of most Seafires with no loss of performance. Most of the Seafire squadrons had only just formed and work-up periods to get them accustomed to small CVE flight decks had been too short, even for pilots transferred from the big fleet carriers. Significantly the commanding officer of *Hunter*'s 834 NAS had drilled his pilots relentlessly in deck-landing techniques and this unit suffered no losses. This example proved, yet again, that rushing units into service

A Seafire F 17 of 771 NAS.

with inadequate preparation to achieve numbers on paper had not produced the desired results.

There were other factors. There was virtually no natural wind during 'Avalanche' and without it, even with the CVEs at their maximum speed, pilots found themselves coping with approach speeds relative to the deck 10 to 15 knots faster than their previous experience. Even those who had carried out their initial deck-landing training on a CVE in the Clyde had to adapt. Higher relative speed increased the Seafire's tendency to 'float' over the wires when the throttle was closed and made barrier crashes inevitable when the aircraft was not handled expertly. The most significant factor, however, was that Admiral Vian and his staff had arrived late in the planning process and accepted without question the unreasonably small 'box' 30nm square in which the whole of Force V was to operate. Even with a reasonable natural wind, five carriers manoeuvring close together in such a tight sea space would have caused accidents, with no wind and ships steaming at high speed it left no margin for manoeuvre. If a recovery commenced as a carrier neared the edge of the 'box' it had to be completed hastily. Aircraft that were already short of fuel had no time to wait until the carriers regained a position on a flying course with adequate sea room to recover them. Circuits had to be exceptionally tight and even then they actually overlapped, visibility was poor and pilots found themselves making finals turns from positions that were less than ideal onto carriers that were about to make drastic alterations of course to remain in the 'box'. The staff had also made the situation worse by tasking small numbers of aircraft from each carrier for every launch cycle. This was meant to simplify deck operations in the cramped CVEs but in practice it meant that patrols over the beachhead were made up with aircraft from several different squadrons. Leaders did not know the pilots flying on their wing and the new pilots were unsettled by leaders with whom they were not familiar. Even with standardised procedures, there were subtle differences of interpretation between squadrons and these made the experiences of new pilots more difficult than they needed to be.

Shortcomings and statistics do not tell the whole story, however. In late 1943 two sorties a day by every serviceable aircraft embarked in a carrier was considered exceptional in both the RN and USN. On successive days Force V flew 2.5, then 3.6 and finally 4.1 sorties a day per serviceable aircraft. This was partially because the engineers were able to devote all their resources to them as the number of available aircraft grew less but also the new pilots were gaining the skills necessary to operate successfully. The Seafire's problems lay more with a lack of

A Seafire FR 47 seconds after landing on *Triumph* in 1949 showing the advantage of power-folding wings.

training and the failure of the staff to plan the force operations to best advantage than the Seafire's weak undercarriage. These were lessons that should have been learnt from Operation 'Torch'.

Seafires played a part the Home Fleet strikes on the German battleship *Tirpitz* in Kaa Fjord during 1944 but by 1945 most Seafire squadrons had deployed to the BPF and the East Indies Fleet. Pacific operations exposed the Seafire Mark III's lack of range and endurance. At first, when only *Indefatigable* had the type embarked, they were used mainly for CAP over the task force with strike fighter missions flown by Corsairs and Hellcats. When *Implacable* joined the BPF, the number of Seafires was doubled and urgent steps were taken to improve their capability. Squadrons in the two carriers created different solutions that were equally effective. *Indefatigable*'s 24 Wing disembarked to Schofields in Australia between operations and obtained Spitfire-pattern 90-gallon drop tanks from the RAAF in large numbers. With these fitted the Seafire Mark III exceeded its authorised MTOW and no official clearance for the tank was ever given but the improvement to the aircraft's radius of action was so great that they were used anyway. With it both the L III and F III had an endurance in excess of 4 hours.

The solution devised by 38 Wing in *Implacable* was even more radical. While disembarked at Ponam in the Admiralty Islands between operations the squadrons evaluated ex-RAAF 90-, 45- and 30-gallon drop tanks but selected USAAF 89-gallon tanks designed for the Curtiss P-40 Warhawk. Squadron trials established the ideal clearances between the top of tank and the fuselage and the bottom of the tank and the deck, bearing in mind oleo compression on being catapulted and local modifications allowed the wing's Seafires to carry this tank despite no official clearance for it ever having been given. Commander C L G Evans DSO DSC RN, the ship's Commander 'Air' and the driving force behind the tank's adoption, contrived to get large stocks from a USAAF depot in New Guinea. These were ferried to Ponam in destroyers sent to New Guinea for the task and there is a delightful, though unsubstantiated, story that the drop tanks were provided in exchange for several cases of whisky from *Implacable*'s wardroom. Such mutually beneficial trades were certainly not uncommon in the Pacific theatre of operations.

The Griffon-engined Seafire 15 was just entering operational service when the war ended but equipped several front-line squadrons in the late 1940s. Seafire FR 47s equipped 800 NAS, the last operational Seafire squadron. When the Korean War broke out in June 1950 it was embarked in *Triumph* and was supplied with the few remaining reserve aircraft from *Unicorn*. *Triumph* was among the first ships in action and its Seafires were used both in strikes against Communist forces ashore and for CAP over the Allied task force which included the USS *Valley Forge*. Seafires flew on 115 strike sorties and made 245 interceptions of unidentified aircraft approaching the task force. Many of these were USAF aircraft that had forgotten to switch on their IFF and one such was a B-29 bomber that approached the force on 28 July 1950. A Seafire flown by Commissioned Pilot White RN was directed to intercept it and, having identified it as 'friendly', he drew alongside it and waved, only to be shot down by the bomber's crew which, despite the British markings, the words 'Royal Navy' painted on the aircraft and the friendly wave, assumed it must be an enemy aircraft because it had an 'in-line' engine. White suffered from

Seafang FR 32.

burns but managed to bail out and was rescued from the sea by an American destroyer. The incident led the RN to paint conspicuous black and white 'identification stripes' on its aircraft and large union flags on the flight decks of its carriers. When informed of the incident, the USN task force commander apparently said that 'the calculated risk of damage to friendly forces must be accepted'. Mr White's comments were not recorded.

Seafang

Supermarine's attempts to improve Spitfire/Seafire performance led to the laminar-flow wing, developed with the aid of the National Physical Laboratory. Its maximum aerofoil thickness was further aft than in earlier wings and it was expected not only to raise the critical speed at which compressibility increased drag, thus increasing maximum level speed by about 40 knots but also to offer an improved rate of roll. A naval variant was included in the design process from the outset and the new two-spar wing allowed an inwards retracting undercarriage to widen the track by 4ft, curing one of the Seafire's inherited faults. There was a better view over the nose for deck landing and powered wing-folding together with a fuselage strong enough to stand the stresses of catapult launch and deck landing. The new wing was mated with a Spitfire fuselage in 1944 and the resulting aircraft was considered to differ sufficiently from the Spitfire to merit a new name, Spiteful. The naval derivative was named Seafang with mark numbers in the block from 30 onwards. Development Seafangs were designated F 31 and the planned operational development FR 32. As in the Seafire provision was made for vertical and oblique cameras aft of the cockpit to give a reconnaissance capability.

The Admiralty issued Specification N.5/45 to cover the Seafang and orders were placed for three prototypes and 150 F 31s in April 1945 with the intention that the F 31s could be flown while development of the FR 32 continued. The end of the war led to the cancellation of one prototype and 124 production aircraft. Only 18 Seafangs were ever delivered to the RN and they were used for trials and development work. The last aircraft were delivered as Type 382 Seafang FR 32s with a 2,350hp Rolls-Royce Griffon 89 engine driving two three-bladed, contra-rotating, variable-pitch metal propellers. Wingspan was 35ft, MTOW 10,450lb but the performance was not the significant improvement over the Seafire FR 47 that Supermarine had anticipated. Both the initial rate of climb at 4,630ft per minute and the service ceiling at 41,000ft were inferior. The maximum speed in level flight of 420 knots was an improvement, however. The armament comprised four 20mm Hispano cannon, two in each wing firing clear of the propeller arc, with 156 rpg. Underwing hardpoints could carry two 1,000lb bombs, one under each wing, or two 5in rockets under each wing.

The Seafang might have replaced the Seafire FR 47 in post-war production but it had a major weakness, a vicious stall that led to a sharp port-wing drop. The first Seafang was delivered in 1946 and test flown by 'Winkle' Brown who described its controls as beautiful and effective in the normal speed ranges but the stall with undercarriage and flaps down in the carrier approach configuration at about 89 knots led to a vicious port-wing drop to about 80 degrees with an incipient tendency to spin. In 1948 he flew an FR 32 in which spring tabs replaced the ailerons' earlier balance tabs. 'Winkle' described the result as near perfection but the unacceptable low-speed stall characteristic was still there. He concluded that the Seafang left a lot to be desired as a deck-landing aircraft and, with the Sea Fury coming into service, it did not represent a sufficient improvement over the Seafire FR 47 to merit production. Deck-landing trials were carried out on *Illustrious* in May 1947 which confirmed that the type's low-speed handling qualities were markedly inferior to both the Seafire FR 47 and the Sea Fury FB 10/11. It is arguable that more was lost by the adoption of the laminar flow wing than was gained but whilst the Seafang was never used operationally, it did contribute to the study of supersonic aerodynamics in Britain and the same laminar-flow wing was used on the Attacker.

Attacker

In 1944 Rolls-Royce had begun work on a jet engine that evolved into the Nene and the MAP tasked Supermarine to design a Spiteful development around it with Specification E.1/44, later amended to E.10/44. The design mated the Spiteful's laminar-flow wings with a barrel-shaped fuselage containing the large centrifugal-flow Nene. The cockpit was in the extreme nose with a bubble canopy and, to avoid complication, the tail wheel of the earlier piston-engined design was retained making this bulky aircraft awkward to taxi. Early in the design process a further specification, E.1/45, was issued for a navalised version and when a pre-production batch of twenty-four was ordered in July 1945, sixteen were for the RN. With the end of the war and laminar flow wing problems evident in the Seafang, this batch was cancelled and Sea Vampire F 20s ordered instead.

The MAP had assumed that using the Spiteful/Seafang laminar flow wing would speed development but the loss of a Spiteful prototype and discovery of low speed handling problems actually slowed development of the new fighter. The fuselage was of metal semi-monocoque construction with the Nene engine positioned aft of the wings and a 'straight-through' jet pipe exhausting under the tailplane. The Attacker was fitted with the differential braking system standard on British aircraft of the period and with its wide-track undercarriage, should have been easy to taxi. However, with the engine mass well aft rather than ahead of the cockpit any turn, once started, developed rapidly when the tail wheel was unlocked. Harsh braking was required to counteract this effect but locking the tail wheel simplified matters and turns of up to 45 degrees were possible without any apparent dragging effect. The rudder was useless for taxiing. Another result of the tail-wheeled layout was the tendency of the downward-pointed jet

Attackers ranged with Firebrands on *Eagle*.

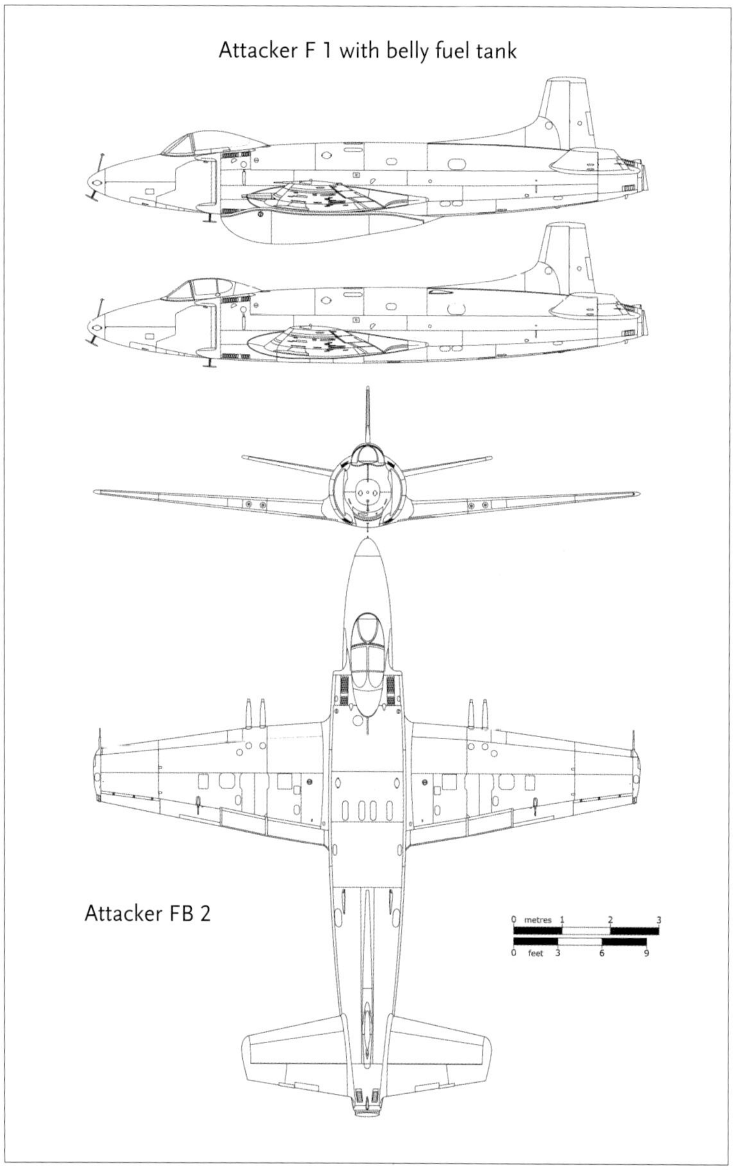

exhaust to lift paving stones that were not adequately cemented into place; something for the next pilot astern in a line of aircraft to beware of. An external power supply from a ground battery trolley was required to start the Nene engine and some care had to be taken to select the high-pressure fuel cock at just the right moment to prevent over-fuelling that could lead to engine resonance at low rpm. The front gun installation in the wings was taken directly from the Spiteful/Seafang design and an installation in the nose under the cockpit would have been better. The space in the wings formerly occupied by radiators was used to provide fuel tanks. The outer wing panels could be folded upwards or spread by hydraulic pressure when the pilot selected the wing-fold lever in the cockpit.

The Type 398 Attacker was one of the first British fighters to be fitted with a Martin Baker ejection seat. The Mark 1 seat had an adjustable seat pan, foot rests on which the pilot's feet were placed to stabilise them during the ejection sequence and integral thigh guards at the sides of the seat to act as protection. Ejection was initiated by the pilot pulling the face-blind handle from its stowed position above his head. Once the seat was clear of the aircraft a small stabilising parachute known as a drogue was automatically streamed to stop the seat tumbling. In early seats the pilot had to release his safety harness, push clear of the seat and pull the 'D'-ring to deploy his parachute. In later versions a barostatic control automatically released the pilot from the seat below 10,000ft and the parachute was deployed automatically. At higher altitudes the pilot was kept in the seat with an emergency oxygen supply keeping him conscious until the barostatic control released him below 10,000ft. A safety pin was placed in the face-blind handle while the aircraft was on the ground to prevent its inadvertent operation.

The first of three Attacker prototypes flew in February 1946 and soon encountered control problems in high-speed flight that had not been anticipated. Carrier qualification trials were carried out on *Illustrious* in October 1947 and, while generally successful, they revealed that the Attacker tended to 'float' after the throttle was closed without the braking effect of a large propeller. This was largely cured by the adoption of the constant power, constant speed approach technique. The Admiralty wanted a single-seat jet fighter that could be put into service relatively quickly with a minimum of modifications and a fully navalised prototype flew in March 1949. A production contract was placed in November 1949 and the two surviving prototypes carried out a further series of thirty-three deck landings on *Illustrious*. As production Attackers became available in 1950, two aircraft carried out the final deck-landing clearance trials on *Illustrious* in November. These included 197 deck landings as well as clearance for the use of RATOG and catapult launches.

Attackers only ever operated from the trials carrier *Illustrious* and the new *Eagle*. Both were straight-deck carriers and the former operated with a clear deck that allowed the aircraft to bolt if it failed to catch a wire. For operations from *Eagle* a new type of barrier had to be developed to prevent aircraft that missed the wires crashing into aircraft parked in Fly 1. Piston-engined aircraft relied on the mass of the propeller, engine and its bearers in front of the cockpit to protect the pilot from the impact of a barrier engagement but in the Attacker the cockpit was in the nose with nothing substantial in front of it; engagement in the standard wire barrier could crush the pilot so a new, nylon barrier was designed with vertical nylon chords which left a gap for the fuselage to pass through, retardation being applied to the wings.

Attacker FB 2 data

Length:	37ft 1in
Wingspan:	36ft 11in (28ft 11in folded)
Height:	9ft 6½in
MTOW:	12,210lb
Engine:	One 5,000lb static thrust Rolls-Royce Nene 3 centrifugal turbojet
Fuel:	Avcat. 395 gallons internal plus optional 270-gallon ventral tank. Total 665 gallons
Performance:	Maximum level speed 512 knots, Mach 0.73 Service ceiling 45,000ft. 7 minutes to 30,000ft without ventral tank
Endurance:	Up to 3 hours with ventral tank
Armament:	Four 20mm Hispano cannon, two in each wing, with 156 rpg. Provision for two 1,000lb bombs under wings or up to eight 3in R/P on Mark VIII launchers, four under each wing

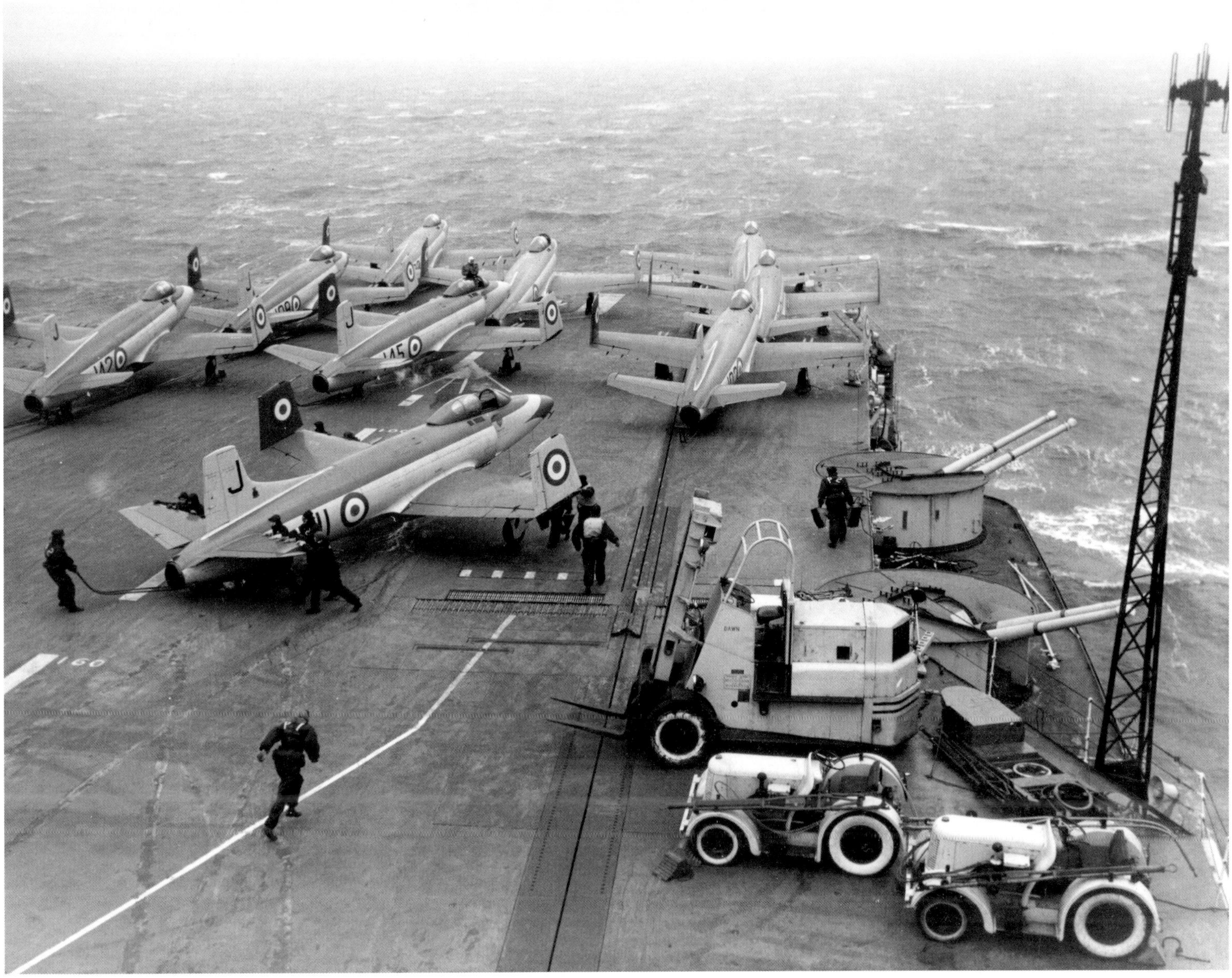

Attackers parked in *Eagle*'s Fly 1 after a recovery.

A total of 120 Attackers were delivered to the RN comprising three prototypes, 63 to F 1 or FB 1 standard and 54 to FB 2 standard.

Between 1951 and 1956 Attackers equipped or partially equipped shore-based squadrons for training, development and fleet requirements tasks including 700, 702, 703, 718, 736, 767 and 787 NAS. The unnumbered, civilian-manned FRU at Hurn used Attackers between 1955 and 1957.

Between 1951 and 1954 Attackers of all three marks equipped 800, 803 and 890 NAS. They were shore-based at Ford and embarked in *Eagle* for deployments to the Home and Mediterranean Fleets.

Between 1955 and 1957 Attackers were issued to the RNVR Air Branch and served with 1831, 1832 and 1833 NAS. They were already being re-equipped with Sea Hawks after only a little over a year when the Air Branch was disbanded in March 1957.

The first operational RN squadron to re-equip with jet fighters was 800 NAS which re-formed at Ford in August 1951 followed by 803 NAS in November. 890 NAS formed in April 1952 but its existence was short as it disbanded in December and transferred its aircraft and personnel to the other two to create two twelve-aircraft squadrons rather than three eight-aircraft squadrons.

The introduction of the FB 1 and 2 variants capable of carrying bombs and rockets led to a change of role for the Attacker force from the interceptor to the strike/ground attack role. The most obvious external feature that identified the FB 2 was its more heavily framed cockpit canopy. The type had proved a disappointment in the fighter role since performance deteriorated badly above 30,000ft and its rate of climb was poor. During high-speed combat manoeuvres the wings were found to flex, putting the guns out of alignment and making the Attacker a poor gun platform. By 1954, after just over two years, it was replaced in front-line service by the Hawker Sea Hawk which had the same basic Nene engine but much better all-round performance. The Attacker earned a place in history as the first operational RN jet fighter but it was a poor performer that was replaced as soon as possible and most pilots were glad to see it go.

Supermarine Type 510 landing on *Illustrious* in 1950.

Type 510

Realisation that swept wings offered advantages in high-speed flight led the MoS to issue specifications for a range of new aircraft in 1946 and E.41/46 called for a swept-wing development of the Attacker. Two prototypes were ordered and the Admiralty secured an agreement that one would be modified for deck-landing trials. Designated Type 510 by Supermarine, the first prototype flew in December 1948. The sole navalised Type 510 had a wingspan of 32ft 8in and MTOW of 12,200lb. Its 5,000lb static thrust Rolls-Royce Nene 2 centrifugal turbojet gave a maximum level speed of 568 knots. In dives it achieved Mach 0.93 but at that speed the aircraft became port-wing low and full starboard control deflection was required to correct it. Test flying revealed that the swept wings gave considerably better performance than the Attacker at medium altitude and at speeds approaching the transonic region but at high altitude turning performance was limited by the Nene's low thrust. However, sweep back was found to induce longitudinal instability near the stall at typical deck-landing speeds.

After being fitted with an arrester hook and attachment points for RATOG, the naval prototype carried out deck-landing trials on *Illustrious* in November 1950. It was the world's first swept-wing aircraft to land on an aircraft carrier and twelve deck landings were carried out by Lieutenant Commander D G Parker DSO DSC RN, Lieutenant J Elliot and M J Lithgow a former RN pilot now Supermarine's chief test pilot. RATOG had to be used for every take-off since the ship's BH 3 hydraulic catapult lacked sufficient end-speed. Depending on aircraft weight, which got lighter as fuel was used, the approach speed for a deck landing was between 124 and 134 knots. The ship steamed at 25 knots into a 25-knot wind giving an entry speed into the wires relative to the deck of over 70 knots which was close to the arresting system's limit. Despite this the landings, using the constant speed and rate of descent technique, were all judged as good, the rebound characteristics of the oleos being described as excellent. On conclusion of this trial the aircraft was returned to Supermarine for use in non-naval development work.

Type 505

While it was interested in flexible or 'rubber' flight deck technology, the Admiralty asked industry to propose suitable undercarriage-less fighters and Supermarine's response was the single-seat Type 505 with two Rolls-Royce AJ-65 axial-flow turbojet engines, later developed into the Avon. Swept wings were considered but rejected and a thin, straight wing was adopted with the two engines mounted side by side in a semi-monocoque fuselage. A 'V' tailplane was chosen to give strength in the fine thickness/chord ratio surfaces and it was also thought they would interfere less with the jet efflux than conventional tail surfaces. Lateral control was by wide chord ailerons and there were to be leading-edge slats and air brakes at one third chord under the wings. The Type 505 was only produced in mock-up form and, had a prototype been completed, it would have flown initially with a fixed nose wheel undercarriage attached,

Supermarine Type 508 carrying out deck trials in *Eagle* during 1952.

later to be removed for 'rubber deck' trials when necessary. Loss of Admiralty interest in the flexible deck and fighters without undercarriages led to Supermarine modifying the design into the Type 508.

Type 508/529

Supermarine modified its Type 505 design into the Type 508 with a retractable nose-wheel undercarriage. It resembled the earlier design but the Admiralty required the lowest possible speed for deck landing and this led to the wing thickness/chord ratio being raised from 7 per cent to 9 per cent to incorporate the main oleos and improve low-speed performance. Wing area was increased with main spars which now passed under the engines to provide anchorages for the undercarriage.

Three Type 508 development aircraft fitted with arrester hooks were ordered to meet Admiralty Specification N.9/47 and the first flew in 1951. It carried out deck-landing trials in *Eagle* in May 1952 and was used for deck-handling trials in both *Bulwark* and *Centaur* during 1955–6. Two 6,500lb static thrust Rolls-Royce Avon axial-flow turbojets gave a maximum level speed of 540 knots. Wingspan was 41ft and MTOW 18,459lb. The second prototype was modified during construction to become the sole Type 529. It differed in having power-folding wings with the hinge-point well outboard of the main oleos. It carried out deck-landing trials in *Eagle* during November 1953 but ended its days as a gunnery target at Shoeburyness after damage suffered in its trials programme.

Supermarine Type 525 taking off at the Farnborough Air Show in 1954.

Type 525

The third development aircraft ordered under N.9/47 was more extensively modified and designated Type 525, effectively a prototype Scimitar. It retained the two Avon engines but emerged in April 1954 with swept wings and a conventional swept tailplane. Like the other development aircraft it was designed to take four 20mm cannon under the nose but they were never fitted. It was slightly smaller and lighter than the Scimitar which evolved from it but it was used for the trial installation and testing of its blown flap system. In July 1955 whilst flying from the A&AEE it crashed, killing the pilot, whilst carrying out low-speed handling trials having departed controlled flight into an irrecoverable flat spin.

Scimitar

In 1951 the Admiralty issued Specification N.113D, 'D' standing for development, for a single-seat, swept-wing strike fighter to replace the Sea Hawk. Supermarine successfully tendered a modified Type 525, designated Type 544, and three prototypes were ordered in 1951. They differed from the Type 525 in having more powerful Avon engines which required larger air intakes and had a longer nose. The fuselage cross section was redesigned on the area principle to improve performance in the transonic speed range and, for the same reason, an all-moving, anhedral slab tailplane was fitted in place of the 525's fixed tail surfaces with elevators. It was the first British naval aircraft to be fitted with 'blown flaps', high-pressure air bled from the engine compressors blown over the flaps to delay the onset of turbulence over the wing at high angles of attack. In the Scimitar a thin jet of high-pressure air was fed through a narrow slot along the trailing edge of the wing just ahead of the flap hinge and a phenomenon known as the Coanda effect caused this to follow the contour of the flap carrying the free stream air with it to prevent boundary layer turbulence and separation. In practice this reduced the deck-landing speed by about 15 knots; reduced the angle of attack to improve the pilot's view for deck landing and improved control and stability at low airspeed. It was given the name Scimitar in 1956. An early problem was encountered with pitch-up at high Mach numbers caused by shock-induced separation of the airflow over the wing leading to a high-speed tip-stall, aggravated by increased downwash over the all-flying tailplane. This was resolved by fitting 'saw-tooth' steps in the wing leading edges augmented by boundary layer fences and Kuchemann-shaped wingtips but the greatest improvement followed the inversion of the tailplane, converting ten degrees of dihedral to ten degrees of anhedral. When it entered operational service in 1958 the Scimitar was the largest, heaviest and most powerful fighter the RN had ever operated.

Besides the considerable changes made to the Scimitar's airframe during its protracted development, its role also changed. Originally conceived as a fast-climbing interceptor fighter capable of engaging hostile bombers at high altitude with front guns, by the time prototypes were flying the NAFDU, 787 NAS, had briefed the Admiralty that a gun-armed fighter lacking radar stood only a minimal chance of destroying an incoming high-altitude bomber. The solution lay with radar-equipped fighters armed with guided missiles and the Admiralty opted for the Sea Vixen to carry out the high-level intercept role. Test pilots found that the Scimitar had an exhilarating performance up to

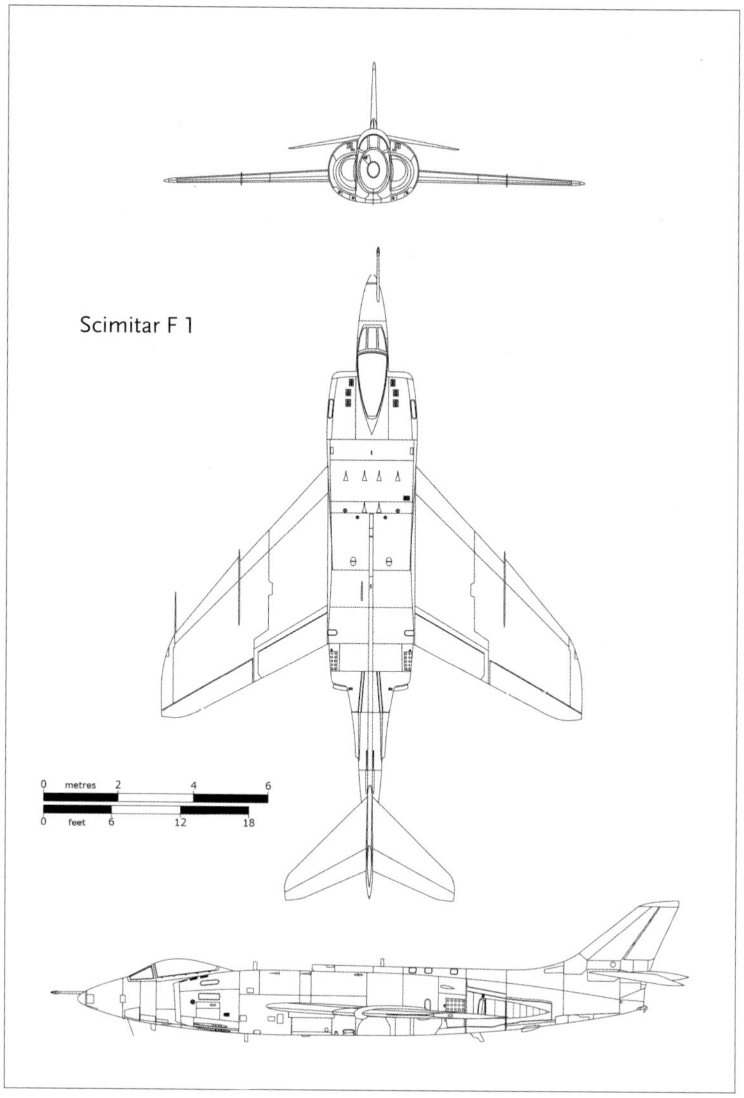

25,000ft but it fell off significantly above that. The Scimitar was, therefore, developed as a strike fighter rather than an interceptor.

It was the first RN aircraft to have fuel tanks integrated into the structure rather than having flexible bags inserted into the airframe. Spaces in the wings and fuselage were sprayed with sealant during construction and linked by extensive pipes and connectors. Leaks were commonplace and, when parked in a hangar, Scimitars needed dustbins rather than drip trays placed under them to collect seepage. Each fuel cell had its own booster pump which could be selected on or off by the pilot. After its complicated development history the Scimitar was not an easy aircraft to maintain. Engine replacement was relatively straightforward but a number of components such as pipe unions or electrical connections could only be reached by mechanics with long arms who had developed the knack of feeling for them with an appropriate tool. There was a delightful myth that Supermarine began constructing every Scimitar by hanging a hydraulic pump and its pipe unions from the ceiling and then building the aircraft around them. It was the first aircraft in which fault diagnosis, especially for the electrical system, used a number of test sets which had themselves to be maintained and fully understood by ship and squadron maintenance personnel.

The biggest advance the Scimitar brought to RN fighter squadrons was in both the variety and quantity of weapons it could carry. The

Scimitar F 1s of 803 in *Victorious*' Fly 1 with Gannet AEW 3s and a Sea Vixen.

four 30mm Aden Mark 4 cannon in the lower fuselage had a rate of fire of 1,200 rounds per minute and an effective range up to 400 yards. They gave approximately 8 seconds of fire and rounds were loaded in the order high-explosive, semi-armour-piercing and incendiary. Alan Leahy recalled that firing all four created sufficient noise and vibration to loosen a pilot's teeth. They also loosened the aircraft's 'plumbing' and practice firing was usually limited to two guns. Target tracking and aiming was achieved using a Mark 8 gyro gunsight which received accurate range information from a radar-ranging unit in the aircraft's nose. Below 25,000ft the Scimitar was easy to manoeuvre in order to track targets; above that height less so.

The Scimitar was the first RN aircraft capable of carrying a nuclear weapon, the 2,000lb Red Beard, a 25-kiloton device designated TMB to mask its true nature. It was carried on the port inboard pylon, balanced by a 250-gallon drop tank on the starboard inner for the outbound flight. Red Beard was delivered using LABS. This was a pre-planned method in which the pilot aimed towards the target at 600 knots and low level, pulling up at an identified IP and following the LABS indicator in the cockpit accurately. At the ideal moment the system released the bomb which followed a ballistic trajectory to the intended target about 4nm away. Detonation could be an air burst or on impact and it was believed that this technique gave the aircraft time to get clear of the blast; thankfully, this never had to be put to the test. An alternative, used against a target of opportunity or when the IP was obscured was an OTS attack. In this case the pilot overflew the target, pulled to the vertical above it and released the bomb which climbed to about 16,000ft and then fell back onto it. This was more dangerous for a variety of obvious reasons and gave the pilot less chance of a getaway. Nuclear-armed Scimitars had to be modified with LABS and there were usually only four within a squadron. They were cleared to launch from a carrier with a live Red Beard but prohibited from deck landing with it because it was a large shape with minimal clearance and a scrape caused by a burst tyre might cause partial detonation. Inert replicas could be carried for peacetime training with runs against suitable ranges; the 28lb practice bomb was designed to have the same ballistic properties as Red Beard.

Another of the Scimitar's 'firsts' was the ability to carry an AGM; the USN-designed AGM-12 Bullpup. It weighed 570lb, contained a 250lb warhead and, unlike the complicated British air weapons of the era, could be treated as a round of ammunition with very little pre-flight testing. The pilot controlled it using radio-command guidance with a thumb switch fitted to the port side of the cockpit which allowed him to give up, down, left and right commands. The missile accelerated to Mach 2 after launch and had a nominal range of 10nm, in theory keeping the aircraft clear of close-range anti-aircraft fire. In practice the pilot had to fly the aircraft in a steady dive with the gunsight aiming point steady on the target whilst gathering the flares at the rear of the missile onto the target as quickly as possible. It was difficult to assess how far the missile had to run to impact. Scimitars could carry up to four Bullpups but only one could be launched at a time.

Sidewinder was another USN guided weapon acquired by the RN for use on the Scimitar. Designated AIM-9 by the USN, it weighed only 160lb and was both simple and effective. Unlike the British Firestreak it was treated as a round of ammunition and its gyro-

A Scimitar of 800B NAS with a flight-refuelling pod on the starboard inner pylon about to launch from *Eagle*'s waist catapult.

stabilised, infra-red homing device was tested by groundcrew shining a torch at it, a serviceable Sidewinder gave the pilot a 'growl' in his headphones exactly as it would when locked onto a target during an interception. It gave the Scimitar a reasonable intercept capability against medium-level targets but had to be fired in their stern sectors.

Bombs and rockets were all aimed using the Mark 8 gunsight with a depressed sightline. By contemporary standards they could be delivered accurately and pilots practised engaging moving targets by bombing and rocketing the splash targets towed astern of carriers and their escorts and accompanying RFAs. Another innovative system enabled the Scimitar to be used as an air-to-air tanker with a Mark 20A flight refuelling pod 'plumbed' onto the starboard inner pylon. This was usually combined with 250- or 200-gallon tanks on the other pylons to give the maximum fuel 'giveaway' and squadrons usually maintained two aircraft as tankers to extend the range of strike aircraft or to be on deck alert to support aircraft that were low on fuel at the start of recovery. 800B NAS was embarked in *Eagle* as a specialist tanker unit to support the Buccaneer S 1s of 800 NAS which could not be launched with maximum fuel. An alternative nose section could be fitted to allow Scimitars to operate in the PR role with two oblique and one vertical camera.

The first Scimitar deck-landing trials were carried out on *Ark Royal* during 1956. A total of 148 deck landings and catapult launches were carried out in which it was found that the ideal approach speed was 124 knots at a weight of 28,000lb. The aircraft was easy and positive to control with a good view of the deck for the pilot. It was a more

Scimitar F 1 of 803 NAS airborne from *Hermes* with a Bullpup ASM.

complex aircraft than its predecessors and prior to the formation of the IFTU a number of courses with industry had to be organised to teach aircraft artificers and mechanics how to use the range of sophisticated test rigs. Like other aircraft of its generation it used a Palouste low-pressure air starter.

Scimitar F 1 data

Length:	55ft 3in
Wingspan:	37ft 2in (20ft 6½in folded)
Height:	17ft 4in
MTOW:	34,200lb
Engine:	Two 11,250lb static thrust Rolls-Royce Avon 202 turbojets
Fuel:	Avcat. 1,065 gallons internal plus optional 250-, 200- or 100-gallon drop tanks and Mark 20A flight refuelling pod
Performance:	Maximum level speed 640 knots, Mach 0.966 Service ceiling 46,000ft. 6 minutes to 40,000ft
Endurance:	Range with maximum external fuel over 1,200nm. On 17 June 1958 a Scimitar flew non-stop from London to Malta, 1,150nm
Armament:	Four 30mm Aden Mark 4 cannon with 120 rpg. Four underwing hardpoints, each capable of taking stores up to 2,000lb. These included a single 2,000lb Red Beard nuclear bomb, 1000lb, 500lb free-fall bombs, Bullpup ASM, Sidewinder AIM, 2in rocket pods, rails for up to sixteen 3in rockets or Glowworm illuminant rockets

The RN received three prototypes and seventy-six production Scimitars. The Admiralty originally ordered 100 to Specification N.113P, 'P' standing for production, but the last twenty-four were considered unnecessary once the Buccaneer entered service and cancelled.

Between 1957 and 1965 Scimitars equipped 700, 700X, 736, 764 and 764B NAS in the development and strike fighter training roles, operating mainly from Ford at first and then Lossiemouth. They were also used by the civilian-manned, un-numbered fleet requirements unit based at Hurn until 1970.

Front line units that operated the Scimitar between 1958 and 1966 included 800, 800B, 803, 804 and 807 NAS. They operated from the aircraft carriers *Victorious*, *Hermes*, *Centaur*, *Ark Royal* and *Eagle*.

Alan Leahy, who commanded 803 NAS, once told me that in his opinion the combination of the Scimitar and *Victorious*' Type 984 radar created 'the best day fighter system in the business'. Four of his 100 deck landings on the type were at night and he regarded these as 'four too many' but he had wonderful memories of the Scimitar. Other pilots including Colin Casperd and Michael Doust described its performance as 'thrilling'. Keith Leppard, who commanded 807 NAS, described it as a rugged and versatile aircraft with an exceptional rate of roll at low level. He acknowledged that it lacked radar and had a complicated fuel system that tended to leak but against this it had first class low-speed handling and provided an excellent transition from the Sea Hawk into the swept-wing era. The Scimitar gave the RN an

A Scimitar F 1 of 803 NAS landing on *Victorious* in 1959.

Bomb-armed Scimitars of 803 NAS with Sea Venoms in the background on *Victorious* starting-up in a snow squall.

important range of new weapons at the height of the Cold War. Carriers with the type embarked served in the Home, Mediterranean and Far East Fleets. None ever had to use their weapons in anger but they played an important deterrent role with the NATO Strike Fleet and their embarked presence in *Victorious* and *Centaur* played a key role in preventing Iraqi aggression against Kuwait in 1961 and in defending Malaysia against Indonesian aggression between 1963 and 1966. Scimitars were also used as probes under Gannet radar control during several Beira Patrol periods of operation from *Ark Royal* and *Eagle*. 807 NAS in 1959 and 800 NAS in 1961 gave displays of formation aerobatics at Farnborough air shows that were described by the press as spectacular.

Supermarine proposed several developments including the Type 562 which would have had AI-23 radar and 500-gallon nacelle-type wing tanks that would have increased total fuel capacity to 2,360 gallons and doubled the radius of action. The Type 564 proposed the substitution of de Havilland Gyron Junior engines for the Avons and in 1957 the Type 567 was a proposed single or two-seat development with tip tanks and a projected MTOW of over 50,000lb. Among the last proposals were the Type 575 and Type 576 which incorporated extra fuel in an elongated 'hump' aft of the cockpit. Maximum radius of action with a Red Beard at low level was expected to be 520nm and in the fighter role tip-mounted rocket motors were designed to accelerate the aircraft to Mach 1.4 at 55,000ft. The Admiralty considered all these proposals and discussed them with Supermarine but none were taken forward.

TELLIER

Flying boat

The Admiralty purchased two French Tellier flying boats in 1917. They were two-seat biplanes powered by a 200hp Hispano-Suiza pusher engine driving a two-bladed wooden propeller to give a maximum level speed of 70 knots. Wingspan was 51ft 2in and MTOW 3,960lb. The pilot occupied a small cockpit forward of the engine and the gunlayer sat in the nose armed with a single belt-fed 0.303in Vickers machine gun. Both were delivered to the RNAS in April 1918 and used for gun and camouflage trials at Isle of Grain. They saw no operational use and were soon deleted.

THOMAS BROTHERS

T 2

Manufactured at Ithaca, New York, the T 2 first flew in 1914 and the Admiralty ordered twenty-four for use as training aircraft. They were two-seat biplanes powered by a single 90hp Curtiss OX-5 engine driving a two-bladed wooden propeller to give a maximum level speed of 72 knots. Wingspan was 36ft and MTOW 1,972lb. They were delivered 1915 but by then the design was obsolete. Five were wrecked when their canvas storage hangar was blown away in a storm and the remainder were probably never even erected before being deleted in 1916.

VICKERS

HM Airship Number 1

The first aircraft of any kind to be ordered by the RN, its development began with a carefully orchestrated letter dated 21 July 1908 from the DNO, Captain R H S Bacon RN, who had responsibility for the development of new weapon systems. He had supervised the introduction of submarines from 1900 and on his advice the Admiralty had agreed an exclusive contract for Vickers to design and build them. He continued to work closely with the firm and recommended that a similar arrangement for airships would hasten their development and introduction into service. It is likely that Bacon had agreed the way forward with the First Sea Lord, Admiral Fisher, and Vickers when he wrote the letter since only two days later, on 23 July, Fisher wrote to the Prime Minister, H Asquith, proposing the construction of a developmental rigid airship and Treasury approval was given in principle on 4 August 1908. The estimated cost of £35,000 was slightly less than half the cost of a destroyer and just under 10 per cent of the cost of a light cruiser. The Treasury gave its final approval for the project on 23 February 1909. Vickers agreed to build an airship construction shed in Cavendish Dock close to its shipyard at Barrow-in-Furness.

The Admiralty specification required it to fulfil the duties of an aerial scout, maintaining 40 knots for as close to 24 hours as possible. Boat-shaped control cars were to enable it to float on the sea surface and it was to be capable of being moored by the nose to a support vessel, either whilst 'flying' above the surface or floating on the water. As far as possible it was to be capable of staying out in all weathers, to carry W/T equipment and have sufficient facilities for the crew to live on board without suffering hardship. It was to have an operational ceiling of at least 1,500ft and was to be constructed as cheaply as possible for initial experimental use. The cruiser *Hermione* was to be refitted to act as an airship support vessel with a plant for producing hydrogen, accommodation for spare crews and a mooring mast. In Admiralty records the first airship was often referred to as the '*Hermione* Airship' but the Press gave it the nickname 'Mayfly' because journalists were unable to comprehend why its construction took so long. The 'R' designation for rigid airships was not introduced until R-26 in 1918; rigids from Number 1 to 25 simply had a number.

Design work was carried out by a team of Vickers submarine engineers and naval officers. Much of it was without precedent, making progress slow at first. Duralumin was selected for the rigid frame, its

HM Airship Number 1 being moved from its shed towards the mooring mast in Cavendish Dock, Barrow-in-Furness in May 1911.

first use in a military aircraft of any type. The seventeen hydrogen-filled gas bags were each made of a different fabric to see which was best and the outer covering was of silk made waterproof by a substance with the trade name Ioco. It could not be sewn and sheets had to be glued together, a process which took both time and acquired skill to perfect. The material intended for the bottom of the airship was dyed yellow to make it more visible from below and the upper half was painted with aluminium dust to reflect the sun's rays and prevent heat absorption. Unfortunately the dust was found to weaken the silk as much as Ioco strengthened it and a further process had to be devised in which the fabric was dusted with aluminium powder after being Ioco-ed. The area of outer skin aft of the engines was made of a fireproof material and the control surfaces were covered with two layers of silk stuck together using a process pioneered by Short Brothers. At Admiralty insistence the design included an anchor and cable so that the airship could be moored and even a sea-boat.

Two crews were appointed in January 1910 and underwent comprehensive training at Short Brothers Battersea works. When *Hermione* arrived at Barrow in September they joined her and carried out all the fabrication work on the gas bags and the outer cover to fulfil the Admiralty's side of the construction agreement. The control cars were made of copper-sawn Honduras mahogany and the forward car contained the control bridge. Both cars contained a single 180hp Wolseley engine, its radiator and control systems. At the time the Wolseley Motor Company was owned by Vickers. As originally designed the forward engine drove two propellers on outriggers through gearing and the after engine drove a single propeller. Equipment included a telephone exchange that connected the two cars and a W/T installation that was expected to have a range of about 600nm.

Number 1's first inflation was completed on 22 May 1911 and she was walked out of her shed by 300 sailors and marines. Once clear, she was towed to a specially-designed mast in the centre of the dock and moored to it, ballast was dropped to make it buoyant, hovering nose into wind. A number of acceptance trials were carried out and on 23 May she successfully rode out a gale of 45 knots. She was considered too heavy to carry out the full programme of trials, however, and was returned to the shed and deflated for remedial work to reduce weight. The keel, crew cabin and any equipment not needed in flight including the anchor, cable and sea-boat were removed and the heavier car was moved from aft to forward. The control car was lightened and moved aft to replace it. In August Number 1 was still found to be too heavy and a further 1,195lb of equipment was removed. By 24 September 1911 it had been re-inflated and was extracted from the shed by electric winches. Things went badly wrong as the nose was pulled towards the centre of the dock and witnesses heard cracking sounds amidships as the airship broke in two with only the outer fabric holding the halves together. It was thought that a crosswind had caught the airship and rolled it onto its side but it is also possible that steadying ropes put an uneven strain on the hull which caused it to fail. Whatever the initial cause, considerable further damage was done cramming the damaged hull back into its shed. The Admiralty Air Department did not regard Number 1 as a write-off and the damage undoubtedly looked worse than it was. Her construction had, by then, cost in excess of £70,000 but the airship's fate was decided by a Board of Enquiry chaired by the conservative Rear Admiral Sturdee who was opposed to technical innovation and reform. Winston Churchill, the new First Lord, was known to be an advocate of winged aircraft rather than airships and when the Board decided that the project should be terminated and Number 1 scrapped he refused to allow the full findings to be made public. They were subsequently lost so the reason for the hull's failure will probably never be known for certain.

HM Airship Number 1 data

Length:	512ft 3in
Diameter:	48ft
Height:	61ft 10in
Envelope capacity:	663,518ft^3
Engines:	Two 180hp Wolseley 8-cylinder, water-cooled engines driving three wooden propellers
Fuel:	Avgas. 250 gallons
Gross lift:	20.7 tons with gas bags 100% full
Disposable lift:	1.1 tons after being lightened
Performance:	Estimated maximum level speed 40 knots
Endurance:	24 hours specified
Armament:	None

The planned trials programme gives insight into the Admiralty's first thoughts on the use of aircraft. After confirming its flight performance Number 1 was to evaluate the airborne location of minefields and submarines and then to determine how best to monitor ports and enemy fleet movements from the air. Next, the practical use of aerial photography and the potential for airships to carry both offensive and defensive armament would have been evaluated. At Churchill's insistence the Admiralty Airship Department was disbanded in 1912 but it was re-formed a year later when German Zeppelins began to show their value and the need for such an RN capability was recognised as urgent. Number 1 was the largest and most technically complex aircraft of its day and, whilst the need to overcome developmental problems as they arose should have been better appreciated, it was certainly was not the ill-considered failure that some critics labelled it

HM Airship Number 9

Once reformed in 1913, the Admiralty's Airship Department ordered Number 9, the next sequential airship number, from Vickers. The shed in which Number 1 had been built was considered too small and was replaced by a new airship building facility on Walney Island west of Barrow. Number 9 was ready for erection when war broke out but technical problems and policy changes delayed it. Churchill cancelled it in March 1915 but when he left the Admiralty two months later it was reinstated, construction workers having to be recalled. Further specification changes led to further delays and it was not completed until November 1916. It was the first British rigid airship to fly but was only provisionally accepted by the RNAS a year later due to concerns about inadequate lift. A weight reduction programme included the removal of two 180hp Wolseley/Maybach engines from the rear car and their replacement by a single 240hp Maybach engine salvaged from the wrecked German L-33. Number 9 was finally accepted in March 1917.

HM Airship Number 9. (Philip Jarrett)

HM Airship Number 9 data

Length:	526ft
Diameter:	53ft
Height:	76ft
Envelope capacity:	846,000ft³
Engines:	Once modified, two 180hp Wolseley/Maybach water-cooled engines and one 240hp Maybach driving three wooden propellers
Fuel:	Avgas. 500 gallons
Gross lift:	25.6 tons with gas bags 100% full
Disposable lift:	3.8 tons after lightening
Performance:	Maximum level speed 38 knots
Endurance:	Over 24 hours specified
Armament:	One 0.303in Lewis gun on the gun platform on top of the hull, access gained by a ladder within a tube through the hull. One Lewis gun in the after car. Three 100lb bombs could be fitted to frames attached to the handling rail of the after car; two to port and one to starboard

Number 9 proved to be a disappointment; its armament was little more than a non-rigid could carry and it was cumbersome to manoeuvre. It carried out some patrols over the North Sea, one of which lasted for 26 hours 45 minutes, but by 1918 it was used for training at East Fortune, Cranwell and then Pulham before being deleted in June 1918 after flying for only 198 hours 45 minutes. The forward 20ft of the framework was used to make a bandstand at Pulham.

HM Airship Number 23 and R-26

After ordering Number 9 the Admiralty ordered four airships to an improved design referred to as the 23 Class. Number 23 was built by Vickers which was the design lead for the class; Number 24 was built by Beardmore; Number 25 by Armstrong Whitworth and R-26, the first designated in the 'R' series, was built by Vickers.

The 23 Class was essentially the Number 9 design modified with an extra bay inserted amidships and the ends widened to accommodate nineteen rather than seventeen gas bags, changes that had originally been proposed for the overweight Number 1 in 1911 but not implemented. The external keel below the hull had a cabin 45ft long which contained a bomb room, officers' wardroom, ratings' quarters, a W/T office and a lavatory right aft. Three cars were suspended below the keel and accessed by open ladders. The forward car was partitioned between the control bridge forward and a single Rolls-Royce Eagle engine driving a pair of swivelling, four-bladed wooden propellers. It had a starting handle so that it could be shut down or re-started in flight. The midships car contained two Rolls-Royce Eagles, each driving its own four-bladed wooden propeller mounted on brackets. The after car was similar to the forward car except that the control bridge was only intended for emergency use if the forward car was damaged. The normal crew was sixteen officers and men. The platform on top of the hull was enlarged to take a 2pdr pom-pom and two 0.303in Lewis machine guns. Three other Lewis guns could be fitted, one at the extreme tail; one in a control car window and one aft of the gun platform on the walkway. The gun platform had a small windscreen and gunners were attached to the platform or walkway by safety harnesses.

HMA Number 23 data

Length:	535ft
Diameter:	53ft
Height:	75ft
Envelope capacity:	942,000ft³
Engines:	Four 250hp Rolls-Royce Eagle Series 3
Fuel:	Avgas. 1,200 gallons
Gross lift:	28.5 tons with gas bags 100% full
Disposable lift:	6½ tons
Performance:	Maximum level speed 45 knots
Endurance:	Over 24 hours specified
Armament:	One 2pdr pom-pom, five 0.303in Lewis guns and three or more 100lb bombs

HM Airship Number 23. (Philip Jarrett)

Number 23 was commissioned in October 1917 and carried out some North Sea patrols before being relegated to training and experimental work in 1918. The most interesting experiment was to ascertain whether an airship could carry an aircraft and release it, whilst airborne, either to repel attacking fighters or to carry out its own strike fighter tasks. In November 1918 Number 23 took off from Pulham with a Sopwith 2F.1 Camel suspended under it; it had no pilot but provided proof-of-concept when it glided safely to the ground. Two successful launches by manned Camels followed; both pilots started their engines and landed successfully at Pulham but with the end of the war the concept was not taken forward immediately although later trials were carried out using R-33. Number 23 was deleted and scrapped in September 1919 having flown for 320 hours.

In December 1917 R-26 was the last of the class to be completed and was the only one of its class to incorporate all the design changes found necessary with Number 23. It was delivered to Howden in April 1918 where its disposable lift was found to be 6¼ tons. In June it carried out a North Sea patrol of 40 hours 40 minutes, the longest by any British rigid airship and on 26 November 1918 it flew over German U-boats as they surrendered off Harwich. Deletion and scrapping followed mooring trials in March 1919 by which time it had only flown for 197 hours 47 minutes.

R-80

R-80 was the last rigid airship ordered by the Admiralty and numbered out of sequence because Walney Island was not big enough to build an R-33 class airship. The design team, including Barnes Wallis, was allowed considerable freedom and the result was the best of the naval rigids with a capacity of 1,200,000ft^3 within a perfectly streamlined hull 535ft long and 70ft wide. It was powered by four 230hp Wolseley/Maybach engines, two in a double installation aft of the control bridge driving a single wooden propeller and two in single streamlined power cars amidships. Maximum level speed was 52 knots and disposable lift 17.8 tons. Armament included a 2pdr pom-pom, five 0.303in Lewis guns and eight 230lb bombs. It was not completed until 1920, however, and was deflated as the airship programme ran down. In 1921 it was inflated again to train USN aviators who were to take over R-38 but was then deleted and scrapped in 1924 after flying for only 75 hours

Vickers-built Parseval non-rigid airships

In 1912 the Admiralty placed an order through Vickers for Parseval-designed non-rigid airships and as part of the agreement Vickers received a full set of drawings for the firm's PL-18 design in 1913. The Admiralty contracted for one, P-5, to be built in Germany and two, P-6 and P-7, to be built by Vickers but, in the event, all three were built by Vickers. Vickers also obtained exclusive rights for Maybach-designed engines manufactured by Vickers' subsidiary Wolseley. P-5 had a length

HM Airship R-26.

of 304ft and a capacity of 364,000ft^3 which gave a gross lift of 11 tons. It was powered by two 240hp Renault engines which gave a maximum level speed of 38 knots. Construction was inevitably slowed by the outbreak of war with Germany in 1914 but Vickers persevered and replaced the original engine transmission gear with a new type of swivelling propeller mounting of its own design. P-6 and P-7 had two 180hp Wolseley/Maybach engines but were otherwise identical to P-5.

After construction, P-5 was re-assembled at Howden, completed in November 1917 and used for training rigid airship crews. After a forced landing at East Fortune in February 1918 it was deleted having only flown for 69 hours 5 minutes. P-6 was built at Barrow and completed in December 1916 but then dismantled and re-assembled at Howden where it was used for trials. Remarkably it survived a hangar fire there in February 1918 that destroyed three other airships and in 1919 it was used to search for mines that had broken loose from wartime minefields. It was deleted in October 1919 having flown for 488 hours. P-7 was identical to P-6 but was only used as a source of spare parts for P-6. It may only have flown once.

SS non-rigid airships

In addition to the rigids and Parsevals, Vickers built three SS non-rigid airships at Barrow and rebuilt one. Details of the SS class can be found in the Kingsnorth RN Air Station section and those built at Barrow were SS 32, rebuilt as SS 32A, SS-33 and SS-34.

SS-32 was delivered in April 1916 and rebuilt in October. After re-delivery as SS-32A it was used with its engine removed for experiments in the Cavendish Dock moored to a mast on a raft. It was eventually wrecked by high wind gusts and deleted in 1917. SS-33 operated on anti-submarine patrols from Luce Bay before being deleted in 1917 and SS-34 was also used for mooring experiments in Cavendish Dock before being deleted in May 1917 after the envelope was destroyed in a gale.

FB 5 Gunbus

FB stood for Fighting Biplane and the FB 5 was one of a series of two-seat biplane fighters with pusher engines produced by Vickers for the RFC. The RNAS received twelve from 1914, some of which were transferred to the RFC. Wingspan was 36ft 6in and MTOW 2,050lb. A 100hp Gnome monosoupape rotary, pusher, engine driving a two-bladed wooden propeller gave a maximum level speed of 62 knots. The pilot occupied the rear cockpit with the gunlayer in the nose with a single 0.303in Lewis machine on a pivoted mounting. One FB 5 is known to have served with 1 Squadron RNAS in France in early 1915 but the type was used mainly for experimental work at Eastchurch and Isle of Grain. Some were used for training but the type was found to have little operational value and the surviving examples were transferred to the RFC or deleted by mid-1916.

FB.5 Gunbus.

Wellington of 765 NAS at Lee-on-Solent in 1945. (Philip Jarrett)

Wellington

No Wellingtons were built for the RN but twenty-three were transferred from the RAF for use as flying classrooms or transport aircraft. Designed as bomber for the RAF, Wellingtons had a wingspan of 82ft 6in and MTOW of 36,500lb. Different marks had different engines. Those transferred to the RN included two Mark Is with two 1,050hp Bristol Pegasus XVIII engines driving three-bladed metal variable-pitch propellers to give a maximum level speed of 215 knots. The three Mark IIs were powered by two 1,145hp Rolls-Royce Merlin X engines driving three-bladed metal variable-pitch propellers to give a maximum level speed of 224 knots and the others comprised four Mark X, nine Mark XI and five Mark T XVII all of which were powered by various marks of the 1,675hp Bristol Hercules to give a maximum speed of 224 knots. The T XVIIs were modified as flying classrooms for night-fighter crews with AI radar in the nose and intercept consoles for students and instructors in the cabin area. The rear turret and all other armament options were removed. In some of the other RN Wellingtons the turrets were left in place but the guns were removed from them. RN Wellingtons used as transports had operational equipment removed and replaced by bench seating along the cabin sides.

Between 1943 and 1946 RN Wellingtons served with 716, 758, 762, 765, 778, 782 and 783 NAS although some of these only used one example briefly. They were used in the AI training, instrument training, twin conversion and transport roles and at least one example was used by Yeovilton station flight in 1945. Some were also used for the development of instrument approach techniques, aircrew safety equipment development and twin-engine conversion courses for pilots. The largest single user was probably 765 NAS which used the type in the transport role to ferry RN personnel from outlying stations in the Mediterranean to Hal Far until 1946.

VOUGHT-SIKORSKY

Chesapeake

The Admiralty allocated the name Chesapeake to the Vought-Sikorsky SB2U Vindicator, one of the first monoplanes accepted by the USN. It first flew in January 1936, was made available for export in 1938 and the French Navy ordered a large batch. After the French collapse in June 1940 the British Purchasing Commission in the USA took over the contract and forty-nine examples were delivered to the RN. Vought-Sikorsky was instructed to make significant design changes including an increase from one to four wing-mounted 0.3in Browning machine guns with 500 rpg mounted two in each wing firing clear of the propeller arc. Increased armour plate for the two aircrew and fuel tanks made the aircraft's poor performance even worse. A single front-line unit was formed in July 1941 intended for use from CVEs, but Chesapeakes were found unsuitable for operation from small decks and were issued instead to FRUs based ashore. These found it a useful aircraft because it had a reliable engine and good endurance. It continued to give valuable service in this role until 1944 when the lack of spares became an issue.

Chesapeake data

Length:	33ft 11¾in
Wingspan:	41ft 10¾in (16ft folded)
Height:	14ft 3in with propeller vertical
MTOW:	9,763lb
Engine:	One 825hp Pratt & Whitney R-1535-SB4-G Twin Wasp driving a two-bladed, variable-pitch metal propeller
Fuel:	Avgas. 202½ gallons
Performance:	Maximum level speed 215 knots Service ceiling 16,400ft. 40 minutes to 15,000ft
Endurance:	3 hours
Armament:	Four 0.3in Browning machine guns in wings with 500 rpg. One 0.3in Browning on flexible mounting in rear cockpit. Three 500lb bombs

A Chesapeake shortly after delivery

Between 1941 and 1944 Chesapeakes equipped, or partially equipped, 768, 770, 771, 772, 776, 778, 781, 784 and 787 NAS in the fleet requirements and evaluation roles. They operated from Crail, Twatt, Machrihanish, Speke, Arbroath and Lee-on-Solent.

They were operated briefly by 811 NAS, a composite unit with fourteen Chesapeakes and two Sea Hurricanes, between July and November 1941 but did not embark. 'Winkle' Brown flew the type at Arbroath and wrote that whilst its introduction to the USN had been significant, it been overtaken rapidly by technological development. By 1941 it was obsolescent.

Kingfisher

Designed to meet a USN specification for a floatplane spotter/reconnaissance aircraft operated from battleships and cruisers. Designated OS2U, it served throughout the Pacific War and, during the fast carrier strike operations of 1944–5 was also used as an ASR aircraft by the USN. It was a two-seat monoplane with extensively-glazed cockpits and featured an all-metal structure with mixed metal and fabric covering, the latter over the after half of the wings and all control surfaces. It could be fitted with either a float or fixed, wheeled undercarriage.

Kingfisher data

Length:	33ft 7¾in
Wingspan:	35ft 11in
Height:	14ft 8in as a seaplane, 13ft on wheels
MTOW:	4,619lb
Engine:	One 450hp Pratt & Whitney R-985-SB3 Wasp Junior driving a two-bladed, variable-pitch metal propeller
Fuel:	Avgas. 120 gallons
Performance:	Maximum level speed 150 knots Service ceiling 18,200ft. 12 minutes to 10,000ft
Endurance:	5 hours
Armament:	One fixed 0.3in Browning front gun and one similar gun on a flexible mount in the rear cockpit. Provision for light bombs under the wings

The RN received 100 Kingfishers transferred from the USN under Lend-Lease arrangements, beginning in 1942.

703 NAS formed in June 1942 as the HQ unit for Kingfisher flights allocated to AMCs. By then these operated mainly in the South Atlantic and Indian Oceans searching for blockade runners and protecting trade and so detachments with spare aircraft were positioned at Freetown, Palisadoes and Wingfield. The last Kingfisher flight, embarked in the cruiser *Emerald*, was stood down in 1944. Other units equipped or partially-equipped with Kingfishers included 702, 726, 763, 764, 765, 777, 778, 781, 787 and 789 NAS. These were used mainly in the seaplane training and trials roles but some flew on anti-submarine patrols, especially off West Africa.

Kingfishers operated as catapult seaplanes from the cruisers *Emerald* and *Enterprise*; the seaplane training carrier *Pegasus* and the special service vessel *Fidelity*. AMCs that operated Kingfisher flights included *Canton*, *Cilicia*, *Corfu* and *Ranpura* between 1942 and 1944.

VOISIN

From 1915 the Admiralty procured thirty-seven reconnaissance bombers from the French Voisin Company. RN examples were all built in France of three distinct sub-types known as the Biplane, Type III

The Voisin Pusher Biplanes used in trials with the Hotchkiss 37mm cannon. (Goble Family)

Kingfisher being launched into the water from a slipway in 1942.

LA.S and the Cannon. Of these twelve were Biplanes, twenty-three were Type IIIs and the two known as Cannons were lent by the French Government for use in RNAS gun trials.

The basic Voisin design was a biplane made of steel tubing covered with doped fabric and a pusher engine. Engines of slightly increased power were used in the later models.

Type III LA.S data

Length:	31ft 2in
Wingspan:	48ft 4in
Height:	9ft 8in
MTOW:	2,976lb
Engine:	One 140hp Canton-Une B.9 pusher radial driving a two-bladed wooden propeller
Fuel:	Avgas. 27½ gallons
Performance:	Maximum level speed 60 knots Service ceiling nominally 10,000ft. 25 minutes to 6,500ft
Endurance:	4 hours
Armament:	One 0.303in Lewis machine gun on flexible mount in front cockpit for the observer/gunlayer supplemented by rifles or pistols. Up to 200lb of bombs

Half the first batch of twelve was delivered direct to St Pol where they were used by 1 Squadron RNAS, later 1 Wing. They were soon outclassed by newer designs and all were deleted by 1916. The other six were shipped to the Aegean where they equipped 3 Wing at Tenedos. These were used for a variety of reconnaissance and bombing duties and those that survived were not deleted until 1917.

Some Type IIIs joined 3 Wing at Imbros in 1915. In 1916 two others joined a joint RNAS/RFC unit at Basra to support military operations in Mesopotamia. These were eventually transferred to the RFC. Other Voisins were used by 8 Squadron RNAS for operations in East Africa but some remained in the UK for use by training units at Redcar and Eastchurch. The final example from this batch was used for gun trials with a Davis gun at Isle of Grain.

The two Cannon variants were used in gun trials at both Isle of Grain and St Pol. These had 200hp Hispano-Suiza engines, the most powerful fitted to any RNAS Voisin and their trial installation included a 37mm Hotchkiss gun which must have caused noticeable recoil when it was fired. No further development appears to have followed the trials. The Voisins had a reputation for being robust aircraft but they had a poor performance and were completely outclassed over the Western Front by 1916. Those in the Aegean lasted longer because of the initial lack of air opposition. Most pilots were pleased to see them go.

VULTEE

Vengeance

The A-31 Vengeance was an attack/dive-bomber designed to meet a French Air Force requirement but after the French collapse in 1940 the British Purchasing Commission in the USA ordered substantial batches for the RAF. The USAAF only used the type as a target tug. Vengeances were operated by the RAF, RAAF and Indian Air Force in South East Asia and the South West Pacific with some success. After the purchased batches, many more were provided under Lend-Lease arrangements. No Vengeances were supplied directly to the RN but a significant number were transferred from the RAF and RAAF for use as fleet requirements aircraft in Ceylon and the Pacific. The unique feature of its design was a zero-incidence wing that enabled it to dive vertically without lift from the wing pulling the aircraft off target but this resulted in a nose-up attitude in normal flight which was not popular with pilots, particularly on landing. It also had a distinctive 'W'-shaped wing planform that resulted from an error in calculating its centre of gravity; sweeping back the centre section was an easier fix than re-designing the wing attachment structure. Overall the Vengeance was considered to be a reliable and rugged aircraft that was a good workhorse for target-towing and fleet requirements tasks.

Vengeance Mark II data

Length:	39ft 9in
Wingspan:	48ft
Height:	15ft 4in
MTOW:	14,300lb
Engine:	One 1,700hp Wright Double Cyclone R-2600-A5B-5 radial driving a three-bladed, variable-pitch metal propeller
Fuel:	Avgas. 223 gallons
Performance:	Maximum level speed 240 knots Service ceiling 22,500ft. 12 minutes to 10,000ft
Endurance:	6 hours
Armament:	None in FRU and DDT-spraying roles. Target-towing winch fitted in rear cockpit of TT IV

The RN received 113 Vengeance Mark IIs transferred from the RAF, of which 14 were returned unused. A further twenty-five TT IVs were made available by the RAAF in Australia but only nine of these were taken up.

Between 1945 and 1947 Vengeances were used in the fleet requirements role by 721, 733 and 791 NAS.

721 NAS had its aircraft ferried to the Pacific in *Begum* during

Vengeances of 721 NAS at Ponam in 1945.

1945 and became the resident FRU at Ponam in the Admiralty Islands. It moved to Archerfield in Australia in October 1945 and then Kai Tak in Hong Kong in 1946. The TT IVs were modified to spray DDT and used in an attempt to suppress malarial mosquitoes in Hong Kong during 1946, an unusual tasking for a naval air squadron. These specialised aircraft and their crews formed the anti-malarial air spraying unit, effectively a flight within 721 NAS. 733 NAS operated as a FRU at China Bay in Ceylon in 1947 and 791 NAS operated as a FRU at Sembawang in Singapore until 1947. It also operated a flight of TT IVs on DDT spraying tasks over Singapore.

WESTLAND

N.1B

In 1916 the Admiralty issued Specification N.1B for a single-seat floatplane fighter capable of operation from ships. Two prototypes were ordered from Westland, both designated N.1B. They had a rectangular-section fuselage with four longerons and the wings folded for carrier stowage. Both aircraft were assembled at Isle of Grain in August 1917 but deleted in early 1918 and there was no further development. Wingspan was 31ft 3½in and MTOW 1,987lb. The 150hp Bentley radial engine gave a maximum level speed of 95 knots and armament comprised a single belt-fed Vicker 0.303in machine gun under a hump forward of the pilot's windshield and a single 0.303in Lewis machine gun on an Admiralty-pattern swivel mounting on the upper wing centre-section. Two 65lb bombs could be carried in tandem under the fuselage centreline.

Walrus

By 1918 the Sopwith 1½ 'Ship' Strutter was no longer adequate for the embarked spotter/reconnaissance role because the observer could not spot the fall of shot, identify ships, encode signals, transmit and receive signals. The Admiralty therefore requested a three-seater aircraft capable of carrying a significant load. Numbers of DH9A two-seaters were available and post-war economy led to their selection as the basis of a modified design. Westland was contracted to carry out the work, taking into account a modification already carried out by Armstrong Whitworth in 1920 and given the name Tadpole. The sole Tadpole effectively became the prototype Walrus. The resulting Walrus had three cockpits, all with windscreens and two conspicuous flotation bags, inflated by compressed air bottles inside the fuselage, were mounted along the front fuselage sides, extending back under the wings. The undercarriage incorporated a hydrovane to prevent the aircraft nosing over if it ditched. The cross-axle between the wheels carried jaws to engage the fore and aft retaining wires and other detail design

Westland N.1B Scout Seaplane. (Philip Jarrett)

improvements included a Westland patented fuel dump valve which could empty the main tank quickly and seal it to act as an additional buoyancy aid. The wings could not be folded but were detachable to reduce hangar stowage space. Fuel pumps and the generator that provided electrical power for the W/T set were powered by two small wind vanes mounted on top of the fuselage forward of the pilot's cockpit. Aft of the main wheels there was a semi-glazed pannier in which the observer could lay prone to see the sea surface below.

The type's first flight in 1921 nearly ended in disaster when the pilot found that the nose dropped dramatically when the throttle was closed and could only be raised by opening it. The engineer in the centre cockpit was persuaded to climb into the rear cockpit and then onto the rear fuselage, the change of balance allowing the pilot to close the throttle and land. Unsurprisingly test pilots referred to the Walrus as the vicious beast, a view borne out by the eleven lost in crashes during the types' time in service.

Walrus data

Length:	29ft 9in
Wingspan:	46ft 2in
Height:	11ft 7in
MTOW:	4,998lb
Engine:	One 450hp Napier Lion II water-cooled engine driving a two-bladed wooden propeller
Fuel:	Avgas. 75 gallons
Performance:	Maximum level speed 109 knots Service ceiling nominally 19,000ft. 15 minutes to 10,000ft
Endurance:	4 hours
Armament:	One fixed forward-firing 0.303in belt-fed Vickers machine gun on port side of fuselage and one 0.303in Lewis machine on a Scarff ring on the rear cockpit

In total, thirty-six Walrus were delivered in two batches of eighteen, the first designated Mark Is and the second Mark IIs with what was described as a high-lift wing section and an enlarged rudder.

They served with 3 and 210 Squadrons at first and then with 420, 421 and 423 Flights. Walrus' operated ashore from Leuchars and Gosport on fleet requirements tasks. The only carrier on which they operated was *Argus*. They never proved popular with those unfortunate enough to have to fly them and in 1925 they were withdrawn from service and replaced by Blackburn Blackburns and Avro Bisons.

Lysander

Designed to a 1934 Air Ministry specification for what it described as an Army co-operation aircraft, the Lysander was technically innovative but heavy on the controls, lumbering and slow; easily destroyed by German single-seat fighters over France in 1940. They found their niche later, however, when used to insert agents into occupied Europe at night. Surprisingly, production continued until 1942 and many were modified for target-towing. No Lysanders were built directly for the RN but sixty-seven were transferred from the RAF after 1941. Most were Mark IIIs, some to TT III standard. It was a two-seat monoplane of metal girder construction covered by metal panels in the engine and

Lysander Mark II of 755 NAS. (Philip Jarrett)

cockpit area and fabric elsewhere, including the wings. The high mounted wings gave excellent low-speed handling characteristics and Mark III's 870hp Bristol Mercury XX air-cooled radial engine gave a maximum level speed of 185 knots. Wingspan was 50ft and MTOW of the examples used by the RN was 6,330lb.

Between 1941 and 1944 Lysanders equipped, or partially equipped, 754, 755, 757, 771 and 792 NAS in the radio and navigation training, TAG training, fleet requirements and target-towing roles. They were all shore-based and operated from Arbroath, Worthy Down, Twatt, St Merryn and other airfields.

Wyvern

Originally designated W.34 by Westland, design work started on it in 1943 as a single-seat, piston-engined torpedo strike fighter. In 1944 Admiralty Specification N.11/44 was written around it and it emerged with a 'humped' fuselage that gave the pilot an excellent view from a clear 'bubble' canopy. It was to be powered by a 2,690hp Rolls-Royce Eagle 22 liquid-cooled engine driving two four-bladed, variable-pitch, contra-rotating propellers, the most powerful British aircraft engine at the time and, arguably, the most complicated piston-engine installation ever flown in a British military aircraft. The propellers had a diameter of 13ft and the main undercarriage legs had to be long enough to provide adequate tip clearance. When retracted they had to leave space for the torpedo or other weapons on the centreline and the track was determined by the folded width of the wings. Dowty designed a mechanism that shortened the oleo legs as they retracted to minimise the space they took up in the wings. In 1945 Rolls-Royce stopped Eagle development to concentrate on jet engines but delivered sufficient to complete the prototypes. The first of these flew in December 1946 but the combination of a very complicated engine and the contra-rotating propellers caused difficulties. The name Wyvern was announced in 1947 with the prototypes designated TF 1. In October 1947 the second TF 1 suffered a bearing failure and the enormous drag from the 'discing' propellers caused it to crash, killing the pilot. It was found that the long shaft to the front propeller flexed badly in flight, cutting off lubrication to the pitch-change bearings between the two propellers and leading, ultimately, to failure. Deck-landing trials were carried out in *Implacable* during June 1948 but they were suspended following another propeller failure during the test programme ashore but resumed to complete twenty-two take-offs and landings. Further deck-landing trials were carried out in *Illustrious* during May and June 1949.

Before the TF 1 had even flown, the Admiralty issued Specification N.12/45 for a turboprop-powered TF 2 which Westland designated W.35. Two prototypes were ordered, the first of which was powered by a 4,000shp Rolls-Royce Clyde reverse axial-flow turboprop and the second by an Armstrong Siddeley Python. Both drove large four-bladed, contra-rotating propellers. Both flew but Rolls-Royce was heavily committed to development of the Dart and terminated work on the Clyde. Wyvern development then concentrated on the Python which was longer than the Clyde and required significant fuselage changes. The first Python-powered TF 2 flew in March 1949 and a second in August. One example was displayed at the 1949 Farnborough Air Show but crashed in October after an engine flameout, killing the pilot and the occupants of a house that it impacted.

Admiralty interest in a two-seat trainer version led to a single prototype Wyvern T 3, designated W.38 by Westland, with a deepened rear fuselage to accommodate a second seat in tandem for the instructor. Both pilots had Martin-Baker ejection seats. The T 3 first flew in February 1950 but was written off after a forced landing following engine failure. In December the Admiralty decided that there was no need for a trainer variant and development of the T 3 ceased.

Wyvern S 4 of 831 NAS being catapulted from *Ark Royal*.

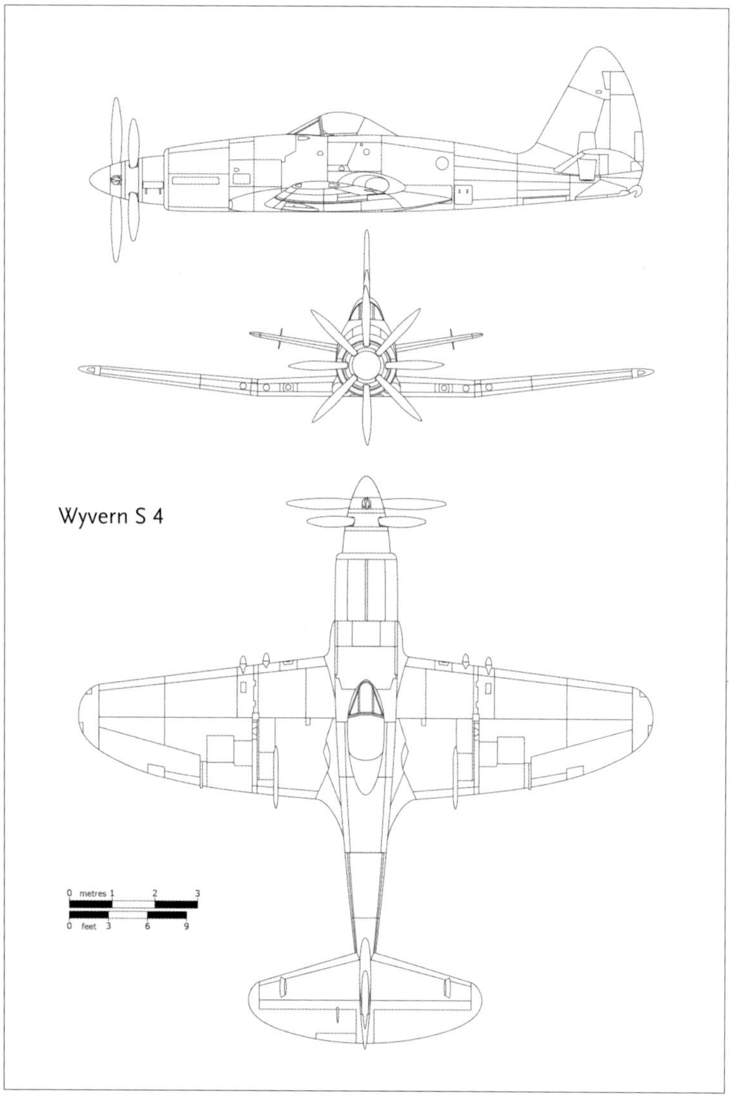

Single-seat development continued with twenty TF 2 pre-production aircraft during which a number of problems had to be overcome. The canopy was strengthened after collapses in flight caused the death of one test pilot and injuries to two others. The biggest problems, however, were associated with engine and propeller control, including a lag in power response following throttle movements and surges when stored energy in the rotating core of the engine or the propellers was transmitted from one to the other. Several solutions were devised and evaluated between 1950 and 1952 including a new inertia control system designed by Rotol which was flown in 1951. A mechanical fault led to initial suspicion that the system might be unreliable but further test flying proved that it had actually solved the problem. In August 1952 it was found that a sustained side-slip caused rudder lock

A Wyvern S 4 of 813 NAS carrying out deck-landing practice, with its hook raised, on *Eagle*.

A Wyvern S 4 firing 3in RP.

at low airspeed and this was cured by fitting finlets to the tailplane. A limited operational clearance was issued for the production aircraft, by then designated Wyvern S 4, in December 1954 but they could only operate ashore until production-standard Rotol control units were fitted.

The Wyvern S 4 had the Gyro Gunsight Mark 4E for weapon aiming and the there was a position in the wing root for either a G-45 gunfire recording camera or an F-46 torpedo release marking camera. In the reconnaissance role oblique F-24 cameras could be mounted aft of the cockpit, viewing through circular clear panels which could be covered when cameras were not fitted. Early production S 4s were fitted with Martin-Baker Mark 1B ejection seats but these were replaced by the Mark 2B which gave automatic pilot separation below 10,000ft.

Service acceptance trials of the Wyvern S 4 took place in 1953 and included deck landings on the USS *Antietam*, the first carrier with a fully-angled flight deck, which was carrying out trials with British naval aircraft in UK waters. Further deck-landing trials were carried out on *Eagle* but marred by an undercarriage collapse after which the propellers hit the deck and shattered, killing an aircraft handler. Final deck-landing clearance was not given until November 1953 after forty-eight accident-free landings were carried out on *Illustrious* using the newly developed mirror landing aid. Development from the initial Admiralty specification to operational clearance had taken a decade and the Wyvern was arguably obsolescent when it equipped its first squadron.

Wyvern S 4 data

Length:	42ft 3in
Wingspan:	44ft (20ft folded)
Height:	11ft 7in
MTOW:	24,550lb
Engine:	One 3,670shp Armstrong Siddeley Python 4 axial-flow turboprop with 1,180lb residual thrust driving two four-bladed, variable-pitch, contra-rotating metal propellers
Fuel:	Avcat. 526 gallons in 7 internal tanks. Two optional 90-gallon drop tanks. Total with all tanks 706 gallons
Performance:	Maximum level speed 290 knots Service ceiling 28,000ft. 5 minutes to 10,000ft
Endurance:	3 hours with drop tanks
Armament:	Four fixed forward-firing 20mm Hispano Mark 5 cannon with 200 rpg, two in each wing firing clear of the propeller arc. Alternative loads included one 18in Mark 15 or 17 torpedo under fuselage centreline or one 2,000lb AP bomb on centreline or up to three 1,000lb MC bombs or a single Mine Type A Mark 7/8/9 on the centreline. Up to sixteen double-tier 3in R/P could be carried under the wings

Wheels down flaps down, hook down; a Wyvern S 4 of 813 NAS landing on *Albion*.

A Dragonfly of Lossiemouth Station Flight in 1959.

Wyvern production amounted to 124 aircraft. Of these, six were W.34 prototypes, seven were TF 1 pre-production aircraft, three were TF 2 prototypes, one was a T 3 prototype, twenty were TF 2 pre-production aircraft of which nine were completed as S 4s, and eighty-seven were built as S 4s.

Shore-based squadrons equipped with Wyverns between 1953 and 1957 included 700,703, 764 and 787 NAS together with the un-numbered Wyvern Conversion Unit. They were used in the trials and training roles at Ford except for 787 NAS which operated in the development role at West Raynham.

Front-line units that operated the Wyvern between 1953 and 1958 included 813, 827, 830 and 831 NAS. Only two of these were usually in commission at any one time and they operated from the aircraft carriers *Albion*, *Eagle* and *Ark Royal.*

The first carrier-based squadron was 813 NAS which embarked in *Albion* in September 1954 for operations in the Mediterranean. It encountered problems with engine flameouts during catapult launches caused by fuel starvation during acceleration. On 13 October Lieutenant B D Macfarlane RN suffered a flameout on the catapult and ditched ahead of the bow. The aircraft passed under the ship as it sank but once clear of the propellers Macfarlane escaped by ejecting underwater, the first time this had ever been done. On reaching the surface he was winched to safety by the planeguard helicopter. The flameout problem made carrier operations hazardous and so 813 NAS disembarked to Hal Far until March 1955 when it returned to the UK for its aircraft to be modified.

In November 1956 *Eagle*'s 830 NAS flew eighty-two combat sorties during Operation 'Musketeer', the Suez Crisis. On Day 1 they flew eighteen sorties against Dekheila airfield and then attacked other airfields, bridges and vehicles. Two aircraft were shot down by anti-aircraft fire but their pilots ejected safely and were rescued by *Eagle*'s SAR helicopter. The last Wyvern unit was the re-formed 813 NAS which eventually disbanded in April 1958.

Dragonfly

Rather than spend years on costly helicopter development, Westland approached Sikorsky for a licence to manufacture its S-51 and an agreement was signed in December 1946, allowing Westland not only to build the basic helicopter but to develop and market it outside the USA and Canada. A batch of S-51s were purchased for use as pattern aircraft and these arrived in 1947. One of them was taken on RN charge for evaluation in 1948 and embarked in *Vengeance* during 1949. This confirmed the type's suitability for the carrier-borne SAR role and the Admiralty ordered six, designated WS-51 by Westland and Dragonfly HR 1 by the RN. Dragonflies were subsequently ordered by the RAF and so RN variants were given odd mark numbers, RAF variants even. Westland had to redraw 2,700 drawings before WS-51 production could start and that took until September 1948.

The Dragonfly had a forward cabin and tail cone made with light alloy, semi-monocoque structures with a metal-clad centre section made

A Dragonfly HR 3 of Lossiemouth Station Flight. It is hovering next to a cairn on Ben Klibreck which marks the spot where XA 103, a Sea Vampire T 22 of 736 NAS, crashed on 17 March 1955 killing Lieutenants P L Beers and J H Knight RN. (Dave Skelton)

of steel tubing under the main rotor pylon which housed the engine and gearbox. A monocoque structure formed the cabin floor, providing support for the extensively glazed cabin. The pilot's seat and simple instrument panel were on the aircraft centreline with a bench seat for three passengers side-by-side behind it. Alternatively the bench could be removed and dual controls fitted with the two pilots seated in tandem. The original 450hp Pratt & Whitney Wasp Junior engine of the S-51 was replaced by a British 500hp Alvis Leonides. Cooling air entered the engine bay through an intake in the front face of the pylon and the engine exhaust pipe projected through the starboard side of the fuselage. The fixed tricycle undercarriage had a castoring nosewheel. Each of the three main rotor blades was built up around a single tubular metal spar with wooden leading and trailing edges which were fabric covered. The first HR 1 flew in June 1949.

Most RN Dragonflies were to HR 3 standard which differed in having more robust, all-metal main rotor blades and a hydraulic-powered control system to ease pilot workload. The rescue winch was on the port side of the main rotor pylon, operated either by a winchman or by the pilot using a control on his collective pitch lever. With a winchman the HR 1 could only rescue a single survivor but the HR 3 introduced a rapid fuel dumping capability that enabled two to be rescued with just sufficient fuel to recover to the carrier deck. Dragonflies replaced Sea Otter amphibians in the aircrew rescue role and they replaced planeguard destroyers by day. They lacked the instrumentation to fly or hover safely at night. When flying was in progress the planeguard helicopter hovered off the port quarter or beam of the carrier ready to be over a ditched aircraft within seconds. Performance was further improved in the HR 5 which had a more powerful engine and better instrument fit. No Dragonflies were built as HR 5s but twenty-five HR 1 and 3 airframes were modified to the new standard.

Dragonfly HR 5 data

Length:	57ft 6½in
Rotor Diameter:	48ft (span 13ft folded)
Height:	12ft 11in
MTOW:	5,900lb
Engine:	One 540hp Alvis Leonides 523/1 air-cooled radial engine mounted with the drive-shaft running upwards into the main rotor gearbox.
Fuel:	Avgas. 84 gallons
Performance:	Maximum level speed 90 knots Service ceiling 12,400ft. 6 minutes to 5,000ft
Endurance:	2 hours
Armament:	None

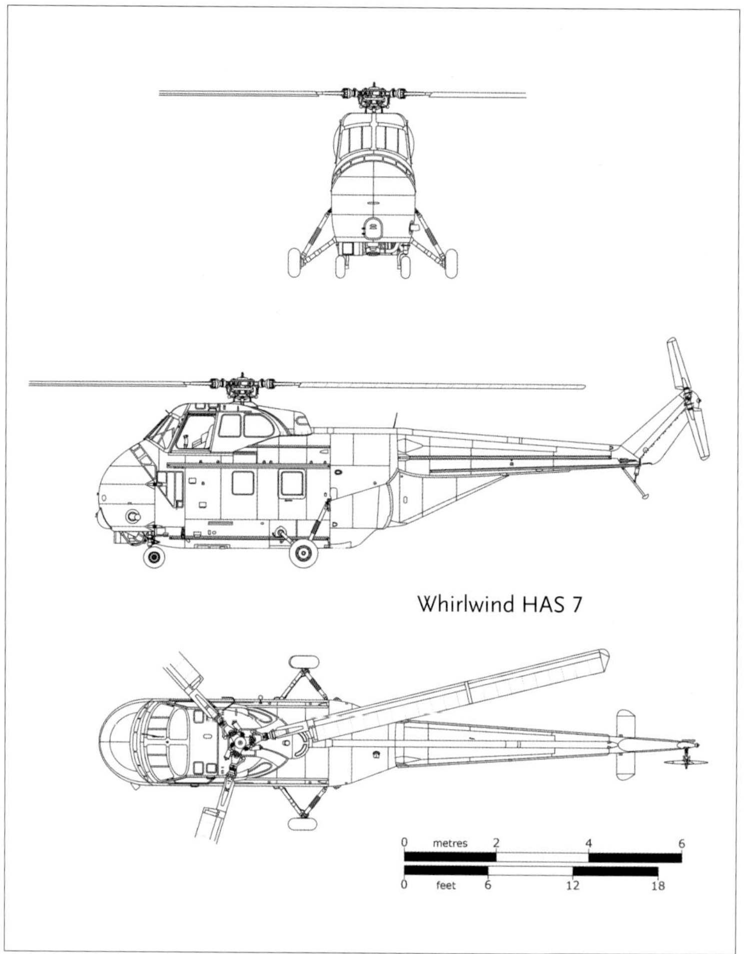

Whirlwind HAS 7

Westland built seventy Dragonflies for the RN and two of the original-pattern aircraft were used for evaluation.

They equipped, or partially equipped, 700. 701, 705, 727, 728, 744 and 771 NAS for use in the trials, training, SAR and fleet requirements roles between 1950 and 1962. In 1960 the two Dragonflies operated by 727 NAS were transferred from Brawdy to BRNC Dartmouth to give air experience to young officers until 1967. This was the last RN unit to operate the type and I was lucky enough to fly in both as a Cadet before they were replaced by Wasps.

Between 1952 and 1961 Dragonflies equipped SAR Flights embarked in the aircraft carriers *Albion*, *Ark Royal*, *Bulwark*, *Campania*, *Centaur*, *Eagle*, *Glory*, *Hermes*, *Illustrious*, *Indomitable*, *Ocean*, *Theseus*, *Victorious* and *Warrior*. RN Dragonflies also spent periods embarked in HMAS *Sydney* in 1951 and 1953 but the RAN did not operate the type.

RN air station SAR Flights that operated Dragonflies between 1952 and 1963 included Anthorn, Brawdy, Culdrose, Eglinton, Ford, Hal Far, Lossiemouth and Yeovilton.

The first RN SAR unit was formed in January 1951 and embarked in *Indomitable.* The second served in *Glory* during Korean War operations where it rescued four aircrew from the sea and a further four who had come down behind enemy lines. Two Dragonflies were embarked in *Campania* for the first British atom bomb test at Monte Bello island off north-west Australia. They collected water samples from the area where the device was exploded in the frigate *Plym* and flew them ashore for analysis. As helicopter roles expanded, two Dragonflies were embarked in the survey ship *Vidal* and one of these placed a Union flag on Rockall. In 1953 the Dutch authorities appealed to the UK for helicopter assistance after devastating floods; 705 NAS Dragonflies were deployed and rescued 734 people, three dogs and a cat in 229 hours' flying. One of them also flew Queen Juliana and Prince Bernhardt over the area to assess damage from the air.

Widgeon

In 1954 Westland produced an improved WS-51 with a wider cockpit capable of seating a passenger to the pilot's left and an improved gearbox. Several were built for export and in 1957 the Admiralty decided to convert twenty-four Dragonfly HR 5s to the new standard designated HR 7 but they were almost immediately cancelled as part of the 1957 Defence Review. Rotor diameter would have been slightly greater than the HR 5 at 49ft 2in but MTOW remained the same.

Whirlwind

Discussions about licence production of the Sikorsky S-55 by Westland began in 1950 and led to an agreement for its license production. Work began immediately to produce drawings of the helicopter it designated WS-55 and a single pattern airframe was purchased from Sikorsky. The WS-55 was a more advanced design than the WS-51 and comprised a rectangular light alloy semi-monocoque structure containing the cabin with a rear cone-shaped pylon for the tail rotor. The pronounced step between the bottom line of the cabin to the tail pylon was filled by a large triangular fillet to smooth the airflow past the fuselage in forward flight. The initial powerplant was the 600hp Pratt & Whitney 1340-40 air-cooled radial engine mounted on an inclined axis forward of the cabin, beneath but slightly forward of the cockpit which had dual controls for pilots seated side by side. A drive shaft from the engine passed between the pilots to the main rotor gearbox aft of the cockpit and a second shaft ran from it to drive the two-bladed tail rotor. Access to the engine could be gained by opening two clamshell doors in the nose and it was at a convenient height for mechanics to reach whilst standing. Fuel tanks were placed in cells under the cabin floor.

Whirlwind HAS 7 of 829 NAS lowering its sonar transducer off Portland in 1965.

A Whirlwind HAR 3 of *Warrior*'s Ship's Flight operating off Christmas Island during the UK nuclear weapon tests in 1958.

The three-bladed main rotor had offset flapping hinges and hydraulically-damped drag hinges and the blades were fabricated around a single metal spar with a metal leading edge and light alloy trailing edge structures. Two blades could be folded aft along the fuselage sides for hangar stowage with the third blade secured over and in line with the tail pylon. The four-wheel, non-retractable, undercarriage comprised two fully castoring front wheels and two main units with an oleo-pneumatic shock-absorber strut and a radius arm. The cabin was designed to seat ten marine commandos or six stretcher cases but could only take off with them at a minimal fuel state. The RN was the first customer and again RN versions were given odd mark numbers and subsequent variants for the RAF even. The first WS-55 Whirlwind flew in August 1953, the first of ten Whirlwinds designated HAR 1. They replaced Sikorsky Whirlwind HAR 21s in 848 NAS and five were deployed to Malaya where the hot and humid operating conditions significantly reduced performance. Two others operated successfully from the Antarctic patrol ship *Protector* during 1955–6 with more equipment and improved flotation gear. Another HAR 1 was used in mine-clearance trials, towing a sledge that would detonate influence mines at a safe distance astern of the aircraft. The aircraft's towing power was found to be marginal, however, and the trials were inconclusive. In another trial, a Whirlwind HAR 1 succeeded in towing a 'Ton' class minesweeper a short distance.

To overcome the HAR 1's lack of power Westland developed the HAR 3 with a single 700hp Wright 12-1300-3 air-cooled radial engine. Initially, thirty-seven were ordered as replacement SAR helicopters but three of these were completed as HAR 5s and a further nine as HAS 7s. Later HAR 3s and all subsequent Westland Whirlwinds had the tail cone drooped by 3 degrees to give greater rotor disc clearance during a harsh flaring manoeuvre, especially during an engine-off landing after autorotation. The three completed as HAR 5s introduced the Series II Whirlwind powered by a single derated 750hp Alvis Leonides 755 air-cooled, radial piston engine. Whilst this delivered more power than the earlier engines it had a fatal weakness. It was originally designed to operate on the horizontal plane on fixed-wing aircraft. Modifications

had been made to suit the vertical application in the Dragonfly but the angled positioning in the Whirlwind meant that lubrication did not flow through the engine as designed. The small batch of HAR 5s was too small to reveal this shortcoming and the same engine was selected for the large production run of HAS 7s that followed.

The Whirlwind HAS 7 was selected after the Bristol 191 was cancelled but was only considered to be an interim type since it was only capable of operating by day since pilots had to hover manually and doing so was demanding, difficult and tiring even in ideal wind and sea conditions. The sensor selected for the HAS 7 was a licence-built version of the USN AQS-4 built by R B Pullin & Co as the Admiralty Type 194 dipping sonar, originally known as ASDIC. The type's primary anti-submarine weapon was the Mark 30 acoustic-homing torpedo carried in a recess under the cabin floor.

The HAS 7 normally flew with a crew of three, pilot, observer and sonar operator, although under difficult conditions, dual controls allowed for two pilots to share the workload. It lacked sufficient lift to carry both sonar and a weapon and the torpedo, when loaded, blocked the hole through which the transducer was lowered. The HAS 7 had, therefore, to operate in hunter/killer pairs with the sonar-fitted aircraft searching for and then tracking a contact before guiding a weapon carrier to attack it. With no radar this could be difficult but observers acquired skill with practice. At first HAS 7s were painted with sky cabin

Whirlwind HAR 9 of *Endurance* Flight over pack ice off Graham Land.

sides and sea grey top but to help other units see the helicopters hovering in sonar contact the top decking was painted yellow. Whirlwinds withdrawn from anti-submarine operations were redesignated as HAR 7s and used in a variety of roles including helicopter pilot training, fleet requirements and SAR.

The engine problem manifested itself from the outset and the HAS 7 fleet was frequently grounded while remedies were sought and implemented. Gannets were kept in operation longer than the Admiralty had intended and the HAS 7 gained an unenviable reputation for unreliability.

HAR 9

No HAR 9s were built as such but those converted retained the same main rotor gearbox, rotor blades and transmission systems to simplify the conversion but the Leonides piston engine was replaced by a single 1,050shp Bristol Siddeley Gnome H 1000 turboshaft. The Gnome was smaller than the Leonides and only one third of its weight but produced 40 per cent more power, greatly improving performance and reliability. It was mounted horizontally and offset to starboard in a new nose assembly lengthened by 30in to provide a more streamlined shape and the space to port was used to house the Lucas fuel system and Hawker-

Whirlwind HAS 7s of 848 NAS from *Bulwark* operating in the commando role north of Aden.

Siddeley Dynamics control computer. In the SAR role the type was usually flown by a crew of three, pilot, winchman and SAR diver, and could recover up to five survivors. HAR 9s entered service during 1966 and remained in use until the mid-1970s. They were also used briefly by carrier SAR flights including *Victorious* and *Hermes*.

Whirlwind HAS 7 data

Length:	41ft 8½in
Rotor Diameter:	53ft (span 13ft folded)
Height:	15ft 7½in
MTOW:	7,800lb
Engine:	One 750hp Alvis Leonides Major 755 air-cooled radial
Fuel:	Avgas. 179 gallons
Performance:	Maximum level speed 95 knots
	Service ceiling 13,000ft. 7 minutes to 5,000ft
Endurance:	2 hours
Armament:	One Mark 30 homing torpedo

Westland delivered 169 Whirlwinds to the RN. Of these 10 were HAR 1s; 27 were HAR 3s; three were HAR 5s and 129 were HAS 7s. Sixteen HAS 7s were converted to HAR 9s.

Between 1954 and 1965 they equipped, or partially equipped, 700, 700H, 701, 705, 719, 728, 737, 771 and 781 NAS based ashore in the trials, helicopter pilot training, ASW development, operational training, SAR and fleet requirement roles and even as an Admiral's 'barge'.

Between 1954 and 1967 Westland Whirlwinds served with 814, 815, 819, 820, 824, 825, 829, 845, 846, 847 and 848 NAS in the anti-submarine and commando assault roles from the aircraft carriers *Albion*, *Ark Royal*, *Bulwark*, *Centaur*, *Eagle*, *Glory*, *Hermes*, *Theseus*, *Victorious* and *Warrior* together with the ice patrol ships *Endurance* and *Protector*.

They were used between 1958 and 1977 by station SAR flights at Brawdy, Culdrose, Hal Far, Lee-on-Solent, Lossiemouth, Portland and Yeovilton.

Early Whirlwinds were used as SAR flights on the operational carriers and from the ice patrol ships. Some HAR 3s were operated by squadrons when their HAS 7s were grounded in order to keep pilots in flying practice as much as possible. Two HAR 3s flew alongside Sikorsky Whirlwinds of 845 NAS during the first airborne commando assault in history at Suez in November 1956.

The operational life of the HAS 7 began in March 1957 when 700H NAS was formed. It was disbanded in September. 845 NAS had re-formed in June 1957 with HAS 7s and embarked in *Bulwark* in August, the first helicopter squadron to form part of a carrier air group. Apart from its operational role it proved that both fixed and rotary-wing aircraft could operate together within a single carrier air group. Far from being a hindrance, the helicopters broadened the ship's capability significantly and in September 1958 *Bulwark* was operating off the Strait of Hormuz when two tankers collided, one of which, the *Melika*, caught fire. Whirlwinds of 845 NAS ferried fire-fighting teams and equipment to her and, once the fire was brought under control, passed a cable which allowed *Bulwark* to tow her to a safe anchorage. The squadron was awarded the Boyd Trophy for 1958 in recognition of its part in this operation.

Engine failures led to the entire HAS 7 fleet being grounded in 1959. Improvements were made but the type never really recovered from its bad reputation. Once they were flying again, HAS 7s from *Victorious*, *Centaur* and *Bulwark* played an important role during the Kuwait Crisis of 1961 ferrying Royal Marines to positions near the Iraqi border and keeping them supplied with water and other vital logistics. From 1960 HAS 7s equipped commando helicopter squadrons operating both from *Bulwark* and *Albion* and sites ashore such as Nangga Gaat in Borneo during operations in the Brunei rebellion and during the Confrontation in Borneo against Indonesia. 846 NAS was awarded the Boyd Trophy in 1963 for its part in these operations. Operating unreliable, single-engined helicopters over the jungle took a particular kind of courage and the Commando Helicopter Force nickname 'Junglies' stemmed from this era.

Albion Ship's Flight Whirlwind HAR 3 bringing casualties to the ship during the Suez Crisis in 1956.

848 NAS Whirlwind HAS 7s from *Bulwark* landing sticks of Royal Marines in the desert during the 1961 Kuwait Crisis.

Statistics show that out of 129 HAS 7s operated by the RN, 51 were lost in crashes or ditchings. Besides these a considerable number made precautionary landings if they could because of a rough-running engine or hydraulic failure; the latter a symptom of incipient engine failure. Everyone who flew the HAS 7 has a story to tell. I flew it during my helicopter conversion course and my own incident involved a precautionary landing following hydraulic failure; I was lucky, many others were not. The HAS 7 used a cartridge starter which was not quite up to turning the engine over if the lubricating oil was cold and stiff. I think the maximum number used for a single start by a member of my course was twelve, my own record was seven. Once the engine was warming up I remember the Whirlwind rocking on its four wheels like a jelly on a plate. In flight there was virtually no feel on the cyclic pitch stick; it felt rather like holding a broom handle balanced on a sharpened tip and care had to be taken not to over control. The stick was also much higher than those of other aircraft to give the pilot leverage if hydraulic power was lost. The collective pitch lever, on the other hand, was very stiff to raise and lower. Rotor speed had to be maintained at a constant 213 rpm and there was a mechanical interlock to increase engine rpm as the collective was raised in order to keep it within limits. It was not that accurate, however, and constant adjustment had to be made with the twist-grip throttle on the end of the collective lever to keep rotor rpm at exactly 213. No matter what else the pilot was doing, his focus never strayed far from the rotor rpm gauge.

A quotation in *The Naval Review* from an un-named author summed up the Whirlwind HAS 7 perfectly; it described it as a perfectly good helicopter ruined by replacing a reliable US engine with a totally unsuitable British engine.

Wessex

When the Admiralty cancelled the Bristol Type 191 in 1956, Westland decided to offer a replacement based on the Sikorsky S-58 which had first flown in March 1954. Sikorsky was approached immediately and agreement was reached to licence-build the S-58 under the same conditions as the Whirlwind. The company had already identified the S-58 as an ideal airframe in which to replace the piston engine with a British turboshaft engine. A single pattern aircraft was shipped to the UK in 1957, a HSS-1N Seabat used by USN anti-submarine squadrons and powered by a single 1,525hp Wright R-1820-84 radial engine

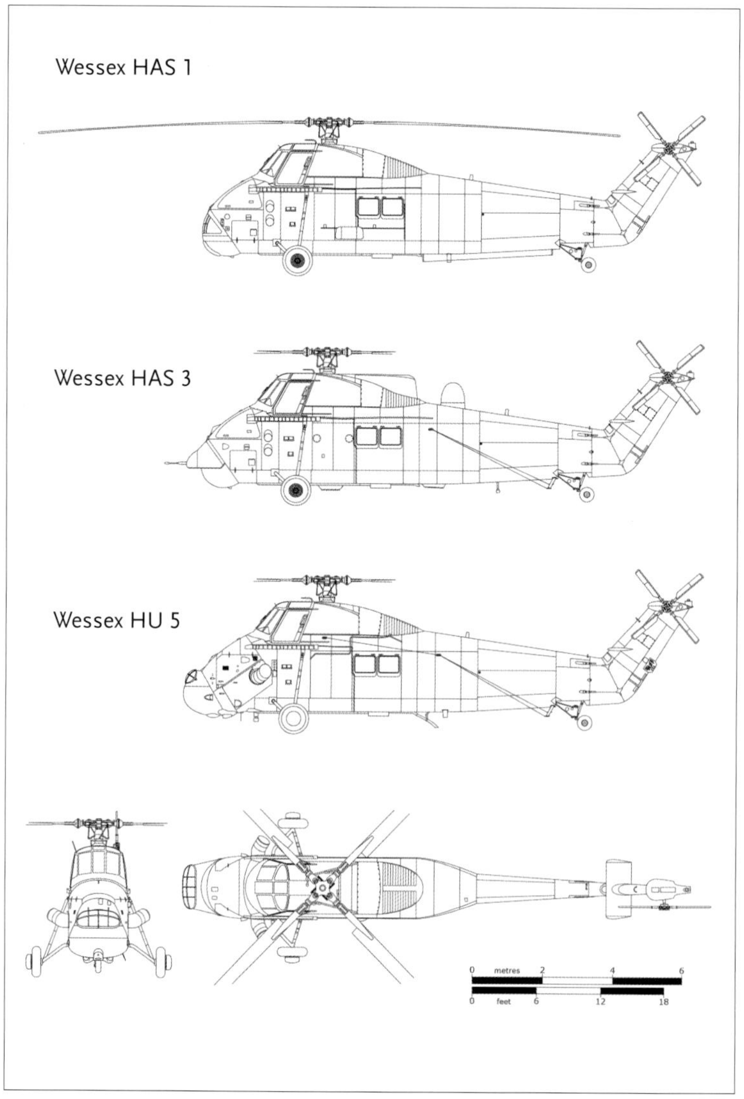

Wessex HAS 1s of 814 NAS landing on *Victorious* in 1966.

designed for the purpose. After reassembly it was test flown in its original form to give base-line performance figures and handling characteristics. Then the engine was removed and replaced by a single 1,100shp Napier Gazelle NG.11 free power turboshaft which had first run in December 1955. It had been designed for helicopter use and could run equally well when mounted in a horizontal, vertical or inclined plane; in this instance it was mounted at an angle of 39 degrees from the vertical to drive the original S-58 main and tail rotor drive systems through the main rotor gearbox. At first the original 'clam-shell' nose doors were retained with a circular hole cut in them under the engine air intake but this was later replaced by a redesigned nose with a refined intake structure. The Napier engine was less powerful but only half the weight of the piston engine and delivered better overall performance. The revised airframe first flew in May 1957 and the results proved sufficiently promising for the Admiralty to order a pre-production batch, the first of which flew in June 1958.

The new helicopter was given the name Wessex. Its fuselage was a semi-monocoque structure made from light alloy with a forged steel structure on which the main rotor gearbox was attached. The tail pylon incorporated a small horizontal stabiliser and the after part could be folded through 180 degrees to port to reduce fuselage length for carrier stowage. The four individual metal main rotor blades could be manually folded to lay aft along the fuselage sides. With both tail pylon and main rotor blades folded the overall length was reduced by 27ft. The drive shaft to the main rotor gear box was through a double epicyclic reduction gearbox and engine exhaust was ducted through outlets, two on each side forward of and below cockpit level. A drive shaft connected the main rotor gearbox to the tail rotor gearbox which drove a four-bladed metal tail rotor. The fixed undercarriage comprised two main units under the cockpit, each consisting of an oleo-pneumatic shock absorber strut and a single radius rod. The tailwheel was fully castoring and self-centring with an anti-swivelling lock.

Dual controls were fitted in every mark of Wessex but they could be flown by a single pilot occupying the right-hand seat. The cockpit was located in front of and above the main cabin and access was normally through large sliding windows having climbed the steps built into the fuselage sides above a step on each undercarriage radius arm. Aft of the cockpit floor, under the pilots' seat pans, the cabin space was open and this allowed either pilot to stand, albeit rather awkwardly, tilt up the seat pan and climb down into the cabin. Alternatively, the cockpit could be accessed from below by pushing up the seat pan from underneath, climbing the steps built into the forward cabin bulkhead and lowering the seat once awkwardly crouched in the cockpit. This method was often used to change pilots during rotors-running refuels, especially in commando squadrons. Access to the cabin space in all models was via a cargo door in the starboard side. Both this and the sliding, cockpit access windows could be jettisoned to help egress in the event of a ditching. Cabin windows could also be jettisoned in emergencies. A hydraulic winch was fitted on the starboard side over the cargo door. It had a maximum load of 600lb and a cable run-out of 100ft. It could be operated by either a winch operator with a control by the cargo door or by the right-hand-seat pilot using a control on the collective pitch lever. The Wessex was also procured for the RAF and mark numbers followed the precedent set by the Dragonfly and Whirlwind; odd numbers RN, even RAF.

HAS 1

The first RN variant was the HAS 1. Flight development work with pre-production aircraft began in July 1958 and individual aircraft were allocated to different aspects of the test programme. The HAS 1 had a flight-control system to hold the aircraft in an automatic hover over the sonar transducer when it was lowered. A cockpit

Wessex HAR 1 of 771 NAS at Culdrose practising diver drops.

indicator showed the aircraft's position relative to the cable to allow pilots to hover manually if necessary. In automatic mode, fork-shaped sensors set 90 degrees apart sensed reaction on the cable if it was drawn out of the vertical by aircraft movement and made delicate control adjustments to correct. The hover height was usually 40ft above the sea surface and could either be maintained manually or by setting a radar altitude hold. The basic sonar fit in the HAS 1 was a developed version of the Type 194 originally fitted in the Whirlwind HAS 7. Range and bearing information were displayed on a paper trace which gave rates of change in addition to raw data. There was no radar and the observer had to maintain his own position as well as target data on a chart board. Like the Whirlwind, the Wessex HAS 1 had its upper surfaces painted yellow to be seen whilst in the hover. Wessex HAS 1s began to equip operational squadrons from 1961

The HAS 1s used AVPIN, to run up the engine to self-sustaining rpm on startup. It was an extremely volatile monofuel and when the pilot pressed the start button a measured quantity was introduced into the starter combustion chamber and ignited. It was carried in two pressurised bottles fitted inside the aircraft's nose giving two starter 'shots'. If an aircraft diverted ashore failed to start, the carrier had the problem of getting a supply of AVPIN to it. AVPIN was considered so dangerous that supplies were kept on the carrier in tanks on angled sledges clear of the edge of the flight deck that could be dumped overboard in the event of a fire on deck.

A batch of HAS 1s was delivered without the sonar equipment or the automatic flight-control system for commando squadrons as a replacement for the Whirlwind HAS 7. They reached operational squadrons from 1962 painted in sand-coloured camouflage overall with a view to desert operations in the Middle East. Once RN commando helicopters began to fly in operations over the Borneo jungle from 1963, however, the paint scheme was modified to a sand and green scheme known as 'sand and spinach'. They also differed from the basic Mark 1 in having panniers which could be fitted to the forward fuselage above the main undercarriage legs capable of carrying a variety of weapons, principally 0.303in or 7.62mm machine guns to suppress enemy fire during an opposed landing operation.

Wessex HAS 1 data

Length:	65ft 10in (38ft 2in folded)
Rotor Diameter:	56ft (span 16ft folded)
Height:	15ft 7½in
MTOW:	12,600lb
Engine:	One 1,450shp Napier Gazelle 13 Mark 161 turboshaft
Fuel:	Avcat. 300 gallons internal plus one or two optional 100-gallon drop tanks
Performance:	Maximum level speed 120 knots Service ceiling 14,100ft. 4 minutes to 5,000ft
Endurance:	2½ hours on internal fuel
Armament:	Two pylons, one on each side of the fuselage, were capable of carrying one Mark 44 or 46 homing torpedo, Mark 11 depth charge or 100-gallon drop tank. 7.62mm machine guns in the commando role

HAS 3

The USN had begun development of the magnificent Sikorsky S-61 Sea King in 1957 and it entered service only a few months after the Wessex. The Admiralty had been constrained by cost limitations when it ordered the Wessex but it was also concerned that a larger helicopter would take up too much deck space. The concept of a developed Wessex incorporating the latest anti-submarine technology was, therefore, initially considered attractive and Westland was tasked to produce an improved variant designated HAS 3 powered by a 1,600shp Napier Gazelle. A compressed-air starter system similar to that used by the Buccaneer, Gannet and Phantom replaced AVPIN and the core of the HAS 3 was a complicated duplex flight-control system designed by Louis Newmark to allow fully automatic control through the transition to the hover, lowering the sonar, auto hover and 'jump navigation' to a new hover position. It certainly allowed safer operation at night or in marginal weather but was slow in operation. Most pilots elected to keep the radar-altimeter height lock in play but fly the manoeuvre between hover positions manually.

The observer's battle-management capability was significantly enhanced by the introduction of an Ecko lightweight search radar but this was mounted aft of the cockpit/main rotor gearbox structure which prevented it from covering an arc ahead of the aircraft. The thimble-shaped radome caused an airflow disturbance which affected the tail rotor and caused an airframe 'twitch' and this had to be smoothed by

Wessex HAS 3 of 737 NAS lowering its sonar transducer off Portland.

Wessex HAS 3 of 814 NAS embarked in *Hermes* during 1968.

fitting a fairing, known as a 'horse-collar', aft of the main rotor gearbox. The space within it was used to house an additional alternator to power the expanded avionic outfit. The new sonar was Type 195M designed by Plessey Marine in which range, bearing and rate information were displayed on a screen. Fuselage side hardpoints could carry a single WE 177 nuclear depth bomb, usually on the port side. Weight constraints usually meant that only the port-side hardpoint was fitted but if both were fitted two Mark 44/46 torpedoes or two Mark 11 depth charges could be carried.

The HAS 3 had the same internal fuel capacity as the HAS 1 with the option of drop tanks but its weakness was weight. New equipment increased basic weight but structural and power-train limitations meant that MTOW remained the same as the HAS 1. Sortie times were limited, even with no weapon and limited internal fuel. The attempt to get a 'quart' of avionics, fuel and weapons into the 'pint pot' of a weight-limited airframe has to be judged a failure. Transit between hover positions at 200ft in a heavy, single-engined aircraft meant that reaction to any form of engine malfunction had to be rapid if the aircrew were stand a chance of surviving the subsequent ditching.

HAS 3 squadrons had to resort to Whirlwind HAS 7 tactics with separate hunter and killer aircraft. All versions of the Wessex were built with pressure refuelling as standard with the refuelling point close to the cargo door and this allowed in-flight refuelling from ships in the screen rather than having to return to the carrier. Time on task could be extended by winching up the fuel hose nozzle and refuelling whilst hovering, HIFR. Sorties could be extended in this way but while HIFR-ing took place the HAS 3 sonar was not in the water. HAS 3s only equipped front-line squadrons embarked in carriers for 4 years but they lasted longer in flights embarked in 'County' class destroyers.

HU 5

Admiralty concern about the danger of operating single-engined helicopters over jungle or other hostile terrain led to the procurement of a twin-engined variant for the commando squadrons. The RAF had already specified the twin-engined Wessex HC 2 and the RN derivative was designated HU 5. A single prototype was ordered in 1962 and first flew in May 1963. The first production aircraft flew in November. The HU 5 was powered by two Bristol Siddeley Gnome turboshafts driving the transmission through a coupling gearbox and different engine air intakes could be fitted to cope with ambient conditions ranging from tropical jungle to the arctic. The transmission system was strengthened to make use of the increased engine power. For the gunship role the weapon panniers used on the HAS 1 were modified to allow the carriage of wire-guided ASM or 2in rocket pods which were aimed using a reflector sight folded down into the right-hand seat pilot's eye-line from the top of the windscreen frame. Given exactly the right angle of dive, airspeed and steady aim it could be an accurate system and I scored a number of hits with it on designated targets around the world ranging from tanks at the Castle Martin range in Wales, USN landing craft on the ranges at Vieques Island and splash targets towed astern of various carriers and RFAs. The belt-fed 7.62mm front guns were also effective although the slight vibration of the pannier in forward flight tended to cause the rounds to spread slightly around the intended mean point of impact. This actually caused a wider field of suppressive fire to be laid down as other helicopters ran in with their assault sticks of Royal Marines. Armour plates could be fitted around the cockpit and belt-fed machine guns could be fitted in the cargo door and one of the port windows of troop carriers to give suppressive fire on the run-in to a landing zone. Hardpoints on the fuselage sides allowed drop tanks, torpedoes or depth charges to be carried; the latter enabling the HU 5's to act as an ASW weapons carrier.

The HU 5 airframe was cleared to lift underslung loads of up to 4,600lb but this would have been impractical with any but the lightest fuel load; a 3,000lb load was more practical, equating to a stripped-down, short-wheelbase Land Rover. Canvas seats along the cabin sides could take a stick of up to sixteen marines. A more practical number was twelve but the actual number carried in an assault would depend on the distance of the carrier offshore and the amount of equipment carried by the stick. The aircrewman sat by the cargo door and was responsible for getting the marines and their kit stowed quickly. Getting the whole stick out of the cabin onto the ground ready for action quickly required constant practice. Four headset connection points in the cabin allowed pilots to brief stick leaders about the landing zone and there were also red/green lights controlled by the pilot; red-on indicated running in stand-by; green-on leave the aircraft.

The HU 5 avionic fit was primitive, comprising only a 12-channel UHF radio and an HF radio for longer-range communication with the fleet. The lack of UHF channels was a major embarrassment on operations and during the 1970s the sets were replaced by multi-channel ARC-52 UHF radios removed from fixed-wing aircraft. Some HU 5s were fitted with obsolescent Rebecca Mark 8 homing beacons to act as navigation leaders for an assault using a beacon set up by a beach reconnaissance party and all were fitted with a UHF homer.

Wessex HU 5s of 845 NAS embarked in *Bulwark* for Exercise Dry Fly in 1971.

Wessex HU 5 data

Length:	65ft 10in (38ft 2in folded)
Rotor Diameter:	56ft (span 16ft folded)
Height:	15ft 10in
MTOW:	13,600lb
Engine:	Two Bristol Siddeley/Rolls-Royce Gnome 112/113 turboshaft engines, each capable of developing 1,320shp for single-engine operation but normally limited to 775shp for twin-engine operation
Fuel:	Avcat. 308 gallons internal plus one or two optional 97-gallon drop tanks. Total 502 gallons
Performance:	Maximum level speed 120 knots Service ceiling 14,100ft. 4 minutes to 5,000ft
Endurance:	2½ hours on internal fuel
Armament:	Two pylons, one on each side of the fuselage, were capable of carrying one Mark 44 or 46 homing torpedo, Mark 11 depth charge or 97-gallon drop tank. Panniers could be fitted on either side of the fuselage by the main oleos capable of carrying up to four Nord SS.11 or AS.12 wire-guided air-to-surface guided missiles, belt-fed 7.62mm machine guns or 2in rocket pods

A Wessex HU 5 of 845 NAS firing an SS-11 ASM over the Borneo jungle.

The RN received 245 Wessex helicopters. These included the single pattern aircraft; 12 pre-production and 128 production HAS 1s; three built as HAS 3s; one prototype and 100 production HU 5s. In addition to the aircraft built as HAS 3s, forty-three HAS 1s were rebuilt by Westland to HAS 3 standard, many of them airframes formerly used in the commando role.

A Wessex HU 5 of 848 NAS with an underslung 105mm howitzer with its parent carrier, *Albion*, in the background.

Between 1960 and 1988 Wessex of all three marks served with a number of trials and shore-based units. These included 700H, 700V, 706, 707, 737, 771, 772 and 781 NAS. They operated in the aircrew conversion, ASW operational training, commando training, fleet requirements and light communications roles, the latter including some aircraft fitted out as Admirals' 'barges'.

Front-line units that flew the three marks of Wessex included 814, 815, 819, 820, 826, 829, 845, 846, 847 and 848 NAS. The eight 'County' class destroyers each operated a semi-autonomous Wessex Flight, HAS 1 at first, later HAS 3. These were parented by 829 NAS at first, later 737 NAS.

Wessex operated from the aircraft carriers *Albion*, *Ark Royal*, *Bulwark*, *Centaur. Eagle*, *Hermes* and *Victorious*. They also operated from a number of ships other than aircraft carriers including *Blake*, *Engadine*, *Fearless*, *Intrepid*, *Devonshire*, *Hampshire*, *Kent*, *London*, *Fife*, *Glamorgan*, *Antrim*, *Norfolk*, *Regent*, *Resource*, *Fort Grange*, *Lofoten*, *Olna*, *Olmeda*, *Olwen*, *Tidepool* and *Tidespring*.

Dedicated Wessex SAR flights operated from Lee-on-Solent, Prestwick and Yeovilton; at other air stations such as Culdrose and Portland SAR capability was provided by aircraft from squadrons including 771 and 772 NAS.

Service trials for the Wessex were carried out by the re-formed 700H NAS from 1960 and the first front-line unit to operate the type was 815 NAS in July 1961. During 1964 the squadron was embarked in *Centaur* and put 45 Commando ashore at the request of the Tanganyikan Government to end a rebellion by mutinous army units. Wessex 1s and 5s were heavily involved in the defence of Brunei and then Malaysia between 1963 and 1966 during the confrontation against Indonesia. They operated both ashore from clearings in the jungle and from both *Albion* and *Bulwark*.

Wessex HU 5s played a significant part in Operation 'Corporate', the liberation of the Falkland Islands in 1982. 845 NAS was the only operational HU 5 unit when the operation began but 847 and 848 NAS were re-commissioned using HU 5s held in reserve and others from training squadrons. Their aircrew came from shore-based squadrons, exchange and non-flying appointments. Over fifty HU 5s were involved, eight of which were lost when *Atlantic Conveyor* was sunk by an Exocet missile on 25 May. They provided essential mobility for the operation alongside the Sea King HC 4s of 846 NAS. The Wessex HAS 3 embarked in *Glamorgan* was destroyed on 12 June 1982 when an Exocet missile hit the ship's hangar and set it on fire. *Antrim*'s HAS 3, nicknamed 'Humphrey', rescued a Special Forces team and the crews of two HU 5s from the Fortuna Glacier in South Georgia in adverse weather. Three days later it depth-charged and damaged the Argentine submarine *Sante Fe* near Grytviken harbour where it was subsequently beached after missile attacks by Wasps. 847 and 848 NAS were disbanded by the end of 1982, leaving 845 NAS as the last operational Wessex squadron. A few Wessex remained in SAR flights aircraft until 31 March 1988 when they were withdrawn from service.

Sea King

The Sea King originated in 1957 when the USN stated a requirement for a helicopter capable of combining the anti-submarine hunter/killer roles. The resulting twin-engined Sikorsky S-61 was a large helicopter

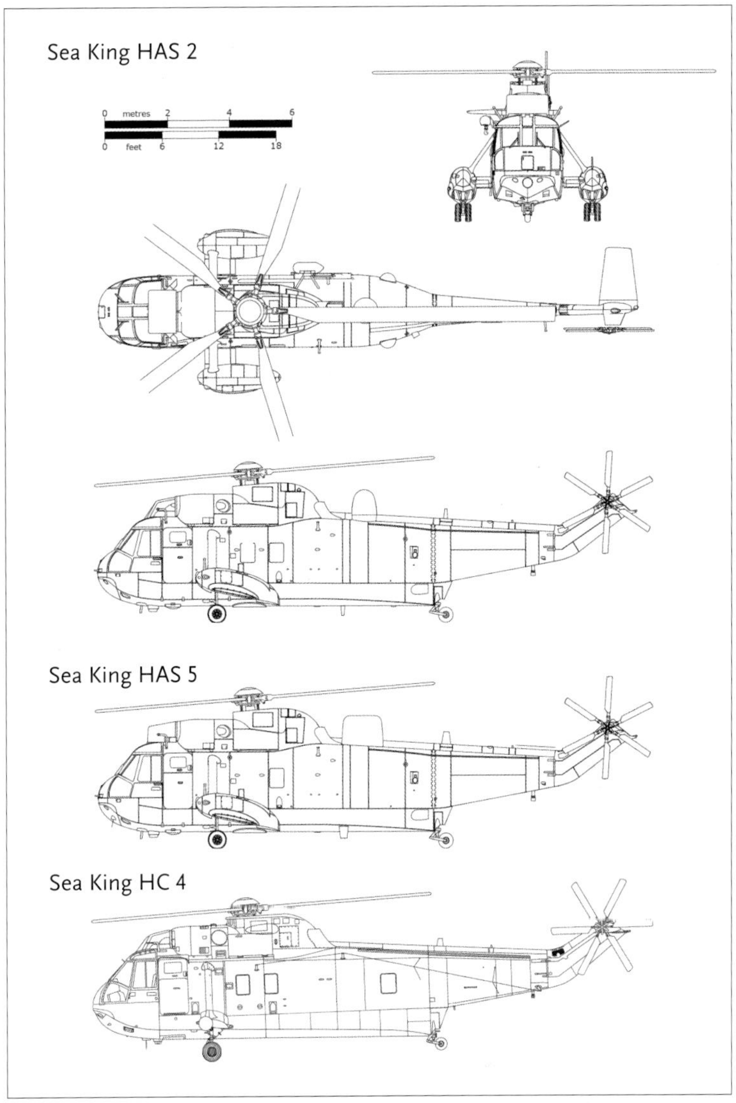

that retained Sikorsky's single-rotor configuration. First flight was in March 1959 and the first USN squadron formed in September 1961, only two months after the first operational RN Wessex HAS 1 squadron. At first the USN designated the Sea King as the HSS-2 but in July 1962 it was re-designated as the SH-3A under the new tri-service system.

Westland had immediately recognised the Sea King's potential and negotiated a licence-manufacturing agreement with Sikorsky in 1959 which allowed it not only to build the improved SH-3D variant under licence but to modify it with British equipment and export it. The RN had pinned its hopes on the Wessex HAS 3 but its failure to combine the hunter/killer roles and its low endurance led it to order Westland-built Sea Kings as an urgent replacement. The first RN contract was placed in June 1966, only 4 months after the cancellation of the CVA-01 aircraft carrier project, and Westland procured four SH-3Ds as pattern aircraft to speed development. The first arrived in 1967 and flew initially with two 1,500shp General Electric T58 engines and other US-built equipment before being stripped down for modification to the UK production standard. The first Westland built Sea King variant was designated HAS 1. It had two Bristol Siddeley (later Rolls-Royce) Gnome turboshaft engines, licence-built derivatives of the T-58, mounted side-by-side on top of the forward part of main cabin with

A Sea King HAS 1 of 824 NAS lowering its sonar transducer with its parent carrier, *Ark Royal*, in the background.

the main rotor gearbox aft of them. They had a Hawker Siddeley Dynamics full-authority electronic engine control system and the main rotor comprised five metal blades with power folding and spreading. Initially the tail rotor had five metal blades, driven through intermediate and tail rotor gearboxes and shafts, the latter covered by a spine which ran along the top of the rear fuselage.

The fuselage comprised a single-step boat hull of all-metal semi-monocoque construction with a cantilevered stabiliser on the starboard side of the tail pylon which could be folded through 180 degrees to starboard in order to reduce the aircraft's length for hangar stowage. The main undercarriage consisted of two twin-wheel units which retracted hydraulically into stabilising sponsons braced onto the fuselage sides. Retraction was intended to keep the wheels clear of the sonar cable when lowered. A fully-castoring, non-retracting tailwheel was fitted at the after end of the boat hull. Pop-out flotation bags were fitted to the outboard sides of the sponsons, activated by salt water switches on ditching. The Sea King hull shape gave more stable ditching characteristics so that the crew could escape and was never intended for regular operation from the sea. The battery access compartment under the cockpit was not completely watertight, water got in through it after a ditching and shorted out the batteries. The high-mounted engines and gearbox actually made the Sea King unstable when floating upright in any but the calmest sea and they invariably rolled over despite the flotation gear keeping them afloat initially. The USN used specially-waterproofed, 'war-weary' Sea Kings with ballast weights low down to teach ditching techniques but the RN never did so.

As in the earlier Sikorsky designs, there was a single cargo door on the starboard after side of the cabin which could be opened in flight. A rescue hoist was fitted above the door which could hoist up to 650lb and the aircraft's pressure refuelling point was located under the cargo

Sea King HAS 1s of 826 NAS landing on *Eagle*.

Sea King AEW 2 of 849NAS.

door so that a hose could be hoisted up and connected to it for HIFR. The Sea King was 7ft longer than the Wessex but the distance between the main and tail wheels was 9ft less so it could land on a smaller deck providing there was room above it for the fuselage and rotor disc. A variant of the Sea King was ordered by the RAF for SAR duties but unlike earlier Westland helicopters, mark numbers were not alternated between RN and RAF versions. Thus the HAS 1 and 2 were RN; the HAR 3 the sole RAF version and marks 4, 5, 6 and 7 were all RN variants.

Anti-submarine variants

The Sea King HAS 1 was flown by a crew of four; two pilots, an observer and an aircrewman. Although it could be flown by a single pilot, two were normal in case there was an engine problem that needed one to operate a manual throttle to match the power demanded by the collective pitch lever input from the unaffected engine. Both pilots could access the rear cabin by moving aft between the seats if necessary; the observer's position was on the port side of the cabin with a large tactical display for the Ecko AW 391 search radar. As in the Wessex HAS 3, the radar scanner was in a radome aft of the main rotor gearbox and had a blind arc ahead but in the hover the observer would ask pilots to rotate the aircraft every few minutes to give an all-round look. The observer had a cabin window to his left but it could be closed by a blind as the radar display had to be viewed in the dark. The Plessey Type 195 Sonar with its 'pit-head' gear and sonar operator's position was to starboard of the observer, both seats facing forward. The HAS 1 had Marconi AD 580 Doppler processing and bathythermographic facilities; flight control and 'jump' navigation between sonar hover positions used a Louis Newmark Mark 31 AFCS. There were up to four hardpoints on the fuselage sides, each of which could be fitted with a single Mark 44 torpedo or Mark 11 depth charge. A single WE-177 nuclear depth bomb could be carried. A belt-fed 7.62mm machine gun could be fitted by the cargo door or in the window to port of the observer's position if required.

The next production variant was the Sea King HAS 2 which first flew in 1976. It had more powerful Gnome turboshafts and more robust main, intermediate and tail rotor gearboxes to take the additional power. It also introduced the 'barn door' engine intake which prevented the ingestion of foreign objects. A six-bladed tail rotor was fitted to improve yaw control in the hover. HAS 2s retained the same weapons system as the HAS 1, some were built new and others were converted from HAS 1 airframes.

The HAS 5 introduced a new ASW sensor suite from 1981. Again some were built new and others modified from HAS 2 airframes and the new equipment required the cabin to be slightly enlarged with a strengthened floor. The new radar was the MEL Sea Searcher with the

Sea King HC 4 of 846 NAS.

scanner in an enlarged, flat-topped radome aft of the main rotor gearbox. Upgraded Type 195M sonar was fitted and a new console, fitted aft of the radar and sonar displays facing to port, contained the GEC Avionics LAPADS lightweight digital acoustic processing equipment for monitoring both active and passive sonobuoys. Sonobuoys were carried on a rotary dispenser in the after cabin or, alternatively, they could be dropped by hand. HAS 5s could monitor their own sonobuoy fields or those laid by other aircraft. Accurate navigation was enhanced by a Decca TANS 9447G linked to a Decca Doppler 71 movement sensor and an electronic warfare capability was introduced with the Racal MIR-2 Orange Crop ESM system. The extra systems added weight and MTOW grew from the HAS 2's 20,500lb to 21,500lb. It also moved the centre of gravity near its after limit and HAS 5s hovered with a greater tail-down attitude than their predecessors. This caused airframe weaknesses and strengthening modifications were introduced to prevent them developing. Wiring to the weapon stations was modified to allow the carriage of Mark 46 torpedoes at first and later the Stingray lightweight anti-submarine torpedo. Other weapon options, including the WE-177 NDB, remained the same. HAS 5s were fitted with a modified starboard sponson which had an integral winch and stowage for a MAD 'bird' which could be towed astern of the aircraft in flight, clear of its magnetic signature. These were bought from Sikorsky since the USN used the same system. MAD was intended to pick up a submarine close to the surface with sufficient accuracy to drop a homing torpedo but the system never proved as popular in the RN as it had been in the USN and was seldom fitted.

In service HAS 5s demonstrated a quantum advance in capability, carrying out wide area searches using passive sonobuoys which did not betray their presence to an enemy submarine, then localising a contact with active sonobuoys and finally using the active sonar in the hover to give precise target data for an attack with torpedoes. The Sea Searcher also gave a surface search capability. The UK Government's decision to delete its tactical nuclear weapons in the 1990s led to the withdrawal of the WE-177 NDB.

Sea King HAS 5 data

Length:	72ft 8in rotors turning (47ft 3in folded)
Rotor Diameter:	62ft (span 16ft folded)
Height:	16ft 10in rotors turning
MTOW:	21,500lb
Engine:	Two 1,600shp Bristol Siddeley/Rolls-Royce Gnome H.1400-1 turboshafts
Fuel:	Avcat. 800 gallons internal
Performance:	Maximum level speed 120 knots Service ceiling 14,700ft. 4 minutes to 5,000ft
Endurance:	Over 4 hours
Armament:	Four pylons, two on each side of the fuselage, each capable of carrying one Mark 46, later Stingray, homing torpedo, Mark 11 depth charge. A belt-fed 7.62mm machine gun could be fitted in the cargo door position

The last anti-submarine variant was the HAS 6 which entered service in 1988. A small batch was built by Westland but the majority were HAS

5s modified in RN air yards. The fuselage was outwardly similar to the HAS 5 but had a new pale grey colour scheme. The rotor blades were to a new Westland design using composite materials which enhanced performance from the same engines. The major change was the incorporation of new sensors including the Plessey/GEC Digital Type 2069 dipping sonar. Information from the dipping sonar and sonobuoys was integrated through a new GEC Avionics AQS-902G-DS digital processor, however, reducing the number of consoles in the rear cabin and moving the centre of gravity forward. This variant complemented frigates fitted with long-range, towed-array sonar systems and several were embarked in those that had suitably-sized flight decks and hangars to give a very effective area capability against hostile submarines. The HAS 6 was gradually replaced by the Merlin from 2000.

Commando helicopters

Westland had developed a transport Sea King variant for export and this formed the basis of a commando assault variant ordered for the RN in 1978 as a Wessex HU 5 replacement. Designated HC 4, it first flew in September 1979. They retained the main rotor-powered blade-fold system of the anti-submarine variant as well as the folding tail pylon but had simplified, non-retracting main oleos attached to short stub-wings with no sponsons. Flotation gear comprised two cool-gas filled inflatable bags, one fitted to each stub wing and fired either manually by the pilots or by submersion actuators. Depending on fuel load the HC 4 could carry up to twenty-seven marines on canvas bench seats or a 5,500lb underslung load. With no radar or sonar consoles the entire cabin was available for the carriage of an equivalent loading of stores when the bench seats were folded up. The cabin could be fitted to take six stretcher cases plus seating for ten 'walking wounded' and an attendant in addition to the aircrewman. There was no rear ramp, however, and everything had to be loaded through the cargo door. The HC 4 was flown by two pilots with an aircrewman in the cabin. In the static-line parachuting role the HC 4 could carry eighteen parachutists in sticks of four or drop parachute loads up to 700lb. Aircrew in the commando squadrons were a mixture of RN and RM with the majority of aircrewmen being the latter. Sea King HC 4s were painted green with black lettering. As with the earlier Wessex and Whirlwind, commando Sea Kings were identified by individual letters not numbers.

A Sea King HAS 5 dropping a depth charge.

Export Sea Kings had defensive aids suites and there is an apocryphal story that the RN retained them because Westland would have charged more for the redesign work to remove them than build HC 4s with them. More likely the RN appreciated the value of defensive aids after the primitive equipment in the Wessex HU 5 was compared unfavourably with USMC helicopters. Defensive aids were constantly upgraded as HC 4s were committed to a series of conflicts throughout their time in service and included an ALQ-157 infrared jammer, Sky Guardian 2000 missile approach warning system and radar-warning receiver, M-130/M-147 chaff and flare dispensers. The cockpit was NVG compatible, initially ANVIS Generation 3 later replaced by Ferranti Nite-OP Gen 3.

Avionics included UHF, VHF, HF and secure speech radios which were constantly updated. Mode 1, 2, 3 and 4 IFF interrogation system was standard. Initially, navigation aids included the Decca Mark 19 area navigation system and Racal/Decca Type 71 doppler system feeding the same Type 9447F/09 TANS, used by the HAS 6 but the HC 4 also had a Decca automatic chart display, VOR/ILS and both UHF and VHF homing and distance measuring equipment. During the first Gulf War Sea King HC 4s were fitted with a GPS navigation system linked to a Racal RNS252 Super TANS computer that was compatible with the existing Mark 19. TANS 252 took GPS inputs and the doppler system to provide accurate information on the aircraft's position, height and velocity. Stored waypoints could be called up or transferred to another aircraft.

During the Falklands Conflict in 1982 Sea King HAS 2s of 825 NAS had their sonar equipment removed and operated in the commando role. After 2000 the number of HC 4 airframes available for operations was reduced by the constant need for upgrades and refurbishment after operations, including those in Afghanistan, and four HAS 6s had their role equipment removed together with other changes to provide aircraft for training and other non-combat-related commando roles in the UK. They were painted green and designated Mark 6CR but lacked defensive aids and other operational features. Externally they could be recognised by the undercarriage sponsons although the oleos were locked in the down position.

AEW/ASaC

When ships were sunk by Argentine low-level air attack in May 1982 off the Falkland Islands, the RN learnt the hard way that the deletion of AEW capability when the Fairey Gannet was withdrawn from service 4 years earlier had been an unforgivable mistake. With great urgency, studies into the feasibility of fitting ARI 5980 Searchwater radar into a Sea King helicopter from the 1970s which had not been taken forward were resurrected in Project LAST. Eleven weeks later two Sea Kings modified for the AEW role were embarked in *Illustrious* in time for her to sail to the South Atlantic. By then the war was over but they marked the first step in restoring this vital capability to the RN. The radar scanner was housed externally in a retractable, inflatable radome on the starboard side of the aircraft at the lower rear part of the cargo door. The cabin interior was stripped of ASW role equipment and filled with the avionics required for the new radar.

After the two prototypes a further eight Sea King HAS 2s were modified and re-designated AEW 2. Unlike other RN Sea Kings, this variant was flown by a single pilot and two observers, one of whom was trained to occupy the left-hand seat on landing and take-off to operate the manual throttle if necessary in the case of an engine control emergency. The fuselage structure, power-folding rotors and engines were unchanged and the original radome was left in position although there was nothing inside it. The main feature of the AEW 2 was its Thorn EMI Searchwater surveillance radar and the inflated kettledrum-shaped 'bag' that contained its scanner. It was lowered and raised hydraulically to give clearance underneath when the aircraft was on the ground and with the bag deflated it took up a minimal amount of space. ASW Sea King crews were already known as 'Pingers' because of their active sonar; HC 4 crew were known as 'Junglies' and now AEW crews became known as 'Baggers' because of their unique radome. When the radome was lowered it was below the airframe and offered a full 360-degree scan stabilised in both pitch and roll. A third electrical alternator had to be fitted to cope with the extra power required by the radar which could alter its beam shapes digitally. 849 NAS re-formed in 1984 to operate the Sea King AEW 2 and initially operated dedicated flights for embarkation in carriers as it had done in Skyraider and Gannet days. These were later reformed as naval air squadrons in their own right. There was no specific pilot training course for the AEW role and they all had to have flown the type in other roles; no aircrewman flew in the AEW role and so 849 NAS was unusual in that it only trained observers. Their training included qualification as a fighter controller and the two usually flew in the AEW 2 with the senior operator on the left and the more junior on the right; each could select and modify his or her own radar picture as required. Like other Sea Kings the AEW 2 could HIFR from a non-flight-deck fitted warship or RFA to extend its sortie time to up to 6 hours. The AEW version of the Searchwater was designated ARI 5980/3 and incorporated improvements in range, scan speed and software to enhance its capability. The Cossor IFF 357-0 Jubilee Guardsman system complemented the radar and ARI 18233 Orange Crop ESM gave a passive detection and identification capability. Two consoles side by

A Sea King ASaC 7 over Afghanistan. (Crown Copyright)

side, were fitted for the observers with the radar controls over the right-hand panel. The radar display units were identical 15in TV-type CRTs on which alphanumeric characters and markers could be overlaid onto the processed radar signal. There was also a B-scope which enabled observers to resolve closely-spaced targets and an A-scope which showed amplitude against range of a selected target to generate a ship profile sufficient for target classification. Decca Doppler 71/TANS was retained for navigation and two AN/ARC-164 UHF sets; a legacy Bendix VHF and Collins HF radios were fitted.

Effective as the Sea King AEW 2 was during the 1980s, it was clear by the early 1990s that improvement was required and this resulted in the Sea King ASaC 7 with the new Cerberus mission system centred on the ARI 500036/0 Searchwater radar. This was a multi-mode, pulse doppler radar with a long-range look up/look down capability against airborne targets together with the ability to track small contacts in cluttered littoral environments, a capability that included the detection of objects as small as a human being on land. Whereas the original radar had used a single narrow beam, the new version introduced multi-bar scanning using three different beams nearly simultaneously to give the observers full volume coverage in which the top pulse envelope beam provided long-range air detection at altitude; the pulse doppler beam below it was used to detect targets under clutter or over land and the bottom beam was used for surface search. An ASaC 7 on barrier could, therefore, provide a task force with both the recognised air picture and the recognised maritime picture at the same time by using Link 16/JTIDS to data link them to other ships and aircraft.

Beams could also be interleaved, for instance pulse envelope and pulse doppler could be interlaced to detect targets at maximum range and then tracked through background clutter. A range scale E was introduced to provide an instrumented range out to 300nm in low PRF pulse envelope mode to enhance long-range situational awareness and improve the recognised air picture still further. The observers accessed the system using touch-screen technology and could even zoom out to look at reported Link 16 contacts beyond their own radar coverage. AN/APX-113(V) combined IFF Mode 4 interrogator and transponder was linked to the system together with an enhanced communications system incorporating two AN/ARC-164(V) UHF radios with secure Have Quick II capability; one AD3400 V/UHF radio and one Collins HF radio. ARI23331/3 wide band secure speech provided the aircrew with a secure, unencrypted intercom net and secure radio communication facilities. For operations from Camp Bastion in Afghanistan ASaC 7s were fitted with the same defensive aids suite as the HC 4.

The ASaC 7 also introduced the Mark 4A aircrew helmet with active noise reduction and the airborne video replay system which recorded all voice channels and both displays for playback on a dedicated ground video replay system. This feature was of considerable value for post-sortie analysis in which something that might have been missed in the air could be studied at leisure as well as for de-briefing and training. Another important tool was the portable load device that allowed the observers to set up all the necessary mission data such as way points, Link 16 participation and electronic warfare information before the flight and then load it into the Cerberus system after start-up. At the time of writing it is fair to say that the Sea King ASaC 7/Cerberus was the most advanced airborne surveillance and control system yet fitted in an RN aircraft. It led directly to the Crowsnest/Cerberus system that can be fitted to a Merlin HM 2.

SAR and Utility

Front-line Sea King squadrons always had an impressive secondary SAR capability and several long-range missions were carried out from Culdrose and Prestwick as well as carriers responding to distress calls. When the Wessex were withdrawn from service in 1988 several HAS 5s had their sonar equipment removed and were modified to HAR 5 standard for use in 771 and 819 NAS as dedicated SAR aircraft. The Sea Searcher radar and navigation systems were retained to give an effective capability out to over 200nm from a shore base. This could be extended by HIFR if a suitable ship was in the right place. Bench seating in the rear cabin allowed up to twenty-three survivors to be carried and HAR 5s usually operated with a crew of five; two pilots, an observer, an aircrewman/winch operator and an SAR diver. Aircraft were maintained at 15 minutes notice to be airborne in daylight hours and 45 minutes at night on every day until March 2016 when the majority of Sea Kings, including the RAF HAR 3 SAR variant, were withdrawn from service and replaced by Coast Guard contractors.

Sea King ASaC 7 data

Length:	72ft 8in rotors turning (47ft 3in folded)
Rotor Diameter:	62ft (span 16ft 4in folded)
Height:	16ft 10in
MTOW:	21,500lb
Engine:	Two 1,600shp Bristol Siddeley (Rolls-Royce) Gnome H.1400.1 turboshafts driving a five-bladed composite main rotor and six-bladed tail rotor
Fuel:	Avcat. 800 gallons internal (817 gallons when gravity refuelled)
Performance:	Maximum level speed 120 knots Service ceiling 16,730ft. 4 minutes to 5,000ft
Endurance:	Up to 4 hours
Armament:	None

Including pattern and development aircraft, the RN received 159 Sea Kings. Of these fifty-six were built as HAS 1s, twenty-one built as HAS 2s, forty built as HC 4s, thirty built as HAS 5s and five built as HAS 6s. A number of these were modified to HAS 5, HAS 6, AEW 2, ASaC 7 and HAR 5 standard during their long and heavily-utilised lives. For example ten were converted to AEW 2 standard and the same ten, plus three attrition replacements and a development aircraft, were converted to ASaC 7 standard.

Between 1969 and 1998 Sea Kings of various marks equipped, or partially equipped a number of shore-based units in the IFTU and training roles. They included 700S, 706, 707, 737, 771 and 772 NAS. Operational units that flew Sea Kings between 1970 and 2018 included 810, 814, 819, 820, 824, 825, 826, 845, 846, 848, 849, 849A, 849B, 854 and 857 NAS. During the ASaC 7 run-down in 2017, 849 deployed three operational flights named Palembang, Okinawa and Normandy as part of tailored air groups when required; the names taken from the squadron's battle honours.

Sea King HC 4s of 846 NAS embarked in *Ocean* rapid-roping Royal Marine Commandos onto a beach in Sierra Leone in 2000.

Sea Kings of various marks operated from the aircraft carriers *Albion*, *Ark Royal* (4), *Ark Royal* (5), *Bulwark*, *Eagle*, *Hermes*, *Illustrious*, *Invincible* and the LPH *Ocean*. At various times they operated from the following flight deck and hangar equipped warships and RFAs other than aircraft carriers, *Albion*, *Argus*, *Blake*, *Brave*, *Bulwark*, *Campbeltown*, *Chatham*, *Cornwall*, *Cumberland*, *Engadine*, *Fearless*, *Fort Austin*, *Fort George*, *Fort Grange*, *Fort Rosalie*, *Fort Victoria*, *Intrepid*, *Iron Duke*, *London*, *Olmeda*, *Olna*, *Olwen*, *Reliant*, *Tidepool* and *Tiger*. During 1982 they also operated from the STUFT cruise ships *Queen Elizaeth 2* and *Canberra*.

Throughout the Sea King's time in service, ASW and AEW/ASaC squadrons were based at Culdrose and commando squadrons at Yeovilton. Sea King SAR flights giving 24-hour coverage were based at Culdrose and Prestwick.

The operational history of Sea King squadrons would fill many volumes. The demonstration of Cold War anti-submarine capability around the world and preparedness for commando operations in Northern Norway were themes that ran throughout the period and Sea Kings proved sufficiently adaptable to absorb new technologies, at extremely short notice in the case of AEW. During Operation 'Corporate', the liberation of the Falkland Islands and South Georgia in 1982, Sea King squadrons demonstrated 90 per cent serviceability and flew around the clock to defend the task force in all weathers. In May 1982, for example, HAS 5s of 820 NAS embarked in *Invincible* flew 1,560 hours, the equivalent of two aircraft airborne at all times throughout the month. 825 NAS was re-formed at short notice to operate in the troop transport role.

Sea Kings formed part of the task forces that fought in Operation 'Granby', the first Gulf War that liberated Kuwait, and in Operation 'Mana' that provided humanitarian support to Bangladesh. Operation 'Haven' involved HC 4s and other UK assets in 1991 providing humanitarian relief to Kurdish refugees stranded between Turkey and Iraq. HC 4s and ASaC 7s operated from Camp Bastion in Afghanistan in support of British and NATO coalition forces in Helmand Province between 2009 and 2014. Both variants had engine and rotor blade

modifications made to enable operation at high take-off weights in hot and high conditions and besides improved defensive aids they had rifle racks fitted for the aircrew so that they could defend themselves after a forced landing if necessary. HC 4s developed a high reputation operating with medical teams at short notice in the emergency CASEVAC role and, overall, operations in Afghanistan were some of the longest running commitments in RN history.

Between 1991 and 1996 HC 4s maintained rotational detachments at Split as both part of the UK Operation 'Grapple' in former Yugoslavia and in support of the lightly-armed UN Protection Force at first and later NATO forces. In fulfilling a variety of roles Sea Kings operating from RN carriers in the Adriatic supported national forces and attempts by the international community to end the conflict ashore. In May 2000 HC 4s took part in Operation 'Palliser' which was intended to stabilise the situation in Sierra Leone which had been ravaged by nine years of civil war.

Operation 'Telic', the second Gulf War in 2003, saw the first deployment of the ASaC 7 only weeks after it had entered service with 849 NAS. Four were embarked in *Ark Royal* but, unfortunately, two of them collided and were lost with seven aircrew. Overall, however, the assault on Iraq was a great success in which HC 4s played a significant part. In September 2011 Sea Kings were embarked in the LPH *Ocean* for operations off Libya in support of UN resolutions.

Serena Brotherton, an observer who flew the ASaC 7, described the Cerberus mission system as being like the latest PlayStation fitted in the back of a vintage car. The large Human Machine Interface screen coupled with the radar provided the operators with a wide surveillance area with detections in excess of 200nm. Two individual touch-screen panels allowed optimisation in a number of roles in a maximum of two touches. Despite the sophistication of the mission system, however, the surrounding analogue instruments meant that you never forgot that you were sat in an airframe that was over 30 years old. A trickle of hydraulic oil down the port window and the occasional drip of gearbox oil onto the console was usually considered a comfort as it meant there was oil in the aircraft. Whether conducting traditional AEW, maritime surveillance or ISR of the battlefield in Helmand Province, Afghanistan, the ASaC 7 really was an observer's dream and the eyes of the fleet. From a pilot's perspective, John Brotherton explained that the role of a pilot was often not dynamic with hours spent on barrier at altitude where the prospect of a 180-degree turn was something to look forward to. It was a true all-weather helicopter able to cope with the hottest of days in Afghanistan and the extreme cold of the North Atlantic with its mountainous seas and challenging deck conditions. The Sea King never let him down in the 5,000 hours he flew in different variants.

Gazelle HT 2 of 705 NAS at Culdrose.

Gazelle

A Sud-Aviation design, the SA-341 Gazelle was conceived as an Alouette replacement and in 1967 it became part of the Anglo-French collaborative helicopter programme alongside the French Puma and the British Lynx. The RN procured the type as a training helicopter to replace both the Hiller 12E and Whirlwind HAS 7 in 705 NAS and it was also procured in large numbers by the Army and RAF. All Gazelles intended for the UK armed forces were assembled by Westland using French and British-made components.

Gazelle HT 2s of 705 NAS 'SHARKS' Display Team.

The RN Gazelle variant, designated HT 2, was an extensively-glazed, dual control helicopter with a bench seat aft of the pilots' seats capable of taking three passengers or a stretcher athwartships. It had a single; three-blade metal main rotor and a fenestron tail rotor enclosed within the tail fin for yaw control. The skid undercarriage could be fitted with small wheels to enable it to be towed on the ground. A stability augmentation system was fitted to prepare pilots for operational helicopter types and a winch could be fitted when necessary for training. Small side doors aft of the main cabin doors could be opened or removed when winching to allow space for bulky objects to be placed in the rear cabin if necessary. A joint IFTU cleared the type for service use after the first example flew in 1972 and 705 NAS began helicopter pilot training with Gazelles at Culdrose in late 1974. During its years of operation with the type, 705 NAS formed a display team called the 'Sharks' in which volunteer instructors performed at air displays in the UK throughout the summer months. RN Gazelle HT 2s were flown by naval pilots but maintained by civilian engineers under contract.

The Royal Marines used twelve Gazelles transferred from the Army designated AH 1 from 1974 in the light observation role to replace the Sioux. They were operated by 3 Commando Brigade Air Squadron until 1995 when it was replaced by 847 NAS although some of the maintenance personnel continued to be supplied by the Army. Gazelle AH 1s of 3 BAS saw action in the 1982 Falklands War and several were shot down. They were finally withdrawn from RM service with 847 NAS in 2005.

Gazelle HT 2 data

Length:	31ft 2¾in rotors turning
Rotor Diameter:	34ft 5½in
Height:	9ft 0¼in
MTOW:	3,747lb
Engine:	One 592shp Turbomeca Astazou turboshaft
Fuel:	Avtur. 120 gallons internal
Performance:	Maximum level speed 140 knots
	Service ceiling 16,730ft. 4 minutes to 5,000ft
Endurance:	Up to 4 hours
Armament:	None

The RN and RM operated forty-seven Gazelles of which thirty-five were HT 2s and twelve AH 1s. Between 1974 and 2005 they were operated by 705 and 847 NAS and by 3 BAS.

In September 1997 all helicopter training was transferred to the JHS at Shawbury; 705 NAS was disbanded and the RN Gazelles put up for disposal. One of the units at Shawbury is identified as 705 Squadron but is not commissioned as a naval air squadron.

Lynx

Westland's WG-13 Lynx was the third of the collaborative helicopter projects agreed between the UK and France in 1967 with production shared between Westland and Aerospatiale. Work on it had begun in 1963 as a twin-engined light tactical helicopter for the British Army but in 1966 the RN identified it as a Wasp replacement. It was originally to have been powered by two 770shp Continental turboshafts but after 1967 the rotor diameter had to be reduced and MTOW increased to meet French Naval requirements and this led to the selection of two 900shp Bristol Siddeley (Rolls-Royce) BS360 Gem turboshafts, a new and untried but technologically-advanced engine in a new airframe. Inevitably this combination led to problems which slowed development and increased cost. The Lynx had an innovative four-bladed, semi-rigid main rotor head which was less bulky and complicated than previous articulated heads and gave excellent manoeuvrability. The fuselage and tail pylon were of conventional semi-monocoque, light-alloy construction with carbon-fibre doors, access panels and fairings to reduce weight. There were sliding cargo doors on either side of the cabin aft of the cockpit which had two seats, the pilot on the right and observer on the left, each with their own side access door. The after portion of the tail pylon could be folded through 180 degrees to starboard to reduce folded length by 8ft 6in and the main rotor blades could be folded aft to lie above the tail pylon. The two Gem turboshafts were mounted side-by-side over the cabin roof aft of the main rotor gearbox and separated from the fuselage, gearbox and each other by firewalls. Fuel was contained in five crash-proof bag tanks under the cabin floor and an additional tank could be installed in the rear cabin for ferry flights.

The main rotor hub and inboard portions of the four flexible arms were a one-piece titanium forging and early marks of Lynx had blades fabricated with a two-channel stainless steel D-shaped box spar to which a GRP rear skin was bonded stabilised by a paper honeycomb filling. Later marks had more advanced technology blades with paddle tips developed under the British Experimental Rotor Programme, BERP, to

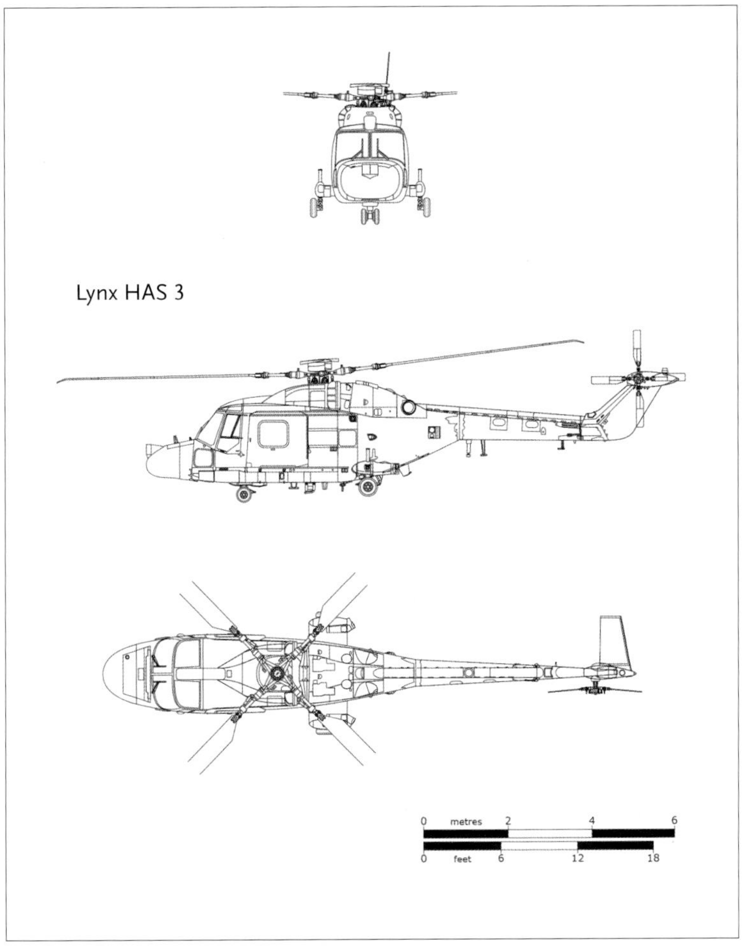

Lynx HAS 3

improve performance. Blades were attached to the hub by titanium root plates and a hydraulic lag plane damper arm designed to reduce what was known as 'air resonance'. The naval Lynx had a fixed tricycle undercarriage and the after wheels could be splayed outward and locked at 27 degrees from the aircraft centreline and the nose wheels could be rotated through 360 degrees. This meant that when the aircraft was held down by the hydraulically-actuated Fairey Harpoon system, which locked onto a grid on the flight deck, the aircraft could be rotated by the pilot into wind for take-off. To help prevent the Lynx from sliding on the wet, pitching and rolling flight deck of a destroyer or frigate, the pilot could lower the collective pitch lever to give 3,000lb of negative thrust. The first development Lynx flew in April 1972 and the first naval prototype a month later. Gem turboshaft problems caused delays but test flying continued using early Gems with limited power output. Deck-landing trials were carried out in *Engadine* and a production contract for the RN variant, designated HAS 2, was signed in May 1974. It entered operational service in August 1976 with 700L NAS, the IFTU, at Yeovilton which was a joint RN/Royal Netherlands Navy unit since both navies were replacing their Wasps with the Lynx.

Rolls-Royce produced a more powerful engine, the Gem 41, for the next production batch, designated HAS 3, which had a strengthened transmission system to absorb the extra power and a number of HAS 2s were modified to HAS 3 standard. The RN Lynx had the Ferranti Seaspray Mark 1 radar with its scanner inside a nose radome which could track small, high-speed surface targets in an arc ahead of the aircraft but the observer had to track them manually. The TANS navigation system, similar to the Sea King's, was fitted as standard. In the MATCH role the Lynx could carry a single NDB, two homing torpedoes or two depth charges. In the strike role the semi-active homing Sea Skua missile was introduced in 1982. More powerful engines allowed an increase in MTOW and HAS 3s were gradually fitted with avionic improvements including the Racal-Decca MIR-2 Orange Crop ESM system. Further improvements led the incorporation of a Racal-designed RAMS 4000 central tactical system and seven HAS 3s were modified to HAS 3CTS standard to evaluate the system as part of the Lynx HMA 8 development programme. It introduced digital target tracking and other new technologies to reduce the aircrew workload. 700L NAS was re-formed in 1990 to develop the new system and the tactics it made possible with aircraft embarked in *Argus*.

The RM 3 Commando BAS received six Lynx AH 1 transferred from the Army in 1982 and when it was re-organised as 847 NAS in 1995 it had six Lynx AH 7s on strength, also Army aircraft on loan as no Army-type Lynx were procured directly by the RN. They could be armed with TOW wire-guided anti-tank missiles and a 0.5in machine gun in the cabin door. They were initially augmented and then replaced by AH 9s. A specialised version of the Lynx for RM use, designated AH 6, was projected which would have had the undercarriage, folding tail pylon and folding blades of the HAS 3 but gunship armament. It was never ordered as cost would have been inflated by the small production run.

The final naval variant of the Lynx was the HMA 8, its changed designation indicating its greatly enhanced strike potential. No HMA 8s were built as such; they were all conversions of HAS 2 and 3 airframes. A redesigned nose housed a Seaspray 3 radar with 360-degree coverage and a turret over the radome contained the GEC Sea Owl E/O device for passive identification of targets by day or night. The HMA 8 also featured a secure speech system, improved ESM and the RAMS 4000 CTS evaluated successfully in the HAS 3CTS. They also introduced GPS navigation to augment TANS. Last, but by no means least, they introduced a four-bag flotation gear system which gave aircrew a far better chance of getting out after a ditching. Early Lynx

Lynx HAS 2 of 815 NAS *Arrow* Flight.

Lynx HAS 3 of 702 NAS practising winching with a stretcher.

Lynx HMA 8 of 815 NAS *Chatham* Flight landing.

were described by aircrew as having the ditching properties of a manhole cover with the nose pitching forward violently, leaving the cockpit well below the surface as the two-bag system was situated well aft. Several upgrades were fitted to HMA 8s including enhanced digital processing for the radar to complement the CTS; improved defensive aids and the second generation anti-jam tactical UHF radio for NATO, SATURN. The whole HMA 8 fleet was eventually standardised under a common modification programme and aircraft that had undergone it were re-designated HMA 8 (SRU).

Lynx HMA 8 data

Length:	49ft 9in rotors turning (35ft 8in folded)
Rotor Diameter:	42ft (span 11ft folded)
Height:	11ft 3in
MTOW:	11,300lb
Engine:	Two 920shp Bristol Siddeley (Rolls-Royce) Gem 42-200 turboshafts
Fuel:	Avcat. 238 gallons internal
Performance:	Maximum level speed 160 knots Service ceiling 12,000ft. 4 minutes to 5,000ft
Endurance:	Up to 3 hours
Armament:	Two Stingray homing torpedoes or Mark 11 depth charges in the ASW role; earlier versions could carry one WE-177 nuclear depth bomb until it was withdrawn in 1992. Up to four radar-guided Sea Skua semi-active homing ASM in the strike role. One 0.5in machine gun could be fitted on a flexible mounting in the starboard cargo door space

The RN received ninety-five Lynx from 1974 onwards of which five were development prototypes. HAS 2s were built in two batches of thirty and HAS 3s were built in batches of twenty, three and seven. No HMA 8s were built as such but a number were modified from airframes originally built as HAS 2s and 3s. No Lynx AH 1, 7 or 9 versions were built for the RN.

Lynx operated with 700L and 702 NAS based ashore, the IFTU and the training unit for both aircrew and maintenance personnel. Lynx HAS 2, 3 and HMA 8 operated with 815 and 829 NAS. At one stage there were more than forty flights deployed. 3 BAS and then 847 NAS operated AH 1, 7s and 9s.

Lynx flights embarked for periods in the aircraft carriers *Ark Royal* (5), *Hermes, Illustrious, Invincible* and the LPH *Ocean*. Ships other than aircraft carriers that embarked Lynx flights included *Active, Alacrity, Albion, Amazon, Ambuscade, Andromeda, Antelope, Ardent, Argonaut, Argus, Argyll, Arrow, Avenger, Battleaxe, Beaver, Birmingham, Boxer, Brave, Brazen, Brilliant, Broadsword, Bulwark, Campbeltown, Cardiff, Cardigan Bay, Charybdis, Chatham, Cleopatra, Cornwall, Coventry, Cumberland, Danae, Daring, Dauntless, Defender, Diamond, Dragon, Duncan, Edinburgh, Endurance* (1), *Endurance* (2), *Engadine, Exeter, Fearless, Fife, Fort Austin, Fort George, Fort Victoria, Glamorgan, Glasgow, Gloucester, Grafton, Hermione, Iron Duke, Jupiter, Kent, Lancaster, Largs Bay, Liverpool, London, Lyme Bay, Manchester, Marlborough, Minerva, Monmouth, Montrose, Mounts Bay, Newcastle, Norfolk, Northumberland, Nottingham, Olwen, Penelope, Phoebe, Portland, Richmond, St Albans, Scylla, Sheffield* (1), *Sheffield* (2), *Sirius, Somerset, Southampton, Sutherland, Wave Knight, Wave Ruler, Westminster* and *York*. A number of STUFT ships were modified with flight decks capable of operating Lynx during the South Atlantic War of 1982.

The first deck landing was carried out by a 700L NAS Lynx flown by Lieutenant Commander G A Cavalier RN on *Birmingham* in February 1977. Later that year the IFTU was absorbed into 702 NAS which became the training unit and, initially, the parent unit for the first embarked flights. The latter task was taken over by 815 NAS in January 1981 and as the number of flights grew it was joined by 829 NAS.

Lynx flights saw action in all the conflicts of the late twentieth century including the South Atlantic War that liberated the Falkland Islands and both Gulf Wars. In the South Atlantic Lynx flew 3,050 hours in 1,863 sorties for the loss of three aircraft which went down with *Ardent, Coventry* and *Atlantic Conveyor*. The Sea Skua missile was rushed into action successfully despite not having fully completed its

A Lynx HMA 8 firing a Sea Skua ASM.

Lynx HMA 8 of 815 NAS *Boxer* Flight folded on deck.

trials programme and Lynx were embarked in carriers after being fitted with systems to decoy Argentine Exocet missiles away from their target. In the 1991 Gulf War Lynx flights were upgraded with defensive aids and FLIR cameras under the fuselage and operated with particular success against Iraqi fast craft in the enemy littoral environment in the Northern Gulf. By February 1991 Lynx had launched twenty-five Sea Skua missiles, eighteen of which hit their designated targets. During these operations in a hostile air environment, Lynx were fitted with improved defensive aids and a FLIR system.

Lynx flights operated around the world on virtually every task the RN undertook ranging from anti-drug-smuggling operations in the Caribbean; humanitarian aid in the same region; operations to defend shipping in the Gulf and deployments to the Pacific. The Lynx was finally withdrawn from service in March 2017 and replaced by the Wildcat.

Lynx HMA 8.

Pre-production Merlin PP 5, ZF 649, was the first to land on an RN warship, *Norfolk*, in 1990.

Merlin

The RN had only expected the Sea King to remain in service until the mid-1980s and working groups were established in 1970 to formulate the requirement for a multi-role fleet helicopter to replace both the Sea King HAS 2 and Wessex HU 5. Westland was tasked to study a number of advanced options but it favoured a large, single-rotor helicopter it designated WG.24. By 1973 this had evolved into the WG.27 with a rotor diameter of 77ft and a fuselage that folded aft of the cabin to meet stowage criteria. The RN requirement changed after the introduction of ships with towed-array sonars and the role of ASW helicopters changed from close-in defence of a task force to long-range localisation and attacks on towed-array contacts. The Lynx lacked localisation capability and range for the task and the Sea King HAS 5 with its increased MTOW would be forced to ditch after a single-engine failure, possibly a long way from any possible rescuer. The naval staff argued, therefore, that only a totally new ASW helicopter able to remain airborne after an engine failure would be effective for work with the towed-array frigate that evolved into the Type 23. These ships should have a flight deck and hangar designed to take what was then referred to as the Sea King replacement, SKR, helicopter. The Type 22 Batch 2 and 3 frigates were also designed with SKR-sized aviation facilities.

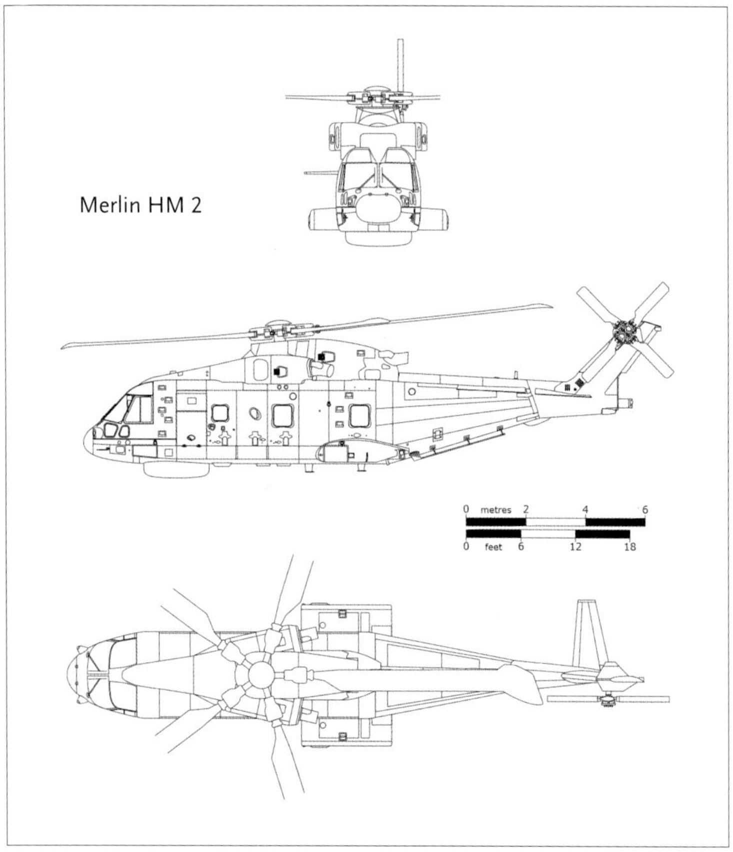

In 1977 the naval staff issued NSR 6646 for the SKR. It was described as urgent and expected to be in service by 1986. Westland offered a series of Sea King developments that it believed to offer value for money, some aspects of which found their way into the Sea King HAS 5 and 6, but none met the requirement for radius of action or time on task. Westland also produced a new design designated WG.31 which met the endurance requirement. By 1979 this evolved into the three-engined WG.34 which was close to the definitive Merlin. It was, however, obvious that it would be very expensive both to develop and operate. Comparisons were made with the USN Sikorsky Seahawk SH-60B, for which Westland had a licence production agreement, and a notional SH-60B with British avionics. The MOD decided that WG.34 offered the most capable solution and authorised development but the cost was too great for the UK to cover alone and a collaborative partner was sought. France and Germany were committed to the NH 90 which the RN had rejected because it lacked the endurance for its concept of towed-array operations. Italy wanted a Sea King replacement but favoured dipping sonar rather than the passive sonobuoys favoured by the RN at the time. The RN wanted its SKR to operate from frigates, the Italian Navy favoured operations from larger warships in less demanding Mediterranean operations but staff discussions led to a compromise design based on the WG.34. The UK and Italian Governments signed a MOU that created a joint company, European Helicopter Industries, to take development forward from 1980. Full development from 1983 followed a project definition phase and a contract for RN Merlins was signed in March 1984. The mission avionics for the first RN variant, designated HM 1, included a

A Merlin HM 1 carrying out a winch transfer to a *Swiftsure* class SSN.

A Merlin HM 2 about to land on a frigate. (Crown Copyright)

A Merlin HM 2 lowering its winchman to a survivor in the water. (Crown Copyright)

Thomson Marconi AQS-903A Barra/Cambs sonobuoy system processor, Marconi Blue Kestrel 5000 surface surveillance radar in a 360-degree radome under the nose and Racal Orange Reaper ESM. Italian influence and a move away from exclusive towed-array work by the RN led to the inclusion of a Thomson Sintra FLASH, Type 2089 dipping sonar. With mission equipment removed up to twenty-six marines could be carried in crash-resistant seating along the sides of the cabin or up to five tons of cargo accessed via a sliding cargo door on the starboard side.

The first RN prototype flew in October 1989 and deck-landing trials were carried out on *Norfolk* in 1990. Serious development problems including two accidents led to a partial redesign and the MOD demanded a prime contractor for mission system integration. This was awarded to an IBM/Westland consortium in 1991. The first production contract was for fifty HMA 1s but this was reduced at the end of the Cold War. The first production example was delivered in 1997 and 700M NAS, the IFTU, formed on 1 December 1998. The first operational unit, 814 NAS formed in June 2000. Following the crash of an HM 1 in 2004 a redesigned tail rotor was fitted to all Merlins. In 2000 GKN, who owned Westland, and the Italian firm Finmeccanica merged their helicopter assets as AgustaWestland and in 2004 Finmeccanica bought out GKN's remaining 50 per cent share. In 2016 the Finmeccanica Group re-branded itself as Leonardo.

Thirty Merlin HM 1s were upgraded to HM 2 standard under a capability sustainment programme. An option to upgrade a further eight was not taken up for cost reasons and the remaining HM 1s remained in extended storage at Culdrose. The upgrade included new mission software architecture, new forward-facing control consoles with 24in colour displays. Surprisingly the less-than-comfortable HM 1 consoles had faced aft for some inexplicable reason. Glass pilots' cockpit displays replaced the earlier instruments and were NVG compatible. Upgraded navigation systems included imbedded GPS and a new air data computer. The Blue Kestrel radar was upgraded with digital signal processing and a new Thales acoustic processing system common to both active and passive sensors was fitted which featured greatly enhanced shallow water detection facilities. The first HM 2 carried out sea trials in 2012 and the last was re-delivered in 2016. Under present plans the HM 2 is to remain in service until 2029 but with no replacement system, manned or unmanned, confirmed in 2024 it is likely to survive for considerably longer. Operational experience in the Gulf and Afghanistan led to new equipment being fitted under urgent operational requirements. These include AN/AAR-57 missile warning systems, AN/ALQ-157 IR jammers, AN/ALE-47 chaff and flare dispensers. L-3 Wescam EO/IR imagers were procured to be fitted to one of the weapon station and M3M 0.5in machine guns can be fitted in the cargo door space.

The Merlins used by commando squadrons have a tortuous background having originally been ordered as an HC 3 variant for the RAF to support the battlefield movement of the British Army. Twenty-five designated as HC 3s were ordered in 1991 with the rear fuselage modified to have a loading ramp capable of taking small vehicles or palletised loads. The RAF went to some trouble to prevent them operating at sea and they differed from the HM 1 and 2 in not having a folding tail pylon or rotor blades and no lashing points. They lacked

Merlin HM 2 'Crowsnest' versions with their radomes lowered. (Crown Copyright)

many other items such as tele-brief wiring. After considerable study into potential Sea King HC 4 replacements, however, the MOD decided to transfer the HC 3s from the RAF to the RN. Seven were modified to iHC 3 standard with lashing points so that they could operate from carriers and all of them were upgraded to a new HC 4 standard by 2022. This involved fitting NVG-capable glass cockpits similar to the HM 2, power-folding main rotor blades and tail pylon, a strengthened undercarriage capable of taking the shock of deck landing, revised fast-roping points and an upgraded defensive aids suite. 846 NAS re-formed with HC 3s in 2014 and 845 NAS in 2015. The first HC 4 was delivered in 2017. Unlike the HC 3s, HC 4s have a pale grey colour scheme identical to the HM 2 although they are still identified individually by letters rather than numbers. The HC 4's projected out of service date is 2030 but no replacement had been identified in 2024.

845 NAS has ten HC 4s available for deployment within tailored air groups. 846 also has ten but has a training flight at Yeovilton which limits the number available for embarkation. The remaining five aircraft are attrition replacements and allow all aircraft to cycle through deep maintenance without diminishing the numbers in the squadrons. Apart from their role within the Commando helicopter force, HC 4s are used as combat SAR and COD aircraft on carrier deployments.

The third Merlin role is airborne surveillance and control but there are no dedicated ASaC airframes, instead the UK Government decided in 2015 that the Sea King ASaC 7 would be replaced by a 'plug-in' Cerberus system fitted to Merlin HM 2s as operational circumstances dictate. Even the kindest defence analysts described this decision as 'budget-led' and it is obvious that the thirty HM 2 airframes are inadequate to support the training of pilots, ASW and ASaC observers, the tailored air group needs of two carriers and the ASW frigates that embark them. Cerberus was based on a newly-packaged version of the Searchwater 2000AEW system fitted in the Sea King ASaC 7. In 2015 the prime contractor for this modification, Lockheed Martin, selected Thales to provide the mission system and IOC was to be in 2018 when the ASaC 7 was withdrawn from service. The manufacturing and development phase began in 2017 but defence cuts and unexpected software problems integrating Cerberus into the existing Merlin software caused delays. Resolution of these issues escalated cost above any savings achieved by the cuts.

Cerberus uses touch-screen technology for two observer consoles and has an artificial intelligence-based tracking system. It incorporates a digital library of data to identify airborne contacts and fuses them with data from integrated ESM. It also has enhanced mission recording and replay for real-time and post-mission analysis and subsequent training simulations. Ten Cerberus 'kits' were ordered, all of which were delivered by 2023 and three pre-IOC Merlin HM 2/Cerberus prototypes were embarked in *Queen Elizabeth* for her CSG 21 Pacific deployment. Cerberus reached IOC in 2023, however, 5 years after the Sea King ASaC 7 was withdrawn from service. Coherence was not helped by disbanding 849 NAS and subsuming ASaC work into 820 NAS which attempts to combine the work of embarked ASW detachments to tailored carrier air groups with the development of ASaC tactics and operational training.

Merlin HM 2 data

Length:	75ft 3in rotors spread (52ft folded)
Rotor Diameter:	61ft (span 18ft folded)
Height:	21ft 4in
MTOW:	32,120lb
Engine:	Three 2,100shp Rolls-Royce/Turbomeca RTM 322 turboshafts
Fuel:	Avcat. 710 gallons in three internal tanks
Performance:	Maximum level speed 167 knots Service ceiling 15,000ft. 4 minutes to 5,000ft
Endurance:	Up to 5 hours on an ASW mission using dipping sonar
Armament:	Four Stingray homing torpedoes or Mark 11 depth charges in the ASW role. One M3M 0.5in machine gun could be fitted on a flexible mounting in the starboard cargo door space and one 7.62mm machine gun in the port cabin window

The RN has received seventy-two Merlins. Of these three were pre-production prototypes, forty-four were HM 1s of which thirty were subsequently modified to HM 2/Cerberus standard, and twenty-five were transferred from the RAF as HC 3s and modified to HC 4 standard.

The only 700-series squadron to operate Merlins was the long running IFTU, 700M NAS, which operated between 1998 and 2008. Training units were recognised as being capable of embarkation and so other units were numbered in the 800 series.

A Merlin HM 2 'Crowsnest' landing with its radome retracted. (Crown Copyright)

Merlin HC 4. (Crown Copyright)

From 2000 to date Merlins of the various marks have served with 814, 820, 824, 829, 845 and 846 NAS. 824 NAS is the training unit and trains pilots for all versions as well as ASW and ASaC observers. It also trains sensor operators for the HM 2's ASW role.

To date Merlins have served in tailored air groups embarked in the aircraft carriers *Queen Elizabeth*, *Prince of Wales*, *Illustrious*, *Invincible*, *Ark Royal* (5) and the LPH *Ocean*. When not embarked, ASW/Cerberus Merlins are shore-based at Culdrose; HC 4s are shore-based at Yeovilton. The Merlin's history is still unfolding but to date ships other than aircraft carriers that have embarked merlin flights for a significant period include *Albion*, *Argus*, *Bulwark*, *Dauntless*, *Defender*, *Duncan*, *Fort Victoria*, *Lancaster*, *Lyme Bay*, *Monmouth*, *Northumberland*, *Richmond*, *St Albans*, *Somerset*, *Sutherland*, *Wave Knight* and *Westminster*.

Embarked Merlins have served all over the world including *Queen Elizabeth*'s CSG 21 deployment to the Pacific. In addition to embarked operations, single-aircraft detachments have taken part in NATO exercises and operations in the Arctic, Eastern Atlantic and Mediterranean. Thus far the Merlin has been a successful but complicated and very expensive asset.

Wildcat

Westland Helicopters continued to develop the Lynx privately and proposals for a Super Lynx were put forward in the 1990s when it became clear that an all-Merlin RN helicopter force was unaffordable. In 2002 the MOD placed a contract for a Lynx replacement designated AW 159 by Westland with Thales contracted to develop communications, navigation and systems management avionics common to both RN and Army variants. Glass cockpits were incorporated and the fuselage was significantly larger than that of the Lynx, making extensive use of composites. It was designed to have a reduced radar cross section with upturned engine exhausts to supress the engines' heat signature. The design was also one of the first to be created digitally, leading to digital construction methods and a 'paperless' maintenance regime for aircraft in service. It is one of the first British aircraft to have digital aircraft histories of individual maintenance, flight data, modification and, ultimately, disposal methods.

In 2006 the MOD placed a single contract, without competitive tender, for forty battlefield reconnaissance versions for the Army, thirty maritime combat versions for the RN and options for the manufacture

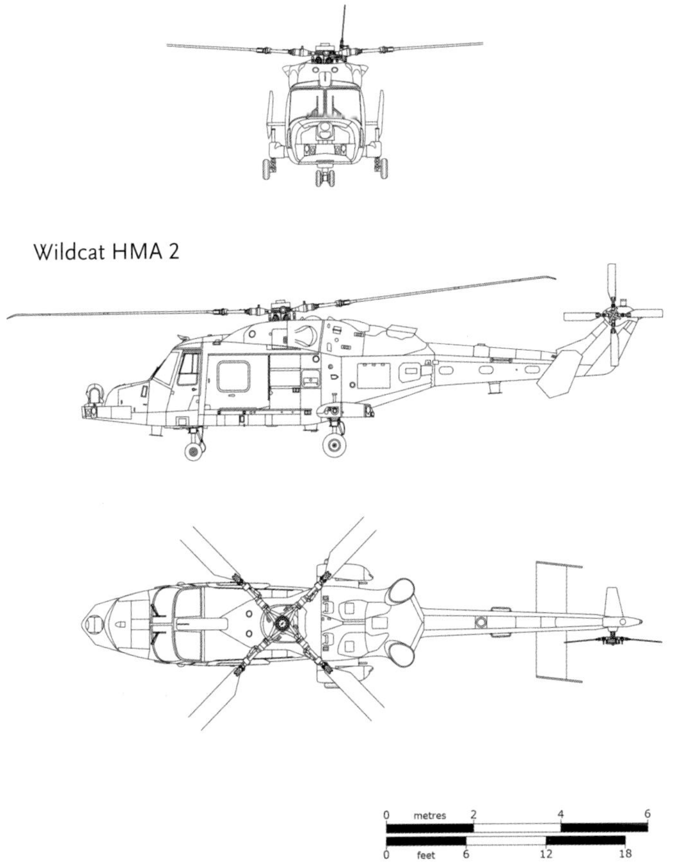

Wildcat HMA 2

Wildcat AH 1 of 847 NAS landing on HMNLMS *De Zeven Provincien*. (Crown Copyright)

of a further five of each. By then it was appreciated that the design differed sufficiently from the Lynx to make a new name appropriate and Wildcat was chosen. The Army variant became the Wildcat AH 1 and the RN variant the HMA 2. By July 2009, however, AW 159 development and production costs had nearly doubled and the orders were reduced.

Wildcat HMA 2 carrying out humanitarian relief work in the West Indies. (Crown Copyright)

Wildcat HMA 2 armed with Martlet ASM on its stub wings over the destroyer *Diamond*. (Crown Copyright)

Wildcat HMA 2 has a SELEX Galileo Seaspray 7000E AESA radar with its scanner mounted in a radome under the nose and an L-3 Wescam MX-15Di EO/IR system in a rotatable turret mounted above it. The AH 1 and the HMA 2 share common defensive aids that warn of incoming radar-guided or IR missiles and fire chaff and flares. Surprisingly, the Wildcat was not at first fitted with Link 16 to transfer data and was, therefore, reduced to reporting contacts by radio. The glass cockpit has four Smiths SDS-5000 10in by 8in multifunction displays and a Smiths airframe monitoring system. Both Army and RN Wildcats are based at Yeovilton and 847 NAS was the first unit to

Wildcat HMA 2 carrying out a winch transfer. (Crown Copyright)

Wildcat HMA 2. (Crown Copyright)

receive AH 1s which, like the Lynx before it, were transferred from the Army production batch.

The HMA 2 was intended to carry two ASM types, neither of which had reached IOC when it entered service; Martlet was the lighter of the two, Sea Venom the heavier. Martlet was designed to counter swarm attacks in littoral waters and it was developed from 2008 by Thales based on the Short Starstreak man-portable SAM. It has a 6.6lb blast HE warhead and is launched from canisters of five, two of which can be carried on stub wings fitted either side of the Wildcat for a total of twenty. The complete missile is 3in in diameter, weighs 28.6lb and accelerates to Mach 1.5 out of the launcher and has a maximum range of 4.3nm. It is guided by semi-active controlled, line-of-sight, laser-beam riding which means that only one target at a time can be engaged. Since each engagement lasts less than 4 seconds, however, this is not regarded as a problem. The loaded canisters are stored as rounds of ammunition, require no pre-use checks and have a shelf life of 15 years. Martel was supposed to be ready for service in 2020 but delays moved IOC to 2021. Wildcats demonstrated Martlet's capability during CSG-21.

Sea Venom weighs 265lb and its development was also meant to be complete by 2020 but delays have meant that IOC was delayed until 2024. The missile was developed by MBDA and uses an imaging IR seeker and terminal guidance, a 'fire-and-forget' system that allows launch aircraft to turn away after firing. Range is 11nm and advanced algorithms select the optimal target within a dense mass of ships. Real-time video imagery transmitted from the missile to the aircraft can be monitored on the observer's tactical display to give 'man-above-the-loop' capability throughout an attack. Guidance is autonomous but in-flight monitoring allows the observer to change targets, make mid-course updates and even to adjust the aim-point selection to give maximum precision and effect. It has a 66lb blast/fragmentation warhead suitable for use against warships up to frigate size or land targets. Optional line of sight laser guidance is provided as a back-up. Missile speed is high subsonic with initial acceleration provided by a booster rocket and a sustainer motor with a ventral nozzle to provide cruise power. Two Sea Venoms can be carried under each stub wing to give a total of four and multiple targets can be engaged simultaneously.

Wildcat HMA 2 data

Length:	50ft 3in rotors spread
Rotor Diameter:	42ft (span 14ft folded)
Height:	12ft
MTOW:	13,200lb
Engine:	Two LHTEC CTS 800 turboshafts each developing 1,362shp
Fuel:	Avcat. 238 gallons in internal tanks plus an optional ferry tank in the rear cabin
Performance:	Maximum level speed 157 knots Service ceiling 15,000ft. 2 minutes to 5,000ft
Endurance:	Up to 3 hours
Armament:	Two Stingray homing torpedoes or Mark 11 depth charges in the ASW role. One M3M 0.5in machine gun can be fitted on a flexible mounting in the starboard cargo door. Up to 20 Martlet ASM in five-round clusters on stub wings or up to four Sea Venom ASM. Fitting the starboard stub wing prevents the fitting of the M3M machine gun

The RN received twenty-eight Wildcat HMA 2s plus six AH 1s transferred from the Army for 847 NAS.

The Wildcat IFTU was 700W NAS, the only 700-series unit to operate the type. 825 NAS is the training and tactical development unit and 815 NAS deploys flights of one or two aircraft to destroyers, frigates that do not embark Merlins and to RFAs. 847 NAS operates in the battlefield reconnaissance and light attack role within the CHF. All three squadrons are based at Yeovilton when not at sea, as are the AH 1s of the Army Air Corps' 1 Regiment. 825 NAS has a number of operational roles in addition to its training and trials tasks which include maritime counter-terrorism.

The Wildcat is in the early stage of what is likely to be a long service career. To date Wildcats have operated around the world including detachments in the aircraft carriers *Queen Elizabeth* and *Prince of Wales*. The first deck-landing trials were carried out by 700W NAS on *Iron Duke* in 2012 during which a total of 390 successful landings were made, 148 at night and 76 using NVGs in a variety of wind and sea states. The first Wildcat flight embarked in *Lancaster* during 2015. Subsequently Wildcats have embarked in *Daring* class destroyers, Type 23 frigates and both 'Fort' and 'Wave' class RFA s. Both Type 26 and 31 frigates are designed with large flight decks and hangars but will operate regularly with Wildcat flights embarked. The type's history is still unfolding.

WHITE & THOMPSON

Biplane flying boat

White & Thompson built a single two-seat Curtiss biplane flying boat powered by a 120hp Austro-Daimler pusher engine as an entry for the 1914 Circuit of Britain Air Race. Wingspan was 41ft 8in and MTOW 1,760lb. After requisition by the Admiralty in 1914 it was used at Calshot and Grain for testing bomb fittings before moving to Felixstowe where it crashed in January 1915.

White & Thompson Bognor Bloater. (Philip Jarrett)

Bognor Bloater

Ten of these two-seat tractor biplanes were purchased by the Admiralty in 1915 with a further two purchased for spares. Of wooden construction with a 70hp Renault engine, they were built at Bognor Regis, hence the name. Four were found to be out of true after delivery and not accepted; one was never delivered. Wingspan was 37ft. After evaluation at Eastchurch some were used there for coastal patrols and others from Great Yarmouth and Killingholme. Never popular, they were deleted by early 1916.

Number 3 Tractor Flying Boat

Eight of these small two-seat flying boats were ordered by the Admiralty in 1914 for coastal anti-submarine patrols. The 120hp Beardmore engine gave a maximum level speed of 75 knots. Wingspan was 45ft and MTOW 2,400lb. The pilot and observer sat side-by-side and the latter had a pintle mounting for a single 0.303in Lewis machine gun. They were operated by 1 Squadron at Dover until 1916 and later some operated from Calshot.

Pusher Flying Boat

Ten of these pusher biplane flying boats were ordered by the Admiralty in late 1916. After evaluation they were considered unsuccessful and most saw very little service. Initially, they had 120hp Beardmore engines but these were replaced in some by 150hp Hispano-Suiza engines. Most were delivered to Calshot in 1917 but deleted in early 1918. Dimensions and MTOW were similar to those of the tractor seaplane.

WIGHT

Navyplane Pusher Seaplane

Eleven of these large seaplanes were ordered by the Admiralty in 1913. Wingspan was 63ft and the 200hp Canton-Une water-cooled radial engine driving a two-bladed wooden propeller gave a maximum level speed of 62 knots. MTOW was 3,500lb. Two were embarked in *Ark Royal* when she deployed to the Dardanelles in 1915 and others were shipped out from the UK to replace them. They were not an unqualified success as take-off was uncertain in choppy conditions. One flew a spotting sortie from *Ark Royal* over the Turkish forts in the narrows when they were bombarded by Allied battleships on 18 March 1915. None remained in service after 1916.

Twin-Fuselage, Twin-Engine Seaplane

This big twin aircraft evolved from an original wheeled design and three were ordered by the Admiralty for evaluation as torpedo strike aircraft in 1915. Each fuselage had a single 200hp Canton Une engine and a single cockpit. Wingspan was 117ft and the airframe was fabricated from wood covered with plywood and fabric. They were evaluated at both Calshot and Felixstowe but found to be under-powered and unable to take off with a torpedo fitted. Some torpedo flights were made with limited fuel but further development was abandoned in 1917.

Wight Twin-Fuselage, Twin-Engine Seaplane. (Philip Jarrett)

Type 840 Seaplane

Following the Admiralty practice of allocating a type number taken from a machine in the first production batch, the Type 840 was a biplane fabricated from wood and doped canvas with a 225hp Sunbeam engine driving a two-bladed wooden propeller giving a maximum level speed of 70 knots. The wings could be folded for hangar stowage; wingspan was 61ft and MTOW 4,453lb. Armament comprised a single 810lb 14in torpedo carried under the centre-section or an equivalent weight of bombs. The type proved effective but was never as popular as the contemporary Short 184. Despite this, large Admiralty contracts for Type 840s were placed from 1915 but Wight proved unable to expand sufficiently to meet them and orders were transferred to subcontractors including Beardmore and Portholme Aerodrome. Fifty were eventually delivered for operational use with others delivered from subcontractors as sources of spare parts. Some were embarked in *Engadine* but the majority were used for coastal patrols from Dundee, Felixstowe, Scapa Flow and Gibraltar.

Trainer Seaplane
Two examples of this small two-seat biplane seaplane were built under Admiralty contract for evaluation in 1916 with side-by-side seating. One had a 100hp Anzani and the other a 100hp Gnome monosoupape; both pusher, rotary engines driving four-bladed wooden propellers. Further details have been lost; both were tested at Felixstowe but not selected for further use before being deleted in 1917.

Bomber
A single two-seat Bomber was ordered by the Admiralty for evaluation in 1916. Wingspan was 65ft 6in, MTOW 5,166lb and the 275hp Rolls-Royce water-cooled engine gave a maximum level speed of 78 knots. Maximum bomb load was four 112lb bombs and the gunner had a single 0.303in Lewis machine gun on a Scarff ring. Its evaluation was reported on positively but the requirement for single-engined bombers was adequately filled by other designs and it was not ordered into production.

'Converted' Seaplane
Evolved from the Bomber, the 'Converted' Seaplane differed in having twin-floats, double-acting ailerons and 'goal-post' king-posts to support the outer sections of the upper wings. Early examples had a 275hp Rolls-Royce engine but later examples were re-engined with either a 322hp Rolls-Royce Eagle VI or 265hp Sunbeam Maori. A tall radiator block was mounted on the fuselage top decking aft of the engine but right in front of the pilot's cockpit.

'Converted' Seaplane data

Length:	44ft 8½in
Wingspan:	65ft 6in
Height:	16ft
MTOW:	5,556lb
Engine:	One 275hp Rolls-Royce Mark II
Fuel:	Avgas. 70 gallons
Performance:	Maximum level speed 74 knots
	Service ceiling 9,600ft. 42 minutes to 10,000ft
Endurance:	Up to 3½ hours
Armament:	One 0.303in Lewis machine gun on Scarff ring in rear cockpit. Up to four 100lb or 112lb bombs on underwing racks

The RN received thirty-seven 'Converted' Seaplanes with further airframes delivered as spares. They were used extensively on coastal patrol work, mainly from Calshot but also from Cherbourg and Portland. Most were deleted after fair wear and tear but several survived until the Armistice. After that the survivors were rapidly withdrawn from service.

One 'Converted' Seaplane operating from Cherbourg and flown by Flight Sub Lieutenant C S Mossop RNAS and Air Mechanic A F

Wight 'Converted' Seaplane. (Philip Jarrett)

Ingledew was credited with destroying the first enemy submarine to be sunk by direct air attack by a British aircraft in the English Channel. The action took place on 18 August 1917 and the first 100lb bomb was seen to hit the boat just ahead of the periscope. A second attack was seen to be unnecessary. The wreck was located in the 1980s and identified as *UB-32* in 2021.

Baby Seaplane
A single-seat biplane seaplane fighter similar to the Sopwith Baby. Three prototypes were ordered by the Admiralty for evaluation. All were of conventional wire-braced wooden structure almost wholly covered by doped fabric. Wingspan was 30ft 8in, MTOW 1,864lb and the 100hp Gnome monosoupape engine drove a four-bladed wooden propeller to give a maximum level speed of 76 knots. Two were tested at Calshot and Isle of Grain in 1917 but the third was never flown. By then the Sopwith Pup had demonstrated the superiority of wheeled fighters operating from ships' flight decks and they were deleted.

Wight Baby Seaplane. (Philip Jarrett)

Quadruplane Fighter
Originally built as a private venture, the single Quadruplane prototype was evaluated in 1917. It was a complicated aircraft that was soon found to be impractical; the lower wing being level with the wheel axles and easily damaged. Testing found it to be structurally unsafe and remedial modifications resulted in an ungainly aircraft that was universally unpopular. It crashed in a cemetery near Martlesham Heath in February 1918 and a second projected prototype was cancelled. Wingspan was 19ft and it had a 110hp Clerget rotary engine driving a two-bladed wooden propeller. Other details have been lost.

WILLOWS

HM Airship Number 2

After flying in 1912 the fourth Willows airship was purchased by the Admiralty, becoming HMA 2. Envelope capacity was 35,000ft^3 giving a gross lift of 1.1 tons and the single 35hp Anzani engine gave a top speed of 22 knots. Endurance was 3 hours. During 1914/15 it was progressively upgraded with a dual-control, three-seat car and used for training. It was the last airship to leave Farnborough when the focus of RNAS airship operations moved to Kingsnorth in January 1915 and once there its envelope was used to create the first SS airship. The remaining components of HMA 2 were scrapped.

SS-2

The second prototype SS airship was designed and built by Airships Ltd but based on Willows' private Venture design Number 6. It proved unsatisfactory and was not taken into service.

WORMWOOD SCRUBS NAVAL AIR STATION

SS class non-rigid airships

Technical details are described under Kingsnorth Naval Air Station but Wormwood Scrubs was a major assembly point for RN non-rigid airships. SS-35, SS-36, SS-37, SS-38, SS-39, SS-40, SS-41, SS-42, SS-43, SS-44, SS-45, SS-46, SS-47, SS-48 and SS-49 were assembled there using components manufactured elsewhere.

SST-12, another of the non-rigid airships assembled at Wormwood Scrubs. (Ces Mowthorpe)

SSP class non-rigid airships

Technical details are described under Kingsnorth Naval Air Station but the car of SSP-2 and the complete SSP-3, SSP-4, SSP-5 and SSP-6 were manufactured at Wormwood Scrubs.

SSZ class non-rigid airships

Technical details are described under Folkestone Naval Air Station but Wormwood Scrubs was the largest centre for SSZ construction. SSZ-21, SSZ-22, SSZ-23, SSZ-24, SSZ-25, SSZ-26, SSZ-27, SSZ-28, SSZ-29, SSZ-30, SSZ-31, SSZ-32, SSZ-33, SSZ-34, SSZ-35, SSZ-36, SSZ-37, SSZ-38, SSZ-39, SSZ-40, SSZ-41, SSZ-42, SSZ-43, SSZ-44, SSZ-45, SSZ-46, SSZ-47, SSZ-48, SSZ-49, SSZ-68, SSZ-69 and SSZ-70 were manufactured there.

SSZ-37, assembled at Wormwood Scrubs, with a coastal convoy over the escort vessel *PC-61*. (Guy Warner)

SSE class non-rigid airships

SSE Class airships were designed at Wormwood Scrubs and two of them, SSE-1 and SSE-3, were built there. The third was built at Mullion Naval Air Station. They were completed in early 1918 with an envelope of 90,000ft^3. SSE-1 was powered by two 90hp Curtiss engines, SSE-2 by two 75hp Rolls-Royce Hawk engines. SSE-3 was transferred to the US Navy to train airships crews. None of them flew for more than a few hours.

SST class non-rigid airships

The larger of the two classes designed and built at Wormwood Scrubs, the SSTs were 165ft long with a diameter of 35ft 6in. They were powered by either two 100hp Sunbeam engines or two 75hp Rolls-Royce Hawk engines; the latter designed specifically for airships. Gross lift was 3.1 tons and disposable lift was one ton. Maximum speed in level flight was 50 knots. Most of the class were only completed in mid-1918, too late to see much war service. The majority were deflated and scrapped in 1919 after only a few hours in the air. Those built at Wormwood Scrubs were SST-1, SST-2, SST-3, SST-4, SST-5, SST-6, SST-7, SST-8, SST-9, SST-10, SST-11, SST-12 and SST-14. There was no SST-13.

WRIGHT

A single Wright-designed sports, pusher biplane built by Short Brothers was purchased by the Admiralty in 1915 from Squadron Commander Ogilvy for use within the naval flying school at Eastchurch. It only operated for a few weeks before being damaged and then written off in January 1916. Wingspan was 39ft, MTOW 1,250lb and it had a 35hp Wright engine driving a two-bladed wooden pusher propeller to give a maximum level speed of 35 knots.

A W-Autonomous Systems HCMC in temporary RN markings for operation from *Prince of Wales* in 2023. (Crown Copyright)'

FIRST STEPS TOWARDS UNMANNED CARRIER AIRCRAFT

In 2023 *Prince of Wales* carried out a series of trials involving unmanned aircraft taking off from and landing on her flight deck. The deck landings were autonomous and perfectly executed.

The UAVs involved were a twin-engined W Autonomous Systems HCMC and a single turboprop-engined General Atomics Mojave. Both were manufacturers' development aircraft, not owned by the RN, used to demonstrate the ability of UAVs to integrate with manned aircraft operations on a carrier deck, a move towards the carrier air groups envisaged by the RN Develop Directorate for the 2030s.

A General Atomics Mojave on *Prince of Wales*' flight deck during trials in 2023. (Crown Copyright)

Bibliography

Official Admiralty Sources

CB 3307(1), Naval Staff History of the Second World War, *The Development of British Naval Aviation 1919-1945* Volume 1 (Admiralty, 1954).

CB 3307(2), Naval Staff History of the Second World War, *The Development of British Naval Aviation, 1919-1945* Volume 2 (Admiralty, 1956).

CB 3053 *Naval Aircraft progress and Operations*, Periodical Summaries published by the Admiralty between 1940 and 1956 with information on aircraft projects.

Flight Deck – The Journal of Naval Aviation. Extracts from editions published quarterly between 1944 and 2000. (Admiralty/Ministry of Defence).

Pilots Notes issued for a wide range of aircraft after 1939.

Unclassified notes on aircraft, aero-engines and manufacturers in the archive of the Naval Aircraft .Department studied by the author while he served in the Departmenr between 1989 and 1982. Unfortunately, it now appears that this archive was lost when the Department ceased to exist.

Published Sources

Abbott, Patrick, *The British Airship at War 1914-1918* (Lavenham, Terence Dalton Ltd, 1989).

Admiralty, *Fleet Air Arm – The Admiralty Account of Naval Air Operations* (London, HMSO, 1943).

Allen, Patrick, *Wessex* (Shrewsbury, Airlife Publishing, 1988).

Allen, Patrick, *Sea King* (Shrewsbury, Airlife Publishing, 1993).

Allward, Maurice, *Buccaneer – Modern Combat Aircraft 7* (Shepperton, Ian Allen, 1981).

Andrews, C F, and Morgan, E B, *Supermarine Aircraft since 1914* (London, Putnam, 1981).

Andrews, C F, and Morgan, E B, *Vickers Aircraft since 1908* (London, Putnam, 1988).

Askins, Simon, *Gannet – From the Cockpit 7* (Ringshall, Ad Hoc Publications, 2008).

Bachelor, Len, *Supermarine Seafires (Merlins)* (Windsor, Profile Publications, 1971).

Balance, Theo, Howard, Lee & Sturtivant, Ray, *The Squadrons and Units of the Fleet Air Arm* (Stapleford, Air-Britain Historians, 2016).

Barnes, C H, *Bristol Aircraft since 1910* (London, Putnam, 1964).

Barnes, C H, *Handley Page Aircraft since 1907* (London, Putnam, 1976).

Barnes, C H, and James, Derek N, *Shorts Aircraft since 1900* (London, Putnam, 1989).

Blackbushe Aviation Research Group, *A History of the Westland Wyvern* (Camberley, BARG, 1973).

Blackbushe Aviation Research Group, *A History of the Douglas Skyraider AEW 1* (Camberley, BARG, 1974).

Bowers, Peter M, *Curtiss Aircraft 1907-1947* (London, Putnam, 1979).

Brew, Alec, *Boulton Paul Aircraft since 1915* (London, Putnam, 1993).

Brown, Don L, *Miles Aircraft since 1925* (London, Putnam, 1970).

Brown, Eric M, Captain CBE DSC AFC RN, *Firebrand – From the Cockpit 8* (Ringshall, Ad Hoc Publications, 2008).

Brown, Eric M, Captain CBE DSC AFC RN, edited by William Green, *Wings of the Navy* (London, Macdonald & Jane's Publishing Group, 1980).

Brown, Eric M, Captain CBE DSC AFC RN, *Wings of the Weird and Wonderful* (Manchester, Crecy Publishing, 2010).

Brown, Eric M, Captain CBE DSC AFC RN, *Seafire – From the Cockpit 13* (Ringshall, Ad Hoc Publications, 2010).

Brown, J David, *Supermarine Walrus I and Seagull V Variants* (Windsor, Profile Publications, 1971).

Brown, J David, *Fairey Barracuda Marks I-V* (Windsor, Profile Publications, 1972).

Brown, J David, *Fairey Fulmar Marks I & II* (Windsor, Profile Publications, 1973).

Brown, J David, *Carrier Fighters* (London, Macdonald and Jane's Publishing, 1975).

Brown, J David, *The Seafire – The Spitfire that went to sea* (London, Greenhill Books, 1989).

Bruce, J M, *British Aeroplanes 1914-1918* (London, Putnam, 1957).

Bruce, J M, *The BE.2, 2a and 2b* (Leatherhead, Profile Publications undated).

Bruce, J M, *The Sopwith 1½ Strutter* (Leatherhead, Profile Publications, undated).

Bruce, J M. *The Sopwith Pup* (Leatherhead, Profile Publications, undated).

Bruce, J M, *The Sopwith Triplane* (Leatherhead, Profile Publications, undated).

Bruce, J M, *The Sopwith Camel F.1* (Leatherhead, Profile Publications, undated).

Bruce, J M, *The Short 184* (Leatherhead, Profile Publications, undated).

Bruce, J M, *Sopwith B.1 and T.1 Cuckoo* (Berkhamstead, Albatros Productions, Windsock Data File #90, 2001).

Bruce, J M, *Warplanes of the First World War – Fighters Volume One* (London, Macdonald, 1965).

Bruce, J M, *Warplanes of the First World War – Fighters Volume Two* (London, Macdonald, 1968).

Bruce, J M, *Warplanes of the First World War – Fighters Volume Three* (London, Macdonald, 1969).

Bruce, J M, Page, Gordon, and Sturtivant, Ray, *The Sopwith Pup* (Tunbridge Wells, Air-Britain Historians, 2002).

Buttler, Tony, *The de Havilland Sea Vixen* (Stapleford, Air-Britain Historians, 2007).
Buttler, Tony, *Sturgeon – Target-Tug Extraordinaire* (Ringshall, Ad Hoc Publications, 2009).
Buttler, Tony, *British Secret Projects 2 – Jet Bombers since 1949* (Manchester, Crecy Publishing, 2018).
Chartres, John, *Sea King – Modern Combat Aircraft 18* (Shepperton, Ian Allen, 1984).
Cole, Christopher, and Cheesman, E F, *The Air Defence of Britain 1914-1918* (London, Putnam, 1984).
Cooper, Geoffrey, *Farnborough and the Fleet Air Arm* (Hersham, Midland Publishing, 2008).
Cronin, Dick, *Royal Navy Shipboard Aircraft Developments 1912-1931* (Tonbridge, Air-Britain Historians, 1990).
Davis, Mick, *Sopwith Aircraft* (Marlborough, The Crowood Press, 1999).
Doust, Michael J, Commander RN, *Buccaneer S 1 – From the Cockpit 6* (Ringshall, Ad Hoc Publications, 2007).
Doust, Michael J, Commander RN, *Sea Hawk – From the Cockpit 3* (Ringshall, Ad Hoc Publications, 2007).
Doust, Michael J, Commander RN, *Scimitar – From the Cockpit 2* (Ringshall, Ad Hoc Publications, 2006).
Doust, Michael J, Commander RN, *Wyvern – From the Cockpit 1* (Ringshall, Ad Hoc Publications).
Draper, Michael I, *Sitting Ducks & Peeping Toms – Targets, Drones and UAVs in British Military Service since 1917* (Stapleford, Air-Britain Historians, 2011).
Duval, G R, *British Flying Boats 1909-1952* (London, Putnam, 1966).
Ellis, Paul, *Aircraft of the Royal Navy* (London, Jane's Publishing, 1982).
Fiddler, Brian P, *Gannet* (Chippenham, Picton Publishing, 1990).
Francillon, Rene J, *McDonnell Douglas Aircraft since 1920* (London, Putnam, 1979).
Francillon, Rene J, *Grumman Aircraft since 1929* (London, Putnam, 1989).
Franks, Richard A, *The Fairey Barracuda* (Bedford, Valiant Wings Publishing, 2023).
Friedman, Norman, *British Carrier Aviation – The Evolution of the Ships and their Aircraft* (London, Conway Maritime Press, 1988).
Friedman, Norman, *Carrier Air Power* (London, Conway Maritime Press, 1981).
Gibbings, David & Gorman, J A, *Scimitar* (Yeovilton, Society of Friends of the Fleet Air Arm Museum, 1988).
Gibson, Chris, *The Admiralty and AEW* (A Project Tech Profile of Blue Envoy Press, 2011).
Green, William, *Famous Fighters of the Second World War* (London, Macdonald, 1957).
Green, William, *Famous Fighters of the Second World War – Second Series* (London, Macdonald, 1962).
Green, William, *The World's Fighting Planes* (London, Macdonald, 1964).
Green, William, *The World Guide to Combat Planes – One* (London, Macdonald, 1966).
Green, William, *The World Guide to Combat Planes – Two* (London, Macdonald, 1966).
Green, William, *Warplanes of the Second World War Volume 6 – Floatplanes* (London, Macdonald, 1962).
Green, William, *Warplanes of the Second World War Volume 5 – Flying Boats* (London, Macdonald, 1962).
Green, William, *Warplanes of the Second World War Volume 2 –* Fighters (London, Macdonald, 1961).
Gunston, Bill, *Fighters of the Fifties* (Cambridge, Patrick Stephens, 1981).
Gunston, Bill, *Harrier – Modern Combat Aircraft 13* (Shepperton, Ian Allen, 1981).
Gunston, Bill, *F-4 Phantom – Modern Combat Aircraft 1* (Shepperton, Ian Allen, 1977).
Gunston, Bill, *Attack Aircraft of the West* (Shepperton, Ian Allen, 1974).
Gunston, Bill, *Early Supersonic Fighters of the West* (Shepperton, Ian Allen, 1976).
Hare, Paul R, *The Royal Aircraft Factory* (London, Putnam, 1990).
Harrison, W A, *Fairey Gannet AEW 3* (Aviation News Mini-Monograph, undated).
Harrison, William, *Fairey Firefly* (Shrewsbury, Airlife Publishing, 1992).
Harrison, W A, *Fairey Barracuda* (Milton Keynes, Hall Park Books, Warpaint #35 undated).
Harrison, W A, *Fairey Swordfish and Albacore* (Marlborough, The Crowood Press, 2002).
Hazell, Steve, *de Havilland Sea Vixen* (Bedfordshire, Hall Park Books, Warpaint #11, undated).
Hazell, Steve, *Fairey Gannet* (Bedfordshire, Hall park Books, Warpaint #23, undated).
Horsley, Terence, Lieutenant Commander RNVR, *Find, Fix and Strike* (London, Eyre and Spottiswoode Publishers, 1943).
Howard, Lee, Burrow, Mick & Myall, Eric, *Fleet Air Arm Helicopters since 1943* (Stapleford, Air-Britain Historians, 2011).
Hurren, B J, *The Swordfish Saga* (Hayes, Fairey Aviation, undated).
Jackson, A J, *Blackburn Aircraft since 1909* (London, Putnam, 1968).
Jackson, A J, *De Havilland Aircraft since 1909* (London, Putnam, 1978).
Jackson, A J, *Avro Aircraft since 1908* (London, Putnam, 1990).
Jackson, James, *The Admiralty and the Helicopter* (A Project Tech Profile of Blue Envoy Press, 2018).
James, Derek N, *Gloster Aircraft since 1917* (London, Putnam, 1971).
James, Derek N, *Westland since 1915*, (London, Putnam, 1991).
Jarrett, Philip, *Fairey IIIF – Interwar Military Workhorse* (Ringshall, Ad Hoc Publications, 2009).
Jarrett, Philip, *Frank McClean – Godfather to British Naval Aviation* (Barnsley, Seaforth Publishing, 2011).
Jarrett, Philip, Series Editor, *Pioneer Aircraft – Early Aviation before 1914* (London, Putnam, 2002).
Jarrett, Philip, *The Royal Naval Air Service in the First World War – Aircraft and Events as Recorded in Official Documents* (Barnsley, Pen & Sword Aviation, 2015).
Jones, Barry, *British Experimental Turbojet Aircraft* (Marlborough, The Crowood press, 2003).

King, Brad, *Royal Naval Air Service 1912-1918* (Aldershot, Hikoki Publications, 1997).
King, H F, *Armament of British Aircraft 1909-1939* (London, Putnam, 1971).
King, H F, *Sopwith Aircraft 1912-1920* (London, Putnam, 1980).
Leahy, Alan, Captain CBE DSC RN, *Sea Fury – From the Cockpit 12* (Ringshall, Ad Hoc Publications, 2010).
Leahy, Alan, Captain CBE DSC RN, *Sea Hornet – From the Cockpit 5* (Ringshall, Ad Hoc Publications, 2007).
Lewis, Peter, *The British Fighter since 1912* (London, Putnam, 1965).
Lewis, Peter, *The British Bomber since 1914* (London, Putnam, 1974).
Lindsay, Roger, *The de Havilland Venom* (Stockton-on-Tees, published privately, undated).
London, Peter, *Saunders and Saro Aircraft since 1917* (London, Putnam, 1988).
Mason, Francis K, *The Fairey IIIF* (Leatherhead, Profile Publications, undated).
Mason, Francis K, *The Hawker Sea Fury* (Leatherhead, Profile Publications, undated).
Mason, Francis K, *The Hawker Sea Hawk* (Leatherhead, Profile Publications, undated).
Mason, Francis K, *The Hawker Hurricane* (London, Macdonald, 1962).
Mason, Francis K, *Hawker Hunter – Biography of a Thoroughbred* (Cambridge, Patrick Stephens, 1981).
Mason, Francis K, *Hawker Aircraft since 1920* (London, Putnam, 1991).
Mason, Tim, *British Flight Testing – Martlesham Heath 1920-1939* (London, Putnam, 1993).
McCandless, Robert, *Barracuda – From the Cockpit 16* (Ringshall, Ad Hoc Publishing, 2012).
McEwen, Mac, *Hunter – From the Cockpit 11* (Ringshall, Ad Hoc Publications, 2009).
Morgan, Eric, and Stevens, John, *The Scimitar File* (Tunbridge Wells, Air-Britain Historians, 2000).
Mowthorpe, Ces, *Battlebags – British Airships of the First World War* (Stroud, Sutton Publishing, 1995).
Norman, J G S, Lieutenant Commander RN, *Firefly – From the Cockpit 4* (Ringshall, Ad Hoc Publications, 2007).
Payne, Donald, *Swordfish – From the Cockpit 10* (Ringshall, Ad Hoc Publications, 2008).
Ransom, Stephen, and Fairclough, Robert, *English Electric Aircraft and their Predecessors* (London, Putnam, 1987).
Ridley-Kitts, Daniel George, MBE, *Military, Naval and Civil Airships* (Cheltenham, The History Press, 2023).
Rowan-Thomson, Graeme, Commander RN, *Attacker – From the Cockpit 9* (Ringshall, Ad Hoc Publishing, 2008).
Sandham-Bailey, Chris, *Sea Harriers of the Falklands War* (Horncastle, Morton's Media Group, 2022).
Scott, Richard, *EYES OF THE FLEET – A History of Rotary-Wing Airborne Early Warning/ Airborne Surveillance and Control in the Royal Navy 1982-2022* (Flying Fish Media UK, 2022).
Smith, Peter C, *Skua! The Royal Navy's Dive Bomber* (Barnsley, Pen & Sword Aviation, 2006).
Stott, Ian G, *The Fairey Swordfish Marks I-IV* (Windsor, Profile Publications, undated).
Sturtivant, Ray, and Page, Gordon, *Royal Navy Aircraft Serials and Units 1911-1919* (Tonbridge, Air-Britain Historians, 1992).
Sturtivant, Ray with Cronin, Dick, *Fleet Air Arm Aircraft, Units and Ships 1920-1939* (Tunbridge Wells, Air-Britain Historians, 1998).
Sturtivant, Ray, ISO, with Burrow, Mick, *Fleet Air Arm Aircraft 1939-1945* (Tunbridge Wells, Air-Britain Historians, 1995).
Sturtivant, Ray, with Burrow, Mick, and Howard, Lee, *Fleet Air Arm Aircraft since 1946* (Tonbridge, Air-Britain Historians, 2004).
Swanborough, Gordon, and Bowers, Peter M, *United States Navy Aircraft since 1911* (London, Putnam, 1990).
Tapper, Oliver, *Armstrong Whitworth Aircraft since 1913* (London, Putnam, 1973).
Taylor, H A, *Airspeed Aircraft since 1931* (London, Putnam, 1970).
Taylor, H A, *Fairey Aircraft since 1915* (London, Putnam, 1974).
Taylor, John W R, *Fleet Air Arm* (London, Ian Allen Limited, 1958).
Thetford, Owen, *British Naval Aircraft since 1912* (London, Putnam, 1982).
Thetford, Owen, *The Fairey Flycatcher* (Leatherhead, Profile Publications, undated).
Till, Geoffrey, *Air Power and the Royal Navy 1914 -1945 – A Historical Survey* (London, Macdonald & Jane's Publishers, 1979).
Treadwell, Terry C, *Submarines with Wings* (London, Conway Maritime Press, 1985).
Vicary, Adrian, *Naval Wings* (Cambridge, Patrick Stephens, 1984).
Warner, Guy, *Lighter than Air* (Barnsley, Pen & Sword Aviation, 2016).
Watkins, David, *de Havilland Vampire – The Complete History* (Stroud, Sutton Publishing, 1996).
Williams, Ray, *Fly Navy – Aircraft of the Fleet Air Arm since 1945* (Shrewsbury, Airlife Publishing, 1989).
Willis, Matthew, *Blackburn Skua & Roc* (Redbourn, Mushroom Model Publications, 2007).
Willis, Matthew, *Fairey Swordfish* (Horncastle, Tempest Books, 2022).
Wilson, Stewart, *Combat Aircraft since 1945* (Bungendore, Australia, Aerospace Publications Pty, 2000).
Wixey, Kenneth E, *Parnall Aircraft since 1914* (London, Putnam, 1990).
Wood, Derek, *Project Cancelled* (London, Macdonald and Jane's Publishers, 1975).

In addition to the titles listed above, I have been able to draw on my collection of over seventy-five biographies and autobiographies of RN pilots, observers and air engineers to add colour and contemporary opinions to some of the aircraft's technical descriptions.